# TEXAS

State Capitals
County Seats

Copyright by C. S. HAMMOND & Co., N.Y.

WESTERN PART
OF
TEXAS
*Same scale as main map*

Fourth Edition

# TEXAS

## The Lone Star State

**Rupert Norval Richardson**

*Distinguished Professor of History*
*Hardin-Simmons University*

**Ernest Wallace**

*Horn Professor of History, Emeritus*
*Texas Tech University*

**Adrian N. Anderson**

*Professor of History*
*Lamar University*

PRENTICE-HALL, INC.   Englewood Cliffs, New Jersey 07632

*Library of Congress Cataloging in Publication Data*

RICHARDSON, RUPERT NORVAL (date)
 Texas, the Lone Star State.

 Includes bibliographies and index.
 1. Texas—History. I. Wallace, Ernest, joint
author. II. Anderson, Adrian N., joint author.
III. Title.
F386.R52  1981      976.4      80-20121
ISBN  0-13-912444-6

*Editorial/production supervision and interior*
 *design by Linda Schuman*
*Cover design by Jorge Hernandez*
*Manufacturing buyer: Edmund W. Leone*

Printed in the United States of America

10  9  8  7  6  5  4

PRENTICE-HALL INTERNATIONAL, INC., *London*
PRENTICE-HALL OF AUSTRALIA PTY. LIMITED, *Sydney*
PRENTICE-HALL OF CANADA, LTD., *Toronto*
PRENTICE-HALL OF INDIA PRIVATE LIMITED, *New Delhi*
PRENTICE-HALL OF JAPAN, INC., *Tokyo*
PRENTICE-HALL OF SOUTHEAST ASIA PTE. LTD., *Singapore*
WHITEHALL BOOKS LIMITED, *Wellington, New Zealand*

# CONTENTS

# PREFACE

The history of Texas is replete with adventure and heroic action. The reader meets with self-denying priests and mail-fisted conquerors of Spain, with filibusters and *empresarios* from beyond the Mississippi, with frontiersmen from Tennessee and planters from Alabama. The Anglo-Americans vied with the Mexicans for supremacy until 1848 and took the country from the Indians by 1875. Thereafter came the struggle for law and order, the lusty cattle industry, the surge of land-hungry farmers seeking virgin soil, the rapid approach of railroads, and the discovery of oil fields. In recent times the challenge of space travel and the explosive growth of urban Texas have continued the tradition of adventure and progress.

Since the last edition of *Texas: The Lone Star State* appeared eleven years ago, much history has been made and much has been written. Minorities, racial and otherwise, have continued their search for equality, justice, power, and position. Protest and dissent were visible elements during the early seventies; political factionalism prevailed throughout the decade, and toward the end of the period there were indications that an era of two-party politics might be near. It was, on the whole, a prosperous time, but a developing energy shortage, economic inflation, and continuation of social tensions combined to produce uncertainty, even anxiety, as Texas entered still another decade.

In addition to adding new materials to bring the text up-to-date, the authors have revised the chapters on the past. The greater part of the book has been rewritten; in several places the organization has been changed to present certain subjects more fully and clearly; and where new scholarship has been available, it has been included to offer new insights and information. We have added new maps and photographs and incorporated recently published books and articles in the bibliographies.

In trying to provide a complete survey of the history and current state of Texas we sought to give a fair amount of space to certain less interesting but important affairs, without neglecting the more colorful and romantic. The general reader or the college student can easily follow chronologically the main course of public affairs, breaking the sequence from time to time for a closer look at important movements and life and society in general. Those who prefer to follow the topical units will find the Table of Contents and the Index useful.

We are deeply grateful to the teachers, students, and general readers whose criticism and constructive suggestions have helped greatly in the work of revision.

*R. N. R.*
*E. W.*
*A. N. A.*

Chapter One

# THE COUNTRY
# AND
# ITS NATIVE PEOPLES

The name Texas comes from *Tejas,* meaning "friends" or "allies," a word applied by Spanish explorers and missionaries to an Indian confederacy, the Hasinai, that they found in this country. The early Spaniards thought of Texas as just the land of the Hasinai (Texas) Indians, that is, the territory between the Trinity and the Red rivers, including part of present-day Louisiana. Early in the eighteenth century, however, the borders of Texas were extended westward to include Spanish settlements that had been planted on the San Antonio River and Matagorda Bay. A definite boundary on the west was first fixed in 1746, when it was declared that the Medina River should separate Texas from the province of Nuevo Santander. Later the boundaries were extended far to the west and north, while a part of the territory on the east was sliced off. A large part of the border of the state consists of natural boundaries: the Rio Grande on the west and south from the thirty-second parallel to the Gulf of Mexico, the Gulf shoreline, the Sabine River to the thirty-second parallel, and the Red River for about three hundred miles on the north. The remainder of the boundary consists of straight lines established by surveyors at one time or another in conformity with various treaties and agreements.

With its 267,339 square miles of territory, extending from the High Plains of the Panhandle to the Gulf of Mexico, Texas is, except for Alaska, by far the largest state in the Union. One can travel eight hundred miles in a straight line within its borders. Texarkana, on the Arkansas border, is closer to Chicago than it is to El Paso, on the Rio Grande. The distance from Brownsville to Mexico City is over one

1

hundred miles shorter than the distance to the city of Texline, a town on the northern fringe of the Texas Panhandle. Orange, on the Sabine River, is closer to the Atlantic and El Paso, on the Rio Grande, is closer to the Pacific than the two cities are to each other.

## THE COUNTRY

A glance at a relief map of the United States reveals that Texas is not physiographically uniform but that it is made up of parts of at least three great physical divisions, namely, the Atlantic-Gulf coastal plain, the Great Plains of central North America, and the Rocky Mountain system. The fact that these great physiographic provinces join within the state means that there is variety and contrast in topography, climate, and resources.

The state is divided into a number of natural regions, determined mainly by soil and climate. The Gulf Coast Plain extends from the shore a little south of Corpus Christi to the Sabine River and inland from about a hundred miles to about two hundred miles. Near the coast the land is low and marshy; inland it is well drained, and there is much heavy soil with a great variety of vegetation. Its better clay and loam soils were once savannas affording excellent grazing, but they now are farmed.

East Texas is a country of forests and farm lands. Its pine lands are the western edge of the great southern pine forest that extends eastward to the Atlantic Ocean. Lumber is exported. West of the pine lands is an extensive area of sandy soils and post oak, extending far into Central Texas. The region produces pork, beef, poultry, and dairy products.

The Central Texas Prairies extend from the Colorado River in the vicinity of Austin northward to the Red River; the same type of terrain continues on into Oklahoma. The prairie is broken by the Eastern Cross Timbers, a thin wedge of trees extending northward from the vicinity of Waco through the Dallas country to the Red River valley. East of this narrow belt of timber is the Blackland Prairie and to the west lies the Grand Prairie. Rich, black soils predominate, now largely cultivated except where too thin, producing grain and cotton and supporting livestock. Dallas, Fort Worth, and ten or so lesser cities lie within this region, and Austin and San Antonio share its trade and draw on its resources.

The Cross Timbers, lying between Fort Worth and Abilene and extending from the vicinity of the Colorado River to the Red River and beyond, is a farming and stock-raising country, producing peanuts, vegetables, dairy products, and poultry. Its soils range from belts of loose, blowing sand to black clays.

The Rolling Plains, or North Texas Plains belt, includes the Abilene, Vernon, and Wichita Falls country. It is separated from the High Plains to the west by the Caprock, a prominent limestone escarpment. Some of the Rolling Plains terrain is highly eroded; other areas consist of spacious prairies. Cotton and maize cultivation is interspersed with cattle raising.

The greater part of the High Plains is arable, and this region, once a sea of grass, is one of the foremost farming sections in the world. Cotton, maize, and several other crops are grown in stupendous quantities, made possible by irrigation from wells. Within the area have grown the cities of Amarillo, Lubbock, Plainview, and a score of thriving towns. In more recent years, declining water supplies have become a source of concern.

Texas contains a number of regions determined by geological makeup and the resultant physiographic forms. Grasses, timber, soils, and other natural resources have affected its history greatly. (Adapted from Stanley A. Arbingast, Lorrin G. Kennamer, and Michael E. Bonnie, *Atlas of Texas,* Bureau of Business Research, The University of Texas at Austin, 1967.)

The Edwards Plateau is a broken tableland, an extension of the Great Plains. In most places its soil is too shallow for farming. It is widely known as a livestock region, and San Angelo, on its periphery, is a leading wool and mohair market. The South Texas Plain consists of highly eroded localities interspersed with prairies. Light loam soils are prevalent, and brush has impinged on much of the grasslands. There is considerable farming and livestock raising. The Winter Garden region south of San Antonio, the lower Rio Grande Valley, and a few other localities produce vegetables and citrus fruits in quantity.

Except for a few relatively small irrigation centers, the vast basin and mountain region, lying mainly west of the Pecos, is livestock country. On the best soils and under favorable conditions, good grass will grow, but yucca, catclaw, and creosote bush dominate much of its surface.

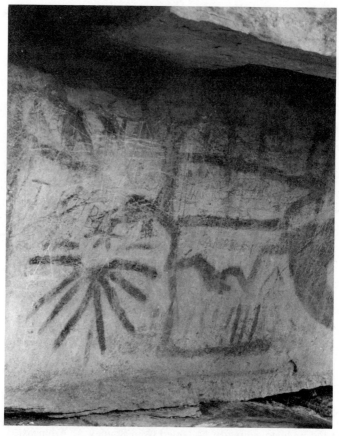

In pictographs like these at Paint Rock, Indians recorded the significant events of their lives. (Texas Highway Department)

With the splendor of its scenery, however, nature compensates for the harsh features of this land. Here are Guadalupe Peak, the highest mountain east of the Rockies, and the wild Chisos of the Big Bend. Under azure skies bald peaks of stone shimmer like giant jewels; silhouettes of massive crags take a thousand fanciful shapes; and myriad-colored canyon walls create an ever-changing vista.

## PREHISTORIC PEOPLE

Texas lies within the three areas in which Indian civilization reached its highest development in North America: the Mayan in Mexico and Central America, the Pueblo of the upper Rio Grande, and the Mound Builder of the Mississippi Valley. Although Texas was a meeting place of these three cultures, it appears that none was ever extensively established within its boundaries, and archeologists differ as to what influence each culture had upon it. However that may be, the archeology of Texas is as diversified as are its natural resources. The ways of life of its early inhabitants differed even more widely from region to region than do those of modern people.

Discoveries during the last half-century indicate that humans have been in America much longer than had previously been believed, and some of the very earliest relics discovered in the New World have been found in Texas. Among the explored sites that indicate the presence of these Paleo-Americans are those near Abilene, Midland, and Plainview, Texas, and Clovis and Folsom, New Mexico—all in the plains country, principally the High Plains, the Llano Estacado. In this region, which E. H. Sellards has named the Llano Complex, the Paleo-Americans hunted and at least occasionally killed in numbers a species of elephant now long extinct. Their spear and dart points, known as Clovis fluted points, were widely distributed. By measuring the remaining radioactivity of organic materials taken from sites where spearheads and fossils of elephants indicate kills, it has been estimated that the Llano people lived some twelve thousand or more years ago.

Somewhat later than the Llano Culture was the Folsom Culture, named after a town in northeastern New Mexico. Here highly finished projectile points were found, characterized by longitudinal flutes or channels in the blade faces. The meat for these people was supplied, in part at least, by huge bison, also long extinct. Folsom fluted points have been found imbedded in the vertebrae of these beasts, and the radiocarbon tests of charred bones taken from an excavation near Lubbock indicate an age of some ten thousand years. Within the city limits of Plainview, shallow excavations have revealed more than two dozen flint tools and skeletons of perhaps a hundred bison, which radiocarbon tests indicate have been there for about nine thousand years.

In the Trinity River gravel beds near Malakoff and Trinidad, three stone images were found that may be thirty thousand or more years old, but the evidence is too scanty to warrant certainty.

About 5000 B.C. either the Paleo-American culture gave way to another culture, or the way of life of these people changed. Perhaps the ending of the ice age and the disappearance of the elephants, the great bisons, and other animals that they had hunted were factors in the change. Also, other peoples may have migrated to America during the centuries following 5000 B.C. These changes brought in the Archaic peoples. They were hunters and gatherers of natural products, as their predecessors had been, but instead of a few well-made stone implements they had a great variety of stone points and tools. At least twenty-seven types of dart points have been found in the Edwards Plateau. They also made use of polished stones. Pestles and mortars indicate that they relied more on seeds for food than did their predecessors.

In time the Archaic peoples domesticated the dog, they began to settle in more favored localities, and they grew corn (which probably was brought in from the south after about 2500 B.C.) and other foods. The making of pottery and the building of more substantial abodes followed.

## THE INDIANS

The history of any American commonwealth may well begin with its native peoples. It was in part the hope of finding Indians who could be exploited that brought the early Spanish expeditions into Texas. The desire for trade with the natives was a great factor in bringing other adventurers into the country, and the yearning of zealous priests to win over the natives to the Christian religion constituted a powerful motive for extending the influence of the Europeans. The Indians were the best teachers the white frontierspeople had. From them they learned of crops and effective means of tillage; of foods, their preparation and preservation; and of wild game, their habits and the methods of taking them.

Indeed, the Indians more than the white people determined the nature of frontier institutions. If the Indians were friendly, the white people explored and settled the country rapidly; if they were docile, it was easy to exploit them or, at least, to ignore their rights. If the Indians were organized in weak and fragmentary tribes, the whites easily drove them away; but if they were powerful and warlike, they retarded the advance of the intruders for decades, and even for centuries. Furthermore, the Indian largely determined the type of warfare that was carried out. The Caddo of the timber, the Comanche of the plain, and the Apache of the mountain all had different tactics, and the Euro-Americans had to meet them in a fashion suited to the conditions that prevailed.

It is true that both the Spaniards, who approached from the west and south, and the Anglo-Americans, who came from the east, had already developed pioneering institutions before they reached Texas, but these institutions proved unsatisfactory in certain important respects. For instance, we shall see that the Spanish mission system, which had been designed for compact pueblos or for Indians brought together in colonies, failed among the Caddos of eastern Texas, who lived in scattered hamlets and refused to move to the missions. Likewise, the Anglo-Americans, who had learned to meet Indians who fought on foot, had to develop new tactics for coping with the mounted Indians of the plains, who struck, fought, and retreated with the advantages of surprise and swiftness.

The first Europeans found many Indian tribes in Texas and a great variety of native cultures—the Caddoan peoples of eastern Texas; the Karankawas along the Gulf Coast; the Wichita and Tonkawa groups of tribes in Central Texas; the Coahuiltecans, consisting of a number of small tribes who lived south of San Antonio; and the Apaches, who lived in the western part of the state but were forced during the eighteenth century to share their country with the Comanches.

Most of the Indians of East Texas belonged to the great Caddoan family and were included in two confederacies: the Caddo, located in Arkansas, Louisiana, and the part of Texas near present-day Texarkana; and the Hasinai, on the upper Angelina and Neches rivers. In Texas history the Hasinai confederacy is the more important of the two. It was in this confederacy that the Spaniards first established missions in the interior of Texas. Probably a dozen tribes belonged to the confederacy, the more important being the Nabedache, the Nacogdoche, the Hainai, the Nasoni, and the Neche. In about 1690, when the first Spanish missionaries arrived, these tribes together probably numbered from three thousand to five thousand persons. It seems that each tribe had its own chiefs and tribal government but owed a measure of allegiance to the *caddi,* that is, the chief of the Hainai tribe and head chief of the confederacy. More powerful than the grand *caddi,* however, was the *chenesi,* or the head priest, who kept the fire temple. The fire in it was never extinguished, and from it the fires of all the confederacy were lighted.

These Indians lived in domelike houses, reinforced with stakes, thatched with twigs, daubed with mud, and covered with grass. According to the descriptions left by early French and Spanish chroniclers, the furnishings suggest beauty as well as comfort. In the houses were many-colored rugs, woven of reeds; beds, made of reeds resting on a framework of poles and covered with buffalo hides; reed baskets, filled with beans, acorns, and nuts; jars, filled with corn and covered over with ashes to keep out the weevils; and corn, shucked and hung where exposure to smoke would drive away the weevils. We are told that each year these

Wichita grass covered arbor and houses, Anadarko, Oklahoma. The houses of the Hasinai and Caddo in East Texas were of similar construction. From Earl H. Elam, "The History of the Wichita Indian Confederacy to 1868" (Ph.D. dissertation; Lubbock, Texas, 1971), p. 58. (By permission of the author.)

Indians kept enough seed for two years, lest one crop should be a total failure. Of course, a great part of their food was secured by hunting. Deer and bear were abundant, and hunting parties frequently visited the buffalo range, which was not more than a hundred miles to the west. The Hasinai did not live in large, compact villages similar to the pueblos in Mexico and along the Rio Grande, but rather in hamlets of from seven to fifteen houses divided by woodlands and farms. The diseases and vices of the Europeans took a heavy toll among the Hasinai tribes during the late eighteenth century. Then, when the Anglo-Americans came in the nineteenth century, they drove the Indians from their homes into Central Texas and finally into the Indian Territory. Most of the tribes lost their identity and were referred to by the common appellation "Caddo." Associated with the Caddo in southeast Texas lived the Atakapans, consisting of several small tribes, including the Orcoquisacs and the Bidais. They were hunters, gatherers, and fishermen.

The Karankawa Indians, a small tribe, lived near Matagorda Bay. For their living they depended on the produce of both the sea and the land. To protect themselves from the ever-present mosquitoes, they coated themselves with a mixture of shark, fish, and alligator oils, an effective but unusually foul-smelling repellent. After an initial, peaceful encounter, their relations with the Europeans who came into their midst were usually hostile. They were especially feared for their widely advertised practice of cannibalism, even though the ceremonial type of cannibalism they followed was practiced by most of the Indian tribes of Texas. A few were eventually converted to Christianity or, at least, lived at the Spanish mission, Espíritu Santo, but the large majority was exterminated in wars with the Anglo-Americans during the first half of the nineteenth century.

In south central Texas lived the Tonkawa, a powerful tribe or association of tribes that farmed on a small scale and subsisted mainly on deer and buffalo. They were alternately at peace and at war with the Spaniards during the eighteenth century, and their relations with the Hasinais in the east, the Wichitas and Comanches in the north, and the Apaches in the west were unstable. In the nineteenth century, by the time the Anglo-American colonists arrived, the Tonkawa had been reduced by war and disease to a few hundred, tolerated but generally not trusted by the white frontierspeople. During the last Indian wars in Texas they served well as scouts for the military.

From the Arkansas River in Kansas southward to the vicinity of the present Waco, lived the Wichita tribes. Of these tribes, the Wichita proper (probably identifiable with the Taovayas, or Tawehash of the Spanish era) lived along the Red River and, during the nineteenth century, became talented horse thieves preying along the entire border.

The Tawakoni and Waco tribes lived in north central Texas and belonged to Texas until they were expelled in 1859. In some respects they lived much like their Caddoan kinspeople to the east; in other respects they were like the Indians of the plains. They farmed to a limited extent and from time to time made hunting trips into the plains. They were proud and preferred death to imprisonment.

When the Spaniards first came to Texas, all of the western part of the state from the Panhandle to the Rio Grande seems to have been dominated by the Apache Indians. Probably the Querechos, whom Coronado met on the plains in 1541, were Apaches. They moved with the buffalos, and the herds supplied all their wants. When they struck camp, they packed their belongings on the backs of dogs. The Apaches began to harass San Antonio immediately after that outpost was established in 1718, and their raids continued until late in the nineteenth century.

Among the Apache tribes in Texas were the Lipan, the Natagés, and the Mescalero. Many military expeditions were sent against them, and if we are to believe the reports of the white people, large numbers of Indians were slain; but always enough were left to return and renew the depredations. Missionary efforts among them during the eighteenth century were unsuccessful as were later efforts to exterminate them by aligning against them the friendly tribes of the north. The history of the Jicarilla and the other Apache tribes that frequented the northwestern part of Texas at an early date is mainly linked with that of New Mexico.

Either an Apache tribe or a tribe associated with the Apaches was the Jumano, found by the Spaniards in the seventeenth century in the vicinity of present-day Presidio eastward to the mouth of the Concho. When the Spaniards first knew them, they were enemies of the Apaches and received the white people kindly. Later, however, they became allies of the Apaches and enemies of the Spaniards. The Taovayas (Tawehash) along the Red River also came to be called by the name Jumano, but it may well be doubted that they had any connection with the Jumanos of West Texas.

During later historic times the Great Plains of Texas and a part of the adjacent territory were occupied by the Comanche Indians. They came from the north in the early eighteenth century and drove a wedge between the Apache country in the west and the Caddoan country in the east which extended to the vicinity of Austin and San Antonio. There were several Comanche tribes, or Comanche bands, with the status of independent tribes. Of these tribes or bands the better known were the Penatekas, or Honey-eaters, in the south; the Kotsotekas, or Buffalo-eaters, and Nokonies, along the Red and Canadian rivers; the Yamparikas, or Root-eaters, along the Arkansas; and the Kwahadis of the High

Plains. The Penatekas lived in Texas, and the other Comanche divisions either lived in Texas or visited it from time to time. The Kiowas, loyal allies of the Comanches, occasionally came along with these northern bands.

The Comanches were a nomadic people who never planted crops of any kind. Although each tribe or band regarded a given region as its home and always returned to it after its wanderings, the Comanches never remained for long in any one place. They would break camp on the slightest excuse or on no excuse at all. If a prominent person died, or if an epidemic caused several deaths at a certain camp, the site would be abandoned at once, and the Indians would never return there—a practice that, in spite of its obvious inconveniences, no doubt checked

A great part of Texas was once Comanche country. Pictured here is Quanah Parker, one of the last Comanche war chiefs and the son of Chief Nocona and Cynthia Ann Parker, a captive white woman. (Bureau of American Ethnology)

Comanche camp in 1872. (Bureau of American Ethnology)

the ravages of diseases. More modern people fumigate after an epidemic; the Comanches moved. Superb horsemen and warriors, the Comanches harried the settlements of Texas and other northern Mexican provinces during the Spanish and Mexican regimes and made life unsafe for white people on the Anglo-American frontier until 1875.

## SELECTED BIBLIOGRAPHY

The foremost bibliographies pertaining to Texas are Thomas W. Streeter, *Bibliography of Texas, 1795–1845* (2 vols., Cambridge, Mass., 1956); E. W. Winkler, *Check List of Texas Imprints, 1846–1876* (Austin, 1949); E. W. Winkler and Llerena Friend, *Check List of Texas Imprints, 1861–1876* (Austin, 1963); Seymour V. Connor, "A Preliminary Guide to Archives of Texas," *Southwestern Historical Quarterly,* LX, 255–334; Chester V. Kielman, *University of Texas Archives* (Austin, 1967).

It is well to be acquainted with *Resources of Texas Libraries* by Edward G. Holley and Donald D. Hendrick (Austin, 1968). The most comprehensive work on the history of Texas is the *Handbook of Texas,* edited by Walter Prescott Webb and H. Bailey Carroll (vols. I and II, Austin, 1952), and Eldon S. Branda (vol. III, Austin, 1977). *The Texas Almanac,* published biennially by the *Dallas News,* is a dependable reference.

The greatest collection of writings on Texas history is the *Quarterly of the Texas State Historical Association* (I–XV, Austin) from 1897 to 1912; and its successor, the *Southwestern Historical Quarterly,* beginning in July 1912. Much Texas material may be found also in the *Mississippi Valley Historical Review* (and its successor, the *Journal of American History*) from 1914; the *Journal of Southern History* from 1934; the *Southwestern Social Science Quarterly* from 1920; the *American West* from 1963; and *Texana,* a quarterly journal of Texas history published since 1962 in Waco. Some regional publications contain a great deal of Texas history: the *East Texas Historical Journal* from 1963; *Texas Gulf Coast Historical Publications* from 1957; the *Panhandle-Plains Historical Review* from 1927; and the *West Texas Historical Association Year Book* from 1925.

On natural resources, useful are William C. Pool, *A Historical Atlas of Texas* (Austin, 1975); Harry C. Oberholser, *The Bird Life of Texas* (2 vols., Austin, 1974); Walter Keene Ferguson, *Geology and Politics in Texas, 1845–1909* (Austin, 1969); Jim Bones and John Graves, *Texas Heartland: A Hill Country Year* (College Station, Tex., 1975); Pauline Robertson, *Panhandle Pilgrimage* (Austin, 1978); and Terry Jordan, "Pioneer Evaluation of Vegetation in Frontier Texas," *Southwestern Historical Quarterly,* LXXVI, 233–254. Older but valuable are Elmer H. Johnson, *The Natural Regions of Texas* (University of Texas *Bulletin,* no. 3113, Austin, 1931); Frederick W. Simonds, *The Geography of Texas* (Boston, 1914); W. T. Carter, *The Soils of Texas* (College Station, Tex., 1931); W. A. Silveus, *Texas Grasses* (San Antonio, 1933); and Roy Bedicheck, *Adventures with A Texas Naturalist* (New York, 1947).

A basic source for Texas archeology is Dee Ann Suhm and Alex D. Krieger, *An Introductory Handbook of Texas Archeology,* Texas Archeological Society *Bulletin,* XXV (Austin, 1954). Useful also is E. H. Sellards, *Early Man in America: A Study in Pre-History* (Austin, 1952); T. N. Campbell, "A List of Radiocarbon Dates from Archeological Sites in Texas," *Bulletin of the Texas Archeological Society,* 1959, 311–320; and Jane Holden Kelley, "Comments on the Archeology of the Llano

Estacado," *Bulletin of the Texas Archeological Society,* 1964, 1–17. An authoritative book on archeology and Indians, containing a comprehensive bibliography, is *The Indians of Texas* by W. W. Newcomb, Jr. (Austin, 1961). Rich in source material is Dorman H. Winfrey and James M. Day (eds.), *The Indian Papers of Texas and the Southwest, 1825–1916* (5 vols., Austin, 1966). Some histories of Indian tribes are: Mildred P. Mayhall, *The Kiowas* (Norman, Okla., 1962); Rupert N. Richardson, *The Comanche Barrier to South Plains Settlement* (Glendale, Calif., 1933); Ernest Wallace and E. A. Hoebel, *The Comanches, Lords of the South Plains* (Norman, Okla., 1952); and Charles L. Sonnichsen, *The Mescalero Apaches* (Norman, Okla., 1973).

Chapter Two

# EXPLORATION
# AND OCCUPATION
# 1519–1763

## SPANISH EXPLORATION

Following the exploration of Columbus and his captains, the Spaniards killed or enslaved the natives and established colonies on several islands of the West Indies, including Haiti, Jamaica, Puerto Rico, and Cuba. From bases on these islands, several expeditions explored the regions bordering on the Gulf of Mexico. In 1513 Ponce de León searched for both a fountain of youth and Indian slaves along the coast of Florida, and in 1519 Hernando Cortéz defeated the Aztecs, occupied their principal city, and confiscated their rich supplies of gold and silver. Simultaneously, Texas came within the orbit of Spain's interest. Commissioned by the governor of Jamaica to explore the lands beyond those claimed by Ponce de León and to search for a strait that linked the Atlantic and Pacific oceans, Alonso Álvarez de Piñeda in 1519 mapped the coast of the Gulf of Mexico from Florida to Vera Cruz. Piñeda spent forty days at the mouth of the Rio Grande, his "River of Palms," and recommended that a settlement be planted there. This goal was not attained, however, until more than two centuries later.

The first Spaniards to enter the interior of Texas were Alvar Núñez Cabeza de Vaca and three companions, survivors of the ill-fated Pánfilo de Narváez expedition, which had landed on the west coast of Florida in 1528. Having despaired of finding rumored riches, the 242 stranded survivors, in five overcrowded, crude boats, tried to reach Pánuco by sailing westward along the coast. The party was shipwrecked in November on the coast of Texas, apparently on Galveston Island, and only a few escaped from the sea. After nearly six years of servitude to the Indians, four survivors, including De Vaca and a black man named Estevanico, by persistence and ingenuity, managed to escape into the interior. Thence, after wandering many hundreds of miles, probably by the sites of San Antonio and Presidio, they arrived on May 18, 1536, at the northern outpost of Culiacán, near the Gulf of California.

The tales related by De Vaca created great excitement in Mexico. Although he had not seen them, he had heard from the Indians of large cities in the north, where there was gold and silver in abundance. Viceroy Antonio de Mendoza soon dispatched Fray Marcos de Niza, with Estevanico as a guide, to find the fabled Seven Cities of Cíbola. Upon receiving a report from Fray Marcos that he had indeed seen from afar a great city, Mendoza then commissioned Francisco Vásquez de Coronado, governor of Nueva Galicia on the northwestern frontier, to penetrate the mysterious north country. Starting from Compostela in February 1540, Coronado had in his command three hundred horsemen, seventy footmen, and more than one thousand Indians.

Instead of the splendid Seven Cities of Cíbola, which the conqueror had hoped to find, he reached, near the present Arizona–New Mexico line, humble pueblos inhabited by hostile Indians. Nor did he find anything precious at Tiguex on the Rio Grande, a few miles north of Albuquerque, where he spent the winter of 1540–1541. When spring came, he set out in search of Quivira, a gilded land that an Indian slave told him lay somewhere to the east. He spent many days wandering over the treeless and level plains of Texas and probably crossed Palo Duro Canyon. After seventy-seven days of marching across a land where he had seen "nothing but cows and the sky," he found Quivira—several Wichita Indian villages of grass houses in central Kansas. The chief wore a copper plate around his neck, but there was no gold. Thoroughly discouraged, Coronado returned by way of Tiguex to Mexico and reported to King Charles I that he did not consider the country he had explored of sufficient value to warrant its being occupied by Spaniards. He had found no precious metals, and the natives were either nomads, who lived in lodges make of skins, or semisedentary barbarians, who lived miserably in little villages. His report destroyed for many years to come the interest of the Spaniards in the great northern interior.

While Coronado was searching the southwestern United States for fabulous cities that did not exist, another Spaniard, Hernando de Soto, with about six hundred men was exploring for wealth the region north of the Gulf of Mexico with no better success. After De Soto's death, at the Mississippi River in May 1542, the expedition under the command of Luis de Moscoso de Alvarado set out by land for Mexico. After passing through the piney woods of the Tejas in eastern Texas, it marched for many days through a very poor and thinly populated country, probably as far west as the Brazos River in the Western Cross Timbers. Unable to get in touch with Coronado, of whom they had heard from the Indians, and beset by a lack of food and inhospitable natives, Moscoso and his followers returned to the Mississippi. Here they built seven crude boats and on July 3, 1543, began floating downstream. Eleven weeks later, after having been forced ashore near the present site of Beaumont, where they caulked their disabled ships with cakes of oil that had oozed to the surface, the 311 survivors reached Pánuco. Like Coronado, they had found nothing in the interior that made them wish to return. For half a century thereafter the Spaniards gave little thought to the region now known as New Mexico and Texas.

During the seventeenth century the history of Texas was closely linked with that of New Mexico. By 1563 the frontier of New Spain had been extended to Santa Barbara, on the headwaters of the Conchos, a stream that flows northward into the Rio Grande. Zealous Franciscans laboring in that vicinity heard of Indians living in the upper valley of the Rio Grande who lived like those in Mexico. Accompanied by military commands, they visited the country, and, as a result of their reports, in 1598 Juan de Oñate established a Spanish settlement on the Rio Grande, a few miles north of present-day Santa Fé. Three years later, while searching for Coronado's Quivira, Oñate led an expedition across the Panhandle of Texas. In 1609 Santa Fé had its beginning. This northward advance was followed by the establishment of several missions along the Rio Grande. From one of the missions near present-day Albuquerque, Father Juan de Salas in 1629 accompanied some visiting Jumano Indians southeastward nearly three hundred miles to their village in Texas, possibly on the Pecos or Concho River. Then, in the early 1650s two other expeditions from New Mexico visited and traded with the Jumano in that area. In 1659 a mission was founded on the site of modern Juarez at El Paso del Norte. After the Indian revolt in New Mexico in 1680, the retreating Spaniards and friendly Indians established a pueblo and Mission Corpus Christi de la Isleta, a few miles east of El Paso where the village of Ysleta now is. This was the first permanent European settlement within the present boundaries of Texas.

From El Paso, the Spaniards attempted to expand their missionary activities eastward. In 1683 they established a group of missions and pueblos near the junction of the Rio Grande and the Conchos River in the vicinity of present-day Presidio. Also that year, emissaries of the Jumano Indians, a friendly tribe along the Concho River which the Spaniards had visited, came to El Paso asking for missionaries. The emissaries did not explain, however, that the real reason for the request was to obtain aid against the encroaching Apaches. In response to the

*From Robert S. Weddle,* The San Saba Mission, Spanish Pivot in Texas *(Austin, 1964), p. 4. (By permission of the author and publisher, the University of Texas Press.)*

request, the governor of New Mexico sent Father Nicolás López and a military escort of about thirty soldiers commanded by Captain Juan Domínguez de Mendoza, who thirty years before had been to the Concho country. Starting from El Paso in 1683, the expedition went by the way of present Presidio and Horsehead Crossing on the Pecos. At a site probably on the San Saba River west of present-day Menard, where they arrived in February 1684, Mendoza and López built a combination chapel and fort they called San Clemente. During a six-week sojourn there, the soldiers gathered an abundant number of buffalo hides, and the two priests baptized many Indians. Harassed by Apache Indians, however, Mendoza and López returned to Mexico and sought authorization to take a stronger force and plant a mission in the Jumano country. The petition was never granted, for at about that time reports began to reach New Spain that the French had established a settlement on the Gulf Coast, a flagrant violation of Spanish claims. These intruders had to be found and expelled, and toward that end the best efforts of New Spain were directed.

## FRENCH INTRUSION: LA SALLE

The Frenchman whose settlement in Texas provoked Spain's ire was Robert Cavelier, sieur de La Salle, a trader from Canada. In 1682 La Salle had descended the Mississippi to its mouth and claimed for his king all the country that it drained, even "to the mouth of the River of Palms" (Rio Grande). Returning to France, La Salle obtained from Louis XIV a commission to found a colony at the mouth of the Mississippi as a base for controlling the trade along the river and extending it into the rich mining area of northern Mexico. On August 1, 1684, he set sail with 280 persons in four ships to carry out his plan. Missing the mouth of the Mississippi, perhaps intentionally, La Salle landed at Matagorda Bay on the Texas coast in February 1685. He erected a crude stockade, Fort St. Louis, on Garcitas Creek, in the vicinity of present-day Vanderbilt, and set out to explore the country. After a six-month journey to the south and west, he returned (with only 8 of the 30 men who had started) to find that he was stranded. Not one of his four ships was left. The *St. François* had been lost to Spanish corsairs, the *Amiable* had grounded on the shoals of Matagorda Bay, the *Belle* had wrecked on Palacios Bay, and the *Joli* had sailed back to France. Furthermore, the first crop had failed, the supplies were gone, the Karankawa Indians were making life unsafe, and of the 180 people left behind when the *Joli* sailed for France only 45 were still alive. La Salle thus determined to find the Mississippi and go to Canada for help.

On his third expedition (his second toward the east) La Salle was assassinated on March 20, 1687, by one of a group of dissentients, somewhere in the piney woods of East Texas between present-day Navasota and Jacksonville. The survivors soon scattered. The assassins, after two of the leaders had been murdered in a quarrel among themselves, went to live with the Indians, and one, Jean L'Archeveque, eventually settled in Santa Fé. Six not involved in the conspiracy, led by Henri Joutel, La Salle's faithful lieutenant, finally made their way to Canada. From there, Joutel went to France where he wrote an account of his experiences and tried unsuccessfully to persuade Louis XIV to send aid to the ill-fated colony in Texas.

Meanwhile, Fort St. Louis had been destroyed, and its inhabitants had been slain by or had gone to live with the Indians. Eventually, some became servants in the home of the viceroy at Mexico City, and a few returned by way of Spain to France. Through French pirates whom they happened to capture, the Spaniards learned of La Salle's establishment some six months after it was founded. Several expeditions by both land and sea, however, failed to discover the intruders. At last, on his fourth expedition into Texas, Governor Alonso de León of Coahuila, marching from the vicinity of Monclova and using as guides a Frenchman captured near the Rio Grande and Indians with whom other Frenchmen had lived, reached the ruins of Fort St. Louis on April 22, 1689. Afterward, De León found two of La Salle's men living among the Indians and from them learned the sad history of the colony.

## THE FIRST MISSIONS IN EAST TEXAS

Although fate had removed the French menace from the Gulf Coast, thoughtful and patriotic Spaniards realized that Spain's claim to the region would always be disputed until possession was taken of the area. On his return to Mexico, De León sent to the viceroy a glowing report of the country of the Tejas. The land was fertile; the climate salubrious; and the people were more highly civilized than most primitive groups. Spain should occupy the country at once. Father Damian Massanet, who had accompanied De León and had visited with a Tejas chief, was even more eager for the Spaniards to move into the region. He had promised the Tejas chief that he would return. Thus, the priest and the soldier made a joint petition asking the viceroy, the Count of Galve, to authorize and support a missionary expedition to the Tejas.

Their petition having been officially approved, Father Massanet, accompanied by three other priests, and De León, with a military escort of more than a hundred soldiers, set out from Monclova for Texas in late March 1690. The Tejas chief, with a welcoming party of fourteen Indians, met them at the Trinity, and on May 22, 1690, they arrived at the principal village of the Nabedache, one of the tribes of the Hasinai confederacy. Fields of corn, beans, and melons gave the Spaniards confidence in the value of the country, and the chief demonstrated Indian hospitality by serving his guests tamales and mush. Twelve days later the Spaniards celebrated mass and sang *Te Deum Laudamus* in the first mission in the land of the Tejas—San Francisco de los Tejas, located a few miles west of the Neches River, near the present-day village of Weches in Houston County. On the next day De León and Father Massanet began their homeward trek, leaving behind three priests and three soldiers to man this remote post in the land of the Tejas against further French intrusion.

In 1691 Domingo Terán de los Rios, who had been commissioned as governor of the new province of Texas and Coahuila, with orders to explore and establish additional missions in Texas, was accompanied by Father Massanet and nine priests on a second expedition to the Tejas, where one of the priests had already founded a second small mission, Santísimo Nombre de María, about five miles east of Mission San Francisco on the Neches River. Affairs at the mission were going badly, however. An epidemic had killed many of the Indians, and a priest had died; drought had destroyed the crops; and the Indians had grown first indifferent, then hostile, and in January 1692 Santa María was abandoned.

For several months, Terán explored eastward as far as western Louisiana or Arkansas but, finding no evidence of French in the area, left for Mexico, leaving behind only the stouthearted Massanet, two companions, and a guard of nine soldiers. From Monclova in June 1693, Terán sent Gregorio de Salinas Varona to San Francisco de los Tejas with food and equipment, but Varona considered the cause hopeless and recommended that East Texas be abandoned. By then Father Massanet agreed that it would take the strong arm of the military to sustain the mission, and on October 25, 1693, even before word had been received authorizing the abandonment of the place, the Spaniards set fire to their mission and stole away.

The efforts of De León, Terán, and Massanet had not been altogether in vain. They had acquainted the Spaniards with the geography and the Indians of Texas, and their failure proved that missions in that country could not succeed unless sustained by presidios and settlements.

## OCCUPATION OF EAST TEXAS

Although the administration of New Spain had abandoned the Tejas country, the priests and the captains of the frontier did not forget the land of sturdy oaks and stately pines. One of the priests, Father Francisco

Hidalgo, spent most of his time on the frontier of Coahuila, hoping anxiously for an opportunity to return to Texas. The dedicated missionary had to wait many years.

For a decade after the failure of La Salle's enterprise, France did not press its claim to the lower Mississippi Valley. Costly wars absorbed the energy of Louis XIV. When the Peace of Ryswick in 1696 gave him a breathing spell and word came that the English were threatening to take the Gulf country, the Grand Monarch moved with energy. His expedition under Pierre Le Moyne, sieur d'Iberville, sailed from France to occupy Pensacola Bay. But the Spaniards, aroused by reports of renewed French activity, beat him there. The French expedition then sailed westward and established a post at Biloxi in April 1699. Three years later the French founded Mobile.

In 1712 the crown granted the colony of Louisiana to Antoine Crozat as a commercial monopoly, and Antoine de la Mothe Cadillac became its first proprietary governor. Meanwhile, Philip of Anjou, grandson of Louis XIV, had ascended the throne of Spain, and the Spanish government had given its tacit consent to French occupancy of the Gulf region. Thenceforth Spanish relations with the French were cordial, but the Spaniards were loath to engage in international trade. This trade Crozat sought, and in 1713 he was planning to send an overland expedition to New Spain when he received a strange letter from a former missionary to the Tejas, Fray Francisco Hidalgo at Mission San Juan Bautista south of the Rio Grande near present-day Eagle Pass, suggesting that the French help with missionary work among the Tejas. Cadillac saw in the invitation a possible opportunity for the expansion of trade. Accordingly, he commissioned the Canadian-born Captain Luis Juchereau de St. Denis, a successful trader and commander of a military post, who had been in Louisiana since 1699 and was fluent in Spanish and several Indian languages, to go to the country of the Tejas, find Father Hidalgo, and inaugurate a trading program with the Spaniards on the northern frontier of Mexico. St. Denis, with a large amount of trade goods, proceeded to a village of the Natchitoches on the Red River, where in October 1713 he built a storehouse and then traded leisurely with several Indian tribes and inquired among the Tejas about Father Hidalgo. During the next summer he made his way with a small party, including a survivor of the La Salle expedition, across Texas to San Juan Bautista on the Rio Grande, arriving there on July 18, 1714.

St. Denis's coming excited and alarmed the Spaniards. There were positive orders, without exceptions, against the introduction of foreign goods or the admission of foreigners into New Spain. Both St. Denis and Father Hidalgo were called to Mexico City for explanations. They fared well, nevertheless. The Frenchman, meanwhile, had managed to win a promise of marriage from María Ramón, the granddaughter of Captain Diego Ramón, the commander of the presidio at San Juan Bautista. In Mexico City, after persuading the viceroy to establish missions in East Texas, he obtained a contract to serve as guide to the Spaniards who went there. Father Hidalgo received permission to return to the Tejas. Once again the encroachment of the French had spurred the Spaniards into action, and they were now convinced that missions among the Tejas must be sustained by forts and civil settlements.

To guard the Spanish claim to Texas, the officials in Mexico City, in September 1715, named Domingo Ramón, son of Captain Diego Ramón and the uncle of St. Denis's fiancée, to recruit and lead an expedition composed of civilians, soldiers, and missionaries. While preparations were underway, St. Denis, who had been granted Spanish citizenship, returned to San Juan Bautista and married María. In the party that arrived in the country of the Tejas under the command of Captain Domingo Ramón in June 1716, there were twenty-five soldiers, no less than thirty civilian men and married women, nine priests, St. Denis, and two other Frenchmen. The mission work was divided between the two noted Franciscan missionary colleges, or seminaries, located at Zacatecas and at Querétaro. Fray Isidro Felix Espinosa was in charge of the Querétarans. Father Hidalgo was a Querétaran.

Like that accorded to De León and Massanet more than a quarter of a century before, the reception by the Hasinai was most cordial. On July 3, 1716, the San Francisco mission of 1690 was reestablished but renamed Nuestro Padre San Francisco de los Tejas. It was fitting that Father Hidalgo was placed in charge of this mission. During the next few days three other missions were established: Nuestra Señora de la Purísima Concepción among the Hasinai on the Angelina River about fifteen miles west of the present city of Nacogdoches, Nuestra Señora de Guadalupe de los Nacogdoches at Nacogdoches, and San José de los Nazonis near the north line of Nacogdoches County and two and one-half miles north of the present village of Cushing.

To offset French influence (but at the suggestion of St. Denis, who wanted the missions at sites suitable for French trade), Ramón in December 1716 founded San Miguel de Linares de los Adaes at the site of modern Robeline, Louisiana, about eighteen miles southwest of the French post at Natchitoches. Then, before the end of the year, he established Nuestra Señora de los Dolores among the Ais Indians, at modern San Augustine, Texas. This mission served as headquarters for the three Zacatecan missions, the other two being Guadalupe and San Miguel de Linares. Thus, by the close of 1716, the Spaniards had established six missions, five extending in a line from the Neches River to Adaes, almost within the sound of a cannon shot of the French outpost on the Red River. As quarters for his soldiers, Ramón built Presidio Nuestra Señora de los Dolores de los Tejas on the east bank of the Neches River, across from the Tejas mission.

In summary, St. Denis's motive was commercial rather than political. He sought profitable trade relations with the northern settlements of Mexico and, when he failed, assisted the Spanish in establishing posts where, because of the great distance from the settlements of northern Mexico, the residents would look to the French for their supplies.

Father Antonio de Buenaventura Olivares who, while with the Ramón expedition, had done missionary work among some Indians along the San Antonio River, petitioned for a mission in that area. When confronted with Father Olivares's petition and a request for supplies and reinforcements for East Texas, officials at Mexico City assigned the tasks to Martín de Alarcón, governor of Coahuila and Texas. The site selected for the support station was at present-day San Antonio. There on May 1, 1718, Alarcón founded Mission San Antonio de Valero (its chapel later becoming known as the Alamo), which was entrusted to Father Olivares, and on May 5, about one mile to the north, established Presidio San Antonio de Béxar. The ten families that settled around the presidio constituted the Villa de Béxar, a village destined to become the most important Spanish settlement in Texas.

Fortunately for Spain, the halfway post was established none too soon. The Spaniards in East Texas were desperately in need of supplies, the Indians were refusing to submit to mission life, and France and Spain were at war. The French in Louisiana learned of the war long before the news reached the Spaniards in Mexico. By order of Governor Celeron de Bienville, Corporal M. Blondel with six soldiers from Natchitoches in June 1719 went to the Adaes mission on reconnaissance. The French took the mission and the two residents present, a soldier and a lay brother, but in the confusion caused by the squawking of the excited chickens, the lay brother escaped and fled hurriedly to the Dolores mission, where he reported that the French were invading with a large force. Thereupon, the residents of Dolores rushed westward to the presidio where Captain Ramón was still in command. Since his position appeared untenable against a superior force of French and Indians, who likely would join the French, Ramón decided that the Spaniards should again abandon East Texas. In October the caravan of motley refugees straggled into San Antonio. The French "invasion," or "Chicken War," had revealed that the Spaniards' claim to the country of the Tejas had not yet been established.

Convinced that vigorous action was needed, the viceroy appointed the Marquis de San Miguel de Aguayo, a wealthy citizen of Coahuila who had offered to drive the French out of Texas at his own expense, as governor and captain-general of the provinces of Coahuila and Texas and commissioned him to recruit a force sufficient to drive the French from Texas and to reestablish the missions there. In the early spring of 1721 Aguayo set out for Texas with five hundred men, five thousand horses and mules, and large herds of cattle and sheep. At San Antonio he found that some refugee priests from East Texas had dedicated a new mission, San José y San Miguel de Aguayo. Located on the San Antonio River about five miles from San Antonio de Valero, this soon became the most successful mission in Texas. Accompanied from San Antonio by the friars who had fled from East Texas in 1719, Aguayo, because of floods, did not reach Tejas country until mid-July. The Indians there were friendly and welcomed the Spaniards with evident delight.

St. Denis, who had escaped from Mexico City where he was being detained for contraband trade and who was now commander at Natchitoches, met Aguayo on July 13 and informed him that, inasmuch as France and Spain had made peace, he would withdraw the French forces to Natchitoches. Aguayo reestablished all the abandoned missions (San Francisco a few miles farther east and renamed San Francisco de los Neches) and turned them over to the churchmen with impressive ceremonies. Then, in spite of St. Denis's protests, he established at Los Adaes, in the autumn of 1721, the presidio of Nuestra Señora del Pilár and left in charge a garrison of a hundred men, equipped with six brass fieldpieces and plenty of powder and shot. This place, with its garrison, mission, and small civil settlement, became the capital of Texas. Here at Los Adaes and the neighboring French post of Natchitoches, the prongs of empire touched. The Spanish advance toward the northeast was ended, as was the French penetration westward from the Mississippi.

In the spring of 1722 Aguayo went to the site of La Salle's Fort St. Louis, where he had sent Domingo Ramón with a detachment of soldiers, and directed the construction of a mission, Nuestra Señora del Espíritu Santo Zuñiga, and a presidio, Nuestra Señora de Loreto, both commonly called La Bahía. When he returned to Coahuila, Aguayo left behind 269 soldiers, quartered in presidios at San Antonio, on the Angelina, at Los Adaes, and at La Bahía. Each of the four presidios marked a mission center and altogether they guarded ten missions. As a result of the Aguayo expedition, Spain's claim to Texas was never again challenged by the French.

But the complete and adequate establishment left by Aguayo was not permitted to remain undisturbed for long. King Philip V directed the viceroy of New Spain, the Marquis de Casafuerte, to make reforms in the interest of economy. Consequently, the viceroy sent General Pedro de Rivera y Villalon to make a complete inspection of the frontier posts and recommendations for reforms, keeping in mind the necessity for economizing. As a result of Rivera's recommendation in 1727, the number of soldiers at Los Adaes was cut from one hundred to sixty, and the presidio on the Angelina River was abolished. The abandonment of the presidio led to the removal (rather than the consolidation recommended by Rivera) of three missions, San Francisco, Concepción, and San José, in 1730 to the Colorado River and in the following year to San Antonio. As Spanish influence declined, French influence increased. To Rivera's recommendations also must be charged many of the losses and sufferings endured by the people of San Antonio from raids by the Apaches. At the very time the beleaguered community needed more soldiers to protect its expanding settlements, the military force was reduced.

Franco-Spanish relations on the border of Texas, from Rivera's visit to the cession of Louisiana to Spain in 1762, were quiet and peaceful, generally speaking. Representatives of both nations generally accepted in practice the Arroyo Hondo, a small stream running between Los Adaes and Natchitoches, as the dividing line between the two empires. In the contest for the Indian trade, the French were more successful. By means of the Nassonite post, established by Bénard de la Harpe in 1719 on the Red River a few miles northwest of the present-day Texarkana, the French controlled the Cadodacho and associated tribes in that vicinity. Likewise, they appropriated the trade of the Wichita and the Tawakoni in northern Texas and of the Tonkawa farther south. About 1750 the Taovayas located their villages on the Red River, north of the present town of Nocona, and this place became a center of French influence. As early as 1730 French traders from Louisiana crossed the Sabine River and traded among the Orcoquizac on the Texas coast. Spurred by this threat, the Spaniards in 1756 established the presidio of San Agustín de Ahumada and a mission, Nuestra Señora de la Luz del Orcoquisac, near the mouth of the Trinity in the general vicinity of modern Anahuac and maintained them for about fifteen years. The place was commonly referred to as El Orcoquisac.

**EFFORTS AT EXPANSION**

The Spanish occupation of the Gulf region along the lower Trinity River in 1756 was, in a way, only one part of a general program of expansion in practically all of northern New Spain. These efforts at expansion were prompted by a combination of forces, both external and internal. Spain's northern outposts were threatened all along its frontiers. The French from Canada and Louisiana were edging into Texas and across the Great Plains toward Santa Fé; the English had founded Georgia and were

Mission and (restored) Presidio La Bahía, Goliad. Before he withdrew from the Presidio in one of the bloodiest battles in Texas history, James Fannin buried the ancient hand-poured cannon (shown below) to prevent its being taken by the Mexicans. On the prairie a few miles away, Fannin's force of some four hundred troops was captured and later shot by Mexican firing squads. (Texas Highway Department)

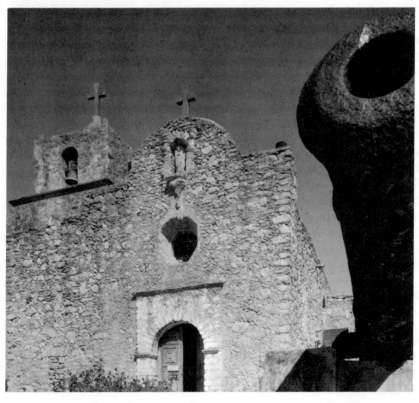

threatening Spanish supremacy in Florida; a number of Indian tribes were menacing the settlements on the frontier; and reports of the discovery of precious metals in the Apache country north of San Antonio made the occupation of that region seem imperative. In Texas, the expansion movement got under way about 1745 and continued, with various interruptions, until the cession of Louisiana to Spain by France in 1762. In addition to the establishment of a post at the mouth of the Trinity River, which has been mentioned previously, there were three other areas of expansion activity: Nuevo Santander, on the lower Rio Grande; on the San Gabriel River, northeast of San Antonio; and on the San Saba and upper Nueces rivers, northwest of San Antonio.

In their northward advance in New Spain, the Spaniards had bypassed the vast coastal area from Tampico to the La Bahía post and the region extending inland to the San Antonio River, San Juan Bautista, Monclova, and Monterrey, in some places three hundred miles. It was occupied by remnants of various tribes and by Indian renegades. The aggressive activity by the English in Georgia and during the War of Austrian Succession aroused fear among Spanish officials that Britain might attempt to plant a settlement somewhere on this nine hundred miles of unguarded coast. The task of subduing the natives and colonizing the region was assigned in 1746 to José de Escandón, a veteran Indian fighter, who had established Spanish authority in the Sierra Gorda hinterland.

After almost two years of exploration, conquest, and preparations, in 1749 Escandón left Querétaro for the region, which had been renamed Nuevo Santander, with more than three thousand settlers, soldiers, and priests. Beginning with the village of Camargo and Reynosa south of the Rio Grande, by 1755 he had placed almost six thousand people in twenty-three settlements, two of which, Dolores and Laredo, were north of the Rio Grande. Dolores, in the present Zapata County, was soon abandoned, but Laredo's population grew quite rapidly. Meanwhile, the Franciscan missionaries of the College of Zacatecas had founded fifteen missions. Of later significance, most of the land between the Rio Grande and the Nueces River was either granted to or appropriated by Spanish ranchers who lived south of the Rio Grande.

Modern Goliad also had its beginning with Escandón. In 1726 Mission La Bahía del Espíritu Santo de Zuñiga and Presidio Nuestra Señora de Loreto, which had been founded by Aguayo, were moved to the Guadalupe River in the vicinity of present-day Victoria. Because of the unhealthy climate and the inability to irrigate the surrounding lands, Escandón had the mission and presidio moved in 1749 to the San Antonio River at the present site of Goliad. Although many miles in the interior, the new establishment continued to be known simply as La Bahía. In

1754, as a result of rivalry between Zacatecan and Querétaran missionaries, Mission Nuestra Señora del Rosario was founded for the Karankawas, about three miles to the southwest. Around these establishments, which were under the jurisdiction of Nuevo Santander until 1755 when the boundary was reset at the Nueces River, grew up one of three principal settlements in Spanish Texas, La Bahía, or Goliad.

Simultaneously, 150 miles northeast of San Antonio, other Spaniards were attempting, less successfully, to expand the mission system. Along the San Gabriel, called San Xavier by the Spanish, near modern Rockdale, lived the Tonkawas and a conglomeration of other small tribes and remnants of tribes, referred to as *Ranchería Grande*. Harassed by both the Apaches and the Comanches, who were taking possession of the Great Plains, in 1745 the Tonkawas asked the Spaniards to send missionaries and soldiers to the San Gabriel. The next year Father Mariano Francisco de los Dolores y Viana petitioned the authorities to approve the request and, without waiting for the answer, began working with the Tonkawas. Between 1748, when the viceroy gave the authorization, and 1751, the Spaniards established along the San Gabriel, in the vicinity of the present towns of Rockdale and San Gabriel, three Franciscan missions (San Francisco Xavier de Horcasitas, San Ildefonso, and Nuestra Señora de la Candelaria) and Presidio San Francisco Xavier, all generally referred to as San Xavier. They were never free of turmoil and strife. Unfaithful neophytes, smallpox, measles, drought, hostile Apaches, and the French trade beset the area. Constant friction between the presidio commander, Captain Felipe de Rábago y Terán, and the priests culminated in the murder of Fray Juan José Ganzabál. Rábago was charged with the murder but never convicted. In the confusion one mission was abandoned, and in the summer of 1755 the new military commander, without authorization, moved the establishment to the upper San Marcos River. Mission San Francisco Xavier, however, was temporarily relocated on the Guadalupe River near present-day New Braunfels, and early in 1757 the entire properties of the San Xavier missions were transferred to Father Alonso Giraldo de Terreros for a new mission to be established on the San Saba River.

The San Xavier enterprise was followed by the most ambitious and the most ill-fated mission extension program undertaken by the Spaniards in Texas—the San Sabá post for the Lipan Apaches. Lipan hostility toward the Spaniards dated back to the early entradas into the Concho River country. Following the founding of San Antonio in 1718, marauding became a regular occurrence. The Spaniards' retaliatory expeditions never resulted in more than temporary relief. The missionaries, particularly the veteran Francisco Hidalgo, urged the substitution of the gospel for the sword. In 1745, the Lipans, hard pressed by the Comanches to their north, were at San Antonio asking for a mission. Four years later a peace treaty was negotiated at San Antonio, and subsequently a mission for the supplicants was built in Coahuila. In 1755, after the Apaches had destroyed the mission, because, the priest argued, it was not conveniently located, Don Pedro Romero de Terreros, a wealthy mine-owner philanthropist, offered to finance a mission for three years for the Apaches in the San Saba region, provided that his cousin, Father Alonso de Terreros, would be placed in charge, that the government would bear all military expenses, that after three years the missions would be operated by the government, and that he would have a monopoly over the mining rights in the area. On May 18, 1756, the viceroy ordered the establishment of a post in accordance with this proposal.

In the spring of 1757 Colonel Diego Ortiz Parrilla, in command of nearly 100 soldiers, 237 Indian servants, women, and children, and 6 Franciscan priests headed by Father Terreros, founded Mission San Sabá de la Santa Cruz, Presidio San Luis de las Amarillas, and a civil settlement on the San Saba River, near present-day Menard. The Apaches came in swarms that summer but never found it convenient to stay. The alliance of the Spaniards with the Apaches had antagonized the Comanches and their Wichita allies, who with an estimated 600 to 2,000 warriors, attacked the mission in March 1758, killing 10 persons, among them Father Terreros and 1 other priest. Father Santísima Trinidad Molina escaped (3 priests had returned to Mexico) and later wrote an account of the attack. In another attack the next year, the hostile Indians killed 19 persons. In accordance with the decision of a military conference in January 1759, Colonel Parrilla started out with a mixed force of about 500, consisting of presidial troops, mission Indians, and 134 Apache warriors. North of the Brazos River the expedition defeated a village of Tonkawas and then continued northward to the Taovayas village near the present Spanish Fort on the Red River. To their amazement, the Spaniards found the Comanches and their Wichita allies entrenched behind a stockade fortification, over which flew a French flag. There, on October 7, Parrilla was beaten by the hostile Indians and hurriedly retreated to San Sabá, leaving behind the cannon that had been ineffective in the battle. Spain had suffered the most humiliating defeat at the hands of Indians in the entire history of Texas.

The mission on the San Sabá was never rebuilt. Missionary activities on behalf of the Apaches were transferred to the upper Nueces River, near the present-day Barksdale, where two missions, San Lorenzo de la Santa Cruz and Nuestra Señora de la Candelaria del Cañon, were established in 1762. For a while these missions prospered, but they were never given any support by the government and were abandoned seven years later. The presidio at San Sabá was strengthened and maintained until 1769.

Thus, Spain's efforts at expansion in Texas, except at Goliad and Laredo on the Rio Grande, were failures. El Orcoquisac, placed at the mouth of the Trinity River to expel French intruders, may have been of some value, but it never developed into a civil settlement or even a mission center of any consequence. The mission efforts on the San Xavier and the San Sabá ended in calamity, proving that Spain's chief pioneering institutions, the mission and the presidio, could not be made effective north of San Antonio.

## SELECTED BIBLIOGRAPHY

A satisfactory bibliography on Spanish Texas for the material available at the time it was published is Henry R. Wagner, *The Spanish Southwest, 1542–1794; An Annotated Bibliography* (Berkeley, Calif., 1924). The history of Texas in its relation to that of the rest of New Spain is dealt with in H. E. Bolton and Thomas M. Marshall, *The Colonization of North America, 1492–1783* (New York, 1921); H. E. Bolton, *The Spanish Borderlands* (New Haven, Conn., 1921); Edward G. Bourne, *Spain in America* (New York, 1904). Of the older histories of Texas, the most satisfactory for the Spanish period are H. H. Bancroft, *History of the North Mexican States and Texas* (2 vols., San Francisco, 1884 and 1889); and Henderson Yoakum, *History of Texas* (2 vols., New York, 1855). A comprehensive history of early Texas is C. E. Castañeda's *Our Catholic Heritage in Texas 1519–1936* (7 vols., Austin, 1936–1958). Some recently published, shorter accounts of the history of Spain in Texas are Odie B. Faulk, *A Successful Failure* (Austin, 1965); O. B. Faulk, *The Last Years of Spanish Texas* (The Hague, 1964); Elizabeth A. H. Johns, *Storms Brewed in Other Men's Worlds* (College Station, Tex., 1975); Hodding Carter, *Doomed Road of Empire: The Spanish Trail of Conquest* (New York, 1963). For another short survey, especially good on the founding of San Antonio, see S. V. Connor, *Texas: A History* (New York, 1971).

A voluminous amount of Spanish source material is available. The best source of primary material is the Béxar Archives, located at the University of Texas. The best collection of translated sources is Charles W. Hackett (ed. and trans.), *Pichardo's Treatise on the Limits of Louisiana and Texas* (4 vols., Austin, 1931–1947). Other useful sources include Juan Agustín Morfi, *History of Texas, 1673–1679* (2 vols., Albuquerque, N.M., 1935); E. Wallace and D. M. Vigness (eds.) *Documents of Texas History; Documentos para la Historia Eclesiástica y*

*Civil de la Provincia de Texas o Nueves Philipinas, 1720–1779* (Madrid, 1961).

There is an abundance of material on early explorers. General accounts are H. E. Bolton (ed.), *Spanish Exploration in the Southwest, 1542–1706* (New York, 1925 and 1959); F. W. Hodge and T. H. Lewis (eds.), *The Spanish Explorers in the Southern United States, 1528–1543* (New York, 1907 and 1959). See also Harbert Davenport and Joseph K. Wells, "The First Europeans in Texas, 1528–1536" (Cabeza de Vaca), *Southwestern Historical Quarterly,* XXII, 111–142, 205–259; Morris Bishop, *The Odyssey of Cabeza de Vaca* (New York, 1933); G. P. Winship, "The Coronado Expedition, 1540–1542," *Fourteenth Annual Report of the Bureau of American Ethnology, 1892–1893,* I, 329–637 (Washington, D.C., 1896); C. W. Hackett (ed.), *Historical Documents Relating to New Mexico, Nueva Vizcaya, and Approaches Thereto to 1773* (2 vols., Washington, D.C., 1923–1926); H. E. Bolton, *Coronado, Knight of Pueblos and Plains* (New York, 1949); David Donoghue, "The Route of the Coronado Expedition in Texas," *Southwestern Historical Quarterly,* XXXII, 181–192; W. C. Holden, "Coronado's Route across the Staked Plains," *West Texas Historical Association Year Book,* XX, 3–20; Francis Parkman, *LaSalle and the Discovery of the Great West* (Boston, 1893); Rex W. Strickland, "Moscoso's Journey through Texas," J. W. Williams, "Moscoso's Trail in Texas," and Albert Woldert, "The Expedition of Luis de Moscoso in Texas," *Southwestern Historical Quarterly,* XLVI, 109–166.

The best available material on the history of early missions and presidios is C. E. Castañeda, *Our Catholic Heritage in Texas;* Robert C. Clark, *The Beginnings of Texas, 1684–1718* (Austin, 1907); C. L. Sonnichsen, *Pass of the North: Four Centuries on the Rio Grande* (El Paso, Tex., 1968); H. E. Bolton, "The Location of LaSalle's Colony on the Gulf of Mexico," *Southwestern Historical Quarterly,* XXVII, 171–189; George L. Crocket, *Two Centuries in East Texas* (Dallas, 1932); Walter F. McCaleb, *Spanish Missions of Texas* (San Antonio, 1954); E. W. Cole, "LaSalle in Texas," *Southwestern Historical Quarterly,* XLIX, 473–500; Robert S. Weddle, *San Juan Bautista: Gateway to Spanish Texas* (Austin, 1968); R. S. Weddle, *The San Sabá Mission: Spanish Pivot in Texas* (Austin, 1964); Lesley B. Simpson (ed.), *The San Saba Papers: A Documentary Account of the Founding and Destruction of the San Sabá Mission* (San Francisco, 1959); B. W. Aston, "Evolution of Nuevo Santander, 1746–1821" (unpublished thesis, Texas Tech University, Lubbock, 1964); James Day and others, *Six Missions of Texas* (Waco, Tex., 1965); Kathryn N. O'Connor, *The Presidio La Bahía del Espíritu Santo de Zuñiga, 1821–1846* (Austin, 1966).

On border relations and efforts at expansion, two scholarly studies by H. E. Bolton are *Texas in the Middle Eighteenth Century* (Berkeley, Calif., 1915), and *Athanase de Mézières and the Louisiana-Texas Frontier, 1768–1780* (2 vols., Cleveland, 1914). Useful also are C. W. Hackett, "Policy of the Spanish Crown Regarding French Encroachments from Louisiana, 1721–1762," in *New Spain and the Anglo-American West* (Los Angeles, 1932); William E. Dunn, "Missionary Activities among the Eastern Apaches . . . ," *Quarterly of the Texas State Historical Association,* XV, 186–200; I. J. Cox, "The Louisiana-Texas Frontier," *ibid.,* X, 1–75; XVII, 1–42, 140–187; W. E. Dunn, "The Apache Mission on the San Saba River . . . ," *ibid.,* XVII, 379–414; Ralph A. Smith (ed. and trans.), "Account of the Journey of Bénard de la Harpe: Discovery Made by Him of Several Nations Situated in the West," *ibid.,* LXII, 75–86, 246–259, 371–385, 525–541.

For an excellent study of the Spanish settlers and their way of life, see Oakah J. Jones, *Los Paisanos: Spanish Settlers on the Northern Frontier of New Spain* (Norman, Okla., 1979).

Chapter Three

# SPANISH TEXAS
# 1763–1821

The Seven Years' War, which began as a colonial struggle in the valley of the upper Ohio River in 1754 between England and France, developed two years later into a major world conflict. Spain, after belatedly entering the war on the side of France, lost Havana in Cuba and Manila in the Philippines, both valuable trading posts. To keep England from taking it and to compensate Spain for its losses, France, before making peace, ceded western Louisiana to Spain. By the Treaty of Paris in 1763 Spain ceded Florida to England for the restoration of Havana and Manila and was permitted to keep western Louisiana. Consequently, some adjustments on its northern frontier were necessary.

## READJUSTMENTS FOLLOWING
## THE ACQUISITION OF LOUISIANA

Louisiana had cost France "eight hundred thousand *livres* a year, without yielding a *sou* in return," and it was to prove no less a burden to Spain. It was a vast domain which the declining Spanish Empire did not have the resources to defend and develop. On the northeast border, the aggressive English along the Mississippi, rather than the tolerant French along the Red River, were now Spain's neighbors. Twenty years later the Republic of the United States had its beginning, and its frontier people were even more restless than they had been as British subjects. Furthermore, on the Pacific slope both the English and the Russians were threatening to appropriate a part of the Spanish Empire. Internal troubles in New Spain (Mexico) were even more threatening than external dangers. In Texas and other northern provinces hordes of Indians were becoming more and more destructive.

Drastic reforms and energetic measures were necessary to meet such problems. Fortunately for Spain, the king at this time was Charles III, one of the ablest men of the Bourbon line. Of the various officials whom he sent to America to carry out his reforms, José de Gálvez, *visitador general,* was chief, and of those associated directly with Texas, the most important was the Marqués de Rubí, inspector of the northern frontier. Accompanied by Nicolás de la Fora (Lafora), his engineer, Rubí set out in 1766 to explore the frontier from the Gulf of California to Louisiana. Entering Texas during the summer of 1767, he visited El Cañon, San Sabá, San Antonio, Nacogdoches, Los Ais, Los Adaes, San Augustín de Ahumada (Orcoquisac), and La Bahía. At the end of his journey in Mexico City, Rubí had traveled about seven thousand miles in less than three years. The inspector discovered what Spanish frontier officers had long been trying to impress on their superiors. The far-flung posts could not be maintained with the resources available. His very comprehensive and informative reports brought forth on September 10, 1772, a royal order, "Regulation for the Presidios," which substantially followed his recommendations.

In short, as it applied to Texas, the new regulation called for: (1) the abandonment of all missions and presidios except San Antonio and La Bahía, (2) the strengthening of San Antonio de Béxar by moving to it settlers from East Texas, and (3) the inauguration of a new Indian program calling for friendly relations with the Comanches and Wichitas and a war of extermination against the Apaches. Thus, Spain had decided to give up not only all attempts to occupy the country north of the San Antonio but also to abandon, except San Antonio and La Bahía, all its establishments in Texas.

It did not take a royal order to bring about the abandonment of San Sabá and El Cañon; the Comanches forced that in 1769. Two years later the presidio at Orcoquisac was abandoned, and shortly thereafter the missionaries left their post in that vicinity. These readjustments took place before the new regulation went into effect.

The abandonment of the East Texas settlements, however, was a different matter. These settlers were removed, not because of the problem of maintaining them, but because they were no longer needed as a barrier against French aggression and could be used to strengthen San Antonio. Baron Juan María de Ripperdá, governor of Texas, super-vised the cruel removal, a task not to his liking. In the summer of 1773 the missions were abandoned, and more than five hundred persons were torn away from their homes and forced to leave behind their growing crops and even their livestock.

Dissatisfied with San Antonio, because of the poor land on which they were located and the Comanche raids on their livestock, the East Texans petitioned to return to Los Ais, where their leader, Antonio Gil y Barbo (Ybarbo), had a ranch. Ripperdá endorsed their petition, but the viceroy consented for them to return no closer to Natchitoches than one hundred leagues. In modern Madison County, where the Nacogdoches road crossed the Trinity River, the refugees in August 1774 laid out the pueblo of Bucareli. Three years later the settlement was the home of 347 persons. Plagued by floods and raids by Comanche Indians, they again moved in 1779, this time without permission, to Nacogdoches. The authorities reluctantly gave their approval, and eventually some scattered to their former homes.

Another part of the new regulation called for the pacification of the northern tribes and a war of "reduction or destruction" against the Apaches. After Louisiana was taken over from the French in 1763, the Spaniards were wise enough to adopt in part the French system and to employ Frenchmen to deal with the Indians. The plan adopted was substantially what Rubí had recommended. The guiding genius in this arrangement was Athanase de Mézières, who was appointed lieutenant governor of the Natchitoches district in 1769. De Mézières, a man of unusual ability who was fluent in several Indian languages, French, Spanish, and Latin and who was the son-in-law of St. Denis and the brother-in-law of the Duke of Orleans, had been seasoned by thirty years of service in Louisiana as a soldier, planter, and Indian trader. By 1771 he had made peace with the Wichita. Then, in the summer of 1772, he visited the Tawakoni villages (near present-day Waco), proceeded up the Brazos about one hundred miles, visited the Wichitas, got in touch with the Taovayas, and then proceeded three hundred miles southward to San Antonio. One Comanche band, possibly the Nokoni, signed a treaty with J. Gaignard, a trader from Natchitoches, at the Taovayas villages in 1774, but the other Comanche bands continued to harass San Antonio. For several years De Mézières and Ripperdá worked on plans to get the northern tribes to join the Spaniards in a campaign against the Apaches. To implement this plan De Mézières was appointed governor of Texas in 1779, but before he took office, death ended the career of the great French frontiersman.

De Mézières's task of pacifying the northern tribes was never completed. A united campaign against the Apaches was never waged, although Comanche war parties occasionally joined the Spaniards on expeditions against the hated Apaches. The military strength of the province was rarely sufficient to cope with the many hostile Indians.

With less than two hundred troops to divide among three or four presidios or outposts, to furnish escorts for traveling parties, and to supply guards for the various missions, there were never enough soldiers. The peace with the Apaches in 1749 brought only a respite; the 1774 treaty with the Comanches was of little benefit; and a treaty in 1785 with the southern Comanches was a mere temporizing measure.

Baron Ripperdá, who came to San Antonio as governor in 1770, sent to his superiors dramatic accounts of the plight of that place and urgent pleas for more troops. Additional troops were sent, but Ripperdá never felt secure. Domingo Cabello, Ripperdá's successor, in 1780 wrote Teodoro de Croix, commandant of the *Provincias Internas* (the northern provinces of Mexico, created in 1776 mainly for the purpose of carrying out the new Indian policy): "There is not an instant by day or night when reports do not arrive from all these ranches of barbarities and disorder falling on us. Totally unprotected as we are, they will result in the absolute destruction and loss of this province." In 1792 Governor Manuel Muñoz complained that peace agreements and presents did not stop Comanche raids and that Apache depredations were chronic. The Indians accepted the gifts but did not stop their marauding expeditions.

A desire to strengthen their influence over the Comanche and Wichita Indians, so that they might serve as a barrier against Anglo-American intrusion, and the imperative military need to connect the three widely separated pivotal points (San Antonio, Santa Fé, and Natchitoches) on the northern frontier with direct routes prompted the Spaniards to make some notable explorations in Texas in the 1780s. In Pedro (Pierre) Vial, a Frenchman who had traded with the Indians along the Red River, Governor Cabello had a man well equipped to find a route from San Antonio to Santa Fé. Starting on October 4, 1786, with a small party, Vial went northward to a few miles east of the present-day Brownwood, then eastward to the Tawakoni village near Waco, thence northwest and north to the Taovayas villages on the Red River in the vicinity of Spanish Fort, and from there by way of the Red and Canadian rivers to Santa Fé, where he arrived in May 1787.

Not satisfied with Vial's report, Governor Fernando de la Concha of New Mexico in July dispatched Corporal José Mares to find a more direct route linking the two outposts. Accompanied by Christóbal de los Santos, who had come to Santa Fé with Vial, Mares went eastward and southeastward by way of Tule Creek and the site of Quanah to the Taovayas villages and thence southward by present-day Jacksboro to San Antonio, where he arrived in October 1787. He had reached San Antonio by traveling about 980 miles, 210 less than Vial but considerably farther than necessary. Guided by friendly Comanches, he started on his return trip in January 1788, determined to go as directly as possible.

Traveling northward and slightly westward, he went by or near the sites of Coleman and Abilene, Double Mountain near Aspermont and the Salt Fork of the Brazos, to the lower Tule Creek, and thence proceeded to Santa Fé by his outgoing route. The distance by this route was 845 miles; had Mares continued up the Brazos by the site of Lubbock, he would have traveled 100 miles less and almost as direct as the shortest modern highway.

The most ambitious journey of all was made by Pedro Vial between 1788 and 1789. Setting out from Santa Fé on June 24, 1788, he pursued a comparatively direct route by the site of Tucumcari and along the Prairie Dog Fork (main) of Red River to the Taovayas villages; thence he went through the vicinity of Gainesville and Greenville to Natchitoches. He left Natchitoches with its 3,000 inhabitants and proceeded to San Antonio, passing by the site of San Augustine and visiting the settlement of Nacogdoches, which at that time had about 250 inhabitants. He estimated that San Antonio then had about 700 inhabitants. In 1789 the tireless explorer returned to Santa Fé by a route that veered eastward from the trail that Mares had followed the year before.

The route from Santa Fé to Natchitoches may have resulted in a slight increase in travel between those two far-flung outposts, but the route from San Antonio to Santa Fé was never used because the inhospitable plains and the Comanches made it impracticable. In 1808 Don Francisco Amangual with the aid of Comanche guides was able to go from San Antonio to Santa Fé with two hundred troops. The expedition, a demonstration in response to an exploring expedition commanded by Lieutenant Zebulon Pike of the United States Army into Spanish territory two years before, was made to impress both the Americans and the Comanche Indians with Spanish strength and mobility. Amangual went considerably to the west of the routes of Vial and Mares. Going first to the old San Sabá post, he then marched by the site of San Angelo and west of Double Mountain, along the eastern side of the Caprock to the Quitaque, across the High Plains by way of present-day Amarillo to the Canadian River, and then westward to Santa Fé. He returned by a still more westerly route which followed the Pecos for some distance.

## READJUSTMENTS FOLLOWING
## THE RETROCESSION OF LOUISIANA

In 1800 Napoleon inaugurated a grand scheme for reestablishing the French Empire in America and wheedled the king of Spain into transferring Louisiana again to France. Then in 1803, realizing that it would be difficult to hold the province in the event of a war with Great Britain, he broke his pledge to Spain not to alienate it and in 1803 sold Louisiana for approximately $15 million to the United States. Texas was once again on the border of New Spain, and an indefinite boundary separated it from the land-hungry Americans. To meet the new situation Spain adopted a threefold imperial policy: first, to hold the territory with its ancient boundaries unimpaired; second, to increase its garrisons and colonize the territory with loyal Spanish subjects; and third, to keep out Anglo-American intruders. Although these three phases are closely related, it seems expedient to develop each of them separately.

A controversy over the western boundary was inevitable. The purchase treaty, rather than naming specific boundaries, provided for the transfer of the territory as it had been prior to its cession to Spain in 1762. President Thomas Jefferson, on the basis of the French claim, held that the territory extended to the Rio Grande, while the Spaniards, with more justification, contended that it did not extend west of the Red River. The Spaniards placed additional troops in Texas, including detachments at the old post El Orcoquisac at the mouth of the Trinity and at points east of the Sabine, and thwarted efforts of the United States to explore the disputed territory. The Thomas Freeman expedition, sent up the Red River in 1806, was stopped at a point near the western boundary of the present state of Arkansas, and Zebulon Pike, who succeeded in reaching the upper stretches of the Rio Grande, was captured by a Spanish force.

The United States, on the other hand, sent troops into Louisiana, drove the Spanish troops from Los Adaes, and made preparations for war. Fortunately, a clash of arms was avoided. In November 1806, General James Wilkinson, in command of the United States forces, made with General Simón Herrera, in command of Spanish troops on the border, what is known as the Neutral Ground Agreement, providing that the Spaniards should remain west of the Sabine River and the Americans east of the Arroyo Hondo until their respective governments had reached an agreement. Strained relations between the two countries were aggravated by the report that Aaron Burr, formerly vice-president of the United States, was planning to lead a filibuster expedition into Texas or some other Spanish province. Burr's force disintegrated, however, before it reached New Orleans. When Wilkinson, who is believed to have been both in league with Burr and in the secret pay of Spain, realized that the Burr expedition was doomed to failure, he readily entered into the Neutral Ground Agreement and hurried to New Orleans, where he made much ado while preparing the place for defense against attack from Burr's force.

The diplomatic controversy concerning the western boundary of the Louisiana purchase was long and involved and was linked with the claims of the United States to West Florida. Because of the confusion incident to the Napoleonic wars in Europe, negotiations were discontinued in 1807 and were not resumed until ten years later. At last, the Adams-De Onís, or Florida Purchase, Treaty was signed in 1819 and became effective by exchange of ratification two years later. By that agreement the United States acquired Florida from Spain and gave up its shadowy claim to Texas. Also, the Louisiana-Texas boundary was fixed as follows: the west bank of the Sabine River from the Gulf to the thirty-second parallel, north to the Red River, along the south bank of that stream to the one hundredth meridian, north to the Arkansas River, along the south or west bank of that stream to its source, north to the forty-second parallel, and along that parallel to the Pacific Ocean.

Notwithstanding all its efforts, Spain had in Texas, at the time the United States acquired Louisiana, only the settlements of San Antonio, Goliad, and Nacogdoches. San Antonio, consisting of five missions, the settlement of Béxar, and the *villa* of San Fernando, had a population of about 2,500; about 1,200 persons lived in Goliad and about 500 in Nacogdoches. Faced with the threat of Anglo-American aggression, Spain renewed its efforts to populate the province. In 1805 it established the *villa* of Salcedo on the Trinity River, opposite the ruins of Bucareli, and the *villa* of San Marcos, eight miles above the site of present-day Gonzales, but in 1809 there were only 16 persons living in Salcedo and 82 in San Marcos. The entire population of Texas at that time was estimated at only 4,155 persons, more than 1,000 of whom were soldiers. There were still very few foreigners in the province. The efforts of officials to introduce foreigners were offset in great measure by the opposition of Nemesio Salcedo, commandant general of the Interior Provinces, who looked with suspicion on all immigrants from Louisiana and stoutly forbade commercial relations with that country.

In September 1820, after the Spanish liberals had forced Ferdinand VII to accept the Constitution of 1812, the *Cortes* issued a decree opening all Spanish dominions to any foreigners who would respect the constitution and laws of the monarchy. But the evening of Spain's empire in America was spent, and the policy would soon become the heritage of the independent Mexican nation.


## THE FILIBUSTERS

During the early nineteenth century, the Spanish authorities were repeatedly harassed by the fear of Anglo-American "filibusters," intruders with political designs. Traders from Louisiana appropriated much of the

Indian trade and offered a market for horses that the Indians stole from the Spanish posts. Some of these traders defied the authority of Spain. The best known was Philip Nolan, whose career is partly shrouded in mystery. Nolan was a bookkeeper for and protégé of General James Wilkinson, commander of the United States forces in Louisiana, whose capacity for double dealing has never been surpassed in American history.

Nolan came to Texas as a trader as early as 1791 and with the permission of the Spanish officials took horses out of the country. On one trip he drove out thirteen hundred; on another he rounded up about two thousand. The Spaniards became suspicious of his motive, and when he returned in the autumn of 1800 with a party of seventeen armed followers, they sent a force of about a hundred soldiers to arrest him. In the fight that ensued near the present-day city of Waco on March 22, 1801, Nolan was killed. His followers were imprisoned in Mexico and later cast dice to see who of the nine survivors would die to satisfy the decree of the Spanish monarch. Some evidence indicates that Nolan was planning a more ambitious expedition against Texas.

The severe reception accorded Nolan did not frighten away other American adventurers. The second Anglo-American filibuster movement into Texas originated from a combination of revolutionary developments within New Spain. At the town of Dolores on September 16, 1810, the priest Miguel Hidalgo, representing the underprivileged classes, raised the standard of revolt against the Spanish government. With a few soldiers and a straggling horde of Indians, the priest captured and sacked Guanajuato, where he set up a government, then captured Guadalajara, and soon added Nuevo Santander and Coahuila to the revolutionists' territory.

The people of Texas at first declared their loyalty to the king but soon became indifferent and critical. Then, on January 22, 1811, Juan Bautista de las Casas, a resident of San Antonio and a former militia captain, along with a few fellow conspirators, quietly seized without a struggle Simón Herrera, commander of the troops, Governor Manuel María de Salcedo, and other officials at San Antonio. Las Casas then proclaimed himself governor of Texas. After his delegations, with equal ease, had taken possession of Goliad and Nacogdoches, he notified Hidalgo of his success. The season of his power was short. On March 2, the loyalists, led by Juan Manuel Zambrano, a native Texas rancher, Erasmo Seguín, and Francisco Ruiz, captured Las Casas and in July reinstated the loyalist authorities. Soon afterward Las Casas was executed. The patriots' cause in Texas was seriously weakened by the charge of the royalists that they were tools of Napoleon who, now that he was master of Spain, believed that a revolution in America would further his designs to obtain control of the Spanish colonies.

Although Hidalgo was captured and put to death, the revolution went on under other leaders. Bernardo Gutiérrez de Lara, a wealthy citizen of the city of Revilla (now Guerrero) went to the United States in 1811 as the envoy of the revolutionists. Although he was not recognized by the United States government, he was well received by some cabinet members and various other persons. The Texas republicans were interested in his plan to organize a filibustering force on the border of the United States, and agents from Béxar and Nacogdoches assured him that Texas would revolt on the approach of his invading army. The nucleus of this army was a number of men recruited by Lieutenant Augustus W. Magee, an adroit young officer who had made a good record on the Louisiana-Texas frontier. Dissatisfied at not being promoted in the United States Army, Magee resigned his commission in January 1812 to accept command of the "Republican Army of the North." Gutiérrez was named as the commander in chief, but Magee was the actual commander.

Starting from Natchitoches with a conglomerate array of more than one hundred Anglo-Americans, Frenchmen, Mexican revolutionists, and Indian allies, Magee occupied with ease Nacogdoches in mid-August 1812. The Gutiérrez propaganda pamphlets, letters, and broadsides had smoothed the way. The Spanish soldiers deserted or fled, and the people drove away their officers and went out in a procession to greet the liberators. Gutiérrez followed the army to Nacogdoches and renewed his propaganda. In November the army laid siege to La Bahía. There Magee became fatally ill, and the offensive was stalled until February 1813 when the Spaniards withdrew to San Antonio. In March Samuel Kemper, who had succeeded Magee, renewed the advance. After defeating a Spanish army of twelve hundred men commanded by Simón Herrera, the invaders occupied San Antonio on April 1, 1813. Five days later Gutiérrez issued a "Declaration of Independence of the State of Texas," a worthy document written according to the best traditions of liberalism. On April 17 he proclaimed a constitution that provided for a centralized, rather than the republican, form of government expected by the Anglo-Americans. The constitution provided for a governor and a *junta* with dictatorial powers. Also, by declaring that the "State of Texas" formed "a part of the Mexican Republic, to which it remains inviolably joined," the instrument destroyed the hopes of the Americans that Texas would become a dependency of the United States.

Disgusted with the course of events, including the executions of Governor Salcedo, General Simón Herrera, and twelve other Spanish officers, some Anglo-Americans left for the United States. After a barrage of propaganda, the Americans replaced Gutiérrez, who a few days afterwards left for exile in the United States, with José Alvarez de Toledo, a revolutionist from Spain, who promised a more independent and liberal government for Texas. Torn by dissension in their ranks, the heterogeneous collection of 1,400 Americans, Mexicans, and Indians at San Antonio was no match for the 1,830 troops that Joaquín de Arredondo, commandant general of the Eastern Interior Provinces, brought against them. On the Medina River, west of San Antonio, on August 18, 1813, the liberals were put to rout. Most of the Americans were slain; those lucky enough to escape fled to the United States. Thus the Mexican state of Texas came to an end after a troubled career of four months.

Arredondo followed up his victory with a purge calculated to rid Texas of all Anglo-Americans and liberal Mexicans. Rebels were shot, their property confiscated, and their wives and daughters imprisoned and forced to labor for the loyalist army. So thoroughly did he do his work that the province was virtually depopulated save for the settlement at Béxar. Indeed, he was unable to put into effect the new liberal Constitution of 1812 because there were not enough suitable persons to fill the offices! No serious effort was again made to populate Texas until 1820, and meanwhile the officials forbade any trade with Louisiana.

But the rich lands of Texas constituted an invitation that offset the harshest decrees of the Spanish government. In 1818 the military had to drive away a band of about 120 Napoleonic sympathizers who, under a Frenchman named Charles Lallemand, had settled on the lower Trinity River. The next year a more serious threat to Spanish sovereignty appeared under the leadership of James Long, a merchant of Natchez, who had married a niece of General Wilkinson. The signing of the treaty of 1819, granting the Floridas to the United States in consideration of the acknowledgment of Spain's claim to Texas, angered many Americans on the southern frontier, who referred to it as the "surrender of Texas." At a meeting in Natchez, plans were formulated for driving out of Texas the few royalist troops, organizing a liberal government, and attracting immigrants by the offer of generous land grants. Under Long's leadership the party set out in June for Nacogdoches, gaining recruits as it advanced until it had three hundred men, among them Gutiérrez. Shortly after their arrival at Nacogdoches on June 23, 1819, the invaders established a civil government, adopted a declaration of independence, and invited immigrants to share with them the blessings of liberty.

To hold various outposts, Long divided his forces and left for Galveston Island to enlist the aid of Jean Lafitte. For several years Galveston had served as the headquarters for various adventurers or buccaneers, including Colonel Henry Perry, a survivor of the Gutiérrez-

Magee expedition, and Luis Aury, who held a naval commission from the Mexican revolutionists, and Lafitte. Lafitte's tenure dated from April 1817, when he set up his "republic" on the island and made it the headquarters for his privateering activities. Long not only failed on his mission, but during his absence a Spanish force under Colonel Ignacio Pérez captured a part of his men and put the others to flight. Long then made his way to New Orleans and with another group of adventurers in 1820 established his headquarters at Point Bolivar on Galveston Bay. With fifty men Long then went to La Bahía where on October 4, 1821, he was warmly received as a revolutionary. Mexico, however, had already won its independence, and a few days later Long and his men were captured and sent to Mexico City. While there on parole, Long was mysteriously shot.

## POLITICAL AND MILITARY ADMINISTRATION

The political system of Texas was similar to that of the other provinces in New Spain. It was subject directly to the viceroy, who in turn referred important matters to the fiscal of the Royal Audiencia and to the *auditor*

Jane Long, wife of Filibuster James Long, became one of the best-known and most beloved women in nineteenth-century Texas. When her husband was arrested and carried to Mexico City, Jane Long, with only her baby, two-year-old daughter, and a black girl, waited at Bolivar Point on Galveston Bay throughout the winter of 1821–1822 for the return of her husband. After receiving word that he had been assassinated, she returned to Mississippi but later settled in Austin's colony. (Southwest Collection, Texas Tech University)

*de guerra.* In important cases, before a final decision was made, a *junta,* or general council, composed of various dignitaries might be called together. All important decisions of the viceroy were subject to royal approval, and, except in emergencies, policies of great consequence were not adopted until the king approved them. In 1776 the Interior (northern) Provinces of New Spain were organized under a commandant general who was responsible to the king and practically independent of the viceroy.

Except for the *villa* of San Fernando de Béxar, which had selfgovernment in some measure, the government of Texas was almost wholly military. At the head of the administration was a governor appointed by the crown. He commanded the army and the militia of the province and had the authority to grant land titles, issue licenses, hear appeals from the alcalde court, supervise fiscal matters, and administer and execute laws and decrees. The terms of the governors varied in length, but the average term was about four years. Inspectors from time to time checked on the governors, and at the end of their term a *residencia* or investigation of their administration was made.

Evidently the presidios frequently were badly managed. The common soldiers received about 450 pesos a year out of which they had to purchase their equipment and maintain themselves and their families. They spent a great deal of time working on the private estates of the officers. The captain of a presidio served as the merchant of the post, sometimes charging the soldiers exorbitant prices for their supplies, in spite of regulations intended to prevent that abuse. Probably the case of Governor Martos y Navarrete (1759–1767), who was charged with making $80,000 in profits on goods sold to soldiers at Los Adaes, is too extreme to be typical, but it suggests the weaknesses in the system. No doubt this graft greatly lowered the efficiency of the commands. In 1737 Governor Franquis de Lugo reprimanded Captain Gabriel Costales at La Bahía for failure to pay and to supply his men adequately, alleging that certain soldiers came to San Antonio from La Bahía practically naked, their arms out of order, and their horses so poor that they were a disgrace.

## THE MISSION SYSTEM

Since there have been many references to the missions and the missionaries, some special notice of the subject is in order. The missionary projects of San Xavier and San Sabá, which received considerable treatment in the secular history of the province, are not representative of the work of the churchmen.

The Spanish mission system as it was introduced in Texas was developed in Mexico, where the Europeans found the Indians living in relatively compact and permanent pueblos. The purpose of the mission was threefold: first, to convert the Indians to Christianity; second, to teach them the habits and customs of Spanish life and make them creditable and self-sustaining subjects of the king; and third, to extend the influence and authority of Spain and to hold the territory in its vicinity against all intruders. It belonged both to the church and the state. Indeed, the missionaries were employees of the king. Although they were selected by the evangelical colleges, their stipends, generally 450 pesos a year, were paid out of the royal treasury, and their appointments had to be approved by the viceroy. The stipends were not used as salaries for the missionaries but by the college to maintain the mission. New missions could not be established without viceregal assent, and the undertaking was a function of both church and state. The government bore the initial expense of founding a mission, and the evangelical colleges maintained it. A mission was generally maintained for about ten years, after which time it was secularized; that is, its lands and property were distributed among the neophytes and its church taken over by the secular clergy. The time limit was not enforced, however, and in Texas the most successful missions continued in operation for many decades.

The missionaries who served in Texas belonged to the Franciscan order, nearly all sent either by the College (seminary) of Santa Cruz de Querétaro, established at Querétaro in 1683, or by the College of Nuestra Señora de Guadalupe de Zacatecas, founded at Zacatecas in 1707.

The chief mission centers in Texas were the East Texas group, extending from the upper Neches River eastward to Los Adaes at modern Robeline, Louisiana; the La Bahía group on the San Antonio River at present-day Goliad; and those at San Antonio. Of the six founded in East Texas in 1716–1717 and reestablished in 1721, three were administered by priests from the College of Querétaro and three by priests from the college in Zacatecas. The three Querétaran missions, as previously noted, were moved first to the Colorado River and in 1731 to San Antonio, but the three Zacatecan missions (Guadalupe, Dolores, and San Miguel) were maintained until the abandonment of East Texas in 1773.

In 1722 Aguayo established and delivered to Father Augustín Patrón, a Zacatecan, La Bahía mission. In 1726 the entire La Bahía establishment was moved about twenty-five miles northwestward to the Guadalupe River. In 1749, in connection with Escandón's settlement of

Nuevo Santander, it was again moved, this time to the site of the present Goliad. Mission Espíritu Santo and Mission Nuestra Señora del Rosario, established nearby by the Zacatecans, were fairly successful.

The last mission established in Texas was in this vicinity. In 1793 Nuestra Señora del Refugio was located at the junction of the Guadalupe and San Antonio rivers. Two years later it was moved to a better site in the vicinity of Refugio, but its faithful Zacatecan padres were no more successful than their predecessors had been in converting and changing the habits of the Karankawas and their neighbors.

It was at San Antonio that Spanish mission activity attained its highest success. San Antonio de Valero, a Querétaran mission founded in 1718, was followed two years later by San José y San Miguel de Aguayo, as already noted, by the Zacatecans. Added to these were the three missions moved from East Texas in 1731 and thereafter commonly called Concepción, San Juan de Capistrano (in East Texas, San José de los Nazonis), and Espada (formerly San Francisco de los Neches). Reports by competent authorities in 1749, 1768, and 1781 agree that San José was the most successful.

In 1768 Father Gaspar José de Solís, inspector of the Zacatecan missions, recorded that "it is so pretty and well arranged both in a material and a spiritual way that I have no voice, words, or figures with which to describe its beauty."

The establishment consisted of a square, approximately 204 yards on each side, enclosed by a stone wall with towers in two opposite corners. Against the wall were 84 quarters built of stone, each supplied with a small kitchen and loopholes for defense. Other structures of stone and mortar inside the enclosure included the church, friary, offices, refectory and arch granary, a workshop for spinning and weaving cotton and woolen cloth, shops for carpentry, iron work, and tailoring, and a lime kiln. The present church, started in 1768 and large enough to accommodate two thousand persons, with its vaulted roof and its famous Rose Window, is reputed to be the finest mission architecture in New Spain. Outside the walls, there was a mill and an irrigation ditch so large that it "seemed to flow like a small river," which ran from the river by the houses to the fields fenced in for more than a league in which were grown corn, brown beans, lentils, melons, peaches (some a pound in weight), sweet and Irish potatoes, sugar cane, and cotton. So abundant were the crops that the mission, with more than 350 Indians in 1768, supplied in part the presidios at San Antonio, La Bahía, San Sabá, El Orcoquisac, and Los Adaes. The Indians were described as energetic, skilled, and versatile laborers who worked even without supervision. They maintained their own guard and patrol for the defense of the

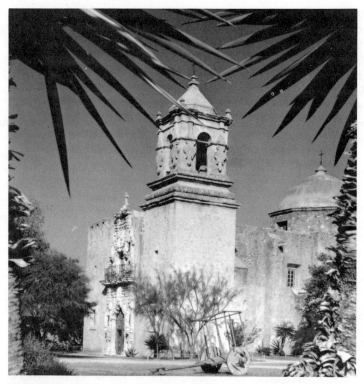
Mission San José y San Miguel de Aguayo, founded in 1720 for the Zacatecan brotherhood in San Antonio, was the center of Spanish mission efforts in Texas. (Texas Highway Department)

establishment and had their own government with much the same officers and courts as a Spanish pueblo. More than 350 Indians lived at the mission, most of whom spoke Spanish.

A typical day for the mission Indians was rather routine. It began with a religious service at dawn followed by thirty minutes or an hour of instruction in the catechism; breakfast; then work in the fields or the shops, or more frequently for the women, work on the looms, at the pottery wheel, or in the kitchen; and school for the children. All work and instruction were under the direction and personal supervision of the priests, or of the soldiers assigned to the mission for such purposes. In the evening all gathered in front of the church for another hour of instruction and the rosary.

The missions enjoyed comparative prosperity, and reports indicate

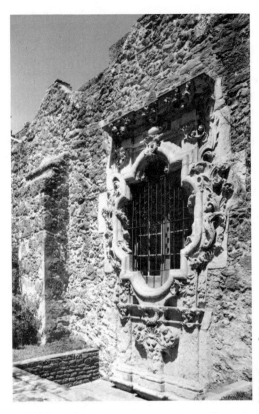

The Rose Window of the Mission San José y San Miguel de Aguayo is renowned as a masterpiece of art. (Texas Highway Department)

that in San Antonio, at least, the padres did effective work. An inspector of the four Querétaran missions in San Antonio in 1745 reported 2,441 baptisms since 1718. At the time of the report 885 Indians, most of whom had been baptized, were living in the missions. They had more than 5,000 head of cattle, about half that many sheep, and large herds of goats and horses. The mission produced annually about 8,000 bushels of corn and quantities of beans, melons, watermelons, sweet potatoes, and cotton.

Life for the religious, however, was hard indeed when the governor or the presidial officials were hostile toward them, a condition that occasionally prevailed. The most serious quarrel of this kind was with the Governor Franquis de Lugo (1736–1737), who seems to have used every device within his power to annoy the missionaries and discredit them with the Indians and the populace in San Antonio. The priests appealed to the viceroy. Franquis de Lugo was reprimanded and later removed, but before they were rid of his presence many of the Indians had fled, and the whole mission field was demoralized.

Soon after Father De Solís made his inspection, the missions began a decline that continued until the close of the Spanish era. In 1773 the Querétarans, burdened with demands from other fields, turned over their four missions in San Antonio to the Zacatecans. There were only 9 missionaries officially active in 1785. Mission Valero (now the Alamo), which had only 42 persons in 1777, all fully acclimated, was secularized in 1793. San José, which had only 138 neophytes in 1781, was secularized in 1794. Concepción, San Juan de Capistrano, and Espada were given up by the missionaries a few years later. Some missionary work continued at San Antonio until 1823, and Mission Refugio continued until 1830.

## ECONOMIC AND SOCIAL LIFE

The first civil settlement in Texas was established in San Antonio by Alarcón in 1718. It consisted of ten families under the protection of a military guard and was called Villa de Béxar. In 1731 fifty-five persons, most of them from the Canary Islands, were moved to San Antonio and located at public expense. The place was now called San Fernando de Béxar. The settlement grew slowly. The population in 1770 was about eight hundred, but this number may not have included persons living on ranches in the vicinity. With the coming of Baron Ripperdá as governor in 1770, San Antonio became the de facto capital, and after the abandonment of Los Adaes three years later, it was officially the seat of government in the province.

The only other civil settlements in Spanish Texas worthy of notice were Goliad, Nacogdoches, and Adaes. After their removal to the site of Goliad in 1749, there grew up around the Mission La Bahía del Espíritu Santo and the presidio of Loreto a settlement and important ranching interests. The population of the community in 1782 was 512. Likewise, Nacogdoches experienced considerable growth after Gil Ybarbo and his exiled Adaesians settled there in 1779. Ybarbo, the lieutenant governor, assigned lands to the people. A commissary for Indian trade was established, and there was considerable illicit trade with Louisiana. A census in 1790 showed a population of 480. Los Adaes, the capital of Texas from 1722 to 1773, was always a small struggling settlement.

The basic economy of the civilian population of Spanish Texas was livestock and farming. Livestock ran unattended, with innumerable wild cattle free for the taking; the fertile soils produced good crops; the countryside and streams contained an abundance of wild game, edible plants, and fish; and so the settlers were inclined to be relaxed and indolent. Sheep were tried but were unsatisfactory in the wet woodlands and among predatory animals. Cattle thrived and, after the transfer of Louisiana to Spain, constituted the principal revenue. The first large herd was driven legally to Natchitoches in 1779. From then until 1803, when the United States obtained Louisiana, an estimated fifteen thousand head of cattle were driven annually to the eastern market. Despite orders to the contrary, smuggling flourished between East Texas and the French after 1716, and apparently much of the revenue derived from the sale of cattle was used to purchase goods, which were considerably cheaper than those brought overland from Vera Cruz.

Most people were farmers. Corn was the staple crop. Other crops included beans, chiles, sugar cane, pumpkins, melons, and gourds. Obviously, not all people were ranchers and farmers. In San Antonio in 1795 approximately one-third of the workers were servants, merchants, tailors, cobblers, teamsters, blacksmiths, and fishermen. There was no lawyer and only one physician listed on the census roll.

Social life in Spanish Texas was simple and closely regulated. The number of clergymen was never large. Not until 1750 did San Antonio get a church, and then by royal aid. Yet, as a result of the few faithful missionaries (only nine in 1785), the people remained devout adherents to their Catholic heritage. The first school, which opened in San Antonio in 1789, was short lived. In 1803 the governor of Texas received orders to see that a school was established near each settlement or presidio, that each boy under twelve was in school, and that each parent paid monthly tuition in the amount of one-fourth peso. Schools were opened soon thereafter in San Antonio and in La Bahía, but the lieutenant governor at Nacogdoches responded that most of the boys there lived on scattered ranches and that consequently it would be impossible to enroll a sufficient number for the teacher to make a living.

Illness and death were not strangers to most households. Outbreaks of the dreaded smallpox and cholera were periodic, and the major remedy was prayer. Although local officials imposed sanitary regulations, there was no pharmacist or civilian physician, and only one hospital (a military one) was ever established.

The behavior and social activities of the people were carefully regulated. Treason, slander of any member of the royal family, murder, arson, or major theft was punishable by death. Whipping, loss of all or half of one's property, or eight to ten years in the galleys was the penalty for robbery or the abuse of a holy person. Yet, despite the toil and scarcity of goods, the lack of adequate spiritual welfare and schools, burdensome taxation and too much government regulation, and isolation and recurring plagues, the Spaniards of Texas led a life of relaxation and enjoyed several kinds of entertainment, particularly the fandangos on the public square (private dances were discouraged and at times were illegal) and horse racing, even on religious holidays, at the risk of twenty-five lashes as punishment for participation.

## MEXICAN INDEPENDENCE

It has been observed already that the abortive rebellion instigated by the priest Hidalgo in 1810 was soon suppressed. The underlying cause of its failure was that the upper classes did not support it, neither did the clergy or the merchants. Yet, the death of Hidalgo did not bring an end to the insurrection. The flames of rebellion were beaten out, but the smoldering embers of discontent remained. Dissatisfaction with the government in Spain was general, now that Napoleon had made Ferdinand VII a prisoner and had placed Joseph Bonaparte, his brother, on the Spanish throne. Even the Mexican clergy, staunch supporters of monarchy, were alienated because they knew that Napoleon was disposed to take many liberties with the church.

Under the leadership of José María Morelos and Vicente Guerrero, the revolution continued. At the end of the wars in Europe, however, it seemed that the royal government would suppress the rebels entirely. In 1819 Viceroy Juan Ruíz Apodaca reported to the king that no additional troops were necessary. At this time, however, the character of the revolution completely changed. Because of an insurrection in Spain, Ferdinand was forced to restore the liberal Constitution of 1812. This move antagonized the privileged classes in Mexico, especially the clergy, who resented certain anticlerical policies of the *Cortes*. Old Spain had become too liberal for New Spain. The upper classes in Mexico threw their support behind Agustín de Iturbide. With a command of 2,500 troops he marched against Guerrero, the liberal leader, not to fight but to negotiate. The two leaders soon came to an agreement known as the Plan of Iguala, proclaimed on February 24, 1821. The plan declared that New Spain was an independent, moderate, constitutional monarchy, guaranteed it the Catholic religion, and proclaimed racial equality. In August, Juan O'Donojú, the last viceroy, recognized the independence of Mexico, and on September 27 Iturbide entered Mexico City. Thus, through a strange combination of liberals and conservatives, the independence of Mexico was attained with little bloodshed.

## FAILURE AND LEGACY

The causes of the comparative failure of Spain in Texas were partly within and partly beyond its control. Its exclusive commercial policy, which prohibited trade even between the different parts of its dominions, was certainly a retarding factor. Strict and tyrannical methods of government, strangely mixed with laxity and the tolerance of graft, were also causes of the failure. Certain unfavorable conditions, chief of which was the hostility of nomadic Indian tribes, were beyond its control. Yet Spain might have changed its pioneeering institutions—the *villa,* the presidio, and the mission—to meet the conditions peculiar to the northern frontier in a better way.

In general it may be said that Spain suffered most because of a lack of realism in its policies and the stubborn adherence to tradition in administration. For instance, it held doggedly to the notion that the pueblo type of mission was suited to Texas, although it soon proved of little value except along the Rio Grande and in the vicinity of San Antonio. It adhered rigidly to the high ideal that Indians should not have firearms and thereby compelled them to trade with its rivals. It never gave up the theory that, since Texas was an extension of New Spain, the province should trade with New Spain only; thus it impoverished its settlements and caused people of enterprise to violate the law. Notwithstanding abundant evidence that conditions were otherwise, Spain clung to the fiction that poorly paid captains of isolated posts would be scrupulously honest, would sell supplies to their soldiers at fair prices, would keep their men employed in the public service, and would not use them for their own gain. The facts that occasional rigid inspections were made and that sometimes the guilty were punished did not ensure honesty.

Spain's achievement in Texas must not be despised, however. It held Texas against all contenders until its empire in America collapsed and left upon it an imprint that will endure throughout the ages. Many streams and towns bear Spanish names. In almost every section there are land titles that go back to Spanish grants. The law shows Spanish influence, particularly that pertaining to the property rights of women. Fortunately, a few specimens of Spanish architecture still remain. In San Antonio some of the chapels of the old missions have withstood almost two centuries of assault by the elements and the occasional ravages of unfriendly hands. Their stateliness and gentle beauty command a reverent interest. They are worthy monuments to the idealism of the Spaniard and fitting symbols of immortality in a transitory world.

## SELECTED BIBLIOGRAPHY

The most useful reference for the period is the *Handbook of Texas*. The general accounts mentioned in the preceding bibliography also apply to this chapter. The best sources on the readjustment following the acquisition of Louisiana by Spain are H. E. Bolton, *Texas in the Middle Eighteenth Century;* H. E. Bolton, *Athanase de Mézières;* C. E. Castañeda, *Our Catholic Heritage in Texas, 1519–1936,* vol. IV; O. B. Faulk, *A Successful Failure;* Noel M. Loomis and A. P. Nasater, *Pedro Vial and the Roads to Santa Fé* (Norman, Okla., 1967). See also E. Wallace and D. M. Vigness (eds.) *Documents of Texas History;* H. E. Bolton, "The Spanish Abandonment and Reoccupation of East Texas, 1773–1779," *Quarterly of the Texas State Historical Association,* IX, 67–137; A. B. Thomas (ed. and trans.), *Teodoro de Croix and the Northern Frontier of New Spain,* 1776–1783 (Norman, Okla., 1941); E. A. H. John, *Storms Brewed in Other Men's Worlds;* Elizabeth Ann Harper, "The Taovayas Indians in Frontier Trade and Diplomacy, 1769–1779," *Southwestern Historical Quarterly,* LVII, 181–201.

For the last years of Spain in Texas, the best scholarly studies are M. A. Hatcher, *The Opening of Texas to Foreign Settlement, 1801–1821* (University of Texas *Bulletin,* no. 2714; Austin, 1927); O. B. Faulk, *The Last Years of Spanish Texas;* D. M. Vigness, *The Revolutionary Decades* (Austin, 1965); N. L. Benson (ed. and trans.), "A Governor's Report on Texas in 1809," *Southwestern Historical Quarterly,* LXXI, 603–615; L. Friend, "Old Spanish Fort," *West Texas Historical Asssociation Year Book,* XVI, 3–27; Kathryn Garrett, "Dr. John Sibley and the Louisiana-Texas Frontier, 1803–1814," *Southwestern Historical Quarterly,* XLVIII, XLIX; Harris G. Warren, *The Sword Was Their Passport* (Baton Rouge, La., 1943). Texas-Louisiana relations of that period are dealt with in Thomas M. Marshall, *A History of the Western Boundary of the Louisiana Purchase, 1819–1841* (Berkeley, Calif., 1914).

On the filibusters, see the general references previously cited and also: K. Garrett, *Green Flag over Texas* (Austin, 1969); D. M. Vigness, *The Revolutionary Decades;* H. S. Thrall, *Pictorial History of Texas* (St. Louis, 1879); M. A. Hatcher, "Joaquin de Arredondo's Report of the Battle of the Medina . . . ," *Quarterly of the Texas State Historical Association,* XI, 220–236; K. Garrett, "The First Constitution of Texas, April 17, 1813," *Southwestern Historical Quarterly,* XL, 290–308; Lois Garver, "Benjamin Rush Milam," *ibid.,* XXXVIII, 79–121; Henry P. Walker (ed.), "William McLane's Narrative of the Magee-Gutiérrez Expedition of 1812–1813," *ibid.,* LXVI, 234–251, 457–479; 569–588; James C. Milligan, "José Bernardo Gutiérrez de Lara, 1811–1841" (unpublished dissertation, Texas Tech University, Lubbock, 1975); E. Wallace and D. M. Vigness (eds.), *Documents of Texas History.*

On the Spanish political and military administration, the best source is H. E. Bolton, *Texas in the Middle Eighteenth Century.* See also M. A. Hatcher, "The Municipal Government of San Fernando de Béxar, 1730–1800," *Quarterly of the Texas State Historical Association,* VIII, 277–352; F. C. Chabot, *San Antonio and Its Beginnings;* Sidney B. Brinckerhoff and O. B. Faulk, *Lancers for the King; A Study of the Frontier Military System of Northern New Spain, with a Translation of the Royal Regulations of 1772* (Phoenix, Ariz., 1965); B. E. Bobb, *The Viceregency of Antonio Mariá Bucareli in New Spain, 1771–1779* (Austin, 1962); Nettie Lee Benson, "Texas Failure to Send a Deputy to the Spanish Cortes, 1810–1812," *Southwestern Historical Quarterly,* LXIV, 14–35; Virginia Taylor (ed. and trans.), *Letters of Antonio Martínez, Last Governor of Texas, 1817–1822* (Austin, 1957); Felix D. Alamaraz, Jr., *Tragic Cavalier: Governor Manuel Salcedo of Texas, 1808–1813* (Austin, 1971); E. Wallace and D. M. Vigness (eds.), *Documents of Texas History;* D. M. Vigness, *The Revolutionary Decades;* O. B. Faulk, *The Last Years of Spanish Texas, 1778–1821.*

For a description of various missions, see C. E. Castañeda, *Our Catholic Heritage,* vol. IV; H. E. Bolton, *Texas in the Middle Eighteenth Century;* F. C. Chabot, *San Antonio and Its Beginnings, 1691–1731;* Margaret K. Kress (trans; introduction by M. A. Hatcher), "Diary of a Visit of Inspection of the Texas Missions Made by Fray Gaspar José de Solís in the Year 1767–'68," *Southwestern Historical Quarterly,* XXXV, 28–76; W. E. Dunn, "The Founding of Nuestra Señora del Refugio, the Last Spanish Mission in Texas," *ibid.,* XXV, 174–184; E. M. Schiwetz (historical notes by Robert S. Weddle), *Six Spanish Missions of Texas: A Portfolio of Paintings* (Austin, 1967); William H. Oberste, *History of Refugio Mission* (Refugio, 1942); K. S. O'Connor, *The Presidio La Bahía del Espíritu Santo Zuñiga, 1821–1846;* Billie Persons, "Secular Life in the San Antonio Missions," *Southwestern Historical Quarterly,* LXII, 45–62; E. Wallace and D. M. Vigness (eds.), *Documents of Texas History;* Mattie Austin Hatcher (trans.), "A Description of Mission Life," in E. C. Barker (ed.), *Readings in Texas History* (Dallas, 1929); Marion A. Habig, *The Alamo Chain of Missions* (Chicago, 1968); James Day and others, *Six Missions of Texas.*

Many writings about Spanish Texas contain references to the economic and social life of the settlers, but the best study is Oakah L. Jones, *Los Paisanos: Spanish Settlers on the Northern Frontier of New Spain* (Norman, Okla., 1979). Other excellent, though shorter or more specialized accounts, are O. B. Faulk, *A Successful Failure;* Fane

Downs, "The History of Mexicans in Texas" (unpublished dissertation, Texas Tech University, Lubbock, 1970); I. J. Cox, "Educational Efforts in San Fernando de Béxar," *Quarterly of the Texas State Historical Association,* VI, 27–63; F. C. Chabot, *San Antonio and Its Beginnings;* Sandra L. Myres, *The Ranch in Spanish Texas* (El Paso, 1969).

# Chapter Four

# ANGLO-AMERICAN COLONIZATION 1820–1835

Simultaneously with the Mexican Revolution, factors in the United States launched a migration movement that was destined to populate Texas and to open the way for the extension of the United States to the Pacific. Most significant of these were the Indian barrier, the Great Plains barrier, the financial panic in 1819, and the land policy. In 1817 Secretary of War John C. Calhoun inaugurated the policy of removing all the Indians from the American frontier to the Louisiana Territory north of Texas and immediately west of the ninety-fifth meridian—in the western extremity of the timberlands and beyond. In 1825 Congress enacted the policy into law. The frontier people may have ignored the line and continued their westward advance, but Texas, with a familiar geographic environment, seemed more desirable than having to contest a mass of eastern Indians who, pressed against the infuriated Plains Indians, could retreat no farther; to defy soldiers under orders to keep them off Indian lands; and to cope with the great American desert. Furthermore, the land laws of Spain and Mexico were more attractive than those of the United States. Even after purchase was made easier in 1820, the public domain was sold by bid in blocks of no less than eighty acres at a minimum cash price of $1.25 an acre, whereas more than fifty times as much could be obtained in Texas free or for a considerably smaller amount with no down payment. However, because of the Panic of 1819, possibly a majority of the farm seekers did not have the necessary $100.00 in cash; thus, some came to Texas.

The history of the movement of settlers is largely the story of two men, Moses Austin and his son, Stephen Fuller Austin. "Of all the men who figured in American history [wrote Professor George P. Garrison], there are no other two who attracted so little attention from their contemporaries and yet did things of such vast and manifest importance, as Moses Austin and his son Stephen. Their great work consisted of the making of Anglo-American Texas, an enterprise planned and begun by the one and carried into execution by the other."

## THE FIRST ANGLO-AMERICAN SETTLEMENT

Simultaneously with the filibusters, another group of Anglo-Americans were peacefully and permanently settling in northeast Texas, in present-day Red River County. These people had no connection with *empresarios,* nor were the first arrivals the result of the above factors. "They came," says R. W. Strickland, an historian of the region, "from Kentucky and Tennessee by way of Missouri and Arkansas. Their fathers had followed Boone and Harrod over the Wilderness Road to Harrodsburg and Bryant's Station or pioneered with Sevier along the waters of the Holston or French Broad." Because of the uncertainty of the western limits of Louisiana Territory, they settled at sites that a later boundary survey placed in Texas. The first arrivals were Indian traders, including George and Alex Wetmore, but in 1815 William Lawrence and William Hensley settled on the Red River, north of present-day Clarksville, at a site they named Jonesborough, for a trader already there. The following year Walter Pool, Charles Burkham, and Claiborne Wright built their cabins at Pecan Point, about thirty miles downstream at the junction of Pecan Bayou and the Red River, previously used as a camping place by French traders. Within two years twelve families and several traders were there. Horse thieves, trafficking in animals taken in Missouri and sold in Nacogdoches, laid out Trammel's Trace, a trail that linked these settlements with the outside world. In 1820 the legislature of the newly created Territory of Arkansas, uncertain of the location of its western boundary (even though the Adams-Onís Treaty had been signed), created Miller County out of all its territory south and west of the Red River. This action speeded immigration, and within a year about eighty families were in the settlement. A few families (including those of Martin Varner, Andrew Robinson, and Jesse Burnam) left to join Austin's first colony, but in 1825 most of the people, ousted from their homes north of the river to make way for the Choctaws, resettled at Jonesborough and Pecan Point. In 1831 Jonesborough became the seat of Miller County. Three years later, an estimated three thousand people lived in the area, and Clarksville had been founded.

    Nevertheless, because of a realistic need to know the proper location of the international boundary or a desire to have the advantage of Mexico's liberal land policy, many settlers felt that they were in Texas and applied to the Mexican government for land titles. They organized a company of militia to aid Texas during the revolution, and Richard Ellis of Pecan Point, whose son represented Miller County in the Arkansas legislature, was president of the convention that on March 2, 1836, declared Texas to be a free and independent nation.

## THE AUSTINS MAKE THE WAY

The Red River communities, however, were never a functioning unit within either Spanish or Mexican Texas, and it remained for the Austins to find a way to settle Anglo-Americans in that province. On December 23, 1820, the fifty-nine-year-old elder Austin, Connecticut born and seasoned by many years of business experience in Virginia and on the Missouri frontier, appeared before Governor Antonio de Martínez in San Antonio and asked for permission to establish in Texas a colony of three hundred families. Austin had moved to Spanish Missouri in 1798, and he now came, he said, as a former Spanish subject who wished to renew his allegiance to the king. Thanks to the aid of his old friend, the Baron de Bastrop (a native of Holland with a self-assumed title who was a large landowner in Spanish Louisiana before moving to Texas), whom he happened to meet in San Antonio, his application was finally endorsed by Martínez and on January 17, 1821, was approved in Monterrey by a board of superior officers, known as the provincial deputation.

Moses Austin died soon after his return to Missouri, and it was left to the son to complete the task begun by the father. Although only twenty-seven years old, Stephen F. Austin was already a man of rich experience. He was well educated. He had served five years in the legislature of Missouri Territory, had been appointed district judge in the territory of Arkansas, and had engaged in a variety of business undertakings. In addition, in Missouri he had operated a farm, had served as a federal territorial judge in Arkansas, and had studied law in New Orleans. More important still, he was, as Professor Eugene C. Barker, his biographer, states, "patient; methodical; energetic; and fair-spoken; and acquainted from childhood with the characteristic social types that mingled on the southwestern border."

With a small party Austin went to San Antonio in the summer of 1821. There Governor Martínez received him cordially, recognized him as the heir to his father's commission, and authorized him to explore the country and to make other arrangements for his colony. News about the project had already traveled far, and on his return to Natchitoches,

Moses Austin. In 1820, when hard times came to Potosi, Missouri, which Austin had founded in 1798, he went to Texas and obtained the governor's permission to settle three hundred families there. (E. C. Barker History Center, University of Texas)

Louisiana, he found nearly a hundred letters from persons who were interested. With the aid of his New Orleans partner, Joseph H. Hawkins, who had represented Kentucky in Congress, he purchased the schooner *Lively* and sent it to Texas with eighteen settlers and essential supplies. Austin returned to Texas by way of Natchitoches and Nacogdoches, where in late December he met a group of waiting colonists. Following the San Antonio road to the Brazos, he found a few colonists already selecting choice lands along the Brazos and Colorado rivers.

The first settler in the colony, Andrew Robinson, who arrived at the Brazos in November 1821, established and operated a ferry at the settlement of Washington on the Brazos. Two or three days later the three Kuykendall brothers and their families joined the Robinsons; others came, among them Josiah H. Bell, whom Austin had known in Missouri; and soon there were settlements in that community and also westward near the site of Independence. At Christmastime Robert and Joseph Kuykendall and Daniel Gilliland followed the La Bahía Road to the Colorado and settled near present-day Columbus. On January 1, 1822,

Thomas Boatright settled on a little stream he called New Year's Creek. Jared E. Groce, planter, lumberman, and capitalist of Alabama, arrived with his fifty wagons and ninety slaves early in 1822 and settled on the east side of the Brazos near the site of Hempstead. In March fifty men on the Brazos and one hundred on the Colorado were building houses and planting corn.

After some delay in the colony, Austin went to the mouth of the Colorado River to meet the *Lively*. He suffered a heavy financial loss and was greatly disturbed when the *Lively* failed to show. He learned later that it had landed by mistake at the mouth of the Brazos and that most of the immigrants on board, discouraged that Austin did not meet them, had returned with the ship to New Orleans.

Despairing of making contact with the *Lively,* Austin went to San Antonio in March 1822 to report to the governor on his progress. There, Governor Martínez informed him that the officials at Monterrey had refused to recognize his authority to introduce settlers under his father's grant, that the new government of the Mexican nation was considering a colonization policy for Texas and the Californias, and that he should go to Mexico City to look after his interests. Leaving the colony in charge of Josiah Bell, Austin, without delay, set out for Mexico.

At the capital, where he arrived on April 29, 1822, Austin found a complex and unstable political situation. He patiently and methodically set to work to secure the approval of the contract, but a quarrel between the "Liberator," Agustín de Iturbide, and the liberal Constituent Congress was approaching a crisis. On May 18 a popular revolution (in reality a mob), which Iturbide prompted, proclaimed him Emperor Agustín I, and on the next day Congress conceded. Then on October 31 Iturbide forced the Congress to adjourn and replaced it with a handpicked *junta* of forty-five members. Austin, who by this time had mastered the rudiments of the Spanish language and some cardinal principles of Mexican politics, talked with each member of the *junta* individually and secured the passage of a general colonization law on January 4, 1823, through which he could secure relief.

Iturbide's power had begun to wane, however, and Austin dared not leave the capital lest a new government undo all that had been accomplished. On March 19 Iturbide abdicated, and the restored Congress acted favorably on a contract for Austin in accordance with the terms of the Imperial Colonization Law. The new executive committee approved it on April 14, 1823. At the same time, Congress voided the Imperial Colonization Law, thereby making Austin the only person to receive a grant under its terms. Under the terms of the contract Austin was responsible for the government of the colony, and four days after its approval he left Mexico City for Monterrey to consult with the commandant general of the Eastern Interior Provinces regarding details of this responsibility.

It was not until early August 1823 that Austin, accompanied by Baron de Bastrop, the commissioner empowered to grant land titles, arrived in the colony. Although Bastrop had been sent at the end of 1822 by the governor to supervise the election of alcaldes and militia officers, conditions were critical. The drought of 1822, the hostile Karankawas, and Austin's long absence had caused a number of people to return to the United States. The crisis ended, however, when Austin assured the colonists that his contract had been validated and Bastrop began issuing land titles.

The seat of government was established on the Brazos River at the Atascosito crossing and was christened by Governor Luciano García as San Felipe de Austin. By the close of the summer of 1824 when he was called away, Bastrop had issued 272 titles.[1] The "Old Three Hundred," as these settlers came to be known, selected the rich plantation lands along the Brazos, Colorado, and Bernard rivers, from the vicinity of present-day Navasota, Brenham, and La Grange to the coast. By the terms of the imperial law each family was to receive one *labor* (177 acres) if engaged in farming, and a *sitio* (a square league or about 4,428 acres) for stock raising. Of course, most of the colonists preferred to be classed as stock raisers, and only about 20 titles called for less than a *sitio*. Special grants were made to a few men as compensation for substantial improvements such as mills. Jared E. Groce, the owner of many slaves, received ten *sitios*. Austin, as *empresario,* received about twenty-two *sitios*. The law required that the land be occupied and improved within two years after the receipt of the deed, that colonists profess the Catholic religion, that for six years they be exempt from the payment of tithes and duties on imports, and that children of slaves born in the empire be freed at the age of fourteen.

## A COLONIZATION PROGRAM

The Imperial Colonization Law, as previously stated, was merely a special arrangement for the relief of Austin. Congress, however, wanted a permanent colonization program and, after a prolonged discussion, on August 18, 1824, enacted a general law on the subject, generally referred to as the National Colonization Law. By this act the government

[1]The remainder, issued in 1827 and 1828, brought the total number of families introduced, including the "families" of single men who formed partnerships to meet the requirements of the law, to 297. Single men were entitled to 1,476 acres (one-third of a square league). Only 7 of the 297 titles actually issued were forfeited.

relegated to the states the administration of the public lands and authorized them to prescribe regulations for settlements, with only a few
reservations. The most important of these were (1) that all state laws had
to conform to the constitution then being framed; (2) that, except by
special approval of the federal executive, foreigners were not to settle
within ten leagues of the coast or twenty leagues of the international
boundary; (3) that no person should hold more than eleven *sitios;* (4)
that no alien should receive a land grant; and (5) that "until after the
year 1840, the general congress shall not prohibit the entrance of any
foreigner, as a colonist, unless imperious circumstances should require
it, with respect to individuals of a particular nation."

By a federal act of May 7, 1824, the two old Spanish provinces of
Coahuila and Texas were united as one state until the population of
Texas should become large enough for the maintenance of a separate
government. The state constituent body was installed in Saltillo on
August 15, 1824, and on March 24 of the following year it passed a
colonization law, known as the Coahuila-Texas Colonization Law. The
law required immigrants to give satisfactory evidence of their Christian
(Catholic) faith, morality, and good habits. Immigrants might receive
titles to land individually or through an *empresario.* Each head of a
family could receive, after the payment of a fee of $30.00, a *sitio* of land
for $62.50 ($87.50 for irrigable land), payable in three annual installments
beginning at the end of the fourth year, and he had to cultivate or occupy
the land within six years. For his services an *empresario* was entitled to
five *sitios* (approximately 22,140 acres) of grazing land and five *labors*
(approximately 885 acres) of farming land for each one hundred families,
up to eight hundred. *Empresario* contracts were to run six years and to
be absolutely void if at least one hundred families had not been settled
before the expiration of that time. Native-born Mexicans might purchase,
for small fees, as much as eleven *sitios.* There were to be no essential
changes in the law for a period of six years. Colonists were exempted
from general taxation for ten years. The national tariff law of 1823,
exempting colonists from payment of custom duties for a period of seven
years, was applicable.

## EARLY *EMPRESARIO* CONTRACTS
## AND COLONIZATION

The boundaries of Austin's colony were not immediately defined. In 1824
they were tentatively located for judicial purposes as extending from the
seashore to the San Antonio–Nacogdoches Road and from the Lavaca
River to the San Jacinto River. On the vacant land in this area, after the

**CHIEF COLONIZATION
GRANTS**

Miles

0       85

Austin's contract called for 300 families under the Imperial Colonization Law of April 14, 1823. Three contracts under the state law, 1825, 1827, 1828, called for 900 additional families in the area of his first colony; and, with Sam M. Williams, he had a contract to settle 800 families north and west of his first colony. He located over 1500 families.

On April 15, 1825, Green DeWitt got a contract for 400 families to be located on the Guadalupe, San Marcos, and Lavaca rivers. He issued 166 titles. The Nashville Company, known by the name of its agent, Sterling C. Robertson, as Robertson's colony, secured a contract for 800 families in 1825. After the revolution it was allowed premium lands for 379 families.

David G. Burnet, Lorenzo de Zavala, and Joseph Vehlein secured colonization rights in 1826 for territory on the eastern border of Texas between the twenty-ninth and thirty-third parallels. These rights were transferred to the Galveston Bay & Texas Land Company, which issued, between September 1834 and December 1835, titles to over 916 leagues.

On March 9, 1826, Arthur G. Wavell, an Englishman, secured a contract for 500 families to be located in northeast Texas. His associate, Benjamin R. Milam, located a number of families, but the United States contended that they were settled east of the boundary set by the treaty of 1819 with Spain, and the contractors never secured premium lands. Power and Hewetson granted almost 200 titles, McMullen and McGloin, 84. The Mexican *empresario*, De León, settled between 100 and 200 families.

location of his first 300 families, in 1825 Austin obtained a contract to settle an additional 500 families. The "Little Colony," which he contracted in 1827 to settle 100 families, was on the east side of the Colorado River, immediately above his original grant. Bastrop became its principal town. The reserve zones of the national law did not apply to Austin's original settlers, and some had located within ten leagues of the coast. Austin subsequently petitioned for and in 1828 received permission to settle 300 additional families in this coastal reserve between the Lavaca and the San Jacinto rivers. Thus, by 1828 Austin had signed four contracts to settle in Texas a total of 1,200 families. By then the population of his colonies was increasing rapidly. It was 2,021 in March 1828 and 4,248 in June 1830. Tabulations after his death indicate that the great *empresario* authorized a total of 1,540 grants to colonists.

In 1825 Green DeWitt, another Missourian and next to Austin the most successful of the *empresarios,* received a state contract to settle four hundred families between the Lavaca River and a line two leagues west of and parallel to the Guadalupe River and between the San Antonio–Nacogdoches Road and the ten-league reserve adjacent to the coast. Gonzales, the main town, was located that same year, but after an attack by Comanche Indians in July 1826 the people moved to the lower Lavaca. Here their troubles did not end, for they were within the restricted zone and became involved in a quarrel with *Empresario* Martín de León. The following year they were ordered to leave. By the summer of 1828 they were back in Gonzales, where they were again harassed by the Comanches. At the expiration of DeWitt's contract on April 15, 1831, 166 titles had been issued to settlers, but the greater part of the land within his grant was still vacant.

Martín de León, whose contract was unique, had fair success as a colonizer. A native of and a rancher in Nuevo Santander, De León, soon after visiting Texas in 1805, moved his operation to the vicinity of San Patricio. During the Mexican Revolution he cooperated with the republicans in San Antonio. In April 1824, after hearing of the Imperial Colonization Law, he obtained from the provincial delegation in San Antonio de Béxar a grant to settle an unspecified number of families (he stated that he had already recruited forty-one families) near the coast and between the Lavaca and Guadalupe rivers. The settlers were predominantly Mexican. Twelve families arrived that fall, and in October De León laid out the town of Guadalupe Victoria on the banks of the Guadalupe. The precise limits of the colony were not fixed, and this gave rise to a quarrel between De León and DeWitt. De León located some settlers clearly within DeWitt's grant, which had been authorized by the Coahuila-Texas legislature with knowledge of the De León grant, and in 1826 the settlers at Gonzales, after an Indian attack, retired to a site within the littoral reserve and within De León's grant. As noted previously, the DeWitt colonists had to leave the reserve, and in 1829 De León received permission to settle another 150 families in the area. When it was learned, however, that he intended to displace some of DeWitt's colonists to enlarge his own colony, the second grant was canceled. Victoria continued to prosper and grow, nevertheless, and by 1833 its population was over 200.

Haden Edwards, another of the early *empresarios,* secured a contract for a colony in eastern Texas, but a quarrel with the Mexican officials in 1826 ended his efforts before much had been accomplished. An account of his troubles and the cancellation of his grant will be discussed in the next chapter.

In addition to the concessions to Austin, DeWitt, and De León, the state of Coahuila and Texas made about twenty-two other contracts with *empresarios* under the law of March 24, 1825, calling in all for about eight thousand families. The great majority of these *empresarios* located no families or only a negligible number. Others were more successful, but their colonists, almost without exception, came during the second period of colonization.

## THE DECREE OF APRIL 6, 1830

The very success of the colonization movement all but destroyed it. The stream of immigration from the United States that had been flowing into Texas in ever-increasing numbers was stopped suddenly by an act of the federal government on April 6, 1830. The decree was the direct outgrowth of reports of General Manuel Mier y Terán, soldier, scholar, and statesman, who in 1828 was sent to survey the eastern boundary as defined in the Adams-Onís Treaty and to investigate the need for new military posts in Texas. The importance of his visit, however, was his reports and recommendations in June and July pertaining to conditions in Texas. Terán reported that Mexican influence diminished rapidly as he proceeded eastward. In Nacogdoches, the Mexican population was of the lowest class and a minority. The Anglo-Americans, including slave holders, honest laborers, criminals, and vagabonds, were taking the country, maintained an English school, were progressive, shrewd, and unruly, and demanded the privileges and rights guaranteed by the constitution. Mexico must act "now" or Texas "is lost forever." Terán proposed that the Mexican government should (1) colonize Mexicans in Texas; (2) colonize Swiss and Germans; (3) encourage coastal trade between Texas and the rest of the republic; and (4) place more troops in

Texas, among them convict-soldiers who would become permanent settlers after their terms had expired.

The report alarmed other high-ranking Mexican officials, including General José María Tornel. Tornel persuaded President Vicente Guerrero, a federalist who had used the military to prevent the installation in 1829 of the constitutionally elected Gómez Pedraza, to exercise the dictatorial powers that Congress had given him and to abolish slavery. On September 15, 1829, Guerrero issued a proclamation to end slavery throughout the nation. The decree threatened the property rights of all Mexicans. Because of its protestations, Texas was excluded from its operation, and soon the decree was voided, but not in time to stave off a Centralist coup d'etat that deposed Guerrero and installed in his place Anastacio Bustamante. To check Anglo-American influence in Texas, the Bustamante government immediately took a more direct approach. Lucas Alamán, minister of foreign relations, urged Congress to adopt Terán's proposals with certain modifications that he suggested. The decree, signed April 6, 1830, contained, in addition, the drastic Article 11, a part of which reads: "Citizens of foreign countries lying adjacent to the Mexican territory are prohibited from settling as colonists in the states or territories of the Republic adjoining such countries," meaning that no more Anglo-Americans could settle in Texas. The article, furthermore, declared suspended "all contracts not already completed and not in harmony with the law," for the establishment of military posts by convict-soldiers, for the settlement around these posts by the families of the soldiers and other Mexican colonists, and for the strict prohibition of any further introduction of slaves.

To the Mexican government, the law was a mandatory act to meet an emergency; to the colonists, however, the law seemed nothing less than a calamity. Austin succeeded in fending off the blow slightly, insofar as his colony and that of DeWitt were concerned, by an ingenious interpretation that permitted them to complete their quota of families without respect to the law. Thus, the population of Austin's settlements increased from 4,248 in June 1830 to 5,665 a year later. DeWitt's contract and one of Austin's soon expired by limitation, however; Austin's other contracts were soon filled, and in November of 1831 Austin had to admit that immigration of North Americans was totally prohibited. He and his secretary, Samuel M. Williams, then secured a grant to settle European and Mexican families, but in this they did not succeed.

As the unfilled *empresario* contracts made under the state law of 1825 expired, the forfeited lands they had encompassed again became available for new grants. Furthermore, the Law of April 6, 1830, sought to encourage European and Mexican families to settle in Texas. In 1832 the legislature of Coahuila-Texas passed an act promoting the same plan.

Under its terms two or three contracts were made, but the results were negligible.

Meanwhile, considerable pressure was exerted for the repeal of the act. The colonists in their convention in April 1833 made repeal of the act their major aim, and Austin, who carried the petition to Mexico City, managed to secure its repeal, effective May 1, 1834.

## THE RENEWAL OF COLONIZATION

After the repeal of the anti-immigration law, the state government renewed several contracts that had been voided in 1830 and made some new contracts. With the legal barrier removed, the stream of immigrants reached unprecedented proportions. One observer reported that during January and February 1835 alone, about two thousand persons landed at the mouth of the Brazos.

Meanwhile, the officials of two companies, the Galveston Bay and Texas Land Company and the Texas Association of Nashville (Robertson Colony) proceeded with colonization plans in disregard of the law of April 6, 1830. On October 16, 1830, Lorenzo de Zavala, Joseph Vehlein, and David G. Burnet pooled their extensive grants in eastern Texas and assigned them to the Galveston Bay and Texas Land Company, a New York City–based organization with James Prentiss, Samuel Swartout, and John T. Mason as its principal promoters and agents. Although the company did not own any land and did not have the right to sell any, it advertised in a fashion similar to that used later by western railroad companies. It sublet huge blocks to subordinate contractors, and it sold scrip, amounting to nearly 7.5 million acres from one to ten cents an acre, to prospective settlers and speculators, many of whom evidently believed that they were buying land. The scrip merely reserved the designated number of acres for the holder who, before obtaining title to any land, still had to comply with all requirements of the Mexican colonization laws, which, at that time, did not permit persons from the United States to settle in Texas. Nevertheless, the company soon sent by sea two groups of emigrants, but Mexican officials would not allow them to locate lands or to settle. Although hesitant because of its irregularities, the authorities finally recognized the company and extended the three contracts. Thereafter came a stream of immigrants, and between September 1834 and December 1835 a total of 936 titles to land were issued in the area north of Galveston Bay.

In 1825 the Texas Association of Nashville, generally known as the Robertson Colony, obtained through Robert Leftwich an extensive grant north and northwest of Austin's grant on which to settle eight hundred colonists. This company also sold land scrip and became involved in considerable controversy and litigation. Since the company agent, Sterling C. Robertson, had made very little progress toward its settlement before the passage of the Law of April 6, 1830, the governor declared the contract forfeited. In 1831 the territory was granted to Austin and his partner, Samuel M. Williams, who proposed to settle on it eight hundred Mexican and European families. The governor, after examining Robertson's claim to having settled more than 100 families before the enactment of the Law of April 6, 1830, restored the colony to the Nashville Company, but Austin and Williams regained the colony in May of the following year. By the time the revolution closed the land offices, more than six hundred families had located in the colony, and the towns of Nashville, Viesca, and Salada had been founded. In 1847, after Robertson's death, a Texas court ruled that his claim to the colony was valid and awarded his heirs premium land for 379 families.

Meanwhile, two Irish colonies, McMullen and McGloin and Power and Hewetson, were being settled in southern Texas. In August 1828 John McMullen and his son-in-law, James McGloin, both natives of Ireland but at the time merchants in Matamoros, Mexico, obtained a state contract to settle two hundred Irish families in a portion of the territory east of the Nueces River and immediately above the coastal reserve. The first group to arrive, fifty-eight in late 1829, remained for a time at the Refugio mission but in October 1831 established Hibernia or San Patricio, the colony's principal town. The contract was voided by the Law of April 6, 1830, but in 1834 it was extended, and by the outbreak of the Texas Revolution, eighty-four land titles had been issued.

Although beset by trouble and misfortune, the other Irish colony was more successful. James Power, a native of Ireland, was engaged in business and mining in Mexico. James Hewetson, also a native of Ireland who, after coming to Texas in 1821 with Stephen F. Austin, settled in Saltillo and Monclova where he was engaged in manufacturing, mining, and the mercantile business. In 1828, by special permission of both the national and the Coahuila-Texas governments, Power and Hewetson obtained a contract to settle two hundred families from Mexico and Ireland in the ten-league littoral reserve between the Nueces and the Guadalupe rivers, and (after a compromise with *Empresario* De León) in a part of the former lands of the abandoned mission of Nuestra Señora del Refugio. Power went to Ireland and in 1834 sailed for Texas with 350 immigrants, but enroute they contracted cholera. Seventy were left in New Orleans, some were buried at sea, and the survivors were forced to abandon their ship, losing all their supplies on the coast. In Texas others were stricken with the deadly plague. Refugio, on the site of the old mission by that name, became their central town, and by the time of the

Texas Revolution, almost two hundred land titles had been granted, many apparently to Anglo-Americans.

A third attempt to establish a colony of Europeans was a complete failure. Dr. John Charles Beales, a surgeon from England who moved to Mexico in 1829, and Dr. James Grant, a physician from Scotland who after two years in Texas settled in Parras, Coahuila, and after that was a member of the legislature of Coahuila and Texas, in 1832 contracted to settle eight hundred European families in the region between the Rio Grande and the Nueces River. The first group of colonists, including English, German, Spanish-Americans, and Anglo-Americans, landed at Copano Bay and traveled by ox wagon to Las Moras Creek, near present-day Brackettville, where in March 1834 they established a settlement they named Dolores, in honor of Beales's Mexican wife. Beales brought at least one other group of colonists to Dolores, but because of crop failure, Indian hostility, and Santa Anna's invasion of Texas, the settlers abandoned the colony. During the flight all the settlers in one wagon train were killed or taken captive by Comanche Indians.

## COLONIZATION IN RETROSPECT

The Texas colonization era ended legally with the decree by the Texas provisional government in November 1835 that closed the land offices. An act of the Congress of the republic in June 1837 declared that all *empresario* contracts had ceased on the day of the declaration of independence, March 2, 1836. It may be stated in review that the majority of the twenty-five or more colonization contracts for Texas were without results of any consequence. Preeminent among the *empresarios* stands Austin, who settled almost as many families as all the others combined. After Austin, the most successful during the early period, that is, before the passage of the Law of April 6, 1830, were DeWitt and De León. Of the later colonizers the Galveston Bay and Texas Land Company and Robertson's Nashville Company were most successful. In colonizing Europeans, Power and Hewetson made the most progress; but their relatively small accomplishments sustain the statement made by the English historian, William Kennedy, that "the North Americans are the only people who, in defiance of all obstacles, have struck the roots of civilization deep into the soil of Texas."

The colonists were distributed from the Sabine to the Nueces, but an overwhelming majority were located east of the Guadalupe and south of the old road from San Antonio to Nacogdoches. About 3,500 land titles were issued through the different *empresarios,* and a few titles were granted without the aid of proprietors. Estimates of population

Stephen F. Austin, the Father of Texas, earned his title by his outstanding efforts as the greatest colonizer of the state. (University of Texas Library) Also shown, a replica of his home near Sealy. (Texas Highway Department)

vary. In 1834 the Mexican soldier and statesman, Juan N. Almonte, after a visit to Texas, placed the population at 24,700 including slaves, or at a little more than 20,000 for the Anglo-Americans and their slaves.

Who were these people? Whence had they come and what were the forces that brought them? The evidence available indicates that they were, in the main, farmers and people of some means, although many had left behind them debts they could not pay. That they were honest and law abiding is evidenced by the small amount of crime committed in the colonies. The *empresarios* were required to see that lawless persons did not remain. Among the settlers literacy was high for that date. Of more than 266 of Austin's "Old Three Hundred," only 4 could not write. Data kept by Austin for his colony show that the majority of his people came from Louisiana, Alabama, Arkansas, Tennessee, or Missouri, in the order named. A total of 699 registered from the trans-Appalachian states as compared with a total of 107 from the Atlantic Seaboard. However, most adults living west of the mountains at that time had been born in the seaboard states. The settlement of Texas by Anglo-Americans, stated simply, was merely a part of a phenomenal movement of thousands and thousands of people, who, with gun and axe in search of a better life, had cleared the forests and built communities on the Piedmont, in the Great Valley, and along the tributaries of the Ohio, the Mississippi, and beyond. They came to be with relatives and friends, to escape conflicts with the law or with some individual, to drown their sorrows, to regain their health, or to satisfy their curiosity. They came because of the panic of 1819 and financial adversity and because they wanted virgin soil to replace their eroded and worn-out farms, but the overwhelming majority came to get free or cheap land.

The land system in the United States was modified in a way that made it difficult or impossible for some people to obtain land. The least amount of the public domain that could be purchased was 80 acres, and the minimum price was set at $1.25 an acre, cash. By comparison, in Texas the head of a family could obtain 4,428 acres of land free in Austin's first colony and afterward for only little more than the cost of 80 acres in the United States.[2]

---

[2]The total cost of land varied from time to time and in the different colonies. The Coahuila and Texas Colonization Law of 1825 required a payment to the state of $30.00 for each *sitio* of grazing land, $2.50 for each *labor* ($62.50 for each *sitio*) without the facility of irrigation, and $3.50 for each *labor* ($87.50 for each *sitio*) that could be irrigated. The variation in the cost was largely in the fees. The fee to Austin ranged from nothing to $60.00, to his land commissioner $15.00, to S.M. Williams for clerical work $10.00, and for stamped paper $2.00—a maximum total of $117.00 for a *sitio* of grazing land or $149.50 for nonirrigated farm land. Austin stated with pride that he never had turned a man away because he was poor.

## COLONIAL INSTITUTIONS

When they crossed the Sabine River, the Anglo-American colonists entered a country whose government, religion, customs, and attitudes differed greatly from those they had known before. They ran their own affairs with a minimum of interference from Mexican officials, and they modified Mexican institutions as much as possible to conform to Anglo-American patterns. As H. Yoakum states: "They brought with them here, as household gods, their own first lessons in politics, morals, religion, and business, and they wished not to unlearn those lessons to learn others."

On October 4, 1824, the Constituent Congress, which had assembled in November 1823, framed and published a constitution much like that of the United States. Perhaps the greatest difference was that the Mexican instrument established the Roman Catholic church as the official religion. In this congress Erasmo Seguin represented Texas, and the farmers of Austin's colony loyally subscribed several hundred bushels of corn to help pay his expenses. The legislature for the state of Coahuila and Texas was organized in Saltillo on August 15, 1824, and Baron de Bastrop represented Texas. Most of its efforts before March 11, 1827, went toward framing a state constitution which was published at that time. The constitution provided for twelve deputies. Of these, Texas was allotted only one, but the number was later increased to three. The deputies, like the members of the national congress, were to be chosen by an indirect electoral process.

In 1825 Texas was made a department within the state of Coahuila and Texas, to be presided over by a political chief who was appointed by and responsible to the governor. This officer, a kind of subgovernor, was to reside in Béxar, watch over public tranquility, inflict punishments, command the local militia, see that the laws were enforced, and make reports to the governor. Later, Texas was divided into three departments, with headquarters and political chiefs in San Antonio, Nacogdoches, and San Felipe.

The most important unit of local government was the municipality, which included one or more towns and adjacent territory. It might cover thousands of square miles. The *ayuntamiento,* or governing body of the municipality, had broad duties that suggest the combined functions of a modern city commission and a county commissioners' court. At its head was an alcalde, the chief executive officer, whose duties were similar to those of sheriff, judge, and mayor of a city. The *regidores,* like members of our own city commissions, had certain legislative powers as well as some administrative responsibilities. Each municipality had a *sindico* (an attorney and the state's representative), an *alguacil* (sheriff) appointed by the alcalde, and a secretary appointed by the *ayuntamiento*. Each subdivision of a municipality, known as a district or precinct, had its *comisario*, a sort of subalcalde, generally thought of by Anglo-American colonists as a justice of the peace, and also a *sindico* for the district. Austin's first colonists were given local self-government by the order of Governor José Trespalacios in November 1822, when alcaldes were elected by the settlers on both the Colorado River and the Brazos River. New districts were created from time to time, so that when constitutional government was established in 1828, Austin's colony had seven. At that time the municipalities of Texas were Béxar, La Bahía or Goliad, Nacogdoches, and San Felipe (Austin's colony). The municipalities of Brazoria and of Gonzales were created in 1832; by the close of 1834 there were thirteen. Municipal taxes were light and payable largely in kind. The early colonists, it will be recalled, were exempted from state taxes, church tithes, and national customs duties.[3]

Into this pattern of government the *empresario* system was fitted. The duties of the *empresario* were numerous and trying. He had to deal not only with state and national governments that were often unsympathetic but also with the Anglo-American pioneers who, though sturdy, worthy, and well meaning, were prejudiced, stubborn, jealous of their freedom, and disposed to find fault with those in authority. Austin's burden was much greater than that of his fellow proprietors, for his colony was seven years old before regular constitutional government was established. He was responsible for selecting his colonists, their good character, and, although Bastrop, his land commissioner, actually issued the titles, for surveying the land and all business connected with obtaining and recording titles. At first, Austin was responsible for the government of the colony. Indeed, he was a lawgiver, for he wrote civil and criminal codes for the alcaldes, based on the Mexican laws but adapted to conditions in the colonies. He was commander in chief of the militia and responsible for defense and the maintenance of satisfactory relations with the Indians.

In addition, he had many informal obligations even more burdensome than those required by law. Prospective colonists expected entertainment at his home, and frequently he was called on to settle petty disputes. Many persons regarded him as a collecting agent; others expected him to make for them purchases and loans. With the establish-

---

[3]The Imperial Colonization Law exempted the colonists for six years from tithes, excises, or taxes of any kind whatever. By decree of September 29, 1823, Congress exempted from duties for seven years all merchandise from any country. In its colonization law of 1825 the state exempted colonists from taxes for ten years. The Law of April 6, 1830, permitted for two years the importation of provisions, lumber, tools, and so forth, free of duty. In 1832 the exemption on certain articles was extended again for two years.

ment of constitutional government in 1828, the greater part of Austin's governmental responsibilities ceased, but there was no letup of the informal ones.

During its early history, DeWitt's colony was apparently governed similarly to Austin's. In 1826 the *empresario* appointed James Norton as alcalde, an irregular act, but the governor approved it. At first, the colony was under the jurisdiction of Béxar, but in 1828 in response to a petition it was placed under the jurisdiction of San Felipe, where it remained until the municipality of Gonzales was organized in 1832.

The Anglo-Americans, with a love for legislating that equaled the love of the Mexicans for regulating, passed many local laws but had little interest in enforcing them, primarily because the court system was most unsatisfactory. In all important cases the alcalde or *comisario* was required to send a record of the testimony to a higher official at Saltillo and wait for the return of his decision. Even if there were no errors, the sentence had to be approved by the supreme court before the decree could be executed. Such a system would have been intolerable except for the facts that there was very little crime in the colonies and that most offenders could be dealt with outside of the courts. Austin drove a number of undesirables from his colony; the *ayuntamientos* compelled some to leave; and occasionally the people persuaded certain ill-disposed persons that their health and happiness would be greater elsewhere. An act passed in 1834 provided for jury trials in both civil and criminal cases and for an appellate circuit court for Texas, but certain features were impracticable and it never went into effect.

For the first colonists, hostile Indians added to other perils. The Karankawas on the coast pillaged and murdered in small bands. In the interior, the Tonkawas were generally nominally at peace with the whites, and along the Brazos River above the San Antonio Road, the Wacos and Tawakonis were periodically dangerous and always troublesome. In eastern Texas a few hundred Cherokees and Choctaws from east of the Mississippi and bands of indigenous sedentary Indians kept the colonists on the alert.

For defense against the Indians the colonists had to depend mainly on their own resources. The militia in Austin's colony was first organized in the fall of 1822. From time to time new districts were created, until, by the close of 1824, six companies had been organized. By 1830 the Indian menace for Austin's colony was a thing of the past. Béxar, Gonzales, and Goliad, however, did not fare as well as those to the east. In 1830 DeWitt wrote the governor that unless troops were sent to his colony, his settlements would be broken up. The settlers managed to hold out, although troops were not sent until the following year, and then only fifteen came. A six-pounder cannon loaned to Gonzales in 1831 for protection against the Indians was destined to be the cause of the first bloodshed in the Texas Revolution.

The status of slavery in colonial Texas is hard to describe. The Imperial Colonization Law recognized slavery but forbade the slave trade and declared that slaves born in the empire should be free at the age of fourteen. The state constitution of 1827 recognized existing slavery and permitted the introduction of slaves for six months after its promulgation, but no person born thereafter could be a slave. Meanwhile, the Mexican government began to undo with its left hand what it had done with its right: It legalized the domestic slave trade by providing that a slave might "change" his or her master "if the new master would indemnify the old," and a state law of 1828 legalized slave importation by recognizing labor "contracts made in foreign countries. . . ." Afterwards, upon entering Texas, blacks were nominally servants under contract, but actually they were still slaves. Mention has been made already of President Guerrero's proclamation in 1829 abolishing slavery and its repeal because of opposition throughout the country. The decree of April 6, 1830, recognized existing slavery but prohibited the further introduction of slaves. An act of the state legislature in 1832 strengthened the antislavery laws and limited to ten years the contracts with slaves and day laborers. Thus, by 1832, the introduction of slaves was positively barred, and peonage contracts were limited to ten years.

Although many slaves had been brought to Texas, their ratio to whites declined in the later colonial years. In 1825 Austin's colony had 443 slaves and 1,347 whites. In 1834 Juan Almonte estimated the number of slaves in the Department of the Brazos (composed of Austin's colonies) as 1,000, out of a total population of about 10,000. The subject of slavery does not appear extensively in the discussions and protests of the colonists preceding the revolution, but the uncertain status of the institution frequently caused anxiety and, no doubt, frightened away many prospective immigrants.

Judging from letters of inquiry sent to Austin and from other sources, it seems that a few potential colonists stayed away from Texas because of their hostility to Catholicism. By constitution and law, Roman Catholicism was the religion of Mexico, to the exclusion of any other. The Catholic faith was supposed to accompany Mexican citizenship, and heretics were subject to banishment and other punishment. Although he always stated these facts plainly to prospective colonists, Austin emphasized them less and less as his colony grew, and other proprietors apparently took much the same attitude. In fact, very few of the colonists were Catholics by faith, and not many were so even by name.

Most of the settlers apparently had little interest in formal religion. One observer, while praising them for the small amount of crime in

Texas, added that, in respect to the gospel, conditions were "bad—bad! superlatively bad." Another wrote from the Colorado River country in 1831 that there was little regard for the Sabbath which "is generally spent in visiting, driving stock, and breaking mustangs."

The people had more cause to complain of spiritual neglect than of persecution. Repeatedly, Austin petitioned the authorities to send a priest to his colony to christen children, legalize marriage contracts, and perform various other services that were expected in a Catholic country. But he was put off with promises and excuses, the chief reason being, it seems, that there was no provision for paying a priest as long as the colonists were exempted from taxes and tithes. Finally, in 1831 Father Michael Muldoon, an Irish priest, arrived. He was good natured, loyal, and kind, but apparently he did not always live up to the Anglo-American standards of piety for the ministry. In Nacogdoches, where there once had been a Catholic church and where many Catholics still resided, the established church under Father Antonio Diaz fared better.

In spite of official opposition and the indifference of the colonists, the Protestants made considerable progress in colonial Texas. In 1820, Joseph E. Bays, a Baptist preacher who came from Missouri to Louisiana with Moses Austin, soon was preaching in Texas. William Stevenson, a Methodist who had preached at Pecan Point in the winter of 1818–1819, continued to preach despite warnings from Austin and James Gaines, alcalde of the Sabine district.[4] A little later several missionaries came, including Sumner Bacon, a Cumberland Presbyterian who traveled through Austin's and DeWitt's colonies distributing Bibles, and Thomas J. Pilgrim, a Baptist credited with organizing the first Sunday school in Texas.

After the colonists drove out the Mexican garrisons in 1832, Protestant camp meetings became common. One on Caney Creek in 1835 had five ministers present. Horatio Chriesman, the alcalde, and Dr. James B. Miller, the political chief, presumably encouraged the meetings and helped to support the ministers. A few churches also were organized during this period. In 1834, a state law, in violation of the constitution, afforded a measure of religious tolerance. It stated that no person should be molested on account of his or her religious or political opinions, provided he or she did not disturb the public order.

There was no system of public education in colonial Texas. A public school was established in San Antonio as early as 1746, and shortly after 1813 the Spaniards erected a building there to provide for

---

[4]Pecan Point (in present-day Red River County) was a part of the regular circuit of the Missouri Conference from 1818 to 1825. At different times Thomas Tennant, Green Orr, and Joseph Reed rode that circuit. Freeman Smalley, a Baptist, preached there in 1822.

seventy pupils. Books were purchased for a primary school in San Antonio in 1828, but Colonel Almonte, who visited Texas in 1834, lamented that the school once maintained by the *ayuntamiento* of Béxar had been discontinued. He added, however, that there were schools in Nacogdoches, San Augustine, and Jonesborough. A small private school in Austin's colony was taught by Isaac M. Pennington as early as 1823, and there were other teachers. Harrisburg had no school in 1833, but a little later a school with about ten pupils was begun in a nearby community.

The chief industries in early Texas were farming and trade. Farming will be discussed in a later chapter. A few trade centers were established at an early date. San Felipe became a thriving town, but in 1830 it still had only one house that was not built of logs. By 1832 Brazoria had approximately forty houses and was perhaps the leading shipping town. Soon, however, it shared some of its trade with the new town of Matagorda, at the mouth of the Colorado. Galveston, with the best harbor on the Texas coast, remained uninhabited during most of the colonial era. The old Spanish town of Nacogdoches, which had only thirty-six inhabitants when Austin saw it in 1821, grew into a business center with stores well supplied with dry goods, notions, and foodstuffs. San Antonio, or Béxar, although the most populous town throughout the entire period, did not grow as rapidly as some of the newer towns.

Two conditions hampered business severely: the lack of money or banking facilities and the absence of roads and other means of transportation. The account of George B. Erath, an Austrian-American, is typical. Erath traded clothes which he had brought from Germany for cattle and hogs and he traded a horse for corn. His partner gave an ox for a sow valued at five dollars, a feather bed for three cows and calves, a gun for a mare, and another gun for a cow, calf, and yearling. The *ayuntamiento* recognized the paucity of money by permitting a man to pay two-thirds of his local taxes[5] in kind, and it gave an official stamp to bovine currency by stating that a cow and calf should be valued at ten dollars. Interest rates were exorbitant.

Save for small quantities of salt, some horses, and occasional illicit purchases of tobacco, there seems to have been virtually no trade between Texas and Mexico. In 1821 on his first visit to Texas, Stephen F. Austin found a good trade already established between Natchitoches, Louisiana, and Goliad. Although Natchitoches continued to be a favorite trading post of Texans and most shipments into the colonies by land originated there, trade by sea with New Orleans increased throughout the period.

[5]The tax exemptions did not apply to local taxes.

Map of Texas, 1835. (Southwest Collection, Texas Tech University)

Inadequate ports constituted a great handicap to shipping. Galveston was not convenient to the principal settlements. Even small vessels had to be partly unloaded to cross the bar in order to reach Brazoria and other points on the lower Brazos. Likewise, Matagorda Bay had its perils, and small schooners had difficulty in reaching either the mouth of the Lavaca or the town of Matagorda at the mouth of the Colorado.

Austin stated in 1829 that the chief possibilities for export from Texas were "cotton, beef, tallow, pork, lard, mules, etc." Almonte, whose data are the best extant but probably are little more than a collection of guesses, valued Texas exports for 1833 at $500,000. Of this, cotton made up $353,000; "furs" (probably hides of all kinds), $140,000;

and cattle, $25,000. His estimate on cotton certainly is too high, but it may have been offset by miscellaneous items which he ignored and his failure to credit the Department of the Brazos[6] with the shipment of cattle. The importation for that year, Almonte said, amounted to $630,000.

It is well to remember that most families brought with them quantities of goods that are not considered in these estimates. These imports supplied approximately twenty thousand colonists with necessities and a few, a very few, with luxuries: The exports proved to be the great potential wealth of the land. Of great political importance, also, is the fact that these imported goods—almost wholly from the United States—kept alive the interest of the Texans in the land of their birth.

## SELECTED BIBLIOGRAPHY

Material on Texas colonization is comparatively abundant. Of the older accounts, the best is H. Yoakum, *History of Texas*. His text, along with some supplementary material, is reproduced in Dudley G. Wooten, *A Comprehensive History of Texas* (2 vols., Dallas, 1897). Other general accounts are William Kennedy, *Texas* (2nd ed., London, 1841; Fort Worth, 1925); H. H. Bancroft, *History of the North Mexican States and Texas;* John Henry Brown, *A History of Texas, 1685–1892* (2 vols., St. Louis, 1892–1893); Louis J. Wortham, *A History of Texas* (5 vols., Fort Worth, 1924); Clarence R. Wharton, *Texas under Many Flags* (5 vols., Chicago and New York, 1930); and H. S. Thrall, *Pictorial History of Texas;* S. V. Connor, *Texas: A History.*

The most useful reference is the *Handbook of Texas*. Rich collections of source materials are E. C. Barker (ed.), *The Austin Papers* (3 vols.); vols. I and II were published as *The Annual Report of the American Historical Association,* 1919, II, and 1922, II (Washington, D.C., 1924 and 1928); vol. III (Austin, 1926); Malcolm D. McLean (ed.), *Papers Concerning Robertson's Colony in Texas* (6 vols., Fort Worth and Arlington, Tex., 1974–1979); E. Wallace and D. M. Vigness (eds.), *Documents of Texas History;* Juan N. Almonte, "Statistical Report on Texas," 1835 (trans. C. E. Castañeda), *Southwestern Historical Quarterly,* XXVIII, 177–222.

The most scholarly studies are E. C. Barker, *The Life of Stephen F. Austin* (Nashville and Dallas, 1925); E. C. Barker, *Mexico and Texas, 1821–1835* (Dallas, 1928); and D. M. Vigness, *The Revolutionary Dec-*

---

[6]It will be recalled that at this time Texas was divided into three departments: Béxar, with headquarters in San Antonio; the Brazos, with headquarters in San Felipe; and Nacogdoches, with headquarters in the town of Nacogdoches.

*ades*. For the decree of April 6, 1830, see Ohland Morton, *Terán and Texas* (Austin, 1948).

Articles on colony planting are to be found in the *Quarterly of the Texas State Historical Association* (I–XV) and the *Southwestern Historical Quarterly* (XVI–). Among them are: "Journal of Stephen F. Austin on His First Trip to Texas, 1821," VII, 286–307; W. S. Lewis, "Adventures of the *Lively* Immigrants," III, 1–32; L. G. Bugbee, "What Became of the *Lively?*" III, 141–148; L. G. Bugbee, "The Old Three Hundred," I, 108–117; E. C. Barker, "Notes on the Colonization of Texas," XXVII, 108–119; Mary Virginia Henderson, "Minor Empresario Contracts for the Colonization of Texas, 1825–1834," XXXI, 295–324; XXXII, 1–28; Robert W. Amsler, "General Arthur G. Wavell: A Soldier of Fortune in Texas," LXIX, 1–21, 186–209; Andrew Forest Muir, "Humphrey Jackson, Alcalde of San Jacinto," LXVIII, 362–366; Charles A. Bacarisse, "The Union of Coahuila and Texas," LXI, 341–349; Henry W. Barton, "The Anglo-American Colonists under Mexican Militia Laws," LXV, 61–71; Roger N. Conger, "The Tomás de la Vega Eleven-League Grant on the Brazos," LXI, 371–382. R. W. Strickland, "Miller County, Arkansas Territory, the Frontier That Men Forget," *Chronicles of Oklahoma*, XVIII, 12–34, 154–170; XIX, 37–54, is the best account available of the settlement of extreme northeast Texas. Excellent studies of the colonies in southern Texas include W. H. Oberste's comprehensive *Texas Irish Empresarios and Their Colonies* (Austin, 1953); Leroy P. Graf, "Colonizing Projects in Texas South of the Nueces, 1820–1845," *Southwestern Historical Quarterly*, L, 431–448; Carl Coke Rister, *Comanche Bondage* (Glendale, Calif., 1955), about Beale's colony; A. B. J. Hammett, *The Empresario Don Martín de León: The Richest Man in Texas* (Victoria, Tex., 1971).

On colonial institutions, there are in the *Southwestern Historical Quarterly:* E. C. Barker, "The Government of Austin's Colony, 1821–1831," XXI, 223–252; supplemented by the "Minutes of the *Ayuntamiento of San Felipe de Austin,* 1828–1832, XXI, 299–326, 395–423; XXII, 78–95, 180–196, 272–278, 353–359; XXIII, 69–77, 141–151, 214–223, 302–307; XXIV, 81–83, 154–166. Useful also is E. C. Barker, "The Influence of Slavery in the Colonization of Texas," *Southwestern Historical Quarterly,* XXVIII, 1–33. J. H. Kuykendall, a colonist, gathered a series of interesting and valuable reminiscences of colonists; they are printed in the *Quarterly of the Texas State Historical Association* VI, 236–253, 311–330, and VII, 29–64; others, somewhat similar, are found in V, 12–18; XIII, 44–80; XIV, 24–73. Worthy of special mention are *Travel and Adventures in Texas in the 1820's: Being the Reminiscences of Mary Crownover Rabb* (Waco, Tex., 1962); and "Reminiscences of Mrs. Dilue Harris," *Quarterly of the Texas State*

*Historical Association,* IV, 85–127, 155–189, 387, written in part from a journal kept by Mrs. Harris's father, Dr. Pleasant W. Rose. Noah Smithwick, *The Evolution of a State* (Austin, 1900), written when the author was ninety years old, is rich in detail and very accurate. The best descriptive book of Texas written by a contemporary is Mary Austin Holley, *Texas* (Baltimore, 1833; Lexington, Ky., 1836). Mrs. Holley's text is included in M. A. Hatcher, *Letters of an Early American Traveller: Mary Austin Holley. Her Life and Works,* 1784–1846 (Dallas, 1933). For another biography of this remarkable observer of the Texas scene, see Rebecca Smith Lee, *Mary Austin Holley: A Biography* (Austin, 1962). Religion in early Texas is best discussed in W. S. Red, *The Texas Colonists and Religion, 1821–1836* (Austin, 1924).

Chapter Five

# THE DEVELOPMENT
# OF THE TEXAN
# REVOLUTION
# 1827–1835

"This is the most liberal and munificent Govt. on earth to emigra[n]ts—
after being here one year you will oppose a change even to Uncle
Sam—." Thus wrote Stephen F. Austin in 1829 to his sister and brother-
in-law, urging them to come to Texas. As late as 1832, to his partner and
boon companion, Samuel M. Williams, he wrote: "My standing motto—
'Fidelity to Mexico'—ought to be in every man's mouth and
repeated. . . ." Yet, three years later, Austin, the most loyal of all of
Mexico's adopted sons, was leading troops in rebellion against that
government. This reversal in sentiment did not take place in one week
or even in one year but was the natural reaction to ethnic and cultural
differences and to a long chain of developments that all together led from
fidelity through alienation to rebellion. The development of the Texan
Revolution may be considered under six topics, namely: (1) underlying
causes, the most important of which were the ethnic and cultural
differences between the Mexicans and the Anglo-American colonists, the
Edwards or Fredonian Rebellion, the efforts of the United States to buy
Texas, the Emancipation Proclamation of 1829, and the Law of April 6,
1830; (2) the quarrel between the Texans and the customs and military
officials, climaxed by the insurrection at Anahuac in 1832; (3) the
conventions of 1832 and 1833 and developments resulting from them; (4)
Santa Anna's abrogation of the Constitution of 1824 and other acts of
tyranny; (5) confusion in the seat of state government from early in 1833
to the spring of 1835; and (6) Santa Anna's effort to enforce his will upon
Texas.

## UNDERLYING CAUSES

A study of the Texan Revolution reveals striking resemblances to the American Revolution: Both can be traced to the disposition of the superior government to assert its authority after the colonists had learned to expect from it laxity and neglect. Customs duties and officious customs collectors played important parts in both stories. The Texans resented Mexican troops quartered among them, just as their forebears hated the British red coats in the days of Samuel Adams. In this connection the grievances of the Texans were even greater than those of the English colonists from whom most of them were descended: first, because the Mexican government even more than the British used the military to enforce civil law, and, second, because the Texans looked upon the Mexicans as an inferior race with whom they had little in common. The Anglo-Americans were aggressive and self-reliant individualists, rebels against centralist authority, and tenacious adherents to the doctrine that their civil liberties could best be preserved by constitutional and local self-government. Furthermore, they were violently averse to the subordination of the civil to the military power and to any connection whatsoever of church and state. They came to Texas with a long heritage of successful experience in self-government.

The Mexicans, in contrast, were sensitive, subtle, and indirect in their ways and adherents to the Roman Catholic religion. After three hundred years of subjugation to Spain, they were not prepared for self-government. Nevertheless, they promulgated a federal republican constitution that provided for a political system that the majority neither well understood nor regarded as sacrosanct. To the Anglo-American colonists, the constitution was not satisfactory: It did not guarantee trial by jury or the right of the accused to bail, it established Roman Catholicism as the official religion, and it did not adequately curb military power. Such contrasts, accentuated by a difference in language, naturally bred mutual suspicion, misunderstanding, and distrust, and consequently the two peoples made poor yokefellows.

Because the Mexicans were preoccupied with political instability at home and the Anglo-American colonists were busy building homes and clearing farms, it was five years after Austin arrived with the first colonists before the first clash between the two cultural groups occurred. In 1825 Haden Edwards secured an *empresario* grant that permitted him to locate colonists in a large area of eastern Texas. Within the boundaries of the grant were (1) the descendants of settlers who had returned to Nacogdoches in 1779 with Ybarbo, (2) a settlement of about thirty families on the San Jacinto which had been incorporated into Austin's first colony, (3) some who held or were entitled to grants, (4) a number of Anglo-American squatters, and (5) remnants of several Indian tribes. Edwards made an arbitrary ruling that all claimants must prove title or else pay him for their lands. This ruling alarmed and antagonized the settlers, many of whom, because of the inconvenience, had been careless in seeing that their land titles were in order. Also antagonizing the old settlers was Edwards's involvement through his son-in-law, Chicester Chaplain, in an election for an alcalde of the district, which also included the twenty-league reserve where there were a large number of Anglo-American squatters. Austin cautioned Edwards not to antagonize the Mexican officials, but his advice went unheeded. Edwards's enemies likewise took their cause to the higher officials. Finally, on June 3, 1826, the president of Mexico ordered Edwards's expulsion. It was not until October 20, however, that the vice-governor, Victor Blanco, angered by a "disrespectful" and "sarcastic" letter from Edwards's brother, Benjamin, transmitted the order that Haden Edwards's grant had been canceled and that he must leave the country. On December 16, with between fifteen and thirty armed men, Benjamin Edwards rode into Nacogdoches and proclaimed the Republic of Fredonia. He was unable, however, to generate any support from the Anglos, and an alliance with the Cherokee Indians by which Texas would be divided between them and the Fredonians failed to materialize. On learning of the approach of troops from San Antonio and militia from Austin's colony, the insurgents abandoned Nacogdoches and on January 31, 1827, crossed the Sabine into the United States. The Fredonian uprising had a greater impact on Mexican sentiment than it deserved. Mexican officials concluded that the Fredonians had intended to add Texas to the United States and became increasingly suspicious of the Anglo-Americans.

The Mexican mind linked inseparably the Fredonian affair with the effort of the United States to acquire, by purchase or otherwise, all or part of Texas. In 1825, President John Quincy Adams, who had often asserted that the Louisiana Purchase extended to the Rio Grande, through Joel R. Poinsett, envoy to Mexico, inaugurated efforts to obtain for the United States a "more suitable" boundary. Poinsett was authorized to offer Mexico one million dollars for the removal of the line to the Rio Grande. President Andrew Jackson raised Adams's offer to five million and continued the effort through Poinsett and Poinsett's successor, Anthony Butler, with no results other than to aggravate the Mexicans' suspicions concerning both the United States and the Anglo-American colonists. "The Yankees have failed to take Texas through rebellion," said the Mexicans, "and now they are trying to purchase it. Soon they will renew their efforts to acquire it by violence." The fact that such charges were altogether unfair, both to the United States government and to the Texan colonists, did not lessen their effectiveness in promoting discord.

In turn, a feeling of anxiety and suspicion was aroused among the Anglo-American colonists as a result of President Guerrero's proclamation of emancipation of slavery on September 15, 1829. Upon receipt of the decree, the Mexican political chief at San Antonio petitioned and obtained an exemption for Texas, but the colonists, nevertheless, were left with a feeling that their interests were not safe.

Greater than the emancipation proclamation in promoting ill feeling was the decree of April 6, 1830. It will be recalled that this law prohibited further colonization by people from the United States and provided for the collection of customs duties and for the garrisoning of troops in Texas. Alamán, who drafted the bill, feared that when the Americans became a preponderant majority they first would petition for changes or reforms, then create disturbances, and finally, by violence or diplomacy, take possession of the province. The law caused exactly what Alamán had hoped to prevent by it; out of it grew the chain of events, listed above, that led from disturbances and petitions to rebellion and independence.

## DISTURBANCES OF 1831 AND 1832

In keeping with its program "to maintain the integrity of Mexican territory" as set forth in the Law of April 6, 1830, the federal government sent a customs collector to Texas in May of that year and soon thereafter began to send more troops. The selection of officers for these duties was exceedingly unfortunate. The customs collector for ports east of the Colorado was George Fisher, a Serbian adventurer, once a citizen of the United States and a Mexican citizen since 1825. He not only took his position seriously, but he also was arbitrary and impractical.

Fisher, in November 1831, located the customhouse in Anahuac at the head of Galveston Bay, where a new military post had been established and placed under the command of Colonel John D. Bradburn, a stubborn, tactless Kentuckian who had gone to Mexico in 1817. Bradburn decreed that all ships leaving Texas from the mouth of the Brazos and certain other ports must clear through Anahuac. Since doing this sometimes required an overland journey of about two hundred miles or by sea a longer and more dangerous journey, the order provoked great dissatisfaction. When in December 1831 some shippers ignored the order and ran by the guard on the lower Brazos, shots were exchanged, and one soldier was seriously wounded. A deputy collector was then placed at Brazoria, but the colonists still protested, and after September 1832 the government collected little, if anything, in custom duties in Texas until the spring of 1835.

Ill will over tariffs was closely linked with a far more serious conflict between the Anglo-Texans and Bradburn, who in several ways infuriated the people. Bradburn's most unpopular offense was the arrest, early in 1831, of Francisco Madero, general land commissioner of Texas, who proposed to issue land titles to settlers, including those who had come independently of any *empresario* and perhaps some colonists of the Galveston Bay and Texas Land Company. When Bradburn ordered Madero to desist, on the ground that the issuance of the titles would be in violation of the Law of April 6, 1830, Madero explained that he had been commissioned by both the state and federal governments to issue the titles and ignored the order. Thereupon, Bradburn had him and his surveyor, José María Carbajal, arrested. Furthermore, Bradburn annulled for a time the *ayuntamiento* of the town of Liberty which Madero had established by the authority of his superiors, used slave labor for public works without compensating the owners, impressed supplies for his garrison, placed the border reserve under martial law, and arrested attorneys William B. Travis and Patrick Jack who began, it seems, deliberately to annoy him with mysterious messages about an armed force that was coming from Louisiana to recover the runaway slaves that Bradburn had refused to release.

The prolonged imprisonment of Travis and Jack brought the colonists to resistance. William H. Jack, brother of Patrick, having tried unsuccessfully to secure his brother's release, returned to San Felipe and called on his fellow colonists to join him in an attack on Bradburn. In early June men began to gather in Liberty, and soon John Austin (who may have been distantly related to Stephen F. Austin) from Brazoria arrived with 90 men, and by June 10 Bradburn was besieged by 160 angry Texans. After some negotiations, during which time Bradburn strengthened his post, the colonists withdrew a few miles to Turtle Bayou and sent John Austin to Brazoria for a cannon with which to assault the fort.

Meanwhile, in Mexico, Antonio López de Santa Anna, in support of liberalism and the Constitution of 1824, was leading a rebellion against President Anastacio Bustamante, a military dictator who ignored the constitution. At that time Bradburn was serving under Bustamante. While waiting for Austin to return, the Texans on Turtle Bayou, aware of these two developments, prepared a formal statement of the causes for their resistance. Thus, on June 13, in "The Turtle Bayou Resolutions," they asserted their loyalty to the constitution and to Santa Anna and the liberals. The resolutions were to serve them well.

As soon as he learned of the situation in Velasco, Colonel José de las Piedras, commander of the garrison in Nacogdoches, rushed to the troubled scene with some of his troops. Seeing that Bradburn's arbitrary action was the cause of the trouble, he agreed to release the prisoners to the civil authorities for trial, to replace Bradburn, to end martial law, and to endeavor to secure indemnity for the owners of the property that Bradburn had taken illegally. Bradburn soon resigned, the Texans dispersed, and the garrison declared for Santa Anna and sailed away.

The situation on the Brazos was even more serious. John Austin returned to Brazoria, secured the cannon (also reenforcements of more than a hundred men), and started by boat for Anahuac. At Velasco at the mouth of the Brazos, Colonel Domingo de Ugartechea, commander of the fort there, tried to prevent his passage. In the ensuing battle ten Texans and five Mexicans were killed, but Ugartechea was forced to surrender the garrison and withdraw his troops to Matamoros.

The resistance movement spread rapidly, and the colonists determined to drive every soldier from the settlements. In August Anglo- and Spanish-American settlers defeated Piedras and his troops in a bloody battle and forced them to abandon Texas. The post of Tenoxtitlan on the upper Brazos was also abandoned, leaving the Anglo-American part of Texas completely free of Mexicans, and on August 30 Ramón Músquiz, the political chief in San Antonio, tardily declared for Santa Anna.

Had it not been for the developments in Mexico that favored the Texans and the adroit work of Austin and a few others, these events would surely have brought severe retribution upon Texas. In early July in Matamoros, Colonel José Antonio Mexía was in command of the Santanista forces. Nearby was Colonel José Mariano Guerra in command of the Bustamante troops. When Mexía overhauled a mail packet from Brazoria and learned of the disturbances in Texas, he proposed to Guerra that they declare a truce and pool their resources to save Texas for the Mexican confederation. Guerra agreed, and soon Mexía with about four hundred soldiers was off for Texas. Fortunately for the colonists, he took along Stephen F. Austin, who had come by way of Matamoros on his return from the legislature in Saltillo. It is safe to conjecture that Austin spent many hours amplifying and emphasizing to Mexía what he had already written to the Mexican authorities concerning affairs in Texas. His argument was stated thus: "There is no insurrection of the Colonists against the Constitution and Government, neither do they entertain ideas endangering even remotely the integrity of the territory." They had not resisted the Mexican government but had fought Bradburn, a petty tyrant who took his orders from Bustamante, the very man Mexía was trying to overthrow. They were loyal Santanistas and had declared themselves so in the beginning. Mexía gave the colonists their cue in a letter of July 16 to John Austin, written after a conference with and, no doubt, in the presence of Stephen F. Austin. Mexía stated:

> But if, as I have been assured by respectable citizens, the past occurrences were on account of the colonists having adhered to the plan of Vera Cruz . . . you can in that case assure the inhabitants that I will unite with them to accomplish their wishes, and that the forces under my command will protect their adhesion to said plan.

The colonists, who knew of the coming of the expedition, prepared for Mexía a most lavish reception. He was saluted at the mouth of the Brazos by a salvo of cannon, entertained in the home of John Austin, and assured by reception committees of the loyalty of the Texans. At Brazoria the general was given a dinner and ball; the crowd was "large, cheerful, and convivial," and drank many toasts to Santa Anna. Under such conditions there was nothing for Mexía to do but to return to Mexico. He could not make war on the people who were on his side of the contest and who were treating him like a king.

## THE CONVENTIONS OF 1832 AND 1833

Although the insurrection of 1832 was eminently successful, the colonists were not willing to leave matters where they stood. They wanted some concessions from the Mexican government and some assurance that the abuses would not be repeated. Accordingly, on August 22, just a month after Mexía had sailed away, the *ayuntamiento* of San Felipe issued a call to the districts to send delegates to a convention to meet in San Felipe on October 1, 1832. Sixteen districts responded (not counting Goliad, whose delegation arrived too late for the proceedings) and sent fifty-eight delegates. Stephen F. Austin was elected president. Several resolutions addressed to the federal and state governments were prepared and adopted; still others related to local affairs. In lengthy and urgent memorials, the convention petitioned the national government for the repeal of that part of the Law of April 6, 1830, prohibiting Anglo-American immigration and for the admission of Texas as a state to the Mexican confederation. It also asked Congress to exempt the colonists from tariff duties on necessities for three years and to allow customs officers to be appointed by the alcaldes of the respective jurisdictions. It asked the state to issue land titles to settlers east of Austin's colony, to create additional *ayuntamientos* there, and to set aside land for school purposes. Locally, it provided for a committee, together with the *ayuntamiento* of Nacogdoches, to investigate the affairs of the Cherokee and other Indians in East Texas, and it approved a uniform plan for organizing the militia and suggested plans for defense against the Indians. The convention adjourned on October 6 and forwarded its petitions through the political chief in San Antonio.

For reasons not entirely clear, its petitions were never presented to the state and federal governments. The governor instructed the political chief to remind the Texans that the convention was a violation of the constitution and the laws. Santa Anna frowned on it, for he saw in it a tendency of the foreigners in Texas to declare themselves independent of the republic.

The Texans were not in the least intimidated by the official disapproval. In the convention they had set up a central committee and subcommittees for the different districts. These organizations were known as committees of "safety, vigilence, etc." to keep up "a regular and stated correspondence with each other, on all subjects relating to the peace and safety of the frontier. . . ." In January 1833, when it was apparent that Santa Anna would become president, the Central Committee of Safety and Correspondence issued a call for a second convention

Antonio López de Santa Anna. The reactionary dictatorship of this opportunistic general and politician provoked the Texas Revolution. His harsh treatment of the men of the Alamo and Goliad made his name hated in Texas. Defeated and captured by Sam Houston at San Jacinto, he nevertheless became president of Mexico twice again before his death in 1876. (Southwest Collection. Texas Tech University)

to meet in San Felipe on April 1. A larger number of discontented delegates was in attendance this time, evidenced by the selection of William H. Wharton, rather than Austin, as president of the convention. Only about one-third of the delegates had attended the first convention. The petitions were much the same as those prepared the previous year. The convention asked for the repeal of the anti-immigration law, adopted an exceptionally well-written memorial by David G. Burnet setting forth reasons why Texas should be a state separate from Coahuila, accepted a constitution drafted by a committee chaired by Sam Houston, who had come to Texas that year, and designated Austin to carry the petition to Mexico City.

On April 22, 1833, Austin set out on the long, expensive trip to Mexico City to present to the supreme government the petitions of the convention. When he arrived there on July 18, President Santa Anna was not at the capital, and Valentín Gómez Farías, the vice-president who advocated a number of ultraliberal reforms, was the acting president. Although Santa Anna had overthrown Bustamante and won the presidency on a platform that called for liberalism and the restoration of the Constitution of 1824, he was doubtful that the wealthy and powerful elite would accept such a program. Thus, he decided to "recuperate his health at his estate" until Gómez Farías presented his reform program to Congress. If the proposed reforms proved popular, he could assume the presidency and claim the credit; if, on the contrary, they aroused strong opposition, he could assume the presidency and oppose them. Austin conferred with Vice-President Gómez Farías who, although suspicious of the intentions of the Texans, received him cordially. The ministry submitted to the house of deputies the petition asking for a state government. Then a cholera scourge suspended all business in the capital, and Austin, impatient at the delay, on October 1 told Farías bluntly that unless the government remedied "the evils which threaten that country [Texas] with ruin," the people of Texas would organize a state government without its approval. Farías took this statement as a threat; the two men quarreled, and Austin, while still in a huff, wrote the *ayuntamiento* in San Antonio, urging that body to take the initiative in a plan to organize a state government.

A little later the proprietor was reconciled to Farías, and on November 5 he had a conference with Santa Anna (now exercising the executive power) and his cabinet. He found Santa Anna sympathetic and friendly. The president would not approve separation from Coahuila, but he did assent to almost every other request. He agreed to the repeal of the prohibition on immigration; he would refer to the treasury office a request for better mail service and a modification of the tariff; and he promised to urge the state government to give Texas trial by jury.

Before he left the city on December 10, Austin actually witnessed the repeal of the law against immigration, which was to take effect six months later. On his way back to Texas he stoppped on January 3, 1834, to see the commandant in Saltillo on a matter of business. There he was placed under arrest and then taken back to Mexico City. The cause was his letter of the preceding October to the *ayuntamiento* in San Antonio, written, as Austin said, "in a moment of irritation and impatience," suggesting that it take the initiative in the organization of a state government without waiting for the approval of the central government. The letter had found its way to the governor and finally back to Gómez Farías just after Austin had left Mexico City.

For some time Austin was kept *incommunicado* in the Prison of the Inquisition. He could get no trial, for no Mexican court would accept jurisdiction of his case. Two attorneys, Peter W. Grayson and Spencer H. Jack, were sent to his aid by the people of Texas, bearing many petitions for his release, but all they accomplished was to get him out of prison on bail on Christmas Day 1834. He was finally released through an amnesty law and left Mexico City in July 1835.

## SANTA ANNA AND THE NATIONAL SCENE (1833–1835)

Born in Jalapa in 1795, Santa Anna became a cadet at the age of fifteen and thereafter was a professional soldier. In the various contests over the supreme authority in Mexico he supported consistently the constitution and popular government. When Bustamante came into power, Santa Anna retired and remained out of the public eye for nearly two years. In January 1832 he prompted the garrison in Vera Cruz to start a revolt, soon became its leader, and finally forced Bustamante to capitulate. He was easily elected president for the term beginning April 1, 1833. He was not inaugurated on that date, however, but let Vice-President Valentín Gómez Farías, an ultraliberal but woefully lacking in political wisdom, assume the powers of the office. Farías was permitted to exercise the executive power on several occasions. From April 1, 1833, to January 28, 1835, the presidency was exchanged seven times by these two men.

Meanwhile, the reforms to which both men were pledged were being carried out by Farías and a liberal congress. Church appointments were placed in the hands of the state; the clergy was forbidden to discuss political matters; forced collections of tithes were suspended; and plans were inaugurated to reduce the size and the influence of the army. It has been stated previously how Texas profited from this liberal movement.

Obviously, the powerful clerical and army personnel, sustained as they were by the wealthier classes, did not permit these reforms to proceed without challenge. Quietly and surreptitiously they organized and found a leader, strange to say, in Santa Anna himself. The wily politician had permitted Farías to launch a trial balloon of liberalism, while he, in the eyes of the public, was a mere spectator. Seeing that the opposition was very powerful, he realized that, as its leader, he could make himself dictator. In April 1834 he returned to the capital and took over the supreme power from Farías. This time he repudiated liberalism, dissolved Congress, forced Farías into exile, dismissed all except one of Farías's cabinet, disbanded legislatures and *ayuntamientos,* declared void the laws against the privileges of the clergy, and in various other ways imitated Napoleon Bonaparte, whom he greatly admired. A new, subservient congress supplemented and legalized what Santa Anna did, and in October 1835 the Constitution of 1824 and federalism were replaced by the *Siete Leyes,* which provided for a centralized system of government. The new document converted the states into departments, ruled by a governor appointed by the president, and substituted an appointive council for the state legislature. The dictatorship of Santa Anna had been legalized—but in an illegal manner. Armed rebellion began over a decree that ordered the reduction of the number of militia to one soldier for every five hundred inhabitants and the surrender of excess arms. At word of this, the people of Zacatecas, spirited and known for their love of free institutions, rose in rebellion, but Santa Anna defeated five thousand state troops led by their governor and permitted his soldiers to plunder the state capital.

## AFFAIRS IN TEXAS AND COAHUILA (1833–1835)

During 1833 and 1834 the state government was generous with Texas. The legislature repealed the law that had prohibited any but native-born Mexicans from engaging in retail merchandising. It divided Texas into three political departments, the capitals to be Béxar, San Felipe, and Nacogdoches. Texas was allowed three deputies out of the twelve that comprised the state congress. The English language was recognized for official purposes, and religious toleration was granted. The court system, which had been the most constant object of complaint, was completely revised. A superior court was created for Texas and trial by jury was established. As stated previously, the new court proved defective, but it, like the other concessions, was an honest attempt to satisfy the colonists.

Except for the disturbances of 1832, when they declared for Santa Anna as a kind of afterthought, the Texans had managed to avoid entanglements in Mexican civil wars. Beginning with 1834, however, these wars came closer to home. The two principal sources of strife and agitation were the quarrel between Saltillo and Monclova over the location of the state capital and the squandering of the public lands of Texas through sales to speculators.

The quarrel over the state capital began in March 1833, when the legislature removed the seat of government from Saltillo in the south-eastern corner of Coahuila to Monclova in the north. Later, Saltillo set up a rival government, but Santa Anna gave his nod to Monclova and the government remained there. In April 1835 the legislature criticized Santa Anna severely, and the dictator sent his brother-in-law, Martín Perfecto de Cós, to break up the state government. On the approach of the national forces Governor Agustín Viesca sought to transfer the government to Béxar but was arrested on his way by Cós's troops. Other officers and a swarm of land speculators fled to Béxar. By August both the Saltillo and the Monclova factions accepted as governor Rafael Eca y Músquiz, who then moved the capital back to Saltillo.

Most Texans were disgusted with their state government because of its unwise and dishonest land sales. Speculation in Texas lands had been common ever since the passage of the state colonization law of 1825, which permitted a native Mexican to purchase as much as eleven *sitios* for a nominal sum. This speculation was eclipsed, however, by reckless legislation in 1834 and 1835. Representatives John Durst, from Nacogdoches, and J. M. Carbajal, from San Antonio, were implicated in and probably profited from this business. An act of April 19, 1834, authorized the governor to dispose of as much as four hundred *sitios* of land for the purpose of maintaining the militia in defense against the Indians. Another law, that of March 14, 1835, empowered the governor to dispose of four hundred more *sitios*. The final act in this extravagant series was passed on April 7, 1835, authorizing the governor "to take of himself whatever measure he may think proper for securing the public tranquility. . . ." Apparently the governor thought the situation called for the frittering away of additional large blocks of land.

The operations of the partnership firm of Williams, Peebles, and Johnson are typical. In consideration for four hundred *sitios* of land they agreed to place and maintain in the field one thousand men for the defense of the state. Without supplying a single soldier, they issued to about forty persons certificates calling for the entire four hundred *sitios*. The constitutional convention of 1836 nullified some of these grants but validated others apparently no more meritorious.

As a result of the imbroglio at the capital, the rank and file of Texans failed to see clearly that the basic issue was Santa Anna's intent to discard the constitution and establish himself as a dictator. The land speculators brought alarming reports to the effect that Santa Anna was planning to invade Texas, but most people believed that their talk was merely a cloud to screen their own bad conduct.

One citizen wrote:

> Williams, Johnson, Carbajal, Bowie and others cry, "Wolf, wolf, condemnation, destruction, war, to arms, to arms!" Williams says, "I have bought a few leagues of land from the Government; but if they don't bring the Governor to Bexar, I shall not be able to get my titles." What a pity. . . .

As late as midsummer of 1835, most Texans would have endorsed the statement of George W. Smyth, land commissioner in Nacogdoches, who wrote in May of that year that he was confident that there would be no war and added: "Come what may I am convinced that Texas must prosper. We pay no taxes, work no public roads, get our land at cost, and perform no public duties of any kind."

Yet there was a small but active war party and, on the other extreme, a peace party, likewise small, active, and persistent. The great majority of Texans stood between these two extreme groups, indifferent at first but finding their complacent attitude more and more untenable. Developments during the summer of 1835 favored the war party.

## SANTA ANNA FORCES THE ISSUE

The first violent action that led directly to revolution was associated with Anahuac, the seat of the disturbances of 1832. Indeed, the story of Texas during the early summer of 1835 reads strangely like that of 1832. In January 1835 Santa Anna sent a small detachment of soldiers to Anahuac to enforce the collection of customs there and in Galveston. The collector at Velasco on the Brazos collected tonnage duties only, while the officers at Galveston and Anahuac, backed by the garrison, insisted on the payment of all duties. Andrew Briscoe, a merchant of Anahuac, and others became disgruntled and declared that no more duties should be collected at that port until collections were enforced equally throughout Texas. As a result of a misunderstanding, a Texan was wounded at Anahuac, and Briscoe and another citizen, De Witt C. Harris, were imprisoned. Meanwhile Cós had heard of the threatening attitude of the people at Anahuac and had determined to reinforce the garrison. He wrote Captain Antonio Tenorio, its commander, to be resolute and of good cheer, that reinforcements were coming. It happened that the courier bearing Cós's letters and other communications in a similar vein stopped at San Felipe on June 21. There was much excitement in the community. The people knew of the breaking up of the state government and of the arrests of Governor Viesca and the citizens at Anahuac. Already excited over these events, the San Felipe war party seized and opened the courier's dispatches. Although the reaction to this extreme measure was sharp, the clique that favored drastic action met, elected J. B. Miller, political chief of the Department of the Brazos, to take the chair, and passed resolutions authorizing W. B. Travis to collect a force and drive away the garrison in Anahuac. With some twenty-five or thirty hotspurs armed with rifles and a small cannon mounted on a pair of sawmill truck wheels, Travis appeared before the post and demanded its surrender. Tenorio made no resistance and on the morning of June 30 surrendered some forty-four men. The prisoners were paroled and treated kindly by the colonists.

This act of Travis and his band was looked upon with pronounced disfavor by the great majority of the people, and it was formally condemned by meetings in no less than seven communities. At a meeting on June 28, the people of Columbia emphatically denounced it as an act calculated to involve the citizens of Texas in a conflict with the central government. They pledged their loyalty to Mexico, and through a committee they asked the political chief to send to Cós assurances of the people's loyalty. More general gatherings in San Felipe on July 14 and 15 adopted resolutions of similar tenor, and J. B. Miller, as if to atone for his alignment with the radicals a few weeks earlier, wrote an apologetic letter to Cós. Then a conference of committees from Columbia, Mina (Bastrop), and San Felipe, meeting in San Felipe from July 17 to 21, sent D. C. Barrett and Edward Gritten with conciliatory letters to Cós in Matamoros. The peace party was asserting itself. The agitators were on the defensive.

Cós was not in a compromising humor. He called for the arrest of Lorenzo de Zavala, a distinguished political refugee and enemy of Santa Anna, who had lately arrived in Texas. Then, at the suggestion of Dr. J. H. C. Miller, a busybody who belonged to the extreme peace party, Colonel Ugartechea, commander at Béxar, sent to Cós a list of offenders: F. W. Johnson, who had been prominent in land speculation; Robert M. Williamson, the Patrick Henry of the Texas Revolution, commonly called "Three Legged Willie"; W. B. Travis; and Samuel Williams. Cós insisted that the colonial officials arrest these men and turn them over to the military for trial. He refused to meet with the peace commissioners (who had gone as far as San Antonio on their way to confer with him) until this was done. To the Anglo-Americans, who believed that a person should be tried only by a jury composed of his or her peers, it was unthinkable to turn their fellow citizens over to the mercies of a Mexican military tribunal. Cós, who managed to secure and read copies of the various inflammatory speeches and utterances of the Texans, particularly a Fourth of July address by R. M. Williamson, became adamant. On August 17 he wrote Henry Rueg, political chief in Nacogdoches:

> The plans of the revolutionists of Texas are well known to this commandency: and it is quite useless and vain to cover them with a hypocritical adherence to the federal Constitution. The constitution by which all Mexicans may be governed is the constitution which the colonists of Texas must obey, no matter on what principles it may be formed.

Thus did the season for conciliation pass.

In the American Revolution it was the committees of correspondence which began in Massachusetts in 1772 under the tutelage of Samuel Adams that kept the people in touch with developments and finally made possible organized resistance. Similar organizations existed during the Texan Revolution, and without them the colonists could not have been aroused to the point of resistance or have been organized with any degree of effectiveness.

Mina (Bastrop) on the frontier led the communities by appointing on May 8, 1835, its Committee of Safety and Correspondence for the general diffusion of information. Organizations in Gonzales and Viesca

William Barret Travis (an artist's conception). A lawyer from Alabama who came to Texas in 1832, Travis was an ardent advocate of the revolt against Mexico. As a colonel in the revolutionary army, he was in command of the small force that died trying to hold the Alamo against Santa Anna in March 1836. James Bowie and David Crockett were among those who died with him. (Texas State Library)

were formed a few days later. Before the end of the summer apparently every precinct had such an organization. Holding over from the convention of 1833 was the central committee which served as a guide and clearing body for the local committees.

These committees brought together representatives of the municipalities for a consultation. Apprehensive about the recent developments, on July 4 the Committee of Safety at Mina issued an address to the *ayuntamientos* of the Department of the Brazos, urging a consultation of the representatives of the several communities. Within ten days the *ayuntamientos* of Columbia and a citizens' meeting in San Felipe likewise had called for a consultation. It was the people of Columbia who actually called the general meeting. At a gathering of the citizens on August 15 with William H. Wharton, the staunch champion of action, presiding, the Committee of Safety and Correspondence was instructed to issue a call for a consultation of all Texans. Three days later the committee framed an address in which it asked that each jurisdiction elect and send five delegates to a consultation to be held in Washington on October 15. The tenor of its message is revealed in the sentence: "The only instructions which we would recommend to be given to our representatives is to secure peace if it is to be obtained on constitutional terms, & to prepare for war—if war is inevitable."

Some three weeks later Stephen F. Austin, free at last and home again, gave the consultation his approval. He accepted the chairmanship of the Central Committee of Safety of San Felipe and by common consent became the leader of the revolution. The news came that Cós was on his way to Béxar with reinforcements. This destroyed the last hope of peace, and on September 19 the central committee reinforced the call for a consultation and added: "War is our only resource. There is no other remedy. We must defend our rights ourselves and our country by force of arms."

## SELECTED BIBLIOGRAPHY

The general accounts cited in Chapter 4 are helpful, but the *Handbook of Texas* is the best single reference. The best accounts for this particular period are D. M. Vigness, *The Revolutionary Decades;* William C. Binkley, *The Texas Revolution* (Baton Rouge, La., 1952); and Frank W. Johnson, *A History of Texas and Texans* (E. C. Barker and E. W. Winkler, eds., 5 vols., Chicago and New York, 1914). Of the more intensive studies, the best are: E. C. Barker, *The Life of Stephen F. Austin;* E. C. Barker, *Mexico and Texas, 1821–1835;* E. C. Barker, "The Organization of the Texas Revolution," *Publications of the Southern*

*History Association,* V, 1–26; E. C. Barker, "Public Opinion in Texas Preceding the Revolution," *Annual Report of the American Historical Association for 1911,* I, 217–228; O. Morton, "Life of General Don Manuel de Mier y Terán, As It Affected Texas-Mexican Relations," *Southwestern Historical Quarterly,* XLVI, 22–47, 239–254; XLVII, 29–47, 120–142, 256–267; XLVIII, 51–66, 193–218; Merton L. Dillon, "Benjamin Lundy in Texas," *Southwestern Historical Quarterly,* LXIII, 46–62; Llerena Friend, *Sam Houston, the Great Designer* (Austin, 1954); *The Texans* (Time-Life Books, 1975); Ohland Morton, *Terán and Texas: A Chapter in Texas-Mexican Relations;* E. C. Barker, "The Battle of Velasco," *Quarterly of the Texas State Historical Association,* VII, 326–328.

The most comprehensive collection of source material on the Texas Revolution has been compiled and edited by John H. Jenkins, *The Papers of the Texas Revolution, 1835–1836* (10 vols., Austin, 1973). Other source materials may be found in Robert E. Davis (ed.), *Dairy of William Barret Travis, August 30, 1833, June 26, 1834* (Waco, Tex., 1966); E. C. Barker, *The Austin Papers;* C. A. Gulich, Katherine Elliott, and Harriet Smither (eds.), *The Papers of Mirabeau Bonaparte Lamar* (6 vols., Austin, 1921–1927); E. C. Barker, contributor of a series of important documents in the *Publications of the Southern History Association,* V, 451–476; VI, 33–40; VII, 25–31, 85–95, 200–206, 238–246; VIII, 1–22, 104–118, 343–362; IX, 87–98, 160–173, 225–233; and E. Wallace and D. M. Vigness (eds.), *Documents of Texas History.* For proceedings of the Texas convention, see H. P. N. Gammel (comp.), *Laws of Texas* (10 vols., Austin, 1898), I.

Accounts of the disturbances of the early 1830s are E. C. Barker, "Difficulties of a Mexican Revenue Officer in Texas," *Quarterly of the Texas State Historical Association,* IV, 190–202; Edna Rowe, "The Disturbances at Anahuac in 1832," *ibid.,* VI, 265–299; N. D. Labadie, "Narrative of the Anahuac, or Opening Campaign of the Texas Revolution," *Texas Almanac, 1859,* 30–36; Duncan W. Robinson, *Judge Robert McAlpin Williamson: Texas' Three-Legged Willie* (Austin, 1948); Forrest E. Ward, "Pre-Revolutionary Activity in Brazoria County," *Southwestern Historical Quarterly,* LXIV, 212–231; Boyce House, "An Incident at Velasco, 1832," *ibid.,* 92–95.

Concerning the "OPQ" letters, see "Some Texas Correspondence," *Mississippi Valley Historical Review,* XI, 99–127. Almonte's report on Texas has been translated and edited by C. E. Castañeda in the *Southwestern Historical Quarterly,* XXVIII, 177–222. For affairs at the state capital, see E. C. Barker, "Land Speculation as a Cause of the Texas Revolution," *Quarterly of the Texas State Historical Association,* X, 76–95.

Concerning Santa Anna and national affairs, see Frank C. Hanighen, *Santa Anna: The Napoleon of the West* (New York, 1934); Wilfred H. Callcott, *Santa Anna* (Norman, Okla., 1936); H. H. Bancroft, *The History of Mexico* (6 vols., San Francisco, 1883–1888).

The best study of this particular period by a Mexican historian is Vito Alessio Robles, *Coahuila y Texas desde la consumación de la independencia hasta el tratado de paz de Guadalupe Hidalgo* (2 vols., Mexico, D.F., 1945–1946).

Chapter Six

# THE TEXAN
# REVOLUTION
# 1835–1836

It has been said that Americans never fought better than they did in Texas, and with a measure of truth it might be added that they never managed their affairs worse. By way of excuse for their mistakes it must be pointed out that they all were comparative newcomers and knew little about one another. Except for Austin, they had no leader at the beginning of the contest, and most of their people were without political experience. As an aid to the reader, the following account of the Texan Revolution is divided into eight sections: (1) fighting for the Constitution of 1824, from October 2, 1835, through the surrender of General Martín Perfecto de Cós in San Antonio on December 9; (2) the Consultation and the provisional state government, from the creation of the Permanent Council on October 11, 1835, until January 17, 1836, when the revolutionary government collapsed; (3) defeat and death, from January until the massacre of Fannin's men on March 27; (4) creation of the republic, from March 1 through 17, when a convention declared the independence of Texas, established an *ad interim* government, and drafted a constitution for the republic; (5) the San Jacinto campaign, from March 6 to April 21, when the defeat of Santa Anna made independence a reality; (6) the navy in the revolution; (7) the adjustments after San Jacinto, particularly the immediate relations with Santa Anna and the problem with the army; and (8) aid from the United States.

## FIGHTING FOR THE CONSTITUTION OF 1824

The Consultation of delegates from the *ayuntamientos* had been called to meet on October 15, 1835, but the events outran the plans. In September General Cós, determined to chastise the Texans for opening his official mail and for refusing to turn over the men he had demanded, began embarking troops for Texas. Colonel Domingo de Ugartechea, commander of troops in San Antonio, sent five cavalrymen to Gonzales, seventy miles to the east and the farthest west of the Anglo-American towns, to get the six-pounder cannon provided to *Empresario* DeWitt about four years before for defense against the Indians. Convinced that the request for the cannon was to weaken resistance against Santa Anna's military dictatorship, Alcalde Andrew Ponton hid the cannon, told the Mexicans he had no authority to give it up, and sent out dispatches calling for aid. Upon receipt of the news, some Texans on their way to intercept General Cós, who with four hundred troops had landed at Copano, turned aside to Gonzales. Meanwhile, Ugartechea sent Lieutenant Francisco Castañeda with about 100 troops to seize the cannon. On September 29 the Mexican force encamped on the west bank of the Guadalupe River, a short distance above the town. Then, on October 2, Colonel J. H. Moore, with about 160 Texans, the disputed cannon loaded with chains and scrap iron and strung with a banner inscribed "COME AND TAKE IT," crossed the river and attacked the Mexican troops, killing one and sending the others scurrying for San Antonio. The Texas Revolution had begun.

Not all the volunteers who had set out to intercept General Cós turned aside to Gonzales. One company from Matagorda, under Captain George M. Collinsworth, after learning at Victoria that Cós with his troops had left Goliad for San Antonio and after being joined by Ben R. Milam, who was returning from imprisonment in Mexico, captured Goliad and its approximately twenty-five presidial defenders. The capture of Goliad and its well-supplied stores was significant: It enabled the Texans to maintain the siege of San Antonio and prevented Cós from obtaining additional supplies and reinforcements by sea.

Meanwhile, more volunteers continued to arrive at Gonzales and raised the cry "On to San Antonio," but there was no organization and they could not agree on a commander. Fortunately, at the urgent request of a group of officers, Austin arrived and was unanimously selected. On October 12, the ragtag army, numbering about three hundred, started for San Antonio, where Cós with Ugartechea's command and reinforcements that had arrived ahead of the Texans, had twelve hundred or more troops. On October 28 James Bowie and James W. Fannin, Jr., while making a reconnaissance with ninety men, were attacked near Mission Purísima Concepción de Acuña by a Mexican cavalry force of about four hundred. After a brief skirmish, in which the enemy lost sixty men and the Texans only one, the volunteer army encamped at the mission.

On November 18 Austin received word that he had been relieved of his command by the Consultation and named to go with a commission to seek aid in the United States. Before Austin left on November 25, the volunteers voted down the question of storming Cós, but four hundred pledged to remain and elected Edward Burleson as their chief commander. On the next day, a skirmish known as the Grass Fight, in which the Texans again were victorious, occurred on the outskirts of town. That afternoon Erastus (Deaf) Smith, a scout, returned to camp with word that a pack train was approaching the city. Concluding that it was Ugartechea returning from Matamoros with reinforcements and pay for the troops, the Texans set out to capture it, and Cós, in turn, sent out troops with artillery. After a short but furious fight, the Mexicans retreated to safety inside the town, leaving about fifty killed. The Texans had two wounded. The pack train turned out to be a foraging party sent out by Cós to get grass for the horses.

Despite their success in the Grass Fight, the resolve of the poorly clothed and inadequately fed Texans to maintain the siege began to weaken in the winter cold, and a few days later the staff of officers decided to abandon the siege and go into winter quarters at Goliad. Before the withdrawal began, however, Ben Milam, upon returning from a scouting expedition on December 4 and learning from a Mexican deserter and from some San Antonians that Mexican morale and supplies

Benjamin Rusk (Ben) Milam, a native of Kentucky, had been a member of Dr. James Long's filibuster expedition into Texas in 1820 and an officer in the Mexican Army. Because of his opposition to Santa Anna's centralist government in Coahuila, he was captured by troops of General Martín Perfecto de Cós but escaped and in the fall of 1835 joined the Texas army at Goliad. On December 5, when the Texans were ready to give up the siege of General Cós at San Antonio (Béxar), Milam called for and led one group of volunteers that attacked the Mexicans. Two days later he was killed by a rifle ball, but on December 10 Cós capitulated. (Southwest Collection: Texas Tech University)

were very low, defied the order to withdraw by calling out, "Who will go with old Ben Milam into San Antonio?" Three hundred men volunteered. Before daylight on the morning of December 5, the Texas volunteers led by Milam began the assault.

After being subjected to artillery and small arms for three days (Milam was killed by enemy fire on the third day), the Texans began a house-to-house assault. On December 9 Cós hoisted a white flag. Under the capitulation agreement Cós gave to the Texans all the public property, money, arms, and supplies in San Antonio; in return, Cós and his men were permitted to return south of the Rio Grande after agreeing never again to oppose the restoration of the Constitution of 1824. The Texan victory in San Antonio was a brilliant achievement. About four hundred citizen soldiers had taken a town held by more than three times their number in an advantageous defensive position. Their success, however, made them over optimistic.

## CONSULTATION AND PROVISIONAL STATE GOVERNMENT

While these developments were taking place in the field, the political scene had shifted several times. Texas had had two provisional governments, and a third was ineffective and on the verge of dissolution. Ironically, the first is known as the Permanent Council, although it existed formally for only three weeks. Organized on October 11, it consisted of the Committee of Public Safety in San Felipe joined by representatives from other communities, with R. R. Royall of Matagorda as president and a secretary. During its brief existence, the Permanent Council served well. It sent supplies and volunteers to the army in the field; it commissioned privateers; it established a postal system; it ordered the land offices closed and surveying discontinued; it authorized an agent, Thomas F. McKinney, to go to the United States and borrow $100,000; and it appealed to the citizens of the United States for men, money, and supplies. It kept the people of Texas informed about the revolution and spurred them to greater exertion.

The Consultation, which had been delayed because of the situation at Gonzales and which had changed its place of meeting from Washington to San Felipe, finally had a quorum on November 3, when fifty-five delegates from twelve municipalities of the departments of the Brazos and Nacogdoches appeared.[1] Dr. Branch T. Archer, from Brazoria and

[1]Each municipality was entitled to send seven delegates. The municipalities of the Department of Béxar, except the municipality of Béxar, later elected delegates, some of whom participated in the general council that grew out of the Consultation. Ninety-eight men were named as delegates but only fifty-eight took part in the Consultation.

a former member of the Virginia legislature, was elected president of the Consultation and previewed the decision of the majority in his keynote speech with the statement that Texas was "laying the cornerstone of liberty in the great Mexican republic," and was not "battling alone for her rights and liberties." A committee, composed of one delegate from each of the twelve municipalities and headed by John A. Wharton, could not agree, however, whether it should declare that the colonists were fighting for independence or for their rights under the Constitution of 1824 and returned the issue to the house. After three days of debate, described by Gail Borden, Jr., a participant, as "lengthy and animated yet coolness and moderation pervaded throughout . . . ," the Consultation voted on November 6 for a "provisional government, upon the principles of the Constitution of 1824," and then thirty-three to fifteen against a declaration of independence. On the next day it accepted Wharton's committee report reflecting the majority view. The declaration adopted was, however, a compromise between the majority and the advocates of an immediate separation. It spoke of Santa Anna's tyranny and of the "natural rights" of the people of Texas, declared that the Texans were fighting to maintain the federal Constitution of 1824, and stated that they offered their assistance to all Mexicans who would join them in resisting military despotism. The fifth article is especially suggestive of more extreme action. The colonists, it stated, "hold it to be their right . . . to establish an independent government," but they would "continue faithful to the Mexican government so long as that nation is governed by the constitution and laws that were formed for the government of the political association." Another act of the body that constituted a definite step toward separation was the election of B. T. Archer, William H. Wharton, and Stephen F. Austin as commissioners to the United States to obtain aid. The delegates must have known that their kinspeople east of the Sabine would not send men and money to Texas merely to have a part in a domestic Mexican squabble. In fact, the cause of the friends of the constitution was already lost. That instrument had been superseded on October 3 by a decree of Congress which established a centralist form of government for the nation, including the replacement of states with departments controlled by the president.

The Consultation gave its official endorsement to most of the work of the Permanent Council, adopted a plan for the creation of an army and elected Sam Houston commander in chief, and drew up a plan for a provisional government. The plan provided for a governor, a lieutenant governor, and a general council to be composed of one member from each municipality. All officials were to be chosen from the members of the Consultation, the governor and lieutenant governor by the whole body, and members of the council by the delegations from the several municipalities. The most unfortunate part of the instrument was that it failed to delineate clearly the powers of the council and of the governor. The Consultation voted to sustain the army then before Béxar but declared that the volunteers were not obliged to submit to its control, thereby confessing its weakness and transmitting to its successor an army over which it had no control.

The Consultation deprived Texas of the valuable services of its two most essential men. Austin, who should have been placed at the head of the provisional government, was sent away "in honorable exile" to the United States, and Houston was made a commander in chief without any army. Henry Smith, who had served as political chief of the Department of the Brazos, was elected governor, and James W. Robinson of Nacogdoches was chosen lieutenant governor. The Consultation adjourned on November 14, to reassemble on March 1, 1836, unless called sooner by the governor and council. For about a month, nevertheless, the new government worked creditably. It created and filled offices and completed the framework of the political structure, provided for the organization of a post office and a navy, and gave support to the army in the field.

Internal discord, however, soon made it helpless. The crises came over a matter of policy. Like the Consultation, the council favored the

Henry Smith, who was one of the first to advocate Texas independence, was named governor of the Provisional State of Texas (of Mexico) by the Consultation in November 1835. (Southwest Collection, Texas Tech University)

Constitution of 1824 and cooperation with the Mexican liberals against Santa Anna. Thus, it approved a campaign to be led by Frank W. Johnson, aided by James Grant, against Matamoros, believing that its seizure would encourage the people there to resist Santa Anna. Both the governor and General Houston opposed it. After the council had repeatedly passed measures over his veto, Governor Smith determined to cow it into submission or to dismiss it. For a test of his strength he chose the occasion of the receipt of a letter from J. C. Neill, commanding the troops in Béxar, complaining that Johnson and his fellow officer, James Grant, had on leaving with their troops for Matamoros stripped the garrison of supplies and clothing. On January 10, 1836, his message, vilifying certain members of the body in most intemperate language, was read to the council. Either the council should apologize for its evil ways, said the governor, and agree henceforth to cooperate with him or adjourn until the first of March. The council replied in language quite as severe as the governor's, declared the office of governor vacant, and inaugurated Lieutenant Governor Robinson as acting governor. Smith refused to deliver up the archives and continued to receive much mail addressed to the executive. The council could not secure a quorum after January 17, and thereafter, until a new convention assembled on March 1, the only semblance of government was Robinson and an advisory committee, and its results were negligible.

## A WINTER OF DEFEAT AND DEATH

Developments in the field during the early part of 1836 were fully as discouraging as those at the seat of government. Even before San Antonio de Béxar fell, Dr. James Grant, an Englishman who was a citizen and land owner in Coahuila, began extolling the advantages of an expedition against Matamoros and beyond. In late December, after being named commander in chief of the expedition by F. W. Johnson, then in command in San Antonio, Grant left San Antonio, taking with him four hundred of the volunteers, most of the food and medical supplies, and virtually all of the munitions. On January 3, however, Johnson informed the council that he had decided the Matamoros campaign would be a mistake. Four days later the council named Colonel James W. Fannin, in command in Velasco, to serve as its agent to raise volunteers and supplies and to invade Mexico. By then Johnson had decided that he wanted to lead the expedition. Proceeding to the seat of government in San Felipe, on January 14 he obtained from the council, but not the governor, approval of his plan. He then left for Goliad to take command of the expedition.

Meanwhile, General Houston, who was trying to assemble the troops of the regular army in Goliad and Refugio and to keep Copano port open, set out for those places on January 8. In Refugio on January 20, Johnson told him that the council had deposed Governor Smith and commissioned Colonel Fannin and himself as its agents to raise men and supplies and to take Matamoros. Since the council had ignored the military government established by the Consultation by superseding the commander in chief with its own agents and plan of action, Houston took a furlough from the army until March 1.

He then went to eastern Texas to carry out a previous order to negotiate a treaty with the Cherokee Indians. On February 23, he and John Forbes signed a treaty that assured the Indians title to their lands in return for remaining at peace with the Texans, but the treaty was never ratified by the government of Texas.

Before he left the army, however, Houston succeeded in persuading most of the volunteers with Johnson and Grant to abandon the Matamoros project. The remainder, no more than a scouting party, moved into the area of San Patricio. Fannin landed at Copano on February 2 with about two hundred men and moved inland by way of Refugio where he learned that Santa Anna's invasion of Texas was underway. He thereupon decided against the Matamoros campaign and moved to Goliad, which he considered to be of strategic importance. By then he had assembled about 450 troops, most of whom were recent arrivals from the United States. These men, who had been recruited to help make Texas a Mexican state and to restore the Constitution of 1824, were to live long enough to learn that Texas had declared its independence; the defenders of the Alamo, however, never knew that Texas had declared its independence.

On October 27, 1835, President Santa Anna concluded at a meeting with his advisors that the Anglo-American colonists in Texas no longer wished to remain a part of Mexico and decided that he would lead personally an expedition against them. Then, in Saltillo on January 25, he held a grand review of the army, a dazzling spectacle. Having learned of the plans of the Texans to invade Mexico, he sent Colonel José Urrea with fifteen hundred cavalrymen to Matamoros with orders to march from there along the coast into Texas by way of Refugio and Goliad. He then proceeded to the Rio Grande, where he joined General Joaquin Ramírez y Sesma, who commanded his left flank with about fifteen hundred men. Santa Anna now had a total force of about six thousand troops on the march into Texas. On February 16, the main army began crossing the Rio Grande with twenty-one cannons, eighteen hundred pack mules, thirty-three four-wheel wagons, and two hundred two-wheel carts, and headed for San Antonio, about 150 miles distant, in disregard of General Vicente Filisola's plea to march directly for San Felipe. The self-styled "Napoleon of the West" wanted to avenge the defeat of Cós. The vanguard of the army reached San Antonio on February 23, to the great surprise of Travis who did not expect it until after the grass was green and the weather warm.

In late December 1835, after Grant and Johnson stripped the garrison of men and supplies for the Matamoros expedition, J. C. Neill was left in command of that post with about one hundred poorly equipped men. The council was disposed to hold San Antonio at all costs, but on January 17 General Houston ordered Bowie, who had accompanied him to Goliad, to take some men to San Antonio, destroy the fortifications, and retreat to Gonzales, taking with him the cannon and as many supplies as possible. Once there, however, with about twenty-five men, Bowie decided to remain. In disregard of Houston's order, Governor Smith ordered Lieutenant Colonel William Barret Travis, recruiting officer in San Felipe, to recruit one hundred men and go to the relief of San Antonio. Travis, with only thirty-one men, reached San Antonio on February 3.

A few days later, Neill gave Travis command of the garrison and left for home because of illness in his family. The volunteers, however, refused to accept the arrangement and elected Bowie as their commander;

James (Jim) Bowie, born in Tennessee, at nineteen moved to Louisiana and engaged in the illicit slave trade with Jean Lafitte. Migrating to Texas in 1828, in 1831 he married Ursula María de Veramendi, daughter of the vice-governor (governor 1832–1833) of Coahuila and Texas and engaged in business in Coahuila. In 1832 Bowie helped drive the Mexican troops from Texas and in 1835 joined the Texas volunteers and commanded the volunteers in San Antonio when William B. Travis arrived with a few regular army troops. Forced by illness to relinquish command to Travis, the bedridden Bowie was killed on March 6, 1836, when Santa Anna's troops stormed the Alamo. (Southwest Collection, Texas Tech University)

Travis remained in command of the regulars. The stalemate was not for long; Bowie, already seriously ill, was compelled to leave the command to Travis.

A few other troops arrived, some already famous. James B. Bonham, a native of South Carolina, an Alabama lawyer, and the organizer of the Mobile Grays, left his company in Goliad to join his long-time friend, Travis, in the Alamo. The most famous was David Crockett, excongressman from Tennessee and a bitter political enemy of Andrew Jackson, who with about a dozen of his "Tennessee boys" rode into San Antonio unexpectedly on February 8. The new arrivals strengthened the determination of the men to ignore the orders to abandon the garrison. As Amelia Williams, historian of the Alamo, stated, "the place, moreover, seemed to cast some sort of spell over the Texas leaders." "We consider death preferable to disgrace which would be the result of giving up the Post which has been so dearly won," wrote Travis.

When the advance units of the Mexican army reached San Antonio, a number of civilians swarmed into the Alamo. Almaron Dickenson, a blacksmith who had prepared eighteen cannons for service in the Alamo, galloped to his eighteen-year-old wife, Suzanna, and fifteen-month-old baby, pulled them up behind him, and galloped back into the Alamo. When the gates to the fortress were closed, there were 150 fighting men, quartered along the east and west walls, and about 24 noncombatants crowded into the old church.

Travis sent out appeals for help phrased in language forceful and dramatic to Goliad, Gonzales, the convention in Washington on the Brazos, the people of Texas, and all Americans in the world. The messengers risked their lives to maintain communication.

On February 23, when the Mexicans were first sighted, Travis sent two of his scouts, Dr. John Sutherland and John W. Smith, to Andrew Ponton, alcalde of Gonzales, with a plea for men and provisions. The men, he added, "are determined to defend the Alamo to the last." On the next day, while the Mexican artillery was bombarding the Alamo, he sent out a stirring appeal "To the People of Texas and All Americans in the World," which has been described as "the most sublime document in American history." In it he stated that "The enemy has demanded a surrender at discretion," but "*I shall never surrender or retreat* . . . VICTORY OR DEATH." During the night of February 25, Juan N. Seguin, a prominent San Antonian, on Bowie's fast horse, rode through the Mexican sentries and raced for Gonzales with another urgent plea for aid, this one written in desperation. In response to Travis's appeal, Fannin started for San Antonio with most of his men on February 26 but the next day returned to his newly renamed Fort Defiance at Goliad. Bonham twice went out and twice came back. His return through the fire of the enemy at 11:00 A.M. on March 3, after it was evident that the Alamo was a deathtrap, should qualify him to head the list of Texas heroes. Yet, a roll call of the immortals would include also the names of Albert Martin and the thirty-two men from Gonzales who, in response to Travis's appeal and with courier John W. Smith as guide, slipped past the Mexican lines and into the Alamo at 3:00 A.M. on March 1. On March 3 Travis sent out his last appeal for help, this one to the convention that he knew was scheduled to be in session in Washington on the Brazos.

Although at least two hundred shells had fallen inside the works, the Texans had not lost a person, and their spirits were still high. It was better, Travis believed, to meet the enemy "here than to suffer a war of devastation to rage in our settlements." With this and a number of other notes, John W. Smith slipped out through the south wall. Travis hoped that the convention would issue a declaration of independence, but ironically he and the other defenders of the Alamo died officially fighting for a federalist government under the Constitution of 1824, without knowing that such action had been taken.

On March 4 and 5 the Mexican cannon were moved closer and became more effective. Then, just before dawn on March 6, with the band playing *Degüello* (no quarter), Santa Anna took the fortress by storm, the defenders fighting until death. On orders of Santa Anna the bodies of 182 Texans (183 according to a report by a Mexican officer) were stacked on layers of wood and burned. The Mexican dead, variously estimated from 1,000 to 1,600, were buried in the cemetery until it was filled, and the remainder were dumped into the river. The Texans had not died in vain; their sacrifice delayed Santa Anna and gave their countrymen a few more precious days to prepare for his advance. After his victory at the Alamo, Santa Anna devised a three-column advance eastward through the settlements to complete the subjugation of Texas. Urrea, reinforced by a detachment of about 600 troops from San Antonio and after disposing of Fannin, was to march by way of Victoria and Matagorda Bay to Brazoria and perhaps as far as Anahuac. General Antonio Gaona with 725 men was ordered to march to Nacogdoches by way of Bastrop and the upper crossing on the Trinity River. The main army, with General Joaquin Ramírez y Sesma leading the advance unit, would proceed eastward by way of Gonzales and San Felipe. Santa Anna and General Vicente Filisola, next in command, left San Antonio on March 31 after the departure of the troops.

Meanwhile, General José Urrea on the southern front, with no more than one-fourth of the Mexican army under his command, was killing more than twice as many Texans as Santa Anna's troops were at the Alamo. Leaving Matamoros on January 18, Urrea marched rapidly

The Alamo. The Texas revolutionaries took the town of San Antonio in December 1835, and three months later about 180 men led by Travis, Bowie, and Crockett died trying to hold the Alamo against Santa Anna's several thousand troops. Their heroic resistance made "Remember the Alamo" the rallying cry of the revolutionary army. (University of Texas Library)

up the coastal road and on February 27 at San Patricio, on the Nueces River near present-day Corpus Christi, surprised Johnson, who at the time had with him about thirty-five men. All the men were killed or captured, except Johnson and four or five of his companions, who managed to escape. Twenty miles further up the road, on March 2, Urrea destroyed Dr. Grant and his scouting party of about thirty men and then continued toward Goliad.

At Goliad, Fannin was displaying the indecisiveness and ineptitude as a military commander that qualified him for a rating as the poorest in the Texas army. As previously stated, on February 26 he started with 320 men for San Antonio, at Travis's urgent appeal, but two miles out had transportation problems and on the next day returned to Goliad. On March 14 he received an order to fall back to Victoria from General Houston, who had been named ten days before by the convention to command all troops in Texas. Unfortunately, he delayed in order to wait for the return of two detachments of troops, variously estimated from less than 100 to 180 under Amon B. King and William Ward, that he had sent to aid in the evacuation of settlers in the vicinity of Refugio. Neither King nor Ward returned, and the delay cost Fannin and most of his men their lives. King and his thirty-three men had been captured near Refugio and, except for some Germans, were shot on March 16. Ward and his men had escaped from Refugio but were surrounded and captured on March 22 by Urrea near Victoria, where Ward had anticipated rejoining Fannin, and were impounded with the other prisoners at Goliad.

Fannin, with his main force, began his retreat on March 19, the day after Urrea, augmented by 600 troops from San Antonio, reached Goliad. That afternoon when a wagon loaded with ammunition broke down and the oxen needed to graze, Fannin camped on the prairie instead of pressing onward two or three miles to timber and to badly needed water. He was quickly surrounded by Urrea's cavalry, which was hurled back, but the next morning, when the main Mexican force arrived on the field with cannon, Fannin surrendered. The survivors contended that they surrendered as prisoners of war to be treated in accordance with international policy, but the original document in the Mexican archives shows that they capitulated "subject to the disposition of the Supreme Government." In this battle the Texans had 9 killed, 51 wounded, and 234 others captured; Urrea had at least 50 killed and 140 wounded, with some sources estimating more than 200 killed. The prisoners were returned to Goliad, kept in confinement for a week, and then, on orders of Santa Anna, about 350 (including Ward and 82 of his men) were shot. Four physicians, some nurses, and several needed workmen were spared, and 28 escaped from the firing squad. Unlike the Texans who died at the Alamo in defense of their constitutional rights, those massacred at Goliad knew that they were fighting for independence from Mexico and for the newly created republic.

## THE BIRTH OF THE REPUBLIC

On March 1, 1836, the contesting governors and council, despised and impotent because of quarrels and bickerings, were supplanted by a convention. Realizing that a reconvening of the Consultation would not be adequate to meet the emergency, the council had passed on December 14, 1835, over Governor Smith's veto, an act calling for the election of delegates to a convention "with ample, unlimited, or plenary powers as to the form of government to be adopted." The delegates, elected on February 1, convened on the morning of March 1 in Washington on the

Brazos, a new town about thirty-five miles upstream from San Felipe. It was a dismal place, a visitor from Virginia recorded, the cold rain the night before had left the one street ankle deep in mud, and the cotton cloth, stretched across the openings for windows in the unfinished blacksmith building in which they met, only partially excluded the chilling wind.

The condition that confronted the delegates when they assembled that cold morning called for courage and statesmanship of the highest order. Urrea's lancers were slashing their way toward Goliad, Santa Anna's legions were wearing out the heroic garrison at the Alamo, and Travis was pleading for aid. There were no troops at Washington and none between Washington and San Antonio, 150 miles away. The life of every delegate was in danger; indeed, all Texas was in peril and the outlook was well-nigh hopeless. Yet several features contributed to the effectiveness of the convention. Among the fifty-nine men who signed the declaration of independence were a few with broad experience and several of superior ability. Robert Potter and Samuel Carson had served in the Congress of the United States from North Carolina, and Richard Ellis and Martin Parmer had helped to frame state constitutions before they came to Texas. Other men of less experience, but of equal or greater ability, were Thomas J. Rusk, James Collinsworth, and George C. Childress. Collin McKinney, then seventy years old, but destined to outlive many of his colleagues, and James Gaines, who had known Texas since the days of Magee and Gutiérrez, did not make outstanding records, but they supplied such wisdom as comes only with age. One of the most distinguished and influential members was Lorenzo de Zavala, a former member of the Mexican Congress and a staunch opponent of Santa Anna's centralism. Sam Houston, a delegate from Refugio, was, no doubt, the most influential member, but he left the convention in less than a week to take command of the army. Of the fifty-nine delegates who attended the convention, fifty-two were from the United States (forty-five from the South and seven from the North; two had been born in Texas).

On the first day the convention elected as president Richard Ellis of Pecan Point in present-day Red River County (then Miller County, Arkansas), who had been a member of the Alabama constitutional convention and supreme court. It named H. S. Kimble, who returned immediately to his home in Tennessee, as secretary, and selected a committee to be chaired by George C. Childress, who only recently had brought five thousand dollars from the citizens of Tennessee to aid the Texas cause, to draft a declaration of independence. On the next day, March 2, it adopted a declaration of independence written by Childress, perhaps before the convention assembled, that followed the main features of the document written by Thomas Jefferson sixty years earlier.

The convention then began preparing a constitution for the new nation. The completed document, adopted at midnight on March 16, was a composite of excerpts from the constitutions of the United States and several states. Some unique features were: The term for the president was to be three years (the first constitutional president to serve two years only), and he was not to succeed himself; the president was not to lead armies in the field except with the consent of Congress; ministers of the gospel were not to hold office; each head of a family in Texas was to be granted a headright of a league and a *labor* of land;[2] and the institution of slavery was legalized, but the African slave trade was made piracy.

The convention also constituted itself the government of Texas and took steps to meet the emergency. Its most important work in that connection was the appointment on March 4 of Sam Houston as "Commander in Chief of all the land forces of the Texan Army, both regulars, volunteers, and militia, while in actual service." On Sunday, March 6, when Travis's last message from the Alamo arrived, the impetuous Potter moved that the delegates adjourn and go to the relief of the Alamo, but, after a long speech by Houston who insisted that the establishment of a government should have priority, it was rejected. Houston then left the convention to rally a force to fight for the independence of the new nation. The last act of the convention, performed as the candles burned short on the night of March 16–17, was the selection of an *ad interim* government to direct the infant republic until the constitution could be adopted and a regular government inaugurated. David G. Burnet was elected president over Samuel P. Carson by a vote of twenty-nine to twenty-three; Lorenzo de Zavala, vice-president; Samuel P. Carson, secretary of state; Bailey Hardeman, secretary of the treasury; Thomas J. Rusk, secretary of war; Robert Potter, secretary of the navy; and David Thomas, attorney general. They were sworn in at 4:00 A.M., and a few hours later the convention adjourned.

## FIGHTING FOR INDEPENDENCE

From the convention Houston went directly to Gonzales, where on his arrival on March 11 he found 374 men without two days' provisions, many without arms, and others without any ammunition. He had contemplated uniting with Fannin and going to the relief of the Alamo, but, when word of its fall came that evening, he dispatched an order to

---

[2]The convention also provided for land bounties to soldiers in amounts of 320 to 1,280 acres, varying with the lengths of service, but this was not incorporated in the constitution.

David G. Burnet was *ad interim* president of the Republic of Texas, March 16 to October 22, 1836, and vice-president, 1838–1841. A native of New Jersey, Burnet previously had commanded the launch that fired the first shot in the war for Venezuelan independence, had lived for almost two years with the Comanche Indians in West Texas while recovering from tuberculosis, and in 1826 had obtained an *empresario* grant in East Texas. In 1866 he was named to represent Texas in the United States Senate but was never seated. (Southwest Collection, Texas Tech University)

Fannin to fall back to Victoria. He immediately organized the First Regiment of Texas Volunteers with Edward Burleson in command. On the thirteenth he learned from his scouts and Suzanna Dickenson, who had been in the Alamo during the battle, that General Joaquin Ramírez y Sesma with about seven hundred troops was marching toward Gonzales. Knowing that with his small, untrained, and poorly equipped force he could not defend the town, he had it burned and that night began his retreat. A rear guard shepherded the frightened settlers, who hurriedly abandoned their homes and fled eastward with the retreating army. On the afternoon of March 17, the day the convention adjourned, he arrived at Burnam's (Burnham's) Ferry on the Colorado, near La Grange. By then he had about six hundred men. After getting the refugees and the troops across, he destroyed the ferry and encamped a short distance downstream at Beason's Crossing, barely ahead of the arrival of units of the Mexican army on the west bank of the swollen river. Hounded by his own men to let them fight, Houston considered making a stand at the Colorado, but upon the arrival of news that Fannin had capitulated, he decided to withdraw to the Brazos, for he realized that a victory over Sesma would not end the war and that a defeat would mean the total subjugation of Texas. Thus, on March 26 he left for the Brazos, arriving late the next day at San Felipe, a village of five stores and twenty-five or thirty houses. Here, Captains Moseley Baker and Wiley Martin refused to retreat further. Houston thereupon assigned Baker with his company to guard the crossing at San Felipe and Martin to guard the crossing at Fort Bend, about thirty miles downstream. The remainder of the troops sloshed upstream, less than twenty miles in three days, and camped on the west side of the Brazos across from the large plantation of Jared E. Groce, who furnished the army with large quantities of supplies and food. Here, Houston remained for nearly two weeks, reorganizing and drilling the army.

The incessant floods, mud, and cold weather also created misery and hardships for thousands of refugees and problems for Santa Anna and his troops. Probably as many as a thousand families lived along the Colorado and Brazos along the paths of the armies. News of Houston's retreat, coupled with that of the fate of the Alamo and Goliad, carried eastward into the settlements by fleeing civilians and soldiers who left with or without leave to look after their families, created widespread fear. The frontier began to fold back upon itself. Loading their wagons, oxcarts, or sleds, or taking such simple belongings as could be carried on horseback or even on foot, the people set out in a desperate rush to keep ahead of the Mexican army. It was a season of heavy rain. Streams were swollen, ferries became jammed, epidemics prevailed, and the misery and suffering were indescribable. Stern Captain Mosely Baker wept at the sad sight he witnessed as the people trudged by his camp opposite San Felipe. In her reminiscences, Dilue Rose Harris states that there were five thousand people at Lynch's Ferry at the mouth of the San Jacinto when her family arrived there on April 10.

The government fled with the people. As the Mexican forces advanced, Texan headquarters were removed from Washington to Harrisburg (now within the city of Houston) and from Harrisburg to Galveston Island. Houston complained at the government for retreating, and Burnet in turn berated Houston. "The enemy are laughing you to scorn," he wrote, "you must fight them. You must retreat no farther. The country expects you to fight. The salvation of the country depends on you doing so." In commenting on his own conduct Houston wrote Rusk on March 29, "I consulted none—I held no councils-of-war. If I err, the blame is mine."

Meanwhile, Burnet sent Secretary of State Carson to Fort Jessup, Louisiana, to appeal for aid to General Edmund P. Gaines, who commanded a strong force of United States troops, but at that time Gaines's troops did not cross the Sabine.

Having left General Filisola at the Colorado with a detachment of troops to help get the artillery and supplies across the swollen Guadalupe, Santa Anna with Sesma and a part of the army on April 7 reached San Felipe, which Baker had burned. With the ferry destroyed and his slow rafts an easy target for Baker's riflemen on the opposite shore, Santa Anna was unable to cross. By going upstream Houston had left the government at Harrisburg and the lower settlements without any protection. Thus, Santa Anna decided first to lay waste that region and to deal with Houston later. Sending orders to Filisola, Urrea, and Gaona to march their commands to Fort Bend, near present-day Richmond, he led an advance detachment of Sesma's troops to that place. When all the units arrived, he would have at his command a force of about 3,400, more than three times the size of Houston's.

Meanwhile, on April 12 a messenger from Fort Bend reached Houston's camp with word of Santa Anna's plan. This was the opportunity Houston wanted. With the aid of the steamboat *Yellowstone* he moved his command across the river where it received the famous "Twin Sisters," two cannon donated by the people of Cincinnati, that would soon help win Texas independence. Not far ahead the road forked, one leading to Louisiana, the other to Harrisburg. The men, especially Moseley Baker, who had rejoined the main command, threatened to mutiny if Houston took the road toward Louisiana. They were unaware, of course, as most historians have been since, that on the night before reaching the fork Houston wrote a friend that he was on his way to meet Santa Anna. Houston took the road to Harrisburg. On April 18, while he was camped near the ruins of the town, Deaf Smith, the faithful and effective scout, brought in as captive a Mexican courier with dispatches that revealed Santa Anna's plans and movements. Houston thereupon crossed his army on rough rafts to the south side of Buffalo Bayou, left his baggage and sick men with a small guard hidden in the woods, and during the next night proceeded with slightly more than nine hundred men across the wooden bridge over Vince's Bayou to Lynch's Ferry. Taking possession of the ferry, he pitched camp soon after dawn on April 20 with the bayou at his rear, the San Jacinto on his left, and open prairie on his front and right flanks.

Until he reached Harrisburg, Houston apparently had no definite plan. His general plan had been to retreat eastward to gain the advantage of being nearer a source of supplies in the Texas settlements and in the United States, to draw the enemy farther and farther away from his base of supplies, and to avoid battle until the enemy made a mistake. On the afternoon of April 20, Santa Anna made the mistake of camping where organized retreat was impossible.

A sharp skirmish occurred during the afternoon. Upon finding the Texans in control of the ferry, the surprised Mexicans hauled a cannon to some nearby timber and began firing at the Texans. Colonel Sidney Sherman with a small force of cavalry attempted to take the cannon but was momentarily trapped by the Mexicans. In this encounter, the action of Mirabeau B. Lamar, who had arrived only a few days before, resulted in his appointment to command a unit of cavalry. That night, the Texans slept and the next morning had a good breakfast. Santa Anna, on the other hand, prepared for an attack and kept his men on the alert. When General Cós arrived the next morning with 542, or perhaps more, tired and hungry troops, Santa Anna, convinced that the Texans did not intend to attack, permitted all, except for a small guard, to eat and to retire to their tents for sleep and rest.

Informed that Cós had arrived by way of Vince's bridge, Houston sent Deaf Smith to destroy it, leaving neither army with an escape route. Finally, about noon on Thursday, April 21, aware that the men were becoming increasingly impatient, Houston told his officers to prepare for battle. At 3:30 that afternoon, he formed his troops in a line that extended one thousand yards along the edge of the woods. From left to right, the line order was the Second Regiment under Sherman, the First Regiment under Burleson, and artillery under George W. Hockley, a four-piece band, four companies of infantry under Henry Millard, and sixty-one cavalrymen under Lamar to move out first and distract the Mexicans and to prevent them from breaking away to the prairie. The Texans moved quietly, hidden from view by a rise in the terrain, until they were within two hundred yards of the Mexican barricades. Then the "Twin Sisters" fired a blast of broken horseshoes and shrapnel directly into the Mexican camp; the four-piece band began playing an inappropriate popular love song, "Will You Come to the Bow'r I Have Shaded for You"; Colonel Sherman struck the enemy on his left; and the line, center and right, charged directly into the breastworks of the camp, shouting "Remember the Alamo!" and "Remember Goliad!" The surprised and frightened Mexicans fled in panic. General Manuel Fernandez Castrillón tried to rally the confused Mexican soldiers, but, despite General Rusk's attempt to save him, other Texans riddled his body with bullets. Santa Anna and some of his staff escaped into the woods, hoping apparently to reach his main army at Fort Bend.

The carnage at San Jacinto was indescribable. The battle, according to Houston's official report, lasted only eighteen minutes, but the pursuit, killing, and capture of the enemy continued longer. The Texans, determined to exact full vengeance, could not be restrained. Arriving at the scene where a terrible slaughter was underway, an officer who ordered the men to stop was told, according to Austin's nephew, "Colonel, if Jesus Christ were to come down from heaven and ordered me to quit shooting Santanistas, I wouldn't do it sir!" After peering for a moment down the barrel of the speaker's cocked rifle, the officer rode away. According to Houston's official report four days later, 630 of the enemy were killed, 208 were wounded, and 730 were taken prisoner, including

General Cós and Santa Anna who were captured the next day. Only a few Mexicans escaped.[3] Nine Texans were killed and thirty-four wounded, including Houston whose right leg just above the ankle was shattered by shot in the midst of the battle.

The shape of the terrain, the Mexican custom of taking a siesta, the utter contempt in which Santa Anna held the Anglo-American troops, the torrential floods, and Santa Anna's mistakes in strategy afford the only explanation as to why a smaller army advancing three-fourths of a mile across an open prairie on an April afternoon had been able to surprise and in just eighteen minutes win a significant battle—and, as it eventually turned out, independence.

## READJUSTMENTS AFTER SAN JACINTO

The defeat of Santa Anna's forces saved the Texan cause for the time, but it did not assure independence right away. Mexico was still belligerent; there were in Texas about two thousand Mexican troops that might

[3]The exact size of the Mexican army at San Jacinto has never been determined. In his report Houston accounts for nearly 1,400 men, but it is difficult to reconcile this number with the Mexican accounts. See Johnson, *Texas and Texans*, I, 448. In their *Heroes of San Jacinto* (1932), Kemp and Dixon have verified the names of 918 participants on the Texan side.

have to be reckoned with; and Houston was helpless and soon to take a steamer to New Orleans for the treatment of his ankle. The Texan army was, furthermore, almost as badly disorganized by victory as was the Mexican army on the Brazos by the reports of defeat and death brought on the night of April 21 by a few dragoons who had managed to escape from the San Jacinto battlefield. The testing time was not yet over. The immediate problems before the government were: first, to restore order and establish among the people a sense of security and competence; second, to strengthen, supply, and keep control of the army; and third, to secure from Mexico the recognition of Texan independence, or at least to empty the country of Mexican troops.

Order and confidence returned gradually as the people learned of the completeness of the victory and observed that the government again was functioning. Many persons who had taken part in the "runaway scrape" went back to their homes at once. Government headquarters were removed from Galveston to Velasco where better quarters could be secured. The *Telegraph and Texas Register*, whose plant at Harrisburg had been destroyed during the invasion, resumed publication in Columbia in August. On July 23, President Burnet issued a proclamation calling for a general election to be held on the first Monday in September to establish a constitutional government.

The gravest problem that confronted the *ad interim* government after San Jacinto was that of controlling the army. The subject was, however, inseparably linked with that of disposing of the prisoner Santa Anna and arriving at some understanding with the Mexicans. Shortly after he had been brought to Houston's headquarters on April 22, the Mexican president entered into an armistice in consequence of which he wrote General Vicente Filisola, second in command to retire with his troops to Béxar and to order Urrea to fall back to Victoria "pending some negotiations . . . by which the war is to cease forever." This order was not necessary. Even as Santa Anna wrote, the Mexican forces were in retreat, and the messenger did not overtake Filisola until April 28. Then, in Velasco on May 14, Burnet negotiated two treaties with Santa Anna, one public and one secret. By the terms of the public treaty an end was declared to hostilities; the Mexican army was to retire at once beyond the Rio Grande, and all Texan prisoners were to be released by the Mexicans, the Texans agreeing to release a corresponding number of Mexican prisoners. The chief purpose of the secret treaty was to get from Santa Anna the pledge to use his influence on the Mexican government to secure the execution of the treaty already made and, also, to establish a permanent treaty whereby Mexico would acknowledge the independence of Texas and the boundary of Texas would not extend beyond the Rio Grande. The Texan government in turn pledged to release Santa Anna at once, giving him an escort to Vera Cruz.

There was widespread clamor that the dictator be put to death, but Burnet courageously determined to carry out the treaty and return him to Mexico. On June 4, after General Santa Anna, his secretary Caro, and Colonel Almonte were aboard the armed schooner of war *Invincible*, a group of disgruntled and ambitious army officers, led by General Thomas J. Green, who had just arrived from the United States with a force of volunteers, compelled Burnet, despite Santa Anna's protest, to remove the Mexicans from the vessel and place them again in confinement.

Developments during the next few weeks did not improve Santa Anna's position. Word came that the Mexican senate had annulled his treaty and had declared that the government would continue the war. Three Texan emissaries, sent to Matamoros under a flag of truce and bearing passports from Filisola to see if all prisoners had been released, were arrested and added to the Mexican prison rolls. On June 17, Rusk wrote from the army that Urrea was advancing on Goliad. It was left to President Houston finally to dispose of the prisoner.

Burnet's difficulties with insubordinate troops were not confined to volunteers at the seat of government. After the Battle of San Jacinto, Thomas J. Rusk reluctantly took command of the Texan army and followed the retreating Mexicans as far as Victoria. Word that Santa Anna was to be released provoked an army mass meeting and an insolent and threatening letter to Burnet. Thinking that army morale might be improved by a change of commanders, Burnet sent Mirabeau B. Lamar on about July 1 to replace Rusk, but neither the men nor officers would accept him. When a plan of the army officers to arrest and bring Rusk before the army for trial failed, Burnet sought to absorb the energies of the army by encouraging an expedition against Matamoros. This was not carried out. He then sent word to agents in New Orleans to send no more short-term volunteers and passed the problem of the army on to his successor, Houston.

## AID FROM THE UNITED STATES

Expenditures of the Texan revolutionary government were strikingly small. Figures in the audits read more like those of a retail store than of the government of a sovereign state. Virtually every device for raising money known in that day was tried. Donations, including one of $7,000 from a committee in New Orleans and two of $5,000 each from persons in the United States, amounted to about $25,000. Many loyal persons pledged land, slaves, and other property to be sold for the benefit of the cause, but little money was raised in that way. Receipts from the sale of land and other property were negligible. Treasury notes, issued to the amount of $150,000, were almost worthless from the date of their issue. The most substantial receipts, about $100,000, came from loans negotiated in the United States by Commissioners Austin, Archer, and Wharton. The revolution was financed largely by those who advanced supplies to the infant government on faith and by the troops who willingly served for little other compensation than the promise of land bounties. By August 31, 1836, the government debt was $1.25 million.

War supplies came mainly from New Orleans. The firm of William Bryan and Company, Texan agents in that city, often used their own funds and impaired their private credit in the interests of the struggle. Also, the Texan merchant, Thomas F. McKinney, who declined the office of commissary general, worked faithfully in a private capacity toward supplying the troops, and to that end he spent large sums of his own money. The records show shipments of flour, rifles, powder, lead, clothing, and other necessary supplies for the army, without which it could not have continued the struggle.

From east of the Sabine came men as well as supplies. As early as October 26, the Permanent Council addressed the citizens of the United States with an impassioned appeal to come to the aid of "suffering Texas." From New Orleans to Cincinnati friends of the colonists held meetings, raised funds, and sent out forces of volunteers of "armed emigrants." The chief recruiting stations were Louisville, Cincinnati, and New Orleans. Some of the best-known volunteer organizations were the two companies of "New Orleans Greys," in one of which were represented five foreign countries and twelve different states; the Georgia Battalion, composed of men from Georgia and Alabama and strengthened by recruits who joined them on the way to Texas; the "Mobile Grays," originally some thirty men under Captain David N. Burke; the Alabama "Red Rovers," almost seventy men under Captain Jack Shackelford, who arrived at Matagorda early in 1836 armed with 81 muskets from the arsenal of the state of Alabama; the "Mustangs," from Kentucky and Tennessee; and some fifty Tennesseans, among them David Crockett, who arrived in Nacogdoches on January 12, 1836.

For most of these valiant young Americans fate held a tragic ending. A majority of the men who died in the Alamo recently had come from the United States, as was true of the forces of Johnson and Grant, and Fannin's men were, almost without exception, newcomers. After all, the Texan colonists did the most effective fighting. It was they who drove the Mexicans out of Texas in 1835, and they constituted an overwhelming majority of Houston's army at San Jacinto.

The most successful work in recruiting troops abroad for Texas was that of Thomas J. Chambers. Authorized by the council to raise for Texas an "Army of the Reserve," Chambers in February 1836 proceeded to Natchez, Mississippi, and thence to points in Tennessee, Kentucky, and Ohio. Report of the victory at San Jacinto made it comparatively easy, both to secure volunteers and to raise the means to equip them. By December 1836 he had sent 1,915 well-equipped volunteers and, also, quantities of ammunition and other supplies. These forces arrived too late, however, to participate in the battles of the revolution.

## THE TEXAS NAVY

In conveying men and equipment, as well as preventing the free movements of troops and supplies by the enemy, the Texans were greatly aided by the navy. In fact, it seems safe to say that without the support rendered by the navy, the Texans never would have won the war. The first battle in the revolution occurred at sea on September 1, 1835. The Mexican war schooner *Correo*, commanded by Thomas M. Thompson, who had antagonized the Anglo-Americans by his arbitrary seizures of ships and cargoes in the vicinity of Velasco, fired upon the *San Felipe*, an armed trading schooner owned by Thomas F. McKinney and commanded by William A. Hurd, which was bound for Brazoria with a cargo of munitions. After a two-hour fight the *Correo* was captured and taken to New Orleans. In October the Texas government commandeered the *San Felipe*, but soon thereafter it was grounded in Matagorda Bay.

Mexican war and transport ships continued to operate along the coast, and consequently the provisional government on November 25 provided for the purchase of four schooners and for granting a letter of marque to privateers until the navy materialized. Meanwhile, the citizens in the coastal communities had bought and equipped the schooner *William Robbins* with which W. A. Hurd, after being granted a letter of marque, sailed to Paso Cavallo and took the Mexican man of war *Bravo* and a prize it had just taken. Sentiment in the United States, however, was so strongly against privateering that the Texans had to discontinue the practice. Thus, the Texas commissioners in January 1836 proceeded to purchase as authorized four naval vessels: the 60-ton *William Robbins*, rechristened the *Liberty*; the 125-ton *Independence*, a former United States revenue cutter purchased in New Orleans and sent to sea under Captain Charles E. Hawkins; the 125-ton *Invincible*, which had been built in Baltimore for the African slave trade; and the 125-ton, 8-gun *Brutus*, purchased from John K. and Augustus C. Allen in 1835 and fitted out as a privateer. The *Brutus*, after being delayed in New Orleans, was commissioned in early March and placed in command of William A. Hurd. About the same time President Burnet commissioned Hawkins to the rank of commodore and placed him in command of the first Texas navy.

In cruising along the coast and convoying shipments from New Orleans, the vessels rendered excellent service. The *Brutus* maintained a blockade along the Texas coast until it was lost in a storm in October 1837. The *Liberty* took as a prize the fine Mexican schooner *Pelicano*, whose cargo consisted largely of munitions for the Mexican army (packed in barrels of flour and apples and consigned to New Orleans in the hope of escaping the blockade). It took other less noteworthy prizes and escorted the *Flora* with the wounded Houston aboard to New Orleans, but in July it had to be sold because the Texas government could not pay the bill for its repair. The *Invincible* cruised along the Gulf Coast, taking prizes until August 26, when it ran aground and was destroyed in Galveston harbor while engaged in a fight with two Mexican vessels. During the early months of the year the *Independence* captured a number of small Mexican vessels along the Texas coast and then sailed for New Orleans where Hawkins died. On its return, after a four-hour fight, it was captured in sight of Galveston. As the Mexican army advanced, the Texas ships centered their activity on keeping the port of Galveston open, thereby allowing the Mexicans uncontested use of the forts at the mouth of the Brazos and at Copano Bay. Anticipating that the Mexicans might send troops and supplies through these ports, General T. J. Rusk ordered Major Issac W. Burton with about thirty mounted men to patrol the coast. Sighting a Mexican vessel in Copano Bay, Burton on June 3 managed to decoy the captain and some crew members ashore, seized them, rowed out in their boat, and took the ship (loaded with supplies for the Mexican army) without resistance. Two weeks later, when two other ships loaded with supplies appeared, the "Horse Marines," as Burton and his rangers became known, managed to take both without a casualty.

## SELECTED BIBLIOGRAPHY

A great deal has been written about the Texan Revolution. Of the older general histories, all cited at the beginning of the references for Chapter 4, good accounts may be had in J. H. Brown, H. H. Bancroft, W. Kennedy, H. Yoakum, D. G. Wooten (reprint of Yoakum's text), C. R. Wortham, and H. S. Thrall. Yoakum gives much source material. Thrall has many biographical sketches; Wortham devotes a volume to the revolution; Juan N. Almonte, *Noticia Estradistica Sobre Tejas* (Mexico, 1835); Vicente Filisola, *Memoirs of the History of the War with Texas* (typescript trans. Verona Griffith, Library, Texas Tech University, Lubbock, Tex.; Mexico, 1848).

Of the newer general histories, two are superior: W. C. Binkley, *The Texas Revolution*; and D. M. Vigness, *The Revolutionary Decades*; two others of great value are Vito Alessio Robles, *Coahuila y Texas en la Epoca Colonial* (Mexico, 1938); and A.J. Houston, *Texas Independence* (Houston, 1938).

Several biographies are extremely valuable in connection with the revolution. The best is E. C. Barker, *The Life of Stephen F. Austin*. Others are L. Friend, *Sam Houston, the Great Designer;* Marquis James, *The Raven: A Biography of Sam Houston* (New York, 1929); E. Wallace, *Charles DeMorse, Pioneer Editor and Statesman* (Lubbock, Tex., 1943); Herbert P. Gambrell, *Mirabeau Bonaparte Lamar* (Dallas, 1934); Herbert P. Gambrell, *Anson Jones: The Last President of Texas* (New York, 1948); Mary Whatley Clarke, *David G. Burnet* (Austin, 1969); Herman Ehrenberg, *With Milam and Fannin* (trans. Charlotte Churchill and ed. Henry Smith; Austin, 1974); Hobart Huson, *Captain Phillip Dimmitt's Commandancy of Goliad* (Austin, 1974); Ernest C. Shearer, *Robert Potter, Remarkable North Carolinian and Texan* (Houston, 1951); Archie McDonald, *Travis* (Austin, 1976); W. N. Bate, *General Sidney Sherman: Texas Soldier, Statesman and Builder* (Waco, Tex., 1974); Cleburn Huston, *Deaf Smith, Incredible Spy* (Waco, Tex., 1973); J. A. Atkins, *David Crockett, the Man and the Legend* (Chapel Hill, N.C., 1956); John Henry Brown, *Life and Times of Henry Smith, the*

*First American Governor of Texas* (Dallas, 1887); R. N. Richardson, and others, *Heroes of Texas* (Waco, Tex., 1964).

The source materials for the revolution are voluminous. The most comprehensive is John H. Jenkins (ed.), *The Papers of the Texas Revolution.* Other comprehensive collections are E. C. Barker (ed.), *The Austin Papers*; Amelia W. Williams and E. C. Barker (eds.), *The Writings of Sam Houston* (8 vols., Austin, 1938–1943); C. A. Gulick, Katherine Elliott, and Harriett Smithers (eds.), *The Papers of Mirabeau Buonaparte Lamar* (6 vols., Austin, 1921–1927); W. C. Binkley (ed.), *Official Correspondence of the Texan Revolution, 1835–1836* (2 vols., New York and London, 1936). Useful also is C. E. Castañeda (ed. and trans.), *The Mexican Side of the Texan Revolution* (Dallas, 1928); E. Wallace and D. M. Vigness (eds.), *Documents of Texas History*; John H. Jenkins (ed.), *Recollections of Early Texas: The Memoirs of John Holland Jenkins* (Austin, 1958).

Shorter studies dealing primarily with the early phase of the revolution include "General Austin's Order Book for the Campaign of 1835," *Quarterly of the Texas State Historical Association* XI, 1–55; Fred H. Turner, "The Mejia Expedition," *ibid.*, VII, 1–28; E. C. Barker, "Proceedings of the Permanent Council," *ibid.*, IX, 287–288; E. C. Barker (ed.), "Journal of the Permanent Council," *ibid.*, VII, 249–278; E. C. Barker, "The Texan Declaration of Causes for Taking Up Arms against Mexico," *ibid.*, XV, 173–185; E. C. Barker, "The Tampico Expedition," *ibid.*, VI, 169–186; Ralph Steen, "Analysis of the Work of the General Council of Texas, 1835–1836," *Southwestern Historical Quarterly*, XL, 309–333; XLI, 225–240; E. C. Barker, "Don Carlos Barrett," *ibid.*, XX, 139–145; R. S. Lee, "The Publication of Austin's Louisville Address," *ibid.*, LXX, 424–442; Raymond Estep, "Lorenzo de Zavala and the Texas Revolution," *ibid.*, LVII, 322–335; Miles S. Bennett, "The Battle of Gonzales, the 'Lexington' of the Texas Revolution," *Quarterly of the Texas State Historical Association*, II, 313–316; E. C. Barker, "The Texas Revolutionary Army," *ibid.*, IX, 227–261; *The Texans* (Time-Life Books, 1975); Katherine Hart and Elizabeth Kemp (eds.), "E. M. Pease's Account of the Texas Revolution," *Southwestern Historical Quarterly*, LXVIII, 79–89.

On the war in the field, see: E. C. Barker, "The Texan Revolutionary Army," *Quarterly of the Texas State Historical Association*, IX, 227–261; E. C. Barker, "The San Jacinto Campaign," *ibid.*, IV, 237–345; John E. Roller, "Captain John Sowers Brooks," *ibid.*, IX, 157–209, contains letters from a soldier with Fannin; Ruby C. Smith, "James W. Fannin, Jr., in the Texas Revolution," *Southwestern Historical Quarterly*, XXIII, 79–90, 171–203, 271–284; Harbert Davenport, "Captain Jesus Cuellar, Texas Cavalry, Otherwise Comanche," *ibid.*, XX, 56–62; Amelia Williams, "A Critical Study of the Siege of the Alamo . . . ," *ibid.*, XXXVI, 251–287; XXXVII, 1–44, 79–115, 157–184, 237–312; M. L. Bonham, Jr., "James Butler Bonham: A Consistent Rebel," *ibid.*, XXXV, 124–136; H. Davenport, "The Men of Goliad," *ibid.*, XLIII, 1–41 (an interpretation of the entire Texan Revolution); H. M. Henderson, "A Critical Analysis of the San Jacinto Campaign," *ibid.*, LIX, 344–362; Jewel D. Scarborough, "The Georgia Battalion in the Texas Revolution: A Critical Study," *ibid.*, LXIII, 511–532; Thomas I. Miller, "Fannin's Men: Some Additions to Earlier Rosters," *ibid.*, LXI, 522–532; James Presley, "Santa Anna in Texas: A Mexican Viewpoint," *ibid.*, LXII, 489–512; Walter Lord, *A Time to Stand* (New York, 1961); Lon Tinkle, *Thirteen Days to Glory* (New York, 1958); Sam H. Dixon and Louis W. Kemp, *The Heroes of San Jacinto* (Houston, 1932).

For an account of the convention of 1836 see R. N. Richardson, "Framing the Constitution of the Republic of Texas," *Southwestern Historical Quarterly*, XXXI, 191–220; J. K. Greer, "The Committee of the Texas Declaration of Independence, *ibid.*, XXX, 239–251; XXI, 33–49, 130–149; Henderson Shuffler, "The Signing of Texas' Declaration of Independence: Myth and Reality," *ibid.*, LXV, 310–332; L. W. Kemp, *The Signers of the Texas Declaration of Independence* (Houston, 1944).

On developments after the Battle of San Jacinto, see W. C. Binkley, "Activities of the Texan Revolutionary Army after San Jacinto," *Journal of Southern History*, VI, 331–346.

Concerning the attitude of President Jackson toward the Texan Revolution, two points of view are presented in E. C. Barker, "President Jackson and the Texas Revolution," *American Historical Review*, XII, 797–803; and R. C. Stenberg, "The Texas Schemes of Jackson and Houston, 1829–1836," *Southwestern Social Science Quarterly*, XV, 229–250.

J. E. Winston has published in the *Southwestern Historical Quarterly* a series of articles on aid from the United States. See XVI, 27–62, 277–283; XXI, 36–60; XVIII, 368–385; and XVII, 262–282. See also C. Elliott, "Alabama and the Texas Revolution," *ibid.*, I., 316–328.

On the Texan navy, see Alex Dienst. "The Navy of the Republic of Texas," *Quarterly of the Texas State Historical Association*, XII, 165–203, 249–275; XIII, 1–43, 85–127; Jim Dan Hill, *The Texas Navy* (Chicago, 1937); George G. Haugh (ed.), "History of the Texas Navy," *Southwestern Historical Quarterly*, LXIII, 572–579.

Chapter Seven

# THE REPUBLIC
# OF TEXAS
# 1836–1846

The history of the Republic of Texas may be divided logically into two major sections: domestic affairs and foreign relations. Because of the many problems with which the newborn republic had to cope and the contrasting policies of Presidents Houston and Lamar, each of these sections in turn is subdivided into a number of topics. Domestic affairs is treated under the following subjects: the election of 1836, Houston's first administration, Lamar's administration, Houston's second administration, the land policy of the republic, contracts of immigrant agents, and immigration and the extension of settlement. The section on foreign relations divides itself naturally into four topics: early efforts to obtain recognition by and annexation to the United States, relations with European nations, relations with Mexico, and the annexation of Texas to the United States.

## THE ELECTION OF 1836

Even after the Texan victory at San Jacinto, the *ad interim* government had to cope with many critical problems. Arrogant military officers defied the government's orders and threatened to replace it with military dictatorship. Money was scarce; families were destitute; crops had been planted too late, if at all, to yield well; and the government lacked adequate power to deal with problems either at home or abroad. Consequently, in desperation, President Burnet and his cabinet, without waiting until December as the convention had proposed, on July 23 issued a proclamation setting the first Monday of the following September as the date for the election. The three major issues were to be decided: first, ratification of the constitution; second, the election of the constitutional officers who would take office provided the voters approved the constitution; and third, whether the new government should seek annexation to the United States.

The ratification of the constitution and a favorable vote on annexation were unquestionably certain; thus the major interest in the election centered on the selection of a president. Since there were no political parties in Texas at the time, the candidates had to depend largely on their general popularity. Henry Smith, the first to announce openly for the presidency, sought to vindicate his policies as head of the provisional government. Austin entered the race at the solicitation of William H. Wharton, B. T. Archer, and others. Despite his distinguished and unselfish service to Texas, Austin had become exceedingly unpopular. His early opposition to independence, his support of the government in saving Santa Anna from a firing squad, and the charge that he had not served Texas well while in the United States adversely affected his popularity. It was soon evident that Sam Houston was the people's choice. Just eleven days before the election he formally accepted the nomination by numerous groups throughout the nation. In the election Houston received 5,110 votes, almost 80 percent of the total, Smith 743, and Austin only 587. Mirabeau B. Lamar was elected vice-president. The constitution was accepted overwhelmingly. Only 233 voters were in favor of giving the Congress the power to amend it, and only 93 voted against the mandate requiring the new president to negotiate for annexation to the United States.

## HOUSTON'S FIRST ADMINISTRATION (1836–1838)

*Ad interim* President Burnet convened the First Congress in Columbia on October 3 and on the next day delivered to it his message embodying recommendations for legislative consideration. There was a growing demand, however, for Houston and Lamar to take office without waiting until the second Monday in December, as provided in the constitution. On October 22 Burnet resigned, and Houston took the oath of office as the first constitutionally elected president of the Republic of Texas. In his impromptu inaugural address, Houston spoke only briefly of his program. The extensive frontier created a major problem. Toward the Indians he called for a policy of treaties and friendship, commerce, and nonaggression. It was necessary to maintain a well-organized and disci-

The capitol of Texas, Columbia, 1836. (Southwest Collection, Texas Tech University)

plined army for defense against an invasion by Mexico, and he was of the opinion that the union of Texas with the United States would soon take place. Houston stated that he chose his cabinet "with a total disregard to personal preference" and "for the furtherance of the interests of the Country." Austin, long the leader of conservative Texans, who had opposed, until after the revolution was well under way, separation from Mexico, was made secretary of state, and Henry Smith of the radical or Wharton faction was appointed secretary of the treasury. Austin died about two months after taking office and was replaced by Dr. Robert A. Irion, a native of Tennessee who had come from Vicksburg to Nacogdoches in 1832. William H. Wharton, a leader in the revolutionary movement and close friend of President Andrew Jackson, was sent to represent the republic in Washington. Thirty-year-old James Collinsworth, a lawyer who had come from Tennessee to Texas in 1835 and in 1836 had nominated Houston for commander in chief of the army, was appointed chief justice. The chief justice, acting with the four district judges provided for in the law, constituted the supreme court. Congress created twenty-two counties, corresponding in most cases to the Mexican municipalities. By 1845 the number had been increased to thirty-six. Each county was to have a court with a chief justice and two associate justices, who were to be selected by a majority of the county's justices of the peace. Because Mexico did not ratify the Treaty of Velasco, the First Congress had to define the limits of the republic before it could establish counties. Thus, on December 19, 1836, it set the boundary at the center of the Rio Grande from its mouth to its source, north to the forty-second parallel, and east and south along the Adams-Onís Treaty line to the Gulf.

National defense and frontier protection were of major concern during Houston's first administration. In response to threats of a Mexican reinvasion and to fear of hostile Indians, Congress in December 1836

President's mansion, Houston, 1837. (Southwest collection, Texas Tech University)

authorized an army of 3,587 troops and 280 mounted rangers, a chain of forts and trading houses on the frontier, the enrollment of all able-bodied males between the ages of twenty-one and fifty in a militia organization, and the creation of a new navy.

Houston, however, was more interested in getting rid of the army he already had than in increasing its size. As previously stated, the army became insubordinate when it heard of plans to release Santa Anna and refused to accept Lamar, who was sent to replace Rusk as commander. It wanted to take Matamoros. Its morale did not improve when Houston named Rusk secretary of war, and the command devolved upon Felix Huston, a military adventurer who had recruited at his own expense almost five hundred volunteers in the United States. In the fall of 1836, President Houston appointed Felix Huston to the rank of brigadier general and Albert Sidney Johnston, one of the most capable officers that had come out of West Point, to the newly created rank of major general and sent him to take command of the army. When Johnston arrived at the camp, however, Huston challenged him to a duel, wounded him severely, and stayed in command. The clever Houston, however, solved the problem in an unusual way. In May 1837, while Huston was at the seat of government lobbying for authorization to lead a campaign into Mexico, President Houston furloughed or disbanded all but six hundred of the troops, offering free transportation to New Orleans to those who desired to return to the United States or 1,280 acres of land free to those who would accept a discharge and settle in Texas. To offset

First capitol at Houston, 1837. (Southwest Collection, Texas Tech University)

the reduction in the strength of the army, Congress then provided for a corps of rangers which Houston organized into six companies. Some names famous for their daring, fearlessness, and heroism associated with this initial group included John Coffee ("Jack") Hays, Samuel H. Walker, Ben McCulloch, W. A. ("Bigfoot") Wallace, and John S. ("Rip") Ford.

By keeping troops out of the Indian country and using such limited means as were available, Houston managed to avoid serious Indian wars. The most threatening situation was relations with the Cherokees, who had begun moving into Texas as early as 1819. The Spanish government had given them a vague grant to lands in the vicinity of Nacogdoches. In February 1836, when the Texans needed their friendship, commissioners Sam Houston and John Forbes, by authority of the Consultation, negotiated with them a treaty providing for permanent titles to their lands. When the senate, contrary to Houston's admonition, refused to ratify the treaty, the Cherokees and their associated tribes threatened to make trouble. To add to the confusion and uncertainty, Vicente Cordova, a Mexican citizen of Nacogdoches and an agent of the Mexican government, in the summer of 1838 led a band of nearly six hundred Mexicans and Kickapoo Indians in a rebellion in the Angelina River vicinity. In November General Rusk with a force of volunteers marched against the insurgents. Cordova fled, but the following winter he succeeded in inciting some of the tribes to renew hostilities. The Cherokees did not participate in this affair, but the president was both uneasy about their attitude and solicitous of their rights. His efforts to protect them did not avail, however, and as a result of Lamar's harsh Indian policy, they were expelled in 1839.

Public expenses in Houston's first administration amounted to nearly $2 million. There was a wide breach between expenditures and income. A tariff, ranging from a duty of 1 percent on breadstuffs to 50

Sam Houston. Elected governor of Tennessee in 1827, Houston seemed to have a secure political future when two years later he resigned and moved to what is now Oklahoma to rejoin the Cherokee Indians by whom he had been adopted in his youth. Houston came to Texas in 1833 and became a member of the conventions that declared Texas independent of Mexico and set up a provisional government. Criticized for retreating before the Mexicans, Houston regained popular favor when he defeated Santa Anna at San Jacinto in April 1836 and was elected the first president of the republic. (E. C. Barker History Center, University of Texas)

percent on silks, was the most productive tax. Tonnage dues and port fees, a direct property tax, poll taxes, business taxes, and land fees each added a little. Inasmuch as this small income was in the form of audited drafts, the treasury received but little money. These claims, incidentally, had depreciated to fifteen cents on the dollar, when an act of June 12, 1837, provided that they might be exchanged at par for 10-percent bonds. The poverty of the government at times was embarrassing. For a period, Secretary of the Treasury Henry Smith could not attend to his duties because he had no stationery and no funds with which to buy any. Houston could secure supplies for the army only by pledging his personal credit.

Under such conditions the government resorted to the expedient of issuing paper money. Acts of 1837 required the president to issue promissory notes of the government to the amount of $650,000, payable twelve months after the date of issue and yielding 10 percent interest. The notes circulated readily, were not reissued, and suffered little or no depreciation. However, a succeeding issue, "the engraved interest

The home the Houstons built in Huntsville, Texas, in 1847. (C. C. Springfield, Huntsville)

notes'' already had depreciated to a valuation as low as sixty-five cents on the dollar several months before November 3, 1838, when the estimated amount in circulation was $812,454.

The constitutional provisions that the first president serve two years only and that no president succeed himself made Houston ineligible for reelection. Long before the election it became evident that Vice-President Lamar would be president. He was the choice of the senate and was endorsed by various persons and groups. The opposition, that is, the Houston party, was never able to find a candidate. Rusk was solicited, but he refused to run. The Houston followers then decided to support Kentucky-born Peter W. Grayson, a San Felipe lawyer who had been one of the attorneys to obtain Austin's release on bail in Mexico City, who had been Austin's aide-de-camp in the campaign against San Antonio in 1835, and who had served as attorney general of the republic and as commissioner to Washington under both *ad interim* President Burnet and President Houston. In eastern Tennessee, while on an official mission to the United States, he took his own life. The Houston party then selected as its candidate thirty-year-old James W. Collinsworth, a hero in the Battle of San Jacinto, one of President Burnet's commissioners to Washington, and chief justice of the supreme court, but too young to meet the constitutional age requirement. In July 1836 he jumped from a boat in Galveston Bay and drowned, apparently a suicide victim. A few weeks before the election, the Houston party agreed to support Robert Wilson of Harrisburg, a steamship and sawmill owner and operator, an associate of A. C. and J. K. Allen in the promotion of the town of Houston, and a member of the Texas senate until expelled in 1838; but the vote for Lamar on November 16 was almost unanimous. David G. Burnet was elected vice-president.

## LAMAR'S ADMINISTRATION (1838–1841)

In his inaugural address and in a ten thousand–word message to Congress in December 1838, Lamar indicated that the conservative policies of the two preceding years would be abandoned for a more ambitious public program. Only a few of his proposals, however, were actually adopted.

An act of January 20, 1839, provided that each county should be given three square leagues of land for primary schools and that fifty square leagues should be set aside for two colleges or universities. A year later a law gave an additional square league to each county, one-half of the proceeds of which were to be used for the benefit of a county academy and the remainder to be distributed among the common school districts. Congress also made land grants to several private institutions. Lands were cheap, and many years were to pass before Texas had even the semblance of a system of public education; but these foundation laws link Lamar, who urged their enactment, eternally with the schools of Texas. A second piece of legislation to leave Lamar's trademark permanently on Texas, likewise regarded as very liberal and worthy for its day, was the Homestead Law. This measure, enacted on January 26, 1839, was the first legislation of its kind passed by any country against seizure for debt. Its property exemption, unknown in English common law, may have been influenced by Spanish law.

The question concerning the seat of government was carried over from Houston's regime. Burnet had selected Columbia as a temporary capital, and there the first administration under the constitution had its beginning. In December 1836 Congress voted to move the seat of government to the new town of Houston in May 1837, with the stipulation that a permanent location would be designated by 1840. Because of sectional rivalry, the site had not been selected when Lamar became president. Prompted by Lamar, Congress in January 1839 authorized the appointment of a new committee to select a site between the Colorado and Brazos rivers and north of the "Old San Antonio Road" and decided that it should be named for Stephen F. Austin. The commissioners chose a site near the small settlement of Waterloo on the Colorado River at the foot of the Balcones Escarpment, where there was an abundance of good

Mirabeau Buonaparte Lamar came to Texas from Georgia to join the revolutionaries in 1835 and took part in the Battle of San Jacinto. During his term as the second president of the republic (1838–1841), he secured foreign recognition of Texas's independence. He had hoped to make the republic self-sufficient, but his ill-advised expeditions to New Mexico left Texas in financial difficulties. (E. C. Barker History Center, University of Texas)

water. At that point they believed the roads linking the Red River with Matamoros and Santa Fé with the Gulf of Mexico would intersect. Edwin Waller designed the town which was named Austin, and in October of that year President Lamar and his cabinet proceeded to the new capital. Four months later the town claimed a population of 856.

Upon assuming the presidency, Lamar immediately inaugurated a drastic change in Indian policy. He told Congress that the Indians were tenants at will and had no possessory rights to the land, and thus the white people could take the land whenever they so desired. The Indians must either conform to Texas laws, leave the nation, or be exterminated.

Albert Sidney Johnston, the secretary of war, G. W. Bonnell, commissioner of Indian affairs, a majority of Congress, and many others agreed with him and urged an aggressive frontier policy. Consequently, Lamar's administration was marked by the bloodiest Indian wars Texas had known. Yet the fact must be kept in mind that Lamar had inherited these wars; hostilities had already begun when he became president. The Cherokees and associated tribes in eastern Texas had been put off with promises for too long, and they were in an ugly humor. Farther west, the Wacos, Tawakonis, and Comanches, seeing the surveyors penetrate their hunting grounds deeper each season, were already on the warpath.

The Cherokees were the first to be uprooted as a result of Lamar's hostile Indian policy. As noted previously, the senate in October 1837, influenced by Vice-President Lamar, rejected Houston's Cherokee treaty. As a result, the Cherokees were resentful, and some joined with Vicente Cordova, a former alcalde of Nacogdoches, in plotting an uprising in eastern Texas on behalf of the Centralists in Mexico. When in 1838 the plot became known, Rusk marched into Cherokee country, and Cordova and a band of his followers fled to Mexico. Raiding against the whites, however, continued. In May 1839, Texas volunteer militia, operating near Austin and assuming every Indian was an enemy to be slain, encounte˙ᴣd and killed Manuel Flores, who with a party of twenty-five marauders had committed several murders between Seguin and Austin. Convinced from papers found on his body that the Cherokees were in treasonable correspondence with the Mexicans, Lamar and his cabinet determined to expel them. After the Cherokees had refused to accept compensation for their crops and to move peacefully, Rusk and Burleson marched into their country, defeated them in the Battle of the Neches on July 16, near the present city of Tyler, and drove the survivors across the Red River into Indian Territory. The Shawnees and some other groups then abandoned the area, and the peaceful Alabama and Coushatta were moved to other land in Texas.

More prolonged and bloody was the war with the Comanches, whose tactics of surprise attacks and flight before the whites could strike back made them the most formidable enemy of the frontierspeople. Disturbed by the westward advance of the Texans, some southern Comanches early in 1838 asked for peace. President Houston, however, refused their demand for a boundary, and when Lamar became president, they were waging a destructive war upon the exposed frontier. Congress promptly provided Lamar with punitive military forces. On February 14, 1839, J. H. Moore with three small companies of volunteers attacked a Comanche village at Spring Creek in the valley of the San Saba and was repulsed. Captain John Bird lost his life, and his company of thirty-five men was threatened with annihilation near present-day Belton by an aggregation of Indians, among whom Comanches predominated.

Realizing that Lamar was bent on their destruction, early in 1840 the southern Comanches requested a peace council. The overture was accepted, provided the Comanches would bring to the council in San Antonio all their white captives. On March 19, 1840, the Comanches, sixty-five men, women, and children, arrived for the council, bringing only one captive—Matilda Lockhart, a badly mutilated fifteen-year-old girl who had been captured near Gonzales in 1838. When the Texans, who had hidden troops in an adjacent room, attempted to take the Comanche warriors as hostages, a battle erupted in which 35 Comanches were killed and 29 were taken prisoner. The Texans had 7 killed and 8 wounded. When they heard of this affair, other Comanches killed their white prisoners. That summer they raided Victoria and on August 8 pillaged and destroyed Linnville, near the town of Port Lavaca. As they moved homeward, heavily loaded with booty, the Comanches were intercepted and defeated at Plum Creek near Lockhart on August 12 by the Texans commanded by General Huston, Colonel Burleson, and Ben McCulloch. The Comanches escaped with most of their plunder, but Colonel J. H. Moore led an expedition into the Indian country and, aided by Lipan Apaches, on October 23 surprised and destroyed the raiders' village on the Colorado River, probably in the vicinity of the present Ballinger, killing an estimated 130 Comanches and regaining a large amount of the plunder and livestock taken on the Linnville raid. The Comanches thereupon withdrew far from the Texas frontier. By the end of 1840 Indian wars in Texas had practically ceased.

Lamar's Indian policy cost $2.5 million and perhaps the lives of several scores of whites and a larger number of Indians. The justice of his campaigns may be questioned but not their effectiveness. Lamar and his troops opened to settlers the rich Indian lands of eastern Texas, emptied the area of most of its Indians, and made the western frontier comparatively safe for the advancing settlers.

The financial affairs of the republic, bad enough at the start, grew constantly worse during the Lamar administration. Tariff duties, which were already quite moderate, were lowered almost to a free-trade basis. Direct taxes and license taxes were levied but were difficult to collect and brought small returns, especially since they were paid in depreciated currency. Total receipts for the three-year period were $1,083,661, and expenditures were $4,855,213.

Since the autumn of 1836, the government had been trying to borrow $5 million, but all that it managed to secure was a loan of $457,380 from the Bank of the United States in Pennsylvania, negotiated by James Hamilton, who had been appointed by Lamar to seek loans for the republic. Lamar himself favored a gigantic Texas bank to be owned and operated by the government, but he never could get Congress to create it. It could not have been placed in operation without the proceeds of the proposed $5 million loan.

The administration resorted to the favorite expedient of moneyless governments—the issue of government paper money. When Lamar assumed office, there was outstanding more than $800,000 of treasury notes, already depreciated by 15 to 50 percent. Then by the acts of 1839, 1840, and 1841, Congress authorized government noninterest-bearing notes, known as "red backs," which were issued in the amount of $3,552,800. The last act placed no limit on the quantity of such notes other than the amount of appropriations that Congress might vote. By

November 1841 they were quoted at from twelve to fifteen cents on the dollar.

## HOUSTON'S SECOND ADMINISTRATION
## (1841–1844)

So radically different from the policies of Houston were those of Lamar that the voters soon came to be divided into two distinct camps: the administration group and the opposition led by Houston. It was natural, therefore, that Houston, who since the end of his presidential term had served in the house of representatives, should become the candidate to succeed Lamar. The forces opposing Houston supported David G. Burnet, formerly president *ad interim,* vice-president, and for a period while Lamar was away, acting president.

A few issues to which the press and campaign speakers referred occasionally were the Franco-Texienne bill, which Houston had favored but which his followers now regarded as dead; economy and retrench-ment; certain laws to check land speculators and grant land titles to *bona fide* settlers; protection of the frontier; and the removal of the seat of government. Issues were incidental, however, for the contest took the form of gossip, scandal, and vituperation against the two candidates. The saga of San Jacinto was too widespread and the unpopularity of the Lamar administration too great for the race to be really close. Houston received 7,915 votes to Burnet's 3,616. Edward Burleson, running as an independent and not altogether acceptable to the Houston forces, was elected vice-president.

The election of Houston and a conservative congress marked a sharp transition from the ambitious and costly program of the Lamar administration. The Sixth Congress carried economy to the point of parsimony. Offices thought to be unnecessary were abolished; the number of clerks was reduced; and salaries were lowered below a living wage. The Fifth Congress had failed to make any appropriation for the regular army, and military expeditions after 1841 were confined to the mainte-nance of a few companies of rangers. The navy continued to call for outlays, and its ships were badly in need of repairs. Congress met this situation in January 1843 by a secret act ordering them to be sold. However, the people of Galveston were enthusiastic about the little fleet of four vessels which had helped to protect Texas from Mexico. They were in sympathy with its commander, Edwin W. Moore, who had been insubordinate, had been declared a pirate, and then had been dishonor-ably discharged by Houston. By force they prevented the auction of the four vessels. In June 1846, in conformity with the joint resolution of annexation, the ships of the Texas navy were transferred to the United States Navy.

Total expenditures for Houston's administration of three years was only a little more than $500,000. All currency laws were repealed by an act authorizing the issue in quantities not to exceed $200,000 in "exchequer bills," which were made the only currency receivable for taxes. Even under these favorable conditions the notes depreciated in value.

President Houston returned to the pacific Indian policy of his first administration. In September 1843 a treaty was signed at Bird's Fort with the Waco, Tawakoni, and other sedentary tribes. On October 9, 1844, about nine miles east of present-day Waco, President Houston and Chief Buffalo Hump for the Penateka Comanches, after failing to agree on a common boundary line, signed the Treaty of Tehuacana Creek providing for trade and friendship. Both treaties were ratified by the senate; that with the Comanches was the last treaty with Indians made by the Republic of Texas.

In keeping with these treaties, the Texan government granted to Torrey's Trading House, which looms large in the saga of the Texas frontier, and to another trading post on the west fork of the Trinity that was not long maintained, a monopoly of the trade with the Indians on the northwestern frontier. As a result of Lamar's successful military campaigns and Houston's peace policy, the period from late 1840 until after annexation to the United States was relatively free of Indian wars.

During his second administration President Houston succeeded in settling a feud in East Texas between the "Regulators" and "Moderators" that had become almost as serious as the Indian problem. The feud was inherent in the Neutral Ground Agreement and in the twenty-league border zone where by 1836 several thousand Anglo-Americans were living without benefit of law other than that imposed locally. The killings started in 1840 in Shelby County but spread to neighboring counties. The Regulators, avowedly organized to suppress crime, were opposed by the Moderators, who organized to stop the Regulators from burning homes, ordering families to leave their homes, and other excesses. Soon the opposing factions, including many well-meaning men, numbered about 150 each, and a reign of terror spread over Shelby County until President Houston ordered 600 militia to the scene and, partly by force and partly by persuasion, succeeded in disbanding the organizations.

In 1844 President Houston saw his administration vindicated by the election of a Houston party man to succeed him in the presidency. Although Dr. Anson Jones, who had been a successful physician in Brazoria, a surgeon in the San Jacinto campaign, a member of Congress, and secretary of state, publicly criticized some of the president's policies and wrote in his *Memoranda* that Houston did not prefer him as his successor, that he was regarded as the administration candidate, and that his success was a measure of Houston's popularity. The comparatively high tariff, the removal of the government from Austin (which Jones condemned), Houston's Indian policy, and his failure to secure the release of the Texans imprisoned at Perote came in for much censure. Vice-President Edward Burleson was the candidate of the opposition, and although he denied any such connection, his opponents dubbed him the Lamar party candidate. Jones carried the east, that is, the country east of the Trinity, and Burleson carried the west. The vote was 7,037 for Jones to 5,668 for Burleson.

## LAND POLICY OF THE REPUBLIC

The public land policy of the government, because of its absorbing interest, to the people throughout the entire period of the republic and because of its far-reaching consequences, merits special treatment. The old Texans had hardly returned from the army or from the "runaway scrape" before their kinspeople from east of the Sabine began to join them. On May 16, 1837, the *Telegraph and Texas Register* stated:

> Crowds of enterprising emigrants are arriving on every vessel, and so numerous have our citizens already become, that we confidently believe Houston alone could, in case of a second invasion, furnish an army of able-bodied men, nearly equal to that now encamped on the banks of the La Baca.

It was reported that during the following summer and fall, 6,000 immigrants crossed the Sabine at one ferry. Accounts indicate that in 1840 more immigrants arrived than had in any previous year and that the volume was sustained in 1841 and in the early part of 1842. The Mexican invasion of 1842 checked the flow sharply, but by 1844 the fear of invasion had ceased and a veritable stream of homeseekers was arriving almost daily. On October 30 the editor of the *Northern Standard* (Clarksville) stated: "Even now as we write, four wagons are passing the office, from Green County, Illinois, with 'Polk, Dallas, Oregon, and Texas' painted on the covers." Trains of immigrants gathered at the ferry crossings and had to wait for hours, while the children amused themselves counting the conveyances. The white population, which was estimated in 1836 by Henry M. Morfit, Jackson's special representative in Texas, at 34,470, including Mexicans, had reached 102,961 by 1847; the slave population, estimated at 5,000 in 1836, had reached 38,753. Adding the 295 free blacks, the total population of Texas was 142,009.

The explanation for this phenomenal migration is to be found in the liberal land policy of the republic and the early state government and in the Anglo-American lust for free or cheap virgin land. The government was generous with its public lands. The constitution specified that heads of families (blacks and Indians excepted) living in the republic on March 2, 1836, might receive free a first class headright of a square league and a *labor* of land (4,605 acres) and that single men above seventeen years of age might receive one-third of a square league (1,476 acres). Those who previously had received a smaller amount were entitled to an additional quantity equal to the difference. The recipients of constitutional grants were not required to live on their land. To be included in the constitutional proviso, the Congress of the republic, and afterwards the state legislature, enacted measures that extended the land grants to others. Congress provided for a Second Class headright of 1,280 acres for heads of families and 640 acres for unmarried men who arrived in Texas between March 2, 1836, and October 1, 1837, and met certain prescribed conditions; a Third Class headright of 640 and 320 acres, respectively, for family heads and single men who came to Texas between October 1, 1837, and January 1, 1840; and a Fourth Class headright of 640 and 320 acres, respectively, for those who came between January 1, 1840, and January 1, 1842, and put at least 10 acres into cultivation. Altogether, the republic granted 36,876,492 acres in headright certificates. The purpose of the First Class headright was to reward those who had aided in the struggle for independence; the objective of the others was to encourage immigration.

In their determination to make Texas a nation of homeowners, the lawmakers went even further. They enacted a limited homestead law in 1838 (which preceded by a quarter of a century similar legislation by the United States government), passed the following year the Homestead Exemption Act, exempting from seizure for debt the home, 50 acres of land, and certain improvements, and placed into the Constitution of 1845 a more liberal exemption article. Furthermore, in 1845 Congress gave settlers who had been living on vacant public land for three years and had made certain improvements the first option to purchase (for the most part at fifty cents an acre) up to 320 acres. In 1853, the preemption act became, in fact, a free homestead grant but with the maximum number of acres reduced the next year to 160. Except for the years from 1856–1866, the law, with some details changed from time to time, continued in force until 1898. Altogether, under the preemption and homestead laws Texas granted 4,847,136 acres. Additional lands were granted to permanently disabled veterans, to those who had participated in the Battle of San Jacinto, and to the heirs of the men who had fallen in the Alamo and in the Matamoros and Goliad campaigns. Soldiers who served the republic after the revolution were granted lands varying in quantity from 320 acres for serving three months to 1,280 acres for serving twelve months.

The law of December 1837 provided for a board of land commissioners in each county, before whom claimants had to appear to obtain certificates designating the amount of land to which they were legally entitled. Certificate holders would then engage a surveyor who was authorized to "locate" and survey the land out of the unappropriated public domain for a fee usually amounting to one-third of the land. The surveyor's field notes were then approved by the county or district surveyor and certified to the commissioner of the General Land Office who, if convinced that the requirements of the law had been met, issued a patent.

The system, drawn partly from the Old South and partly from the Spanish and Mexican practice, had the merit of costing the public little, as the people who got the land paid the cost. There were, of course, some forgeries and other kinds of fraudulent claims, but the most unfortunate result was that the aim of the lawmakers to place the land in the possession of actual settlers was only partly attained. No residence requirements were attached to certificates issued to old settlers and to soldiers for military service. Speculators and men who made a business of locating lands went into the Indian country far ahead of the settlements and surveyed and secured title to these lands, so that *bona fide* settlers who came later found the best country already taken. An examination of a land map of any county in Central Texas will reveal that the choicest land, that along the streams, passed into private ownership from ten to thirty years before the county was actually settled.

## CONTRACTS WITH IMMIGRANT AGENTS

Contracts with immigrant agents was another phase of the land system of the republic. In its eagerness to secure citizens and to increase its income, the government abandoned the headright system for contracts to immigrant agents much like the *empresario* agreements under the Mexican regime. These contracts were authorized by an act of Congress in February 1841 and by a general colonization law on February 5, 1842. Most important were those made with W. S. Peters and Associates, afterwards known as the Texas Emigration and Land Company; Charles F. Mercer; Henri Castro; and with Fisher and Miller, afterwards transferred to the German Emigration Company. Although the contracts with these companies differed in certain details, they were alike in all essentials. A given area was designated as "the colony," and within the boundaries thus indicated all unappropriated public domain was closed to entry by others until the proprietor had completed his contract or it had been declared forfeited. The contractor was allowed ten premium sections for each one hundred families. He also might secure additional compensation from his colonists for surveying the land, erecting cabins, moving the colonists to Texas, and supplying certain necessities. The republic, and afterward the state, retained alternate sections, and it was from the sale of these that it expected to secure a money income.

However, the day of the *empresario's* usefulness had passed. It was no longer expedient to close from public entry thousands of square miles of public domain while an *empresario* or proprietary company appropriated the best lands. It was natural that persons holding land certificates would oppose these colonization contracts in every way possible. Accordingly, early in 1844 Congress passed over Houston's veto a bill repealing all laws authorizing colonization contracts and requiring the president to declare forfeited all that had not been complied with strictly.

During the debate on the Franco-Texienne Company proposal to settle a colony of Frenchmen on the Texas frontier, Congress received a request from a Louisville group, headed by W. S. Peters, for a grant on which to settle a colony of Americans. Preferring the alternative, it approved the request in February 1841. As finally amended, the contract with W. S. Peters and Associates (the Texas Emigration and Land Company) set aside for the colony more than 16,000 square miles, bounded on the north by the Red River, on the east by a line extending from the Red River east of present-day Dallas to the vicinity of present-day Ennis, west about 150 miles (between the present-day cities of Cisco and Abilene), and north to the Red River. The settlers, mostly from the Ohio River Valley and Missouri and nonslaveholders, began arriving in 1841. They received Third Class headrights free, even without any survey cost. The company, however, met with difficulties posed by dissatisfied colonists, by holders of certificates eager to locate on vacant lands within its boundaries, and by an unfriendly government. By order of the constitutional convention of 1845, the attorney general instituted proceedings to cancel the contract, but the subsequent legislation and litigation is too vast to describe here. A legislative committee found that by July 1848 the company had introduced 2,205 families, located along the eastern side of the grant.

Three *empresario* contracts were awarded under the general colonization law of 1842. One with Charles F. Mercer, signed just before the act of Congress of January 30, 1844, discontinued *empresario* contracts, called for the location of families in a large area lying mainly south and east of Peters's colony and in that colony, subject to Peters's prior rights. Mercer and Associates met with difficulties similar to those that confronted Peters and the Texas Emigration and Land Company. On October 25, 1848, R. E. B. Baylor, judge of the third judicial district, declared the contract void because of the failure of Mercer to meet all of its requirements. Thereafter came legislation and litigation until finally in 1882, the Supreme Court of the United States denied the Mercer associates any compensation whatsoever.

A most energetic *empresario* was Henri Castro, a Frenchman. Castro advertised his colony extensively in Europe and by March 1, 1843, about 300 colonists, mostly from the Rhine provinces of France, had set out for Texas under his direction. The area assigned to him was the Indian-inhabited country between the Nueces and the Rio Grande, a region made more dangerous by threats of another Mexican invasion. One tract was about fifty miles southwest of San Antonio and another in Starr County on the lower Rio Grande. Castro laid out the town of Castroville, the first permanent settlement between San Antonio and the Rio Grande, in September 1844, and by 1847 he had introduced 2,134 colonists.

Of great importance in bringing about a large migration of Germans to Texas was the contract with Henry F. Fisher and Burchard Miller. In February 1842 and in January 1844 Fisher and Miller in return for a grant of about three million acres lying between the Llano and Colorado rivers contracted to introduce six thousand colonists. Before introducing any settlers, however, they sold their grant to the *Adelsverein* (Society for the Protection of German Immigrants in Texas), organized in 1842 by a group of German noblemen for the purpose of promoting German immigration to Texas. A German settlement had been made in Texas as early as 1838 when Friedrich Ernst founded Industry in Austin County, but German immigration on a large scale is associated with the *Adelsverein*. Its agent, or commissioner general, Prince Carl of Solms-Braunfels, who visited Texas in 1844, purchased for the society the Fisher and Miller lands and, in addition, an extensive area north of San Antonio and a tract on Matagorda Bay. Early in 1845 the society's first settlers established New Braunfels, named for the prince. During the next year the society founded Fredericksburg, about eighty miles north of New Braunfels but outside the Fisher and Miller grant. In fact, before settlement could be made on this tract it was necessary to pacify the Penateka Comanches who had occupied the area for half a century. John O. Muesebach (Baron Ottfried Hans Freiherr von Muesebach), Solms-Braunfels's successor, made a treaty with this Comanche division in March 1847 in which for presents worth three thousand dollars the Indians agreed to share their country with the Germans. Fredericksburg grew rapidly, and by 1850 its population was 754. Several other German settlements were made in that general vicinity, but the society never succeeded in inducing a great number of settlers to go into the Fisher and Miller grant. It was too far from the coast and the attitude of the Indians was too uncertain. Sisterdale, Boerne, Comfort, and other settlements were established. By 1860 Germans constituted a majority of the population in three counties of the Austin and San Antonio section and a substantial part of the population in six other counties in the general vicinity.

## IMMIGRATION AND EXTENSION OF SETTLEMENT

The settled area of Texas in 1836 lay approximately south and east of a line running from San Antonio along the old road to Nacogdoches and extending north to the Red River. Each year after 1836 witnessed the extension of settlements into the unappropriated area. At first the most rapid advance was from the northeast, where the settlements around Pecan Point and Jonesborough on the Red River near Clarksville served as a base. This section was comparatively unaffected by the threat of Mexican invasion; it had wood, rich soil, and good grass; and in 1835 after Captain Henry Shreve had finished removing the raft that obstructed navigation on the Red River, it had an outlet for its commodities. On the Texas side of the river were a dozen landings, which were visited periodically by steamboats during the high-water season from December to July. Although the boats frequently were held up for weeks because of the shallow river, navigation at its worst was more practicable than overland transportation.

In the van of the advancing column of farmers were Indian traders, among them Samuel Fulton and Robert Cravens, who built a trading house at the mouth of Sander's Creek in Lamar County in 1833. Better known were Holland Coffee and Silas Colville who had traded for years in Indian Territory and had established a trading house at Preston Bend in the northern part of Grayson County in 1837. The town of Preston, laid out in 1840, was for a few years an important gateway to Texas and through it came many immigrants.

From Bowie, Red River, and Lamar counties, settlers pushed southward into both the timbered country of Hopkins, Wood, and Van Zandt counties and the prairies of Hunt, Collin, and Kaufman. Dr. Daniel Rowlett and his party from Tennessee came by steamboat to Jonesborough in 1835, continued their journey the following spring, and settled in the present Fannin County. From the Red River settlements pioneers entered Hunt County in 1839, and five years later Ben Anderson's store constituted the beginning of Greenville. The supplies for the new town were hauled from Jefferson. In 1842 settlers moved into Collin County, then a part of Fannin, and a little later the Hopkinses made settlements in the county that bears their name. The first settlers of Kaufman County, Dr. William P. King and a company of forty Mississippians, came by ox train and made a settlement near the town of Kaufman in 1841.

Meanwhile, the advance from the northeast had reached the upper Trinity. John Neely Bryan, a Tennessean who came through Arkansas and by way of the Red River settlements, pitched his lonely cabin in 1841 near the three forks of the Trinity in Peters's Colony. Three years later his widely advertised town of Dallas had only two families and two small cabins. Peters's Colony headquarters at nearby Farmer's Branch was the larger settlement, but after 1846, when it became the county seat, Bryan's Dallas gained ascendancy.

While settlers were advancing from the northeast, a similar extension was in process from the southeast along the lower Trinity, Brazos, and Colorado valleys. Parker's Fort, near the Navasota River in Limestone County, had been the center of a settlement established in 1834. The "runaway scrape," followed by the massacre of a number of citizens at Parker's Fort[1] by Indians in 1836 caused the section to be all but depopulated. The dauntless pioneers soon returned, however, and in December of the following year, the region between the Trinity and the Brazos, north of the San Antonio and Nacogdoches Road, was organized as Robertson County. In 1839 a blockhouse was built on Boggy Creek in the present Leon County, and within a year settlers began to move in. The pacification of the Indian tribes by President Houston in 1843 hastened the settlement of the counties along the Trinity, and by the close of 1846 Limestone, Navarro, and other counties in that vicinity had been organized. Navigation of the Trinity River was of some aid to these settlers, but most of their corn and cotton had to be hauled overland to Galveston.

The hostility of the Indians retarded the settlement of the valley of the Brazos above the San Antonio and Nacogdoches Road. A blockhouse near present-day Belton afforded some protection, but it was not until after the Indian treaty of September 29, 1843, that white people were able to live even in partial security in Bell County. The settlement of McLennan County was preceded by the establishment in 1842 of the Torrey Brothers and Associates' trading house on Tehuacana Creek, about eight miles southeast of the present-day city of Waco. In 1845, Neal McLennan, a Scotsman, settled on the South Bosque, a little above

---

[1]Young Cynthia Ann Parker, together with others, was captured on this occasion. She grew to womanhood among the Comanches, became the wife of a chief and the mother of Quanah, the last great chief of the Comanches. In 1860 she was recaptured and returned to her white relatives, but her affections remained with the Comanches.

the site of the old Waco Indian village. Other settlers came, and in 1849 George B. Erath surveyed the Waco village, and the city of Waco had its beginning. Three years later, George Barnard, who had been associated with the Torreys, established an Indian trading post farther up the Brazos River in present-day Hood County. The advance of settlers into that area was not far behind.

Because of Indian hostility, settlements along the Colorado River advanced slowly for some time. Hornsby's Bend above Bastrop long was the most advanced point. It was in this vicinity in 1833 that Indians scalped and left for dead Josiah Wilbarger, a man of rugged physique and iron will, who lived for twelve years thereafter. A few farmers had, however, reached the vicinity of Austin when the town was laid out in 1839.

The hostility of the Mexicans as well as the Indian depredations retarded the advance of settlements in southern Texas. For some time after the Mexican invasion of 1836 the counties of San Patricio, Victoria, Goliad, and Refugio were depopulated to such an extent that no district court was held in them. However, in 1839 Henry L. Kinney and William Aubrey established a trading post in the vicinity of Corpus Christi at the mouth of the Nueces River. Other traders joined them, and the place became a trading center. The coming of Taylor's army in 1845 stimulated its growth, and the impetus continued after the close of the war with Mexico. The area between the Nueces and the Rio Grande was not organized into counties until after the Mexican War, and for sometime thereafter its population was overwhelmingly Spanish-American.

In summary, the frontier line of settlement in 1846, when a state government replaced that of the republic, extended from Corpus Christi to San Antonio in the southwest, and northward through New Braunfels, Fredericksburg (settled in 1846), Austin, Belton, Waco, Dallas, and Collin County to Preston on the Red River near the present city of Denison. The main reason for such a phenomenal extension of settlement, in the face of danger from Indian attacks and Mexican invasion, was the liberal land policy of the republic.

## RELATIONS WITH THE UNITED STATES, 1836–1839

The foreign relations of the republic cannot be understood without giving consideration to the diplomacy of the Texan Revolution. The opinion of most Texans on the subject may be summarized thus: Texas should leave nothing undone to secure the maximum aid from the United States; it should seek recognition by the United States and, if possible, bring about

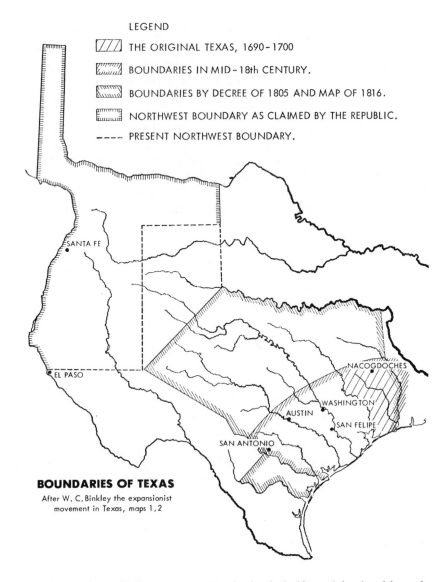

SANTA FE

EL PASO

NACOGDOCHES

WASHINGTON

AUSTIN

SAN FELIPE

SAN ANTONIO

**BOUNDARIES OF TEXAS**

After W. C. Binkley the expansionist
movement in Texas, maps 1, 2

the intervention of that government in its behalf; and it should at the
very earliest date possible be acquired by the United States, either by
purchase from Mexico or by annexation after independence had been
attained.

The commissioners, Austin, Archer, and Wharton, traveling slowly
but working zealously in the Texan cause as they proceeded from city to
city, arrived in Washington late in March 1836. They were soon replaced
by other representatives, but little was accomplished. James Collinsworth

and Peter W. Grayson, the last commissioners sent by Burnet, did learn in an informal interview with President Jackson that he had sent Henry M. Morfit, a secret agent, to Texas to secure information.

The vote in the election of September 1836, all but unanimous in favor of annexation, constituted a mandate to Houston to promote that end. Santa Anna, seeking some means to secure his freedom, suggested that he be allowed to go to Washington to interview President Jackson in the interest of a transfer of Texas to the United States. Houston, who was seeking some excuse to get his prisoner out of Texas, accepted the suggestion; and, in spite of the protests of Congress, Santa Anna started with an escort for Washington on November 26. Jackson realized that the exdictator's proposal to sell Texas to the United States was now impractical. At Jackson's order Santa Anna was carried to Vera Cruz aboard the United States frigate *Pioneer.*

Houston sent William H. Wharton, with comprehensive instructions from Secretary of State Stephen F. Austin, to secure the recognition of Texas and to bring about its annexation to the United States. Memucan Hunt was sent to assist Wharton. To the great disappointment of the Texans, President Jackson, with the report of Morfit before him, in a message to Congress in December, advocated delay in recognizing Texas independence. His reasons were doubt as to the ability of Texas to maintain its independence, fear of offending Mexico, and belief that recognition would be regarded as a preliminary step toward annexation. In a private interview Wharton learned, however, that President Jackson would approve recognition if Congress would recommend it. By diligent work and with the aid of various friends, Wharton and Hunt got an item in the appropriation bill providing expenses for a diplomatic agent to Texas whenever the president should deem it expedient. The last official act of President Jackson was to appoint Alcée LaBranche *charge d'affaires* to the Republic of Texas.

Recognition now attained, Texas pressed for annexation. On August 4, 1837, Hunt formally made the offer. John Forsyth, the United States secretary of state, answered three weeks later, saying that treaty obligations with Mexico prevented the United States from entertaining the subject. Having failed to get annexation by treaty, the issue was introduced in the United States Congress in the fall of 1837 along with a stream of memorials and petitions. Opposition to the annexation of Texas was very strong. John Quincy Adams, in the House of Representatives, spoke in opposition to annexation during the scheduled hours for its debate each day from June 16 to July 7, when Congress adjourned, thereby blocking a vote on the measure. Pursuant to Houston's orders, Anson Jones, then representing Texas in Washington, announced the "formal and absolute withdrawal" of the offer. The congress of Texas, on January 23, 1839, with President Lamar's sanction, ratified the withdrawal, and annexation was not again an issue until 1843.


## RECOGNITION BY EUROPEAN POWERS

In the summer of 1837 President Houston, convinced that the United States would not consider annexation, obtained authority from Congress to open diplomatic negotiations with the European powers. He then sent Secretary of State J. Pinckney Henderson as minister plenipotentiary to Great Britain and France to secure recognition and negotiate commercial treaties. Lord Palmerston, British minister of foreign affairs, was disappointingly indifferent. England was opposed to slavery; British capitalists had millions invested in Mexican bonds; and England was not interested in aiding a state that probably would soon join the American Union. Early in 1838 Henderson did, however, secure a convention with Great Britain that provided for trade between that country and Texas. He then took up negotiations with the French ministry. Because of its intervention in Mexico (the Pastry War) at the time, France was interested in having a treaty of friendship with Texas. Furthermore, the withdrawal that autumn of the offer of Texan annexation to the United States and the avowed purpose of Lamar to maintain an independent nation appreciably strengthened Texan diplomacy. President Lamar commissioned James Hamilton, a former governor of South Carolina with successful experience in diplomacy and business, to negotiate a foreign loan. Hamilton and Henderson and the French minister of foreign affairs on September 25, 1839, signed a commercial treaty which was ratified the following January. Thus, France was the first European nation to recognize the independence of Texas. Henderson thereupon returned to Texas, but Hamilton remained in Europe as the representative of the Lamar administration, and on September 18, 1840, he signed a treaty with the Netherlands.

Meanwhile, Palmerston had become convinced that a treaty with Texas would serve Britain's interest. On November 13, 14, and 16, respectively, he and Hamilton signed a treaty of commerce and navigation, a treaty obligating England to mediate with Mexico for Texas independence (Texas to assume, if successful, $5 million of Mexico's debt to British bondholders), and a treaty giving England great liberty in suppressing the foreign slave trade. Because of the hesitancy of the Texas senate to agree to the third treaty, ratifications were not exchanged until June 1842. Hamilton was never able to secure the loan in Europe.

Thus, before the close of Lamar's administration in December 1841, France, the Netherlands, Great Britain, and Belgium (in 1841) had recognized the independence of Texas, and favorable commercial treaties had been secured from France, Great Britain, and the Netherlands.

## RELATIONS WITH MEXICO

As stated previously, President Burnet and Santa Anna on May 14, 1836, signed the Treaty of Velasco which specified that Mexican troops were to be withdrawn south of the Rio Grande and that the boundary between the two countries would be established in a later treaty but that the territory of Texas would not extend beyond the Rio Grande. The Mexican Congress, however, on May 20 rejected the Treaty of Velasco and announced that it intended to subdue the rebellious Texans. President Houston, convinced that Mexico was too involved in internal difficulties to carry out the threat, furloughed most of the army.

When Lamar became president in December 1838, Mexico's threatening attitude seemed likely to lead to war. Aware of this possibility, Lamar in his first message to Congress stated: "If peace can only be obtained by the sword, let the sword do its work." He would, however, meet with alacrity any move for peace. Indeed, he sought to secure some understanding with Mexico on satisfactory terms. To this end he sent three different agents to Mexico and solicited and secured the diplomatic aid of the United States and Great Britain, all to no avail.

Conditions seemed propitious. France, in order to enforce the collection of its subjects' claims against Mexico, resorted to arms (the Pastry War) and kept Mexican ports blockaded for the greater part of 1838 and until March 1839. Anastacio Bustamante, again in power, was a weak executive, and the federalists in several northern states were defying his government.

Lamar sent Secretary of State Barnard E. Bee to Mexico in May 1839 with the authority to offer the Mexican government as much as $5 million if it would recognize Texan independence and the Rio Grande as a boundary. Richard Pakenham, British minister to Mexico, supported the Texan cause, but to no avail. Bee never got beyond Vera Cruz and did not accomplish anything of consequence. In New Orleans, on his return home, Bee met James Treat, a soldier of fortune, who claimed that he had information that his friend Santa Anna, who was now back in power as a result of the Pastry War, wanted a treaty and that he could negotiate it. Favorably impressed, Bee with the aid of James Hamilton convinced Lamar to send Treat to Mexico. In November 1839 James Treat arrived in Mexico City as the confidential agent of the Texan government. He remained there ten months while the Mexicans gave him just enough encouragement to keep him from leaving. The most important factor in changing the attitude of the Mexicans was the Texas navy, contracted by the Houston administration and delivered in the spring of 1840. Under its commander, Edwin Ward Moore, it was cruising the Gulf by June and threatening Mexican shipping and Mexican ports. It was well, thought the Mexicans, to continue to encourage Treat as long as his presence would keep the Texas fleet from their ports.

When at last Treat left without accomplishing anything, Lamar recommended war to compel Mexico to recognize Texas. Congress, however, took no action. Then came news of the second treaty of November 1840, whereby Great Britain agreed to mediate between Mexico and Texas, and if successful, Texas would assume $5 million of the Mexican foreign debt to protect the British subjects who held Mexican bonds.

Consequently, Lamar early in 1841 sent his last emissary, Secretary of State James Webb, to Mexico. Despite pressure exerted by Pakenham the Mexicans refused to receive him, and in June he returned to urge his government to begin hostilities immediately. Lamar then entered into an alliance with the Mexican state of Yucatán, then in revolt against the central government, whereby the government of Yucatán agreed to help maintain the Texan navy. But the alliance proved of little consequence because shortly after it was made Yucatán renewed its allegiance to Mexico.

Mexico's smouldering malice was fanned into active hostility by the expansionist efforts of the Texans. Like many of his contemporaries, Lamar dreamed of a Republic of Texas extending westward to the Pacific. He gave first attention, however, to the territory actually claimed under the terms of the law passed by the First Congress, which fixed the boundary on the south and west at the Rio Grande. He sought to promote trade with the settlements along the Rio Grande, but such an arrangement was not practicable at that time. Several colonizing schemes were given more or less serious consideration. The most important was the Franco-Texienne Company bill in January 1841, which would have authorized the introduction of eight thousand French families and the establishment of twenty forts to be located in such a way as to create a shield between the hostile Indians and the outermost Texas settlers. It would have created a semiautonomous state on the border, thereby threatening the unity of Texas. The bill, supported by Congressman Sam Houston and Count Alphonse de Saligny, the French minister to Texas, passed the house of representatives, but it was never considered by the senate, probably because of opposition by Lamar and Burnet.

On the east side of the upper Rio Grande were most of the settlements that had long comprised the Spanish province and later the Mexican territory of New Mexico. These communities came within the jurisdiction of Texas as defined so generously by Congress, and Lamar proposed to occupy them. His resolution was strengthened by reports from that country that the hold of the Mexican government was weak and that the people desired a union with Texas. After Congress had refused to authorize the expedition, President Lamar, on his own responsibility, proceeded to raise and equip it. At his invitation merchants with a supply of goods made up a caravan to go along, and Lamar bid the party adieu at its camp near Austin on June 21, 1841. Colonel Hugh McLeod commanded the military escort of 270 men, and William G. Cooke, ex-Senator José Antonio Navarro, and Dr. Richard F. Brenham went along as commissioners of the Texan government. William G. Dryden, a citizen of Santa Fé who had been in touch with Lamar, was to act with the commissioners after the expedition reached New Mexico. The commissioners were instructed to take possession of Santa Fé and to set up a government under the authority of Texas, but to use force only if convinced that the majority of the population favored the Texans. In fairness to Lamar, it should be remembered that the best information he could secure indicated that the Texans would be welcomed.

The story of the expedition was written by George Wilkins Kendall, editor of the New Orleans *Picayune,* who went with the party for an outing. The vacation he had anticipated turned out to be a desperate experience with heat, hunger, thirst, hostile Indians, and unfriendly Mexicans; his narrative is a classic of travel and adventure. Misfortune dogged the trail of the party as it traveled thirteen hundred miles, first northward to present-day Wichita Falls and then northwestward by way of Quitaque, to arrive in New Mexico exhausted and at the mercy of the Mexicans. The survivors were made prisoners and marched in most brutal fashion to Mexico City and thence to Perote and other prisons, where they were confined until April 1842.

In the Texan Santa Fé expedition Lamar had sown the wind, and it was for Houston, his successor, to reap the whirlwind. Partly because he did not wish Mexico's claim on Texas to expire by limitation and partly in retaliation for the ambitious move of the Texans, Santa Anna sent an army into Texas in March 1842. The invaders took San Antonio, Goliad, and Refugio but retired after a day or two, having done little damage. The most unfortunate result was the panic that the affair caused in West Texas, resembling the "runaway scrape" of 1836. President Houston declared a public emergency and ordered the archives of the government removed to Houston. Some citizens of Austin, led by Mrs. Angelina Belle Eberly, a hotel proprietor, obtained a cannon and refused to permit their removal, thus creating the comical and grim "archive war."

The republic had no regular army, but the militia by the hundreds rushed to San Antonio, and Houston sent W. H. Daingerfield as agent to the United States to secure men, money, and supplies for the invasion of Mexico. He called Congress to assemble in Houston on June 27, delaying the call, as he stated in confidential communications, because he could not "trust their wisdom" in the crisis. When Congress met, it voted for a declaration of war and appropriated ten million acres of land to meet the expense. Houston, determined to avoid a war if possible, wisely pronounced this amount totally inadequate and vetoed the bill.

There was another invasion in September 1842 when General Adrian Woll held San Antonio for nine days before retiring on September 20 with a number of prisoners, including a district judge and other officials. Again the militia was called out and gathered at San Antonio. About the middle of November, 750 men under the leadership of General Alexander Somervell started for Laredo. After occupying that town on December 8, a part of the force disbanded and returned home. The remainder then marched down the Rio Grande until December 19, when Somervell ordered them to return to Gonzales. About three hundred of the men refused to obey Somervell's orders, organized under Colonel W. S. Fisher, and on Christmas morning marched to Mier on the south side of the Rio Grande. There, after a desperate battle with General Pedro Ampudia, they surrendered on December 26. Then followed their march as prisoners into Mexico, their break for liberty, their recapture, and the drawing of the black beans to determine which one-tenth of the number would be shot. The survivors were finally imprisoned in the dank Castle Perote with the men of the Texas Santa Fé expedition and the prisoners from San Antonio who had been taken away by Woll. After many months of confinement they were released by Santa Anna, partly because of the efforts in their behalf by Waddy Thompson, United States minister to Mexico.

Another Texan expedition against the Mexicans at this time ended only a little less tragically than that against Mier. In the spring of 1843 Colonel Jacob Snively organized a force of 180 men in North Texas and by authority of the president led it to the Santa Fé Trail in an attempt to seize rich Mexican caravans going from Missouri to Santa Fé across northern Texas. The members of the expedition, after defeating a Mexican force of a hundred soldiers near the Arkansas River, quarreled and split into three parties. Snively and a part of the men were captured and disarmed south of the Arkansas by an escort of United States troops, and, as a result, had to return home. Since the seizure was within the limits claimed by Texas, the United States eventually reimbursed Texas for the arms taken.

While resisting the popular clamor for war with Mexico, Houston was exerting every effort to secure peace and the recognition of independence. After Woll's invasion in 1842, he urged the governments of Great Britain, France, and the United States to "require of Mexico either the recognition of the Independence of Texas, or to make war upon her according to the rules established and universally recognized by civilized nations." A month later Waddy Thompson urged recognition and offered the good services of his government in the interest of peace. Nothing came directly from these efforts; but early in 1843 Santa Anna released James W. Robinson, formerly lieutenant governor of Texas, from Castle Perote and sent him to Texas to open negotiations with that government. Robinson conveyed to Houston Santa Anna's offer of peace if Texas would recognize Mexican sovereignty. Houston had no intention of accepting the offer, but it gave him an opportunity to bargain and to play for time while he corresponded with the Mexicans through British diplomatic agents. He proclaimed a truce on June 14, 1843, and both nations later appointed commissioners who signed an armistice on the following February 15. A revival of the movement to annex Texas to the United States, however, brought an end to this armistice four months later.

## ANNEXATION ACHIEVED

Perhaps the most important result of the ill-fated Santa Fé and Mier expeditions was that they greatly augmented the interest of the people of the United States in Texas. The result was to revive the subject of Texan annexation, which had been dormant since 1838. Houston had sounded out the United States government on the subject in March 1842, when his appointee, James Reily, succeeded Barnard Bee as *chargé d'affaires* at Washington. The United States did not respond at the time, but fear of growing British influence caused President John Tyler on October 15, 1843, to open negotiations for annexation by treaty. Houston agreed on two conditions: The United States must place its armed forces in position to prevent a foreign invasion of Texas during the negotiations, and the negotiations must be kept secret. A. P. Upshur, Tyler's secretary of state, would not agree to the demands, but he was killed accidentally in February 1844. John C. Calhoun, his successor, who was fearful of aggressive British imperialism, quickly assented to Houston's demands, and on April 12 he and Isaac Van Zandt, the Texas minister in Washington, and J. P. Henderson, who had been sent to aid Van Zandt with the negotiations, signed a treaty. The treaty provided for the annexation of Texas to the United States as a territory and for the United States to assume Texas's public debt, but on June 8 it was rejected by the United States Senate. New England and the free soilers opposed it. Furthermore, some senators were disinclined to make such an important decision on the eve of a national election.

The subject of annexation then went before the American people in the political campaign that year. Martin Van Buren, the leading Democratic candidate, lost the nomination to James K. Polk, a "dark horse," because he refused to endorse annexation. In the election James K. Polk defeated Henry Clay, the Whig nominee, who opposed immediate annexation.

President Tyler in December told Congress that Polk's election was a mandate from the people for immediate annexation and recommended that Congress, rather than the executive, take the necessary action. On February 28, 1845, Congress passed a joint resolution providing for annexation. The terms of the resolution were: (1) Texas would enter the Union as a state if the terms of the resolution were approved by its delegates in an official convention; (2) all questions concerning the international boundary were to be adjusted by the United States; (3) Texas must cede to the United States its public property, including navy, posts, fortifications, and armaments; (4) Texas would retain all its public domain to be applied to its public debt and other liabilities; (5) as many as four additional states, by the consent of Texas, might be formed out of its territory; (6) slavery would be prohibited in any state formed out of the territory north of parallel 36° 30'; and (7) the president, should he prefer, could withhold the joint-resolution proposal and negotiate in its stead another treaty of annexation.

Tyler signed the joint resolution on March 1 and through his agent, Andrew Jackson Donelson, promptly submitted the offer to the Texan government. James K. Polk, who was inaugurated president on the day after instructions had been sent to Donelson, also pressed the offer on Texas and urged that there be no delay. Indeed, it was now the American government's turn to be anxious about the subject, while Jones and his colleagues could be tantalizingly independent.

England and France opposed annexation and sought to maintain an independent Texas. Captain Charles Elliot and Count de Saligny, representing England and France, respectively, induced President Jones on March 29 not to commit the government for ninety days, during which Elliot would go to Mexico and secure a treaty guaranteeing Texan independence on the condition that the republic agree never to unite with the United States. Meanwhile, Jones on April 15 called Congress to meet on June 16. Public sentiment for annexation was so overwhelming, however, that the new president realized he could not delay action.

Without waiting for Congress to assemble, on May 5 Jones issued a call for a convention to meet in Austin on July 4. When Congress convened, he submitted to it both the proposal of annexation to the

United States and the preliminary treaty with Mexico that Elliot had secured on May 19 and rushed to Washington on the Brazos, the capital at that time. Congress rejected the Mexican treaty, unanimously recommended the acceptance of the offer by the United States, approved the president's proclamation calling for the election of delegates to a convention, and adjourned. The convention then met on July 4, named T. J. Rusk as its president, adopted with only one dissenting vote (R. B. Bache of Galveston) an ordinance accepting the terms of annexation, and on August 27 completed a state constitution. On October 13, the voters approved annexation and ratified the constitution by a vote of 4,254 to 257 and 4,174 to 312, respectively. The constitution was accepted by the United States Congress, and President Polk on December 29, 1845, signed the act that officially made Texas a state of the United States.

At a special election on December 15 new state officials were named, and on February 19, 1846, at a ceremony in front of the Texas capitol, President Jones relinquished executive authority to Governor J. P. Henderson. In concluding his address Jones uttered the memorable words: "The final act in this great drama is now performed; the Republic of Texas is no more."

## SELECTED BIBLIOGRAPHY

Of the older general histories that have been previously cited, good accounts of the Republic of Texas are included in H. H. Bancroft, J. H. Brown, W. Kennedy, H. Yoakum, H. S. Thrall, L. J. Wortham, and F. W. Johnson. The most useful reference is the *Handbook of Texas*. The best recent account is S. V. Connor, *Adventure in Glory* (Austin, 1965). Emphasizing certain phases are William R. Hogan, *The Texas Republic: A Social and Economic History* (Norman, Okla., 1946); Stanley Siegel, *Political History of the Texas Republic, 1836–1845* (Austin, 1956); Stephens B. Oates (ed.), *The Republic of Texas* (Palo Alto, Calif., 1968); John E. Weems, *Dream of Empire: A Human History of the Republic of Texas, 1836–1846* (New York, 1971); Joseph Schmitz, *Texan Statecraft, 1836–1845* (San Antonio, 1941); E. T. Miller, *A Financial History of Texas* (Austin, 1916); and Edward M. Neusinger, "The Monetary History of the Republic of Texas," *Southwestern Historical Quarterly,* LVII, 82–90; Anson Jones, *Memoranda and Official Correspondence Relating to the Republic of Texas, Its History and Annexation, Including a Brief Autobiography of the Author* (Chicago, 1966); W. P. Webb, *The Great Plains* (New York, 1931). The best biographies of the period are those of Sam Houston, previously cited. A. K. Christian, "Mirabeau B. Lamar," *Southwestern Historical Quarterly,* XXIII, 153–170, 231–270; XXIV, 39–80, 87–139, 195–234, 317–324; H. P. Gambrell, *Mirabeau Bonaparte Lamar;* H. P. Gambrell, *Anson Jones;* John N. Cravens, *James Harper Star: Financier of the Republic of Texas* (Austin, 1950); Joe B. Frantz, *Gail Borden, Dairyman to a Nation* (Norman, Okla., 1951); and E. Wallace, *Charles DeMorse: Pioneer Editor and Statesman.* Useful also are John J. Linn, *Reminiscences of Fifty Years in Texas* (New York, 1883); and *A Biographical Directory of Texas Congresses and Conventions* (Austin, 1941).

On domestic affairs the following are useful: Charles P. Roland, *Albert Sidney Johnston: Soldier of Three Republics* (Austin, 1964); Mary A. Maverick, *Memoirs* (San Antonio, 1921); W. P. Webb, *The Texas Rangers* (Boston, 1935); J. Schmitz, *Texas Culture in the Days of the Republic, 1836–1846* (San Antonio, 1960); Tom Henderson Wells, *Commodore Moore and the Texas Navy* (Austin, 1960); E. W. Winkler, "The Seat of Government of Texas," *Quarterly of the Texas State Historical Association,* X, 140–171, 185–245; E. W. Winkler, "The Cherokee Indians in Texas," *ibid.,* VII, 94–165; Nancy N. Barker, *The French Legation in Texas,* vol. II: *Mission Miscarried* (Austin, 1973); D. H. Winfrey, "The Texan Archives War of 1842," *Southwestern Historical Quarterly,* LXIV, 171–184; G. F. Haugh (ed.), "History of the Texas Navy," *ibid.,* LXIII, 572–579; Anna Muckleroy, "The Indian Policy of the Republic of Texas," *ibid.,* XXV, 229–260; XXVI, 1–29, 128–148, 184–206; Jesse Guy Smith, *Heroes of the Saddlebags* (San Antonio, 1951); W. Eugene Hollon and Ruth L. Butler (eds.), *William Bollaert's Texas* (Norman, Okla., 1956); D. H. Winfrey (ed.), *Texas Indian Papers, 1825–1843* (Austin, 1959); D. H. Winfrey (ed.), *Texas Indian Papers, 1844–1845* (Austin, 1960); Earl H. Elam, "The History of the Wichita Indian Confederacy to 1868" (unpublished dissertation, Texas Tech University, Lubbock, Tex., 1971).

Sources and specialized studies relating to the land policy, immigration, *empresario* contracts, and extension of settlement are numerous. On these subjects, county and regional histories are essential, and indispensable to their effective use is H. B. Carroll, "Bibliography of Texas Counties," *Southwestern Historical Quarterly,* XLV, 74–98, 260–275, 343–361. Two good works of a regional nature are Lucy A. Erath (ed.), "Memories of Major Bernard Erath," *ibid.,* XXVI, 207–233, 255–280; XXVII, 27–51, 140–163; and James K. Greer, *Grand Prairie* (Dallas, 1935). The best studies on the land policy are A. S. Lang, *Financial History of the Public Lands in Texas* (Waco, Tex., 1932); and Thomas L. Miller, "Texas Land Grants to Veterans," *Southwestern Historical Quarterly,* XLIV, 342–437; Thomas L. Miller, *The Public Lands of Texas, 1519–1970* (Norman, Okla., 1972).

The best source of information on immigration to Texas is the United States census returns for 1850 and the Texas census of 1847, bound with *Laws Passed by the Second Legislature* (Houston, 1848). There is much information in E. E. Braman, *Braman's Information about Texas* (Philadelphia, 1857); and Jacob DeCordova, *Texas, Her Resources and Public Men* (Philadelphia, 1858). Barnes F. Lathrop's *Migration into East Texas, 1835–1860* (Austin, 1949) is an impressive study. B. M. Jones, "Health Seekers in Early Anglo-American Texas," *Southwestern Historical Quarterly*, LXIX, 287–299, shows that many of the immigrants came to Texas because of their health.

Studies dealing with colonizers, their settlers, and their lands include R. L. Biesele, *The History of the German Settlements in Texas, 1831–1861* (Austin, 1930); S. V. Connor, *The Peters Colony of Texas, A History and Biographical Sketches of the Early Settlers* (Austin, 1959); Irene M. King, *John O. Meusebach, German Colonizer in Texas* (Austin, 1967); Terry G. Jordan, *German Seed in Texas Soil: Immigrant Farmers in the Nineteenth Century* (Austin and London, 1966); S.V. Connor, "A Statistical Review of the Settlement of the Peters Colony, 1841–1848," *Southwestern Historical Quarterly*, LVII, 38–64; Nancy Eagleton, "The Mercer Colony in Texas, 1844–1883," *ibid.*, XXXIX, 275–291; XL, 35–57, 114–144; and Julia N. Waugh, *Castroville and Henry Castro* (San Antonio, 1934). On Lamar's efforts to extend the jurisdiction of Texas over Santa Fé, see W. C. Binkley, *The Expansionist Movement in Texas* (Berkeley, Calif., 1925); W. C. Binkley, "New Mexico and the Texan Santa Fé Expedition," *Southwestern Historical Quarterly*, XXVII, 85–107; George W. Kendall, *Narrative of the Texan Santa Fé Expedition* (London, 1845); H. Bailey Carroll, *The Texan Sante Fé Trail* (Canyon, Tex., 1951); N. Loomis, *The Texan-Santa Fé Pioneers* (Norman, Okla., 1958).

On foreign relations of the Republic of Texas, the most important source material is G. P. Garrison (ed.), *Texan Diplomatic Correspondence* (3 vols.), in *The Annual Report of the American Historical Association for 1907 and 1908* (2 vols., Washington, D.C., 1908 and 1911); a good survey is J. Schmitz, *Texan Statecraft*.

Definitive and impressive studies dealing with special phases of the subject include: E. D. Adams, *British Interests and Activities in Texas* (Baltimore, 1910); J. M. Nance, *After San Jacinto: The Texas-Mexican Frontier, 1836–1841* (Austin, 1963), a comprehensive study; J. M. Nance, *Attack and Counterattack: the Texas-Mexican Frontier, 1842* (Austin, 1964), another impressive study; J. H. Smith, *The Annexation of Texas* (New York, 1912). Some other specialized studies of significant value are: David M. Fletcher, *The Diplomacy of Annexation: Texas, Oregon, and the Mexican War* (Columbia, Mo., 1973); Milton Lindheim, *The Republic of the Rio Grande: Texas in Mexico, 1839–1840* (Waco, Tex.,

1964); Thomas J. Green, *Journal of the Texan Expedition against Mier* (New York, 1845); Joseph D. McCutchan, *Mier Expedition Diary: A Texan Prisoner's Account* (ed. J. M. Nance, Austin, 1978); Ethel Z. Rather, "Recognition of the Republic of Texas by the United States," *Quarterly of the Texas State Historical Association,* XIII, 155–256; Annie Middleton, "Donelson's Mission to Texas in Behalf of Annexation," *Southwestern Historical Quarterly,* XXIV, 247–291; E. C. Barker, "The Annexation of Texas," *ibid.,* L, 49–74; Frederick Merk, *Slavery and the Annexation of Texas* (New York, 1972); Alfred J. Watkins and Arnold Fleischmann, "Annexation and Population Growth in Texas Cities," *Texas Business Review* (September 1978), pp. 173–178; Nancy N. Barker, "The Republic of Texas: A French View," *Southwestern Historical Quarterly,* LXXI, 181–193; L. B. Friend (ed.), "Sidelights and Supplements on the Perote Prisoners," *ibid.,* XLVIII, 366–374, 489–496; LXIX, 88–95, 224–230, 377–385, 516–524; Ralph A. Wooster, "Texas Military Operations against Mexico, 1842–1843," *ibid.,* LVII, 465–484; and D.M. Vigness, "Relations of the Republic of Texas and the Republic of the Rio Grande," *ibid.,* LVII, 312–321.

# Chapter Eight

# EARLY STATEHOOD
# 1846–1861

During the decade and a half between the annexation of Texas and its union with the Confederacy, Texas experienced the most rapid growth in its history. Its population increased more than fourfold and its assessed property more than eightfold. That its cultural progress did not keep pace with its material developments was the result of frontier conditions rather than the lack of innate qualities in its people.

Many episodes and developments, both impressive and significant, made the period between annexation and the Civil War rich in history. There is, however, no single theme to which these events can be related with continuity. Thus, this chapter has a topical orientation. The establishment of a new constitutional government obviously was a development of lasting influence. Even more significant was the defeat of Mexico and its recognition of the right of Texas to join the American Union and of the Rio Grande as the boundary. The boundary controversy between the United States and Texas over a part of New Mexico developed into a national crisis. Closely associated with the dispute was the settlement of the debt incurred by the Republic of Texas. Political affairs also call for special treatment, for it was during the period that political parties became active, that Union and state rights factions took the place of old party alignments and that, like an approaching storm, the controversy over slavery and secession grew increasingly ominous. Meanwhile, the army had made extensive explorations across the unknown western part of the state, and immigrant homeseekers, who came year after year in ever-increasing numbers, joined with other thousands of land-hungry, "old" Texans to push their settlements into the Western Cross Timbers.

Finally, the explorations and the intrusion of the whites into the homeland
of the Comanche Indians created a problem that taxed the combined
efforts of both the federal and state governments until they were
interrupted by secession and the Civil War.

## THE ESTABLISHMENT
## OF STATE GOVERNMENT

The Texas Constitution of 1845 was well designed and well written. It
was characterized by Daniel Webster, the great statesman from Massachusetts, as the best of all the American state constitutions. Since it was
used as a working model by the framers of the Constitution of 1876, it is
in a measure still the fundamental law of the state. Its framers probably
constituted the ablest assembly that has ever served the state. Thomas
Jefferson Rusk, its president, had made substantial contributions to the
Constitution of 1836. J. Pinckney Henderson had served in Houston's
cabinet and as minister to England and France, and Isaac Van Zandt had
been a member of the Texas Congress and later was sent as envoy to the
United States. R. E. B. Baylor, a jurist of superior ability, had also
served as the representative from Alabama in the Congress of the United
States. N. H. Darnell had been speaker of the Texas house of representatives; Abner S. Lipscomb had studied law in the office of John C.
Calhoun and had been chief justice in Alabama; and Hiram G. Runnels
had been governor of Mississippi. José Antonio Navarro, a member of
the convention of 1836, was the only native Texan. Tennessee contributed
eighteen members, Virginia eight, Georgia seven, Kentucky six, and
North Carolina five.

The framers drew extensively from the Louisiana constitution,
which had just been completed, and to some extent from the fundamental
laws of other states. Their own Texas Constitution of 1836 seems,
however, to have been used as a working model. The governor was to
be chosen by the voters for a term of two years but was not eligible to
serve more than four out of six years. Subject to the approval of the
senate, the governor was to appoint the secretary of state, the attorney
general, the three justices of the supreme court, and the district judges.
The comptroller and treasurer were to be chosen by the legislature.
Thus, of state officers, only the governor, lieutenant governor, and
members of the legislature were elected by the voters. In 1850, however,
the state provided for the popular election of the attorney general,
comptroller, and treasurer.

Under the republic, the lawmakers had met annually, but the new
constitution called for biennial sessions. Representatives would serve for

two years and would be apportioned among the several districts according to the number of free inhabitants. Senators were to be apportioned on the basis of the number of qualified electors and would serve for four years. From the old constitution was carried over the prohibition against ministers of the gospel holding a seat in the legislature. The instrument disqualified from holding public office any person who might thereafter participate in a duel either as principal or as second.

Its hostility toward corporations, so prevalent in that day, took the form of requiring a two-thirds vote of both houses to create any kind of a private corporation and of forbidding the incorporation of any bank. It required that all property be taxed in proportion to its value, except such as the legislature might exempt by a two-thirds vote, and that the aggregate amount of debt that the legislature might incur not exceed $100,000. Married women were made secure in their right to own property. Exemption from foreclosure of a homestead for debt not in excess of two hundred acres was allowed.

The election of officers for the new state was held on December 15, 1845. On that day J. Pinckney Henderson was chosen governor over Dr. James B. Miller by an overwhelming vote, and for lieutenant governor Albert C. Horton beat N. H. Darnell by a slender majority. On receiving information that President Polk had signed the act admitting Texas, President Jones called the legislature to assemble in Austin on February 16, 1846, for the purpose of organizing a state government. Three days later in a formal ceremony Jones officially transferred the government to the newly elected state officials.

Governor Henderson promptly named John Hemphill chief justice of the state supreme court, and the first legislature elected Thomas J. Rusk and Sam Houston to the United States Senate. To Houston fell the short term, and he was twice reelected. Rusk also was reelected and served until his death in 1857.

Changes and adjustments incident to the transition from republic to state consumed much of the effort of officers in Texas during Henderson's administration. The postal system was taken over by the United States, and arms, buildings, and other public property were transferred to the general government.

## THE WAR WITH MEXICO

The annexation of Texas, although not the only cause, resulted in a war between the United States and Mexico in which Texans had a significant role. The causes, too complicated for more than a partial treatment here, simply stated were: (1) the annexation of Texas, (2) the desire of the

United States to have a port in California, (3) the refusal of the Mexican government to settle claims by citizens of the United States, (4) the instability of the Mexican government, and (5) the location of the boundary.

Upon learning of the renewal of negotiations for the annexation of Texas in 1843, President Santa Anna notified the United States that his government would regard its accomplishment as equivalent to a declaration of war against the Mexican republic. On March 6, 1845, as a consequence of Tyler's approval and Polk's acceptance of the resolution of annexation, Juan N. Almonte, the minister of the Santa Anna government in Washington, announced that Mexico would defend its rightful territory (Texas) by every means within its power and asked for his passport. Before the end of the month the rupture was complete. In midsummer, however, when the Mexican Congress refused to follow the recommendation of the secretary of war to declare war on the United States, President Polk and his cabinet concluded that the new moderate government of President José Herrera wanted an amicable solution of the issues. After ascertaining that it would accept an envoy from the United States who came with full powers to settle "the question" in dispute, President Polk in November 1845 sent John Slidell with full power to settle "all questions" in dispute. Slidell was instructed to buy as much of California and New Mexico as possible and to assume the claims of the United States against Mexico in return for Mexican recognition of the Rio Grande as the boundary between the two countries.

The claims issue was over debts owed by Mexico to citizens of the United States dating back to 1816. France had collected its debts by means of the Pastry War in 1838, and Great Britain was threatening to use force to collect its debts. In a claims convention in 1843 Mexico agreed to pay the claims in twenty quarterly installments but refused to do so when it learned later that year that negotiations for the annexation of Texas had been renewed. The amount of the unadjusted claims was officially estimated in December 1845 at $6,465,464.

When he reached Mexico in December, Slidell was informed that Texas was the only question in dispute and that friendly relations could not be reestablished until it had been restored to Mexico. At the end of the year the ultra-Centralists overthrew President José Herrera and installed Mariano Paredes as president, a man who was strongly anti-American. In March when Polk learned that Slidell would not be received, he ordered General Zachary Taylor, who was encamped at the mouth of the Nueces River, to move his troops to the Rio Grande. The Nueces had been set by the Spaniards in 1775 as the boundary between Texas and Nuevo Santander; and although it still contended that it was the boundary, in actual practice, Mexico, beginning with the capitulation of General Cós at San Antonio in December 1835, had adhered to the Rio Grande as the boundary, and the Republic of Texas by legislative act had designated it as its southern and western boundary. General Taylor, during the last week of March 1846, reached a site opposite Matamoros and began the construction of Fort Brown. On April 12 General Pedro Ampudia, in command of the Mexican forces at Matamoros with instructions to commence hostilities, notified Taylor that, unless he retired beyond the Nueces within twenty-four hours, force of arms would decide the question. Thus, Mexico made the boundary location, rather than the annexation of Texas, the major issue in the controversy. On April 23 President Paredes proclaimed a "defensive" war against the United States, and on the next day Mexican troops crossed the Rio Grande and defeated a smaller detachment of United States dragoons. On May 9, when he received news of the skirmish and before he learned of Taylor's victories on May 8 and 9 over a much larger Mexican army at Palo Alto and Resaca de la Palma, President Polk and his cabinet decided to ask Congress for a declaration of war. Over the objections of the Whigs and abolitionists, Congress on May 13, on the basis that Mexico had "shed American blood on American soil," declared war.

Taylor immediately opened an offensive to drive the Mexican forces toward Monterrey. He asked Governor Henderson for two regiments of

John Coffee (Jack) Hays, a surveyor by profession, became captain of a Texas Ranger company in 1840. As colonel in command of the First Regiment, Texas Mounted Volunteers, during the Mexican War, he participated with distinction in the battles of Monterrey and Mexico City. (Southwest Collection, Texas Tech University)

infantry and two of cavalry, and the legislature gave the governor a leave of absence to take command of the Texan troops who were mustered into the service of the United States. Before the end of May the Mexican troops had abandoned Matamoros to Taylor; on September 25 Taylor took possession of Monterrey; and on February 23 and 24, 1847, he defeated and put to flight a much larger force under Santa Anna at Buena Vista. The Texans performed a key role both at Monterrey and at Buena Vista. At Buena Vista Taylor's campaign ended, for it was doubted that an extended supply line across the deserts and mountains could be kept open.

Polk sent another army, commanded by General Winfield Scott, to land at Vera Cruz and march to Mexico City. Scott captured Mexico City in September, and Santa Anna fled the country. In both campaigns a number of Texans won distinction. One organization, that of John C. (Jack) Hays, made up largely of rangers, lawmen, and frontier Indian fighters and commanded by such fearless and daring men as Ben McCulloch, Samuel H. Walker, and John S. (Rip) Ford, attained renown. With their deadly six-shooters the Texas Rangers in both campaigns served as efficient scouts, were the advance units, and kept the supply lines open. Approximately five thousand Texans were in military service during the war. In the Treaty of Guadalupe Hidalgo on February 2, 1848, which ended the war, Mexico accepted the Rio Grande as the boundary; in return, the United States agreed to assume the claims of its citizens against that nation up to $5 million. It also ceded to the United States for a payment of $15 million the provinces of New Mexico and upper California. The Texas claim to that part of New Mexico east of the Rio Grande soon created a national crisis.

## THE TEXAS–NEW MEXICO BOUNDARY CONTROVERSY

It will be recalled that by an act of December 19, 1836, the Texas Congress claimed as the southern and western boundary of the republic the Rio Grande from mouth to source and thence a line running northward to the forty-second parallel. The claim was exceedingly ambitious. It took in a vast stretch of territory not included in the Texas of Spanish and Mexican days; it cut into the Mexican states of Tamaulipas and Coahuila, according to their boundaries as they had been drawn by the Spanish decrees of 1805 and 1811; it included territory claimed by the state of Chihuahua; and it proposed to attach to Texas the capital and most of the principal settlements of New Mexico. The Texans had made no settlements of consequence beyond the Nueces, and the expedition sent in 1841 to assert jurisdiction over the Santa Fé country had met with disastrous failure.

The Texan claim to the upper Rio Grande was based on the Treaty of Velasco made on May 14, 1836, with the prisoner Santa Anna (which indefinitely indicated that the Rio Grande would be the boundary), on the provision in the resolution of annexation that prohibited slavery in any state formed out of the territory of Texas north of 36°30', on the withdrawal of Mexican troops to the south side of the Rio Grande in both 1836 and 1842, and on the right of the victor to take as much territory of the defeated nation as possible. Also, on December 31, 1845, the United States established a customs district that included Corpus Christi and the territory west to the Rio Grande, and the United States declared war on Mexico on the basis that it had shed American blood on American soil—on the north side of the Rio Grande.

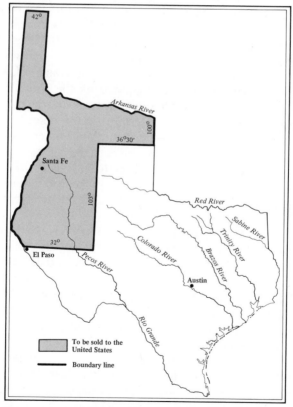

Pearce Plan, 1850. (From *The Howling of the Coyotes: Reconstruction Efforts to Divide Texas,* by Ernest Wallace, published by Texas A&M University Press)

The war with Mexico soon brought a series of developments that complicated the question of the territorial rights of Texas. In August 1846 Stephen W. Kearny, in command of the Army of the West, occupied New Mexico and established a civil government there with the approval of his superiors and without regard to the claims of Texas. On June 4, 1847, Governor Henderson reminded Secretary of State James Buchanan of the Texan claims. Buchanan replied by stating that the question would have to be settled by Congress, but he assured the governor that the temporary civil government would not affect the claim which, he believed, Texas justly asserted to all territory east of the Rio Grande. Their fears thus quieted, the Texans awaited the outcome of the war.

The Treaty of Guadalupe Hidalgo, ratified by the Senate of the United States on March 10, 1848, made the lower Rio Grande the international boundary and put an end to the claims of the Mexican states to territory north and east of that river. Since all of New Mexico was ceded to the United States, the treaty did not in any way settle the claims of Texas to a part of New Mexico. The Texans expected that with the ratification of the treaty all territory east of the Rio Grande would be turned over to them. Meanwhile, the question of the extension of slavery was injected. The Wilmot Proviso, introduced in Congress, would have prohibited slavery in any territory acquired by the United States as a result of the war with Mexico. Although the proviso was not adopted, it united the men of the South in a determination to open to slavery any territory that might be organized out of the Mexican cession. The free-soil men soon became aligned against the extreme claims of Texas. If the boundaries the state claimed were permitted to stand, slave soil thus would extend at least as far westward as the Rio Grande. Divided between these two factions, Congress found itself unable to pass any laws whatever concerning New Mexico.

Texas, however, acted promptly and decisively. Its legislature, by an act of March 15, 1848, created Santa Fé County with boundaries including practically all of that part of New Mexico that it claimed. Five days later it voted to ask the United States to sustain through its army the state officers who were to be sent there. Judge Spruce M. Baird was dispatched to organize the new county and to serve as its judge. Far from sustaining the Texan judge, the military and certain civilian leaders conspired to oppose him and used the press to excite the people against him. Just before his arrival, in November 1848, a convention was held in Santa Fé, and petitions were adopted asking that New Mexico be created a territory. On his arrival Baird was informed by Colonel John M. Washington, commanding officer in Santa Fé, that he would sustain the government established in New Mexico by General Kearny "at every peril'' until ordered to desist either by the executive or the legislative power of the United States. Baird left the territory for Missouri in July 1849.

Whatever chance the Texans had for securing the support of the federal forces in New Mexico vanished with the end of Polk's administration on March 4, 1849. President Taylor favored granting statehood to both California and New Mexico.

Meanwhile, the press and the officials of Texas were growing restive over the situation. In November Governor George T. Wood suggested to the legislature that Texas assert its claim "with the whole power and resources of the state," but neither the governor nor the legislature took any decisive action. Then Peter Hansborough Bell, who had defeated Wood in 1849 by advocating a more aggressive policy regarding the disputed territory, urged that the legislature send to New Mexico a force sufficient to maintain the authority of Texas. In response, the legislature, on December 31, designated new boundaries for Santa Fé County and created three additional counties to the south of it between the Pecos and the Rio Grande. Then, by authority of an act passed four days later, another commissioner, Robert S. Neighbors, was sent to organize the counties. Neighbors went armed with an address by the governor to the citizens of the four counties, urging them to lend him such "assistance and protection" as might be necessary. He organized El Paso County without meeting with resistance, but on arriving in New Mexico he found the majority of the people antagonistic and the military not disposed to aid him. The people, moreover, soon were absorbed in efforts to organize a state government for New Mexico, and President Taylor opposed the Texan efforts. Neighbors thereupon returned to Texas, and his report to the governor, made public early in June 1850, caused great excitement. At mass meetings in Austin and other places there were protests, threats of secession, and proposals that the state assert its claim by military force. Governor Bell called a special session of the legislature to meet on August 12.

Before the legislature assembled, the situation had become even more critical. The people of New Mexico had adopted a constitution for their proposed state with boundaries so extended as to include most of the disputed territory and also some territory unquestionably Texan. President Taylor had died, and his successor, Millard Fillmore, reinforced the army in New Mexico and stated flatly that he would send troops against the Texas militiamen if they attempted to occupy the country. Fillmore did, however, favor a settlement of the controversy and threw the support of his office behind the compromise measures then before Congress. After assembling in August, the legislature heard the governor's message declaring that Texas must assert its rights *"at all hazards and to the last extremity,"* and debated measures to organize the militia and send it into New Mexico.

The crisis finally was brought to an end by the action of Congress. As Congress grappled with the problem, one plan after another was considered and discarded. Senator Thomas H. Benton, on January 16, 1850, proposed that all the territory west of the 102° longitude and north of the Red River be ceded to the United States for a payment of $15 million and that the remainder of Texas be divided into two states, the division line to be along the Colorado River from the Gulf to the ninety-eighth meridian and along that meridian to the Red River. When Benton's proposal proved unacceptable, John Bell proposed the division of Texas into three states, at the Trinity and Colorado rivers with the thirty-fourth parallel being the northern boundary west of its intersection with the Red River. But even the lure of four additional seats in the Senate was not sufficiently attractive to win the support of the Texas delegation. A committee of thirteen with Henry Clay as chairman then reported the Omnibus bill, a compromise proposal for settling five controversial issues before Congress, including the Texas boundary. By this plan Texas would receive $10 million for the cession of all its lands west and north of a straight line beginning at the Rio Grande twenty miles above El Paso and extending northeast to the intersection of the one hundredth meridian and the Red River. This plan also failed, not necessarily because a majority of the senators were opposed but because a majority was opposed to one or more provisions in the overall bill and because of President Taylor's opposition. After President Taylor died on July 9, Millard Fillmore, his successor, although determined to use force to repel any force the Texans sent to New Mexico, favored a compromise.

Also diligently working for a compromise was a group who held Texas bonds payable from revenue obtained from custom duties. This group maintained that the United States government, having taken over the collection of customs after annexation, was responsible for the revenue debt. Finally, the bill written by James A. Pearce of Maryland, which had the support of the entire Texas delegation and of moderate men North and South, was accepted by the Senate and passed by the House on September 6. It fixed the northern and western boundary of Texas as it now stands, providing that it should begin at the intersection of the 100th meridian and the parallel of 36°30', run west along that parallel to the 103rd meridian, follow that to the 32nd parallel, extend along that parallel to the Rio Grande, and follow that stream to its mouth. Texas was to renounce all claims to territory beyond the boundaries described, for which it would be paid $10 million. As amended before final passage, the bill provided for the organization of the territory of New Mexico. It was one of a series of laws known as the Compromise of 1850.

At first there was considerable sentiment in Texas against accepting the proposition; but a majority of the voters seemed to take the point of view of the La Grange *Monument* that, although the measure was not all the state desired, it was "doubtful whether ten years' trading would give Texas a better bargain than she can now make." At a special election the voters accepted the proposition by a majority of two to one, the legislature in special session approved it, and Governor Bell signed the act of acceptance on November 25, 1850.

## SETTLEMENT OF THE DEBT OF THE REPUBLIC

It will be recalled that according to the joint resolution of annexation, the public lands of Texas were to be used, so far as was necessary, for the settlement of the public debt of Texas. The debt was complex in nature and created considerable ill will against the general government because of the terms of the boundary act. It consisted of two major types of obligations, ordinary (nonrevenue) and revenue debt. The ordinary debt consisted of the claims of participants in the Texas Revolution or suppliers of the Texas army, nearly all representing at most a few

Peter H. Bell, a native of Virginia, fought at San Jacinto, was a Texas Ranger, and fought under General Zachary Taylor in the war with Mexico. He was governor of Texas from 1849 to 1853, and in the controversy that developed over the claims of Texas to the Rio Grande as its western boundary he represented the state's interests with force and energy. (E. C. Barker History Center, University of Texas)

hundred dollars each. The revenue debt consisted of principal and interest owed to holders of Republic of Texas securities. Under the terms of the boundary act, as interpreted by United States officers, the revenue debts were preferred obligations, for which import duties of the old Texan government had been pledged as security. To make sure that these were paid, the federal government retained $5 million in bonds. The state soon paid the ordinary or nonrevenue debt out of the $5 million delivered to it and had about $3.75 million in bonds left.

The revenue debt, however, was slowly paid. The state proposed to scale the debt, to which many creditors objected; some creditors neglected to file their claims; and the United States officials would not pay any claims until all were in. Final settlement was made by an act of February 28, 1855. Congress estimated that the bonds held for Texas, together with accrued interest, amounted to $6.5 million. It added to this amount $1,250,000 to reimburse Texas for damages resulting from depredations committed by Indians of the United States in Texas since 1836; thus, there was a total of $7,750,000 in cash to be distributed *pro rata* among the creditors who had not yet been paid. The legislature accepted the offer in February 1856. The $7,750,000 prorated among the holders of the $10,078,703 revenue debt gave each creditor about 77 cents on the dollar. The state contended that such scaling was equitable since the republic had not received par value for the obligations at the time they were issued.

Of the $3.75 million in bonds that remained after the nonrevenue debt had been paid, $2 million was set aside as an endowment for the public schools, the greater part of which amount was, in turn, loaned to railroads to aid construction. For six years, beginning in 1852, the state remitted to the counties nine-tenths of its taxes. The constitution required that the remaining tenth be applied to the use of the schools. The counties, in turn, used the remitted tax money for the construction of public buildings and various other purposes. Thus, Texas was able to endow its public schools, promote internal improvements, construct public buildings, and maintain all the while a very low tax rate.

## STATE POLITICS DURING THE ERA

While Governor Henderson was commanding Texas troops during the Mexican War, Lieutenant Governor Horton served as governor. Henderson returned in November 1846 and resumed his duties as chief executive. He declined to run for reelection and was succeeded on December 21, 1847, by George T. Wood, a Trinity River planter who had gained popularity as commander of a regiment of volunteers in the campaign against Monterrey. Wood's vote was substantially greater than that of his leading opponent, Dr. J. B. Miller. The chief objects of public attention during the Wood administration were frontier defense, the public debt, and the claims of Texas to the disputed territory east of the Rio Grande. While Wood was governor, Texans for the first time participated in an election for president of the United States. They supported Lewis Cass, the Democratic candidate. Wood was a candidate again in 1849 but was defeated by Peter Hansborough Bell. Wood charged his defeat to the indifferent support given his candidacy by Senator Houston. The anti-Houston forces, among them J. P. Henderson and William B. Ochiltree, opposed him actively. The fact that his opponent advocated a more aggressive policy in asserting Texas's claims to a part of New Mexico may account also for Wood's defeat.

Bell was a veteran of San Jacinto and of the war with Mexico. The first term of his administration was marked by the crisis over the Texas–New Mexico boundary, the exploration of routes across Texas, the establishment of a line of military posts along the frontier, and a popular mandate to keep the capital at Austin. In his campaign for reelection in 1851, the growing jealousy of the South over state rights was reflected. None of his opponents—John A. Greer, M. T. Johnson, T. J. Chambers, or B. H. Epperson (who ran as a Whig)—was in sympathy with the abolitionists, but Bell was known as the most pro-Southern of them all. Subjects of general interest in Bell's second administration were the scaling and paying of the public debt; the land claims of certain emigrant agents and their colonists, growing out of contracts made during the period of the republic; and frontier defense. Bell's firm stand against the United States, his aggressive frontier policy, and most of his other measures in general met with public approval. A few weeks before the expiration of his second term, Bell resigned to fill the vacancy in Congress caused by the death of David S. Kaufman.

In 1853 several candidates sought to be governor. W. B. Ochiltree, a Whig, expected to win because of a large personal following. To secure the defeat of Ochiltree, M. T. Johnson and another candidate, J. W. Henderson, withdrew and urged their followers to support Elisha M. Pease. Thus Pease, an "old" Texan, especially popular in the southern and western part of the state, was elected.

Pease's platform called for founding a public school system, encouraging internal improvements, and removing the Indians from Texas. The most important act of his administration was the school law of 1854. By its terms the state set aside $2 million of the indemnity bonds that it had acquired from the United States in the settlement of 1850 as a permanent endowment for public schools. Income from the fund was distributed each year on a per-capita basis to supplement the receipts from the one-tenth of the annual revenues that the constitution had reserved for the schools. The legislature set aside $100,000 of the United States bonds for endowment of a university, but the proceeds later were absorbed in the state revenue fund. A number of charters were granted to railroad companies, and two Indian reservations were authorized by the legislature.

The Pease era is also important in politics because of the rise of political parties in the state and the beginning of party nominations by conventions. No party delineation had existed during the republic and but little during the first years of statehood. Voters generally aligned themselves with the Houston or the anti-Houston leaders. As early as May 1846 an effort was made to organize the Democratic party, but without results. Both the Whigs and the Democrats held conventions from time to time, but the attendance was small. The Democratic convention in 1855 drew delegates from only twelve counties. Shortly

The Pease Mansion was bought by Elisha Marshall Pease, a New England Yankee who came to Texas in 1835 and settled in Bastrop (then called Mina). An outspoken advocate of independence, Pease was a member of the Committee of Safety in Mina and took part in the convention of 1836. Under his administration as governor (1853–1857) railroads were encouraged, taxes reduced, the state debt paid off, the state university planned, and a new capitol erected. A Unionist, Pease was appointed provisional governor again in 1867 but resigned because of disagreements over Reconstruction. (Texas Highway Department)

after it adjourned, however, a new rival organization, mysterious and baffling in its tactics, came into existence.

Resentment of the powerful political influence wielded by foreigners, especially Irish, had inspired on the Atlantic Seaboard a strong nativist movement. Organized initially in a series of secret societies, the followers soon merged into the American or Know-Nothing party. The new party opposed foreigners holding office and was decidedly anti-Catholic and pro-Union. It obtained many of its followers from the disintegrating Whig party. First appearing in Texas in 1854, it elected that year a complete slate of city officers in San Antonio. In the following spring its candidate was elected mayor of Galveston, and several newspapers were carrying articles in its support. Under the guise of a river improvement convention, the Know-Nothings met in convention in Washington on the Brazos, June 11 to 13, agreed on a slate of candidates headed by Lieutenant Governor D. C. Dickson, formed a state organization with R. E. B. Baylor as "grand president," and made plans to extend the order to every community through "subordinate councils" and "committees of vigilance." It got a major boost when Houston publicly expressed sympathy with the aims of the organization.

In less than a week after the Washington convention, the editor of the *State Gazette,* the principal Democratic organ, called a "bombshell" meeting of Democrats in Austin. This gathering denounced all secret political factions and pledged its support to Pease for governor and H. R. Runnels for lieutenant governor. This meeting gave wide publicity to the Know-Nothing secret convention and drew the line of cleavage between that group and the Democrats. Other Democratic contestants for governor were persuaded to withdraw to avoid splitting the party vote. During a hard-fought campaign Dickson severely attacked the governor for his espousal of the "state plan" for building railroads, his alleged hostility toward the proposed Pacific railroad, and his failure to protect the frontier. Pease beat Dickson by a substantial majority, but the Know-Nothings managed to elect about twenty representatives and five senators to the state legislature. It was stated that the Know-Nothing order supported Lemuel D. Evans, who was elected to Congress, but Evans denied any connection with the party.

In 1856 the Know-Nothing party held a state convention, open to the public, but its disintegration was by that time clearly evident, and it soon passed out of existence. Its most important effect was to force the Democrats to perfect their party organization and to adopt the practice of nominating candidates by conventions. When the Democrats convened to nominate candidates and select presidential electors, ninety-one out of ninety-nine counties were represented. With candidates for governor, lieutenant governor, and commissioner of the General Land Office to be nominated, attendance was even better the next year. That convention named Hardin R. Runnels, a wealthy planter of Bowie County, as candidate for governor, and Francis R. Lubbock, who had been an active party worker, for lieutenant governor.

Of greater importance even than party alignments was the distinct cleavage that appeared between the Houston and anti-Houston factions. More and more the Houston group referred to themselves as Jackson Democrats or Unionists, while the opposition was often called Calhoun Democrats. Since 1836 Sam Houston twice had been president of the republic and thrice United States senator. His record had been the subject of both praise and blame, but his supremacy had never been successfully challenged. He antagonized the extreme proslavery leaders in 1848 by voting for the creation of the free-soil territory of Oregon and by refusing to sign John C. Calhoun's protest against what he termed the aggression of the free states. The speeches and debates of Houston and of Rusk (whose record was only slightly less offensive than Houston's to the pro-Southern extremists) created much excitement in Texas in 1849. Then Houston's vote against the Kansas-Nebraska bill (the bill that opened to slavery territory that had been closed to it by the Missouri Compromise) in 1854 was regarded as treason to the South, and Democrats throughout Texas condemned him most bitterly. His affiliation with the Know-Nothing movement in 1855 likewise made him vulnerable. Apparently believing that he would not again be elected to the United States Senate, he determined to test his strength in a gubernatorial contest before the voters. Accordingly, in May 1857 he announced for governor as an independent, running on his record as a Jackson Democrat or Unionist. Louis T. Wigfall, a proslavery extremist and staunch champion of state rights, debated Houston wherever possible, and when Houston avoided debate, Wigfall and J. P. Henderson followed the old veteran from place to place, answering his arguments. Runnels and the regular Democratic ticket won an overwhelming victory. It was the only defeat in a major contest before the voters that Houston ever suffered. The legislature elected Chief Justice John Hemphill to take his seat in the United States Senate. In 1857 Senator Rusk met death by his own hand, and the same legislature chose J. P. Henderson to fill the vacancy. Soon thereafter Henderson died, and Matthias Ward was appointed to succeed him. Wigfall was chosen to succeed Ward in 1858.

During the Runnels administration, 1857 to 1859, frontier defense and the national controversy associated with slavery were all-absorbing subjects, and other issues were eclipsed by the excitement and hatred that they created. The frontier defense problem is treated later in this chapter, and the national controversy and the election of 1859, because of their inseparable connection with secession, also are discussed later.

Colonel John S. (Rip) Ford, a South Carolinian by
birth, came to Texas in 1836. In the course of a long
career he practiced medicine in San Augustine, edited
the *Texas Democrat* and later the *State Times* in
Austin, and served in both the Congress of the Republic of Texas and the state senate. He attained
renown as a ranger, defeating the Indians in two
notable engagements, and as an officer in the Confederate army, commanding the troops that won the
Battle of Palmito Ranch, the last land engagement of
the war. His nickname Rip came from his practice of
introducing death notices during the war with Mexico
with "Rest in peace," which in the stress of battle
became "R.I.P." (E. C. Barker History Center, University of Texas)

## EXPLORATIONS

At the close of the Mexican War, Texas, west and north of a line through
Denton, Dallas, Waco, Austin, Fredericksburg, San Antonio, Castroville,
and Laredo, was an unknown Indian country. During the next twelve
years, as a result of the efforts of the Texans and the army to find and
survey wagon and rail roads across the region and to locate and supply

new military posts on the southern border of the nation, the region was extensively explored.

In the summer of 1848 a group of enterprising citizens of San Antonio, anxious to divert the rich Missouri-Chihuahua trade to their city, persuaded John C. Hays, the famed Texas Ranger, to try to find a practical wagon road to El Paso. Hays with a party of citizens and Texas Rangers went by way of the Llano and Devils rivers, but beyond the Pecos River, lost and with supplies exhausted, he gave up and returned to San Antonio, most of the men suffering great hardships while on the expedition.

The next expedition was jointly sponsored by the army and by the citizens of Austin, who wanted to make their city the eastern departure point on a road to California. In March 1849 Robert S. Neighbors, a noted Indian agent, with orders from General William J. Worth in San Antonio, and John S. (Rip) Ford, a famous Texas Ranger who represented the citizens of Austin, set out with a party to find a practical wagon road between San Antonio and El Paso. They went by way of the Middle Concho, Horsehead Crossing on the Pecos River, and the Davis Mountains, and returned by way of Guadalupe Pass, the Pecos and Middle Concho rivers, and Fredericksburg. At about the same time Captain W. H. C. Whiting made an army reconnaissance to El Paso. He returned by way of the Davis Mountains, Devils River, and the head of Las Moras River at present-day Brackettville. The leaders of both expeditions reported favorably on their return routes. Army officers then surveyed and tested the practicability of the two routes. Lieutenant Francis T. Bryan surveyed the Neighbors-Ford return route, and Lieutenant Colonel Joseph E. Johnston moved a train of 250 wagons in one hundred days from San Antonio to El Paso by Whiting's return route. Both routes were marked: the "upper," leading northward to Brady's Creek, westward to the Pecos at Horsehead Crossing, up that stream to the mouth of Delaware Creek, near the present Texas–New Mexico line, and westward through Guadalupe Pass to El Paso; the "lower," used more extensively, westward from San Antonio, following the route of Highway 90 to Fort Clark, now Brackettville, northwest, crossing the Pecos west of Ozona, and following the general direction of Highway 290 to El Paso. Many emigrants, California bound, used these routes.

Meanwhile, the military was exploring and marking wagon roads across the state farther north. Captain Randolph B. Marcy in April 1849 escorted a party of immigrants to Santa Fé by following the Canadian River across the Texas Panhandle. On his return, Marcy passed through Guadalupe Pass, crossed the Pecos a little south of the present Texas and Pacific Railroad crossing, followed the route of the railroad to the vicinity of Colorado City, and then bore slightly northward by the present towns of Stamford, Haskell, Newcastle, Jacksboro, Henrietta, and Preston, north of Sherman. This route, known as the Marcy Trail, afterward became, as far west as the Clear Fork of the Brazos and then with a south-westward deviation by way of the Middle Concho, a major road for emigrants to California and other pioneers.

In 1853, Congress made an appropriation for surveying practical routes for railroads to the Pacific. The southernmost of these surveys, made in part by Captain John Pope, followed substantially the Marcy Trail. Many years were to pass before the railroad was built, but the exploration and surveys must be credited in part to the Southern Overland Mail Service that was extended through that section in 1858.

In an attempt to solve the transportation and supply problems in the desert Southwest, the army experimented with camels. After his proposal to build a transcontinental railroad along a southern route had been blocked by sectional politics, Secretary of War Jefferson Davis in 1856 and 1857 introduced seventy-five camels into Texas and headquartered them near present-day Kerrville, the eastern terminus of the projected camel route. Tests were begun immediately, some as far as California, but with the outbreak of the Civil War the camels were abandoned and eventually vanished.

## IMMIGRATION AND EXTENSION OF SETTLEMENT

It has been stated previously that the frontier line of settlement in 1846 extended from Corpus Christi to San Antonio on the southwest and northward approximately through New Braunfels, Fredericksburg, Austin, Waco, and Dallas, to Preston on the Red River, and that the total population in Texas in 1847, including blacks but not Indians, was estimated at 142,009. If the liberal land policy and the expectation of annexation had stimulated immigration, annexation and the continuation of the liberal land policy brought a veritable stream of homeseekers. The lure of cheap land in Texas was second only to that of gold in California. During 1845 the newspapers in Missouri, Arkansas, and Louisiana bore strong evidence of migration to Texas. There was a lull in 1846 and 1847 due to the Mexican War, but the news of the United States victory started the wave anew. One day in December 1848, 300 immigrants crossed the ferry at Washington on the Brazos, and during November 1849 more than 5,000 on their way to Texas crossed the Arkansas River at Little Rock. A year later, the editor of the *Northern Standard* at Clarksville, the northeastern gateway to Texas, wrote: "For the last two weeks scarcely a day has passed that a dozen or more movers' wagons have not passed through our town." The census of 1850 showed 154,034 whites, 58,161 slaves, 397 free blacks, for a total of 212,592 or an increase of almost 50 percent since 1847.

Year after year the number grew increasingly larger. In December 1858 the editor of the Clarksville *Standard* declared that no fewer than fifty wagons of immigrants were passing through Clarksville each day. By 1860 the population of the state had jumped to 604,215, almost three times that of 1850. Of this number, 182,921 were blacks.

Of the 1860 population, almost three-fourths had been born outside of Texas. A majority of the immigrants had come from the states of the Old South, Louisiana, Arkansas, and Missouri. Tennessee had contributed 42,265, more than any other state; Alabama was the next with 34,193. A few had been born in northern states. The foreign born, numbering 43,422, represented almost every country of Western Europe. The Germans and Mexicans constituted by far the largest foreign-born elements, being represented by 20,553 and 12,443, respectively.

Immigrants from Europe, other than the Germans who in 1860 constituted a majority of the population in three counties in the San Antonio–Austin area and a substantial part in six other counties, included French, Czechs, and Norwegians. La Réunion, a French colony, was established in 1855 near Dallas by followers of Victor Considerant, a disciple of the socialist, F. C. M. Fourier. The colonists soon lost their enthusiasm for the frontier and cooperative enterprise, however, and drifted away to other communities. A few Czechs had come to Texas during the period of the republic; after the revolutions of 1848 in Central Europe, many others escaping Austrian tyranny followed them. Among them were a number of liberal intellectuals who exercised considerable influence on the early development of Texas. A small Norwegian settlement was planted in Henderson County in 1845, but settlers from Scandinavia did not come in numbers until nearly a half-century later.

Obviously, the liberal land policy and the tremendous population increase resulted in a significant extension of settlements during the fifteen years of early statehood. The counties of Nueces, Webb, Starr, and Cameron were created in 1848. Their populations seem to have been overwhelmingly Mexican. Election returns for Nueces County showed a total of forty-four voters, thirty-seven of whom had Spanish names. Along the Rio Grande, far removed from the main Texas settlements, were a number of communities, including Laredo and Eagle Pass, whose populations likewise were largely Mexican. In 1850 this area and the counties of Cameron, Starr, and Webb had about thirteen thousand people. Higher up on the Rio Grande were several settlements, including Presidio and El Paso, with about four thousand persons.

Thousands of new arrivals, joined by other thousands of "old"

Texans, advanced the frontier westward deep into the Western Cross Timbers despite Indian hostility and the less favorable physical environment. By 1849 the newly established towns of Sherman, Farmersville, Dallas, Waxahachie, Ennis, Waco, and Fredericksburg marked the western limits of white settlement. During that year the federal government completed the establishment of a line of military posts, generally a few miles in advance of the settlements, to deter the Indians from raiding the whites. Villages sprang up at once near Fort Worth and Fort Croghan (Burnet), but because the infantry sent to the posts were unable to offer protection, the rush to the frontier came to a temporary halt in 1850 with the establishment of Gainesville, Belton, and Uvalde County.

Under pressure to open up new lands for settlers, the federal government in 1851 and 1852 moved its military posts westward more than a hundred miles. As soon as the posts were established, there was a rush to settle the intervening lands. Within two years settlements had been made at Bandera, San Saba, Meridian, Gatesville, Cleburne, and Stephenville; and at the end of another four years Comanche, Hamilton, Weatherford, Jacksboro, and Palo Pinto had been founded.

In 1860 the western extremity of settlement extended irregularly from Henrietta on the north through Belknap, Palo Pinto, Brownwood, Llano, and Kerrville, to Uvalde. The advance halted here, not only because of the outbreak of the Civil War and the lack of timber and water, but also because of the inability to cope with the hostile Plains Indians.

## THE INDIAN FRONTIER

The people of Texas believed that once annexation had been completed the United States would put an end to Indian depredations, but they were soon disillusioned. Troubles with Indians continued for more than thirty years and at times were even worse than they had been during the republic. The three sources of frontier defense were the United States Army, state troops, and the frontier citizens.

The United States made a treaty with the Penateka Comanches, the band nearest the whites, in 1846, but because of the outbreak of the Mexican War, Texas was left to defend its own frontiers. Soon after the outbreak of the war, five companies of mounted Texas Rangers were stationed along the frontier from the West Fork of the Trinity to Castroville. They were not able to prevent a series of Indian raids, most severe in South Texas, and during 1847 four additional companies were placed in service between San Antonio and the Rio Grande. Other than these nine companies of state troops, the frontier had no protection until after the war.

When the United States began withdrawing its troops from Mexico, it sent seven companies of regulars to replace the state troops. It has been stated previously that in 1849 the War Department put into effect a permanent line of defense. It established between the Rio Grande and the Red River eight military posts to deter the Indians from going into the settlements. From south to north these forts were Duncan at Eagle Pass; Inge, near Uvalde; Lincoln, fifty-five miles west of San Antonio; Martin Scott, at Fredericksburg; Croghan, near Burnet; Gates, on the Leon River; Graham, on the Brazos River; and Worth, fifty-four miles due north of Fort Graham, at the present city of Fort Worth. So rapid was the advance of settlements, however, that within less than two years the line of frontierspeople's cabins had passed beyond this cordon. Consequently, beginning in 1851 they were replaced by seven new forts generally along an irregular line about one hundred miles to the west.

**LINE OF DEFENSE 1849**

From north to south they were Belknap, on the Brazos at the present town of Newcastle; Phantom Hill, fourteen miles north of present-day Abilene; Chadbourne, on Oak Creek in present-day Coke County; McKavett, on the San Saba River about twenty-four miles above present-day Menard; Terrett, on the North Llano; Mason, at the present town of that name; and Clark, at the present Brackettville. Still a third chain of posts, located along or near the Rio Grande, was built for a double purpose, namely, keeping out marauding parties from Mexico and preventing Indians from the United States from harassing the settlements of northern Mexico. Several other posts also were built in strategic points.

A close correlation existed between the number of troops and the extent of marauding operations by the Indians. During 1853, for instance, there were 3,265 soldiers in Texas, the greatest number at any time before the Civil War, and the frontier was comparatively tranquil. During the following year, after many troops had been withdrawn and the

**TEXAS IN 1860**

Showing Military Posts & Roads

Miles

0     85

country between the Colorado and the Red rivers was defended by only four small companies of infantry and two of dragoons, conditions became so bad that General Persifor F. Smith called on Governor Pease for state troops. At Fort Chadbourne there were only twenty men, and they were commanded by the post surgeon.

Meanwhile, the Indian agents were working faithfully, in spite of great handicaps, to keep the Indians peaceful. The ablest of these agents was Robert S. Neighbors, who had served the Republic of Texas as an Indian agent and afterwards continued in the service of the federal government, except from 1849 to 1853, until his death in 1859.

In an effort to provide better for the Indians and to restrain them, two reservations were established in Texas in 1855. The state contributed the land, twelve square leagues (approximately 53,140 acres). Surviving members, in all about a thousand, of the Caddo, Anadarko, Ioni, Waco, Tonkawa, Tawakoni, and other small tribes, were located on a reservation of eight square leagues at the junction of the Brazos and Clear Fork rivers, near present-day Graham. A reservation of four square leagues (17,713.6 acres) for the Penateka Comanches was established on the Clear Fork in present-day Throckmorton County, but only about five hundred Penatekas, not much more than half of that Comanche band, could be persuaded to move onto the reservation. Some of the remainder united with the northern Comanche bands and became even more troublesome.

Conditions near the Indian country improved greatly in 1856. The change seems to have been caused in part by the reservations, but probably it should be credited more to the presence of the greatest aggregation of fighting men that ever represented the United States Army in the Old West—the Second Cavalry, whose roll of officers included Albert Sidney Johnston, Robert E. Lee, George H. Thomas, George Stoneman, and John B. Hood. Johnston and a part of his regiment were ordered to Utah in 1857, and the depredations again became severe. During the following year both the state and federal forces carried the war to the Indians. In April, with a force of 215 rangers and friendly Brazos Reservation Indians under their agent, Shapley P. Ross, John S. Ford crossed the Red River into present-day Oklahoma and on May 12 decisively defeated a large band of Comanches in the Canadian River valley near the Texas-Oklahoma line.[1] In September of the same year, Major Earl Van Dorn led a cavalry force from Texas against the Comanches in the Indian Territory and on October 1 defeated a band of

---

[1]As incorrectly located at that time, the 100th meridian, which north of Red River separates the Panhandle of Texas from Oklahoma, was approximately sixty miles east of the true location; thus, Ford may have believed that he was in Texas, but apparently he gave the question of boundary no consideration.

that tribe and Wichitas near present-day Rush Springs, Oklahoma. In this campaign also, about 125 friendly Indians from the Brazos Reservation, under the command of Lawrence Sullivan Ross, son of the Indian agent and later governor of Texas, gave substantial aid. Later that year Van Dorn carried his war even farther north and defeated another band of Comanches in southern Kansas.

Meanwhile, in spite of the loyal aid the Indians of the Brazos Reservation had given the troops, the people of the frontier, joined by many persons in the interior, charged that the reservation Indians were taking part in raids on the settlements and demanded that they be removed from Texas. Swarms of angry settlers repeatedly threatened the lives of the reservation people, and only the presence of federal troops prevented a massacre. In the late summer of 1859 the Indians of both reservations were moved to the valley of the Washita River in Indian Territory.

Soon after the removal of the reservation Indians, trouble developed on the lower Rio Grande frontier. In the fall of 1859 Juan N. Cortina and a large band of followers crossed the Rio Grande and harried Brownsville and the entire lower Rio Grande valley. Two companies of state troops, under the command of John S. Ford, went to the aid of a contingent of federal troops and after a lively campaign forced the bandit raider to limit his activities to the south side of the Rio Grande.

The removal of the reservation Indians did not bring peace to the frontier. The northern Comanches and the Kiowas, aroused by the attacks from Texas, retaliated that autumn with devastating raids on the exposed settlements. Dissatisfaction over this situation constituted a major factor that led to the defeat of Runnels and the election of Houston as governor that year. Although aggressive warfare against the Indians had been contrary to Houston's nature, he had promised to quiet the Indians, and this time neither the whites nor the Indians were in a mood to resort to treaties. Thus, he had to act. By a series of orders he authorized and sent to the frontier by the end of March 1860 seven ranger companies, consisting of more than 500 men. Also, the chief justice in each frontier county was authorized to raise a company of not more than 25 minutemen, and for a time that spring 23 such companies were available for service. The state force must have numbered more than 1,000 on active duty. At the same time there were 2,651 federal troops in Texas, and 842 others were on the way to the state. Such a sizable force of mounted troops temporarily frightened the Indian raiders away from the frontier, and in May the minutemen were disbanded, but four companies of rangers were ordered to scout for hostile Indians without regard to state boundaries. Although the rangers remained in Indian Territory for nearly a year, they had little noteworthy success except for the defeat of an encampment of Indians in what is now the Panhandle of Oklahoma. One expedition penetrated the Indian country as far as Kansas but failed to accomplish anything of consequence. Meanwhile, the federal troops were likewise active, and by the end of 1860 it appeared that Texas might have peace on its western frontier. However, Texas was on the eve of secession, and the final settlement of its Indian problem was to require another fifteen years of tough campaigning after the close of the Civil War.

## SELECTED BIBLIOGRAPHY

For a good bibliography on early statehood, see Ralph A. Wooster, "Early Texas Statehood: A Survey of Historical Writings," *Southwestern Historical Quarterly,* LXXVI, 121–141. For source material, see the *Houston Papers;* the *Handbook of Texas;* and E. Wallace and D. M. Vigness (eds.), *Documents of Texas History.*

The best general accounts of the period are S. V. Connor, *Adventure in Glory;* E. Wallace, *Texas in Turmoil* (Austin, 1965); O. M. Roberts, *A Political, Legislative, and Judicial History of Texas, 1845–1895,* in D. G. Wooten (ed.), *A Comprehensive History of Texas, 1685–1897* (2 vols., Dallas, 1898); and previously cited, older works by H. H. Bancroft, J. H. Brown, H. S. Thrall, F. W. Johnson, and L. J. Wortham.

Biographies that are essential for an understanding of the period include those of Sam Houston, previously cited; William Seale, *Sam Houston's Wife; A Biography of Margaret Lea Houston* (Norman, Okla., 1970); H. P. Gambrell, *Anson Jones;* Claude Elliott, *Leathercoat: The Life of James W. Throckmorton* (San Antonio, 1938); W. J. Hughes, *Rebellious Ranger: Rip Ford and the Old Southwest* (Norman, Okla., 1964); E. Wallace, *Charles DeMorse: Pioneer Editor and Statesman;* J. K. Greer, *Colonel Jack Hays* (New York, 1952); Ben H. Procter, *Not without Honor: The Life of John H. Reagan* (Austin, 1962); A. L. King, *Louis T. Wigfall: Southern Fire-eater* (Baton Rouge, La., 1970).

On the constitution of 1845, see a study by F. L. Paxson in *Southwestern Historical Quarterly,* XVIII, 386–398; and another by A. Middleton, *ibid.,* XXV, 26–62; also see *Debates of the Convention of 1845* (Houston, 1846).

For a background study of the war with Mexico, see Charles H. Harris, III, *Mexico Views Manifest Destiny, 1821–1846* (Albuquerque, N.M., 1976). For the war, several excellent studies are available, including: S. V. Connor and O. B. Faulk, *North America Divided: The Mexican War, 1846–1848* (New York, 1971); W. P. Webb, *The Texas Rangers;* John E. Weems, *To Conquer a Peace: The War between the United*

*States and Mexico* (New York, 1974); N. W. Stephenson, *Texas and the Mexican War* (New Haven, Conn., 1921); Otis A. Singletary, *The Mexican War* (Chicago, 1960); Justin H. Smith, *The War with Mexico* (2 vols., New York, 1919); J. K. Greer, *Colonel Jack Hays;* Ernest C. Shearer, "The Carvajal Disturbances," *Southwestern Historical Quarterly,* LV, 201–230; and H. W. Barton, "Five Texas Frontier Companies during the Mexican War," *ibid.,* LXVI, 17–30; E. Wallace, *Charles De Morse: Pioneer Editor and Statesman.*

The controversy over the Texas–New Mexico boundary and the settlement of the debt of the Republic of Texas are dealt with in W. C. Binkley, *The Expansionist Movement in Texas;* E. T. Miller, *A Financial History of Texas;* Holman Hamilton, *Prologue to Conflict: The Crisis and Compromise of 1850* (Lexington, Ky., 1964); Holman Hamilton, "Texas Bonds and Northern Profits: A Study in Compromise, Investment, and Lobby Influence," *Mississippi Valley Historical Review,* XLIII, 579–594; Kenneth F. Neighbours, "The Taylor-Neighbors Struggle over the Upper Rio Grande Region of Texas in 1850," *Southwestern Historical Quarterly,* LXI, 431–463; and C. A. Bridges, "Texas and the Crisis of 1850" (unpublished manuscript, University of Texas library, Austin); S. V. Connor, *Adventure in Glory.*

On the politics of the era, besides the biographies and the general works mentioned above, there is F. B. Sexton, "J. Pinckney Henderson," *Quarterly of the Texas State Historical Association,* I, 187–203; Louis F. Blount, "A Brief Study of Thomas J. Rusk," *Southwestern Historical Quarterly,* XXXIV, 181–202, 271–292; Ralph A. Wooster, "Membership in Early Texas Legislatures, 1850–1860," *ibid.,* LXIX, 163–173; R. A. Wooster, "An Analysis of the Texas Know-Nothings," *ibid.,* LXX, 414–423; S. H. Sherman, "Governor George Thomas Wood," *ibid.,* XX, 260–268; Roy Sylvan Dunn, "The Knights of the KGC in Texas, 1860–1861," *ibid.,* LXX, 543–573; G. L. Crockett, *Two Centuries in East Texas;* E. W. Winkler (ed.), *Platforms of Political Parties in Texas* (Austin, 1916), indispensable to a study of Texas politics; Francis R. Lubbock (C. W. Raines, ed.), *Six Decades in Texas* (Austin, 1900); Norman G. Kittrell, *Governors Who Have Been, and Other Public Men of Texas* (Houston, 1921); James T. DeShields, *They Sat in High Places: The Presidents and Governors of Texas* (San Antonio, 1940). With special reference to education, see J. J. Lane, *History of Education in Texas* (Washington, D.C., 1903); Frederick Eby, *The Development of Education in Texas* (New York, 1925); and J. C. Jeffries, "Sketches of Old Baylor," *Southwestern Historical Quarterly,* LVI, 498–506.

For accounts of exploration, see Grant Foreman, *Marcy and the Gold Seekers* (Norman, Okla., 1936); "Marcy's Report on His Return from Santa Fé," *West Texas Historical Association Year Book,* I, 30–54; M. L. Crimmins, "Captain John Pope's Route to the Pacific," *Military Engineer* (March–April, 1931); W. J. Hughes, *Rebellious Ranger: Rip Ford and the Old Southwest;* W. Turrentine Jackson, *Wagon Roads West* (Berkeley, Calif., 1952); A. B. Bender, "Opening Routes across West Texas, 1848–1856," *Southwestern Historical Quarterly,* XXXVII, 116–135; W. H. Goetzman, "The United States–Mexican Boundary Survey, 1848–1853," *ibid.,* LXII, 164–190; T. L. Connelly, "The American Camel Experiment: A Reappraisal," *ibid.,* LXIX, 442–462; E. B. Lammons, "Operation Camel: An Experiment in Animal Transportation in Texas, 1857–1860," *ibid.,* XLI, 20–49; W. H. Goetzman, *Army Exploration in the American West* (New Haven, Conn., 1959); and Chris Emmett, *Texas Camel Tales* (Austin, 1969).

For land policy, immigration, and the extension of settlements, most of the sources and studies cited under these subjects in the preceding chapter are also valuable for the period of early statehood. In addition, see W. C. Holden, *Alkali Trails* (Dallas, 1930); W. J. Hammond and Margaret F. Hammond, *La Réunion, A French Settlement in Texas* (Dallas, 1958); Ermance V. Rejebain, "La Reunion: The French Colony in Dallas County," *Southwestern Historical Quarterly,* XLIII, 472–478; H. R. Marsh, "The Czechs in Texas," *ibid.,* L, 236–240; Rondel V. Davidson, "Victor Considerant: Fourierist, Legislator, and Humanitarian" (unpublished dissertation, Texas Tech University, Lubbock, Tex., 1970); R. N. Richardson, *The Frontier of Northwest Texas, 1846–1876: Advance and Defense by the Pioneer Settlers of the Cross Timbers and Prairies* (Glendale, Calif., 1963); James Day, *Jacob de Cordova: Land Merchant of Texas* (Waco, Tex., 1962); B. P. Gallaway, "The Physical Barrier to Settlement in the Western Cross Timbers Frontier," *West Texas Historical Association Year Book,* XLII, 51–58; Mrs. William L. Cazneau (Cora Montgomery), *Eagle Pass or Life on the Border* (Austin, 1966); Alwyn Barr, *Black Texans: A History of Negroes in Texas, 1528–1971* (Austin, 1973).

Of the large body of material dealing with the frontier and the Indians, the following are among the most useful: R. N. Richardson, *The Comanche Barrier;* W. P. Webb, *The Texas Rangers;* C. C. Rister, *The Southwestern Frontier* (Cleveland, 1928); D. H. Winfrey, *Texas Indian Papers, 1846–1859* (Austin, 1960); E. Wallace and E. A. Hoebel, *The Comanches;* W. C. Holden, "Frontier Defense, 1846–1860," *West Texas Historical Association Year Book,* VI, 35–64; Kenneth S. Neighbours, "Indian Exodus out of Texas in 1859," *ibid.,* XXXVI, 80–97; A. B. Bender, "The Texas Frontier," *Southwestern Historical Quarterly,* XXXVIII, 135–148; M. L. Crimmins (ed.), "Colonel J. K. F. Mansfield's Report on the Inspection of the Department of Texas in 1856," *ibid.,*

LXII, 122–148, 215–257, 351–387; "W. G. Freeman's Report on the Eighth Military Department," *ibid.*, LII, 227–233; Lena Clara Koch, "The Federal Indian Policy in Texas, 1845–1860," *ibid.*, XXXVIII, 223–234, 259–286; XXIX, 19–35, 98–127; W. J. Hughes, " 'Rip' Ford's Indian Fight on the Canadian," *Panhandle-Plains Historical Review,* XXX, 1–26; J. K. Greer (ed.), *A Texas Ranger and Frontiersman: The Days of Buck Barry in Texas, 1845–1906* (Dallas, 1932); T. R. Havins, *Beyond the Cimarron: Major Earl Van Dorn in Comanche Land* (Brownwood, Tex., 1968); Kenneth F. Neighbours, *Robert Simpson Neighbors and the Texas Frontier* (Waco, Tex., 1975); Kenneth Neighbours, *Indian Exodus: Texas Indian Affairs* (Quanah, Tex., 1973); E. H. Elam, "The History of the Wichita Indian Confederacy to 1868"; Roger N. Conger and others, *Frontier Forts of Texas* (Waco, Tex., 1966).

Chapter Nine

# PIONEER
# INSTITUTIONS

By 1861 when the scourge of war ended all progress, the pattern of Texan civilization had been formed, and the state's cultural institutions had been established. In many respects they were like those of the Old South, whence a majority of the population had come, but there were many variations and a few distinct differences. Texas, in fact, belonged to both the Old South and the New West. Basic to the state's economy were the slaves and cotton of the South, but, whereas in the old states the frontier was a thing of the past, in Texas it still affected all the people either directly or indirectly. Typical of the frontier, men outnumbered women, and in contrast to the Old South, the number of immigrants from Mexico and Europe was comparatively high.

Although most Texans were small subsistence farmers, owning few or no slaves, plantation owners and townspeople contributed more to the ideals and cultural institutions of the time. Of particular concern was the improvement of the primitive frontier-transportation system. Otherwise, Texans worried about epidemics and disease and amused themselves in rather conventional fashion. Although they acquired a reputation for lawlessness, they also made more positive and longer-lasting achievements in such areas as education, literature and the arts, and religion.

## THE PEOPLE

Although the customs and values of the Old South dominated pioneer institutions in some areas of the state, the broad and diverse culture of antebellum Texas reflected the influence of people from many other parts of the world. Most made their homes on farms, but in 1860 foreigners constituted more than a third of the free population in five of the six largest towns. Whether on farms or in the cities, Europeans, Mexicans, and blacks all made their contributions.

German immigrants concentrated their numbers in the hill country of Central Texas, where they built strong, rugged homes often made of stone, but by 1860 one-fifth of the population of Houston, Galveston, and San Antonio were Germans. The townspeople were usually merchants or craftsmen, but some were known nationally for their achievements in science, medicine, and the arts. Immigrants from Poland, the Scandinavian nations, and other Western European countries added to the cultural mixture.

By 1860 the second largest group of foreign-born people living in Texas were the Mexican-Americans. The years following the revolution were often filled with bitter experiences for the Mexican people of Texas. Even though many had served in the revolutionary cause and some were notable leaders, prejudice and discrimination often characterized their treatment. Land titles were sometimes challenged. Most of the Mexican people who had lived around Nacogdoches for generations left their homes, and many who lived in South Texas lost their holdings.

Few returned to East Texas, but the Mexicans resumed their migration to South Texas in large numbers in the 1850s. Most lived off the land on farms and ranches, but some were attracted to the towns. Regardless of where they lived, most held proudly and with determination to the more essential parts of their cultural heritage—their religion, their language, their customs and tradition. Most were poor and lived simply in humble homes, but some were prominent and influential public figures. Santos Benavides, a mayor of Laredo, rose to the rank of general in the Civil War; José Navarro, a hero of the revolution, participated in the writing of the Constitution of 1845 and thereafter served in the Texas legislature.

Although most of the black people who made up one-third of the population of Texas in 1860 were slaves, some were free. Free blacks lived in Texas under Spanish rule with apparently some semblance of legal equality. More came under Mexican rule, and some won their freedom for their service in the revolution. In 1850 the census numbered 397 free blacks, but in 1860 the number decreased to 355. No doubt, the restrictions placed on free blacks in Texas discouraged growth in their numbers. In the republic, free blacks could not vote or own property. After statehood additional restrictions were imposed, especially with respect to punishments assessed for the conviction of crimes.

Most free blacks were farmers or farm laborers and were quite poor, but a few were relatively well-to-do landowners, either with or without special legislative sanction. The most famous of them was William Goyens of Nacogdoches, although the Ashworth family of Jefferson County may have been more wealthy. Both owned slaves, as did two other black families.


## OCCUPATIONS

Occupations of antebellium Texans included both the ordinary and the unusual. Merchants increased rapidly during the fifties, numbering 2,223 by 1860, while 3,541 persons found employment as domestic servants. Four Texans described themselves as "catchers of wild horses," a conventional occupation of the times. Less expected were four toymen, six daguerreotypists, three actors, forty-five artists, five clockmakers, and six dancing masters.

The professions were represented surprisingly well. In 1850 the town of Marshall, serving a wide area but with a relatively small population of 1,189, had 28 lawyers and 11 doctors. Certainly, there was no shortage of lawyers; the 428 located in Texas in 1850 doubled in number by 1860. Physicians, though often poorly trained, were likewise plentiful, their number increasing to 1,471 by 1860. But at the same time Texas had only 65 dentists, most of whom traveled from town to town to carry out their practice. There were 758 clergymen but, as one might expect in a frontier society, only 8 architects.

Manufacturing and the crafts provided a living for some. The census of 1860 reported 3,449 persons employed in 983 manufacturing establishments. More than 400 worked in grist and saw mills, and an equal number of wheelwrights suggests the manufacture of wagons, carriages, and other vehicles. A plant in Houston manufactured hats; a factory in Harrison County produced textiles. In the crafts the 1,361 carpenters of 1850 doubled in number by 1860, and there were many brick and stone masons, blacksmiths, and saddle and harness makers.

By far the most common occupation was farming. In 1850 approximately 25,000 of the 43,000 persons who listed occupations called themselves farmers, and no doubt many others were similarly engaged. Farmers and farm laborers accounted for more than half of the 105,491 occupations of 1860. Appropriately, improved land in farms increased from 639,111 acres in 1850 to 2,650,781 acres ten years later, and during the same period the value of farms increased more than fivefold, reaching a total of about $88 million.

For the marketplace, the most important crop was cotton. Except for occasional years when pests ravaged the crops, the output increased each year. It reached 58,072 bales in 1849–1850 and 431,463 a decade

Early settlers of Comanche County in west central Texas: a representative group of sturdy ranchers, farmers, and an occasional lawyer, doctor, or preacher who probably migrated from counties in eastern Texas or directly from Tennessee, Alabama, Arkansas, or Louisiana during the period between 1854 (the year of the first settlement) and 1880. (E. C. Barker History Center, University of Texas)

later. During the period of the republic, cotton farming had been confined to the river valleys of the Coastal Plain and to eastern Texas from the upper Neches River northward, where there was limited production. By 1860 these regions still produced the greater part of the crop, but cotton farming was being extended into Central Texas, even though the notion still prevailed that it was a bottomland crop not suited to the black prairies.

Although cotton was the money crop, in early Texas corn was indispensable. To a very large extent it sustained both the people and their animals. Reports claimed that an average yield in early years was 40 to 80 bushels to the acre and that as much as 110 bushels had been grown without the application of manure.

Other food crops included sweet potatoes, wheat, and sugar cane. Next to corn in importance were sweet potatoes, grown not only by the small subsistence farmer but also on the large plantations. Less abundant was wheat, not grown at all in southern Texas and a secondary crop elsewhere. During the period of low prices for cotton that followed the Panic of 1837, the planters near the coast turned to raising sugar cane. The industry grew until 1852, but because of occasional droughts and freezes it declined thereafter.

During this period there was some organized effort to improve farming. Agriculture societies were formed as early as 1843, but apparently their efforts were not long sustained. The first exposition known actually to have been held was the Corpus Christi fair of 1852. At Dallas in 1858 the first recorded state fair in Texas was held. Formally chartered in 1886, it has become one of the leading annual exhibitions of the nation. Thomas Affleck, long active in the improvement of agriculture in the South, in 1858 established Glenblythe near Brenham as a model for Texas plantations.

Efforts to improve livestock breeds began at an early date. Purebred livestock was introduced during the Mexican regime; English-bred hogs, sheep, horses, and cattle were imported in 1840. In a land of horses, many were highly bred, some of racing stock. One stallion in the fifties was valued at $6,000. But cattle accounted for most of the value of Texas livestock, placed at $42,825,447 in 1860.

## SLAVERY AND THE PLANTATION SYSTEM

In antebellum Texas, slavery and cotton cultivation expanded together; the largest cotton-producing counties contained the largest slave population. Slaveholders, only about one-third of the state's farmers, produced 90 percent of the cotton crop.

Estimated at 5,000 in 1836, the slave population increased at an accelerated pace after Texas became independent. The census of 1860 showed 182,566 slaves and 430,891 white persons. Since 1850 the slave population had increased 214 percent and the white population only 180 percent.

Slaves represented a substantial proportion of Texas capital. In 1850 the average value of a slave assessed for taxes was $362, while in 1860 this amount reached $672; the aggregate value of all slaves was about 20 percent greater than the value of the farms of Texas. On the market, field hands brought from $1,200 to $2,000 and "plow boys" from $1,000 to $1,500. Good hands could be hired out at from $200 to $300 for the year. Some enthusiasts contended that a good field hand who produced eight bales of cotton could pay for himself in a year.

Rapidly expanding agriculture created a demand for slaves that was never satisfied. Apparently most of the slaves were brought in by immigrants, and most sales were private transactions involving neighbors only. Yet dealers in Galveston and Houston kept on hand slaves of all ages and held regular auctions; in most communities there were sale or auction days. During the late 1850s there was considerable demand for the reopening of the African slave trade, a move supported by a number of prominent Texans and even by some church groups. The illicit African slave trade, meanwhile, brought in hundreds, perhaps thousands, through Galveston and other coastal points. Free blacks were sometimes enslaved, either through kidnapping or legal subterfuge.

Slave quarters on the plantation generally consisted of a one-room or a two-room cabin for each family, located along a street or around an empty square and near the overseer's house. The food of the slaves was much like that of the poorer whites; bacon and corn bread were the basis of the diet. Some, however, raised gardens and kept poultry. On the best plantations food was served from a common kitchen, especially during the planting and harvesting season. Clothing generally consisted of two suits each year, seldom made of homespun for the planter considered ready-made articles more economical. Medical attention in most cases was perhaps as good as that available to sick white people. Often slaves were not forced to work on Saturday afternoon and Sunday, and sometimes they were permitted to earn spending money of their own.

In Texas as elsewhere, those in bondage longed for freedom. Slaves frequently ran away. Some returned voluntarily, but others were arrested and returned, while still others made their way to Mexico or to Indian Territory. It is estimated that more than four thousand escaped to Mexico. During the decade preceding the Civil War, there was growing uneasiness about slavery. Vigilance committees became common, and the punishment of slaves charged with disobedience became more severe.

Although most slaves worked on plantations, urban slavery expanded as Texas towns grew. By 1860 Houston and San Antonio each contained more than one thousand slaves, and smaller towns numbered slaves in the hundreds. Many of the urban slaves were household servants, but others worked in flour mills, sawmills, or other factories, while some were carpenters, blacksmiths, or skilled in other crafts.

Those who profited most from slavery, the planters, made up a small minority of the population. In 1860 there were 21,878 slaveowners in Texas, only 5.7 percent of all slaveowners in the nation. Only 2,163 of these owned 20 or more slaves, and only 54 owned 100 or more. More than half of all the slaveholders owned 5 or fewer. Only about 10 percent of the slaveholders and less than 5 percent of all farmers operated on a scale large enough to necessitate hiring an overseer, thereby coming within the planter class.

The influence of the planters was, however, far out of proportion to their number. Nearly all were leaders in their communities, and many exercised statewide influence. More than any other group they stamped upon early Texas society its distinguishing characteristics.

A study of those planters with more than a hundred slaves revealed wide variations in wealth but several relatively consistent characteristics. Property holdings of forty-seven great planters ranged from $60,000 to more than $600,000, cotton production from less than 250 bales to more than 800, and livestock holdings from $1,400 to more than $53,000. Although all but three were cotton planters, their agricultural practices were surprisingly diversified. Practically all owned cattle and hogs, about half of the group raised sheep, every planter grew corn, more than three-fourths grew sweet potatoes, and a somewhat smaller proportion planted other food crops. The Texas plantation was far from self-sufficient, but it was likewise far from complete dependency on outside sources for many staple products.

The wealthier planters lived better than any other people of their day. They had food in great abundance and variety, and elaborate meals were frequently assembled from garden, woods, and stream, with hot breads, cakes, jellies, preserves, and rare delicacies from New Orleans. As they acquired more property, the planters replaced their log cabins with larger and better constructed buildings of cedar, walnut, or pine, and occasionally of brick. Many of these houses were built during the decade preceding the Civil War. Later generations have sought to imitate their sturdiness, simple lines, and ample proportions. Tastes varied from time to time, but a desire for luxuries remained constant. In 1831, cottonades and candle molds were in especial demand; sideboards, tables, and jewelry were bought in quantity during the forties and fifties; and in 1848 one merchant apparently had difficulty in filling an order for a "Bathing Tub and Pea Fowl Brush."

## LIFE ON THE FARMS

For most rural Texans the plantation system was something only to be observed and perhaps envied. For them their existence depended upon their own labor, their houses were simple, and their luxuries were few.

The houses built by country people were only slightly better than those of colonial times. Here and there was to be found a frame dwelling well designed and carefully built, but the prevailing type in the middle of the century was still the log cabin. The double log cabin, or dog-run house, was the most popular. It consisted of two rooms under a continuous, gabled roof, separated by an open space or dog run. Commonly, a porch extended across the entire front. In addition to serving as a sleeping place for the dogs (and for overflow guests) and providing a space for family and friends to sit in during warm weather, the dog run and the porch served as catchalls for saddles, bridles, harnesses, chests, boxes, guns, and a dozen other things. The logs were hand hewn and dovetailed at the corners. As the family grew, a lean-to might be added to the back of one or both rooms. Also a kitchen and perhaps a smokehouse might be built, but they were separate from the main house. Spaces between the logs were chinked with boards and daubed with clay or mortar. The roofs were of clapboards held securely in place by weight poles. Chimneys commonly were made of sticks, covered with mud. Floors, if any, were puncheon. While traveling in eastern Texas in 1855, Frederick Law Olmsted stopped for the night at a comparatively comfortable house, but he could "look out, as usual, at the stars between the logs." Traveler Rutherford B. Hayes, the future president of the United States, described a house he saw in Texas whose walls you "could throw a cat through at random." Olmsted frequently made note of houses having glass windows, but he mentions them in such a way as to indicate that they were the exception rather than the rule. The Germans built better houses than the Anglo-Americans, frequently using stone in their construction. There was much building during the sixth decade of the century, and houses made of lumber became more common. Often such houses were flimsy, boxlike affairs, not as good as the sturdy log cabins they displaced.

For a country that might have produced fruits, vegetables, cereals, and honey in bountiful quantities, and where cattle were abundant, the diet of most early Texans was strangely monotonous. Even by 1860 many farm families lived as the earliest Texans did, almost wholly on salt pork, corn bread, and syrup. The most common vegetable was the sweet potato. Many people tasted fresh meat only occasionally and a large percentage of them did not have milk and butter. Except in the northern counties, wheat bread was almost unknown in the poorer homes. Water was obtained from a nearby spring or stream or occasionally from a well or cistern.

The farm was substantially, though not totally, self-sufficient. Candles or lard-burning lamps supplied light. Ash hoppers and pork fat supplied materials for soap; corn was ground in steel hand mills; and cotton was carded, spun, and woven into cloth. Within less than five years one Texan recorded in his diary that he made a wheel, a coffin, a reel, a churn, a cradle, a bucket, a pump auger, an ox yoke, and a pair of shoes, in addition to working at the loom, hewing puncheons, and graining deerskins. Isaac Van Zandt, a man of distinction, made in emergencies a saddle, a pair of shoes, candles, and a baby's cradle. Toward the end of the period, however, imported manufactured cloth and ready-made clothing were rapidly supplanting homemade materials.

## THE TOWNS

> A person coming into Texas, direct from the Northern States might, perhaps, be surprised upon seeing many places called towns in Texas. He would, probably, as has been frequently the case, inquire, "where is the town?"

Thus did Melinda Rankin, a missionary from New England, comment on Texas municipalities in 1850. In truth, the state had no towns to spare. Galveston, with 4,177 inhabitants, was the largest. San Antonio, Houston, New Braunfels, and Marshall followed in the order named. No other towns had populations of as many as a thousand. Austin, long buffeted by hostile Indians and the threat of Mexican invasion, was the home of only 639 persons. Through trade with Mexico and growth as an army center, San Antonio had forged ahead by 1860 and showed a total of 8,236 persons. Galveston came second, Houston third, and Austin fourth. Sixteen other towns, making twenty in all, are shown in the eighth census to have had a population of 1,000 or more each.

Civic improvement came but slowly. Observers found Houston streets filled with "bottomless" mud and San Antonio streets almost impassable in bad weather. In 1857, however, Galveston paved its most traveled street with shells, and San Antonio spent twelve hundred dollars on street improvements and also built some bridges. About the same time San Antonio organized a "fire association" and in 1860 installed gas lights.

The best buildings in a town generally were the hotels. Dr. Ferdinand Roemer found the hotel in Houston "a rather pretentious two-story building," but the interior was so neglected as to remind him that he had reached the "borders of civilization." Service was poor and one was expected to occupy a room with several strangers. The pride of San Antonio was the Menger Hotel on Alamo Plaza, which was opened in 1859. The building of fine-cut stone, two and one-half stories high, together with its carpets, decorations, and beautiful furniture cost $16,000. Only wealthy people and professional travelers patronized hotels; the rank and file put up at the wagon yards.

By 1860 one could purchase in the larger Texas towns almost any article to be had in the stores and warehouses in the East. Advertisements indicate that merchants kept in stock all kinds of farm machinery, carriages, wagons, building supplies, furniture, kitchen supplies, many kinds of cloth and clothing, jewelry, gold and silver plate, a large assortment of processed foods, ice, quantities of drugs and cosmetics, and liquors; indeed, an almost endless list of items. There were jobbers and wholesalers in Texas, but many merchants made their purchases in New Orleans or in other cities.

The Texas capitol building, in Austin, 1853 until destroyed by fire in November 1881. (Southwest Collection, Texas Tech University)

The scarcity of money and lack of banking facilities constituted a handicap for business during the period of the republic and early statehood, just as it had in colonial times. This condition was aggravated by the provision in the Constitution of 1845 prohibiting the chartering of banks. Although various firms carried out certain banking functions, only one bank was incorporated in Texas before the Civil War. This was the Bank of Commerce and Agriculture, opened in Galveston by McKinney and Williams in 1847, under an old charter of the state of Coahuila and Texas.

During the early years of the republic quantities of depreciated bank notes from the United States circulated in Texas, and the paper money issued by the Texan government was even less dependable. Promissory notes were sometimes used as money, with the most common hard money consisting of hammered Spanish dollars (old Spanish dollars with the royal effigy defaced) and Mexican dollars. Later the quality of bank notes brought in from the East improved.

## TRANSPORTATION

"No one walks in Texas if the distance is more than a mile," said Dr. Ferdinand Roemer, who visited the country in 1846. Nevertheless,

Texans found inadequate transportation facilities in the vast land to be one of their more difficult problems, one that for a long time retarded development in the state. Travelers and merchants depended on coastal and river traffic, roads, stage lines, and freight contractors. Railroad construction began in the fifties.

Invaluable for foreign and interstate traffic were the coastal outlets. The most serviceable ports were Galveston and Matagorda. Houston did considerable business through Buffalo Bayou, and Indianola, founded by Prince Carl of Solms-Braunfels in 1844, near the present Port Lavaca, came to be the principal port of West Texas. It was destroyed by a storm in 1875, rebuilt, and destroyed again in 1886.

Some areas relied on the rivers. The Brazos was navigable as far as Brazoria, and occasionally boats went even higher up the river. Red River was navigable to Shreveport and under favorable conditions to Pecan Point and Jonesborough. Through Big Cypress Bayou, Caddo Lake, the Red River, and the Mississippi, Jefferson had water connection with New Orleans. In seasons of abundant rain small boats ascended the Sabine to Sabinetown near San Augustine; the lower Trinity would carry boats of shallow draft; and some cotton was shipped down the San Jacinto. Buffalo Bayou afforded good navigation to Houston. Because of a raft that closed its channel near the Gulf, the Colorado was useless for navigation.

The great majority of Texans depended on such roads as existed. The chief roads, or routes of travel that were called roads, were the old military road, from Red River through Dallas, Waco, and Austin; the old San Antonio–Nacogdoches Road, passing through Bastrop and Crockett; the road from Indianola to San Antonio; and a road from Dallas and vicinity southward to Houston. The roads, which were bad even under favorable conditions, became impassable quagmires in wet weather. Olmsted, who entered Texas from the east, pronounced the road in Leon County "little better than a cowtrack." He described the road from Victoria to Lavaca as "a mere collection of straggling wagon ruts, extending for more than a quarter of a mile in width, from outside to outside, it being desirable in this part of the country, rather to avoid the road than follow it." Yet, all roads were not so nearly impassable. Rutherford B. Hayes, in the winter of 1848–1849, recorded in his diary, "Rode 14 miles on good dry roads on the banks of the Brazos [near Columbia]."

Freight contractors and stage lines provided public transportation. Using strong, heavy wagons of *bois d'arc*, "shaped like boats," with iron axles, wheels five and a half feet high, and tires six inches wide, freighters hauled loads averaging seven thousand pounds. These huge wagons, pulled by teams of ten to twenty mules or horses or from twenty to thirty oxen, sometimes moved in long trains, occasionally mixed with the smaller carts generally used by Mexican freighters. Freight rates varied with the weather and season, averaging about one cent per mile for each one hundred pounds but more in bad weather.

Of the many vehicles used for public conveyances, the stage coach was the most popular. The quality of the coaches, at least on certain lines, was greatly improved during the fifties. Described as large, airy, and strong in contrast with the "ordinary hacks" used in the eastern states, they carried as many as nine passengers in the inside and a few on the outside. On the San Antonio–San Diego and the Southern Overland Mail Lines, the famous Concord coaches were used. Travel was nevertheless uncomfortable, sometimes dangerous, and usually expensive. Mud, high water, cold weather, Indian attacks, and robberies combined at times to make travel hazardous. The usual charge for a passenger was ten cents a mile, but some contractors doubled the charges in wet weather.

Interstate stage traffic was fast and dependable. In August 1857 a semimonthly mail and passenger service was opened between San Antonio and San Diego, California. The scheduled thirty-day trip cost two hundred dollars; during the first year there was not a single failure to complete the journey. Still better service was that inaugurated in 1858 by the Southern Overland or Butterfield Mail Lines, which skirted the settlements of North Texas on its route from St. Louis and Memphis on the east to San Francisco on the west. Stages ran each way twice weekly and completed the journey of about 2,700 miles in twenty-five days or less.

Federal mail subsidies were largely responsible for the long stage lines. Mail contracts supplied the large expenditures necessary for stage stands, coaches, road repairs, and labor. Mail service otherwise was substantially improved by 1861, though it did not even approximate present-day standards. Wet mail and late mail were common causes of complaint, and post offices were scarce. Not until 1850, for instance, did San Antonio have one.

During the fifties the railroads began both to compete with and to feed the stage and freight lines. Late in 1852 construction on the first railroad line in Texas was begun in Harrisburg, nine miles south of Houston. It was the Buffalo Bayou, Brazos, and Colorado, commonly called the Harrisburg Railroad and now a part of the great Southern Pacific system. By 1855 it had been extended thirty-two miles, from Harrisburg on Buffalo Bayou to Richmond on the Brazos, and five years later it was built into Alleyton near the Colorado. Several other lines were built in the Houston area, and by 1860 there were railroads linking Victoria to Port Lavaca and Shreveport to Marshall. With a combination of rail and steamship service, passengers could travel between New Orleans and Galveston in twenty-two and a half hours.

With all its inconveniences, railroad travel was far superior to travel by other conveyances. Reflecting the contrast of the old and the new, the Harrisburg Railroad advertised in 1860 "The River Bottom and Wet Prairies are NOW BRIDGED, and what was (and is now on some routes) a journey of days is now performed in the same number of hours." Charges were five cents per mile for passengers and about one cent per mile for each hundred pounds of freight.

## HEALTH

Early-day Texans claimed that their state was the most healthful in America; yet it seems to have been a good place for doctors.

From time to time epidemics took a heavy toll. In the spring of 1833 cholera took eighty lives at Brazoria and nearly depopulated Velasco. The dreaded scourge returned in 1834, ravaging Nacogdoches and taking ninety-one lives in Goliad. Later cholera epidemics in 1849, 1850, and 1852 particularly endangered the slave population. In 1846 an epidemic, which may have been typhus, killed scores of people in New Braunfels and Fredericksburg, and also many German immigrants in Indianola on their way to the settlements. Yellow fever appeared from time to time and, next to cholera, was the most dreaded disease. The people suffered from many ailments, chills and fever, inflammation of the eyes, summer complaints, rheumatism, biliousness, measles, whooping cough, and smallpox.

Although intelligent persons did associate cholera with filth, claims for nostrums and cures were even more extravagant than in our own day, and stores were filled with patent medicines ranging from cancer cures to cough remedies. One merchant said he believed the people used quinine in the same way they used corn meal. They bought it and took it whether they were sick or not. Warning of an impending cholera epidemic, the San Antonio board of health in 1834 prescribed a cleanup campaign and also recommended a copper amulet to be hung around the neck. Another prescription (almost 100 percent effective, it was claimed!) consisted of water from the boiled peyote cactus, a little lime, and a few drops of laudanum. Later "cures" were little, if any, more specific than those of earlier years. Brandy, cayenne pepper, and mustard were favorite remedies.

There was, however, some progress in medical science. Although it did not hold a second meeting for sixteen years, the state medical association was organized in 1853, with Dr. Ashbel Smith and Dr. J. W. Throckmorton among its more prominent members. In 1854 the distinguished surgeon Dr. Ferdinand Charles von Herff of San Antonio performed a major operation using chloroform.

## AMUSEMENTS

The people of Texas brought to their new homes the traditional amusements of the Anglo-American frontier. Athletic contests in which trained teams participated were almost unknown, but there were house raisings, log rollings, shooting matches, bear hunts, wolf hunts, quilting bees, and a dozen other activities in which work, sport, and play were mixed. Dancing was popular in the country and in town, but the most active church people objected to it. Traveler Rutherford B. Hayes described a dance which began at two o'clock in the afternoon and lasted until half-past four the next morning. Men and women came on horseback ten or fifteen miles through mud and rain. Hayes found "fewer wallflowers and more life than is usually found in our gatherings."

Balls and formal dinners frequently were given in honor of some distinguished visitor or on some other special occasion. Apparently everybody joined in the patriotic celebrations on July 4, March 2, and April 21. Barbecues, patriotic songs, processions, and fervid oratory were the favorite forms of entertainment. Organizations, such as the Sunday School Union or the Sons of Temperance, sponsored and directed the programs on these occasions. Christmas and New Year's were times for dances, torchlight processions, and other amusements. Thanksgiving was celebrated at various dates, according to the proclamation of the president of the United States. The most popular sport, both among rustics and townmen, was horse racing. Every community had its racetrack. The track at Velasco was famous in Texas and well known in New Orleans.

Interest in cultural entertainment was creditable. Most towns had amateur theatrical organizations. As early as 1838 San Augustine had its "Thespian Corps." The distinguished lawyer, W. B. Ochiltree, was a member, and John Salmon Ford, famous as an editor, soldier, and statesman, wrote a play for it. Houston and Galveston each had an active lyceum during the fifties. San Antonio, with its large German population, was a center for artists. The German Casino Association owned a fine building there that was used for theatrical performances, concerts, lectures, exhibits, and dramatic readings. In almost every community, literary societies sponsored debates on ponderous subjects; there were many lectures, both pay and free, and vocal and band concerts. Professional troupes gave performances in all the larger towns. A complete program consisted of a song, a dance, a farce, and a drama. Some of the farces were "Limerick Boy," "The Irish Tiger," and "The Widow's Victim." Among the dramas were "Cross of Gold," "The Maiden's Vow," and "William Tell."

## CRIME, VICE, AND REFORM

Early Texas society, like that of our own day, presented to observers many facets. It was clean and wholesome, base and immoral, or at some level between these two extremes, depending on the point of view of the person describing it.

At an early date Texas acquired a reputation for crime and lawlessness, a reputation not altogether undeserved. The high standards required of citizens by the *empresarios* were not maintained in later years, and many renegades drifted in. The *Houston Telegraph* of January 19, 1842, lists several homicides, and the editor states that they are so frequent as to "foster opprobium upon the national character." Dueling continued, although the provision against it in the Constitution of 1845 reduced the practice. More frequent was the informal duel, where enemies simply "shot it out" at first meeting.

As late as the republic, the criminal code was harsh, and several offenses might be punished by death. One rather notorious woman was sentenced to death for forgery, but President Lamar pardoned her. Whipping and branding were not infrequent. There was no penitentiary until 1849. Jails were small and crowded, and jail breaks were common. Law enforcement was lax, a condition that explains why vigilance committees occasionally used direct methods. In 1852 such an organization hanged twelve or fifteen persons in the vicinity of San Antonio, and it was claimed that its work was highly effective in reducing crime.

More common were lesser vices. Gambling was quite prevalent. Gamblers were held in low esteem, but public disapproval apparently was not strong enough to stop their operations. In 1842 the Harris County grand jury brought seventy-seven indictments for "playing at cards." The number found by grand juries after 1848 was decidedly smaller, but the decline probably was due more to greater laxity on the part of the officers than to any change in the habits of the people. Betting on horse races was very common, and occasionally men of some means lost all their property in a single day at the tracks. Drinking was widespread and drunkenness common. In some communities, at least, it was customary for candidates to set before voters an open barrel of whiskey. "Profaneness, gaming, and intemperance are prevailing vices against which we have to contend," wrote Martin Ruter, the Methodist missionary of Texas, in 1838.

Beyond a doubt, the temperance movement, which entered from the East shortly after annexation and enlisted the services of prominent churchmen, brought some change. The Sons of Temperance, a national organization opposing the use of alcohol, was organized in Texas in 1848 and in a little more than a year claimed three thousand members. During the following year it was stated that a majority of the members of the legislature belonged to it. Sam Houston, whose excessive drinking had often been a matter of public comment, had mended his ways and now worked in behalf of the organization. In 1851 a traveler found local organizations of the Sons in nearly every town and in many rural communities.

Meanwhile, there was some legislation on the subject of alcoholic drink. The republic had found it a troublesome subject and enacted laws requiring the licensing of dealers and a bond guaranteeing that they would keep orderly, reputable houses and prevent gambling and quarreling on their premises. A law in 1854 went much further. It permitted the electors of a county, by majority vote, to forbid the licensing of the sale of liquor in quantities of less than a quart, a provision aimed at the saloon. The champions of temperance were not satisfied with such a measure and, in a large convention in Huntsville, advocated a "thorough Maine Liquor Law." Of the forty-one counties in which the subject was submitted to the voters, restriction of sale was adopted in thirty-five. The law was declared unconstitutional, however, and never went into effect.

## EDUCATION

By 1850 there was a strong sentiment for a public school system. People generally were taking a greater interest in education; the agitation of the slavery question was producing an acute sectionalism; and proud Texans were loath to send their children to schools in the North. Even if the parent had to pay tuition, the state, they thought, should contribute funds to make the schools better. In a preceding chapter it was stated that in 1854 the legislature set aside $2 million in United States indemnity bonds for schools. The law provided for dividing the counties into school districts, but two years later this method of organization was abolished. Thereafter, any group of people might set up a school, employ a teacher, and draw from the state fund each child's money. The share of each child was pitifully small: only sixty-two cents in 1854 and a dollar and a half in the following year. Under the terms of the law it was not even necessary that the people of a community organize and start a public school in order to receive state funds. A parent might select a private school, pay his or her children's tuition, and at the end of the year receive from the county treasurer the amount of state funds to which he or she was entitled. In fact, this was done in most cases, with the result that only a few public schools were established.

The most important institutions of learning in Texas before the Civil War were not a part of the public school system. Some were private, wholly under the control of one or two men; others were community enterprises, and some were under the control of lodges or religious denominations. The Constitution of 1836 did not prohibit private or denominational schools from receiving public aid, and several of these early schools were given land grants by the republic. There was no classification and no uniformity of standards. Although with two or three exceptions, their work was confined to elementary and secondary levels; they were called, indiscriminately, institutes, academies, colleges, and universities.

The churches regarded Christian education as an important church function, and they began to establish schools at a very early date. Martin Ruter, the Methodist missionary, had not been in Texas six months when he wrote: "My labor in Texas will be devoted to forming societies and circuits, establishing schools, and making arrangements for a college or university." Schools not under church control generally maintained religious environments. Most of the teachers were preachers. For instance, of the fourteen Presbyterian ministers who came to Texas as missionaries during the republic, nine engaged in teaching. As late as 1866, of the teachers who attended the Texas teachers' state convention, eighteen were ministers and seventeen laymen.

The first Protestant denominational school was Rutersville College (named for Martin Ruter), which was established by the Methodists near La Grange. Its preparatory and female departments were opened in January 1840 and its collegiate department for young men in 1841. It was chartered by the republic and endowed with four leagues of land. For a few years the community was the leading school center in Texas, but in about 1850 the school began to decline rapidly. The University of San Augustine opened in 1842 with a grammar school, a female department, and a college and was widely known for a few years. Associated with it, in 1845 and for some time thereafter, as president of the board of trustees and lecturer in law was Oran M. Roberts, a young lawyer and farmer and a recent graduate of the University of Alabama. Perhaps the most prosperous and best-known school in its day was McKenzie College, founded near Clarksville in 1841. Like others of that day, the school simply grew up around a great teacher, in this case, J. W. P. McKenzie. For a period it had as many as three hundred boarding students.

Baylor University, a Baptist school, chartered in Independence by the republic in 1845, attained a position of leadership at an early date. It granted sixteen degrees in 1858 and twenty-two in 1859, more in each year than all other schools in Texas combined. Waco University was founded in 1861. The two schools were consolidated as Baylor University and were located in Waco in 1886. The female department of Baylor University became Baylor Female College in 1866 and was moved to Belton in 1886.

From annexation to the beginning of the Civil War, the legislature granted charters to 117 schools and incorporated, in addition, 9 educational associations. There were 40 academies, 30 colleges, 27 institutes, 7 universities, 5 schools, 3 high schools, 2 seminaries, 1 collegiate institute, 1 orphan asylum, and 1 medical college. Of these, only 3 have survived with anything like a continuous history: Austin College, founded in 1849 in Huntsville through the influence of Dr. Daniel Baker and moved to Sherman in 1879, Ursuline Academy of San Antonio, and Ursuline Academy of Galveston.

Through their emphasis on discipline, as well as on the knowledge they dispensed, these old schools were great civilizing agencies. "Course of study full, instruction thorough and discipline strict," ran a typical advertisement of the fifties. "A strict discipline rigidly enforced," stated another. The curricula emphasized ancient and modern languages and philosophy. San Augustine University, however, required laboratory work in science and maintained a chemical laboratory and mineralogical cabinet. Even the simplest subjects were described in awe-inspiring terms. Surely, parents would be impressed and children terrified on reading that in the city schools of Houston in 1841 were being taught "English, French, Spanish, and Latin, grammatically and etymologically, on the most approved and expeditious principles." Apparently, some of the teachers taught everything they had studied, and some, like the Reverend Marcus A. Montrose, graduate of Edinburgh, had had liberal training. At San Augustine University he taught mathematics, Latin, Greek, history, navigation, astronomy, rhetoric, logic, political economy, natural philosophy, chemistry, botany, and geology. In fact, for a period, he alone made up the faculty of the university, although he must have been assisted by some of the more advanced students.

Evidently a large majority of early-day Texas youths received their training either in their homes or in "old field schools," unknown beyond the confines of a single community. In spite of the handicaps that confronted teacher and pupil, such training must have been efficient. In 1850 a little less than 6 percent of the white men of Texas and 8 percent of the white women were illiterate. By 1860, illiteracy had decreased to

Founded by Colonel R. T. P. Allen, the Bastrop Military Institute was incorporated in 1858 by a board of trustees elected by the Methodist Episcopal Church. The school offered preparatory and collegiate courses of study to such students as Joseph D. Sayers and Sam Houston, Jr. After being closed during the Civil War, Bastrop became the Texas Military Institute in 1868. (Texas Highway Department)

less than 4 percent among the men and slightly more than 5 percent among the women.

Unlike most southern states, Texas did not have a law prohibiting the education of slaves. Few, however, were educated, and at the end of the Civil War, more than 95 percent were illiterate.

Newspapers in surprising numbers served the people of antebellum Texas. By 1840 no less than thirteen newspapers were being published, one or two of which were semiweeklies. The federal census of 1860 reports three daily, three triweekly, and sixty-five weekly newspapers, and three monthly publications. The circulation of the weekly papers was 90,615, a number sufficiently large to have reached practically every person in the state.

The most venerable publication was the *Telegraph,* revived in Columbia after the Texan Revolution and moved to Houston in 1837. A neighbor of the *Telegraph,* the *Daily News* of Galveston, started in 1842 as a "puny four-page sheet . . . born in a one-room, unpainted shack on the Strand" but lived to become the oldest business institution in Texas. Both the *Dallas News* and the *Galveston News* of our own day trace their lineage to this paper. The *State Gazette* of Austin, established in 1849, was edited from 1853 to 1861 by John Marshall, a Calhoun Democrat, associated for a part of the time with William S. Oldham. Marshall and Oldham were brilliant, aggressive men, and their paper was noted for its opposition to Sam Houston. Beginning in 1842 Charles DeMorse, soldier, statesman, and editor, published in Clarksville the *Northern Standard.* Its files, unbroken until 1861 and renewed in 1865, constitute the richest source of information extant on early civilization in northeast Texas. Robert W. Laughery's *Texas Republican* in Marshall was well edited and influential. Worthy also were the *Weekly Herald* in Dallas and the *Chronicle* in Nacogdoches.

The newspapers of early Texas do not meet the standards of our own day. Apparently little or no use was made of such news-gathering agencies as the Associated Press, which was organized in 1848. Also, not until the late fifties was there sufficient telegraph mileage to distribute the news well. News from the outside generally came through New Orleans. Many social activities were ignored. It was not deemed good taste to print the names of ladies in newspapers, except under very unusual conditions. Yet, more clearly and fully than any other source, these papers describe for us the way of life of that era. They were, furthermore, replete with political news and sharp editorial comment on public affairs, and the people who read them were well informed on important current issues.

Texans who wanted to read beyond the offerings of newspapers could turn to other writings. Travel accounts were popular. Mary Austin Holley, a cousin of Stephen F. Austin, wrote down in vivid style her impressions of the new land. Her second work, more complete than the first, was published in 1836 as *Texas*. Matilda C. F. Houston, an English woman who visited about 1843, wrote *Texas and the Gulf of Mexico,* an informative account of the Galveston-Houston region. In 1849 a German scientist, Dr. Ferdinand Roemer, published *Texas,* a perceptive description of the frontier as it was at that time. A few years later came Frederick Law Olmsted, a landscape artist and engineer with broad interests. His *Journey through Texas* described the state as he saw it through critical eyes.

Other writers turned to history. George Wilkins Kendall, founder and associate editor of the New Orleans *Picayune,* who accompanied the Texan Santa Fé expedition of 1841, recorded in his history of the journey experiences that represented practically every element of adventure and peril that could have befallen people on the Southwestern frontier. William Kennedy, an Englishman, published his *Texas* in 1841. Fourteen years later, Henderson Yoakum brought forth *A History of Texas,* a truly remarkable study which received wide circulation.

Fiction, with adventure as a major theme, attracted the interest of a few authors. Possibly the most successful was the Irishman, Mayne Reid, who wrote *Headless Horseman,* a tale based on a southwest Texas legend. In poetry Mirabeau B. Lamar's "Daughter of Mendoza" was popular, as was James Lytle's "Ranger's Song" and Reuben Potter's "Hymn of the Alamo."

Apparently, the number of books and magazines increased rapidly during the fifties. The bookstore of Francis D. Allen of Galveston, for instance, advertised books: "Standard, Classical, Scientific, Mechanical, School, Historical Law, Medical, Theological, Agricultural, Poetical, Biographical, Voyages, Novels, etc." One item especially mentioned was Henderson Yoakum's *History of Texas,* which had come off the press a few years before. Richardson and Company sold ten thousand copies of the *Texas Almanac* for 1857, increased the output of the 1858 issue, and published thirty thousand copies of the 1859 issue, featuring such items as a biographical sketch of General Rusk and an account of the Texan Revolution. In the census returns for 1850, twelve libraries were listed; the returns for 1860 showed 132. Magazines that were read extensively were *Harper's, Blackwood's Edinburgh Review, Westminster Review, London Quarterly,* and *Godey's Lady's Book.*

Artists who recorded the scenes and people of antebellum Texas numbered literally in the dozens. José Sanchez, a Mexican army officer who visited Texas in 1828, did sketches of some of its scenes and people. James Strange painted creditable portraits of the captives Santa Anna and Juan Almonte. Some of the Germans who located in Texas in the 1850s were artists of truly superior talent. Among these were Herman Lungkwitz and Richard Petri. Lungkwitz was known more for his landscape scenes, Petri for his Indians. Carl G. von Iwonski did portraits and groups of people. In San Antonio, Lousia Heuser Wueste was another popular artist who specialized in portraits.

A contemporary of the German artists, Frenchman Theodore Gentilz of Castro's colony, painted the Indian peoples. Another French artist, Eugenie Lavender, won acclaim at the French court before she came to Texas in 1851. Best known of her work was "Saint Patrick," in the cathedral in Corpus Christi.

## RELIGION

Of all the forces affecting early Texas society, none had a greater influence than the churches. As previously stated, itinerant Protestant preachers began their work during the colonial period. It was not until after Texas had its independence, however, that a well-organized missionary program was launched. Methodists and Baptists were in the van; Presbyterians were not so numerous, but their influence was great, and other denominations were active.

When news of the defeat of Santa Anna reached the general conference of the Methodist Episcopal Church in session in Cincinnati, Ohio, in May 1836, church leaders were quick to realize that it meant the opening of a mission field rich with opportunities. Martin Ruter, already distinguished by years of service in the church, volunteered as a missionary to Texas, then and there. Eighteen months later he crossed the Sabine at Gaines' Ferry and entered Texas. Two other Methodist missionaries had preceded him by a few days; the three worked feverishly, building churches, forming circuits, and organizing classes. In 1840, the Texas Conference was organized with 1,878 members and 25 local preachers. With 30,661 members and 244 traveling preachers, the Methodist church in 1860 was, by far, the strongest in Texas.

Since Baptists recognized the authority of the local congregation as superior to that of any other body in church matters, it was easy for them to establish churches under frontier conditions. There were preachers and deacons among the immigrants, and they frequently organized churches without the aid of a visiting missionary. The sect encountered difficulties, however, because of the presence of two factions, missionary and antimissionary. The first antimissionary church in Texas was the Pilgrim church, brought intact in 1834 by immigrants from Illinois under Daniel Parker. The first missionary Baptist church was organized in Washington early in 1837, and at once it sent an appeal to organized Baptists in the United States to send missionaries. "Dear brethren, we ask you again," said the fervent Texans, "come over into Macedonia and help us!'' People in the East read the appeal, and responded. Churches and associations were organized rapidly, and a state convention was formed in 1848. By 1860 there were approximately 500 Baptist churches in Texas. The denomination had 280 church buildings, as compared with 410 for the Methodists. Baptists, however, led all denominations in number of church publications.

Presbyterian mission work was begun in 1837 under the especial patronage of the Synod of Mississippi. Joining the earlier missionaries, in 1840 came Daniel Baker, whose name looms large in the annals of Texas. Already, Presbyterian churches had been established near Independence, and in Houston, Austin, and Galveston. In 1857 the Presbyterians had 2,261 members in Texas and by 1860 had seventy-two church buildings.

Other churches were active. The Episcopal church sent R. M. Chapman of New York as a missionary to Texas in 1838, and by 1860 there were nineteen Episcopal church houses in Texas. The Christian church grew rapidly during the decade before the Civil War. In 1850 it owned only five buildings; ten years later it had thirty-nine. The Catholics maintained churches in Nacogdoches, San Augustine, and probably in other Texas communities continuously from colonial times. A Catholic church was established in Houston shortly after the Texas Revolution, and by 1860 there were thirty-three Catholic church buildings in the state.

The church people brought with them to Texas practices that had been developed in the United States and tried for a century—protracted meetings, basket meetings, and camp meetings. Sermons were usually long and fervent. The ladies gave suppers, ''refreshment parties,'' ''fairs,'' and bazaars to raise money for the church. The Protestant leaders advocated a strict observance of Sunday but evidently did not succeed in bringing it about. Melinda Rankin complained that the day was ignored by many people, and in Crockett, Olmsted found all the stores open on Sunday and was told that it was the merchants' best day.

Sunday schools, which apparently were maintained by the more active churches of all Protestant denominations, constituted powerful agencies for biblical and moral training as well as for enlarging the intellectual horizons of the people. The best Sunday schools had libraries. The union school in Brownsville had one thousand volumes and another in Austin had thirteen hundred. It was stated that wherever a Sunday school was established, it generally was followed by Bible classes, temperance societies, and educational interests, and that it served as a ''focus where all good influences have converged.''

In the society of early days the churches were the greatest civilizing agencies. They brought the people together, clean and in their best apparel. At church the men exchanged greetings and talked on subjects ranging from the weather and crops to the political issues of the day. Here chatted farmers' wives and daughters, tired of drudgery and starved for companionship. The churches, moreover, set the moral standards for many of the people. They attacked immorality of every type; their leaders praised or condemned almost all conduct and every institution. It cannot be said that they always had their way on moral issues, but even the most reckless individual dared not ignore them.

The effectiveness of the early churches must be credited in large measure to the quality of their leaders, worthy and courageous men with a selfless devotion to duty. Some were educated, representing the highest culture of their day: Martin Ruter, who committed his church to the cause of education in Texas; Daniel Baker, founder of Austin College; and James Huckins, who wrote his sermons in a beautiful, forceful style. The majority had little schooling; they were men of the people who brought spiritual comfort to the most destitute places. One of these, Noah Byars, the gunsmith in Washington on the Brazos who became a preacher, organized in all sixty churches.

Closely associated with the churches and next to them the most influential social agencies were the lodges. Freemasonry had barely been planted before the Texas Revolution uprooted it. With typical Anglo-American resilience the Masons reestablished their order within less than a year. The order was supported by many distinguished Texans, including Anson Jones and Sam Houston. By 1860, 252 lodges had been organized, one for practically every community, and the order numbered nearly ten thousand members. Children of poor Masons were provided assistance for attending school, and the lodge maintained or sponsored a score or more schools. The Independent Order of Odd Fellows was introduced into Texas from Louisiana in 1838, chiefly through the efforts of Jacob De Cordova, publisher and land agent. It grew slowly at first, but there was rapid expansion in the fifties, and by 1860 there were 74 active lodges and more than three thousand members. A noteworthy service for that age was the protection it offered members in the form of sick benefits and benefits for the orphans of deceased members.

## SELECTED BIBLIOGRAPHY

Much has been written about Texan pioneers. Good general references are J. D. De Cordova, *Texas: Her Resources and Public Men;* the *Texas Almanac* (Galveston) from 1857 through 1862; C. C. Rister, *Southern Plainsmen* (Norman, Okla., 1938); W. Gard, *Rawhide Texas* (Norman, Okla., 1965); L. B. Friend, "The Texas of 1860," *Southwestern Histor-*

*ical Quarterly,* LXII, 1–17; Earl Fornell, *The Galveston Era* (Austin, 1961); and R. N. Richardson, *The Frontier of Northwest Texas, 1846–1876.*

For contemporary accounts, see Marilyn McAdams Sibley, *Travelers in Texas, 1761–1860* (Austin, 1967); and "Bishop Morris in Texas, 1841–1842," *East Texas Historical Journal,* III, 149–168. Gilbert J. Jordan, "W. Steinerts' View of Texas in 1849," *Southwestern Historical Quarterly,* LXXX, 57–78, 177–200, 283–301, 399–416; LXXXI, 45–72; Levi Lamoni Wight, *The Reminiscences and Civil War Letters of Levi Lamoni Wight: Life in a Mormon Splinter Colony on the Texas Frontier* (Davis Bitton, ed., Salt Lake City, 1970); Adolphus Sterne, *Hurrah for Texas! The Diary of Adolphus Sterne, 1838–1851* (Archie P. McDonald, ed., Waco, Tex., 1969); A. F. Muir (ed.), *Texas in 1837: An Anonymous Contemporary Narrative;* Mary Austin Holley, *The Texas Diary, 1835–1838* (J. P. Bryan, ed., Austin, 1967); R. S. Lee, *Mary Austin Holley: A Biography* (Austin, 1962); Frederick L. Olmsted, *A Journey through Texas* (1857; James Howard, ed., Austin, 1962); F. R. Lubbock, *Six Decades in Texas;* Charles Michael Gruener, "Rutherford B. Hayes' Horseback Ride through Texas," *Southwestern Historical Quarterly,* LXVIII, 352–360; and Melinda Rankin, *Texas in 1850* (Boston, 1950).

Some studies of life and institutions are W. R. Hogan, *The Texas Republic;* and his "Pamelia Mann, Texas Frontierswoman," *Southwest Review,* XX, 360–370; Kent Keeth, "Sankt Antonius: Germans in the Alamo City in the 1850's," *Southwestern Historical Quarterly,* LXXVI, 183–202; Susan Jackson, "Movin' on: Mobility through Houston in the 1850's," *Southwestern Historical Quarterly,* LXXXI, 251–282; Jane Dysart, "Mexican Women in San Antonio, 1830–1860: The Assimilation Process," *The Western Historical Quarterly,* VII, 365–373; J. B. Frantz, *Gail Borden;* W. P. Webb, "Christmas and New Year in Texas," *Southwestern Historical Quarterly,* XLIV, 357–379; J. W. Schmitz, *Texas Culture in the Days of the Republic, 1836–1846* (San Antonio, 1960); Dorothy Kendall Bracken and Maurine Whorton Redway, *Early Texas Homes* (Dallas, 1956); Kenneth W. Wheeler, *To Wear a City's Crown: The Beginnings of Urban Growth in Texas, 1836–1865* (Cambridge, Mass., 1968); Roy B. Broussard, *San Antonio during the Texas Republic: A City in Transition* (El Paso, Tex., 1968); Caroline Remy, "Hispanic-Mexican San Antonio, 1836–1861," *Southwestern Historical Quarterly,* LXXI, 564–570; A. F. Muir, "Intellectual Climate of Houston during the Period of the Republic," *ibid.,* LXII, 312–321; William Seale, *Texas Riverman* (Austin, 1966); and D. H. Winfrey, *Julian S. Devereux and Monte Verdi Plantation* (Waco, Tex., 1962).

Scholarly analysis of population characteristics may be found in three articles by R. A. Wooster: "Notes on Texas' Largest Slaveholders, 1860," *Southwestern Historical Quarterly,* LXV, 72–79; "Foreigners in the Principal Towns of Ante-Bellum Texas," *ibid.*, LXVI, 208–220; and "Wealthy Texans, 1860," *ibid.*, LXI, 163–180. See also Randolph B. Campbell and Richard G. Lowe, *Wealth and Power in Antebellum Texas* (College Station, Tex., 1977); "Slave Property and the Distribution of Wealth in Texas, 1860," *Journal of American History,* LXIII, 316–324; and "Wealthholding and Political Power in Antebellum Texas," *Southwestern Historical Quarterly,* LXXIX, 21–30.

For economic developments, see Robert L. Jones, "The First Iron Furnace in Texas," *Southwestern Historical Quarterly,* LXIII, 279–289; Charles H. Dillon, "The Arrival of the Telegraph in Texas," *ibid.,* LXIV, 200–211; and Randolph Campbell and Richard Lowe, "Some Economic Aspects of Antebellum Texas Agriculture," *Southwestern Historical Quarterly*, LXXXII, 351–378. William Seale emphasizes architecture in "San Augustine, In the Texas Republic," *Southwestern Historical Quarterly,* LXXII, 347–358. A. L. Carlson tells the history of Texas banking in the *Texas Monthly,* IV, 481–499, 615–641; V, 74–102. See also Mary Rena Green, *Sam Maverick, Texan, 1803–1870* (San Antonio, 1952). Transportation in early Texas has received considerable study. See Ralph Moody, *Stagecoach West* (New York, 1967) for a general treatment; also J. W. Williams, "The Butterfield Overland Mail Road across Texas," *Southwestern Historical Quarterly,* LXI, 1–19; and Emmie Giddings Mahon and Chester V. Kielman, "George H. Giddings and the San Antonio–San Diego Mail Line," *Southwestern Historical Quarterly,* XLI, 220–239. River travel is examined in Pamela Puryear and Nath Winfield, Jr., *Sandbars and Sternwheelers: Steam Navigation on the Brazos* (College Station, Tex., 1976). For railroads, good studies are C. S. Potts, *Railroad Transportation in Texas* (University of Texas Bulletin, no. 119; Austin, 1909); and S. G. Reed, *A History of Texas Railroads* (Houston, 1941). See also P. Briscoe, "The First Texas Railroad," *Quarterly of the Texas State Historical Association,* VII, 279–285; A. F. Muir, "Railroads Come to Houston, 1857–1861," *Southwestern Historical Quarterly,* LXIV; 42–63, and his "The Destiny of Buffalo Bayou," *ibid.,* LXVII, 19–22; and Eugene O. Porter, "Railroad Enterprise in the Republic of Texas," *ibid.,* LIX, 363–371.

On slavery and plantations, see Abigail Curlee, "The History of a Texas Slave Plantation, 1831–1863," *Southwestern Historical Quarterly,* XXVI, 79–127; and "A Glimpse of Life on Antebellum Slave Plantations in Texas," *Southwestern Historical Quarterly,* LXXVI, 361–383. General studies relating to slavery include Alwyn Barr, *Black Texans: A History of Negroes in Texas, 1528–1971* (Austin, 1973); Billy D. Ledbetter, "White over Black: Racial Attitudes in the Ante-Bellum Period," *Phylon,* XXXIV, 406–418; Karl E. Ashburn, "Slavery and Cotton Production in Texas," *Southwestern Social Science Quarterly,* XIV, 257–271; and E. Fornell, "Agitation in Texas for Reopening the Slave Trade," *ibid.,* LX,

245–259. For studies of a more limited area, see Randolph Campbell, "Human Property: The Negro Slave in Harrison County, 1850–1860," *Southwestern Historical Quarterly,* LXXVI, 384–396; and "Slaveholdings in Harrison County, 1850–1860: A Statistical Profile," *East Texas Historical Journal,* XI, 18–27. M. L. Dillon ably presents the activities of an early abolitionist in Texas in *Benjamin Lundy and the Struggle for Negro Freedom.* Later effects of the slavery issue are discussed in Wesley Norton, "The Methodist Episcopal Church and the Civil Disturbances in North Texas in 1859 and 1860," *Southwestern Historical Quarterly,* LXVIII, 317–341. Legal aspects are considered in A. E. Keier Nash, "The Texas Supreme Court and Trial Rights of Blacks, 1845–1860," *Journal of American History,* LVIII, 623–642. Also see Ronnie C. Tyler (ed.), *The Slave Narratives of Texas* (Austin, 1974).

Pioneer medicine is dealt with in George Plunkett Red, *The Medicine Man in Texas* (Houston, 1930); J. V. Haggard, "Epidemic Cholera in Texas, 1833–1834," *Southwestern Historical Quarterly,* XL, 216–230; P. I. Nixon, *A Century of Medicine in San Antonio* (San Antonio, 1936), *The Medical Story of Early Texas* (San Antonio, 1953), and *A History of the Texas Medical Association, 1853–1953* (Austin, 1954). See also Ashbel Smith, *Yellow Fever in Galveston* (Austin, 1951); B. M. Jones, *Health Seekers in the Southwest, 1817–1900* (Norman, Okla., 1967); and Paul J. Scheips, "Albert James Myer, an Army Doctor in Texas, 1854–1857," *Southwestern Historical Quarterly,* LXXXII, 1–24.

The best history of education in Texas remains F. Eby, *The Development of Education in Texas;* but see also C. E. Evans, *The Story of Texas Schools* (Austin, 1955); Mrs. Jonnie L. Wallis (ed.), *Sixty Years on the Brazos* (Los Angeles, 1930), an account of a schoolboy in old Washington; William M. Baker, *The Life and Labours of the Reverend Daniel Baker* (Philadelphia, 1859); F. B. Baillio, *A History of the Texas Press Association* (Dallas, 1916); Murl L. Webb, "Religious and Educational Efforts among Texas Indians in the 1850's," *Southwestern Historical Quarterly,* LXIX, 22–37; H. B. Carroll, *Masonic Influence on Education in the Republic of Texas* (Waco, Tex., 1960); James David Carter, *Masonry in Texas: Background, History, and Influence to 1846* (Waco, Tex., 1958); John C. English, "Wesleyan College of San Augustine," *East Texas Historical Journal,* III, 141–148; and James A. Tinsley, "Genesis of Higher Education in Texas," *Proceedings of the Philosophical Society of Texas* (1968). A glimpse of early schools may be had in Emily Jones Shelton, "Lizzie E. Johnson: A Cattle Queen of Texas," *Southwestern Historical Quarterly,* L, 349–366. See also Jefferson Davis Bragg, "Baylor University, 1851–1861," *ibid.,* XLIX, 37–65; and "Waco University," *ibid.,* LI, 213–224.

For studies on the arts see Pauline A. Pinckney, *Texas Artists of the Nineteenth Century* (Austin, 1967); William W. Newcomb, Jr., *German Artist on the Texas Frontier: Friedrich Richard Petri* (Austin, 1978); and "German Artist on the Pedernales," *Southwestern Historical Quarterly*, LXXXII, 149–172.

On religion and the churches, see C. E. Castaneda, as listed in Chapter 2; and *The Historical Magazine of the Protestant Episcopal Church*, September, 1941; Macum Phelan, *A History of Early Methodism in Texas, 1817–1866* (Nashville, 1924); W. S. Red, *A History of the Presbyterian Church in Texas* (Austin, 1936); J. M. Carroll, *A History of Texas Baptists* (Dallas, 1923); L. R. Elliott (ed.), *Centennial Story of Texas Baptists* (Dallas, 1936); Mary Angela Fitzmorris, *Four Decades of Catholicism in Texas, 1820–1860* (Washington, D.C., 1926); G. L. Crocket, *Two Centuries in East Texas;* Stephen Daniel Eckstein, *History of the Churches of Christ in Texas, 1824–1950* (Austin, 1963); George H. Paschal, Jr. and Judith A. Benner, *A Hundred Years of Challenge and Change: A History of the Synod of Texas of the United Presbyterian Church in the U.S.A.* (San Antonio, 1968); R. Douglas Brackenridge, *Voice in the Wilderness: A History of the Cumberland Presbyterian Church in Texas* (San Antonio, 1968); and Carter E. Boren, *Religion on the Texas Frontier* (San Antonio, 1968).

# Chapter Ten

# SECESSION AND WAR
# 1860–1865

Ninety percent of the white immigrants to Texas had come from the Old South, bringing with them pronounced opinions on their institutions and rights. Thus, as the rancorous controversy over slavery divided the nation into well-defined camps, it was natural that the state should join the proslavery group.

Other issues demanded attention, however, and it was not until 1857 that the electorate became aligned in conservative and radical or Unionist and state rights groups. In that year the state rights faction gained control of the Democratic party. The Whig party was no more; gone also was the Know-Nothing organization which had been basically Unionist in spite of its zeal for state rights. Henceforth the friends of the Union had no organization. Houston's defeat by Runnels in 1857 may be attributed in part to that fact. During the next two years the regular Democrats became more aggressive and gravitated toward the position of the extreme proslavery group east of the Mississippi. The legislature authorized the governor to send delegates to a Southern convention if it should be deemed expedient. John Marshall, chairman of the state Democratic committee, kept up a barrage of editorials in the *State Gazette* advocating the reopening of the African slave trade. The party convention of 1859 refused to endorse a proposal so extreme, but it did favor the acquisition of Cuba "as a measure which self-protection imperatively demands"; it applauded the decision of the Supreme Court in the *Dred Scott* case, holding that Congress could not legislate slavery out of the territories; and it nominated Runnels for reelection.

Against this organization, Houston, running as an independent on a platform endorsing the Constitution and promising allegiance to the Union, threw into the contest all the strength of his personal popularity and skill as a campaigner. Ex-Governor Pease supported him, as also did J. W. Throckmorton, B. H. Epperson, and other old-time Whigs. Touring the state in a buggy, wearing an old linen duster, on hot days sometimes appearing without a shirt, the old warrior made a mighty appeal to the people. In this his last political battle, he defeated Runnels by nearly 9,000 votes, 35,257 to 27,500. By a much narrower margin, Edward Clark, running with Houston as an independent, managed to defeat Lubbock for lieutenant governor. No doubt various factors affected the results of the election. Houston's personal popularity weighed heavily, as did also the dissatisfaction of the people on the frontier who charged Runnels with neglecting to protect them. The conclusion seems inescapable, nevertheless, that the state rights leaders had moved too rapidly for the majority of the voters.

Events thereafter strengthened the hands of the extreme pro-Southern faction. John Brown's raid on Harper's Ferry in October 1859 antagonized and alarmed the people and may have accounted in part for the choice by the legislature of Louis T. Wigfall to represent Texas in the Senate. At the Democratic state convention at Galveston in early April 1860 the state rights leaders, having gained complete control, abandoned restraint. Texas as a sovereign state had the right, they stated, "to withdraw from the confederacy, and resume her place among the powers of the earth as a sovereign and independent nation." The platform deplored "the unnatural efforts of a sectional party at the North to carry on an 'irrepressible conflict' against the institution of slavery" and implied that the election of a Republican president would bring about a dissolution of the Union. This body sent to the national Democratic convention in April in Charleston H. R. Runnels, Francis R. Lubbock, Guy M. Bryan, R. B. Hubbard, and Tom Ochiltree, all staunch champions of the slaveholder's cause. At that convention, when Stephen A. Douglas and the Northern Democrats insisted on a platform endorsing the theory of popular sovereignty in the territories and denouncing the *Dred Scott* decision, the delegates from Texas and seven other Southern states withdrew. The Charleston convention, after thirty-four ballots without nominating a presidential candidate, adjourned to meet in Baltimore on June 18. In Baltimore, the Northern Democrats nominated Douglas for president and Herschel V. Johnson for vice-president. The Southern Democrats then met in Richmond, chose as their candidates John C. Breckinridge of Kentucky and Joseph Lane, and adopted a platform that supported the *Dred Scott* decision. At its national convention, which met in Chicago on May 18, the Republican party adopted a resolution that slavery could not legally exist in a territory and selected Abraham Lincoln and Hannibal Hamlin as its nominees.

Since none of these tickets was to their liking, a group of pro-Union Southerners, including some of the large slaveholders, organized the Constitutional Unionist party, dedicated to the principle that secession would be ruinous to the South and that its only hope lay in fighting for its rights in the Union, and held a convention in Baltimore. On the first ballot Sam Houston received 57 votes as against 68.5 for John Bell of Tennessee. Bell was nominated on the second ballot, and Edward Everett was chosen as his running mate. Houston permitted his name to go before the country as "the People's candidate," but on August 18 he withdrew formally.

During the eventful year of 1860 public excitement in Texas reached the stage of hysteria. Severe fires, of incendiary origin it was alleged, broke out in Dallas, Denton, Waxahachie, Kaufman, and various other points in North Texas. The fires were charged to abolitionists and linked with stories of slave uprisings, poisonings, and assassinations—generally greatly exaggerated if not wholly unfounded. Vigilance committees sprang into action. In Dallas three blacks were hanged in the presence of a large crowd; three white men, presumably abolitionists, were hanged in Fort Worth because they had been "tampering" with slaves. By 1860 a growing spirit of intolerance pervaded the entire state.

A secret order known as the Knights of the Golden Circle was introduced into Texas in 1860 and soon had established a number of local lodges or "castles." The plans of the organization seem to have been to make slavery more secure in the South, particularly by incorporating into the Union additional slave states from Mexican territory. Two poorly organized filibuster movements against Mexico in 1860 never got beyond the borders of Texas. The Knights did, however, supply organized forces that took an active part in the secession movement.

While in the grip of this psychosis, the people were obliged to make a fateful decision at the polls. The Lincoln-Hamlin ticket was not placed on the ballot, and the Douglas-Johnson candidates received only 410 votes; 15,463 Texans voted for Bell and 47,548 for Breckinridge. The pro-Southern faction had won an overwhelming victory in the state and had suffered a humiliating defeat in the nation.

## SECESSION

Lincoln's election drew the issue sharply. The Unionists had no organization but among them were able men: Sam Houston, David G. Burnet,

E. M. Pease, J. W. Throckmorton, John and George Hancock, E. J. Davis, and A. J. Hamilton. The burden of their argument was that the election of Lincoln, although unfortunate, did not warrant secession and that the South could better protect its interests in the Union than out of it. Houston wrote: "Mr. Lincoln has been constitutionally elected, and, much as I deprecate his success, no alternative is left me but to yield to the Constitution."

But each day the conservatives lost ground, and the radicals grew stronger. The party soon to be in power had been born in opposition to the extension of slavery, and its leader, now the president-elect, had said publicly that slavery must ultimately be abolished. Southern leaders had given warning that Lincoln's election would mean the dissolution of the Union; to yield at this late date would, they thought, constitute a surrender of their rights. Some of their utterances showed a lack of restraint, but they were effective in the crisis. The editor of the Navarro *Express* wrote: "The North has gone overwhelmingly for Negro *Equality* and Southern Vassalage! Southern men, will you submit to the degradation?"

Various petitions, editorials, and letters were directed at Governor Houston, urging him to convene the legislature or call a convention. These steps he refused to take, being determined to make no move that would give aid and comfort to the secessionists. The radicals took matters into their own hands and proceeded with haste and determination. In Austin on December 3, a group of leaders, including George M. Flournoy, O. M. Roberts of the supreme court, Guy M. Bryan, W. S. Oldham, and John Marshall, drew up an address to the people of Texas calling on the voters of each representative district to select, at an election to be held on January 8, two delegates to a state convention. Similar resolutions were adopted in several other meetings throughout the state. The elections were held, and the convention met as called on January 28, 1861. Meanwhile, on December 17 Houston had issued a call for the legislature to convene on January 21, 1861, in a special session. The legislature ignored Houston's claim that the recent election was illegal and authorized the convention to act for the people, subject only to the condition that the question of secession be submitted to the voters.

The convention lost no time in dealing with nonessentials. With O. M. Roberts as president, it approved on the second day, by a vote of 152 to 6, a resolution stating: "It is the deliberate sense of this Convention that the State of Texas should separately secede from the Federal Union." A committee on Federal relations then drew up an ordinance of secession which declared that the ordinance of 1845 by which Texas had accepted annexation "is hereby repealed and annulled." The proposed

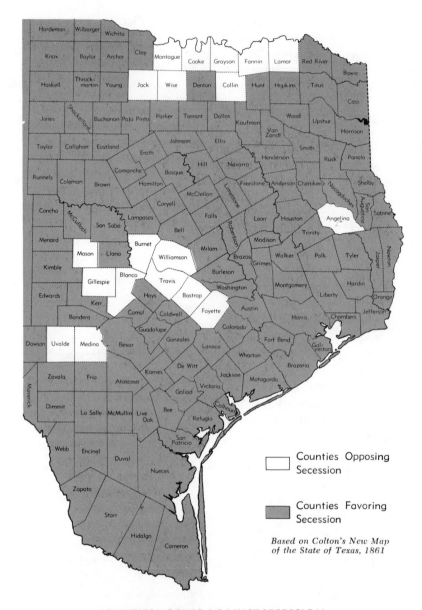

Counties Opposing Secession

Counties Favoring Secession

*Based on Colton's New Map of the State of Texas, 1861*

**COUNTIES VOTING AGAINST SECESSION**

From Ernest Wallace, *Texas in Turmoil* (Austin, 1965), p. 70. Reprinted with the permission and assistance of Steck-Vaughn Company, publisher.

ordinance was to be submitted to the voters on February 23 and, unless rejected by a majority of the votes cast, was to take effect on March 2, exactly twenty-five years after independence had been declared. The vote on the ordinance was taken at noon on February 1 in the presence of packed galleries. The scene had its dramatic incident. As the roll of delegates was called, only very infrequently was the response "No." Among those who voted thus was J. W. Throckmorton who, while voting, violated the no-discussion rule. A hiss and applause followed, to which he made the memorable retort: "Mr. President, when the rabble hiss well may patriots tremble." The final vote was 166 to 8.

On the following day the convention drew up a "declaration of causes." It alleged that (1) the general government had administered the common territory of the Union in such a way as to exclude the Southern people from it; (2) because of the disloyalty of the people of the North and the "imbecility" of their government, incendiarism and outlawry were rampant in Kansas; (3) the United States had failed to protect Texas against Indian and Mexican bandits and had refused to reimburse it for expenditures made in defending itself; (4) the people of the North had become hostile to the Southern states and "their beneficent and patriarchal system of African slavery, preaching the debasing doctrine of the equality of all men, irrespective of race or color"; (5) the slaveholding states were now in a minority, unable to protect themselves against the fanatics of the North who preach a "higher law" than the Constitution; and finally, (6) the extremists of the North had elected as president and vice-president "two men whose chief claims to such high positions are their approval of these long continued wrongs, and their pledges to continue them to the final consummation of these schemes for the ruin of the slave-holding states."

In South Carolina and the old Gulf states the separating movement had attained even greater momentum than it had in Texas. In Charleston on December 20, 1860, a special state convention had formally dissolved the union between South Carolina and the federal government. Soon Mississippi, Florida, Alabama, Georgia, and Louisiana followed; representatives of these commonwealths were about to form a government in Montgomery, Alabama. Technically, Texas could not act until the voters had spoken at the polls. Before it adjourned on February 5, the convention, nevertheless, sent seven delegates "in order that the views and interests of the people of Texas may be consulted with reference to the Constitution and provisional government that may be established by said convention."

The Texas convention adjourned to meet again on March 2, after the election. It projected itself during the interim by leaving in session a powerful select group called the Committee on Public Safety. The legislature adjourned also, to convene again on March 18.

In the brief period between adjournment and the election many of the delegates took part in the campaign on the ordinance of secession. Judge Roberts issued an appeal to the voters to support secession, and twenty thousand copies of the "Declaration of Causes" were distributed. In the cause of secession, state rights journals of long standing, such as the *Telegraph* (Houston), the *Galveston News, State Gazette* (Austin), and *Texas Republican* (Marshall) were soon joined by more conservative papers such as the *Dallas Herald.* The thin line of Unionists made a noble fight. Twenty-four opponents of secession, from the convention and the legislature, issued an address to the people of Texas urging that they oppose secession, at least until further efforts to reach a compromise. The speakers against secession, including Houston, Throckmorton, John Hancock, and others, had the editorial support of several newspapers, including the *Southern Intelligencer* (Austin), the *Bastrop Advertiser,* the La Grange *True Issue,* and the *Weekly Alamo Express.*

The secessionists amassed a vote of 46,129; their opponents, 14,697. Ten counties in the vicinity of Austin showed antisecession majorities, a fact to be attributed to the large German population, to several Unionist newspapers, and to the efforts of such leaders as Sam Houston, A. J. Hamilton, and John Hancock. Throckmorton and a few associates managed to carry eight counties in northern Texas, where there was a large immigrant population from the northern and border states. With only a few exceptions, the heavy slaveholding counties yielded huge majorities for secession.

By their vote on February 23, the electors approved secession; they had taken no action on joining the Confederate States of America. In the minds of most people, however, the two steps seem to have been inseparably linked. The convention reassembled on March 2. Three days later it "approved, ratified, and accepted" the provisional government of the Confederate States of America by a vote of 109 to 2 and directed the Texas delegates in Montgomery to apply for admission to that government. The application was not necessary; already the Confederate Congress has passed an act to admit Texas.

The stride of the secessionists was too rapid for Governor Houston. Thus far he had followed them reluctantly; but when the convention called on him, along with other state officers, to take the oath of allegiance to the Confederacy, he insisted that it had no authority and defied it. Thereupon, the convention on March 16, 1861, declared the office of governor vacant and made Lieutenant Governor Edward Clark governor. President Lincoln offered to aid Houston if he would oppose the convention with force, but the governor, unwilling to bring on civil war, rejected the proposal. The convention ratified the constitution of the Confederacy on March 23 and three days later adjourned *sine die*.

While the convention was directing the course of secession, it did not neglect the state's interest in respect to military affairs. Distributed along the frontier at twenty-one widely separated posts were about 2,700 Federal troops under the command of Major General D. E. Twiggs, with headquarters in San Antonio. Twiggs, a Georgian in sympathy with the South and, in anticipation of the crisis, asked his superiors for instructions, but no orders were given him. Then, he submitted his resignation, but before he turned his command over to his successor, Colonel C. A. Waite, he was confronted with a critical situation. The Committee on Public Safety, acting under authority of the secession convention, boldly demanded that he surrender to its representatives all public arms and munitions of war under his command. When Ben McCulloch, military commander representing the convention, led an armed force into San Antonio, Twiggs and the commissioners came to terms. It was agreed that the Federal troops, 160 in number, should evacuate San Antonio and surrender to representatives of the committee all federal property, that the troops should retain their side arms, camp and garrison equipage, and the facilities of transportation, all to be delivered upon their arrival at the coast. On February 18 Twiggs agreed to the evacuation of all other forts in Texas under similar terms. Henry E. McCulloch received for the Texans the surrender of the northern posts, and John S. Ford took over the posts in the southern part of the state. Thus did the convention by a series of bold strokes and without the firing of a shot put out of action more than 10 percent of the regular army of the United States and acquire military supplies and other property valued at $3 million. In Texas, secession was off to a good start.

After the firing on Fort Sumter, April 12, 1861, and President Lincoln's call for volunteers to suppress the insurrection, both the Texan and Confederate authorities took the position that they were no longer bound by the terms of evacuation made in February. The Federal troops who were still in Texas at the time were held as prisoners of war until paroled or exchanged.

## AT THE BATTLEFRONTS

Texas was a border state in the Confederacy, exposed to attack from the north, west, and south. In May 1861, the immediate threat of invasion from the north was removed when W. C. Young, a former sheriff and a resident of Cooke County, led a volunteer regiment of Texas cavalry across the Red River and took Forts Arbuckle, Cobb, and Washita without firing a shot, thereby making an invasion from the north unlikely.

The problem of protection from the Indian raids that had troubled Texas for a century and a half was never adequately solved by the state and Confederate governments. A Texas regiment under John S. Ford was taken over by the Confederate government and assigned the task of guarding the Rio Grande frontier from Fort Brown, near the Gulf Coast, to Fort Bliss, near the site of El Paso. During 1861, however, companies of minutemen bore the brunt of Indian warfare. Early in 1862 they were replaced by the Frontier Regiment, a state organization under James M. Norris. Norris established a chain of sixteen posts along the frontier from the Red River to the Rio Grande and a regular patrol along the line. The Frontier Regiment was reorganized in 1863, with J. E. McCord as commander. Since the patrols had not been successful, McCord replaced them with scouting expeditions in hope of surprising the Indians. In December 1863 the frontier defense system was again changed. The Frontier Regiment was transferred to Confederate service; a part of it, under the command of Colonel James Bourland, was assigned to defend the frontier along the Red River, and the remainder was sent to the Houston area. To offset the loss, the men in the frontier counties were enrolled in companies, and at least one-fourth were to be in the field at all times. Early in 1864 a total of 4,264 men were enrolled in these militia companies. Bourland's troops gave some aid, but most of the burden for frontier defense fell on the state troops. In the northern district, where the situation was the most critical, Governor Pendleton Murrah commissioned James W. Throckmorton as brigadier general and placed him in command.

Afterward, for the duration of the war, there was only one destructive raid in Texas. In October 1864 about 200 Comanches and Kiowas attacked "Fort Murrah" and the Elm Creek settlement, both near Fort Belknap in Young County, killing 16 persons and capturing 7 others. Because the troops and militia were unable to provide protection, groups of people along the frontier moved into stockades, "forting up" they called it. About 125 people northeast of present-day Albany joined together at "Fort Davis," one of the largest such places. Ironically, a shameful blunder by the Texans resulted in the bloodiest battle with the Indians during the Civil War. In January 1864, at Dove Creek, a few miles south of the present San Angelo, 370 state troops attacked about 1,400 friendly Kickapoos who were migrating from Indian Territory to Mexico and were repulsed with heavy losses. During the last two years of the war, deserters added to the threat of hostile Indians by creating confusion on the frontier.

The most aggressive campaign in which Texans participated was that into New Mexico. John R. Baylor, commander of a detachment of Texas troops, after having occupied the federal posts between Brownsville and El Paso, marched into New Mexico and on August 1, 1861, issued a proclamation establishing the territory of Arizona, which was to comprise that part of New Mexico lying south of the thirty-fourth parallel. Later, with Baylor as governor, a constitutional government was established, and for a short while Confederate troops occupied the country as far west as Tucson. Simultaneously, General H. H. Sibley, with three regiments of Texans, sought to drive the Federals out of New Mexico. He defeated a force of over 3,800 at Valverde on February 2, 1862, and took Albuquerque and Santa Fé. On March 28, however, at Glorietta Pass the Federals checked his advance and destroyed his supply train. As a result of this and other disasters, he was obliged to retire from the territory. When he returned to San Antonio in the summer of 1862 with the shattered remnant of his troops, the territorial government retreated with him. Thus ended the dream to extend the Confederacy to encompass a port on the Gulf of California and the gold and silver mines of the West.

Defense of the Texas coast constitutes one of the most brilliant chapters in the story of the Confederacy. In July 1861 the Federal blockade was extended to include Texas. Before a formidable enemy force, state and Confederate troops evacuated Galveston in October 1862. Then John B. Magruder, fresh from the Peninsula campaign before Richmond and now in command of the Department of Texas, determined to recover the town. With two riverboats armored with cotton bales and 300 veterans of Sibley's New Mexico campaign serving as marines, he moved against it by sea. A land force was concentrated at Virginia Point, opposite Galveston. On January 1, 1863, the combined forces took Galveston with a loss of 26 killed and 117 wounded. The Federals suffered the loss of two warships and 414 men killed or captured. Four Federal gunboats made their escape.

Fighting also took place around Sabine Pass, the outlet for both the Sabine and the Neches rivers. In September 1862 a Federal blockade patrol forced the Confederates to abandon it. After retaking Galveston, the Confederates on January 21 reoccupied it and fortified it as well as their limited means would permit. Admiral David G. Farragut and General N. P. Banks then made plans for a major campaign against Texas that would begin with the retaking of Sabine Pass. Four gunboats and seventeen transports bearing about 1,500 troops for the initial landing attacked it on September 8, 1863. To meet his formidable force, Lieutenant Dick Dowling had two small gunboats and a garrison of 46 men! Yet he disabled and captured two enemy craft, took about 350 prisoners, and turned back the entire expedition. His victory was a severe blow to the morale of the North and augmented doubts about the efficiency of the Federal navy. The *New York Herald* credited it, together with the Federal defeat at Chickamauga, with lowering the credit of the United States to the extent of raising the price of gold by 5 percent.

Banks's next thrust was more successful. With a combined naval and land force of about seven thousand men, he moved against the lower Rio Grande, where the Confederate garrisons were pitiably weak. Beginning by taking the island of Brazos de Santiago off the mouth of the Rio Grande on November 1, 1863, seizures were extended to include Brownsville, Corpus Christi, Aransas Pass, Indianola, and other points, until Galveston and Sabine Pass were the only ports left to the Confederates.

In the spring of 1864 Banks made his last campaign against Texas. From Alexandria, Louisiana, 25,000 well-equipped veterans, sustained by a powerful flotilla of gunboats, moved up the Red River. Banks planned to unite this army with 15,000 men under General Frederick Steele, who was moving southward from Little Rock. It was expected that the combined forces would crush all opposition and extend their operations over all of northern Louisiana, southern Arkansas, and eastern Texas. The Confederate shops at Marshall and Henderson and the rich East Texas farm country constituted choice prizes. With a large part of his best troops drawn away to sustain the flagging Confederate cause in the East, General E. Kirby Smith, in command of the Trans-Mississippi Department, worked desperately to form an army to cope with Banks. Magruder in Texas sent him every man he could spare; and as the regiments hastened eastward, old men and beardless boys were enlisted to offset losses by death, disease, and desertion. With 8,000 cavalrymen, Sterling Price stopped Steele at Camden, Arkansas. Richard Taylor, in immediate command of the army that faced Banks, had a force made up largely of troops from Texas, Louisiana, Arkansas, and Missouri, including Walker's division of Texas infantry and Tom Green's brigade of cavalry. On April 8, with 11,000 effective troops, he attacked and all but routed Banks's army at Mansfield, Louisiana, fifty miles below Shreveport, taking 2,500 prisoners. The Confederates were repulsed on the following day at Pleasant Hill, but Banks hastily retreated to the east side of the Mississippi.

In the summer of 1864, the Confederate forces under John S. Ford recaptured Fort Brown and forced the Federals in South Texas to withdraw from the mainland. The last battle of the Civil War was fought when the Federals in the spring of 1865 attempted to recapture Fort Brown. On May 13 at Palmito Ranch near Brownsville, Ford with a force of three hundred met and defeated two black regiments and a company of unmounted Texas (Union) cavalry. From the 111 prisoners he took in

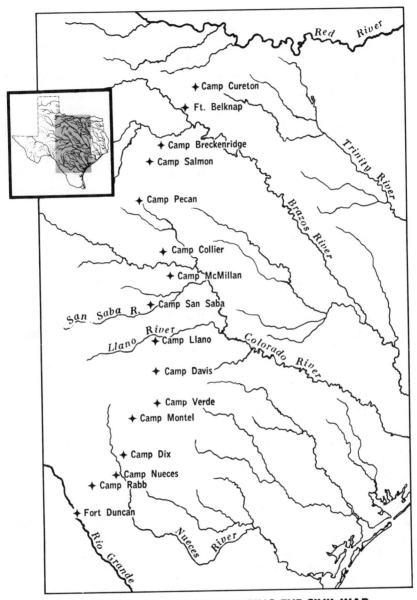

**TEXAS MILITARY POSTS DURING THE CIVIL WAR**

From Ernest Wallace, *Texas in Turmoil* (Austin, 1965), p. 70. Reprinted with the permission and assistance of Steck-Vaughn Company, publisher.

that engagement, Ford learned that General Robert E. Lee had surrendered more than a month before.

Even after Joseph E. Johnston had surrendered the last major Confederate army on April 18, 1865, Governor Murrah, General E. Kirby Smith, and other leaders insisted that the war be continued in the West. That was the decision on May 13 of the conference of the representatives of Trans-Mississippi states held in Marshall after Grant had insisted on the same terms of surrender that were granted to General Lee. Thereafter, Smith, Magruder, and Murrah made various unsuccessful efforts to secure more favorable terms. Meanwhile, the armies of the West melted away, and General Smith, left without an army, formally surrendered the Trans-Mississippi Department in Galveston on June 2.

## SUPPLYING MEN

In Texas there was a pronounced tradition that young men should join the colors in an emergency, and as early as September 30, 1861, ten regiments of Texas troops had already been organized. It was thought at first that Texans would not be needed east of the Mississippi. Early in 1862, however, Governor Lubbock received a call for fifteen regiments of infantry, and these, he stated in his memoirs, were made up of volunteers "in a few months." He thought Texas had about twenty thousand men in military service before conscription went into effect.

The first Confederate conscription act was passed on April 16, 1862, applying to men from eighteen to thirty-five years of age. In September of that year the age limit was raised to forty-five, and a later act extended the limits from seventeen to fifty. On December 25, 1861, the state provided for the enrollment and organization of the militia; an act of March 7, 1863, provided that the militia might be transferred into Confederate service for a period of not more than a year. A state act of May 28, 1864, provided for the transfer of state troops to Confederate service, except officers of the state government and privates not subject to the Confederate conscription laws.

There were liberal exemptions, especially for officeholders and persons supposedly indispensable to the professions, agriculture, and industry. Certain Texans were exempted also for frontier defense. The law, furthermore, permitted the hiring of substitutes. Beyond a doubt the law exemption policy and the provision permitting a man to hire a substitute had a bad effect on the morale of the troops and the people behind the lines.

Texas contributed significantly in manpower to the Confederate military effort. It furnished one general (Albert Sidney Johnston), three major generals (S. B. Maxey, John A. Wharton, and Tom Green), thirty-two brigadier generals, and ninety-seven colonels. It is impossible to determine the number of men who saw military service either as state or Confederate troops during the war. Even Governor Lubbock, who should be a dependable authority for the period when he was chief executive, gives figures that are difficult to reconcile. In February 1863 he stated that Texas had in actual service 68,500 men, including 6,500 state troops. His figures evidently included a number of duplications, particularly among those who volunteered for state duty and afterwards entered Confederate service. According to the census of 1860, white males in Texas between the ages of eighteen and forty-five numbered 92,145. Some 58,533 men were recruited in the cavalry alone. Probably two-thirds of those who served remained west of the Mississippi.

Texans fought on every battlefront, and a host of witnesses vouched for their valor. For mobility and heroic daring, the organization named after B. F. (Frank) Terry was unsurpassed; Ross's Texas Brigade fought well on both sides of the Mississippi; Hood's Texas Brigade broke the Federal lines in the Second Battle of Manassas and at Gaines' Mill, Virginia, and became the first division of Longstreet's famous corps. The war exacted a cruel toll on Texas's population, not to mention the havoc wrought upon its economic and social structure. The number killed and wounded will probably never be known, but the roll of the names that can be counted is truly astounding.

## THE STATE AND THE CONFEDERACY

Party activity ceased during the war. Unionists, pacifists, and defeatists were obliged to keep their counsel, for secessionists were completely in the ascendency. No party nominations were made in 1861. In the race for governor, Francis Richard Lubbock, who had served as lieutenant governor during Runnels's administration, defeated Edward Clark, the incumbent, by only 124 votes. John M. Crockett, mayor of Dallas, was elected lieutenant governor. At the same election, congressmen were chosen to represent the state in Richmond. Louis T. Wigfall and W. S. Oldham were elected to the Confederate senate. John H. Reagan accepted an appointment as postmaster general in President Jefferson Davis's cabinet.

State efforts during Lubbock's administration were centered on winning the war. The governor supported the Confederacy with all his power, and most legislation pertained to defense. A military board consisting of the governor, comptroller, and treasurer was authorized to dispose of the bonds of the United States then held by Texas or to use other means in purchasing military supplies. Other acts suspended all laws for the collection of debts, validated bonds issued for military purposes, authorized special county taxes for war purposes, appropriated money for equipping troops, and authorized the receipt of Confederate notes and treasury warrants for taxes.

Confederate reverses, Lincoln's Emancipation Proclamation, and "signs of a latent dissatisfaction at the existing state of things if not a positive disloyalty to the Confederacy" caused Lubbock to call an extra session of the legislature for February 2, 1863. That body doubled taxes and appropriated $600,000 for the use of needy families of soldiers and $200,000 as a hospital fund for sick and wounded Texans in the Confederate armies.

In 1863 Lubbock entered the Confederate service and did not stand for reelection. The race soon became a contest between T. J. Chambers (candidate for the fourth time) and Pendleton Murrah, a Harrison County lawyer. Murrah, more emphatic than Chambers in his promise to support the Confederate cause in every way possible, defeated Chambers by a vote of 17,511 to 12,455, the total vote being only a little more than half that cast in the preceding election. F. S. Stockdale, who had helped draft the ordinance of secession, was elected lieutenant governor. The election results revealed no special dissatisfaction with the course of events in Richmond.

Every war governor proclaimed his loyalty to the Confederacy and his determination to work with it harmoniously. The Texas Supreme Court upheld the constitutionality of the Confederate conscription law. It declared constitutional the act abolishing substitution in the army, even though it violated the obligation of contract. Brigadier General P. O. Hébert, a West Point valedictorian and former governor of Louisiana, who had succeeded Earl Van Dorn as commander of the Department of Texas, created considerable resentment when in May 1862 he proclaimed martial law for the entire state in order to enforce the conscription law and allowed the Federals to occupy Galveston and Sabine Pass. He was replaced, however, in November by Brigadier General John B. Magruder, fresh from the Peninsula campaign against General George B. McClellan. Magruder, except for a few months in the fall and winter of 1864–1865, retained that post without any conflict with the Texans.

The most serious clash of authority grew out of the Texas law of 1863, which provided for organizing into companies for defense all men of military age in frontier counties and for exempting them from conscription under the Confederate laws. Obviously the proposed exemption was in conflict with the Confederate constitution, but Murrah insisted on its enforcement. Then, when General E. Kirby Smith, desperately in need of troops to repel Banks in Louisiana in the spring of 1864, called

Oran M. Roberts (above left): judge, secessionist leader, governor, and professor of law at the University of Texas where he was awarded the title "the Old Alcalde." Thomas J. Rusk (above right): secretary of war during the Texas Revolution and one of the first two United States senators from Texas. Ashbel Smith (left): Yale graduate, physician, secretary of state of the Republic of Texas, Confederate colonel, and a leader in education. (University of Texas Library)

on Murrah through Magruder to send more men, the governor quibbled over certain relatively unimportant matters until it was too late for the state troops to be of service. In defense of Murrah it should be said that as the war progressed, the Trans-Mississippi states were thrown more and more on their own resources, and it was natural that he should hesitate to transfer men from state control to the Confederate authorities.

As the war proceeded, complaints of neglect of the West by the Confederate government became more emphatic. The governor of Arkansas stated in June 1862 that if the western states were not to be protected, the sooner they knew it the better. At the request of President Davis, Governor Lubbock and Governor Claiborne F. Jackson of the Confederate government of Missouri met in Marshall, Texas, in July 1862 and framed a request to the Richmond government for a commanding general for the Trans-Mississippi West, for money, and for arms and ammunition. The government in Richmond gave them a commanding general and a fiscal agency for the department. E. Kirby Smith, commander of the Trans-Mississippi Department, called another conference of western state representatives in Marshall for August 15, 1863. The conference, presided over by Governor Lubbock, favored more friendly relations with the French in Mexico, agreed on a plan of exchanging cotton for supplies in Mexico, suggested that Confederate notes be reissued for meeting military expenses, and recommended that in his department General Smith "assume at once and exercise the powers and prerogatives of the President of the Confederate States."

In connection with the purchase of cotton and the plan of exchange approved by the Marshall conference, another sharp conflict arose between state and Confederate authorities. Pursuant to an act of Congress, the Confederate government in 1863 began to impress cotton to be hauled to the Rio Grande and exchanged for necessary supplies. The Marshall conference approved a plan, which Smith had already put in operation, whereby the Confederacy was to acquire and dispose of cotton through a bureau with headquarters in Shreveport. Under this arrangement the planter or other holder was asked to sell half of his cotton, after which the other half would be exempt from impressment. Owners were to be paid for their cotton in certificates redeemable in cotton bonds or by such other methods as the Confederate Congress might provide. To compete with Smith's bureau the Texas Military Board under Governor Murrah's "state plan" would contract for all of a planter's cotton, transport it to the Rio Grande, and there give half of it back to the owner, paying for the other half in state bonds. Obviously, the Confederate Cotton Bureau could not compete with the state under such a system, and the importation through Mexico and Texas of arms and other materials equally vital would have to cease. Through an act of

February 6, 1864, the Confederate Congress seized control of the situation by prohibiting the exportation of cotton, tobacco, and certain other commodities, except under regulations made by the president. At a conference in July 1864 Governor Murrah and General E. Kirby Smith arrived at an understanding, and thereafter Murrah cooperated to the fullest extent.

The financial condition of the state during the war is difficult to describe accurately. Most of the transactions were made in depreciated Confederate currency and equally depreciated state treasury warrants. Net expenditures—that is, warrants actually paid by the treasurer from August 31, 1861, to June 8, 1865—amounted to $4,863,790.55, more than three-fourths of which was attributable to the war. Total net receipts for the same period were $8,161,298. About 40 percent of the receipts had been derived from a wide variety of taxes, 8 percent from the sale of bonds, 38 percent from profits on the penitentiary, and 14 percent from miscellaneous sources. In the treasury on August 1, 1865, was $3,368,510 (most of which was in the form of worthless money), and there was a debt of about $8,000,000. In its desperation the state government had used special trust monies, such as the school fund and the university fund, to the amount of almost $1,500,000. A commentary both on the confusion of the times and the poverty of the state is the fact that when

John H. Reagan served Texas, the United States, and the Confederate States of America with distinction. He resigned as United States senator to accept the chairmanship of the first railroad commission of Texas in 1891. (University of Texas Library)

certain persons looted the state treasury on the night of June 11, 1865, all that they found of value and negotiable was $5,000 in specie.

Far greater than the burden of state taxes was the burden of Confederate taxes, which during the four years from 1861 through 1864 amounted in Texas to $37,486,854.

## THE PEOPLE AT HOME DURING THE WAR

Union sentiment in Texas was very strong. The rank and file of Union sympathizers may be classified into three groups: (1) those who accepted the decision of the state electorate as binding upon them and sustained heartily the efforts of the Confederacy; (2) those who tried to remain neutral; and (3) a few who left the state or tried to do so. J. W. Throckmorton, who became a general in the Confederate armies, is, perhaps, the most widely known representative of the first class. Of those who remained neutral, the best known were Sam Houston, David G. Burnet, E. M. Pease, George W. Paschal, Morgan C. Hamilton, and Edward Degener. Also in this class belong many Germans in the settlements along the lower Brazos River and north of San Antonio, who, although never reconciled to secession, served the state and Confederacy as superb soldiers. A third group, headed by A. J. Hamilton, John Hancock, John L. Haynes, James P. Newcomb, and Edmund J. Davis, energetically served the Union.

Unionist sentiment was strongest along the lower Rio Grande, among the Germans, and in the northwestern counties. The lower Rio Grande area, where escape to Mexico was easy and whose Mexican population refused to support the Confederacy, became a site for many Unionist refugees and for the recruitment of volunteers for the United States Army. For protection against Indians and for avoiding conscription, the Germans in 1861 organized the militant Union Loyal League (five hundred members in Gillespie, Kerr, and Kendall counties only) but later were forced to disband. A few left the state, but one group of sixty-five on its way to Mexico in August 1862 had thirty-four killed by the Texas militia. Another fifty were hanged, and others were killed before German resistance in the western area was broken. In Colorado, Austin, and Fayette counties, Germans and some Anglo-Americans organized to resist the draft, but General Magruder declared martial law over the area, arrested the leaders, and quelled open resistance.

The antiwar sentiment in the northwestern part of the state was also troublesome. There in 1862, a secret organization, popularly referred to as the Peace party, was organized. The aims of its members were to avoid the draft, to provide a spy system for the Northern army, to desert, if drafted, during battle, and to prepare the way for an invasion of North Texas by federal troops. Spies visited its meetings, and soon the excited people were repeating in whispers reports that its leaders were planning arson, murder, and a general reign of terror. The Confederate military forces joined civilians in a grim campaign to destroy the movement in its infancy. About 150 men were arrested and tried in Gainesville by "people's courts," which were neither military nor constitutional. Some confessed; 40 were hanged, most of them on no other charge, it seems, than membership in the organization. The Wise County people's courts were more deliberate; only 5 men were hanged there. In Grayson County 40 men were arrested, but J. W. Throckmorton interceded with a plea for justice; a court of investigation reviewed their cases, and all but one were released.

Many outspoken critics of the war were arrested, in most cases by the military under laws that had suspended the writ of *habeas corpus*. Of such cases the best known is that of Dr. Richard R. Peebles, from near Hempstead, and four other prominent citizens who were arrested in October 1863 on charges of plotting treason against the Confederate government. Peebles and two associates were exiled to Mexico.

Numbers of Unionists managed to leave Texas early in the war and many others made their way to Matamoros where they were rescued by Federal ships. Others hid themselves in isolated places, where soon they were joined by deserters from the state and Confederate forces.

By February 1863 the problem of desertion had become so serious that General Magruder was urging Governor Lubbock to aid him in suppressing it. Eight months later, Henry E. McCulloch, in command of the northern submilitary district, estimated that there were one thousand deserters in his territory and declared that he did not have sufficient troops to arrest them. He offered them special inducements to join the army and succeeded thus in enlisting three hundred, but he found that these "bush soldiers" had a weakness for returning to the brush! Soon deserters were so numerous in Wise, Denton, and neighboring counties that they intimidated loyal citizens. Sterner measures apparently brought about improvement in 1864, but during the last few weeks of the war conditions grew distinctly worse.

The story of the disloyal and dissatisfied minority must not be permitted to obscure the fact that the overwhelming majority of Texans at home and at the front supported until the end the waning Confederate cause.

The war forced radical readjustments in farming. The demand for cotton declined and that for food crops increased. Newspapers urged the planting of more corn. There was some agitation for laws to compel changes in acreage to meet the emergency, but no such legislation was enacted. From time to time there was a shortage of farm labor, and the families of poor soldiers frequently found it difficult to work their farms. Crops were good during the years of the war, and except in a few isolated cases, no one suffered from lack of food. Salt, an absolute necessity for livestock and the preservation of meat, became so scarce that a soldier's salary for a month would not buy a sack; the Grand Saline in Van Zandt County, the Brooks salines, and a few other sources supplied most of the state. The frontier people visited Ledbetter's Salt Works, near the site of Albany, the salt flats along the upper Brazos, and the salt lakes in the vicinity of El Paso.

There was never enough medicines and hospital supplies. In 1864 a serious effort was made by the military authorities to encourage the growing of poppies for opium, and the press frequently called the attention of the public to shrubs and plants of medicinal value. Through ladies' aid associations loyal women did their best to supply bandages and other equipment for the wounded; much clothing also was contributed. Relief committees received donations and distributed funds and goods for the benefit of the wives and children of soldiers. In 1863 it was said that the citizens of Houston were contributing nearly $3,000 a week to this purpose. People soon learned to make various substitutions in food and clothing. The ashes of corncobs served as soda; parched sweet potatoes, rye, and okra were substitutes for coffee; women learned to make hats and fans out of shucks and straw; and the spinning wheel again came into use. The people took great pride in their self-sufficiency. Governor Lubbock was inaugurated in a homespun suit, and the "homespun dress that Southern ladies wear" became a theme of song and story.

The shortage of manufactured goods was a great handicap. An arsenal, which turned out a few cannon, and a cap and cartridge factory were established in Austin. Many corporations for the manufacture of goods were chartered, but most of them never reached production. The largest cloth factory was at the penitentiary in Huntsville. Iron foundries were opened near Jefferson and Rusk, and the tanning industry increased rapidly. Likewise, the output of wagons, ambulances, harnesses, and saddles increased sharply. By 1863 many newspapers were forced to suspend publication for want of paper.

As the Federal blockade became more effective, the flow of imports and exports to and from the South was reduced to an intermittent trickle. Cotton, the chief export commodity, was hauled to the Rio Grande over different routes and in such quantities that one observer declared that "the chaparral would be almost white in places from the lint detached from passing bales." In spite of the costs and hazards of the trade, men would undertake it, for cotton in 1862 at the Rio Grande brought from 20 to 72 cents per pound, and in 1864 the price in New York ranged from 72 cents to $1.90 per pound. On their return the cotton wagons brought sugar, coffee, cloth, nails, and sometimes medicines and military supplies.

Imported consumer goods were in great demand, but there never was enough to go around. After the arrival of a shipment, stores were more badly crowded than the present-day bargain counters on the morning of a special sale. Mrs. Maverick of San Antonio related that she "went and stood wedged up and swaying about till near 12," when, at last, she managed to get "one bolt of domestic cloth, one pr. shoes and 1 doz. candles for $180.00." Although that particular merchant's stock had cost $60,000 in specie, she thought it would be exhausted within a week. As the value of the currency declined and prices soared, there was much complaint about "unfair and unjust speculators."

Men of nonmilitary age and women made brave efforts to keep up the morale of their communities, in spite of the reports of Confederate reverses and the tragic news from sons and husbands that they received from time to time. There are accounts of Christmas celebrations as in ordinary times, of parties and receptions for returned soldiers, and of "war meetings" with stirring speeches and "dinner on the grounds." It was the zeal and courage of the people behind the lines, quite as much as the efforts of the men in the field, that sustained for four years the Confederate cause against overwhelming odds.

## SELECTED BIBLIOGRAPHY

The best general accounts of Texas during the Civil War are in D. G. Wooten, F. W. Johnson, J. H. Brown, H. H. Bancroft, and E. Wallace, *Texas in Turmoil,* all previously cited. Two excellent but brief surveys of Texas in the Civil War are Allan C. Ashcraft, *Texas in the Civil War: A Resume History* (Austin, 1962); and Robert L. Kerby, *Kirby Smith's Confederacy: The Trans-Mississippi South, 1863–1865* (New York, 1972).

The chief sources for secession are E. W. Winkler (ed.), *Journal of the Secession Convention of Texas, 1861* (Austin, 1912); and *War of the Rebellion, Official Records, Union and Confederate Armies* (130 vols., Washington, D.C., 1880–1900). Accounts of some merit by participants, in addition to O. M. Roberts's in D. G. Wooten's work, are F. R. Lubbock, *Six Decades in Texas;* and E. L. Dohoney, *An Average American* (Paris, Tex., 1907). The best studies on secession are: C. W. Ramsdell, *Reconstruction in Texas* (New York, 1910); C. W. Ramsdell, "The Frontier and Secession," reprinted from *Studies in Southern History and Politics* (New York, 1914); C. W. Ramsdell, *Behind the*

*Lines in the Southern Confederacy* (Baton Rouge, La., 1944); A. L. King, *Louis T. Wigfall: Southern Fire-eater;* Laura W. Roper, "Frederick Law Olmstead and the Western Texas Free Soil Movement," *American Historical Review,* LIV, 58–65; C. Elliott, *Leathercoat: The Life of James W. Throckmorton;* Anna Irene Sandbo, "Beginnings of the Secession Movement in Texas," *Southwestern Historical Quarterly,* XVIII, 41–73; A. I. Sandbo, "The First Session of the Secession Convention of Texas," *ibid.,* 162–194; R. A. Wooster, "Analysis of the Membership of the Texas Secession Convention," *ibid.,* LXII, 322–335; C. A. Bridges, "The Knights of the Golden Circle," *ibid.,* XLIV, 287–302; Dunn, "The KGC in Texas, 1860–1861," *ibid.,* LXX, 543–573; C. Elliott, "Union Sentiment in Texas, 1861–1865," *ibid.,* L, 449–477; Frank H. Smyrl, "Unionism in Texas, 1856–1861," *ibid.,* LXVIII, 172–195; Floyd F. Ewing, "Origins of Union Sentiment on the West Texas Frontier," *West Texas Historical Association Year Book,* XXXII, 21–29; Floyd F. Ewing, "Unionist Sentiment on the Northwest Texas Frontier," *ibid.,* XXXIII, 58–70.

Accounts of Texas troops in the war include Robert Lee Kerby, *The Confederate Invasion of New Mexico and Arizona, 1861–1862* (Los Angeles, 1958); B. F. Galloway (ed.), *The Dark Corner of the Confederacy* (Dubuque, Ia., 1972); Harold Simpson (ed.), *Texas in the Civil War* (Hillsboro, Tex., 1965); C. P. Roland, *Albert Sidney Johnston: Soldier of Three Republics;* O. B. Faulk, *General Tom Green: Fightin' Texan;* W. J. Hughes, *Rebellious Ranger: Rip Ford and the Old Southwest;* Ludwell Johnson, *The Red River Campaign: Politics and Cotton in the Civil War* (Baltimore, 1958); E. Wallace, *Charles DeMorse: Pioneer Editor and Statesman;* C. Elliott, *Leathercoat: The Life of James W. Throckmorton;* Stephen B. Oates, *Confederate Cavalry West of the Mississippi River* (Austin, 1961); James L. Nichols, *The Confederate Quartermaster in the Trans-Mississippi* (Austin, 1964); J. B. Hood, *Advance and Retreat* (New Orleans, 1880); Victor M. Rose, *Ross' Texas Brigade* (Louisville, Ky., 1881); V. M. Rose, *The Life and Services of General Ben McCulloch* (Philadelphia, 1888; Austin, 1958); Walter P. Lane, *The Adventures and Recollections of General Walter P. Lane* (Marshall, Tex., 1887); August Santleben, *A Texas Pioneer* (New York, 1910), in the Union service; Xavier Blanchard DeBray, *A Sketch of the History of DeBray's (26th) Regiment of Texas Cavalry* (Waco, Tex., 1961); Harold B. Simpson (ed.), *Touched with Valor: Civil War Papers and Casualty Reports of Hood's Texas Brigade* (Hillsboro, Tex., 1964); Marcus J. Wright, *Texas in the War, 1861–1865* (Harold B. Simpson, ed., Hillsboro, Tex., 1965); W. H. Watford, "Confederate Western Ambitions," *Southwestern Historical Quarterly,* XLIV, 161–187; S. B. Oates, "Recruiting Confederate Cavalry in Texas," *ibid.,* LXIV,

463–477; Alwyn Barr, "Texas Coastal Defense, 1861–1865," *ibid.*, LXV, 1–31; A. Barr, "The Battle of Calcasieu Pass," *ibid.*, LXVI, 59–67; Allen W. Jones, "Military Events in Texas during the Civil War, 1861–1865," *ibid.*, LXIV, 64–70; C. C. Jeffries, "The Character of Terry's Texas Rangers," *ibid.*, LXIV, 454–462; F. H. Smyrl, "Texans in the Union Army, 1861–1865," *ibid.*, LXV, 234–250; Charles C. Cumberland, "The Confederate Loss and Recapture of Galveston, 1862–1863," *ibid.*, LI, 109–130; E. C. Barker and Frank Vandiver, "Letters from the Confederate Medical Service in Texas, 1863–1865," *ibid.*, LV, 378–401, 459–474; Theophilus Noel, *Autobiography and Reminiscences* (Chicago, 1904); W. C. Holden, "Frontier Defense in Texas during the Civil War," *West Texas Historical Association Year Book,* IV, 16–31; Harry M. Henderson, *Texas in the Confederacy* (San Antonio, 1955); John P. Dyer, *The Gallant Hood* (New York, 1950); R. N. Richardson, *The Frontier of Northwest Texas;* Richard Taylor, *Destruction and Reconstruction* (Richard B. Harwell, ed., New York, 1955).

For a scholarly account of two prominent Texans who served as officers in the Union Army, see Ronald N. Gray, "Edmund J. Davis: Radical Republican and Reconstruction Governor of Texas" (unpublished dissertation, Texas Tech University, Lubbock, Tex., 1976); and John L. Waller, *Colossal Hamilton of Texas: A Biography of Andrew Jackson Hamilton* (El Paso, Tex., 1968).

Phases of home life and public affairs during the Civil War are dealt with in Mrs. E. M. Loughery, *War and Reconstruction in Texas* (Austin, 1914); Thomas North, *Five Years in Texas* (Cincinnati, 1871); Grover C. Ramsey (comp.), *Confederate Postmasters in Texas, 1861–1865* (Waco, Tex., 1963); Alma D. King, "The Political Career of William Simpson Oldham," *Southwestern Historical Quarterly,* XXXIII, 112–133; C. W. Ramsdell, "The Texas State Military Board, 1862–1865," *ibid.*, XXVII, 253–275; Robert W. Shook, "The Battle of the Nueces, August 10, 1862," *ibid.*, LXVI, 31–42; Carland Elaine Crook, "Benjamin Théron and French Designs in Texas during the Civil War," *ibid.*, XLVIII, 432–454; Thomas L. Miller, "Texas Land Grants to Confederate Veterans and Widows," *ibid.*, LXIX, 59–65; Sam Acheson and Julie Ann Hudson O'Connell (eds.), "George Washington Diamond's Account of the Great Hanging at Gainesville, 1862," *ibid.*, LXVI, 331–414; Thomas Barrett, *The Great Hanging at Gainesville* (Austin, 1961).

Scores of county histories deal with certain phases of the war. Brief biographies of the governors of Texas may be found in J. T. DeShields, *They Sat in High Places; The Presidents and Governors of Texas.* Many excellent unprinted studies are available in the university libraries in Texas.

# Chapter Eleven

# RECONSTRUCTION
# 1865–1874

The decade following the end of the Civil War is generally called the Reconstruction period. During those years the victorious North endeavored to make changes in Southern society that would assure the permanency of its major objectives of the war—the preservation of the Union, the abolition of slavery, and the establishment of government of, by, and for all the people. The war had preserved the Union by force, but the restoration of the Southern states on a constitutional basis was yet to be achieved. It had ended slavery, but it had not solved the future political, economic, and social status of the freed slaves; it had promoted the cause of democracy, but after the war, military government in time of peace created a problem never before experienced by the Americans. Furthermore, the war had left a heritage of violence and hatred that lingered to trouble the postwar years, particularly in Texas where there were many Unionists and where the spirit of frontier individualism was still prevalent.

In addition, Texas faced a few unique problems, particularly because of its isolation and vast distances. By 1865 thousands of refugees, white and black, had entered Texas, and some contributed to the turbulence that followed the war. Furthermore, for a time, anarchy prevailed. After the surrender of the Confederate Trans-Mississippi Department, Generals E. Kirby Smith and John Magruder, Governor Pendleton Murrah, and many other prominent ex-Confederates fled to Mexico. Lieutenant Governor Fletcher S. Stockdale became governor but was unable to restore law and order. And because of the great distances, the lack of transportation facilities, and the French involvement in Mexico, federal troops did not reach some interior areas until seven months after the end of the war. Meanwhile, considerable confusion prevailed as to the status of the new freedmen. Most ex-Confederates, it seems, recognized that emancipation was an accomplished fact, but they anticipated that the freed slaves would become a new peonage caste somewhere between that of slavery and that of their own.

For convenience, the following account of Reconstruction in Texas, which lasted for two months less than nine years, is divided into three periods. The first, "Presidential Reconstruction," includes Johnson's provisional government from June 19, 1865, to August 20, 1866, when President Andrew Johnson declared the insurrection in Texas at an end and the provisional civil government established by the Constitution of 1866, but unacceptable to Congress, in combination with the military, August 20, 1866, to March 2, 1867. The second, "Congressional Reconstruction," began in March 1867, when Congress took over the Reconstruction program, and lasted until April 16, 1870, the date that "all civil authority" was remitted to the officers of the state. The third, "Radical Republican Government under the Reconstruction Constitution," lasted from April 16, 1870, until January 17, 1874, the date that Richard Coke, Democrat, succeeded E. J. Davis, Republican, as governor of Texas.

## PRESIDENTIAL RECONSTRUCTION

### Johnson's Provisional Government, June 19, 1865, to August 20, 1866

From the time federal armies first conquered segments of the Confederacy, Northern leaders were divided over how reconstruction should be accomplished. President Lincoln held that secession was illegal and that reconstruction was thus the responsibility of the executive branch of the government. The radicals, though members of Lincoln's own party, on the other hand, maintained that the Confederate states, by secession, had forfeited their statehood, and, since Congress alone had the power to admit new states, it also had the power to reconstruct.

Lincoln acted first. On December 8, 1863, he set forth his plan of reconstruction. Basically, the plan provided that when as many as 10 percent of the number who had voted in 1860, with a few exceptions, took the oath of allegiance to the United States and accepted all official acts regarding slavery, they could establish a state government. In conformity with this plan, he accorded restoration to Tennessee, Louisiana, and Arkansas. He also granted legitimate status to the refugee loyalist government of Virginia, and in July 1864 by a pocket veto he killed the Wade-Davis bill in which Congress had countered with its own, far less lenient, plan for reconstruction. Nothing further was done to reorganize Southern state governments until after the end of the war.

On May 29, 1865, President Andrew Johnson prescribed in two proclamations a process of reconstruction for the remaining Confederate states that was essentially the same as Lincoln's. The Amnesty Proclamation excluded fourteen classes, including high-ranking military and civil officers and persons whose taxable property was worth over twenty thousand dollars; the second proclamation provided for the reconstruction of civil government in North Carolina. During the next few weeks the president issued proclamations identical to the latter for each of the remaining six former Confederate states. On June 17 the Texas Proclamation was issued, in which A. J. Hamilton, a staunch Unionist and former congressman, was named provisional governor.

On June 2, the same day that General E. Kirby Smith formally surrendered, General Philip H. Sheridan assumed command of the Military Division of the Southwest, which included Texas, and established his headquarters in New Orleans. As soon as ships were available, he sent troops to Texas. On June 19, 1865, General Gordon Granger with 1,800 troops occupied Galveston and in the name of the president of the United States issued a proclamation that declared that the slaves

A native of Alabama, Andrew Jackson Hamilton moved to Texas in 1846, became a Unionist in the Civil War, and was appointed provisional governor of Texas in 1865. (Courtesy of Texas State Library)

were free;[1] that all acts of the Texas government since secession were illegal; and that officers and men of the late Confederate army should be paroled.

By the end of the year an estimated fifty thousand federal troops were in Texas. Some were sent into the interior, but a larger number were concentrated along the Rio Grande as a counter to the French in Mexico. The troops were supposed to restore the authority of the United States and to preserve order. They met with no organized resistance; in fact, a few commanders, including the colorful George A. Custer, who reached Austin with a detachment of troops in November 1865, became quite popular among the townfolk. Because of their small number, the great distances, and the confusion following the collapse of the Confederate armies, the troops were not able to eliminate lawlessness, but, no doubt, they had a salutary effect.

Governor Hamilton arrived in Galveston on July 21 and proceeded slowly to Austin. His reception was quite cordial. On August 9 he began establishing a new state government. He appointed James H. Bell, a former member of the supreme court, as secretary of state and William Alexander as attorney general, both Union men. As rapidly as practicable, Union men, with a few exceptions, were appointed to the district, county, and precinct offices throughout the state. In keeping with President Johnson's plan of reconstruction, the governor called for an election, on January 8, 1866, of delegates to a constitutional convention to convene on February 7. Under the president's plan four conditions had to be met before he would accept the work of the convention: the abolition of slavery; the establishment of the civil status of the newly freed blacks; the repudiation of the ordinance of secession; and the repudiation of debts, both state and Confederate, incurred in behalf of the war.

When the convention assembled, two old factions, Unionists and secessionists, faced each other under new conditions. John Hancock, I. A. Paschal, and Edward Degener were sitting opposite such confirmed rebels as H. R. Runnels and O. M. Roberts. Between them was a group, larger than either, inclined to be conservative and to avoid any permanent alignment with the opposing factions. J. W. Throckmorton, a moderate who had been both a Unionist and an ex-Confederate brigadier, was chosen president.

The convention spent much time in trying to decide what disposition to make of the ordinance of secession. Obviously, it was no longer in

---

[1]Although Lincoln's preliminary Emancipation Proclamation had been announced on September 22, 1862, Texas blacks have observed June 19 as the date of their emancipation. Beginning in 1980, June 19 became a legal holiday in Texas.

effect, but was it null and void from the date it was enacted, or did it become null and void as a result of the war? The question was never answered. By a vote of fifty-five to twenty-one the convention finally simply acknowledged the supremacy of the Constitution of the United States and declared void the ordinance of secession without reference to time.

The most important subject with which the convention dealt was the status of blacks. The questions of abolition and civil rights were combined in a single ordinance. The convention agreed that slavery no longer existed and that it could not be reestablished in Texas, but it formally refused to approve the Thirteenth Amendment to the Constitution of the United States, claiming that it already had been ratified and declared in force. The convention also failed to grant to blacks equality before the law. After a sharp debate, it provided for their security in person and property, but it abridged their right to testify in court in cases in which blacks were not involved. Furthermore, it denied them the right to vote and to hold office. Although more generous toward the freed slaves than the fundamental law of most other former Confederate states, the new constitution failed to comply with the wishes of even President Johnson, who wanted the right of suffrage extended to at least all adult black males who could read and write.

The convention was expected to repudiate the war debt; otherwise, it would be tantamount to recognition that secession and the war were legitimate. It went further and canceled all the state debts incurred during the war. This measure brought much criticism from the conservative press, for the state had incurred obligations in no way connected with carrying on the war. In defense of nullification it was pointed out that the debt had been acquired in violation of the Constitution of 1845 and that nearly all warrants were in the hands of speculators. Men of both parties voted for repudiation.

Before it adjourned, the convention approved all laws and all acts of officers of the Confederate state government not in violation of the Constitution of 1845 and without any direct relation to the war. The work of the convention was done through the passage of a series of ordinances. At first it delegated unto itself legislative and constituent power supreme and final; but on March 27, after it had declared secession null and void, had canceled the war debt, and had fixed the status of freed slaves, it voted to submit to the electors amendments to the Constitution of 1845. Among the changes proposed was a plan to lengthen to four years the terms of most officers, to give constitutional status to county courts, and to provide for a possible division of the state.

In an election on June 25 to choose constitutional officers, the Unionists or radicals supported E. M. Pease for governor, and the conservatives stood behind J. W. Throckmorton. The contest was heated, but the candidates did not differ as widely as their followers. Throckmorton upheld the reconstruction policy of President Johnson and opposed black suffrage in any form. Pease adopted a mild tone. He favored, as a matter of expediency, granting the right to vote to those who could read and write. His followers, however, charged the conservatives with disloyalty and with planning to drive the Union men from the state. Throckmorton received 49,277 votes to Pease's 12,168. By a comparatively close vote the amendments to the constitution were ratified.

### Provisional Civil Government, August 20, 1866, to March 2, 1867

The newly elected Eleventh Legislature, conspicuously conservative, convened on August 6, 1866; three days later Governor Throckmorton and Lieutenant Governor G. W. Jones were inaugurated, and on August 20 President Johnson proclaimed the insurrection in Texas at an end.

The legislature had the task of naming two United States senators. By a decisive vote, it chose over the leading Unionist candidates the elderly David G. Burnet, a Unionist in 1861 who had come out of retirement to denounce vehemently the radicals, and O. M. Roberts, who had been the president of the secession convention. Neither Burnet nor Roberts could take the "iron-clad" test oath required of all United States officials by an act of July 2, 1862. Neither the senators-elect nor the three elected to the House of Representatives were seated. Then, following the suggestion of Governor Throckmorton, the legislators did not act on the Thirteenth Amendment to the Constitution of the United States and refused by an overwhelming vote to ratify the Fourteenth. Ignoring the warning of John H. Reagan[2] that the radical Republicans were gaining control of the government and would demand racial equality in the South, they proceeded to pass laws on the subject of apprenticeship, vagrancy, and labor contracts, all of which were calculated to keep at least some of the freed slaves in a state of peonage. Neither the apprentice nor the vagrancy acts met with strong opposition, but the labor law was especially offensive to champions of black rights. Its tenor

---

[2]John H. Reagan, postmaster general of the Confederacy, spent several months after the war in a Northern prison. There he came to realize that if the South were to avoid a most severe reconstruction program it must safeguard the rights of the freed slaves. His open letter of August 1865 suggesting limited black suffrage was received in Texas with derision. A later letter, written from his home near Palestine, only added to the irritation produced by the first.

may be judged by the provisions that laborers should not leave home without permission or have visitors during working hours and that they must be obedient and respectful. The laws were harsh and unjust, but in some states, the "black codes," which had replaced the old "slave codes," were even more harsh.

More and more the radical Republicans distrusted the ex-Confederates. Numerous reports told of the mistreatment of former slaves and of insults to Union men. The spirit of rebellion in the South had not been broken, said the men of the North. The radicals would provide guidance for the freed slaves in their own way; they would reconstruct the South under a plan that would destroy the political power of the old slavocracy and place all government in the hands of loyal men.

The agencies used by the radicals to carry out their program included the Freedman's Bureau and the army. The Freedmen's Bureau, created pursuant to an act of Congress of March 3, 1865, was clothed with the authority to take control of all affairs relating to freed slaves, refugees, and abandoned lands in the conquered states. In December of that year the bureau was set up in Texas under General E. M. Gregory, assistant commissioner. Toward the end of the summer there was much complaint that the freedmen were breaking their contracts. Gregory set to work with enthusiasm. He admonished the blacks to work; he required that labor contracts be registered with the bureau; and he did his best to dispel the notion that each freedman would be given "forty acres and a mule" out of the lands of former masters. The bureau did some relief work among freed slaves and provided night schools for several thousand of them. Its most important work was, however, to supervise contracts and protect the freed slaves from unscrupulous employers. Another activity, which offended many white citizens, was its intervention in the courts in cases in which freed slaves were involved.

Governor Throckmorton contended that President Johnson's proclamation of August 20, 1866, declaring the insurrection in Texas at an end, reestablished the supremacy of civil over military authority. However, with the president's prestige diminishing each day and the strength of the radical Republicans increasing, the governor was able to restore traditional civil government only in part. While the provisional government had been in existence, army officers had exercised extensive power, and they continued to exercise a great deal of authority after the inauguration of a civil regime.

The governor set to work to make the best of the situation. He sought to restore law and order, to secure the removal of the military from the centers of population to the frontier, to bring an end to the courts of the Freedman's Bureau, and to limit the jurisdiction of the military courts strictly to military cases. To a limited extent, he succeeded in getting a distribution of the troops for the protection of outlying communities. Less effective, however, were his efforts in behalf of the civil courts. There were in Texas three kinds of courts: the military, which claimed jurisdiction in all cases involving soldiers and federal employees; the Freedman's Bureau, which claimed jurisdiction in all cases relating to the freedmen; and those established in accordance with the Constitution of 1866, which claimed jurisdiction in all criminal and in most civil cases. Although the bureau was helpful in forging the new relationship between the black worker and his or her white employer, its partisan actions in intervening in the normal procedures of law, often with the support of the military, at times disregarded justice. A bureau agent arrested and fined D. L. McGary, editor of the Brenham *Banner*, for unnecessary abuse and ridicule of the bureau, its wards, and its agents. McGary refused to pay the fine and went to jail. Throckmorton, through J. B. Kiddoo, head of the bureau in Texas, secured his release, but the unrepentant editor continued his criticism of the bureau. The agent who arrested McGary later was indicted for lawless acts in Guadalupe County but was released by federal troops.

In spite of the furor and rancor it caused, the Freedmen's Bureau operated a system of schools for blacks that had a salutary effect. In January 1866 it had 16 schools attended by 1,041 students, and in June the numbers had increased to 100 schools and 4,447 students. When the bureau ceased operation in 1870, the black enrollment in schools had grown to 6,499 pupils.

In an age filled with racial tensions, it was to be expected that trouble would frequently develop where black troops were stationed. For a while, black troops at Victoria controlled the county jail and made it impossible to hold in prison there a freedman or a Union man. They burned Brenham, and neither the soldiers nor their officers were ever brought to justice. Only occasionally was a soldier turned over to civil authorities for trial for violating the laws of the state, and a few Union men, even criminals, received favorable treatment from the troops. Nevertheless, the troops were necessary, for lawless persons who hated both the blacks and the Unionists added to the problems of the military, the bureau, and the governor.

## CONGRESSIONAL RECONSTRUCTION

The radical Republicans in Congress watched the progress of Johnson's reconstruction program with rising resentment and hostility. It was moving too rapidly to suit them; it was turning the state governments of the late Confederacy back into the hands of the former slaveholders; it threatened to place the freed slaves and the ex-Union men at the mercy of ex-rebels; and it would add to the Democratic party a phalanx of eleven states, at least a part of which would return with a greater representation in Congress than when they seceded. Through pride and failure to comprehend fully their own peril, the men of the South had strengthened the cause of the radicals. They had honored with high office prominent leaders of the Confederacy. Several states had passed black codes calculated to reduce the black to serfdom. They had failed to prevent occasional race riots and many acts of lawlessness, and, with the exception of Tennessee, they had refused to ratify the Fourteenth Amendment.

In the election of 1866 the radical Republicans gained control of Congress and thus could carry out their own reconstruction program. Ignoring all that had been done by the president and the states, they proposed to place the government of the late Confederate states in the hands of those who professed loyalty to the radical cause, depending largely on a relatively small number of whites and the support of blacks. They would disfranchise the people who had always run the government, but whose loyalties were now suspect, and place in control freedman and Unionists, who were, in many instances, politically inexperienced. In short, they proposed to change the basic structure of Southern society.

The First Reconstruction Act, passed over the president's veto on March 2, 1867, contained the heart of their program. It declared inadequate and illegal the existing governments in the Southern states; it divided the South into five military districts; it granted the commanding generals authority superior to state laws and civil officials; it called for a constitutional convention, the delegates to be elected by voters of both races, exclusive of those disqualified as former rebels; it required that the convention frame and the qualified voters ratify a new constitution that granted blacks suffrage and that otherwise was acceptable to Congress; and it required that the legislature elected under the new constitution should ratify the Fourteenth Amendment.

The commanding generals might continue with the civil officers as they were or replace them by their own appointees. General Philip H. Sheridan, then stationed in New Orleans as commander of the Military Division of the Southwest, was given charge of the Fifth District made up of Louisiana and Texas, and under him General Charles Griffin was made commander of the subdistrict of Texas.

Throckmorton pledged to Sheridan and Griffin his cooperation, but the generals expected more than he was willing to concede. Griffin first became offended with the governor when Throckmorton refused to comply with a request that he pardon the 227 black convicts in the penitentiary. A bureau official had visited the prison and accepted the statement of the prisoners that their offenses were trivial. The radical press and Unionists both sought to undermine Throckmorton's influence. On July 19, Congress passed an act that removed the last doubt as to the power of the commanding generals to remove all civil officers, and on July 30 Sheridan declared Throckmorton "an impediment to reconstruction," removed him, and appointed in his stead ex-Governor E. M. Pease.

Meanwhile, Griffin had brought the civil government completely under his control. A rule that jurors take the "iron-clad" test oath[3] barred most men otherwise qualified to serve and threw the courts into confusion. It was in connection with the registration of voters, however, that Sheridan and Griffin were most rigorous in their demands. The Reconstruction Act of March 2 had disfranchised only those persons who were excluded by the Fourteenth Amendment. The Reconstruction Act of March 23 imposed this same restriction more emphatically by requiring the voter to take an oath to the effect that he had never held a state or federal office or taken an oath to support the Constitution of the United States and thereafter engaged in insurrection or rebellion against the Union. Sheridan, with the backing of General Ulysses S. Grant, applied this regulation most rigidly, even after the attorney general of the United States ruled that the law excluded only those who had taken an oath to support the Constitution of the United States and afterwards had supported the Confederacy. For instance, persons who, without having been required to take the oath, had served in such capacities as mayors of cities, school trustees, or even sextons of cemeteries, and had later taken part in the rebellion were disfranchised.[4]

Texas was fortunate in the selection of provisional governors. We have seen that A. J. Hamilton, the first military governor, was a Texas citizen seasoned by years of public service. E. M. Pease was even better prepared. Long a resident of the state, he had served four years as its chief executive. He was, says Ramsdell, "the most moderate of all those who had the confidence of the military authorities; and . . . his advice carried weight as Throckmorton's could not."

After Throckmorton's removal came the dismissal of other state and many local officers. On September 15 Griffin died of yellow fever, and his successor, General J. J. Reynolds, removed "rebel officials" in large numbers. In November, General W. S. Hancock succeeded Sheri-

---

[3]"That I have never voluntarily borne arms against the United States; . . . have voluntarily given no aid, countenance, counsel, or encouragement to persons engaged in hostility thereto; . . . have not yielded a voluntary support to any government . . . hostile or inimical thereto."

[4]The Reconstruction Act of July 19, 1867, gave to local registration boards broad discretionary powers to register or reject an applicant.

dan as commander of the fifth military district. Hancock, a Democrat and more generous than Sheridan, notified civil officials to return to their normal functions and permitted the registration of about five thousand additional voters.

When the registration of voters for the election of delegates to a constitutional convention had been completed, the rolls showed about 59,633 white and 49,479 black voters. It was estimated that the number of men disfranchised was not more than 7,500 to 10,000. The Republicans, organized in the Union League and in the Grand Army of the Republic, sought to gain the votes of the freedmen. The Ku Klux Klan, which in Texas operated under various names, by threats, intimidation, and occasional violence sought to destroy the political influence of the blacks and some Unionists.

The election was held in each county seat for five consecutive days, February 10–14, 1868. The law required that a majority of the registered voters had to participate in the election in order to make it effective. The Democrats proposed to stay away from the polls, hoping thereby to defeat the reconstruction program. As some stated, they preferred "Yankee rule to Negro rule." Unfortunately for the plan, some of the Democratic leaders lost confidence in it and at a meeting early in January advised their followers to vote against a convention and for delegates who would oppose black suffrage. The vote was 44,689 (7,757 white and 36,932 black) for the convention and 11,400 (10,622 white and 818 black) against it, the total being a little more than half of the total registration. Thus, the conservatives lost the election and failed to invalidate it.

The convention assembled in Austin on June 1, 1868. Of its ninety-four members (including four replacements as a result of deaths and resignations), two had served in the constitutional convention in 1845, six in that of 1866, and one in the German National Assembly in Frankfurt. Ten were blacks, including one replacement and George T. Ruby from Galveston, the well-educated, carpetbag president of the Union Leagues in Texas. It has not been possible to identify the exact number of carpetbaggers (Northerners who came South after the war for political office, for economic gains, or to work among freed slaves). Of those whose length of residence is known, thirteen had been in Texas three years or less, and only eight of them were true carpetbaggers. It is possible that a few others, whose length of residence is unknown, could be so classed. Thus, the blacks and carpetbaggers together constituted a much smaller proportion of the total than in the reconstruction conventions in other Southern states, but they provided a sizable block that voted almost solidly with the radicals. Of the original ninety delegates, no more than twelve were conservatives, including eight to ten Democrats, one of whom, L. D. Evans, had gone to the North for the duration of the war and voted with the radicals on division of the state, and seventy-eight were Republicans, irrevocably divided on the major issues. A. J. Hamilton, the leader of the moderate Republicans, had the unwavering support of supreme court justices Colbert Caldwell and Livingston Lindsay, of all the Democrats, and of a number who had been in the army or Congress of the Republic of Texas, in the convention of 1845 or 1866, or in the Confederate or Union army during the Civil War. Several had judicial experience. Of the radical Republicans, the most prominent in the convention were Edmund Jackson (E. J.) Davis of Corpus Christi, a former judge and the president of the convention, who had organized in South Texas a regiment of Union cavalry and attained the rank of brigadier general; Morgan Hamilton, the wealthy brother of A. J. Hamilton and the military-appointed state comptroller; James P. Newcomb, the most pronounced antisecessionist newspaper owner and editor, who had left San Antonio for California at the outbreak of the war; J. W. Flanagan, an opponent of secession, who had been a judge, a member of both houses of the legislature and of the convention of 1866, and a consistent advocate of the division of the state; George T. Ruby, president of the Union Leagues of Texas; and George W. Whitmore, a Smith County lawyer, who was vice-president of the Union Leagues of Texas. The radicals proposed to adopt an ordinance in favor of *ab initio* (that the ordinance of secession was null and void from its passage and that consequently all official acts of the state from that date until congressional reconstruction government was established were null and void), disfranchisement of all those who had voluntarily aided or abetted the Confederate States government, and the division of the state.

The first serious debate in the convention was over *ab initio*. The proposal was defeated, and in its stead a declaration was adopted by a vote of forty-five to twenty-eight that validated all acts that were "not in violation of the Constitution and the laws of the United States, or in aid of the rebellion. . . . " The *ab initio* supporters then set out to delay the restoration of constitutional government in the eastern part of the state and to create a new state or states out of the western section where there were relatively large numbers of Unionists. Their efforts to divide the state provoked the most time-consuming and most bitter debate in the convention. Furthermore, the convention assumed considerable responsibility beyond the writing of a constitution and spent much time chartering railroads, gathering evidence of lawlessness in East Texas, debating proposals for the sale of a portion of the state to the United States, and dealing with the inappropriate conduct of its own members. With the constitution almost completed, the delegates of all factions decided to delay its completion until after the presidential election—the radicals, because they did not like the constitution as it was being prepared and felt that a Republican victory would strengthen their chances for disfranchisement and division; the moderates, because they feared that, if the constitution was completed in time, the Democratic nominee might be elected president of the United States; and the Democrats, because they were opposed to any constitution that might be drafted by the convention and were optimistic that the Democrats would win the election and bring an end to military and Republican rule in Texas. Having delayed the completion of the constitution until it ran out of funds, the convention provided for the collection of a special tax to finance another session and, then, on August 31 recessed until the first Monday in December. During the recess, Grant, the Republican nominee for president, won an overwhelming victory.

Thus, when the convention reconvened in December, the radicals, convinced that they would have support from Washington, began a determined fight to divide the state. In January 1869 the convention, after refusing to accept a "Constitution of the State of West Texas," voted in favor of division of the state and to send a delegation to Washington to lobby for division and against the immediate restoration of eastern Texas to statehood because of the excessive violence there against freed slaves and Unionists. Ironically, to the lawlessness some members contributed more than their share.

The moderate-conservative coalition gained the ascendancy, however, and on February 3 the delegates approved a constitution for engrossment. Having lost every major controversial issue—*ab initio,* the establishment of a State of West Texas, and disfranchisement—Davis on February 5 and 6 engineered the breakup of the convention before the final vote on the completed document. The A. J. Hamilton faction, however, took control, recovered the records, turned them over to the commanding general, and adjourned the convention on February 8. The constitution as adopted was prepared in final form by a committee of three appointed by the commanding general and signed by forty-six delegates, including Davis (by order of the commanding general) and only seven other radicals.

The constitution, as finally adopted, disfranchised only persons disqualified by the Constitution of the United States, and it permitted male black suffrage by providing that the right of suffrage should not be affected by "race, color, or former condition."[5] It provided for much centralization of authority. The governor would hold office for four years and would appoint the secretary of state, the attorney general, and the judges of the courts. County courts were abolished. The convention did more for public education than any like body that had preceded it, by

[5]Seventeen states still permitted only white men to vote.

providing that all proceeds from the sale of public lands would be added to the permanent school fund and that the available fund would be used for the education of all children from six to eighteen years of age, irrespective of race and color. The schools were granted, in addition, proceeds of a poll tax and not less than one-fourth of the revenue from the annual state taxes. All in all, the Constitution of 1869 was not a bad instrument.

Preparation for the vote on ratification and the election of officials produced a flurry of activity. As previously noted, the radicals tried to prevent the final completion of the constitution, and failing, they tried to get President Grant and Congress to reject it. Unsuccessful in this, they did an about-face, endorsed it, and nominated Davis for governor and J. W. Flanagan for lieutenant governor. To oppose the constitution meant defeat, and to join the moderate Republicans would destroy their party. In opposition, the moderate Republicans and the Democrats supported A. J. Hamilton as their candidate for governor. The conservatives made a valiant fight, but the odds were against them. Through the Union League the blacks were aligned solidly with the radicals. General J. J. Reynolds, military commander in Texas, stacked the registration boards with Davis men, and many Democrats refused to take part in the election because they believed that Congress would not recognize the new government if Hamilton were elected or because they simply would not vote for any Republican.

The election was held on Tuesday, November 30 and the three days following. There was little violence, but there were many irregularities. General Reynolds never made public the returns (and they have never been found), but the vote that he certified on January 8, 1870, was 39,901 for Davis and 39,092 for Hamilton. Hamilton always believed that he was counted out; there well may have been fraud on both sides in the election. The constitution was adopted by a huge majority—72,466 as against 4,928. The radical Republicans elected three congressmen; the fourth Texas congressman, J. C. Conner, a Democrat, was an army officer and carpetbagger.

When Reynold's alliance with the radicals became known in September 1869, Governor Pease resigned in protest. Reynolds then proceeded to rule the state without a governor until January 8, 1870, when he appointed the successful candidates for state office to the respective offices for which they had been elected to serve as provisional officers until their constitutional terms began. He convened the legislature on February 8. That body promptly ratified the Fourteenth and Fifteenth Amendments and elected Morgan Hamilton and J. W. Flanagan to the United States Senate. On March 30, 1870, President Grant signed the act of Congress admitting Texas senators and representatives; the executive officers of Texas dropped the qualifying title "provisional"; and on April 16, 1870, General Reynolds formally brought military rule to an end by remitting authority to the civil officers.

Texas had been restored to the Union, but for many it was not until four years later when a government was established under the control of Democrats that Reconstruction would be ended.

## RADICAL REPUBLICAN GOVERNMENT
## UNDER THE RECONSTRUCTION CONSTITUTION

Pursuant to Governor Davis's call, the Twelfth Legislature met in special session from April 26 to August 15, 1870. It was in session twice during 1871, from January 10 to May 31 and from September 12 to December 2. Sixteen of the 30 senators, including 2 blacks, and 50 of the 90 members of the house, including 9 blacks, were Davis supporters. Thus, the governor had most of his program enacted into law. In his first message to the lawmakers, Governor Davis stated that the army was not adequately protecting the northern and western frontier against Indian raids and stressed the need for legislation providing for a ranger force for defense. The legislature immediately approved his recommendation for a force of 20 companies, totaling 1,220 men, but, because of insufficient funds and War Department disapproval, the organization never materialized. The legislature then authorized the establishment of companies of minutemen for frontier defense, but they were never very effective.

After providing for the ranger companies, the legislature moved rapidly to enact into law Davis's other recommendations. Five of the measures, called "obnoxious acts" by the Democrats, obviously for political gain, were controversial. Determined, if possible, to suppress the violence and lawlessness in the state, the governor also had urged the creation of a militia system and a state police organization, both under his control. The militia bill came up for consideration first. The Democrats and some Republicans feared such a force would put too much power in the hands of the governor. To prevent a vote on the militia bill, thirteen senators, some of whom wanted as a requisite the passage of a railroad subsidy bill, were arrested after they intentionally broke a forum. Four of the senators were returned to the senate to make a quorum, and the bill was then approved. The measure provided for the enrollment of all able-bodied males between the ages of eighteen and forty-five in a state milita under the command of the governor, who was empowered to use it to maintain law and order when local officials and the state police failed to do so. The opponents of the measure charged that the arrest of the senators was an act of despotism. Despotism, however, lay not in the arrest, inasmuch as the legislature had the power to compel attendance of its membership to assure a quorum for action, but in holding and denying the right to vote to some and in releasing and allowing the others to vote, an action surely of doubtful propriety. The house, likewise, evidenced lack of restraint almost as lamentable when on May 10, 1871, it removed its speaker, Ira H. Evans, primarily because of his opposition to certain measures of some of the members. Having passed the militia bill, the legislature, with far less opposition, then enacted into law a companion proposal by Davis for the control of lawlessness. This measure provided for the creation of a state police, consisting of 258 men and officers under the control of the governor, empowered to operate anywhere within the state. All local law officers were to aid the state force when called upon and were subject to removal for hindering the state police in the execution of the laws.

The other three controversial and unpopular acts of the legislature in the summer of 1870 were unrelated, but each increased the power of the governor. By the so-called Enabling Act, approved on June 28, the legislature authorized the governor to fill offices made vacant by the act readmitting Texas into the Union, including state, district, county, and city. One citizen estimated that Davis appointed, either directly or indirectly, 8,538 temporary or permanent employees as officers. Regardless of the accuracy of this tabulation, the act provided a tremendous amount of patronage. In another of the series of unpopular acts, provision was made for a state printer, an official state journal, and for the printing of public notices and other official matters in a newspaper in each judicial district. This act, although providing for a better informed citizenry, practically assured Davis some support from a subsidized press, but it aroused the ire of the Democratic editors. The fifth so-called "obnoxious act" postponed until November 1872 the regular election, which for members of congress should have been held in the fall of 1870 and for state officers in 1871. The reason given for the measure was that it made the dates for state and congressional elections coincide; the effect was to assure by an additional year the term of the radical officers elected in 1869.

Of all actions associated with the E. J. Davis administration, those remembered with the greatest resentment pertained to the activities of the state police and the imposition of martial law. The reason, at least partially, was caused by the political power struggle between the conservatives and radical Republicans. The police force had among its number some renowned lawmen, including L. H. McNelly's Special Force of Rangers, but unfortunately it also had within its ranks some criminals and other persons too weak to exercise authority with restraint. On several occasions they arrested men without justification and insti-

A native of Florida, Edmund Jackson Davis moved to Texas in 1838, became a brigadier-general in the Union forces, and returned to Texas after the war to become a Radical Republican leader. After serving one term as governor, he was defeated in his bid for reelection, but he remained active in politics until his death in 1883. (Courtesy Texas State Library)

gated or permitted riots. More than any other practice, the use of black policemen, who constituted about 40 percent of the force and who not long hence had been slaves, seemingly angered the conservative whites. The reputation of the police also suffered when in 1872 its chief, Adjutant General James Davidson, absconded with more than $37,000 in state funds. Nevertheless, the state police rendered valuable service in the interest of law and order. Even the conservative press occasionally praised the men for chasing outlaws and for their dealings with desperate criminals. For the fourteen months that ended September 17, 1871, the police reported 3,475 arrests; during the same period eight of its men had been killed in the line of duty.

Less widespread, but more severe when it did apply and more unpopular among the majority of conservative whites, was Davis's declaration of martial law. The killing of a citizen by a black policeman had led to an "armed insurrection" in Limestone and Freestone counties. The governor in the fall of 1871 declared martial law and sent three hundred militia to the region. The cost of occupation was met by a tax of three cents on each one hundred dollars of property valuation in the occupied area. There is some evidence, including a sizable majority vote in the house of the legislature, that the necessity of martial law in this instance was at least open to question. Davis also declared martial law, apparently with more justification, in Hill and Walker counties. Although postwar conditions indicated a possible need for a state militia and Davis's supporters insisted that he exercised great restraint in its use, the majority of white citizens undeniably resented the governor having such extensive power.

The Twelfth Legislature, apparently in response to strong and possibly unethical pressure from railroad lobbyists, promoted railroad construction. This issue, likewise, must be kept in perspective. The state was immensely large and without much water transportation; there was very little rail mileage in existence at the end of the war; the population was expanding into new areas rapidly; having retained its public lands, Texas, rather than the federal government, had to provide its own support to lines within the state; and finally, a tabulation of the vote on five railroad bills show that support was favored by a majority of Democrats and moderate Republicans, and opposed by a majority of radical Republicans. The legislators authorized cities to vote bonds as an aid. In a law later declared unconstitutional, they promised to the International Railroad Company, which was to build across the state, 8 percent state bonds to the amount of ten thousand dollars for each mile constructed. Many radicals opposed these grants, and it was over Davis's veto that a similar provisional grant was made to the Southern Pacific and to the Southern Transcontinental Railway. Since the Constitution of 1869 prohibited the legislature from granting lands to railroads, the extensive domain could not be used as a subsidy for construction. This restriction was removed in 1873 by a constitutional amendment, and in later years, a legislature controlled by Democrats substituted land grants for the bond subsidies. Other vetoes by Governor Davis at the time and later substitution of lands for bonds saved the state from being burdened by a huge, long-term debt for railroad construction.

The radicals enacted considerable legislation that was creditable. They designed a constructive program of social and economic legislation for Texas which under more favorable conditions might have been successful. They sought to provide a public road system and levied taxes for that purpose. They enacted a homestead law. They were generous in appropriations to provide state troops to supplement the inadequate frontier defense provided by the federal forces. Theirs was the first administration to envision a genuinely public, free school system. In making attendance compulsory and levying taxes adequate for the maintenance of the schools, they were half a century ahead of their time. The system was most unpopular, however, because it was costly and highly centralized.

Before it had been completed, the political structure of the radicals showed signs of disintegration. The Republicans had gained control of the state by a slender margin, and their victory was due to the demoralized state of the Democratic opposition. Their power rested mainly on black suffrage, a support that was soon cut away by the persuasion and intimidation of the opposition. Most of their legislative program was extremely unpopular.

Democrats and conservative Republicans united in attacking the radicals. In September 1871 the representatives of ninety-four counties met in Austin as a taxpayers' convention to protest the extravagance of the administration. Such men as A. J. Hamilton, Morgan Hamilton, and E. M. Pease united with ex-Confederates to argue that the Davis administration was flagrantly violating the constitution and laws and was bankrupting the state. At a special election in October 1871 (which Davis was pressured into calling because the legislature, in violation of the constitution, had postponed the general election until November 1872), the Democrats elected all four of their candidates for Congress; this in spite of Davis's supervision of the polls by peace officers and militiamen. In 1872 Horace Greeley, the Democratic nominee for president, outran President Grant in Texas by almost twenty thousand votes, and the Democrats again won all the seats in Congress and gained control of the legislature. It was at this election, incidentally, that the voters again chose Austin as the permanent capital.

When it assembled in Austin on January 14, 1873, the Thirteenth Legislature proceeded to repeal the basic laws of the radical program. It began by enacting a new printing law which withdrew official patronage from radical newspapers. It repealed, over the governor's veto, the hated police act, limited the power of the governor to declare martial law, and reduced drastically the appointive powers of the governor. It simplified requirements for the registration of voters and provided for precinct voting and one-day elections. The centralized school system of the radicals was reshaped by a law abolishing the board of education and school supervisors and reducing the power of the state superintendent. Before it adjourned, the legislature provided for a general election of state officers for the first Tuesday in December 1873.

The election brought the final test of the strength of the radicals. Davis and R. H. Taylor headed the Republican ticket, running against Richard Coke and R. B. Hubbard, the Democratic nominees. The campaign was hard fought, with both sides resorting to fraud and intimidation. The Union League threatened blacks who voted the Democratic ticket; the Democrats ordered blacks to stay away from the polls; and white men under age voted. Coke's vote was reported as 85,549 to 42,663 for Davis. The other state contests and most county contests were won by the Democrats.

The radicals made their last stand before the courts. They sought to invalidate the election on the ground that it was unconstitutional since, pursuant to the terms of the law passed by the Thirteenth Legislature, the polls were open for one day only while the constitution called for four-day elections. The state supreme court, in what became known as the "semicolon court case," upheld their contention.[6] Its decision, however, was ignored by the general public, and Coke and Hubbard were inaugurated late at night on January 15, 1874. Davis appealed to Grant, but the president advised that it would "be prudent as well as right" to accept the verdict of the voters. Davis refused to recognize the new administration, and certain members of the Thirteenth Legislature sought to organize that body as the constitutional lawmaking agency. For several days it seemed that bloodshed was inevitable. Davis was supported by some of his state police and black militia.

Citizens, armed and grim, under such leaders as Henry E. McCulloch and John S. ("Rip") Ford, sustained Coke. A local militia company, the Travis Rifles, also took the side of the new governor. At last, after he had received another message from the attorney general of the United States, stating positively that President Grant would not sustain him against Coke, Davis retired under protest.

Public indebtedness and taxation had increased under the radicals. Money appropriated under the printing act, the police law, the school law, frontier defense, and for the expenses of long legislative sessions amounted to millions. Through state taxes there was raised in 1871 and the three years following nearly $4 million. Besides the state *ad valorem* taxes and other levies, there were large increases in local taxes. In 1871 these combined rates amounted in some instances to as much as $2.17 on $100.00 of valuation, an increase of 1,450 percent over 1866. Meanwhile, it had become necessary to resort to borrowing, and the public debt was increased by more than $2 million.

## EFFECTS OF RECONSTRUCTION

Although Texas did not suffer to the extent of other southern states, the nine years that followed the collapse of the Confederacy proved destructive to the fortunes of many wealthy plantation owners and difficult for smaller landowners and farmers. The war itself had bankrupted numbers

[6]The justices, all Davis appointees, based their decision on the grammatical force of a semicolon in an article of the constitution: "All elections for state, district, and county officers shall be held at the county seat of the several counties until otherwise provided by law; and the polls shall be opened for four days. . . . " The court ruled that the semicolon in the article had the force of a period, and, therefore, the legislative statute establishing one-day elections was unconstitutional. Thus, the election was null and void.

of persons; and those who held on to their estates through the war found themselves land poor, sometimes without sufficient livestock and without slaves to provide labor. Of all the problems, that of securing labor was the greatest on those lands where slaves had once provided it. A new system of labor and land management acceptable to both black and white people had to evolve. In the meantime, thousands of acres lay idle. Land values fell to 20 percent of 1860 prices. Cotton, practically the only money crop, declined in value from thirty-one cents per pound in 1866 to seventeen cents in 1870, and to thirteen cents in 1875. The total production of cotton declined from 431,000 bales in 1859 to an average of 343,000 bales for the years from 1866 to 1870, both inclusive.

Improvement came gradually. Work for wages gave way to leasing or renting, when black labor was involved, and by 1870 the sharecropping system was becoming common. Under this practice, landowners supplied the laborers with all houses and farming equipment and took as their share from one-half to two-thirds of the crop. Improvement in the agricultural situation is reflected in the production of cotton, which by 1873 was exceeding 500,000 bales per year. Following the discovery that cotton would thrive on the rich uplands of North Texas, the increase in acreage was rapid. Immigration stimulated the production of all farm commodities. During this period southern and western Texas became comparatively prosperous from the pouches of gold brought back by drovers who took each year hundreds of thousands of cattle to northern markets. The industrial development of the country is reflected in the railroad mileage, which increased from 395 in 1865 to 1,650 in 1874.

Economic losses through the war and Reconstruction were soon overcome, but the effect on political and social institutions was more enduring. The people did not forget that radical Republicans in Congress had imposed on the South a program designed, it seemed to the white majority, more for political purposes than for the general welfare. Thus, the Republican party in the state was all but destroyed by the reaction against the Davis administration, and a one-party political system consequently prevailed for a century.

Perhaps it was the black people of Texas who suffered the most from the effects of Reconstruction. Blacks achieved some gains—the beginnings of an educational system, land ownership for a few, a degree of civil equality, and some political influence for a time—and they bore the responsbility of freedom as well as anyone might have been expected. But the tide of racial prejudice would have been strong under the best of circumstances, and many whites associated civil rights for black people with their memories of the hated radical government and reacted accordingly. In the decades to come, segregation, political and economic discrimination, and eventually disfranchisement would become a way of life for the black people of Texas.

## SELECTED BIBLIOGRAPHY

The best extensive studies of Reconstruction are C. W. Ramsdell, *Reconstruction in Texas;* and E. Wallace, *Texas in Turmoil.* Good sketches of Reconstruction may be read in S. S. McKay, *Seven Decades of the Texas Constitution in 1876* (Lubbock, Tex., 1942); L. J. Wortham, *A History of Texas;* F. W. Johnson, *Texas and Texans;* and O. M. Roberts, *A Political, Legislative, and Judicial History of Texas, 1845–1895.* Excellent biographical studies of participants in the Civil War and Reconstruction include B. H. Procter, *Not without Honor: The Life of John H. Reagan;* C. Elliott, *Leathercoat: The Life of James W. Throckmorton;* W. J. Hughes, *Rebellious Ranger: Rip Ford and the Old Southwest;* E. Wallace, *Charles DeMorse: Pioneer Editor and Statesman;* J. L. Waller, *Colossal Hamilton of Texas: A Biography of Andrew Jackson Hamilton;* Ernest Wallace, *The Howling of the Coyotes: Reconstruction Efforts to Divide Texas* (College Station, Tex., 1979); R. N. Gray "Edmund J. Davis: Radical Republican and Reconstruction Governor of Texas"; Betty J. Sandlin, "The Texas Reconstruction Constitutional Convention of 1868–1869" (unpublished dissertation, Texas Tech University, Lubbock, Tex., 1970).

Other useful book-length studies are W. C. Nunn, *Texas under the Carpetbaggers* (Austin, 1962); W. C. Nunn, *Escape from Reconstruction* (Fort Worth, 1956); Marion H. Farrow, *The Texas Democrats* (San Antonio, 1944); and D. Richardson, *Texas as Seen in 1870* (Shreveport, La., 1870).

Of the writings of participants, see O. M. Roberts, "The Experiences of an Unrecognized Senator," *Quarterly of the Texas State Historical Association,* XII, 87–147; John H. Reagan, *Memoirs, with Special Reference to Secession and the Civil War* (W. F. McCaleb, ed., New York, 1906); and A. W. Terrell, *From Texas to Mexico in 1865* (Dallas, 1933).

Valuable specialized studies published as articles include William L. Richter, "Texas Politics and the United States Army, 1866–1867," *Military History of Texas and the Southwest,* X, 159–186; William L. Richter, " 'We Must Rub Out and Begin Anew'; The Army and the Republican Party in Texas Reconstruction," *Civil War History,* XIX, 334–352; Dale A. Somers, "James P. Newcomb: The Making of a Radical," *Southwestern Historical Quarterly,* LXXII, 435–448; W. A.

Russ, Jr., "Radical Disfranchisement in Texas," *ibid.*, XXXVIII, 40–52; Louise Horton (ed.), "Samuel Bell Maxey on the Coke-Davis Controversy," *ibid.*, LXXII, 519–525; C. Elliott, "The Freedman's Bureau in Texas," *ibid.*, LVI, 1–24; George Shelley, "The Semicolon Court of Texas," *ibid.*, XLVIII, 449–468; Billy Bob Lightfoot, "The Negro Exodus from Comanche County, Texas," *ibid.*, LVI, 405–416; O. A. Singletary, "The Texas Militia during Reconstruction," *ibid.*, LX, 23–35; J. R. Norvell, "The Reconstruction Courts of Texas," *ibid.*, LXII, 141–163; and J. E. Ericson, "Delegates to the Texas Constitutional Convention of 1875: A Reappraisal," *ibid.*, LXVII, 22–27.

The most essential documents may be found in W. L. Fleming (ed.), *Documentary History of Reconstruction* (2 vols., Cleveland, 1906–1907); H. P. N. Gammel, *The Laws of Texas;* and E. Wallace and D. M. Vigness (eds.), *Documents of Texas History.*

There are many miscellaneous studies pertinent to the period. Some of the most valuable are James A. Baggett, "The Rise and Fall of the Texas Radical, 1867–1883" (unpublished dissertation, North Texas State University, Denton, Tex., 1972); Robert W. Shook, "Federal Occupation and Administration of Texas, 1865–1870" (unpublished dissertation, North Texas State University, Denton, Tex., 1970); William Lee Richter, "The Army in Texas during Reconstruction" (unpublished dissertation, Louisiana State University, Baton Rouge, La., 1970); Alwyn Barr, *Black Texans: A History of Negroes in Texas, 1528–1971;* Paul D. Casdorph, *A History of the Republican Party in Texas, 1865–1965* (Austin, 1965); Allen W. Trelease, *White Terror: The Ku Klux Klan Conspiracy and Southern Reconstruction* (New York, 1971); Lucille B. Bullard, *Marion County, Texas, 1860–1870* (Jefferson, Tex., 1965); Traylor Russell, *Carpetbaggers, Scalawags, and Others* (Waco, Tex., 1970). The *Texas Almanac* for the years of the Reconstruction period contains a voluminous amount of statistical, factual, and even descriptive information. W. P. Webb has a chapter on the state police in *The Texas Rangers.* Sam Acheson, *35,000 Days in Texas* (New York, 1938), a history of the *Dallas News,* brings out the flavor of the Reconstruction era; John C. McGraw, "The Texas Constitution of 1866" (unpublished dissertation, Texas Technological College, Lubbock, Tex., 1959) is an excellent reference. E. Wallace, *Ranald Slidell Mackenzie on the Texas Frontier* (Lubbock, Tex., 1965), covers the frontier Indian problem from 1871 to 1879. For an account of E. J. Davis's appeal to the courts, see J. H. Davenport, *The History of the Supreme Court of the State of Texas* (Austin, 1917). Short biographical sketches of the governors of the Reconstruction era are in J. T. DeShields, *They Sat in High Places.*

For a somewhat different viewpoint of Reconstruction, see Carl H. Moneyhon, *Republicanism in Reconstruction Texas* (Austin, 1980); Barry A. Crouch and L. J. Schultz, "Crisis in Color: Racial Separation in Texas during Reconstruction," *Civil War History,* XVI, 37–49; Edgar P. Sneed, "A Historiography of Reconstruction in Texas: Some Myths and Problems," *Southwestern Historical Quarterly,* LXXII, 435–448; Ann Patton Baenziger, "The Texas State Police during Reconstruction: A Reexamination," *ibid.,* LXXII, 470–491; Philip J. Avillo, Jr., "Phantom Radicals: Texas Republicans in Congress, 1870–1873," *ibid.,* LXXVII, 431–444; Allen Hornsby, Jr., "The Freedmen's Bureau Schools in Texas, 1864–1870," *ibid.,* LXXVI, 397–417; and John M. Brockman, "Railroads, Radicals, and the Militia Bill: A New Interpretation of the Quorum-Breaking Incident of 1870," *ibid.,* LXXXIII, 105–122.

Chapter Twelve

# THE TRIUMPH
# OF DEMOCRATIC
# CONSERVATISM
# 1875–1890

With the election of the Democratic legislature of 1872 and of Governor Coke in 1873, political power came into the secure grasp of those seeking to redeem the state from radical rule. Only the judiciary remained a Republican stronghold, and it proved to be a temporary one. Legislative maneuvering soon removed several district judges, who were replaced with Democrats; a constitutional amendment created a new supreme court with five positions; and within a month after his inauguration, Coke named five Democrats to fill the vacancies, including Oran M. Roberts as chief justice.

The triumph of the redeemers initiated more than a decade of conservative government. Reflecting the attitudes shared by most white Texans, these conservative Democrats sought where possible to wipe out the last vestiges of radical rule, the most obvious being the Republican-written Constitution of 1869. Suffering under the miseries of the Panic of 1873 they promoted public economy and retrenchment, sometimes to the point of parsimony, but simultaneously they encouraged the distribution of the public lands and the construction of railroads. Initially preoccupied with the legacies of Reconstruction, such as crime and public indebtedness, they soon found another perplexing challenge. Agrarian unrest, provoked by the emergence of a commercial economy characterized by falling prices, tight credit, and strangling freight rates, would be a persistent problem.

Although the conservative Democrats failed to cope successfully with the problems of unhappy farmers and although their policies otherwise were sometimes shortsighted, the period was not without substantial progress. Certainly, old enmities were being forgotten. When U. S. Grant and Phil Sheridan visted Texas in 1880, they were received cordially, and Sheridan apologized for having once said that if he owned Texas and hell he would "rent out Texas and live in hell." Crime was reduced; personal and property rights were made comparatively secure; new institutions were established; foundations were laid for a public school system; and finally, the low prices and the business stagnation that followed the Panic of 1873 gave way in the early eighties to a period of temporary prosperity.

## THE CONSTITUTIONAL CONVENTION OF 1875

Upon winning control of the legislature in 1872, the Democrats agreed with something approaching unanimity that there must be a new constitution. Critics found the Republican origins of the Constitution of 1869 a sufficient cause to discard it, but they offered more substantial reasons. They wanted elected judges, shorter terms, and fewer courts. Advocating a return to the old law, they sought repeal of the road tax and the maintenance of roads by personal service under overseers in the various communities. They hoped to abolish voter registration regulations and to require that all executive officers be elected to two-year terms. Taking the Constitution of 1845 as a working model, they advocated a biennial legislature with severely limited powers, especially concerning taxation and indebtedness, and a governor with substantially reduced authority.

After an effort to remodel the constitution in 1874 through a legislative commission failed, the legislature, on the advice of Governor Coke, submitted the question of a constitutional convention to the people. On the first Monday in August 1875 the voters approved the convention and elected three delegates from each of the thirty senatorial districts.

Perhaps the evaluation made by the San Antonio *Herald* of the convention delegates who assembled in Austin on September 6, 1875, was as sound as any generalization could be. "We know," observed the newspaper, "that the convention has relatively but a few able men in its composition, but those we deem very able, with sound clear judgment." Certainly the roll of delegates bears impressive testimony that the old Texans were again in the ascendancy. Seventy-five were Democrats, and only fifteen, including six blacks, were Republicans. Forty-one were farmers, and twenty-nine were lawyers. Eight had participated in the secession convention of 1861; nineteen had served in the Texas legislature, two in the Congress of the United States, one in the Confederate Congress, and one in the cabinet of Jefferson Davis. More than a score had held high rank in the Confederate army, and three had been officers in the United States Army. One had served in the constitutional convention of 1845 and another in the convention of 1866, but significantly, none had sat in the convention of 1869.

Among the more distinguished were John S. Ford, noted editor and Texas Ranger; John H. Reagan, postmaster general of the Confederacy and congressman-elect to the United States House of Representatives; Lawrence Sullivan Ross, famed Indian fighter destined to become governor of the state and president of Texas A & M College; Charles DeMorse, gifted editor and ex-Confederate colonel; and Thomas Nugent, who became a leader in the farmers' revolt of the 1890s.

Particularly influential in the convention proceedings was a bloc of 40 or more delegates who were members of the Patrons of Husbandry. This powerful and militant farmers' organization, better known as the Grange, had been introduced into Texas in 1873 by the establishment of a subordinate Grange in Salado in Bell County. Spurred by the Panic of 1873, membership climbed rapidly, until by 1876 the order claimed 45,000 members. Although the Grange as such did not take part in politics, Grangers frequently acted collectively for or against certain issues or candidates. In the convention, constitutional provisions reducing taxes and expenditures, crippling the public school system, prohibiting the state from chartering banks, and restricting corporate and railroad practices reflected the ideals of the Grangers.

From the beginning, the convention manifested a determination to promote measures of economy and retrenchment. Hinting of frugal principles to be incorporated into the fundamental law, the delegates voted themselves only five dollars per day, although members of the legislature had been receiving eight, refused to have the proceedings of the convention printed because of the expense, and even refused to employ a stenographer when they could not secure one for less than ten dollars a day. Surely, few would quarrel with a delegate's remark that "if future State Governments prove burdensome and onerous, it ought not to be the fault of the Convention."

## THE CONSTITUTION OF 1876

In keeping with a trend in the making of state constitutions in evidence since the early nineteenth century, the Constitution of 1876 is longer than the fundamental laws that preceded it, and it contains many provisions that the framers of the earlier instruments left to the discretion of the legislatures. It changed the framework of government in several important respects. The legislature was to be composed of two houses, the senate to consist of thirty-one members and the house of representatives never to exceed 150. The term of senators was reduced from six to four years. In calling for biennial sessions instead of annual sessions, as under the Constitution of 1869, the framers returned to the practice of a longstanding tradition. Lawmakers would receive a mileage allowance and five dollars a day for the first sixty days of each regular session and two dollars a day thereafter. Like the Constitution of 1845, the new instrument severely limited the powers of the legislature. It was forbidden to incur indebtedness to an amount greater than $200,000, and the maximum tax rate, except for the payment of debt, was set at a low level. An important limitation was the requirement that all property be taxed in proportion to its value. The duration of all offices created by the legislature was two years. A reaction against conditions of the war and reconstruction periods was reflected in the statement that the writ of *habeas corpus* "is a writ of right" that shall never be suspended.

The article describing the executive department provided for seven officers: a governor, lieutenant governor, secretary of state, comptroller, treasurer, commissioner of the land office, and attorney general. All, save the secretary of state, were to be elected by the voters. The maximum salary, that of the governor, was set at four thousand dollars a year, one thousand dollars less than he was then receiving. In vain did John H. Reagan, Charles DeMorse, and others plead for higher salaries, contending that such parsimony would, in the long run, prove costly. Terms of the executive officers were fixed at two years, with no prohibition against reelection.

The governor's powers and duties were set forth in considerable detail. He might convene the legislature in special session, call out the militia and declare martial law to suppress insurrection, and fill various vacancies by appointment, subject to approval of the senate by a two-thirds vote. He was given power to veto laws and veto items in appropriation bills, but his veto might be overridden by a two-thirds vote of both houses. It was declared that the governor, as the chief executive of the state, should cause the laws to be "faithfully executed," but the powers granted to him were not equal to such great responsibility. He was given no control over local officers and other elective state executive officers.

The judicial article reflected a reaction against the courts of the Reconstruction era. When the convention met, there were sixteen hundred undecided cases before the supreme court, and many regarded a number of the judges appointed by Governor Davis to be notoriously incompetent. Accordingly, the new consitution provided that all judges be elected by popular vote, with terms of four years for district judges and six years for judges of higher courts. The number of district courts was reduced to twenty-six. Establishing a dual system of appellate courts, the convention provided for a supreme court, with power to review civil cases only, and for a court of appeals, with appellate jurisdiction over all criminal cases and certain classes of civil cases.

Following the leadership of some northern states, the convention forbade consolidation of competing railroads and authorized laws to prevent unjust discrimination and to establish maximum freight and passenger rates but made no provision for a commission with regulatory powers. To promote the construction of new mileage, the legislature might grant public land to railroads up to an amount not in excess of sixteen sections for each mile of road constructed. It was forbidden, however, to grant state funds or bonds to railroads. The convention also provided for homestead grants of 160 acres to heads of families and half that amount to single men over eighteen years of age.

Suffrage provoked a heated debate in the convention. The most serious contest was over the proposal, supported largely by the East Texas delegates, to make payment of a poll tax a prerequisite for voting, the chief purpose obviously being the indirect disfranchisement of blacks. A substantial majority, including all but one of the Republicans, defeated the move. Otherwise, nobody objected to permitting aliens to vote, if they had resided in the state one year and had declared their intention of becoming citizens.

Women's suffrage produced a brief but bitter scene. In the constitutional convention of 1868 supporters of women's suffrage had made a serious bid for the right of women to vote, but the convention had eventually defeated the move. In 1875 a similar petition was referred to a committee where it provoked an angry denunciation and was never voted out.

Economy was evident in the discussion over the state-supported immigration bureau. The convention divided along sectional and political lines, with western and Republican delegates fighting for continuation, while others, led by the frugal Grange, successfully demanded its demise. Thus, a useful public institution was destroyed at the very time it was most needed to bring settlers to the millions of acres of public domain.

More controversial and more affected by demands for economy were provisions regarding public education. Texas had never had a satisfactory public school system, measured even by the standards that prevailed in the nineteenth century. Even now, in the convention some contended that education was a private duty, that no man should be taxed to educate another's child. Supporters of public education overruled that argument, but provisions for education were not as generous as those under the Constitution of 1869. Indeed, possibly the radical

Republicans of 1869 had been too ambitious, but surely the conservative Democrats of 1876 were too cautious. The convention authorized the legislature to contribute to the support of the public schools a poll tax of one dollar and not more than one-fourth of the *ad valorem* and occupation taxes. Rejecting the centralization prevailing under the radicals, it abolished the office of state superintendent, eliminated compulsory attendance, established segregated schools, and made no provision for local school taxes. Apparently the delegates saw no inconsistency between these provisions and their declaration that the legislature should "establish and make suitable provisions for the support and maintenance of an efficient system of public free schools." But an aroused *Galveston News* acidly observed that the convention, after "decreeing universal suffrage, had now also decreed universal ignorance."

The convention was more generous with school endowments, a fact that accounts in part for the small support provided for maintenance. It set aside as a perpetual fund all monies, lands, and other property previously granted to the schools and a large portion of the public lands. All told, the land granted amounted to about 42.5 million acres, and the permanent school fund invested in securities at that time was $3,256,970. Largely as a result of the sale of land, oil royalties, and leases, this endowment had grown to about $2 billion by 1980.

To the University of Texas, yet unborn, the convention gave with one hand and took away with the other. By a law of 1858 the school would have been entitled ultimately to about 3.2 million acres, a part of which had already been located and surveyed within the rich domain of north central Texas. The delegates repealed this provision and gave the university a million acres of land to be selected from the public domain unappropriated at that time, an exchange very disadvantageous both as to the quantity and the quality of the land. Only additional grants by the legislature and the fortuitous discovery of oil on some of the lands kept the university from suffering severely.

## ADOPTION OF THE FUNDAMENTAL LAW

Ratification of the Constitution of 1876 was accomplished without effective opposition but without impressive enthusiasm. Only one delegate expressed hearty approval, declaring that the constitution was "the noblest instrument ever submitted to the verdict of a free people." The six Republicans remaining in the convention joined five Democrats in a vote against adoption, and many delegates were opposed to portions of the document. Nevertheless, by a vote of fifty-three to eleven, the convention adopted the constitution on November 24, 1875. Arrangements had been made previously to submit it to the voters for their approval.

Anticipating some criticism, the convention issued a statement praising its handiwork and explaining that its economies would save the state $1.5 million annually. Significantly, the delegates felt obliged to defend at length the measures on public education, the part of the constitution that had been attacked by the press more severely than any other. The statement pointed to the extravagance of the former school system and the poverty of the state, emphasizing the generous permanent school fund.

Some opposition to ratification did develop. By a vote of 674 to 176, the state Democratic convention evaded endorsement, and the Republican convention denounced the document in a unanimous vote. Opponents claimed that the constitution crippled education; that its provision eliminating the immigration bureau would retard development; and that in failing to make the payment of a poll tax a prerequisite to voting, the document would surrender to black rule in a large number of counties. However, Governor Coke and much of the state press, together with the powerful Grange, backed ratification. In a mood for change, the voters probably would have ratified a much poorer instrument. The vote for adoption in a remarkably quiet election was 136,606 to 56,652.

All in all, the constitution complied with public opinion quite faithfully. Biennial sessions of the legislature, low salaries, no registration requirement for voters, precinct voting, abolition of the road tax, a return to the road-working system, a homestead exemption clause, guarantees of a low tax rate, a more economical school system with schools under local control, a less expensive court system, and popular election of officers—all these were popular measures with Texans in 1876.

The constitution, a logical product of its era and a fairly adequate pattern for government for the period in which it was made, was nonetheless an enduring fundamental law with many unfortunate features. Limitations on the powers of the legislature have made necessary many amendments to the original instrument, most of them giving the legislators additional power. Possibly the constitution did not give the governor enough power. It is true that he is regarded as the political leader of the commonwealth and that his influence may be very great, but he does not have the power to modify appreciably the policies and practices of other elective officers, and many appointive officers are wholly beyond his control.

Changes to meet the needs of an evolving society have come through amendments submitted to the voters by the assent of two-thirds of the members of each branch of the legislature at a regular session and approved by a majority vote of the electors. Thus, it is state policy to fix in the constitution by amendment the ceilings on taxes, on salaries, and on various expenditures, to define precisely the powers, rights, and prerogatives of various state agencies, and to assume that state legislatures are not to be trusted—all of which makes necessary more and more legislating by the people themselves. Although during the first half-century of the instrument few amendments were added, adoptions have come in an ever-increasing pace in recent times. Of 99 submitted up to September 1928, only 43 were adopted. Up to 1980, however, 386 have been submitted, and of this number 235 have been approved by the voters, an average of about 2 per year since 1876.

Efforts to effect a complete revision have accomplished little. No provision was made in the document for calling another constitutional convention, and legal authorities have generally agreed that this can be done only by the approval of the voters after the question has been submitted to them by a vote of two-thirds of the members of both houses. At different times there has been considerable agitation for a new constitution, but when the question was submitted to the voters in 1919, only 9 percent of them were sufficiently interested to express an opinion, and in 1975 voters turned down an extensive revision prepared by the legislature.

## POLITICS AND PERSONALITIES, 1875–1890

For nearly a decade and a half following the adoption of the Constitution of 1876, politics were characterized by the same tone of conservatism that prevailed in the convention. Democrats, who won state and local elections with monotonous regularity, differed on various particulars, but most generally agreed that economic retrenchment was more necessary than aggressive reform. Appropriately, in a state whose population was predominantly rural, political conflicts focused on the problems of the farmer, and elected officials concentrated on such matters as law enforcement, debt retirement, and disposal of public lands.

Although the composition of the state legislatures varied and the number of black representatives declined thereafter, the legislature elected in 1878 may be viewed as fairly typical of the age. Business and professional men, mostly attorneys, accounted for sixty-four members, and forty-four were farmers or were involved in activities related to farming. More than 90 percent were native-born southerners, eleven were born in Texas, and at least half had served in the Confederate army. Blacks in the delegation numbered five. Nine of the legislators were members of the Grange, and ten formerly had endorsed Whig policies. An overwhelming majority were Democrats, but there were nine Republicans and seven independents.

Throughout the period the Republican party, torn by factional quarrels even when in power, continued to deteriorate as an effective political organization. The party elected various local officials, a few state legislators, and occasionally even a congressman, but by and large it found little success at the ballot box. Temporarily, Republican leaders joined with agrarian reform groups in a marriage of convenience to oust the Democrats, but usually they concentrated on establishing their power within the party in order to assure their control over federal patronage in Texas. Factional conflicts of this type were intensified by differences over the role of the blacks in the party. Without the black voters the party faced little but frustration and defeat, but white Republicans found black leadership and control unpalatable, if not totally unacceptable. Nevertheless, after the death of E. J. Davis in the mid-1880s, the most powerful figure in the party was Norris Wright Cuney, a black customs collector in Galveston and one of the more perspicacious politicians of his time.

Cuney's influence reflected the continued activities of blacks in politics. After regaining power, white Democrats evaded the disfranchisement of blacks, feeling that the black vote could be controlled or outnumbered. But in fourteen counties located along the Gulf Coast and in East Texas, blacks constituted a majority of the population, and in thirteen others they amounted to nearly one-half. Thus, several counties for a time were controlled by a black electorate. Beginning with Harrison County in 1878 and followed subsequently by others, notably Fort Bend County in 1888, white Democrats used organization, intimidation, and other means, sometimes extralegal, to eliminate these local pockets of black power. But extensive curtailment of black suffrage through sophisticated laws awaited a later day. Meanwhile, blacks participated in politics, often without effectual strength but sometimes holding office. Primarily, they operated in the Republican party but they also formed a significant portion of the strength of another, the Greenback party.

The Greenback party, a threat more serious to Democratic suzerainty than the Republican challenge, was a voice of agrarian discontent calling for various reforms. It was particularly powerful in a West settled recently by poor farmers who had remained poor. Unlike the Grange, which was operated usually within the Democratic party, the Greenbackers formed their own party. Organized originally in the Midwest as early as 1874 to protest the resumption of the payment of gold for greenbacks (paper money without specie backing), the Greenback party wanted "more money and cheaper money" and argued that a gold monetary standard was deflationary and an undue hardship on debtors, a status common to many farmers. Advertising an intention to protect the poor man against bankers and bondholders, the party demanded that the federal government issue more greenbacks as legal tender and redeem all treasury notes and outstanding bonds with such money. In Texas, Greenbackers advocated an income tax, a better school system, a reduction of salaries of state officers, the abolition of useless offices, the regulation of railroads, and various other reforms. Several of these proposals were adopted during the progressive era of the early twentieth century.

Introduced into Texas in 1877, the party had its first campaign the following year, electing two senators and ten representatives to the legislature and indirectly assisting the election of a number of Republicans. Its strength declined somewhat in the election of 1880, but the Greenbackers regained new hope in 1882 with the arrangement of an independent coalition with the Republicans. The move gave the Democrats their biggest fright of the decade, though Democratic candidates, with only rare exceptions, swept the election on all levels. Efforts to perpetuate the independent coalition through the election of 1884 were only partially successful, and thereafter the coalition and the Greenback party faded from Texas politics.

Indeed, between 1875 and 1890 major state offices were controlled by a parade of conservative Democrats. Sam Bell Maxey, an "ultra-simon-pure-secession-anti-reconstruction Democrat," was elected to the United States Senate in 1874, to remain there until 1887. The Granger favorite, Governor Coke, was reelected in 1876, only to resign in December of that year to accept the other seat in the United States Senate, where he remained until 1895. When Lieutenant Governor Richard H. Hubbard, a Georgia-born ex-Confederate officer who succeeded Coke as governor, sought reelection on his own in 1878, he found a crowded field. Critics proffered charges impugning Hubbard's integrity and wisdom, while James T. Throckmorton, who had served as governor in the early days of Reconstruction, and W. W. Lang, master of the state Grange, also vied for the nomination. A deadlocked convention brought about the selection of Oran M. Roberts, an elderly ex-Confederate colonel, then chief justice of the supreme court and known affectionately as the Old Alcalde. Frugal and legalistic but strong-willed and aggressive, Roberts easily defeated W. H. Hamman, his Greenback opponent, an accomplishment he repeated in 1880, winning over both Hamman and E. J. Davis, the Republican nominee.

When in 1882 Roberts refused suggestions that he accept a third term, the Democratic nomination went instead to Judge John Ireland of Seguin. A native of Kentucky, ex-member of the Know-Nothing party, and ex-Confederate colonel, Ireland was an intense and intelligent man of integrity, often called "Ox-Cart John" in tribute to his opposition to railroad land grants. His opponent, George W. ("Wash") Jones of Bastrop, was a delightful addition to the political wars. Jones had been a Unionist but had served as a Confederate colonel. A Democratic lieutenant governor in 1866–1867, he had been elected to Congress as a Democrat in 1878, had won reelection as a Greenbacker in 1880, had welcomed Republican support on all occasions, and was now running as an independent. If party regularity was not one of Jones's virtues, he was, nonetheless, widely respected for his honesty and engaging oratorical talent. He was awkward but kind, earnest but humorous, and shrewd but forthright. The somewhat colorless Ireland, who wisely declined to speak against him on the same platform after an early debate, won the gubernatorial election, but the contest was the closest of the decade, Ireland receiving 150,891 votes to Jones's 102,501. In a repeat race in 1884, however, Jones's votes declined and Ireland's increased substantially.

The practice of electing conservative governors was perpetuated through the end of the decade. With his campaign directed by railroad attorney George Clark, a shrewd and successful conservative political manager, Lawrence Sullivan Ross won the nomination from a field of five candidates and also an easy election in 1886. Agrarian discontent had increased significantly by 1888, but Ross, not a reactionary but certainly no reformer, again won by a margin of almost three to one, this time over Marion Martin, the candidate of an incipient farmers' protest movement.

A number of factors explains the ease with which conservative Democratic elements maintained their political domination. Challenge from outside the party was limited by the lingering memories of Reconstruction and radical Republican government. Republican factionalism and Democratic adoption of some agrarian reform programs advocated by third-party movements likewise reenforced the Democratic domination. No doubt, fraud and ballot-box irregularities sometimes accounted for the Democratic victories. Until 1891 the constitution did not call for voter registration. But even after that date, a voting list in one county contained the names of several national leaders and Jefferson Davis! Radical insurgence within the party was controlled to a degree by nominating practices. Candidates generally were chosen by conventions, primaries not coming into widespread use until near the end of the century. Politicians already in power often found conventions easily manipulated. Finally, essentially conservative policies, such as promotion of railroads, frugal expenditures, and low taxes, were attractive to most Texans, even those who wanted more extensive reforms, such as railroad regulation and augmented state services.

## PUBLIC POVERTY

Poverty-stricken public finances constantly plagued the government of Texas during the decade following the adoption of the Constitution of 1876. When Coke was inaugurated governor in January 1874, the state debt, including some items of doubtful validity, was $3,167,335. The receipts for that year were not sufficient to meet half of the state's expenditures, and state warrants were quoted at sixty-five to eighty cents on the dollar. Industry and commerce, not yet recovered from the Civil War and Reconstruction, were prostrated by the Panic of 1873. Taxes already seemed too burdensome. No new sources of revenue were available, and it seemed that the only way to balance the budget was to reduce the outlay.

With the cooperation of the legislatures, Governors Coke and Hubbard struggled to reduce expenditures, but their economies were offset by increased demands on the treasury—funds for buildings for the new agricultural and mechanical college, pensions for veterans of the Texan Revolution, frontier defense, and interest charges. The treasury did not operate on a cash basis until the spring of 1879, by which time the state's indebtedness had increased to approximately $5.5 million.

Taking office in 1879, Governor Roberts insisted that the legislature balance the state's budget at any sacrifice and made several suggestions toward that end. He would refund state bonds and lower the interest rate, reduce the outlay for veterans' pensions, make the penitentiaries self-supporting, and, most extreme of all, lower the appropriation to the public schools from one-fourth to one-fifth of the general revenue. To increase income he would provide for a better system of tax assessment and collection, and in order to hasten the payment of the public debt, he favored sale of the unappropriated public lands to any person in any quantity desired. For his own part, he discontinued the payment of rewards for the arrest of criminals and followed a liberal policy for reprieves and pardons to relieve the crowded prison system.

The legislature responded readily to a part of Governor Roberts's suggestions. It adopted a law offering for sale in any quantity the public domain at fifty cents an acre, one-half the receipts to go to the permanent school fund and the remainder to be applied to the public debt. It passed laws to improve the collection of taxes, to provide fees for government services, and to broaden and increase occupation taxes. Toward reducing expenditures, it lowered substantially the appropriation for the maintenance of the state frontier force. The legislators exceeded the governor's wishes by discontinuing pensions altogether and substituting instead the grant of one section of land to each indigent veteran, an amount later raised to two sections.

But to complete his program of economy, Governor Roberts resorted to the veto. When lawmakers failed to lower the appropriations to the public schools from one-fourth to one-fifth of the general revenue as he had recommended, the governor vetoed the school item. Sharp criticism was hurled at him, but he stood firmly by his policy of retrenchment. At a special session in June 1879 the legislature reenacted the measure fixing the school appropriation at one-sixth of the general revenue. In 1881, during Roberts's second term, it raised the school appropriation to one-fourth of the general revenue but lowered the tax rate and diverted a part of the public school revenue to the Sam Houston Normal School.

At the end of his administration, the Old Alcalde could report with pride that the public debt had been reduced by more than a million dollars, that the annual interest burden had been cut by a third, and that there was a liberal operating surplus in the treasury. Probably, he found the greatest satisfaction of all in the fact that the *ad valorem* tax rate had been reduced by 40 percent. The achievement was one made at considerable cost, however, for public lands were disappearing into the hands of speculators, and state services, particularly education, were operating at a minimal level.

John Ireland, who took the oath of office in January 1883, differed from his predecessor in several important matters. He opposed the rapid sale of public lands and favored reserving them to meet the needs of homeseekers in future years. He opposed the state's purchasing its own bonds at high prices in order to hasten the extinction of the debt; he urged a more persistent enforcement of the criminal laws; and he promised to follow a less liberal pardoning policy. In the matter of economy, however, he was disposed to continue the Roberts program. The voters themselves in 1883 broke the spell of public parsimony by approving an amendment to the constitution authorizing special state and local school taxes, but the legislature continued to provide funds only with great reluctance, denying, for example, in 1883 and in 1885 appropriations out of the general revenue for the maintenance of the University of Texas.

Surely, the state finances improved substantially during the 1880s, an accomplishment due in part to the sale of public lands, economies in the government, and more effective tax laws. But, in fact, the state's financial record merely indicated the extraordinary increase in wealth and general prosperity. In many significant areas Texas wealth increased from two- to threefold between 1875 and 1890, this growth appropriately reflected on the tax rolls.


## LAW ENFORCEMENT

In respect to government the greatest accomplishment during this period was the victory for law and order. Except in the extreme western part of the state, Indian depredations did not constitute a serious problem after 1875, but there were many other problems. Mexico was in a state of war and confusion, and border troubles were plentiful. Juan Cortina, a folk hero in the eyes of some people but a ruthless murderer in the eyes of others, continued to cause unrest along the lower Rio Grande. The criminal and lawless elements that had become so powerful in the interior of Texas during the Reconstruction era did not yield readily to the authority of the new government, especially along the western frontier.

Often the spirit of rowdyism and the yearning to establish a reputation as a "tough" caused young men who were not criminals at heart to become so in fact. Thus, certain frontier characters would occasionally "take a town" just to see its inhabitants "hunt cover." More desperate and generally more dangerous was the professional criminal. During the seventies and eighties the far-flung ranch headquarters and isolated cow camps afforded concealment and a measure of protection for numbers of renegades and desperados. In 1876 the adjutant general compiled a list of three thousand fugitives from justice and noted that other names were arriving in every mail. In his message to the legislature in 1879 Governor Roberts stated that there was "an amount and character of crime and civil wrong entirely unprecedented in this country."

Stealing horses was one of the most common crimes. The editor of the *Frontier Echo* (Jacksboro) estimated that there had been 100,000 horses stolen in the state during the three years preceding March 8, 1878, that 750 men were regularly engaged in the business, and that not more than one in ten was ever caught and brought to justice. The Northwest Texas Stock Association (which later became the Texas and Southwestern Cattle Raisers' Association), organized in Graham in 1877, devoted considerable effort to suppressing cattle theft, but for several years the results were discouraging, because men of wealth and influence were doing a considerable part of the stealing.

Stage robbery became almost an epidemic between 1876 and 1883. On one occasion near Fort Worth in 1876, highwaymen held up a stage, lined up the passengers along the side of the road, and proceeded to take their money and other valuables. Suddenly a freighter's outfit and a private carriage came up. The new arrivals were made to join the others, and the loot taken amounted to seven thousand dollars. The robbers then shot their own horses and rode away on the animals belonging to their victims.

Feuds presented defenders of law and order with one of their most perplexing problems. For instance, in the spring of 1874 feudists in DeWitt County were defying local officers and making it impossible to convict their friends in court. Their method of avoiding conviction was a simple one. They merely murdered unfavorable witnesses. A bitter feud took place in Mason County in 1875 between the Germans and the Anglo-Americans. Meanwhile, the Horrell and Higgins feud of nearby Lampasas County, which had begun in 1873, grew in intensity. During the chronic quarrel each side committed murders, and the clans were so powerful that local peace officers and even the local courts were helpless to deal with them.

To cope with lawlessness of various types, vigilantes, more or less formally organized, were found in almost every community. Such a group at Denison seems to have been quite active; the Hill County vigilantes warned thieves in open letters; and during one week at Fort Griffin in 1878 vigilantes were credited with shooting one man in his jail cell, hanging another, and being responsible for the disappearance of a third.

But of all agencies suppressing crime in Texas, the Texas Rangers were the most effective. From the Gulf to the Panhandle they terrified evildoers and brought a sense of security to the men who obeyed the law. The dauntless Captain L. H. McNelly and his rangers made it possible to hold court at least in the DeWitt County feuds. Major John B. Jones restored order in the Mason County dispute, though he could not remove the cause of the trouble. In Lampasas County he arrested the leaders of that feud and persuaded them to enter into a peace covenant that temporarily preserved law and order. When Kimble County became notorious as "the worst section of the country there is for men to work in and a better hiding place for rascals than any other part of Texas," the rangers entered the county and soon arrested forty-one men. In 1879 Captain George W. Arrington, a ranger, was sent with a force to the Panhandle where, working with another great hater of cattle thieves, Charles Goodnight, he played a leading part in bringing first order and then law to the High Plains.

The rangers were indeed effective, but not everyone held them in high esteem. In South Texas some of the rangers who rode with great energy and dedication were Mexican-Americans, but other Mexican-

Americans claimed that the organization abused and mistreated their people.

Improvement in law enforcement was not left altogether to the peace officers. Court procedure was made more effective. A law of 1876 made it more difficult for the defense in criminal cases to stack the jury with men who were incompetent, venal, or biased. The number of district attorneys was substantially increased in 1879. When cases continued to stack up in the appellate courts, the legislature in 1879 provided for appointed commissioners of appeals to assist the supreme court and court of appeals by deciding certain civil cases in order to clear the way for criminal matters. This plan was continued until 1892, when the system of courts of civil appeals, still in effect today, was devised.

## THE PUBLIC LANDS

If the establishment of law and order was the state government's greatest accomplishment during this period, the formulation of a wise and far-sighted public land policy may very well have been one of its least satisfactory achievements. In 1876 the state still retained a public domain of 61,258,461 acres. Distribution of these lands brought conflict and confusion and provoked charges of fraud and speculation. In 1881 state officials discovered that railroad land grant commitments exceeded land available for that purpose by 8,000,000 acres. Meanwhile, state policies on sale of school and otherwise unappropriated lands produced a political, if not necessarily an economic, crisis.

Governor Roberts, the Old Alcalde, bore primary responsibility for the crisis. To help defray the cost of public education and to pay the state debts, he persuaded the legislature to pass the so-called Fifty-Cent Law, whereby unappropriated lands could be purchased by anyone for fifty cents an acre in any quantity. The terms allowed the prospective buyer to control the lands for 150 days without paying any part of the purchase price. Receipts from the sale of these unappropriated lands were to be divided equally between the public schools and payment on the state debt. Separate laws provided for sale of school lands at prices of one and two dollars per acre in amounts of up to seven sections per purchaser.

Critics of these land laws declared that they were an open invitation to speculation and fraud, that the heritage of the people was being wasted for an absurdly small return, and that corporations and syndicates would soon own most of the western area of the state. Typical of the critics was the venerable Charles DeMorse who, in indignation over the sacrifice of the public domain, resumed publication of his Clarksville *Standard*. In sympathy with the clamor, the Ireland administration in 1883 put through legislation that established a land board to investigate frauds, terminated the sale of large blocks of land, provided for sale by auction but for minimum prices of two and three dollars per acre according to type, and offered liberal credit terms to *bona fide* settlers.

Actually, the damage done by the notorious Fifty-Cent Law was largely indirect. Less than two million acres of land were sold under its provisions, probably because Land Commissioner W. C. Walsh, who objected strenuously to it, blocked many sales by means that were, if not strictly illegal, certainly unanticipated by the legislature. More important, the law depressed land prices to almost giveaway levels. Much of the acreage that fell into the hands of speculators was not purchased directly from the state but from railroads and Confederate veterans and widows at prices of as little as fifteen cents an acre. Furthermore, the law produced little revenue, less than a million dollars.

Modification of the Roberts administration's land policies did not eliminate Ireland's problems with the public domain. Fence cutting, discussed elsewhere, and the leasing of public lands caused trouble throughout the decade. Efforts to achieve true competitive bidding on state-owned, ranchland leases, expected to yield from four to eight cents per acre, resulted in a nasty quarrel involving the land board, the governor, and the ranchers. Suits to force the ranchers to pay the leases and to abandon lands illegally held were of little value. The cases were tried before West Texas cowboy juries controlled by the ranchers.

The state land board was abolished in 1887, and the entire responsibility of administering the public lands was placed on the commissioner of the General Land Office, subject to the approval of the governor in some matters. In an effort to prevent speculation, each purchaser of agricultural land was required to swear that he desired to "purchase the land for a home." It was also specified that he must reside on the land at least six months each year for a period of three years before the state would pass title to him. These provisions were retained in all subsequent legislation, and, according to the 1908 statement of the commissioner of the General Land Office, John J. Terrell, were the occasion of "untold perjury." Notwithstanding the rigid precautions of the law, in western counties the number of sales exceeded greatly the number of settlers. The greater part of the land went into the ownership of the ranchers, whose use of the land necessarily meant that population growth would be small.

If, in a frontier society, acquisition of a population is of highest priority, and if, in depressed circumstances, reasonable revenue from the disposal of the public domain is a logical objective, Texas public land policy between 1876 and 1890 failed to measure up on either count. The failure is particularly strange, considering the preoccupation of the administration with fiscal prudence and the dominance of farmers in the population.

## PUBLIC IMPROVEMENTS AND EDUCATION

During the decade following 1876, slow but evident improvement was made in the physical plants of the state's institutions. The first hospital for the insane had been built in Austin in 1856, and a sister institution was completed in Terrell in 1885. A state orphans' home was provided in Corsicana in 1887. During the same year the interests of black Texans were recognized in the founding of the school for deaf and blind black youths in Austin. The crowning achievement of the building program is the capitol in Austin, authorized in 1879 and completed in 1888. For this imposing structure of Texas granite, the state exchanged the 3,050,000 acres of land located in the Panhandle that became the famous XIT ranch.

The enforcement of the law soon crowded the penitentiary and focused attention on the state's prison problem. A new penitentiary was completed in Rusk about 1883, with the idea of smelting iron ores in that vicinity, but the results were disappointing. Governor Roberts apparently hoped to relieve the prison burden by a liberal policy of pardons, but his

The Texas state capitol, in Austin, constructed between 1883 and 1888 of native granite and financed by an appropriation of 3,050,000 acres of public domain, is an example of classic architectural style. (Southwest Collection, Texas Tech University)

plan provoked much opposition; his successor, John Ireland, was less generous toward the convicts. In 1871 Texas tried the prison-lease system, under which the state leased the penitentiary to private individuals. The lessees were to employ the convicts in any way they wished, subject only to the mandates of the state inspectors, who were supposed to see that the prisoners were not abused and that the prison property was not damaged. This was perhaps the worst system practiced in modern times. The death rate of convicts doubled, and the number of escapes per year more than tripled. Pursuant to the recommendation of a legislative investigating committee, the lease was terminated in 1876, but the lease system was not abolished until 1883.

The plan of 1883 is described as the contract-lease system. It was better than the old lease plan but far from satisfactory. Under the new arrangement the state retained control of the prison and prisoners, but leased to private operators the shops within the penitentiary walls and also hired out gangs of convicts to railroad construction foremen, planters, and others. The Huntsville industries were not successful, and the iron industry at the Rusk prison proved to be a white elephant in the hands of the state. Meanwhile, intelligent people were coming to realize that as long as the labor of convicts was used to promote the interests of private capitalists, abuses would exist. It seemed, therefore, that the only course left to the state was to buy and operate its own farms. Thus, the Texas prison system began farming as a last resort and without plan or design, but prison farming as well as prison manufacturing was to present difficulties.

The most enduring foundations of this period pertain to public education. Both the state's higher education and the present-day public school system began at this time. The first institution of higher learning was the Agricultural and Mechanical College, established near Bryan in 1876. It is a land-grant college, now named Texas A & M University, and owes its origin to the Morrill Bill passed by Congress in 1862, by which Texas received 180,000 acres of land to establish a college for the study of agricultural and mechanical arts. Texas accepted the offer in 1866, but the school was not opened until 1876, just after the constitutional convention had declared it would be a branch of the University of Texas. A school for black youths under the management of the board of regents of the Agricultural and Mechanical College was established in 1876. At that time no black students sought training in agriculture, and in 1879 the school was reestablished as Prairie View Normal School. It was not until 1899 that agricultural and industrial departments were added for both boys and girls. Sam Houston Normal Institute at Huntsville had its beginning in 1879 when the state matched a donation of six thousand dollars from the Peabody Board and the citizens of Huntsville made available the campus formerly used by Austin College there.

It has been stated in a preceding chapter that the Republic of Texas set aside fifty leagues of land for the endowment of two universities. A bill establishing the University of Texas was passed in 1858, but the Civil War stopped all development, and the project was postponed for another twenty years. The Constitution of 1876 granted a million acres of land to the university and its branches but contained no provisions to compel the actual organization of the school. The State Teachers' Association, organized in 1878 when Governor Roberts called a meeting of the state's teachers under the presidency of Dr. William Carey Crane, was instrumental in developing sentiment for establishing the university. At a meeting of the association in Mexia in 1880, a committee was appointed to present to Governor Roberts a plan for organizing the school. The governor sent the report of the committee to the legislature with his endorsement; the legislature carried out the plan substantially in the law approved March 30, 1881, providing for the establishment of the school. In an election the voters selected Austin as the site for the main university and Galveston for the medical branch. The main university was opened in 1883 and its medical branch in 1887.

Of wider public interest, if not of greater importance than the beginning of teacher education and higher education, was the evolution of the public school system during the early eighties. In keeping with the constitutional pattern, the legislature in 1876 adopted the community school system. This strange institution is without parallel in the history of education in America. The "community" had no boundaries and no means of acquiring and controlling property. After a school had been established there was no assurance that it would be continued, for it had to be reorganized each year.

Governor Roberts's veto of the school appropriation bill in 1879 aroused public sentiment that soon became overwhelming in its demand that the schools be given some income independent of an uncertain share in the general revenue. Among the leaders who promoted an interest in public education were O. N. Hollingsworth, secretary of the state board of education, who initiated the *Texas Journal of Education*; Barnas Sears of the Peabody Board, who had made possible model schools in eighteen communities distributed throughout the state; Dr. Ashbel Smith, a friend of education since the days of Mirabeau B. Lamar; R. C. Burleson, president of Waco University and state agent for the Peabody Board; and William Carey Crane, president of Baylor University. The reforms were actually attained during the Ireland administration by a constitutional amendment adopted in 1883 and a law enacted the following year. The amendment provided for a limited amount of support from the state and also allowed district voters to vote a small local tax.

The following year witnessed the complete rewriting of the school law. The law of 1884 provided for an elective state superintendent of instruction with limited supervisory power over all public schools and placed the schools under the immediate supervision of county judges. It provided that the counties, except the fifty-three that were exempted, should be divided into school districts that should have the privilege of voting for a local tax. It extended the scholastic age to include the years from eight to sixteen, both inclusive; it required that teachers hold certificates; and it prescribed a system of registers and reports.

Progress under the new system was slow. Immigration and a high birth rate caused the scholastic population to increase more rapidly than the available school fund. Especially discouraging was the indisposition of the people to vote for local school taxes. "The chief effect of the law of 1884," says Frederick Eby, "was to lift the responsibility for educational progress from the state as a whole and to place it upon the local communities." Thus, the common country schools remained poor and inefficient, with improvement confined largely to the towns and cities. The legislation of Ireland's day was a noble start, but there lay ahead of the public schools a long and rough ascent which they have not completed even to this day.

## SELECTED BIBLIOGRAPHY

Seth Shepard McKay published several authoritative works on the Constitution of 1876. He wrote *Making the Constitution of 1876* (Philadelphia, 1924); he brought together and edited newspaper accounts of the convention as *Debates of the Texas Constitutional Convention of 1875* (Austin, 1930); and he wrote *Seven Decades of the Texas Constitution* (Lubbock, Tex., 1943). See also his "Some Attitudes of West Texas Delegates in the Constitutional Convention of 1875," *West Texas Historical Association Year Book,* V, 100–106. For other studies, see E. Wallace, *Texas in Turmoil;* S. D. Myers, Jr., "Mysticism, Realism, and the Texas Constitution of 1876," *Southwestern Political and Social Science Quarterly,* IX, 166–184; Ralph Smith, "The Grange Movement in Texas, 1873–1900," *Southwestern Historical Quarterly,* XLII, 297–315; J. E. Ericson, "Delegates to the Texas Constitutional Convention of 1875: A Reappraisal," *ibid.,* LXVII, 20–27; and Oscar Walter Roberts, "Richard Coke on Constitution-Making," *ibid.,* LXVIII, 69–75. The constitution with amendments is published and indexed biennially in the *Texas Almanac.*

A comprehensive and reliable general study of the politics of the period is Alwyn Barr, *Reconstruction to Reform: Texas Politics, 1876–1906* (Austin, 1971). See also E. W. Winkler, *Platforms of Political Parties in Texas;* F. R. Lubbock, *Six Decades in Texas:* S. Acheson, *35,000 Days in Texas;* E. Wallace, *Charles DeMorse;* Paul Casdorph, *A History of the Republican Party in Texas, 1865–1965* (Austin, 1965); and his "Norris Wright Cuney and Texas Republican Politics, 1883–1896," *Southwestern Historical Quarterly,* LXVII, 455–464; B. H. Procter, *Not without Honor, the Life of John H. Reagan;* B. M. Jones, *The Search for Maturity* (Austin, 1965); and Louise Horton, *Samuel Bell Maxey: A Biography* (Austin, 1974).

Useful for politics, economics, education, and a variety of other areas is Lawrence D. Rice, *The Negro in Texas, 1874–1900* (Baton Rouge, La., 1971).

On state finances, the best sources are E. T. Miller, *Financial History of Texas;* A. S. Lang, *Financial History of the Public Lands in Texas;* R. McKitrick, *The Public Land System of Texas, 1823–1910;* and "Memories of a Land Commissioner, W. C. Walsh," *Southwestern Historical Quarterly,* XLIV, 481–497. Also see Thomas L. Miller, *The Public Lands of Texas, 1519–1970* (Norman, Okla., 1972). Considering economic matters primarily is J. S. Spratt, *The Road to Spindletop* (Dallas, 1955).

There is a historical sketch of the Texas penitentiaries by Carl Rosenquist in the *Handbook of Texas,* II, 411–413. See also C. S. Potts, "The Convict Labor System in Texas," *Annals of the American Academy of Political and Social Science,* XXI; W. C. Holden, "Law and Lawlessness on the Texas Frontier, 1875–1890," *Southwestern Historical Quarterly,* XLIV, 188–203; W. Gard, *Frontier Justice* (Norman, Okla., 1949); C. L. Sonnichsen, *I'll Die Before I'll Run* (New York, 1961); and Jack Martin, *Border Boss: Captain John R. Hughes* (San Antonio, 1942).

On the history of education, see F. Eby, *The Development of Education in Texas;* and C. E. Evans, *The Story of Texas Schools.* In this connection see also H. Y. Benedict, *A Source Book Relating to the University of Texas* (Austin, 1917); George Sessions Perry, *The Story of Texas A & M* (New York, 1951); William Hooper, Jr., "Governor Edmund J. Davis, Ezra Cornell and the A & M College of Texas," *Southwestern Historical Quarterly,* LXXVIII, 307–312; W. J. Battle, "A Concise History of the University of Texas, 1883–1950," *ibid.,* LIV, 391–411; George P. Garrison, "The First Twenty-five Years of the University of Texas," *ibid.,* LX, 106–117; and E. Bruce Thompson, "William Carey Crane and Texas Education," *ibid.,* LVIII, 405–421.

Chapter Thirteen

# THE ADVANCE
# OF THE FRONTIER

In 1860 the frontier, except for some settlements along the Rio Grande near Presidio and El Paso, extended along a line from Henrietta southward through Belknap, Palo Pinto, Brownwood, Kerrville, and Uvalde to Brackettville. During the Civil War there was no farther advance. A decade later this line was still the cattleman's farthest westward extension, but many of the earlier settlers, as a result of the ravages of marauding Indians, had retreated eastward. A line drawn from 30 to 150 miles east of it would delineate the area having less than one inhabitant per square mile. Such a line, running from the common boundary of Cooke and Montague counties irregularly to Bandera and to the Gulf a few miles south of Corpus Christi, may be designated as the farmers' frontier. About 40,000 people lived to the west of it in 1870; a decade later the number had increased to 165,000. Within 20 more years the number was nearly 500,000, and by the middle of the twentieth century the area west of the line was the home of about one-third of the population of the state. Although many of these people settled within this vast area as a result of the colonizing efforts of railroad and land companies, the overwhelming majority did so on their own initiative, each trusting in his or her own strength and in a kindly Providence as he or she entered the new country.

Stages in the westward movement included the subjugation and removal of the Indians, the expansion of the range-cattle industry, the conversion of the open ranges into big pastures, the advance of the subsistence farmers, the development of commercial farming, and the growth of industry. The latter two, being dependent upon transportation, had to await the building of railroads and highways to get their products to distant markets. Meanwhile, the stubborn contest between the whites and the Indians for possession of the land and the short interlude before the arrival of the railroads, when cattlemen challenged by only a few bold and hardy subsistence farmers held supremacy over the newly won empire of grass, constitute a colorful and significant segment in the history of Texas and the American West.

## THE DEFEAT AND REMOVAL OF THE INDIANS

After the collapse of the Confederacy, the state organization for frontier defense gradually ceased operation, and for several months thereafter the western settlers were left without protection. The Indians, soon aware of the situation, scourged the frontier as never before in history, driving the line of settlements eastward in some places by a hundred miles. The country west of a line drawn from Gainesville to Fredericks-burg was abandoned by all but a few of the most courageous settlers, who moved into stockades. The worst raids were made on moonlit nights, and the soft summer moon became a harbinger of death. Charred rock chimneys stood guard like weird sentries, symbolizing the blasted hopes of pioneers and often marking their nearby graves. A Waco newspaper in April 1866 claimed that not more than one fifth of the ranches in its vicinity were still occupied, and later that year a large group of citizens in a mass meeting in Denton resolved to abandon their homes unless help arrived before November. Incomplete reports from county judges covering the period from May 1865 to July 1867 showed that 163 persons had been killed by Indians, 43 carried away into captivity, and 24 wounded. These figures did not include Wise and Young counties, whose combined population declined from 3,752 in 1860 to 1,585 in 1870.

Upon the inauguration of the constitutional government in August 1866 the legislature promptly authorized the raising of a thousand rangers, but General Sheridan would not allow it. However, Governor Throck-morton's persistent efforts to persuade Sheridan and the Washington government to place at least a part of the four thousand troops it had in Texas on the frontier met with a measure of success. In September a cavalry detachment was sent to Fredericksburg, and by the end of the year federal troops had reoccupied Fort Mason, Fort Duncan, Fort Inge, Fort Clark, and Camp Verde to provide protection against marauding Apaches and bands from Mexico. Within another year several of these posts had been abandoned for more favorable sites, and the remainder of those maintained before the war had been reoccupied, all on a

Established in 1867, Fort Griffin was an important link in the chain of military posts along the frontier. Troops from this fort were called on to escort government mail, surveying parties, and cattle drives, and to punish Indians for their forays into white settlements. The town that grew up around the fort attained fame as a headquarters for buffalo hunters, cowboys, and frontier adventurers, but it declined rapidly after the fort was abandoned in 1881. (Texas Highway Department)

permanent basis. The line ran from Fort Richardson (in Jacksboro) through Griffin (near Albany), Concho (in San Angelo), McKavett (near Menard on the upper San Saba River), and Clark (near Brackettville) to Duncan (in Eagle Pass). An extreme western line was marked by Fort Stockton (near the present town of Fort Stockton), Fort Davis (near the present town of Fort Davis), and Fort Bliss (near El Paso).

The protection afforded by the military was inadequate. The troops were poorly disciplined and too few in number; many officers were lazy and inept and often were unduly restrained by their superiors; and the policy was strictly defensive—to keep the Indians out of the settlements by scouting maneuvers instead of by attacking their villages. Furthermore, the distance between the posts was too great for the soldiers to prevent the Indians from crossing the line.

In defense of the army, however, it must be said that its delay in establishing permanent posts and in adopting an aggressive policy was partially due to Indian agents who convinced Washington officials that peace could be had by treaty making and the appointment of Quakers as Indian agents. If the Indians could be induced to keep the peace, forts and war would be unnecessary. Consequently, Congress authorized a commission to secure a lasting peace among all the Plains Indians. At Medicine Lodge Creek, Kansas, the commissioners in October 1867 met with the Cheyennes, Arapahoes, Kiowas, Kiowa-Apaches, and Comanches in what seems to have been the most colorful council ever held between Indians and whites in the American West. Satanta, the principal leader of Kiowa raiding parties into Texas, insisted that western Texas belonged to the Kiowas and Comanches and that he did not want to give up any part of it. Ten Bears, a Comanche chief who realized that the Indians must accept the terms offered by the commissioners or be destroyed, blamed the Texans who had taken his country and pleaded that his people might be allowed to continue their nomadic way of life. They argued in vain. According to the Treaty of Medicine Lodge Creek, the Indians present agreed to accept reservations in the Indian Territory and to cease their depredations. The defiant warriors, nevertheless, continued to raid. Some of the Kiowas and about half of the Comanches refused to move onto the reservation. In fact, the Kwahadi Comanche band was not represented at the Medicine Lodge Creek council and did not recognize the treaty. Later that year a government agent who visited them at present-day Quitaque reported that the band had about 15,000 horses, 300 or 400 mules, and innumerable stolen cattle, and that 18 parties were at the time raiding the Texas frontier.

Nevertheless, President Grant, upon assuming office in 1869, was won over by the peace advocates and appointed as Indian agents Quakers who maintained that in dealing with the Indians kindness and reason would be more effective than force. Quaker Lawrie Tatum, a strong devotee of the peace policy who became the new agent at the Kiowa-Comanche reservation, soon found, however, that his wards would not listen to reason unless compelled by armed force. Unrestrained by troops, the reservation became a sanctuary for restless braves who slipped away to plunder in Texas. Beginning in the fall of 1870, they repeatedly raided the Texas frontier, killing fourteen persons during the following spring.

Best known of their audacious raids is the Salt Creek massacre of May 1871 when a band of Kiowas attacked a wagon train between Jacksboro and Fort Griffin, killed or wounded most of the twelve teamsters, and stole the mules. For the Indians the time of the attack proved unfortunate. General of the Army William Tecumseh Sherman, escorted by Randolph B. Marcy, Inspector General of the Army, had passed the site only a few hours before the attack and was in Jacksboro.

The two generals were inspecting the frontier to see for themselves if conditions were as bad as had been reported. Marcy thought they were. He noted in his journal that the Indian raiders, unless punished, would soon have the country between Belknap and Jacksboro totally depopulated. By the time the wounded teamster, who had managed to escape and make his way to Jacksboro, had finished with his description of the tragedy, Sherman likewise was convinced that the Indian menace on the Texas frontier had not been exaggerated. The Indian raiders were followed to the reservation where at least one of their leaders (Satanta) was boasting of his exploits. Sherman ordered the arrest of the raiding chiefs. Satanta and Big Tree were brought back to Jacksboro, tried in accordance with the laws of Texas, convicted of murder, and sentenced to be hanged. Governor Davis, however, commuted the sentence to imprisonment, and the chiefs were paroled in August 1873.

As a result of the Salt Creek massacre, the War Department unleashed its troops against the Indians off the reservation where the peace advocates had no authority. To lead the offensive, General Sherman fortunately had transferred to the Texas frontier Colonel Ranald Slidell Mackenzie, regarded by U. S. Grant as the most promising young officer in the army at the end of the Civil War, and his tough Fourth Cavalry regiment. In the autumn of 1871 Mackenzie led an expedition northwest from old Camp Cooper on the Clear Fork of the Brazos to Blanco Canyon, where he harassed the Kwahadi Comanches under Quanah Parker, the son of Cynthia Ann Parker who had been captured during a raid on "Parker's Fort" in May 1836, but was unable to prevent them from escaping unharmed across the High Plains in a heavy snowstorm. In April of the following year at Howard's Well in Crockett County, Indians, apparently Comanches, killed sixteen members of a wagon train party and afterwards held off two companies of troops who tried to punish them. In July Mackenzie renewed his campaign. After following two routes across the dangerous and unexplored plains in an effort to catch some cattle thieves, on September 29 he decisively defeated on the North Fork of the Red River, a few miles east of the present town of Lefors, a camp of Comanches who had participated in the attack at Howard's Well. As a result of their defeat and the imprisonment of their captured people, the Comanches and Kiowas remained peaceful for more than a year.

With the Comanches and Kiowas seemingly anxious for peace, General Sherman and Lieutenant General Philip H. Sheridan, commander of the Division of the Missouri, sent Mackenzie and his Fourth Cavalry to the Rio Grande border to put a stop to raiding in the area between San Antonio and the Rio Grande by Kickapoo and Apache Indians living in Mexico. By 1873 these Indians, it was estimated, had killed a number of citizens and inflicted damages amounting almost to $50 million. The troops quickly destroyed three of their villages, captured some of the Indians, and established an effective border patrol. By the end of the year, Indian raids along the Rio Grande had ceased, and Mackenzie resumed his job of driving the Indians from northwestern Texas.

Suddenly realizing in the spring of 1874 that reservations and advancing buffalo hunters meant the end of their old way of life, the Indians of the southern plains, led by Quanah Parker, renewed their attacks on the Texas frontier. The new war erupted on June 27 when several hundred Comanche and Cheyenne warriors and perhaps a few Kiowas attacked a buffalo hunters' stockade, known as Adobe Walls, near the present Borger. Superb marksmen among the twenty-eight buffalo hunters in the stockade, armed with their "big fifty" buffalo guns, were more than a match for the Indians. Although repulsed with heavy losses in their initial attack, the Indians were determined to keep white men off their favorite hunting grounds. They again began hitting the isolated settlers along the Texas frontier. When General Sherman learned of the situation, he persuaded President Grant on July 26, 1874, to turn the Indians, even those on the reservation, over to the military, thus putting an end to the Quaker peace policy.

In August, when the deadline for the Indians to enroll at the agencies had passed, the army moved against the remainder. The majority of the proud and stubborn natives took refuge in the wild canyons and breaks along the eastern edge of the *Llano Estacado*. There they were pursued relentlessly by well-mounted, well-armed, and thoroughly seasoned troops, led for the most part by officers who had learned in the school of experience the way of Indian warfare and guided by Indian scouts who could follow a trail like bloodhounds. Altogether, forty-six companies, about three thousand men, marching in five commands from as many directions, converged on the headstreams of the Red River in the eastern Panhandle of Texas where they found the Indian encampments.

Colonel Nelson A. Miles with 750 men moved southwestward from Camp Supply, Indian Territory, toward Palo Duro Canyon. Opposite the junction of Tule and Palo Duro canyons on August 30, he defeated about five hundred Indians, burned their village, and chased those fleeing to the head of Tule Canyon before turning back to scout again the region nearer his supply camp. Major William Price with four companies of cavalry moved from Fort Union, New Mexico, down the Canadian River to join Miles. Near Sweetwater Creek in the eastern Panhandle he won, though terribly scared, a skirmish with a group of Indians in flight from the reservations. From September to November Lieutenant Colonel John W. Davidson with nine companies of troops searched the country between his Fort Sill base and the main fork of the Red River almost to the Caprock without engaging the Indians in battle, but he returned to the reservation over three hundred Comanches who surrendered to him. Simultaneously, Lieutenant Colonel George P. Buell, while scouting up the Red River, destroyed two large Indian villages and a considerable quantity of supplies.

The most effective and dramatic blow to the last bid of the tribes of the southern plains to retain their nomadic way of life, however, was delivered by Mackenzie. After establishing his base at his old supply camp on the upper Brazos River, near the present town of Crosbyton, Mackenzie with about five hundred men, including a detachment of Indian scouts, headed northward along the edge of the Caprock for the headstreams of the Red River. After beating off an attack by Comanches at Tule Canyon and an all-night march, on September 28 in a daring, almost reckless, display of courage Mackenzie led his men down a narrow path to the bottom of Palo Duro Canyon. Here he defeated five villages of Comanches, Kiowas, and Cheyennes, burned their lodges and huge quantities of supplies needed for survival during the ensuing winter, and captured 1,424 horses and mules. Flushed from hideouts which their medicine men had assured them could not be found by the blue-coated troopers, many of the Indians sought safety at the waterholes on the *Llano Estacado*. Mackenzie, however, did not intend that they should find safety anywhere except on the reservation. Early in November he surprised and defeated a band of Comanches near the present town of Tahoka. Most of the Indians, however, had gone already or were on their way to the reservation, and the Red River War was over. By June 1875 the remainder had straggled to Fort Sill and surrendered, the last being a large band of Kwahadies led by Quanah Parker. Very few Indians had been killed or taken captive, but left without lodges and supplies or horses to acquire replacements, they could no longer continue their nomadic existence. Thereafter, only a few ever stole away from the reservation to raid in Texas, and the damage they did was negligible.

On the southwestern frontier, from the vicinity of Laredo to the outskirts of El Paso, another five years was to elapse before the Indian problem was settled. In the eastern portion of that section, the Apaches and Kickapoos from Mexico renewed their destructive forays after Mackenzie and his Fourth Cavalry had been removed. To stop the marauding by Indians based in Mexico, Sherman sent Mackenzie to Fort Clark early in 1878. Mackenzie quickly established at strategic sites a number of subposts, reactivated his system of effective border patrol, and in June led an expedition across the Rio Grande in search of the renegade Indians. The reappearance of this aggressive leader on the border influenced Mexican President Porfirio Díaz, who wanted to attract

United States capital to Mexico, to assist in the efforts to break up the raiding. Before the end of the year, affairs along the Rio Grande border were "most satisfactory."

Further west, the frontier enjoyed comparative peace in 1875, in part because of a successful scouting expedition led by Lieutenant Colonel William R. Shafter, but the next year Victorio at the head of a band of Apaches from New Mexico began raiding in Texas. In 1879 Victorio left the reservation and from his hideouts at isolated watering places on both sides of the Rio Grande made life and property insecure for all who had dared to settle within or attempted to travel across the Trans-Pecos country, despite the protective efforts of the federal troops and the Texas Frontier Battalion. Benjamin H. Grierson, in command of United States troops, and George W. Baylor, with a contingent of Texas Rangers, cooperating with the commander of a Mexican military force, pursued relentlessly the hostile Apaches on both sides of the international border. In October 1880 Victorio, the last of the troublesome leaders of the Apaches, was cornered and killed by Mexican troops, thereby concluding the elimination of the Indian barrier to the settlement of western Texas.

As during the pre-Civil War years, the defense efforts of the federal government were supplemented by the state. In 1871 the legislature authorized the minute-company plan which permitted citizens in twenty-four frontier counties to organize and equip themselves and receive limited pay. The plan, however, was not successful, and in 1874 the state created two organizations of rangers destined to attain renown. The first, the Special Force of Rangers under the command of L. H. McNelly, who always spoke softly but firmly, was sent in the spring of 1875 to the lower Rio Grande where several hundred followers of Juan Cortina were committing daily raids. The ranger captain soon reported that his men had slain near Brownsville an entire party of twelve cattle thieves. On one occasion he crossed the Rio Grande with thirty men, moved against Las Cuevas Ranch, where several hundred bandits and soldiers were established, and recovered some of the stolen cattle. His aggressive and fearless action brought a measure of security to several South Texas counties.

The other famous fighting organization was the Frontier Battalion, commanded by Major John B. Jones, a stern, unassuming, but highly efficient officer whose strongest drink was black coffee and favorite beverage was buttermilk. Although created, like the Special Force of Rangers, to deal principally with lawless white men, the Frontier Battalion took the field in time to have an important part in bringing to an end the Comanche and Kiowa raids in Texas. Jones placed his six companies in camps along the frontier in positions calculated to offer maximum protection. From these camps, scouts and patrols were kept constantly on the move to intercept any Indian raiding party that might be trying to make its way into the settlements. At Lost Valley, near the Jack-Young County line, on June 12, 1875, twenty-seven rangers under the command of Jones himself fought one hundred well-armed Indians for an entire day. In this instance the rangers were obliged to send a runner to Fort Richardson (Jacksboro) for aid, but normally they were able to deal successfully with any Indian force they encountered. During the first six months of its existence the Frontier Battalion had fifteen engagements with Indians, killed fifteen Indians, wounded ten, captured one, followed twenty-eight trails, and recovered livestock valued at five thousand dollars. When the Red River War was over, the Frontier Battalion concentrated its efforts very effectively against lawless white men.

## THE BUFFALO SLAUGHTER

A bizarre but significant episode closely associated with the problem of Indian removal and the advance of the Texas frontier was the extermination of the buffalo, or bison. This large, shaggy animal, which roamed the grassy plains in millions, constituted the Plains Indians' source of existence. In addition to food, clothing, and shelter, buffalo robes provided an important trade commodity. Although 199,870 buffalo robes reached New Orleans in 1828, the peak year, the number of buffalo killed before the end of the Civil War made no apparent reduction in the size of the immense herds nor gave the Indians cause for alarm. Beginning in 1870, however, when experiments showed that buffalo hides could be made into good leather, the demand for hides increased sharply. Buyers gathered at convenient points near the buffalo range and offered good prices for all hides. Hunters, who were superb marksmen, penetrated the plains, beginning near the railroad lines in Kansas, and wrought havoc with the Indians' "cattle."

Having slaughtered most of the buffalo in Kansas, they moved in 1873 from Dodge City to the Panhandle of Texas where they found a massive herd. The attack on their supply post at Adobe Walls in June 1874 only checked their operation for that season. By the end of the year several hunters had taken a long, circuitous route around the Indian country and had entered the range from the east by way of Fort Griffin, near present-day Albany. Before the end of 1875 J. Wright Mooar and his brother John, Joe S. McCombs, and others were hunting in the vicinity of the present towns of Sweetwater, Colorado City, and Haskell. During the 1875–1876 season an estimated fifteen hundred hunters were engaged in their deadly work. The magnitude of their operation is revealed in the volume of business at the supply base. In one day in 1877, the hunters bought at F. E. Conrad's general mercantile store in Fort Griffin, guns and ammunition to the amount of $2,500. Another supply base, Rath City, or Reynolds City, in Stonewall County, had a hide business that alone that year was valued at $100,000. Other bases and camps that became towns included Buffalo Gap, Hide Town (Snyder), and Mobeetie. During two months at the peak of their kill— December 1877 and January 1878—the hunters took at least 100,000 hides from the Texas range. During the following season, however, only a few small herds could be found, and by 1880 the buffaloes were gone.

Frontierspeople long engaged in lively arguments over the comparative effectiveness of the three factors that helped to rid the plains of Indians: the United States Army, the Texas Rangers. and the buffalo hunters. Each made some contribution. The army broke up large-scale resistance to authority; the rangers made raiding too hazardous for even the most reckless warrior; and the buffalo hunters destroyed the Indians' larder and opened the way for the herds of the cattle ranchers.

## THE CATTLE KINGDOM

Before the farmers could establish themselves on the lands vacated after the Civil War by the retreating Indians, except in the Cross Timbers where there was a small supply of timber and water, new inventions and discoveries had to be made. While they impatiently waited for the adaptations for a relatively short interval of less than three decades, the cattle kingdom arose, flourished, and declined on the free or cheap but nutritious grass that covered the plains. Texas is logically associated with cattle. Texans took over from the Spaniards the open-range cattle industry, modified it somewhat, and transferred it from Brownsville to Montana. Besides furnishing a large part of the nation's beef supply, Texas cattle stocked the middle and northern plains. The techniques, the lingo, and other aspects of the culture of the cattle kingdom contributed significantly to the history of the West.

When the first soldiers and priests came, they brought along cattle. The Spanish cattle were the progenitors of the wild cattle that in later years were to be found in various parts of the state, and also of the famous longhorns, a type that evolved in southern Texas and came to be known throughout the West. Apparently, cattle brought in from the Old South in the early nineteenth century affected materially the strain of animals on the range. But whether they were the lanky longhorns of South Texas or the better-built, round-barreled "Texas cattle," they were hardy and able to protect themselves; they made fairly good beef when fat and furnished their own transportation to market. Except for roundups at branding time, they were given no attention and needed none.

The open-range cattle industry had its beginning in South Texas between San Antonio and Brownsville and between Matagorda Bay and Laredo. In climate this region is unsurpassed as a range for cattle that are given practically no care. Some large herds were there during the Spanish era; in 1774 at Goliad, Mission La Bahía Espíritu Santo claimed fifteen thousand and Mission Rosario ten thousand head.

After the retreat of the Mexican army following Santa Anna's defeat at San Jacinto, many Mexicans withdrew from the country between the Nueces and the Rio Grande, and Anglo-Americans gradually entered the region. In a preceding chapter mention was made of H. L. Kinney, an adventurous Irish-American from Illinois, who established a trading post at the site of Corpus Christi in 1839 and soon engaged in ranching. Kinney hired a retinue of followers both to work and to fight, and for many years he was a veritable lord of the marches. The war with Mexico brought a number of prominent Anglo-Americans to this area, among them Captain Mifflin Kenedy and Captain Richard King, who enlarged his initial Santa Gertrudis tract of 75,000 acres into the famous King Ranch of more than a million acres. Many gold seekers on their way to California passed through Corpus Christi and created a limited market for the cattle. In spite of marauding Indian bands and bandits, the cattle increased rapidly, and a few cattlemen prospered. In 1860 there were an estimated 3,786,433 cattle in Texas, six times as many cattle as people.

After the war with Mexico, the range-cattle industry spread into the vast prairie region marked today by such cities as Dallas, Fort Worth, and Denton. John Chisum, later the best-known cattleman in New Mexico, owned a herd in Denton County during this period. By 1861 the cattlemen had extended their domain westward, appropriating the best ranges in the Western Cross Timbers, from San Saba County to Clay County. The Civil War halted their westward march, but in 1867, with the reestablishment of a line of military posts, the rangemen began appropriating the Rolling Plains. By 1876 they had reached or passed the one hundredth meridian, from Kimble County in the Edwards Plateau to Childress County in the eastern Panhandle.

Meanwhile, the industry had swung around the High Plains and was well established along the slopes of the Rocky Mountains and the valleys farther west. The career of Charles Goodnight illustrates this movement. Goodnight went to Palo Pinto County in the Cross Timbers of West Texas in 1857. A few years of trail driving, scouting, and ranger service made him one of America's finished plainsmen. With Oliver

Loving in 1866 he drove a herd by the Concho-Pecos River route to New Mexico, opening the Pecos (or Goodnight-Loving) Trail. He soon drove herds by this route into Colorado and in 1869 established his home near Pueblo. After business reverses had brought losses and the range had become crowded, Goodnight turned again to Texas. He moved his herd southeastward to the Texas Panhandle. The Comanches, who had formed a barrier against white intrusion into that country, had been driven by the soldiers to a reservation, and Goodnight felt confident that he could successfully deal with any small bands that might slip back to their old haunts. He entered the Palo Duro Canyon in 1876 and in partnership with John Adair, an Irish capitalist, established the JA Ranch.

Goodnight had selected a range with a fairly adequate supply of water. The scarcity of water was a great handicap for the cattlemen. Indeed, the plentiful grass was useless without the control of water. Surface water was impounded in tanks where there were creeks and draws, but for several years after the Indians had been removed, ranchers doubted that the millions of acres of fine grass on the High Plains could ever be grazed because of the lack of water. Fortunately, underneath most of the area lay an ample supply. Before it could be used, however, it was necessary to locate this supply and devise methods for making it available.

As early as 1855 Captain John Pope of the United States Army, while surveying for a railroad route, drilled for water on the High Plains. A well near where the Texas-New Mexico boundary crossed the Pecos River showed plentiful water, but at a depth too great to be practical. A few railroads utilized underground water, and in 1881 the Quaker settlers dug a well in Blanco Canyon and found an abundance of shallow water. Within the next two years several good wells were drilled in the San Angelo country and one in Schleicher County. In 1884 a cattleman had six wells drilled on his land in Lubbock County and proved that wells with windmills were practical for watering cattle. Within five years all the High Plains was cattle country.

Texas cattle were much easier to raise than to sell. During the Spanish era they were worth very little and could scarcely be disposed of at any price. Occasionally a herd was driven to Louisiana, notwithstanding the fact that trade with that province was forbidden, and at times dried beef was carried by pack train to cities in Coahuila. After the Texan Revolution, Anglo-Americans entered the business in the lower Nueces country, occasionally drove a herd to the East, and shipped cattle in considerable numbers to New Orleans. Nevertheless, cattle were of so little value that many thousands were slain for their hides and tallow. To conserve these commodities, packing plants were established along the coast of Texas, a dozen or more shipping their products through Rockport alone in the early seventies. A few pens, vats, ropes, pulleys, salt, and containers for the meat products constituted the equipment. Although some of the choicest meat was salted and pickled, millions of pounds, after being cooked to render out the tallow, were fed to hogs or dumped into the sea. Naturally, daring and resourceful men sought to get the cheap Texas steer to the tempting northern market. Before the Civil War a few drovers had proved that trail driving to the railheads in Missouri was practical. Left at the end of the war with very little money and an overabundance of cheap cattle, Texans in great numbers renewed their efforts to reach the affluent markets of the North by means of the long drives. In 1866 an estimated 260,000 cattle were started on the trail for Sedalia and other railroad stations in Missouri from which they could be shipped to eastern markets.

But the Texans met with unforeseen perils. In southern Missouri and eastern Kansas bands of farmers turned them back or broke up their herds, contending that the Texas cattle destroyed their crops and transmitted to their animals the dreaded Texas fever. By following a circuitous route west of the farmers' frontier, some of the herdsmen managed to reach St. Joseph and from there shipped their cattle to Chicago. By midsummer of the next year, however, the Kansas Pacific Railroad had extended its line beyond the farmers' frontier, and in Abilene, Kansas, herds could reach the railroad without interference.

Each year for more than two decades thereafter, thousands of Texas cattle were driven to railroad stations in Kansas to be shipped to eastern markets. During the first few years of the drives, fortunes varied; then the year 1874 and the decade following constituted a prosperous era for the cattle owners. A combination of factors created a strong market. Only a part of the cattle driven out of Texas went directly to the slaughter pens. Men soon discovered that the rich grasses of the northern plains would sustain and fatten cattle, and in the cow towns of Kansas, purchasers of stock cattle competed with those who bought for beef. Also, the process of refrigeration, which made it possible to ship dressed beef across the ocean, came into practice in 1875. By 1882 good steers brought five and one-half cents a pound on the Chicago market, at that time the highest price ever paid in the United States. The boom lasted until 1885 when a severe winter, followed by a drought, forced many owners to sell their animals on a market that already was weak, thereby causing the industry to collapse. Thereafter, trail driving declined rapidly. Vexing quarantine regulations and barbed wire fences made it more difficult and more costly each year.

Estimates of the number of cattle driven over the trails vary. The 1880 census estimates the drives to Sedalia, Missouri, for 1866 at 260,000;

CATTLE TRAILS 1865-1890
——— Chisholm Trail
– – – Dodge City Trail
–·–·– Goodnight-Loving Trail
- - - - Sedalia & Baxter Springs Trail

0        150 Mi.
0        150 Km.

the drives to Abilene, Kansas, 1867–1871, at 1,460,000; to Wichita and
Ellsworth, Kansas, 1872–1875, at 1,072,000; to Dodge City and Ells-
worth, Kansas, 1876–1879, at 1,046,732; to Dodge City, Caldwell, and
Hunneville, Kansas, 1880, at 382,000. More conservatively, Joseph
Nimmo, in *Range and Ranch Cattle Traffic, 1866–1884,* estimates the
total of cattle driven over all the trails from 1866 to 1884 at 5,201,132.

The perils of the trail loom large in the literature of the cattle
kingdom. The monotonous fare on the trail; the lonely night guards; the

storms with their wind, hail, and lightning; the stampedes when the roar of the ten thousand charging hoofs and the clatter of half as many sharp-pointed horns reminded the rider that his life depended on his surefooted horse; cold wind that chilled men to the marrow and blistering sun that scorched the earth; the swirling water of swollen streams; and the hazards of marauding Indians were experiences that caused many a trail driver to swear that he would quit for good at Abilene, Ellsworth, or Dodge City. Yet when it next came time for the drive, he was usually ready to go again.

Trail driving was economical. Eight, ten, or a dozen men with few supplies and only a small amount of equipment could deliver a herd of two thousand or more animals from Texas to the railheads in Kansas at a cost per head of fifty to sixty cents, a small fraction of the charge for shipping by rail. Thus, during the later years many herds were driven past Texas railroad stations and on to Kansas to get them as near as possible to eastern markets before shipping by rail.

There were several major cattle trails to the North, each with a number of branches in Texas used by drovers in reaching the main route. The first was the Sedalia Trail which started near Matagorda Bay and passed through or near Austin, Fort Worth, Denison, and Fort Smith. As a result of unfortunate experiences in Arkansas, the drovers, after crossing the Red River, followed a more westerly course by the Shawnee village to Baxter Springs and around the farmers in eastern Kansas to St. Joseph or to Abilene.

The best known of the group was the Chisholm Trail, opened in 1867 by and named for Jesse Chisholm, a Cherokee Indian trader, which began in South Texas, ran by Austin and Lampasas, passed between Forth Worth and Weatherford, crossed the Red River near present-day Nocona, and ran along or near the ninety-eighth meridian across Indian Territory to Caldwell, Kansas. Here extensions led to Abilene, Wichita, Newton, and other points. As the farmers moved westward, they forced the cattlemen to seek new routes and new shipping termini. For instance, Abilene, Kansas, was the chief shipping point from 1867 through 1871; Wichita to the south and Ellsworth to the west displaced it in 1872; and after 1876 Dodge City received most of the herds on their way to the eastern markets.

The Dodge City or Great Western Trail, formed at Mason by the junction of three important branches that came from the southeast by Lampasas, from the south by San Antonio, and from Bandera to the southwest, led northward through Coleman and Fort Griffin, crossed the Red River near Doan's Store north of Vernon, and then continued in an almost straight line to Dodge City, Kansas. An extension of the trail was used for driving many cattle from Dodge City to stock the vast northern ranges of western Nebraska, Wyoming, and even Montana. Reference has already been made to another major trail farther west that Goodnight and Loving opened in 1866. The Goodnight-Loving (or Pecos) Trail went westward up the Middle Concho, along the Great Comanche War Trail across the waterless stretch to the Pecos River at Horsehead Crossing, and up the Pecos into New Mexico. Within a few years, it had been extended by way of Raton Pass and Denver into Wyoming and Montana.

## THE BIG PASTURE COUNTRY

The open-range cattle industry spread with marvelous rapidity; its decline was even more rapid.[1] The crowded ranges, the westward advance of farmers and railroads, the introduction of barbed wire, and the utilization of drilled wells and windmills for obtaining water econom-

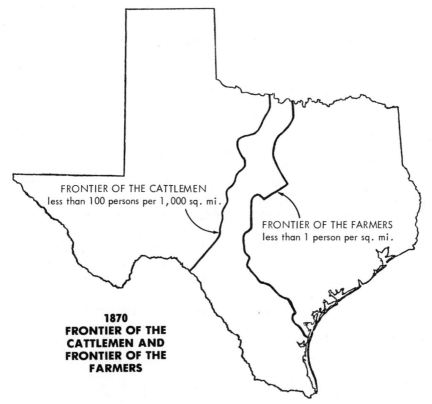

FRONTIER OF THE CATTLEMEN
less than 100 persons per 1,000 sq. mi.

FRONTIER OF THE FARMERS
less than 1 person per sq. mi.

**1870**
**FRONTIER OF THE**
**CATTLEMEN AND**
**FRONTIER OF THE**
**FARMERS**

[1]These statements apply to raising cattle on the unfenced range and not to enclosed ranching and stock farming. The latter continues to be a major industry. There were more beef cattle in Texas in 1976 than in 1885 or 1900.

ically transformed the open range into a country of big pastures. In brief, the open range ceased to exist about 1890 when the ranges had been enclosed by fences. Thus, the forces that promoted fencing call for some consideration.

The very success of the open-range cattle industry led to its destruction. Reports of huge profits attracted eastern and European capitalists as well as many small investors. Numbers of syndicates, such as the Texas Land and Cattle Company, the Matador Land and Cattle Company, the Hansford Cattle Company, the Capitol Syndicate Company, and the Espuela Land and Cattle Company, invested millions in the business. These concerns had the money to buy their lands and to fence them. Furthermore, the ranges soon became crowded. Protracted droughts interspersed by severe blizzards from 1885 through 1887 and quarantine laws of northern states against Texas cattle either decimated many herds or forced owners to sell thousands of gaunt animals, thereby bringing about a disastrous collapse in the cattle market. Fencing seemed to be the logical solution for the problems. Even before barbed wire, which offered a cheap and effective fencing material, had come into use, cattlemen in South Texas were enclosing their better grasslands with smooth wire or with boards.

Fencing was hastened greatly by at least three factors: the extension of railroads into West Texas; the invention and sale of barbed wire; and the discovery of an adequate ground-water supply and the use of windmills to make it available.

The Texas railroad system is described more at length elsewhere in this volume. It must suffice to state here that every large division of West Texas secured a railroad during the decade of the eighties. The network of railroads made practicable the importation of fencing material, though some ranches were still more than one hundred miles from the nearest line, and within another decade the best range lands had been fenced with barbed wire. J. F. Glidden, a farmer of De Kalb, Illinois, invented barbed wire in 1873.[2] Henry B. Sanborn, a salesman for the Glidden wire and later the founder of Amarillo, at first found it difficult to sell his product in Texas, but by 1880 there were a few barbed wire fences in a number of counties, including Clay and Montague in North Texas and Coleman and Runnels farther westward. Three years later practically all the cattle country of South and Central Texas had been enclosed, and fencing was well under way in the Panhandle and North Texas.

Opposition to fencing swelled with its spread. The first lands to be

[2]Other persons were working on the same idea, and it is difficult to apportion credit fairly for the product among the different inventors and promoters.

fenced naturally were those having a supply of surface water. It was soon evident either that the fencing movement had to be stopped or else those who did not fence would be ruined. The commissioners court of San Saba County asked the legislature to prohibit by law the building of barbed wire fences; and in 1888 the stockmen's association of Nolan and Fisher counties approved a resolution that the land west of the one hundredth meridian was "fit only for grazing" and that fences should not be allowed. Some men, however, expressed their resentment more violently by cutting the fences. Public sentiment generally supported the fence cutters. In many cases large proprietors had fenced in land that did not belong to them and had closed public roads. Fences displaced many cowboys who had neither the inclination nor training for another kind of work. Rustlers opposed fences because they made theft more difficult. Furthermore, "nesters" and small farmers who pushed ahead into the cattle country might find themselves entirely surrounded by a fence without an outlet or in turn have their own fences cut by those who resented their bold intrusion into the domain of grass. More significantly, the public resented fencing because the movement was led by large cattle companies mostly owned by eastern and foreign capitalists. This sentiment was well expressed by a contemporary newspaper editor who, after branding fence cutting as an evil, charged it to the fallacious and dangerous policy of the state in selling off its domain in such large tracts, "creating principalities, pashalics, and baronates among a few capitalists and arousing a spirit of agrarianism among the poorer classes."

During 1883 fence cutting occurred in more than half the 171 organized counties of the state. It was most serious along the agricultural frontier, marked by Clay County on the north, Coleman and Brown counties in the center, and Frio and Medina counties farther south. In some areas sentiment was so evenly divided that the local officers and the Texas Rangers were helpless.

To deal with the problem, Governor John Ireland called a special session of the legislature. Early in 1884 it made fence cutting a felony, but required that gates be placed every three miles along a fence. It also made unlawful the enclosing of land not owned or leased. Although in some localities four years later not a fence was left uncut, the legislative enactments, the energetic efforts of a few sheriffs and the Texas Rangers, and a growing public sentiment for law and order combined to put an end, by the close of the decade, to the destructive orgy. The damages to fences has been estimated as high as $20 million, a tremendous financial loss, but even more consequential was the unfavorable publicity that discouraged investments and immigration.

The crowded ranges, the westward advance of farmers and rail-

Cattle were introduced into Texas by the Spanish explorers and counted for the principal wealth of the missions. Herds increased during the Civil War when they were neither tended nor thinned. Barbed wire, first available to Texans in quantity in 1879, revolutionized land values and made it possible to open homesteads in frontier plains areas. In 1977 Texas was still the leading state in the nation in the production of cattle, sheep, and goats. Livestock and their products accounted for more than 50 percent of the agricultural cash income. Shown here, cowboys on the three-million-acre XIT Ranch that was given as payment for construction of the state capitol, and several Herefords, an improved beef breed. (University of Texas Library)

roads, the introduction of barbed wire, and the utilization of drilled wells and windmills transformed the open ranges into big pastures. In the conversion, some of the cattle companies were faced with the problem of consolidating their holdings. A few had managed to secure compact tracts of lands, but many of the large concerns had fenced in land they did not own. They bought a large part of their land from the railroad companies, paying from twenty-five cents to one dollar an acre for it. Interspersed with the sections of railroad were alternate sections of school land, which the ranchmen might lease but could not purchase except in small quantities, for the law limited the amount of school land that one person could buy from the state. The ranchmen bought as much school land as possible, but still there generally was land open to settlers in every large pasture. Immigrants in time sought out and purchased or squatted on these lands. The ranchmen ultimately bought out the "nesters," and a number of big, consolidated ranches emerged.

Most famous among them was the King Ranch which has been mentioned elsewhere. Nearby, Mifflin Kenedy, a former partner of Richard King, established a ranch that encompassed most of Kenedy County. In northwest Texas the JA Ranch under Goodnight's able direction by 1887 had 40,000 cattle and 700,000 acres of land under its control. Thomas Sherman Bugbee, who began grazing cattle in the Texas Panhandle in 1876, eventually expanded his Shoe Bar Ranch to 450,000 acres. Within another decade several other very large ranches were operating in the area. The Matador, a Scottish syndicate, at its peak owned 861,000 acres in Texas; the Spur, a British company adjoining the south side of the Matador, obtained a total of 439,972 acres; and the XIT, a Chicago-based syndicate and the largest of the Texas ranches, located the 3,050,000 acres transferred to it for building the state capitol along the border of New Mexico from Hockley County in the south to the Oklahoma line in the north. J. W. Williams, an authority on the subject, listed nineteen ranches in 1954 with a range of more than 150,000 acres each. The list included the previously mentioned King and Kenedy ranches, the W. T. Waggoner Estate, the West Cattle Company, and the Burnett ranches, all with ranges in excess of 400,000 acres.

On the enclosed pastures, select breeding of animals, impossible under the open-range system, soon came into practice. Durham, Angus, and Hereford cattle replaced the Spanish longhorns, but the Herefords soon dominated. In time the ranchmen began experimenting with crops to supplant their pastures of grass. At first they planted sorghum, then grain sorghum, and eventually wheat on larger and larger farms. In 1976 beef cattle in Texas numbered 15.6 million, about one-eighth of the total for the entire United States, and the cash receipts from this one commodity amounted to more than one-third of the revenue derived from agriculture.

## THE SHEEP AND GOAT INDUSTRY

Closely associated with the advancing frontier and the cattle industry was the raising of sheep and goats. Sheep, like cattle, were brought to Texas during the early Spanish era and were first raised on a large scale in Texas in the country south of San Antonio. In fact, the sheep industry was confined principally to that region until about 1880. Almost without exception, the sheepmen appeared after the cattlemen had established themselves. This fact, as well as the disposition of sheep to eat the grass so short that a cow could not subsist on it, made sheep raising unpopular in the cattle country, and sometimes there were clashes and bloodshed between the sheepmen and cattlemen.

The rapid growth of the sheep industry is reflected by the fact that in 1870 there were 1,223,000 sheep in Texas, whereas in 1880 there were 6,024,000, a larger number than at any time thereafter until 1930. The number, after declining to less than 2,000,000 in the early twentieth century, increased to nearly 11,000,000 during World War II, making Texas the leading sheep-producing state. Since then, however, the number has declined steadily, in 1960 to slightly more than 6,000,000 and in 1970 to less than 4,000,000. In 1976 there were only 2,600,000, but they produced almost $16 million in revenue from wool production.

Angora goats that produce quality mohair were brought to America and to Texas from Turkey in 1849. Goat raising became concentrated chiefly on the Edwards Plateau. In 1976 Texas had 1,120,000 goats, less than half as many as in 1970, that produced more than $24 million in revenue from the sale of mohair.

## THE ADVANCE OF THE FARMERS

In 1870 the extreme western line of the farmers' frontier extended from the common border of Montague and Cook counties irregularly to the vicinity of Bandera and thence to the coast a few miles below Corpus Christi, comparatively close to the cattlemen's frontier. But, as we have seen, within another decade the cattlemen's frontier had left the farmers' frontier hundreds of miles behind. The cattlemen appropriated the choice watering places and best grass lands, but generally there were not enough persons to form communities and establish local governments. The lawmakers created counties (fifty-four by one act in 1876), and geographers marked them on maps in checkerboard fashion; but the herdsmen generally had to wait for the coming of at least a few farmers before they could secure the 150 signatures required to organize a county. For land records and judicial purposes most of these western counties were attached to older counties to the east until a few farmers arrived to augment the adult male population.

Although they advanced more slowly, the farmers came in far greater numbers than did the cattlemen, and their movement gained momentum after the marauding Plains Indians had been confined to the reservations. An estimated 400,000 immigrants entered Texas in 1876, many of whom went directly to the frontier. At the end of the next year the western line of farms ran from Henrietta in Clay County southward through Archer, Young, Stephens, Comanche, Mills, San Saba, and Mason counties. By 1880 it extended from Vernon through Haskell, Jones, Taylor, Runnels, Coleman, and Mason counties. Within the three-year interval farmers by the thousands had settled within the long, triangular region formed by the Red River and these two lines. The increase in population was phenomenal. Jack County, which had only 694 inhabitants in 1870, had 6,626 in 1880. Taylor County was without white population altogether until about 1874, but by 1880 it was the home of 1,736 persons. Apparently, most of the frontier settlers during the 1870s came from older communities in Texas, but other states, particularly of the Old South, were well represented.

During the late seventies and early eighties several colonies of farmers moved to western Texas, some locating far in advance of the other settlements. The best known included a group of four hundred Germans from the vicinity of Indianapolis, who settled in 1878 in Baylor County; Lewis Henry Carhart's Christian Colony, which located in 1879 in the vicinity of the town of Clarendon; a colony of Quakers from Ohio and Indiana, who, under the leadership of Paris Cox, in 1879 established a settlement on the High Plains in Lubbock and Crosby counties; and a colony of German Catholics from Anderson County, who were induced by the Texas and Pacific Railroad to locate in 1881 at the present-day town of Stanton. Unacquainted with the country, the crops and the methods of tillage required, and beset by droughts and plagues of grasshoppers, most of these pioneer farmers did not succeed, but their heroic efforts paved the way for others who came later and profited by their experience.

With the coming of railroads in the eighties, the farmers' frontier abruptly ceased its comparatively orderly and solid advancement. No matter where the rails ran, settlers soon followed. The Texas and Pacific Railroad in 1880 overtook the line of settlements in Taylor County. Within a year Abilene, Sweetwater, Colorado City, and Big Spring were flourishing towns, and the better lands in their vicinity were soon occupied by farmers. A terrible drought in the mid-eighties halted the farmers' advance only for its duration; when it broke in 1887, the tillers of the soil arrived in greater numbers than ever. The mainstream of this new wave of settlers followed the Fort Worth and Denver Railroad along the upper Red River valley and across the Texas Panhandle. Almost by the time the line reached Texline on the border of New Mexico in 1888, Quanah, Childress, Memphis, Clarendon, and Amarillo had become service centers for farmers.

By 1890 the farmers had located in numbers throughout the region east of the one hundredth meridian and near the railroads. A decade then passed before there occurred any significant westward advance. Settlement of the productive area around Lubbock, about midway between the Texas and Pacific and the Fort Worth and Denver railroads, in the Concho valley around San Angelo, and along the Pecos River was delayed until the turn of the century. The advance of agriculture into South and Southwest Texas is likewise a twentieth-century movement.

*SELECTED BIBLIOGRAPHY*

A general survey of frontier defense and the Indian problem may be found in C. C. Rister, *The Southwestern Frontier;* R. N. Richardson and C. C. Rister, *The Greater Southwest* (Glendale, Calif, 1934); and E. Wallace, *Texas in Turmoil, 1849–1876.* Major studies devoted primarily to the subject include R. N. Richardson, *The Comanche Barrier;* E. Wallace, *Ranald S. Mackenzie on the Texas Frontier;* W. S. Nye, *Carbine and Lance, The Story of Old Fort Sill* (Norman, Okla., 1937); C. C. Rister, *Fort Griffin on the Texas Frontier* (Norman, Okla., 1956); J. E. Haley, *Fort Concho and the Texas Frontier* (San Angelo, Tex., 1952); W. H. Leckie, *Military Conquest of the Southern Plains* (Norman, Okla., 1963); R. G. Carter, *On the Border with Mackenzie* (New York, 1961); and Dan Thrapp, *The Conquest of Apachería* (Norman, Okla., 1967); Arlan L. Fowler, *The Black Infantrymen in the West, 1869–1891* (Westport, Conn., 1971); R. W. Shook, "Federal Occupation and Administration of Texas, 1865–1870"; Roger N. Conger and others, *Frontier Forts of Texas;* Paul H. Carlson, "William R. Shafter: Military Commander in the American West" (unpublished dissertation, Texas Tech University, Lubbock, Tex., 1972); H. Allen Anderson, *Fort Phantom Hill: Outpost on the Clear Fort of the Brazos* (Lubbock, Tex., 1976).

Valuable studies of Indian tribes include E. Wallace and E. A. Hoebel, *The Comanches;* M. P. Mayhall, *The Kiowas* (Norman, Okla., 1962); A. M. Gibson, *The Kickapoos: Lords of the Middle Border* (Norman, Okla., 1963); William T. Hagan, *United States-Comanche Relations: The Reservation Years* (New Haven, Conn., 1976).

The Indian side of the story is presented by Thomas C. Battey, *The Life and Adventures of a Quaker among the Indians* (Boston, 1875); and

W. S. Nye, *Bad Medicine and Good: Tales of the Kiowa* (Norman, Okla., 1962).

Considerable source material dealing with the subject is published in J. M. Day and D. H. Winfrey, *Texas Indian Papers, 1860–1916* (Austin, 1961); E. Wallace, *Ranald S. Mackenzie's Official Correspondence Relating to Texas, 1871–1873* (Lubbock, Tex., 1967); E. Wallace, *Ranald S. Mackenzie's Official Correspondence Relating to Texas, 1873–1879* (Lubbock, Tex., 1968); Joe E. Taylor (ed.), ''The Indian Campaign on the Staked Plains, 1874–1875; Military Correspondence from War Department, Adjutant General's Office, File 2815–1874,'' *Panhandle-Plains Historical Review,* XXIV, 1–216; XXV, 1–360.

A few of the many articles dealing with specialized phases of the subject are Adrian N. Anderson, ''The Last Phase of Colonel Ranald S. Mackenzie's 1874 Campaign against the Comanches,'' *West Texas Historical Association Year Book,* XL, 71–82; Frank Temple, ''Colonel B. H. Grierson's Victorio Campaign,'' *West Texas Historical Association Year Book,* XXXV, 99–111; E. Wallace and A. N. Anderson, ''R. S. Mackenzie and the Kickapoos: The Raid into Mexico in 1873,'' *Arizona and the West,* VII, 105–126; G. Derek West, ''The Battle of Adobe Walls (1874),'' *Panhandle-Plains Historical Review,* XXXVI, 1–36; Donald Whisenhunt, *Fort Richardson, Outpost on the Texas Frontier* (El Paso, Tex., 1968); Ernest R. Archambeau, ''The Battle of Lyman's Wagon Train,'' *Panhandle-Plains Historical Review,* XXXVI, 89–102. For a description of military posts where troops were quartered, see Eugener Graham, ''Federal Fort Architecture in Texas during the Nineteenth Century,'' *Southwestern Historical Quarterly,* LXXX, 165–188.

For the story of the shortest-lived frontier industry, see M. Sandoz, *The Buffalo Hunters* (New York, 1954); W. Gard, *The Great Buffalo Hunt* (New York, 1959); and Charles L. Kenner, *A History of New Mexican–Plains Indian Relations* (Norman, Okla., 1969).

Historical literature of the range cattle industry is voluminous. General studies are Ernest S. Osgood, *The Day of the Cattleman* (Minneapolis, 1954); E. E. Dale, *The Range Cattle Industry* (Norman, Okla., 1930); E.E. Dale, *Cow Country* (Norman, Okla., 1942); and James Cox, *The Cattle Industry of Texas and Adjacent Country* (St. Louis, 1895). Bearing especially on Texas is W.C. Holden, *Alkali Trails;* Coleman McCampbell, *The Saga of a Frontier Seaport* (Dallas, 1934); Billy M. Jones, *The Search for Maturity* (Austin, 1965); Robert M. Utley, ''The Range Cattle Industry in the Big Bend of Texas,'' *Southwestern Historical Quarterly,* LXIX, 419–441; Lewis Nordyke, *Cattle Empire* (New York, 1949).

There are several historians of the cattle trails: W. Gard, *The Chisholm Trail* (Norman, Okla., 1954); J. Marvin Hunter and George W.

Saunders (eds.), *The Trail Drivers of Texas* (Dallas, 1925); Harry Drago, *Great American Cattle Trails* (New York, 1965); Andy Adams, *The Log of a Cowboy* (Boston, 1931); Emerson Hough, *The Story of the Cowboy* (New York, 1923); Jimmy M. Skaggs, "The Route of the Great Western (Dodge City) Cattle Trail," *West Texas Historical Association Year Book,* XLI, 131–143; Chandler A. Robinson (comp. and ed.), *J. Evetts Haley and the Passing of the Old West* (Austin, 1978).

    Ranches and cattlemen have been popular subjects for writers. Among the best are Lewis Atherton, *The Cattle Kings* (Bloomington, Ind., 1962); Tom Lea, *The King Ranch* (2 vols., Boston, 1957); William M. Pearce, *The Matador Land and Cattle Company* (Norman, Okla., 1964); J. E. Haley, *The XIT Ranch of Texas* (Chicago, 1929; Norman, Okla., 1953); Cordia Sloan Duke and J.B. Frantz, *6,000 Miles of Fence: Life on the XIT Ranch of Texas* (Austin, 1961); William Timmons, *Twilight on the Range: Recollections of a Latter Cowboy* (Austin, 1962); Ron Tyler and Bank Langmore, *The Cowboy* (New York, 1975); William W. Savage, Jr. (ed.), *Cowboy Life: Reconstructing an American Myth* (Norman, Okla., 1975); Willie N. Lewis, *Tapadero: The Making of a Cowboy* (Austin, 1972); William Curry Holden, *The Espuela Land and Cattle Company: A Study of a Foreign-Owned Ranch in Texas* (Austin, 1970); David J. Murrah, "C. C. Slaughter: The Cattle King of Texas" (unpublished dissertation, Texas Tech University, Lubbock, Tex., 1979); J. E. Haley and W. C. Holden, *The Flamboyant Judge: A Biography* (Canyon, Tex., 1972); J. E. Haley, *Charles Goodnight, Cowman and Plainsman* (Boston and New York, 1936), an excellent biography; J. E. Haley, *George W. Littlefield, Texan* (Norman, Okla., 1943); W. C. Holden, *Rollie Burns: Or an Account of the Ranching Industry on the South Plains* (Dallas, 1932); J. W. Williams, *The Big Ranch Country* (Wichita Falls, Tex., 1954); Laura V. Hammer, *Short Grass and Long-horns* (Norman, Okla., 1943); L. F. Sheffy, *The Life and Times of Timothy Dwight Hobart, 1855–1953* (Canyon, Tex., 1950); L. F. Sheffy, *The Francklyn Land and Cattle Company: A Panhandle Enterprise, 1882–1957* (Austin, 1963); A. Ray Stephens, *The Taft Ranch* (Austin, 1964); Charles Kenner, "John Hittson: Cattle King of West Texas," *West Texas Historical Association Year Book,* XXXVII, 70–81; H. T. Burton, "A History of the J. A. Ranch," *Southwestern Historical Quarterly,* XXXI, 89–115, 221–260, 325–364; XXXII, 26–66; J. M. Skaggs, "John Thomas Lytle: Cattle Baron," *ibid.,* LXXI, 46–60; David B. Gracy, II, "George Washington Littlefield, Portrait of a Cattleman," *ibid.,* LXVIII, 237–258. For cowboy life and lore, see Ramon Adams, *The Cowman Says It Salty* (Tucson, Ariz., 1971).

    Several other phases of the cattle industry have attracted authors. Some excellent studies in this miscellany are W. P. Webb, *The Great*

*Plains;* Frank S. Hastings, *A Ranchman's Recollections* (Chicago, 1921); R. D. Holt, "The Introduction of Barbed Wire into Texas and the Fence Cutting War," *West Texas Historical Association Year Book,* VI, 65–79; Henry D. McCallum, "Barbed Wire in Texas," *Southwestern Historical Quarterly,* LXI, 207–219; W. C. Holden, "The Problem of Maintaining the Solid Range on the Spur Ranch," *ibid.,* XXXIV, 1–19; T. R. Havins, "The Passing of the Longhorns," *ibid.,* LVI, 51–58; T. R. Havins, "Texas Fever," *ibid.,* LVII, 147–162; J. Fred Rippy, "British Investments in Texas Lands and Livestock," *ibid.,* LVIII, 331–341; W. Gard, "The Impact of the Cattle Trails," *ibid.,* LXXI, 1–6; Lowell H. Harrison, "British Interest in the Panhandle-Plains Area, 1878–1885," *Panhandle-Plains Historical Review,* XXXVIII, 1–44; Gene M. Gressley, *Bankers and Cattlemen* (New York, 1966); Jimmy M. Skaggs, *The Cattle Trailing Industry: Between Supply and Demand, 1868–1890* (Lawrence, Kans., 1973); J. B. Frantz and Julian Ernest Choate, *The American Cowboy: The Myth and the Reality* (Norman, Okla., 1955); John I. White, *Git Along Little Dogies: Songs and Songwriters of the American West* (Urbana, Ill., 1975).

The publication of a series of short histories of West Texas ranch families, ed. by Ernest Wallace, is a valuable project of the Ranch Heritage Center, Texas Tech University, Lubbock, Tex.

Two authoritative works on the sheep industry are Edward Norris Wentworth, *America's Sheep Trails* (Ames, Ia., 1948); and Winifred Kupper, *The Golden Hoof: The Story of the Sheep of the Southwest* (New York, 1945); also, see Harold M. Gober, "The Sheep Industry in Sterling County," *West Texas Historical Association Year Book,* XXVII, 32–57. For the correspondence of George W. Kendall, Texas's leading sheep rancher, see H. J. Brown, *Letters from a Texas Sheep Ranch* (Urbana, Ill., 1959).

Preeminent among the accounts of the settlement of West Texas is W. C. Holden, *Alkali Trails;* R. N. Richardson, *The Frontier of Northwest Texas, 1846 to 1876:* B. M. Jones, *The Search for Maturity;* Robert Lee Hunt, *A History of Farmer Movements in the Southwest, 1873–1925* (College Station, Tex., 1935); Francis W. Rathjen, *The Texas Panhandle Frontier* (Austin, 1975). Other writings dealing with various phases of the subject are Mrs. S. C. Miller, *Sixty Years in the Nueces Valley, 1870–1930* (San Antonio, 1930); Stuart McGregor, "Migrations of Population in Texas" (reprinted from the *Dallas News*), *Bunker's Monthly,* September, 1929, 271–279; R. C. Crane, "Early Days in Fisher County," *West Texas Historical Association Year Book,* VI, 124–169; Walter B. Stephens, *Through Texas* (reprint of a series of letters published in the *St. Louis Globe Democrat,* 1892); Mary L. Cox, *History of Hale County, Texas* (Plainview, Tex., 1937); Willie N. Lewis, *Between Sun and Sod:*

*An Informal History of the Texas Panhandle* (College Station, Tex., 1977); Nellie W. Spikes and Temple Ann Ellis, *A History of Crosby County* (San Antonio, 1952); David B. Gracy, *Littlefield Lands: Colonization of the Texas Plains, 1912–1920* (Austin, 1968); Vernon G. Spence, *Judge Legett of Abilene: A Texas Frontier Profile* (College Station, Tex., 1977); and Kathryn Duff, *Abilene on the Catclaw* (Abilene, Tex., 1970).

# Chapter Fourteen

# THE COMMERCIAL REVOLUTION 1870–1930

In the span of a person's lifetime, 1870–1930, the economic transformation of Texas assumed the proportions of a revolution. Most of Texas in 1870 was either unpopulated or inhabited by subsistence farmers who could do little more than produce for their own needs. Transportation facilities were primitive, with only about five hundred miles of serviceable railroads. Industrial production was, for the most part, limited to small shops catering to the demands of self-sustaining communities.

But change, eagerly sought in the name of progress, was accomplished with dramatic speed. By 1904 Texas contained more miles of railroad track than any other state. Settlers rushed forward into western and southern areas. Although subsistence agriculture did not disappear entirely, farmers turned more and more to a commercial market economy, usually concentrating on the production of a single cash crop—cotton. Meanwhile, the pace of industrialization quickened. The value of Texas industrial production by 1901 amounted to more than half of the value of agricultural goods. Commercial agriculture continued to provide a living for a majority of Texans for the next several decades, but after the beginning of oil production at Spindletop, industry became more and more a dominant element in the economy. By the twenties the value of industrial production exceeded that of agriculture. With industrialization came its usual concomitants—the rise of the city and the beginning of organized labor.

## BUILDING THE RAILROADS

To the Texans of the late nineteenth century, the railroads appeared to be the key to progress and prosperity. Farmers and townspeople alike recognized the necessity of a cheap, fast, and dependable means of marketing, one available apparently only through railroads. Without the market afforded by the rails there would have been little point in mining coal at Thurber nor in raising cotton at Sweetwater. Wagon freight rates averaged one dollar per 100 pounds per 100 miles. With cotton bringing about 35 dollars a bale in 1876, wagon freight from north central Texas to Galveston would have absorbed more than half of the value of the crop. Rail freight rates, though often discriminatory, were never after 1879 more than 50 cents per 100 pounds per 100 miles and declined more or less consistently from that figure.

Thus, Texans understandably courted the builders of the roads. Citizens of Brenham, for example, were agreeable to a railroad's demand for a right of way through the county and $150,000 in cash. For a time Fort Worth granted bonuses to all railroads building into the city. For the communities already built and those still existing only in dreams, the railroad meant population and profit. When the railroad bypassed a community, the town was in almost all instances doomed to a certain and often a swift death. Citizens were drawn to the marketplace found in the rail terminals.

In addition to the enticements offered by local communities on their own authority, cities and counties, authorized by an 1871 state law, used public resources amounting to more than two million dollars to subsidize much of the cost of railroad building. In 1856 a law was enacted authorizing the lending of school funds to railroads to the amount of six thousand dollars per mile; under this law nearly $2 million was loaned to the railroads. During Reconstruction, from 1869 through 1871, the legislature voted bonds to railroads, but most of these obligations were later paid in land. In fact, by far the greatest bounty to the railroads came from the public lands. From 1854 until 1882, except for the period from 1869 to 1873 when it was prohibited by the constitution, Texas maintained a policy of liberal land grants. In most cases the amount of land given was sixteen sections for each mile of road constructed. About forty-one railroad companies received state land, first and last, before the repeal of the land-grant act in 1882. The greatest single beneficiary was the Texas and Pacific, which was given 5,167,360 acres. Approximately 32,150,000 acres of the state's public domain were disposed of in this way, an area as large as Alabama.

The wisdom of such generous land grants was, at the time, as it has been since, questionable. Critics have contended that the aid was more generous than necessary, that it caused the building of some lines that were not needed, and that in many instances the land grant actually retarded the development of the country. It must be said, however, that most of the railroads never received any real benefits from their lands. The railroad corporations were undercapitalized; the lands could not be converted into cash; the companies were forced into receivership; and the land was sold at a few cents an acre.

Construction of the bulk of the state's major railroads was accomplished in the span of two decades. Only eleven short railroad lines, with a little less than five hundred miles, had been constructed in Texas before the Civil War. Most of these lines radiated from Houston, and not until 1872 were railroad connections made with other states. The debacle of Civil War brought an end to railroad building, and only one line, the Houston and Texas Central, made any progress before the state was readmitted to the Union in 1870. The pace of construction varied in the next two decades, depending primarily on the general prosperity of the state and the availability of subsidies, but by the close of 1890 the state had 8,710 miles of railroads.

The Gulf Coast was soon connected to northern markets, as the Houston and Texas Central built northward through Dallas, while the Missouri, Kansas, and Texas (the Katy) built southward through Indian Territory. Citizens of Dallas hailed the coming of the rails with a buffalo meat barbecue, and a few months later the two roads met in 1872 in a cornfield where Denison now stands. By the early eighties the International and Great Northern Railway, a part of the Gould system, provided service from Longview in East Texas, through Austin and San Antonio, to Laredo on the Rio Grande where connections were made with Mexican lines. About the same time, leaders of Galveston, frustrated by yellow fever quarantines imposed almost annually by Houston, built around their neighbor to the north, going by way of Richmond toward Fort Worth. By the mid-eighties this railroad was a part of the Atchison, Topeka, and Santa Fe, with connections going in a number of directions.

Two transcontinental roads of particular importance to West Texas were constructed in the eighties. The Galveston, Harrisburg, and San Antonio reached San Antonio in 1877 and six years later connected with the Southern Pacific which was being built eastward from El Paso. These railroads merged and with others formed the Southern Pacific system.

The Texas and Pacific Railway, organized in 1872 with construction beginning at Longview, reached Fort Worth in 1876. Westward construction resumed in 1880, and two years later the westbound Texas and Pacific met the eastbound Southern Pacific at Sierra Blanca. Here the famous agreement made by C. P. Huntington of the Southern Pacific and y Gould of the Texas and Pacific was reached. The two roads publicly

**TEXAS RAILROADS**

——————— Houston and Texas Central
—·——·—— Gulf, Colorado, and Santa Fe
—·—·—·— Fort Worth and Denver City
——————— Texas and Pacific
——————— Southern Pacific
—+—+—+ International and Great Northern

agreed to share the lines from Sierra Blanca to El Paso. Other agreements that were kept a secret for many years called for the distribution of traffic and the pooling of receipts between certain lines of the two great systems and promised that neither side would build lines to compete with the other.

Railroad service for northwest Texas and the Panhandle came with the building of the Fort Worth and Denver City line. Built to Wichita Falls in 1882, the road was extended through Amarillo to Texline in 1888. In 1893 it became a part of the Burlington system.

## SETTLEMENT OF WESTERN
## AND SOUTHERN TEXAS

The conquest of the Indians, liberal land laws, and the building of the railroads combined to provide a momentum to the pace of the westward migration that did not subside until western and southern Texas was populated. As previously noted, by the close of the seventies the Indian barrier to settlements was removed, and by the nineties most areas in the state had been tapped by the railroads. Land laws thereafter were directed toward the interest of people in the western part of the state. The farmers' frontier was seldom very far behind that of the cattlemen. A law of 1897 reduced the minimum price of agricultural lands to $1.50 per acre with terms of one-fortieth down and forty years on the balance. A law of 1901 produced some land rushes and conflicts between cattlemen and farmers. However, a more orderly system was created in 1906 by a law requiring competitive sealed bids, a procedure that brought prices as high as twenty-two dollars an acre.

Actually, these land rushes marked the end of the old controversy between the cattlemen and the farmers. As long as there was free grass or land in quantity to lease, the cattlemen opposed the advance of the farmers. But once they had acquired legal possession of their lands, the ranchmen had no reason to oppose the coming of the farmers or of anybody else who would develop the country and increase the value of all land.

The railroads, which inaugurated costly programs aimed at populating the country, probably accomplished more in that direction than all other agencies combined. They had agents in eastern centers who distributed tons of printed materials; some railroads ran exhibition trains; some erected immigrant depots where people might stay while selecting their lands; some established demonstration farms; and with their transportation rates, all of them favored immigrants. Once settlements were established the people became enthusiastic about the country, and newspapers sometimes proclaimed its wonders in unrestrained language.

At about the turn of the century, when the people of the North Central Plains began to recover from the immigration fever, it spread to the High Plains where it raged intermittently for decades. The best school and railroad lands passed into the ownership of farmers, and the supply was exhausted early in the century. In 1908 the commissioner of the General Land Office reported that trainloads of prospectors, speculators, and investors were invading western counties of the South Plains, eager to buy land at from twelve to twenty-two dollars an acre. Lands held for the support of asylums were sold by 1912, and practically all surveyed school lands were sold by 1920. But already ranchmen had begun cutting up their pastures and selling off land in small tracts. Real estate companies occasionally made a killing from this development, much like those in regions to the east a decade or two earlier. Homeseekers were brought in by the trainloads, and land values sometimes increased from 50 to 100 percent within a few months.

While farmers were establishing themselves on the High Plains, others were moving with equal effectiveness against the domain of the ranchers in southern Texas. They practiced both dry farming and irrigation, but irrigation drew in the greater number, especially in the lower Rio Grande valley.

The growth of this region started with the building of the St. Louis, Brownsville, and Mexico Railroad in 1904. Thereafter the production of fruits and vegetables by irrigation increased rapidly, though irregularly. By 1910 a few commercial citrus fruit orchards had been set, and in 1914 it was discovered that by budding grapefruit and oranges on the native orange stock one could produce a tree adapted to the Rio Grande soil and climate. An amendment to the state constitution in 1917 and subsequent liberal acts of the legislature encouraged the organization of irrigation and drainage districts; thousands of farmers from North Texas migrated to the Rio Grande valley during the decade following World War I.

Indeed, this next decade saw a major land boom in the region. The general prosperity, in which the farmers shared at least in part, and the restoration of order along the Mexican border combined to create conditions ideal for real estate agents. Old irrigation projects were enlarged and new ones were established, so that each season huge blocks of pastureland were marked like gridirons by life-giving ditches. Unlike the promoters of the earlier years, the Rio Grande valley sought only the well-to-do or the rich immigrants. In no other area of Texas was the disparity between wealthy landowner and abysmally poor laborer, usually Mexican-American, as apparent as in the valley. Poor people could not purchase these high-priced lands. From North Texas cities agents ran excursion trains of Pullman cars and diners only, frequently making the passengers their guests, without charge for transportation or meals. At times, land sales on a single excursion of this kind aggregated more than a million dollars. Between 1920 and 1930 the population of the lower Rio Grande valley more than doubled.

## COMMERCIALIZATION OF AGRICULTURE

The revolutionary change in the nature of agriculture that occurred during these decades was in many respects as significant as the expansion of the farmers' frontier. By the seventies there was an apparent trend away from self-sufficiency toward commercialization wherein the farmer produced for the marketplace and in turn purchased many of his necessities.

Although Texans produced a variety of crops for market, cotton dominated the emergence of the commercial agricultural economy. In the late nineteenth century and early decades of the twentieth, the average Texan man was more familiar with the cotton sack and hoe than with the lariat rope and branding iron; he was a farmer, not a rancher. In 1880 farmers on slightly less than 2.5 million acres produced a cotton crop valued at about $57,000,000. In 1928 almost 17 million acres brought a return of $446,687,000. By 1910 approximately half of the cultivated acreage in the state was devoted to cotton, and ultimately it would be grown in 238 of the 254 counties. In comparison, cattle production did not begin to keep pace. Cattle numbers almost doubled between 1880 and 1900, reaching 10 million head, but declined thereafter to slightly more than 5 million in 1930.

Cotton production expanded in the face of innumerable problems and persistent opposition. The vagaries of nature—worms, boll weevils, Johnson grass, root rot, dry weather, wet weather—were enough to try the patience and to test the will of the most determined farmer. Moreover, critics repeatedly questioned the wisdom of expanding production and often the intelligence of the producer. Farm organizations, editors, agricultural colleagues, and self-appointed advisors who volunteered their counsel persistently condemned specialization in general and cotton farming in particular. Cotton farming, they contended, was responsible for oppressive mortgages, exhausted fertility, rising tenancy, and declining income. Diversification, as they used the term, in essence a return to the self-sustaining farm, would ease the burden of the farmer. The cotton farmer paid no heed.

Although some critics argued that ignorance accounted for the cotton farmer's stubborn refusal to restrict his acreage, the reasons were actually more complex and convincing. Prices declined, but cotton almost always returned more income per acre than other crops suited to his labor, land, and machinery resources. Cotton was the most dependable of the southern crops; contrary to popular opinion, it did not exhaust the soil as quickly as many other crops. And the machinery for marketing cotton was more advanced than for other commodities.

Few farmers, whether they raised cotton or other products, found the marketplace with its enticing opportunities an avenue to substantial wealth. Returns fluctuated unpredictably from one year to the next; prices, costs, mortgages, and weather frequently combined to leave the farmer looking anxiously to the "next year" rather than rejoicing in the present one. But between 1880 and 1920 agricultural wealth for the state as a whole increased steadily from decade to decade, even spectacularly, and remained fairly stable during the twenties. From less than one thousand dollars in 1880, the value of the average farm increased to more than seven thousand dollars in 1930. Since the size of the average farm increased only about 20 percent, the expanded value represented primarily new acres brought into production and an increase in value per acre from about five dollars in 1880 to almost thirty dollars per acre in 1930.

To cope with their many problems, farmers turned to organization, hoping thereby to reduce their costs and to control their markets. The early organization of the Grange in the 1870s was followed by the even more ambitious but short-lived Farmers' Alliance a decade later. In 1902 ten Rains County farmers laid the foundation of the Farmers' Educational and Cooperative Union of America. Better known as the Farmers' Union, the organization attempted to control both production and prices, especially for cotton, and for a time exercised some influence in state politics. Financial crisis brought decline to the Farmers' Union on the eve of World War I, though it was revived about midcentury. Two farm groups were formed in the 1920s. The Farm-Labor Union, which limited its membership to "dirt farmers," grew rapidly for a time but declined rapidly after 1925. The Farm Bureau Federation, however, fared better. It grew out of a national base, and though it experienced some difficult years in the late twenties and early thirties, it survived to become an influential, if somewhat conservative, voice of Texas agriculture.

## THE GROWTH OF INDUSTRY

Although Texas possessed vast natural resources, industry in 1870 was still confined primarily to small shops that seldom supplied a market beyond the immediate community. Industrial workers made up less than 1 percent of the population. During the next several decades, however, the pace of industrialization quickened, depending mostly on manufacturing related to agriculture and exploitation of basic natural resources. After the turn of the century a number of organizations were formed to promote the growth of manufacturing.

Processing of agricultural products was one of the major businesses in the late nineteenth century. Into the eighties, flour milling was the leading industry, ranking ahead of lumbering. Meanwhile, the manufacture of products from cottonseed steadily increased in importance, ranking second in the state's industrial economy in 1900. Meat packing, which began in Victoria in 1868, was soon extended to other communities, and a number of small plants added to the output. A small packing plant was built in Fort Worth in 1884; six years later the Fort Worth stockyards were opened; and thereafter the packing business in that city expanded rapidly. The first modern plants in Texas were two establishments located in Fort Worth in about 1901. In later years smaller plants began to operate in Dallas, San Antonio, El Paso, Amarillo, and other cities. Textile manufacturing began before the Civil War when a frontier businessman set up a cotton mill in New Braunfels. A plant manufacturing cotton goods was operated in the penitentiary for a number of years during and after the Civil War. Later, plants were established in Dallas, Sherman, and Post, but they remained comparatively unimportant.

One of the early Texas industries was lumbering. With more than twenty million acres of timberland to supply them, pioneers soon started their sawmills turning. Peter Ellis Bean had a sawmill near Nacogdoches in 1829, and there were several in Texas at the time of Colonel Almonte's visit in 1834. With the coming of the railroads after the Civil War, the lumbering business attained huge proportions. By 1900 Orange and Beaumont had come to be important sawmill centers; in 1900 the mills of Orange alone were cutting 700,000 feet of lumber a day. Production of the Texas mills passed the billion-board–foot total in 1899 and reached a maximum of more than 2.5 billion in 1907. Thereafter, because of the depletion of the forests, the total declined, but Texas continued to rank from sixth to eighth among the states in the production of lumber.

After 1880, mining operations contributed significantly to the industrial economy. Coal deposits existed in many regions of the state, but commercial mining was concentrated in Palo Pinto and Erath counties where Thurber was the center of activity. In 1900 the value of coal mined amounted to more than the combined value of all other mineral products. Commercial coal production continued until the 1920s. Other mineral products of substantial value mined by 1900 included salt in the granite at various sites. In 1912 sulfur was first produced in paying quantities in Texas in Freeport in Brazoria County.

But it was oil that dominated the development of an industrialized Texas. The presence of petroleum in paying quantities was discovered by accident in Nacogdoches County as early as 1867, and in Corsicana about thirty years later. There were a few other early discoveries, but they are of little consequence, except for the fact that they may have stimulated the search for oil. In fact, the petroleum industry in Texas is a twentieth century business. It began at Beaumont, when, on a January day in 1901, a well drilled by Captain Anthony F. Lucas, an oil prospector from Louisiana, roared in with a stream of oil that spouted two hundred feet into the air. This gusher was the first in Spindletop, a field that produced 12,421,000 barrels in 1902 alone. Other Gulf Coast fields raised Texas's oil production to 28,136,189 barrels in 1905, but the output declined for a number of years thereafter.

The discovery of oil at Ranger in 1917 raised Texas oil production to new high levels. The opening of the Ranger field was a matter of worldwide importance, for it added substantially to the oil supply of the United States and its allies during the crisis of World War I. Then came the Burkburnett, Breckenridge, Desdemona, and other discoveries that brought the output almost to 100 million barrels in 1920. The early twenties saw a series of fields along the Balcones Fault, among them the Luling, Mexia, and Powell producing areas.

Throughout the twenties, discovery after discovery in scattered areas of West Texas added to the supply of oil. West Texas fields held potential production of three to five million barrels daily, more oil than the rest of the United States was then producing! Prolific fields on the High Plains in the Panhandle added to the supply, and oil men began to realize that some kind of restriction of production was the only means by which the industry could avoid total collapse.

Closely associated with oil production was that of natural gas. The commercial use of natural gas in Texas dates from the early years of the twentieth century. Corsicana and Marshall were the first towns to secure natural gas distribution systems. In 1910 a pipeline was completed to supply Fort Worth and Dallas. Various other towns and cities secured this service during the next fifteen years, though the gas companies encountered many difficulties, chief of which was that of securing a dependable supply of gas. During the twenties, significant technical improvements were made, and in 1927 the great Panhandle gas field was discovered.

Also allied with oil production were the refining and manufacturing of various petroleum products. It seems that the first oil refinery in the state was constructed in Corsicana in 1890. Flush production at Spindletop, likewise, led to the building of refineries. Most major companies soon operated refining units, and from the earliest history of the industry, there have been numbers of small independent refineries. Forty-three refineries in 1919 produced petroleum products valued at $241,757,313. In the next decade the number of refineries more than doubled, and their capacity in barrels per day tripled.

In Texas, as elsewhere, industries tended to consolidate into a few large companies that controlled a major part of the market. Reflecting the trend toward commercialization, the number of flour mills declined about 50 percent in the last decades of the nineteenth century, but capital investment increased fourfold and the value of the annual production about sixfold. Like the grasslands of West Texas, the timberlands of East Texas came to be owned by comparatively few people. After 1879 timberlands were classified separately from grazing and agricultural lands and (where they had been set aside for the schools) gradually could be bought in small quantities at five dollars an acre. Soon they were purchased by nonresidents. Capitalists of vision, among them, H. J. Lutcher, G. B. Moore, and John H. Kirby, made heavy investments

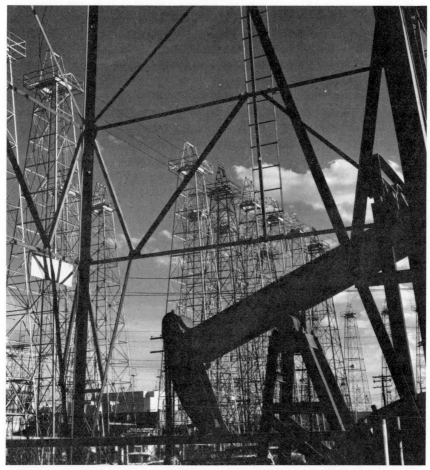

Network of iron and steel. Beginning in the 1920s, Texas led the nation in oil production, and it still has a large share of the nation's oil and gas reserves. Oil field machinery like that pictured above is a familiar sight in many parts of the state. (Texas Highway Department)

which later brought them large fortunes. The Kirby Lumber Company, chartered in 1901 as the first multimillion-dollar industrial corporation in the state, from its formation dominated the lumber business. In some respects the early Texas oil booms in the twentieth century challenged the near-monopoly held elsewhere by the Standard Oil combination. But out of Spindletop and subsequent discoveries came similar gigantic oil companies such as Gulf, Texaco, Exxon, and Mobil.

## THE EMERGENCE OF ORGANIZED LABOR

With the development of a commercial economy clearly underway, some workers in Texas began to look to unity as a means of protecting and advancing their interests. Sometimes organizations such as the Screwmen's Benevolent Association of Galveston, formed originally as a worker's insurance group, evolved into labor unions seeking shorter hours, higher wages, and control of the job. Otherwise, typographers and railroad workers apparently were among the most active leaders in the early formation of unions in the state. By the 1870s railroad brotherhoods in the state were organizing, and there were scattered militant groups to be found in a few other industries. Until the mid-seventies general public sentiment toward labor unions was either neutral or even perhaps sympathetic. However, primarily because strikes on the railroads during the seventies brought inconvenience to the farmer and merchant, public opinion had become definitely antilabor by the end of the decade.

In the 1880s the Knights of Labor, a national organization, represented both an industrial and a political force of consequence. Claiming 300 locals and 30,000 members in the state, the Knights opened their membership to farmers and allowed blacks to join. Probably the Knights organized the highest percentage of nonfarm laborers ever brought into unions in Texas, perhaps amounting for a short time to 50 percent of the nonfarm workers. By 1886 three-fourths of all organized labor in the nation, about 700,000 workers, belonged to the Knights.

Although officially opposing the use of the strike, the Knights resorted to the weapon on several occasions in Texas. Alarming many persons who regarded them as "revolutionary" anyway, the Knights called a strike of the dock workers of the Mallory line in Galveston. About the same time a strike on the railroads controlled by the tycoon, Jay Gould, was called, but the differences were soon adjusted by an agreement favorable to the strikers. However, the Gould organization was apparently determined to crush the Knights. Precipitating the Great Southwest strike of 1886, the Texas and Pacific, a Gould road, fired a foreman in the shops in Marshall in violation of what the workers alleged was a definite agreement. The Knights in response called a strike with about nine thousand men going out, a large number of them in Texas. After a clash in Fort Worth over the movement of a freight train in which blood was shed and property destroyed, Governor Ireland ordered the state militiamen and rangers to the area, and the disturbance soon subsided. Meanwhile, the Texas and Pacific Railway had passed into the hands of a federal receiver, and the strike was ruled in contempt of court. Failure of the Great Southwest strike, charges of responsibility for the Hay Market Square riots in Chicago, and poor business operations thereafter brought a rapid decline in the organization.

A strong militant labor organization in Texas from about 1890 to about 1915 was the United Mine Workers. In the mines of Erath and Palo Pinto counties, working conditions were exceedingly bad and the pay was low. The situation was all the more difficult to improve because a large percentage of the laborers were newly arrived immigrants. In the 1880s the Knights of Labor sought to aid the workers, without success, but in 1890 the Knights formed locals under the United Mine Workers and brought about improvements. For two decades and more—until competition of oil forced the closing of the mines—the United Mine Workers constituted the dominant force in the Texas coal mine region. At its peak, soon after 1900, four thousand miners belonged to the union. Oil workers in the Gulf Coast oil fields were organized by the American Federation of Labor in 1905.

In fact, with the formation of the Texas State Federation of Labor in about 1900, organized labor in Texas for a time had a leader and a spokesman. Although only a fraction of Texas organized labor was affiliated with it, the Texas State Federation of Labor had 783 organizations representing 50,000 members in 1920. Thereafter it declined. Some have laid its decline to the open-shop campaign pursued by business establishments and chambers of commerce of that period, and to the unfriendly open-port law of 1920, enforced vigorously by state officials; others have laid its decline to bad management, including the ill-advised strikes. By 1927, membership in the state federation had declined to 25,000. Efforts to cooperate with farm organizations failed. Laborers generally were faring better than farmers.

## URBANIZATION

Paralleling the emergence of a commercial economy in Texas was the rise of cities. In 1870 only 6.7 percent of the people lived in incorporated urban areas with a population of twenty-five hundred or more. By 1900 urban incorporated centers contained 17.1 percent of the population, and by 1930 the figure had climbed to 41 percent.

The appearance of urban centers is perhaps even more impressive when the growth of individual cities is considered. In 1870, only two towns, Galveston with a population of 13,818 and San Antonio with 12,256, contained more than 10,000 people. Houston counted slightly more than 9,000; Dallas had an estimated 3,000; and Fort Worth was a village of about 500. By 1900 eleven towns claimed more than 10,000 people. San Antonio was the largest city with 53,321, followed by Houston, Dallas, Galveston, and Fort Worth. In 1930 Houston, Dallas, and San Antonio each contained between 200,000 and 300,000, a total of more than 10 percent of the state's population. In addition, there were 33 cities with population figures in excess of 10,000.

Although other factors were involved, transportation facilities and oil accounted for much of the growth of these population islands. Houston, Dallas, and Fort Worth exploited their strategic locations in the railroad network to become leading market centers. In one decade after the Houston ship channel was opened in 1919, the city's population more than doubled. Similarly, cities that lost their advantage in the transportation system either grew slowly, remained stagnant, or declined. Jefferson, once connected to the sea by way of Caddo Lake and the Red River, was a busy port town of more than four thousand in 1870. When clearing debris reduced the level of the lake to a point at which commercial navigation could not be sustained and railroads opened up competitive markets elsewhere, Jefferson's population declined by more than one-fourth.

Oil likewise brought spectacular growth. Port Arthur expanded from fewer than one thousand in 1900 to fifty thousand in 1930. In West Texas, oil discoveries during the twenties actually built towns such as Pampa, Borger, McCamey, and Wink and substantially added to the populations of Amarillo, Abilene, San Angelo, and others.

While growing, Texas cities often acquired a distinct character and identity. San Antonio, perpetuating its early pattern of expansion, retained its military installations and historic sites and sustained a steady growth rate but a somewhat leisurely atmosphere. Dallas became a financial and mercantile center, widely known for its cultural achievements and aspirations. Fort Worth, generally regarded as a city of the west, developed an extensive livestock market and packing facilities, as well as the sobriquet of "Cowtown." Houston, perhaps because of its more varied economy and sprawling explosive growth, could not be given only one label. In all these cities and in a host of smaller ones could be found substantial evidence of the ubiquitous oil industry.

Before the turn of the century the services and conveniences associated with urban life were available in the Texas cities. By 1900 all cities had telephone exchanges, and practically all were linked by telegraph systems. The electric light and power industry was not quite as advanced. Galveston had a power plant in the early 1880s and other cities soon had electric service, but the power these plants generated was insignificant in comparison with the output of our own day. The production of power was a local industry until about 1913, when the Texas Power and Light Company constructed a transmission line from Waco to Fort Worth and Dallas. Soon various small concerns were consolidated, and outlying communities were supplied by high-voltage transmission lines radiating from huge plants. Electric power was no longer a monopoly of the cities, and every town and hamlet could be served by the "high lines." Development was very rapid after the First World War; it was hastened by the availability of oil and gas for fuel and the discovery that lignite could be used for fuel to produce electric power. Meanwhile, the oil industry had made natural gas available to most urban communities.

## THE PORTS

A great stimulus to commerce during this period was the development of a system of deep-water ports. Because the rivers of the state are shallow and bars shut in the estuaries along the 375 miles of coastline, natural ports were poor. Even in the early years when light sailing craft and small steamers prevailed, the ports were not adequate. With the increase in the ships' drafts and the greater demands for safety, the natural ports of Texas became more and more inadequate. The federal government, joined in later years by local navigation districts, spent large sums of money on Texas harbors. As early as 1883 a project was begun to deepen the channel of Galveston Port. Improvements were made from time to time, and by the early twentieth century a twenty-five–foot channel had been provided, and by 1927 it had been increased to thirty-five feet. For many years Galveston ranked second only to New York in exports and was the greatest cotton-shipping port in the world. By 1910 the Sabine and Neches system and the ports of Freeport, Port Aransas, and Houston had been improved.

In the annals of artificial ports, no story is more impressive than that of Houston, the city to which people brought the sea. A channel eighteen and one-half feet deep was made possible by a congressional appropriation in 1899, but it could not be used by ocean-going vessels. About 1908 Houston citizens inaugurated a movement to secure a deep-water channel. A few years later, funds supplied by the Harris County navigation district matched federal appropriations, and improvement was begun in earnest. By 1925, $10.6 million of federal money and local funds to an amount one-third as great had been spent to complete the entire channel, fifty-five miles from the Houston harbor to the outer bar and thirty feet in depth. The channel was deepened in the thirties, as Houston became the leading port in Texas and the second or third largest in the nation.

## CONSEQUENCES OF COMMERCIALIZATION

The development of a marketplace economy significantly complicated the financial, political, and social structure of rural and urban Texas. The

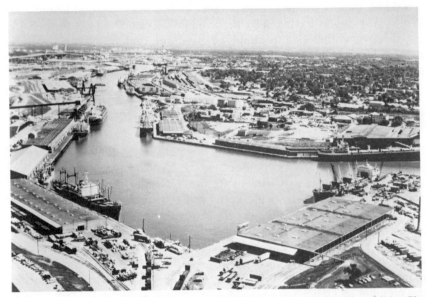

The Houston Ship Channel has contributed much to the development of the City of Houston and the prosperity of the state. Because of it, Houston has become one of the major ports of the world. (Courtesy Houston Chamber of Commerce)

transition added emphasis to some issues in political affairs, while other traditional problems faded away. Moreover, new pressure groups and factions emerged, reflecting not only the changing character of agriculture, but also the emerging industrial and urban community.

More than ever before, the people were subject to the power of economic forces that reached far beyond the boundaries of the state. The Panic of 1893 brought several years of depression in both rural and urban areas, with prolonged suffering unparalleled in previous economic recessions. After ten years of comparative prosperity in the first decade of the twentieth century, cotton prices, generally the barometer of economic health during these years, fell in 1911. An industrial depression in 1913–1914, followed by the outbreak of World War I, brought prices of cotton ruinously low. Despite efforts of the state to support cotton prices with the creation of a public warehouse system, prosperity did not return until forces outside the state brought a rising price level in 1916.

With the approach of the twentieth century, some problems of an older day, such as protection from Indians, disappeared, only to be replaced by more complex questions. Tariffs, rail rates, corporate monopoly, depression, mortgages, declining prices, rising costs, city government, and working conditions for laborers would be major problems of the new age. Resolution of these problems led to the formation of pressure groups, sometimes with conflicting objectives or viewpoints. Particularly active during the nineteenth century and even later were the farmers' organizations. Organized labor for a time wielded substantial influence during the early years of the twentieth century. Business interests, acting individually and collectively, vigorously pursued their own particular objectives. Thus, politics between 1870 and 1930 was to a marked degree the story of the interaction of these often conflicting forces.

## SELECTED BIBLIOGRAPHY

For a general study of economic affairs in Texas between 1875 and 1900, see J. Spratt, *The Road to Spindletop.* Other general works of value are Ralph Steen, *Twentieth Century Texas: An Economic and Social History* (Austin, 1942); B. M. Jones, *The Search for Maturity;* and S. S. McKay and O. B. Faulk, *Texas after Spindletop* (Austin, 1965). Rich in economic information is the *Texas Almanac.* Also see Ralph A. Wooster, "Wealthy Texans, 1870," *Southwestern Historical Quarterly,* LXXIV, 24–35.

The two standard studies on railroads are S. G. Reed, *A History of Texas Railroads* (Houston, 1941); and C. S. Potts, *Railroad Transportation in Texas* (Austin, 1909). See also Ira G. Clark, *Then Came the Railroads* (Norman, Okla., 1958); Vera L. Dugas, "A Duel with Railroads: Houston vs. Galveston, 1866–1881," *East Texas Historical Journal,* II, 118–127; Donald Everett, "San Antonio Welcomes the 'Sunset'— 1877," *Southwestern Historical Quarterly,* LXV, 47–60; and Ralph Traxler, Jr., "The Texas and Pacific Railroad Land Grants," *ibid.,* 357–370. A valuable description of the political intrigue on behalf of railroad construction is John M. Brockman, "Railroads, Radicals, and the Militia Bill: A New Interpretation of the Quorum-Breaking Incident of 1870," *Southwestern Historical Quarterly,* LXXXIII, 105–122.

The abundance of literature on the settlement of western and southern Texas permits listing only a sampling here. Classic studies are W. P. Webb, *The Great Plains;* W. C. Holden, *Alkali Trails;* R. N. Richardson and C. C. Rister, *The Greater Southwest;* and C. C. Rister, *Southern Plainsmen.* See also W. C. Holden, "Experimental Agriculture on the Spur Ranch, 1885–1904," *Southwestern Social Science Quarterly,* XII, 16–23; and Riley E. Baker, "Water Development as an Important Factor in the Utilization of the High Plains," *ibid.,* XXXIV, 31–34. For southern Texas, see J. Lee Stambaugh, *The Lower Rio Grande Valley of Texas* (San Antonio, 1954). On the public land system, see A. S. Lang, *Financial History of the Public Lands in Texas;* and R. D. Holt, "School Land Rushes in West Texas," *West Texas Historical Associa-*

*tion Year Book,* X, 42–57. An account of the transition from ranch to farm is found in D. B. Gracy, II, *Littlefield Lands: Colonization on the Texas Plains, 1912–1920* (Austin, 1968). The effects of drought are portrayed in Richard King, *Wagons East: The Drought of 1886* (Austin, 1965).

The evolution of a commercial economy in agriculture and industry is emphasized in J. Spratt, *The Road to Spindletop,* cited above. However, B. P. Gallaway, "Population Trends in the Western Cross Timbers of Texas, 1890–1960: Economic Change and Social Balance," *Southwestern Historical Quarterly,* LXVII, 376–396; and Neal Baker, Jr., "Red River County, Texas, in the 1920's: A Landlocked Frontier," *ibid.,* LXX, 443–460, suggest that subsistence agriculture remained at least a hope, if not a reality, for some Texans. Also see L. Tuffly Ellis, "The Revolutionizing of the Texas Cotton Trade, 1865–1885," *ibid.,* LXXIII, 478–508; Robert A. Cotner, "Nineteenth Century Farmers, Cotton and Prosperity," *ibid.,* LXXIII, 509–521; and Henry C. Dethloff, "Rice Revolution in the Southwest, 1880–1910," *Arkansas Historical Quarterly,* XXIX, 66–75.

For additional information on industry, see V. L. Dugas, "Texas Industry, 1860–1880," *Southwestern Historical Quarterly,* LIX, 151–183; Edwin L. Caldwell, "Highlights of the Development of Manufacturing in Texas, 1900–1960," *ibid.,* LXVIII, 405–431; Dwight F. Henderson, "The Texas Coal Mining Industry," *ibid.,* LXVIII, 207–219; Robert S. Maxwell, "The Pines of Texas: A Study in Lumbering and Public Policy, 1880–1930," *East Texas Historical Journal,* II, 77–86; William R. Johnson, *A Short History of the Sugar Industry in Texas* (Houston, 1961); Mary Lasswell, *John Henry Kirby: Prince of the Pines* (Austin, 1967); Kenneth Ragsdale, *Quicksilver: Terlingua and the Chisos Mining Company* (College Station, Tex., 1976).

Considering the importance of the industry, the large number of studies on oil is to be expected. C. C. Rister's *Oil! Titan of the Southwest* (Norman, Okla., 1949) is the standard general work, and a colorful account of the first important discovery in Texas is William A. Owens, "Gusher at Spindletop," *American Heritage,* IX, 34ff. Those seeking additional sources should consult Walter Rundell, Jr., "Texas Petroleum History: A Selective Annotated Bibliography," *Southwestern Historical Quarterly,* LXVII, 267–278, which lists and describes more than sixty studies. See also Walter Rundell, Jr., *Early Texas Oil Photographic History, 1866–1936* (College Station, Tex., 1977); and John O. King, *Joseph Stephen Cullinan: A Study of Leadership in the Texas Petroleum Industry, 1897–1937* (Nashville, 1970).

Published materials on organized labor are scarce but are growing in number. Pioneering studies have been made by Ruth A. Allen, who has published *Chapters in the History of Organized Labor in Texas* (Austin, 1941); *The Great Southwest Strike* (Austin, 1942); and *East Texas Lumbering Workers, An Economic and Social Picture, 1870–1950* (Austin, 1961). Dealing primarily with an earlier period but useful for later years is James V. Reese, "The Early History of Labor Organization in Texas, 1838–1876," *Southwestern Historical Quarterly,* LXXII, 1–20; more appropriate to this era is his "The Evolution of an Early Texas Union: The Screwmen's Benevolent Association of Galveston, 1866–1891," *ibid.,* LXXV, 158–185. More information on lumber unionization is available in George T. Morgan, Jr., "The Gospel of Wealth Goes South: John Henry Kirby and Labor's Struggle for Self-Determination, 1901–1916," *ibid.,* LXXV, 186–197.

Increased interest in urban studies is evident in the availability of city histories. *Houston: A History and Guide* (Houston, 1942), compiled by the Federal Writers' Program of the Works Projects Administration in the state of Texas, is useful, but see also for a more specialized aspect of the city, Marilyn Sibley, *The Port of Houston* (Austin, 1968). For twentieth century developments, see James Howard, *Big D Is for Dallas* (Dallas, 1957). A superior study is Lawrence Graves (ed.), *History of Lubbock* (Lubbock, Tex., 1962). Also see Dan E. Kilgore, "Corpus Christi: A Quarter Century of Development, 1900–1925," *Southwestern Historical Quarterly,* LXXV, 435–443; Roger N. Conger, "Waco: Cotton and Culture on the Brazos," *ibid.,* LXXV, 54–60; and Keith L. Bryant, Jr., "Arthur E. Stilwell and the Founding of Port Arthur: A Case of Entrepreneurial Error," *ibid.,* LXXV, 19–40. Among the longer studies are Robert L. Martin, *The City Moves West: Economic and Industrial Growth in Central West Texas* (Austin, 1969); David G. McComb, *Houston: The Bayou City* (Austin, 1969). Donald E. Everett, *San Antonio: The Flavor of Its Past* (San Antonio, 1975); A. C. Greene, *A Place Called Dallas: The Pioneering Years of a Continuing Metropolis* (Dallas, 1975); and Katherine Hart and others, *Austin and Travis County: A Pictorial History, 1839–1939* (Austin, 1975).

# Chapter Fifteen

# IN THE AGE
# OF REFORM
# 1890–1910

By 1890 the demands for reform in political and economic affairs could no longer be ignored or rejected. Texans in the next two decades adopted laws regulating business, expanding education, reforming the electoral system, and making other changes designed to meet the needs of the emerging modern society. In the nineties the primary impetus for reform was the unhappy farmer. Seeking the elimination of economic inequities and the expansion of political democracy, the more militant agrarian radicals organized a third party, the People's or Populist party, while other reformers sought similar goals within the Democratic party.

With the decline of agrarian protest, sentiment for reform subsided temporarily, only to be revived after 1900 with the spirit of the progressive movement. Progressivism of the new century was not merely a renewal of agrarian protest. The strength of the movement was broader, with more emphasis on the role of businessmen, teachers, and professional people, and on new organizations such as the State Federation of Labor and the Texas Local Option Association. The goals were more complex. Business regulation continued to be a primary objective, but progressives also stressed humanitarian reforms, reorganization of municipal government, expansion of education, and other changes affecting not only the rural but also the urban population. In many ways, it was as much an attitude as it was a program. In short, progressivism reflected the growing importance of industrialization and urbanization. Nevertheless, twentieth century Texas progressivism preserved a strong rural influence. Many of the goals and some of the leadership of former years were the same; moreover, a new agrarian organization, the Farmers' Union, was one of the more effective reform pressure groups.

Reform, however, was not the only element determining the course of politics during these years. Except for the Populist challenge, most political conflicts took place within the Democratic party. In the one-party structure, personal and factional rivalry sometimes disregarded ideology for the sake of political expediency, forming alignments not particularly related to the matter of progressive change.

## THE PRELUDE TO REFORM

During the first two decades following the Civil War, the prevailing attitude in Texas toward big business was friendly. We have seen that the Constitution of 1876, though framed by a convention controlled by farmers, contained no provisions hostile to organized wealth. It is true that the Grange and the Greenback party repeatedly criticized the Democratic administration, contending that it was too generous toward corporations and that it failed to control them, but the dominant party continued with its program of encouragement of business with a minimum of regulatory measures. The demand for regulation increased, however, and during the later eighties the number of malcontents grew rapidly.

As in former years, the center of dissatisfaction was among the farmers; this group, let it be remembered, constituted a majority of the people. Since the Civil War the ills of the farmer had been many and real. The price of cotton, the great money crop of Texas, declined from thirty-one cents a pound in 1865 to less than five cents in 1898. It seemed that the more the farmers made, the less they had. The supply of money in circulation, limited anyway, seemed unreasonably diminished when the Coinage Act of 1873 eliminated subsequent coinage of silver into money. Meanwhile, taxes and interest charges on mortgages seldom diminished, and the cost of many other articles the farmer had to buy increased from year to year. It was easy for him to believe that the corporation that held a mortgage on his farm charged him exorbitant interest; that the railroads were overcharging him for hauling his crops; and that the middlemen were appropriating too much for services, some of which he deemed unnecessary.

Amid the disintegration of the first farmers' movement, the Grange, and the Greenback party, arose a second, the Farmers' Alliance. The Farmers' Alliance was founded in Texas in about 1875 and was reorganized in 1879. In 1887 it became a national organization, and soon its strength was estimated at from one to three million members. At a state meeting in Cleburne in 1886, the alliance set forth a political program in a series of "demands." After a preamble that referred to "the shameful abuses that the industrial classes are now suffering at the hands of arrogant capitalists and powerful corporations," the program "demanded," among other measures, that the public school lands be sold only in small grants to actual settlers; that railroad property be assessed at its full value; and that an effective interstate commerce law be enacted. Two years later the alliance called for an antitrust law as well as more effective regulation of railroad rates.

The alliance and, to a lesser extent, the Knights of Labor affected the pronouncements of the Democratic party. The party's platform, as it was framed in 1886, called for the sale of land "in tracts of reasonable size" to *bona fide* settlers only, favored laws correcting various abuses practiced by the railroads, and, most extreme of all, contained a plank that stockholders of a corporation be made liable, within limits, for the debts of the corporation. In 1888 the Democratic convention adopted a stronger plank on railway regulation and called for an antitrust law. Then, two years later the Democratic candidate for governor, running on a platform calling for the abolishment of the national banking system, free coinage of silver, and a state railway commission, received the endorsement of the alliance. All these proposals were the essence of the alliance. At last, the agrarian reformers had triumphed; they felt that they had captured the Democratic party.

Meanwhile, certain Texans worked hard for reforms in the national government. In Congress, Robert Q. Mills, chairman of the Committee on Ways and Means, proposed a tariff reform measure that was passed in the House of Representatives in 1888 and became the Democratic manifesto in the national campaign of that year. More successful as a national reformer was the veteran John H. Reagan, who, as a member of the Senate in 1887, was co-author of the Interstate Commerce Act, which marked the beginning of federal regulation of railroads.

Prohibition was another active reform movement of the period. Introduced into Texas in about 1870 were the United Friends of Temperance and its juvenile society, the Bands of Hope, whose members pledged total abstinence from drink and sought to cultivate public sentiment against the liquor traffic. In 1882 the Women's Christian Temperance Union, which grew rapidly in the state, entered the campaign for prohibition with great fervor. Meanwhile, the Grange had declared against the sale of intoxicating liquor, and the Greenback party had denounced the Democrats for failing to submit the question to the voters. After dodging the issue as long as possible, the legislature submitted to the voters in 1887 an amendment that would replace the local option law of 1876 with statewide prohibition. With both the prohibitionists and their opponents organized, the campaign was heated and bitter, but the amendment was defeated in the election of August 1887 by a vote of 220,627 to 129,270. For the next twenty-four years the forces of moral reform could not muster strength enough to force another prohibition election, but they steadfastly refused to allow the issue to die. Meanwhile, reform was accomplished in a variety of other areas.

## REFORM TRIUMPHANT: JAMES STEPHEN HOGG

For more than a decade, James Stephen Hogg was instrumental in determining the tone of the Texas government. First elected to state office in 1886 as attorney general in the administration of Lawrence Sullivan Ross, Hogg stood in striking contrast to the conservative governor. Thirty-five years old, son of a Texas statesman and Confederate brigadier, and left an orphan at twelve, Hogg had grown to manhood in his native East Texas during the Reconstruction era. He had not passed the intermediate grades when he left Peyton Irving's school in Tyler in 1866. Unaided, he made his way at such jobs as he could secure. Years as a typesetter and printer furnished the background for a sympathetic understanding of the problems of the common people. After serving as prosecuting attorney and spending a few years in private law practice, Hogg was elected attorney general. He realized that the dominant question in Texas was the regulation of corporations. On that issue he soon appropriated the center of the political stage and was elected governor in 1890 on a platform promising correction of the abuses of big business.

Men who knew him were never indifferent to Jim Hogg. Corporation lawyers soon learned that he was a dangerous antagonist, and as a stump campaigner he had few equals. He knew the mind of the common man and how to appeal to it with fluent speech and expressive vernacular. Newspapers of the opposition charged that his frequent "by gatlings" (his nearest approach to profanity) and the earthy epithets he hurled at his enemies "were offensive to the ladies who honored him with their presence," but the ladies and all others continued to go to hear him. First and last he was a commoner. In the scant shade of a picnic arbor he could hold crowds for hours while he berated the railroads and denounced discrimination against farmers. When the heat became severe he would doff his coat, fling off his suspenders, and gulp from time to time water from a pitcher or a bucket. His public record was punctuated with incidents that made good news and kept him ever in the public eye. When the Southern Pacific Railroad in 1894 deliberately stranded seven hundred marchers of Coxey's Army at a West Texas desert station, a Hogg ultimatum defying the awesome corporate power forced the railroad to convey the men across the state.

After he became attorney general in 1887, Hogg first directed his efforts against certain insurance companies that were operating in unlawful fashion. Attorney General Hogg drove about forty of these from the state and compelled certain others to pay taxes and to obey the laws.

Hogg also contributed to the passage of antitrust measures. There had long been a widespread conviction that monopolies or "trusts" conspired to fix prices and to eliminate competition. Farmers' organizations complained of the "cotton-bagging"; there were charges that the packers constituted a "beef combine"; and there was much resentment against land corporations. Agitation on the subject in Congress, moreover, inspired legislation on the state level. Hogg assisted in framing the Texas law. Enacted on March 30, 1889, it was the second antitrust law in the nation, preceded by four weeks by a similar law in Kansas. With labor and farm organizations exempted, the law carried heavy penalties against combinations of any kind for the purpose of restricting trade, fixing prices, or limiting production. The law was extended in 1895 to apply to insurance companies, and subsequent changes in 1899, 1903, and 1907 added to the severity and effectiveness of antitrust regulation.

Hogg's greatest efforts were directed toward regulation of the railroads. The article on railroads in the Constitution of 1876 seems to have been borrowed largely from the Pennsylvania Constitution of 1873. It declared railroads to be public highways and common carriers, authorized the legislature to pass laws to "correct abuses, and prevent unjust discrimination and extortion" in rates and fares, required the railroads to maintain offices where their books were to be open to inspection, forbade the consolidation of competing lines, and authorized the legislature to set by law reasonable maximum rates. The power over the railroads reserved by the state was altogether adequate, except that it did not provide for their regulation by a commission. Under its rate-making authority, the legislature in 1879 set the maximum freight rate, and in 1882 passenger fares were reduced from five to three cents per mile. These regulations were not adequate, however, and apparently little effort had been made to enforce some of them prior to Hogg's administration as attorney general. He found various abuses and proceeded against the railroads with such vigor that he was charged with trying to drive capital from the state. He compelled one railroad that had ceased to operate to revive and continue its service. He forced the dissolution of the Texas Traffic Association, a pool through which nine railroads with headquarters outside the state were controlling all Texas lines save one. He also dissolved the International Traffic Association and the International Weighers' Association, combinations similar to the Texas Traffic Association. Through various suits and official actions he reduced the control that certain out-of-state corporations had over the Texas railroads and compelled the Texas railroads to reestablish their general offices in the state.

James S. Hogg earned a reputation as champion of the people's rights when he served as attorney general and governor of Texas during the last quarter of the nineteenth century, the period when big business was being brought under public control. (University of Texas Library)

The best efforts of Attorney General Hogg were not sufficient, however, to secure effective railroad regulation. Realizing this, Hogg worked aggressively while he was attorney general to secure the enactment of a railroad commission law and while he was governor to sustain the power of the commission after it had been established. Since the constitutionality of such a measure was in doubt, the legislature in 1889 gave up the idea of establishing a commission by law and submitted to the voters a constitutional amendment that would settle all questions as to the legality of such an agency.

At once the commission amendment became a leading political issue. An organization of businessmen, known as the State Freight Rate Convention, endorsed it, and the Farmers' Alliance favored it. In his campaign for governor in 1890, Hogg championed it with the zeal of a crusader. He showed by a series of comparisons and contrasts how unreasonable certain of the Texas rates were; how lumber, for instance, could be shipped from the East Texas forests to Nebraska more cheaply than to Dallas. The opponents of the commission rallied behind Gustave Cooke of Houston, but the Democratic convention nominated Hogg by an overwhelming vote. The convention also endorsed the railroad commission, and the voters adopted the amendment in the November election.

Acting under the leadership of Hogg, the legislature in April 1891 set up a commission with the power to make classifications and to fix rates and fares. As originally established, the commission was to consist of three members appointed by the governor, but by constitutional amendment, which became effective in 1894, the commission was made elective. John H. Reagan resigned his seat in the United States Senate to accept the chairmanship.

The commission enjoyed a measure of success. It secured the reduction of freight rates and claimed credit for the increase of milling and manufacturing in the state and for saving a million dollars on the shipment of cotton in two seasons. The railroads, however, contending that the rates were confiscatory, brought suits in 1892 to restrain the commission from enforcing its orders, and for nearly two years it was impotent. The long fight in the courts ended in victory for the state, and in July 1894 the body again took up the work of rate regulation.

While litigation over rate regulation was underway, the commission acquired additional authority. Realizing that the question of rates was inseparably linked with that of railroad capitalization, Governor Hogg pointed out that the railroads were increasing their obligations on an average of $30 million annually without making any improvements of consequence. Since they would endeavor to maintain rates high enough to pay interest and dividends on this increased capitalization, the increase was, in effect, a charge against the shippers of the state. To correct this evil, the legislature, at Hogg's behest, in 1893 passed a law authorizing the railroad commission to ascertain the value of all property and franchises belonging to each railroad and to regulate and control the issue of securities. The law proved especially effective in enabling the commission to hold down the capitalization of new railroads.

Meanwhile, a bitter political controversy had raged over the railroad commission issue. In the gubernatorial campaign in 1892, the railroads and most leading newspapers supported George Clark of Waco, a railroad attorney. Clark had opposed the commission amendment in 1890 as "wrong in principle, undemocratic and unrepublican"; its only function, he said, was to harass the railroads. Now he accepted the commission as an established fact but insisted that it should be conservative, completely democratic, and elective, and that the law should be liberalized to permit the railroads to appeal to the courts. Hogg defended the commission and attacked his opponent with all of the tactics of the versatile stump speaker that he was. At the famous "Street Car Barn Convention" in Houston in August 1892, the Democrats divided, one group nominating Hogg, the other Clark; and in the autumn the warring factions continued their campaign before the voters. Although one wing of the Republican party supported Clark, Hogg was reelected by a substantial majority.

Other reforms of the Hogg administration, or "Hogg laws" as they were often termed, affected a variety of issues. In response to Governor Hogg's urgent plea, the legislature in 1891 passed a law prohibiting foreigners from owning lands in Texas. The supreme court declared it unconstitutional on a technicality, and in the following year the legislature enacted another alien land law. Another law, which became effective in 1893, prohibited the organization of corporations for the special purpose of dealing in lands and required that such corporations already in existence dispose of their lands within fifteen years. All other corporations were required to sell within fifteen years all land not necessary to enable them to carry on their business. The law was easily contravened and failed to accomplish its purpose. Otherwise, Hogg promoted prison reform, the establishment of a board of pardon advisors, extension of the school term from four to six months, additional revenue for the University of Texas, and a law forcing railroads to segregate facilities for blacks and whites.

Leaving office in 1895, Hogg spent the final decade of his life amassing a fortune, though he did not abandon his interest in public affairs. His zeal as a reformer perhaps diminished somewhat; indeed, his wealth came in large measure from the interests he had sought as a reformer to control. Nevertheless, the position of James Stephen Hogg as the symbol of Texas reform remained deservedly unshaken.

**THE CHALLENGE OF POPULISM**

Reforms either promised or accomplished by Governor Hogg and the Democrats quieted for a time criticism from the Farmers' Alliance, but the Democrats did not go far enough to suit the more militant of the agrarian radicals. Government ownership of railroads and similar proposals found little sympathy among Democratic leaders. Governor Hogg refused even to name a leader of the Farmers' Alliance to the newly created railroad commission. Moreover, Hogg and his followers in the Democratic party refused to endorse the favorite program of the Texas Alliance, a subtreasury plan whereby the general government would make loans to farmers directly, at a nominal rate of interest with farm produce as collateral. In fact, the Democratic leaders in 1891 read out of the party those alliance men who supported the subtreasury plan.

Thus, disenchanted with Hogg and snubbed by the Democrats, before the elections of 1892 the Farmers' Alliance evolved, in effect and purpose, into a new third party, the People's or Populist party, organized not only in Texas but elsewhere over the land by similar dissident groups. The People's party grew rapidly. When the Democratic convention chose Grover Cleveland, the conservative, sound-money champion as its standard bearer in 1892, many of the Democratic faithful were alienated along national lines. The hard times of the early nineties, reinforced by the economic catastrophe of the Panic of 1893, fed the discontent, enlisting thousands of small farmers in the Populist cause. With this formidable strength, the Populists contested each election in Texas for several years, their rivalry with the Democrats at times comparable in bitterness to that of Reconstruction days.

The list of reforms supported by the Populists was lengthy and comprehensive. Some were adopted from earlier reform movements, others from the Democrats, and some were Populist innovations. Demands of the People's party emphasized government regulation of business, public ownership of railroads, free coinage of silver, abolition of the national banking system, and establishment of the subtreasury system. The Populists supported laws to improve the status of the laborer and to implement a graduated income tax. To further democracy, they advocated direct election of United States senators and other federal officers, limiting all officeholders to two terms, and the use of referendum and recall. But Texas Populists, perhaps for political expediency, did not take up the cause of women's suffrage and statewide prohibition.

Populism, however, was more than a platform of an organization; it was also an attitude, a crusade, the determined effort of those who felt oppressed to use the machinery of government to ameliorate their miseries. In a very real sense an example of class consciousness in politics, the Populists at times oversimplified their problems and their solutions, but the problems were real and the solutions were not without merit. It was a rural movement, as almost half of the leaders in Texas were farmers. Strongest among the poorer farmers of East and West Central Texas and among some laboring groups, Populism had little attraction for most business and professional men. Its greatest appeal was to the alienated, to those who felt that they could no longer depend on traditional institutions to protect their interests and to advance their cause.

Basing their program on doctrines of economic and political equality, the Populists struck telling blows at various abuses of the prevailing order. Seventy-five weekly newspapers, among them the *Southern Mercury,* printed at Dallas, carried the gospel of Populism to every part of the state. A corps of stump speakers, led by a few men of superior ability, for example, Thomas L. Nugent, Jerome Kearby, T. P. Gore (who later represented Oklahoma in the United States Senate), and James H. ("Cyclone") Davis, served as ardent evangelists of the new gospel. Many of their leaders were Protestant preachers, who not only appropriated the camp meeting, the hymns, and the religious fervor of the pioneer churches, but took from the Bible many of their utterances and arguments.

As the campaigns became more and more acrimonious, Populists and Democrats resorted to various political tricks. The People's party made a strong bid for the black voters, many of whom were naturally attracted anyway by doctrines suited to their interests. Leaders of both parties, however, sometimes purchased the services of white and black men who were influential in controlling the black vote ('' 'fluence men,'' they were called) and distributed among the black voters many petty bribes. If the Democrats were a little less active and successful in their appeal to the black voter, they were as guilty as the Populists of using corrupt practices to control the Mexican-American vote in South Texas.

Although the Populists did not gain control of the state government, they had some success at the ballot box. The party's maximum strength in the legislature came immediately after the election of 1894, when it had 22 of the 128 members in the lower house and two senators. In the gubernatorial campaign of 1894, Populist Thomas Nugent received nearly one-third of the vote. Two years later Jerome Kearby, aided by the Republicans, threatened Democratic supremacy more seriously than had any candidate since Reconstruction. Kearby polled 238,692 votes to 298,528 for Governor Charles A. Culberson, the Democratic incumbent. More successful in local campaigns, the Populists elected large numbers of county and precinct officers.

After 1896 the Populist party faded quickly from Texas and national politics. With William Jennings Bryan as their standard bearer, the Democrats on the national level had sealed the doom of the third party by appropriating its chief plank, free coinage of silver, and a number of other proposals that the Grange, the Greenback party, the Farmers' Alliance, and the People's party had advocated over the years. Moreover, the wave of prosperity that appeared in Texas near the turn of the century did much to silence the voices of discontent.

While successfully meeting the challenge of Populism, the Democratic administration had cautiously perpetuated the reform programs of Governor Hogg. Between 1895 and 1899 Governor Charles Culberson, former attorney general and son of a well-known United States congressman, signed laws regulating primary elections, strengthening antitrust regulations, adding to the authority of the railroad commission, improving the judicial system, setting aside school lands for a black university, and modifying the collection of delinquent taxes. He occasionally thwarted efforts toward corporate consolidation in the state. In a dramatic move he called a special session of the legislature to outlaw prizefighting in

Texas. But primarily for fiscal reasons, Culberson vetoed a number of measures, many of them furthering the cause of reform. Neither an enthusiast nor an opponent of reform, his administration thus was a logical transition from the preceding reform-minded regime of Governor Hogg to the relatively conservative era that followed.

## REFORM QUIESCENT: SAYERS AND LANHAM

Although the reform impulse was not entirely absent, the years between 1898 and 1906 reflected a noticeable lack of strife and a tone of conservatism. With the Populists fading and the Republicans quarreling, Democratic rule was virtually unchallenged. In the Democratic party much of the tumult usually associated with gubernatorial politics was eliminated by the shrewd and efficient manipulations of Colonel Edward M. House, a well-to-do planter and railroad builder who made politics his avocation and surpassed the professionals in it. A- veteran of the electoral wars who had helped reelect Hogg in 1892 and had directed Culberson's campaigns in 1894 and 1896, House skillfully guided the campaigns of governors Joseph Sayers (1899–1903) and Samuel Willis Tucker Lanham (1903–1907). House, unknown to most Texans, was not a leader of a political machine in the usual sense, but relying on careful, thorough organization and the assistance of a few intimate and powerful friends, he exerted a degree of influence without parallel in Texas politics.

In part, the leadership of governors Sayers and Lanham was responsible for the resurgence of conservatism. Both were genteel, high-minded men; both were ex-Confederates, the last to serve as chief executive of the state; and both had rendered their previous public service mainly in Congress. Both brought to the office mature judgment and high idealism but little imagination; by temperament and training, neither was a zealous crusader for change.

But other forces contributed to the decline of progressive fervor. The conservative mood was a natural reaction to the agitation and drive of the Hogg era, and the Spanish-American War diverted the attention of many Texans. Moreover, an attitude more favorable toward business prevailed. Oil discoveries, including the fabulous Spindletop, excited the hopes of Texans and enticed a welcome flow of capital to the state. Other industries, such as the lumbering companies of East Texas, nearing their peak level of production, bolstered the state's economy. Indicating the growing importance of the commercial community, the proportion of farmer members of the legislature declined from about one-half in the early nineties to about one-third after 1900. Political leaders, such as Colonel House, though surely not subservient to corporate interests, nevertheless did not harbor the suspicious convictions about business common among the agrarian rebels of the nineties. Texas remained a rural land, but the industrial age was fast approaching.

Despite the conservative temper of the times, some worthwhile reforms were accomplished. The legislature adopted several laws protecting labor. An 1899 statute exempted organized labor from antitrust regulations; in 1901 the legislature outlawed the use of blacklists to control union organization and the use of company script that could be spent only at company stores. In 1903, laws limiting the hours of railroad employees and requiring certain safety measures on street railways were passed. The same year the first Texas law regulating child labor was adopted. Unfortunately, enforcement of labor laws was often weak and erratic.

A state banking system, prohibited for many years by the Constitution of 1876, was established during the Lanham administration. In 1904 the voters ratified a constitutional amendment permitting the state to charter banks, and the legislature of the following year established a commission of insurance and banking. Directed by Thomas M. Love, a native of Missouri and a progressive politician of Dallas, the commission supervised the chartering of more than five hundred banks during the next five years.

Tax reform, sought unsuccessfully during the Sayers administration, was partially accomplished in the second Lanham term. The general property tax had provided the greater part of the state's revenue, and valuations had not kept pace with the increasing demands. Railroad properties, for example, were evidently undervalued; the greater portion of intangible properties escaped taxation. In response to Governor Lanham's request, the legislature in 1905 raised taxes on intangible assets of railroads and certain other industries. Laws providing for franchise taxes and levies on gross receipts of express companies, sleeping-car companies, pipelines, and similar concerns also were adopted

Guided by a peculiar mixture of progressive and reactionary goals, the legislature reorganized the state's election system. Prior to 1903, party candidates in some counties were nominated by primaries and in others by conventions. In either case, abuses were widespread. Unscrupulous party officials sometimes failed to give adequate notice of impending conventions; occasionally the meetings were at places and under conditions that made it impossible or impractical for the rank and file of voters to attend. Relying on proxies and other devices, corporation attorneys and other special interests wielded an undue influence. Dates of party primaries were sometimes manipulated to the advantage of particular candidates; ballot-box frauds were common.

There were many abuses in the primary and general elections. Although the constitution authorized the legislature to provide for punishing fraud and preserving the integrity of the ballot, little had been done to eliminate such practices as the purchase of votes, extravagant campaign expenditures, and dishonest election returns. In 1895 the legislature passed a law that regulated primary elections in those counties where they were held, but it was inadequate. The law was changed in 1897 and again two years later, but it did not attack the abuses prevalent in that day. Registration of voters was assured, however, by the constitutional amendment adopted in 1902 which made a poll-tax receipt or exemption certificate mandatory for voting.

During the Lanham years the legislature took hold of the problem in earnest. Two laws, named after Judge Alexander W. Terrell, their author, affected both primaries and general elections. The first became effective in 1903, and the second, repealing the first and passed in 1905, constitutes the foundation of Texas election laws to this day. The first law did not make the primary election mandatory but permitted a political party to determine for itself whether it would nominate its candidates by a primary or a convention. The most important features of the second and more comprehensive law may be stated thus: It set forth in great detail who would be permitted to vote both in primary and general elections; it required candidates to file within ten days after a primary or general election itemized statements of expenditures; it made mandatory a primary for parties that polled at the last general election 100,000 or more votes (the Democratic party); it set forth detailed regulations for the governance of parties and required that primaries be held on the fourth Saturday in July; it provided that county and precinct nominees be determined by the results of the primary, but that the county committee might call a second primary, the voters to make their choice from the two leading candidates; and it required that nominees for state and district offices still be chosen by conventions.

Subsequent legislation modified these rules. In 1907 a law required that, in all cases, the candidate receiving the highest number of votes be declared the nominee. Thus, the primary election had come to be the nominating agency; party conventions were mere canvassing bodies. A 1913 law provided for a second primary in which the voters would select one of the two candidates receiving the most votes, if no candidate for the United States Senate received a majority in the first contest. In 1918 this provision was extended to all state and district contests and made optional in county races.

Although the electoral reforms made at the turn of the century eliminated many abuses, the changes, in some respects, were made at the expense of democracy. The poll tax discouraged poor people of all kinds from voting, but blacks generally fared worse than others. Inspired by a long-standing fear of black suffrage, which was reinforced by the events of the Populist years and the rising tide of racial antagonism prevalent near the end of the century, white politicians deliberately sought to eliminate the black voter from politics. By the early 1900s most Democratic primaries, which were usually tantamount to election, were open only to white voters. For the next several decades, blacks would be denied an effective voice in the politics of the state. Not until the Supreme Court of the United States in 1944 ruled white primaries unconstitutional and in 1966 the poll tax unconstitutional was the black voter assured of his or her place at the polls. Progressive electoral reform, indeed, progressive reforms in general, did little to improve the lives of black people.

Public welfare services and education, which perhaps needed improvement even more than the electoral system, received some attention during the Sayers and Lanham years. The Pasteur Institute for the prevention of rabies was organized in 1903, and the Abilene State Hospital for epileptics began receiving patients in 1904.

Limited improvements were made in education. The legislature in 1901 authorized the state board of education to invest the permanent school fund in the building bonds of independent school districts. Availing themselves of this opportunity, many communities changed their organization from common to independent school districts and erected substantial school plants. Also, most independent school districts erected a local tax for school purposes. By November 1904, about 90 percent of the 381 or more districts then in existence had provided for local taxes.

Unfortunately, country schools, most of which were organized as common school districts, lagged far behind urban programs. Primarily because of conditions in rural schools, Texas in 1901–1902 ranked from twenty-eighth to forty-second among the states of the nation, according to the various tests that were used at the time to determine the adequacy of the school system. In 1900, towns and cities spent $8.35 for the education of each child; the country schools spent only $4.97. The average term of 162 days in town and city schools was almost twice the average of 98 days found in rural areas. A strange and unreasonable restriction in the constitution limited the taxing authority of country districts to less than one-half of that of independent school districts. Emphasizing the tragedy of inadequate rural schools was the fact that they served more than three-fourths of the school-age population.

During this period the state continued its war against the trusts. More stringent antitrust acts were passed in 1899 and 1903, and state attorneys successfully prosecuted a number of violators. Indeed, the Texas antitrust policy was more severe than that of the federal government. Of the 110 prosecutions brought under the Texas statutes up to 1915, 84 were settled by compromise with penalties exacted in 74, totaling $3,324,766. In comparison, federal antitrust laws in effect in about the same period of time brought 187 prosecutions with fines or penalties in 33 cases, amounting to only $548,881.

The most famous Texas antitrust case involved the Waters-Pierce Oil Company, a Missouri corporation with Standard Oil affiliations. In 1897 the attorney general brought suit for violations of the Texas antitrust act. A verdict revoking the firm's permit to do business in the state was upheld by the United States Supreme Court in 1900. Then, claiming that it had reorganized and had severed all ties with the Standard Oil combine, the company secured a new Texas license, though not without the objections of some Texans like Jim Hogg, who questioned the sincerity of the Waters-Pierce officials. Subsequently, a suit brought by the state of Missouri in 1905 revealed that a majority of the stock of the company, though registered in the name of an individual, actually belonged to the Standard Oil Company. Acting quickly, the state of Texas sought and obtained a judgment for ouster and penalties of $1,623,900. When the decision was affirmed by the court of last resort, the corporation paid a fine amounting to $1,808,483.30, the largest ever collected by the state, and the properties of the firm were sold at auction.

Meanwhile, the case had provoked an even greater controversy— Baileyism. While a candidate for the United States Senate in 1900, Congressman Joseph Weldon Bailey, ignoring the possible conflict of interest, urged Governor Sayers and the state attorney general to allow Waters-Pierce to return to the state. Though he did not receive a fee for this service, he was employed by Henry Clay Pierce in other matters. Furthermore, he had borrowed five thousand dollars from Pierce, who, unknown to Bailey, had placed the note on company records.

Almost immediately some questioned the propriety of Bailey's intervention, but not until new investigations in 1905 and 1906 publicly disclosed the relationship between the senator and the oilman did the state divide into angry camps of pro- and anti-Bailey men. Though Bailey was unopposed for reelection in the Democratic primary of 1906, critics argued that the legislature should ignore the primary and refuse to return him to the Senate. Bailey, in response, contended that the whole affair was a conspiracy to deprive the nation of his great services.

By a vote of 108 to 39, the legislature reelected the senator, but meanwhile, a legislative investigating committee was studying the ethics of the colorful figure. The Texas senate, taking the affair out of the hands of its committee, quickly exonerated him, but the house committee was divided in its report. Not satisfied with this victory, Senator Bailey announced that he would make the selection of the Texas delegation to the Democratic National Convention in 1908 a test of his strength; none but Bailey men would go to the convention. Both the Bailey and the anti-Bailey forces waged a contest with heat and rancor that has rarely been equaled in the annals of Texas politics. By an overwhelming vote Bailey and his slate of delegates won. Nevertheless, differences still rankled, and no doubt the controversy would have flared up again in 1912 if Bailey had not voluntarily retired to private life.

## THE REVIVAL OF REFORM: THOMAS M. CAMPBELL

A definite swing away from conservatism was apparent in the gubernatorial contest of 1906. For the first time in more than a decade, Colonel House refused an active role in the contest, and none of the candidates had a decided advantage. Each of the four major contenders favored a war on the trusts, an antilobby law, tax reform, and generous support for the state's institutions. Emerging the victor from a rather evenly divided race was a lawyer from Palestine, Thomas M. Campbell. Generally regarded as the most progressive of the candidates, Campbell had the endorsement of ex-Governor Hogg, who had voiced repeatedly his dissatisfaction with the attitude of the Sayers and Lanham administrations toward big business, and the last minute support of Senator Bailey. Armed with the support of farmers, labor, and various others, Campbell energetically promoted tax reform, insurance regulation, improvements in education, additional laws protecting labor, and a number of other changes. Though sentiment for reform declined in his second term and he was unable to perpetuate the control of progressives beyond his own administration, he, nonetheless, in large measure justified the confidence of Hogg.

Tax reform, begun under Lanham, continued in the Campbell years. Most important was a 1907 "full rendition law" requiring that property be rendered for taxation at its "reasonable cash market value." This law also created an automatic tax board consisting, as amended in 1909, of the governor, comptroller, and treasurer, and gave to the board the power to set the tax rate for general revenue and school purposes within the constitutional limits. The full rendition law very nearly doubled the value of property on the tax rolls, but it also provoked anguished protests, not only from corporate interests but also from land-owning farmers.

Other aspects of Campbell's fiscal program were likewise somewhat controversial. The governor's plea for an income tax had little success; he did obtain a light inheritance tax, but it produced more complaints than revenue. In the interest of economy he vetoed appropriations in 1909 to the amount of $1.7 million; some items were for badly needed improvements. At the end of his administration, the automatic tax board lowered the tax rate to an unrealistic level, leaving a deficit of nearly a million dollars for the next governor. Moreover, it should be noted that the laws of the Lanham and Campbell period did not shift the tax burden extensively. The general property tax continued to produce the greater part of the state's operating revenue, and real estate continued to bear approximately two-thirds of the tax burden placed on property. Not until the coming of the automobile and the development of the oil industry did Texas succeed in placing the larger share of the burden on natural resources and on the production and exchange of goods.

Regulation of insurance companies was a signal accomplishment. Comprehensive codes for life, health, accident, home, and fire insurance were adopted. Furthermore, the Robertson Insurance Law, enacted in 1907, required life insurance companies to invest in Texas securities at least 75 percent of their reserves set aside for insurance policies on the lives of Texas citizens. When they failed to defeat the bill, twenty-one insurance companies withdrew from the state, contending that its requirements were harsh and unreasonable. As a matter of fact, other states had similar requirements; furthermore, of the $40 million in reserves held by the companies, less than $1 million had been invested in Texas. Some of the companies returned after the commissioner of insurance and banking modified certain regulations. Others continued with great persistence to work for the repeal or the modification of the law, but it was not repealed until 1963.

In a related area, the state in 1909 established an insurance program protecting funds deposited in state banks. A few bank failures during the panic of 1907 had centered public attention on the need of greater protection for small depositors. For a number of years the plan worked quite successfully, but numerous failures in the early 1920s put a heavy strain on the system, and it was abolished in 1927.

Progressives made additional improvements in the public school system. Organized in 1907, the Conference for Education in Texas discussed school problems, held mass meetings, scattered information throughout the state, and sought in various other ways to awaken the people to the needs of the schools. Its work was reinforced and extended by the state's Department of Education, the Congress of Mothers, parent-teacher associations, and other agencies. In 1908 the friends of school improvement made certain distinct gains. Noteworthy was the constitutional amendment that permitted common school districts to use funds derived from taxation for the equipment of buildings. Far more important, they abolished the constitutional requirement calling for a two-thirds vote and provided that a simple majority of tax-paying voters might impose a tax on a school district. The greatest victory won that year was the change in the constitution raising the limit of taxation in common school districts. During the first year after these amendments were put into operation, local taxation in the rural districts increased by 35 percent. Local taxation, in fact, between 1905 and 1910 increased by 153 percent.

Reforms in municipal government, a prominent feature of progressive change elsewhere, were most noticeable during the Campbell administration. The commission system of government, first used in Galveston in 1901, was encouraged by the governor who approved thirteen city charters containing the plan. Though demands for similar practices on the state level accomplished nothing, practically every city charter issued under Campbell provided for more direct democracy through the use of the initiative, referendum, and recall.

A number of other progressive measures were adopted. Campbell, who had consistently advocated greater regulation of corporations, in 1907 signed a law strengthing antitrust restrictions. Several laws improving conditions for labor were passed, and the legislature created the state medical board and the state board of health. Campbell also approved laws giving towns of populations of two thousand or more power to regulate utilities, restricting free passes by railroads, promoting pure food, prohibiting nepotism in state administration, as well as laws against lobbying and several acts for the improvement of roads.

Prison reform was the last major change of the Campbell administration. Spurred on by a series of articles on prisons, carried in certain state newspapers in 1908 and 1909, and by the charges of Oscar B. Colquitt during his successful campaign for governor in 1910, Campbell called a special session of the legislature after the election. An investigating committee of state senators and representatives had found conditions in the state penal system intolerable. Convicts had been shot or whipped to death for trivial offenses; women prisoners had been abused; tasks set were unreasonable; food was poor; clothing was inadequate; and the sanitation was abominable. The financial affairs of the system were in such confusion that it was impossible to audit the books.

Acting on the recommendation of the committee, the legislature abolished the contract-lease system whereby the services of convicts were sold to different private employers. Management of the system was placed under the direction of three commissioners appointed by the governor. Stripes were to be abolished except for the worst class of prisoners, sanitation and medical service improved, and each convict paid ten cents a day for his or her labor.

With the close of the Campbell administration shortly after the enactment of these prison reforms, the progressive movement in Texas was, in many respects, nearing an end. Prohibition, absorbing much of the energy of Texans after 1908, would dominate the election of 1910 and political affairs for sometime thereafter. But the progressives in countless ways had already turned the services of government to the benefit of the many rather than the few. In Texas, as elsewhere, they had not succeeded in every instance in their quest of reform. Despite the laws calling for corporate regulation, giant corporations would grow larger and more powerful. Nevertheless, the more obvious abuses had been eliminated, and the most pressing needs had been met.

## SELECTED BIBLIOGRAPHY

General studies dealing with these years are Alwyn Barr, *Reconstruction to Reform: Texas Politics, 1876–1906;* S. Acheson, *35,000 Days in Texas;* B. M. Jones, *Search for Maturity;* and S. S. McKay, and O. B. Faulk, *Texas after Spindletop.*

Very useful are the biographies of figures active in the era. For James S. Hogg, see Robert C. Cotner (ed.), *Addresses and State Papers of James Stephen Hogg* (Austin, 1951) and *James Stephen Hogg, A Biography* (Austin, 1959); and H. P. Gambrell, "James Stephen Hogg: Statesman or Demagogue?" *Southwest Review,* XIII, 338–366. See also B. H. Proctor, *Not without Honor: The Life of John H. Reagan;* C. Nugent, *Life Work of Thomas L. Nugent* (Stephenville, Tex., 1896); Wayne Alvord, "T. L. Nugent, Texas Populist," *Southwestern Historical Quarterly,* LVII, 65–81; S. Acheson, *Joe Bailey: The Last Democrat* (New York, 1932); R. N. Richardson, *Colonel Edward M. House: The Texas Years, 1858–1912* (Abilene, Tex., 1964); Janet Schmelzer, "Thomas M. Campbell: Progressive Governor of Texas," *Red River Valley Historical Review,* III, 52–64; and Pollyana B. Hughes and Elizabeth B. Harrison, "Charles A. Culberson: Not a Shadow of Hogg," *East Texas Historical Journal,* XI, 41–52.

Concerning reforms, on railroad regulation there are M. M. Crane, "Recollections of the Establishment of the Texas Railroad Commission," *Southwestern Historical Quarterly,* L, 478–486; Robert L. Peterson, "Jay Gould and the Railroad Commission of Texas," *ibid.,* LVIII, 422–432; and J. R. Norvell, "The Railroad Commission of Texas: Its Origin and History," *ibid.,* LXVIII, 465–480. The standard work on trust legislation is Tom Finty, Jr., *Anti-trust Legislation in Texas* (Dallas and Galveston, Tex., 1916). See also O. D. Weeks, "The Texas Direct Primary System," *Southwestern Social Science Quarterly,* XIII, 95–120; E. T. Miller, *A Financial History of Texas;* and *The Report of the*

*Prisons Investigating Committee* [first special session of the Thirty-third Legislature] (Austin, 1910). Difficult to classify but a reminder that Texans were concerned about things other than politics and economics is Charles Carver, *Brann the Iconoclast* (Austin, 1957). For reforms in local government, see Bradley R. Rice, "The Galveston Plan of City Government by Commission: The Birth of a Progressive Idea," *Southwestern Historical Quarterly*, LXVIII, 365–408; and Paul E. Isaac, "Municipal Reform in Beaumont, Texas 1902–1909," *ibid.*, LXVIII, 409–430.

On politics and political parties, see Roscoe C. Martin, *The People's Party in Texas* (Austin, 1933); Ralph Smith, "The Farmers Alliance in Texas," *Southwestern Historical Quarterly*, XLVIII, 346–369; E. W. Winkler, *Platforms of Political Parties in Texas;* and S. S. McKay, *Texas Politics, 1906–1944* (Lubbock, Tex., 1952). A number of studies in recent years have examined the role of the farmer. See Lawrence Goodwyn, *Democratic Promise: The Populist Movement in America* (New York, 1976); Robert C. McMath, Jr., *Populist Vanguard: A History of the Southern Farmers Alliance* (Chapel Hill, N.C., 1975); James R. Green, *Grass-roots Socialism: Radical Movements in the Southwest, 1895–1943* (Baton Rouge, La., 1978) and "Tenant Farmer Discontent and Socialist Protest in Texas, 1901–1917," *Southwestern Historical Quarterly*, LXXXI, 133–154; Graham Adams, Jr., "Agrarian Discontent in Progressive Texas," *East Texas Historical Journal*, VIII, 24–28; and Robert Saunders, "Southern Populists and the Negro, 1893–1895," *Journal of Negro History*, LIV, 240–261.

Particularly valuable is a number of manuscripts in various libraries. Bob Holcomb's study of Joe Bailey is in the library of Texas Tech University, and in the library of the University of Wisconsin is James Tinsley's work on the Progressive movement in Texas. In the University of Texas library are Charles Chamberlain, on A. W. Terrell; George P. Huckaby, on Oscar B. Colquitt; R. L. Peterson, on the Railroad Commission; R. L. Wagner, on Charles Culberson; and H. L. Crow, on the Texas penal system.

# Chapter Sixteen

# LIFE
# AT THE TURN
# OF THE CENTURY

Tragedy began life in the twentieth century for Texas when the century opened with a massive hurricane. With the storm came death and destruction, but otherwise the picture of the state was one of progress. More than three million people made their home in Texas in 1900. The number had increased fivefold since the Civil War, and an added indication of the growth of the state was the fact that slightly more than one-fourth of the population had been born in other states. Almost 200,000 had been born in foreign countries; large non-Anglo cultural groups included blacks, Mexican-Americans, and Germans, and there were a number of other cultural backgrounds represented.

Life styles reflected not only the diverse cultural backgrounds but also a rapidly changing pattern of living. For decades Texans had depended primarily on the land for their living and most still did in 1900, but cities were growing and the effects of urbanization were apparent. Likewise, the effects of industrialization were noticeable, particularly in the cities, but also in rural Texas. On the other hand, the literature and art tended to reflect the past, especially the more heroic and romantic past.

## THE GALVESTON FLOOD

Texans experienced a tragic natural disaster in the first year of the twentieth century. In a day before adequate warning devices were available, a gigantic tropical hurricane swept inland over Galveston

Island on September 8, 1900. The magnitude of the storm and the destruction it brought almost defied description. The storm raged for more than twelve hours, with winds of more than 120 miles per hour and tidal waves that completely covered the land. No completely accurate count of the dead was ever made, but estimates of six thousand were commonly heard and many placed the count much higher. When the waters receded, the city was in ruins, with thousands of people left homeless.

Galvestonians were determined to rebuild. The Red Cross provided first aid and emergency care for the survivors; from throughout Texas and the nation people sent food and supplies; the state government allowed the city to retain taxes for use in rebuilding and organized committees to raise money for supplies. But it was the determination of the people of Galveston that was most important in rebuilding the city. Within a short time they had reorganized their city government, and within five years they had built a sea wall on the Gulf side of the island. The wall, seventeen feet high and more than seven miles long, successfully protected the city from storms that struck in 1909, 1915, and 1961.

## LIFE ON THE FARMS AND IN THE TOWNS

Approximately 80 percent of the population lived in rural areas in 1900, with about six out of every ten workers directly involved in agriculture. Horses and mules still provided most of the power; the age of the tractor would not come until the 1920s. But here and there were seen huge steam tractors, and threshing machines, reapers, and new types of plows and riding cultivators were commonplace.

Work patterns on farms had changed little from pioneer days. The farm family was a relatively tight, cohesive unit, and all shared in the work. Daylight to dark was the schedule, with some planting, plowing, and cultivating, while others chopped weeds and tended the livestock. Harvest season demanded the efforts of everyone; many youngsters could not attend school until the cotton crop was at the gin.

In the towns, work schedules were not usually as demanding. Family income in urban areas generally was provided by a business or by the employment of the father, though employment of women was becoming more and more common. In smaller communities where opportunities were available, young people living in towns found summer jobs on nearby farms.

Living conveniences were a mixture of old and new. Farm homes were usually small, warmed by fireplaces or iron heaters with coal or wood cookstoves and kerosene lamps for light. City homes ranged from the simple to the elegant but often offered little more in the way of conveniences than did the farm homes. Although gas and electricity were available in the larger cities before 1900, many homes had neither, depending on ice deliveries for food refrigeration or doing without. The revolution in living conditions produced by electricity was not widespread until the 1920s.

Travel was slow and difficult for both rural and urban Texans at the turn of the century, though the period was one of transition and transportation methods were improving. Long distance travel by railroad was relatively comfortable and safe, but most travel was for short distances for which railroads were either unavailable or impractical. For many families, wagons and buggies were the only choice. There were no paved roads and few bridges; the roads were poorly kept, dusty in dry weather and muddy in wet. A twenty-mile journey required the better part of a day.

In the cities, street construction and maintenance were major problems. Large cities by the end of the century had begun paving the main thoroughfares; Houston, for example, had paved twenty-six miles. Brick was commonly used, though other materials, even wood, also were tried. Streetcars and trolleys powered by electricity appeared by 1890 and were available in the larger cities by 1900.

Two other new inventions hailed the opening years of the twentieth century. In about 1900 the first automobiles were seen in Texas, and the success of the machines was apparent within a short time. Houston was the home of eighty automobiles by 1905 and had already experienced a fatal automobile accident. The state recognized the automobile in 1907 with the adoption of an eighteen-mile-per-hour speed limit. Airplanes attracted attention by 1910, but mostly as a curiosity. Air shows demonstrated the machines in San Antonio and Houston and eventually in most other cities, but airplanes were rare until World War I introduced military aviation to the state.

## LEISURE-TIME LIVING

Even when survival was more uncertain, Texans found opportunities for amusement and entertainment, and these opportunities became more frequent as Texas entered the twentieth century. Visiting with neighbors remained an important social activity, especially on Sunday afternoons. Church socials, the general store, cotton gin offices, sewing circles, and community parties provided many occasions for people to meet and relax together. Children were often a part of these affairs, taking advantage of them to play marbles, various ball games, and other games.

Parker County Courthouse, Weatherford. Such structures built near the turn of the twentieth century, generally on the town square, added a touch of elegance to many Texas county seats and represent rather well the preferred architectural style for the public buildings of that period.

Dancing, one of the most important social diversions throughout the nineteenth century, declined somewhat, primarily because many church groups strongly opposed it.

Holidays were important, especially the Fourth of July and Christmas. Texans often celebrated the Fourth with community picnics and parties, but Christmas was more of an occasion for family gatherings. Among black people, June 19 was a day for celebrating their emancipation from slavery, and Mexican-Americans celebrated two national holidays of Mexico, Cinco de Mayo and Diez y Seis de Septiembre. Less often celebrated, but not entirely ignored, were Thanksgiving and Easter.

Sports, though not nearly as important to the culture as they would become later in the twentieth century, were popular. Horse racing, the most popular sport throughout the nineteenth century, continued to attract large crowds. In 1887 the Texas League of Professional Baseball Clubs was organized, and in the 1890s Texas schoolboys began to play football. A Galveston dock hand, Jack Johnson, won the heavyweight boxing championship of the world in 1908 and held the title until 1915.

Music, theater, and shows provided diversions for many. Sometimes local talent put on the plays or shows, but there were many traveling groups, some with national reputations. At one time or another there appeared on Texas billboards the name of almost every distinguished actor or actress who played in the United States during the late nineteenth and the early twentieth centuries. Among these were Joseph Jefferson, noted for his portrayal of Rip Van Winkle; Edwin Booth, renowned Shakespearean actor; and Sarah Bernhardt, the greatest actress of her generation. Others were Richard Mansfield, Maude Adams, and Ethel Barrymore. Larger towns and many of the smaller ones built theaters for the performing arts in which operas, plays, concerts, and minstrel shows were performed on a more or less regular basis. An opera house was opened in Galveston in 1871, one in Dallas two years after, and others soon followed. Many communities organized bands, some had singing societies; and in Mexican-American communities there were often string orchestras. The traveling circus was a popular show of the time, and in Texas it was the Mollie Bailey Circus. Replete with tigers and elephants, acrobats and clowns, the circus of Mollie Bailey began its tour of Texas about 1880 and lasted for nearly thirty years. Shortly after the turn of the new century, motion pictures were shown in Texas for the first time. The event attracted statewide attention and interest, but Texans would not be able to attend the movies in large numbers on a regular basis until the 1920s.

## HEALTH AND MEDICAL CARE

Disease was a dreaded and frequent occurrence in Texas homes at the turn of the century. Cholera, typhoid, diptheria, and occasionally smallpox epidemics swept the state from time to time. Malaria was common along the coast, and yellow fever was not unknown. Children's diseases, such as measles, whooping cough, mumps, and chicken pox afflicted most families sooner or later.

Professional medical care was limited and often not particularly good. Physicians were few in number and only large towns had hospitals. For a time the state suffered from an abundance of "quack" medical schools which offered quick but poor and improper training. The Medical Association of Texas, organized in 1853, became more active near the end of the century and made the establishment of standards for the training of physicians one of its primary goals. Toward the end of the century, medical care improved somewhat. By 1900 there were several competent medical schools, the best known of these being the University of Texas Medical School located in Galveston.

Texans often relied on their own resources when disease struck.

Neighborhood women, in particular, acted as midwives and sometimes treated the sick. Few of them had formal medical training, but in many instances there was no other care available. Mexican-Americans often turned to a *curandero* when confronted with illness. *Curanderos,* who used herbs and folk medicine in their treatments, generally were given high respect in their communities, and some attracted patients from distant parts of the country. Home remedies were the favorite approach of many families. In the spring, a mixture of sassafras tea, sulfur, and molasses paved the way for a healthy year. Castor oil, quinine, and calomel were also frequently used as home medicines.

## WOMEN AT THE TURN OF THE CENTURY

In 1900 slightly less than half, about 48 percent, of the population of Texas were women. Reflecting the change from a frontier society to that of a more civilized one, the population of women was increasing at a rate more rapid than that of men, but women would not outnumber men in the state for some years.

Although the women of Texas enjoyed more rights than those of many other states, Texas women were less than equal in their legal rights in comparison with men. Not only were women denied the right to vote, but they also were limited in their rights to conduct business. Because of the heritage of Spanish civil law, a woman could own and convey property, make contracts, and sue or be sued. However, if she was married, a woman's property was subject to the management of her husband, even if the property was hers before marriage. She could not dispose of property without her husband's consent, but her husband could, unless the property involved was the family homestead. A husband was required by law to support his wife and was liable for any debts she might incur, while under some circumstances wives were not responsible for their own debts. Single women generally retained more rights than married women, inasmuch as they were legally responsible for their own acts and could legally manage their own property.

Educational opportunities for Texas women of the late nineteenth century were available but limited. By 1890 female students outnumbered males, but few females attended college. The Texas Women's Council, however, stressed improvement in vocational education for girls, and there were other organizations working to improve educational opportunities for women. Business colleges and trade schools appeared, and many of these institutions encouraged the enrollment of women, claiming that many jobs in business were available for women. More traditional forms of women's education persisted, however. Some colleges, such as Baylor University, began to offer courses equal in difficulty to those of men, but often education for women beyond basics in reading and writing were taught at a lower level or consisted of learning the social graces or studying the arts.

At the turn of the century most Texas women followed the role of wife, mother, or homemaker as their career. The percentage of women who married outnumbered that of men. Women tended to marry earlier in life, often to older men, and frequently were widowed at a young age. Divorce was rare. In 1890 slightly more than 2 percent of the female population were divorced.

In 1890, approximately 8 percent (86,015) of the women of Texas were involved in occupations outside the home. Almost half of this number were in occupations related to agriculture, holding jobs as laborers, farmers, planters, or ranchers. The next largest number, 37,210, worked as domestic or personal servants. The remainder of the female work force was scattered among a wide variety of occupations. Among approximately 6,000 women employed in the professions, about 75 percent were teachers. In addition, there were writers and journalists, librarians and ministers, lawyers and physicians, merchants and clerks, seamstresses and copyists, and even gamblers and outlaws. No women held jobs as sailors in 1890, but two claimed to be locomotive engineers.

Organizations to improve conditions for women and for society in general were numerous at the turn of the century. Suffrage and temperance were the most common goals, accounting for a large number of the organizations and for most of the membership. But there were many other women's groups. Literary clubs were organized in small towns and large, with one reported in Clarendon in 1885 and one in Houston the same year. By the 1890s, Houston women had organized the City Federation of Women's Clubs, and in 1897 Waco was the scene of the organization of the Texas Federation of Women's Clubs.

In Belton, women's organizations took an unusual turn with the formation of a women's communal society. The moving spirit for the group, often referred to as the "sanctificationists," was Martha McWhirter, a long-time Belton resident who claimed to have had a vision. Some of the women who gathered together with Martha McWhirter were divorced; others were not, but all were determined to live free, without male support or domination. As the years passed, the group grew in number and prospered, primarily from profits earned in the operation of a hotel, and some of the controversy associated with the early days of the organization faded away. In 1889 the group left Texas, selling their property and moving to Washington, D.C.

## THE ETHNIC CULTURES

Blacks and Mexican-Americans, with about 25 percent of the population, accounted for the majority of the non-Anglo cultures in Texas at the turn of the century. But there was a constant flow of immigrants, especially from Europe, and cultural diversity was one of the most notable features of the state.

Blacks in Texas numbered 620,722 in 1900, or approximately 20 percent of the total population. The ratio of blacks to the general population had declined from about 30 percent at the beginning of the Civil War, but the number was more than twice that of 1860. Most lived on farms, about 80 percent, and about 90 percent lived in the eastern parts of the state. Houston, with blacks amounting to one-third of its population, contained the largest number of urban blacks, with Austin, Dallas, Waco, and Galveston also containing substantial numbers.

Although some were ranchers and cowboys, most blacks who lived on the land were cotton farmers. About 25 percent of the black farmers owned their own land; the remainder were tenants, mostly sharecroppers and usually very poor. Even when the black farmer owned his own land, his situation was often insecure. In 1910 the average value of a black farmer's holdings was about one-fifth the value of a white farmer's.

Urban blacks accounted for about 25 percent of the nonfarm work force at the turn of the century. The greater number held jobs as laborers, and a significant number were employed as domestic or personal servants. Together, these occupations accounted for 80 percent of the black urban workers. Less than 5 percent entered the professions, and an even smaller number were craftsmen. Most black professionals were either teachers or ministers, but Texas in 1900 claimed the largest number of black physicians in the nation, 136. The ratio of black people in the crafts, however, was smaller in Texas than commonly found in other states.

Wages for black workers were low. Apparently, black and white workers who performed the same job were generally paid at the same rate; discrimination occurred in the assignment of the jobs. Wages paid in 1910 ranged from a low thirty cents a day for hotel workers to a maximum of ten dollars per day for certain jobs in mills, but the average pay seems to have been about two dollars daily. Black women received substantially lower wages than did the black men. In fact, women, whether black or white, generally were paid lower wages, even when the tasks performed were the same.

Black workers assumed contradictory roles in the development of labor unions in Texas. In the lumber, railroad, and shipping industries in

One of the major industries of Texas at
the turn of the century, lumbering depended on black workers for a large proportion of its work force.

which labor unions most often were formed, there were large numbers of black workers, and many were involved in the organization of unions. On the other hand, the use of black workers as strikebreakers in labor disputes was not uncommon.

Businesses owned by blacks were few in number and generally quite small. Often operated by the entire family, the business was more often a grocery store, restaurant, tavern, blacksmith shop, or some other type of service agency, and ordinarily was confined to providing for the needs of the black community. However, there were several black insurance companies, most of them connected with black fraternal groups, and there were at least eight black banks in business in the early twentieth century.

Provisions for education for blacks, segregated in their schools by the Constitution of 1876, were inadequate. Black education in Texas for a time compared favorably with that of other southern states, and illiteracy declined from more than 75 percent in 1880 to less than 40 percent in 1900. By 1900, however, Texas ranked fifth among southern states in the enrollment of black students and daily attendance and third in the number of black teachers. There were a number of able black leaders, such as R. L. Smith, a graduate of Atlanta University and an aide to Booker T. Washington, who diligently sought educational gains, and some white leaders recognized the merit of the cause. But often the white community was either disinterested or openly unsympathetic. Generally, black schools labored under the burden of inadequate financial resources and poorly trained personnel. Until the nineties, laws required that funds be divided equitably between white and black schools, but violations of the rule were not unknown. Complaints that many black teachers were deficient in training were often heard. Yet, significant improvement of black faculties could scarcely have been expected. As late as 1900, secondary training for blacks in Texas was not only inadequate, it was practically nonexistent, with only nineteen black high schools in the state. A black student in Texas seeking an education during these years likely could learn the rudiments of reading and writing, but he or she probably would find little opportunity beyond those humble beginnings.

All in all, the situation of black Texans at the turn of the century suggests a mixture of regression and progress. Economically, black Texans were at a disadvantage when compared with their white neighbors. Poverty was common among white Texans, but black people were even poorer. Education for blacks was unequal to that offered whites, and from the 1890s forward, the discrepancy became even greater. The effectiveness of black people in politics declined in the decade before the end of the century and would decline further in the years to come.

Mortality rates for black people were much higher than those for white people, probably influenced by an inadequate diet and lower quality of medical care. Segregation and violence, long a part of life in the black community, continued. In a twenty-one-year period ending in 1903, 199 blacks were lynched; 171 were lynched in the next twenty-four years.

But despite the problems and the inequities, there was also substantial evidence of progress. In 1900, black Texans were only thirty-five years removed from slavery. During those years a number of capable black leaders had emerged; illiteracy had been reduced; and sufficient capital had been acquired to enable some to buy land and others to establish businesses. Perhaps of most significance to the future was the formation of literally dozens, possibly hundreds, of black organizations of all types. Some were religious; others were political. A large number were fraternal and there were many primarily concerned with social affairs. Perhaps most important were the chapters of the National Association for the Advancement of Colored People, the first formed in Houston in 1912. But all were ultimately concerned with the improvement of the black community. These organizations would provide an ongoing level of leadership in the twentieth century.

Much smaller than the black population, but a major ethnic minority, were the Mexican-American people. At the turn of the century, natives of Mexico living in Texas numbered about seventy thousand and were the largest group of foreign born. The number of people of Mexican heritage was many times larger, with some families able to trace their origins back to the days of the Spanish. Well into the twentieth century, 60 percent of the landowners in Cameron, Starr, and Zapata counties were descendants of the original Mexican land-grant recipients. Other Mexican-Americans were recent arrivals, for increasing agricultural production in South Texas attracted workers from Mexico in the 1890s. In 1910, Mexican-Americans made up slightly less than 6 percent of the population, but revolution in Mexico increased the rate of immigration thereafter. Most lived in South Texas and along the Rio Grande. San Antonio was the largest urban center for Mexican-Americans, but other cities, particularly Houston, would prove attractive in the years after the turn of the century.

Mexican-Americans, whether descendants of old settlers or recent immigrants, often found life in Texas to be difficult. Prejudice, poverty, and discrimination were common problems. Sometimes signs declaring "No Mexicans Allowed" were posted in restaurants and other public businesses. In some towns Mexican-Americans could live only in certain areas, and generally only low-paying and physically tiring jobs were available to the Mexican-American worker. Language was sometimes a barrier, for many Mexican-Americans retained the use of Spanish, the language of their heritage. Since schools normally allowed only English to be spoken, Mexican-American students who spoke only Spanish often dropped out at an early age. Nevertheless, Mexican-Americans were not an illiterate people, and by the 1890s several Mexican-American newspapers were being published on a more or less regular basis for the benefit of Spanish-speaking Texans.

In the late nineteenth century, Mexican-Americans exercised only limited influence on state politics, but often they assumed a major role in local politics if the Mexican-American population was large. On the state level only three Mexican-Americans were elected to the legislature in the period between 1865 and 1900. In some instances economic pressure or open coercion was used to prevent Mexican-American voters from going to the polls, but frequently voting was allowed and the vote was controlled to the advantage of local political bosses. Some of the political bosses were Anglos, but others were Mexican-Americans. Although most of the political leadership, whether Anglo or Mexican-American, was quite conservative, sometimes Mexican-American leaders were successful in efforts to correct abuses. When San Pedro Park in San Antonio was closed to Mexican-American people in 1880s, protests forced its reopening. In later years protests against economic discrimination led to the organization of a number of labor unions made up primarily of Mexican-American workers.

Almost fifty thousand Texans in 1900 had been born in Germany, and people of German heritage made up the majority of the population of several counties. Large German communities existed in Houston, Galveston, and San Antonio. More German immigrants arrived in Texas in the late nineteenth century than in the years before the Civil War. In most instances the newcomers settled in communities established by Germans before the war, with Austin, Fayette, Lee, and Washington counties receiving large numbers. Attracted primarily by the lure of cotton-growing lands, German settlers were scattered in isolated communities, known as "folk islands," over Central and West Texas in the late nineteenth and early twentizh centuries. German settlers tended to retain their cultural heritage to a marked degree. Often German was spoken in the daily routine, church services, and occasionally in the schools. There were a number of German newspapers. Foods, holidays, architecture, and other customs made the distinctly German culture quite visible.

Immigrants from Czechoslovakia, then Bohemia and Moravia, made their way to inland areas. Fayette County was a favorite destination, but some chose other locations, usually in communities where the German population was large. Polish settlements founded before the Civil War likewise grew with the new immigration, until by the early

1900s there were some seventeen thousand people of Polish heritage in Texas. Smaller numbers of Swedes joined the tide of settlers, mostly locating near Austin in Travis and Williamson counties.

People from most of the nations in Europe and from some in Asia made their home in Texas during these years. Nederland in Jefferson County was founded by immigrants from the Netherlands. Galveston became the home of a colony of Yugoslavians who made their living by fishing; San Antonio was selected to be the home of a group of Lebanese; and there were sizable numbers of English, Irish, and Italians who settled in the towns and cities. Smaller number of immigrants came from Belgium, Denmark, France, Hungary, Norway, Russia, Scotland, Switzerland, and Wales. By 1900 almost one thousand Chinese lived in Texas, and a small number of Japanese had settled along the Rio Grande.

## LITERATURE AND THE ARTS

The last third of the nineteenth century witnessed a substantial increase in Texas writings and some improvements in quality, and these achievements carried over into the early twentieth century. The best works pertained to adventure. Some were reminiscences dealing largely with the time of the Texan Revolution and early statehood and were of genuine historical value. Z. N. Morrell, a pioneer Baptist preacher who came to Texas in 1836, wrote *Flowers and Fruits of the Wilderness,* a lively narrative of his long career on the frontier. Likewise, in his reminiscences of *Fifty Years in Texas,* John J. Linn gave much information about the Texan Revolution. Equally interesting is Noah Smithwick's *The Evolution of a State.* John C. Duval's *Early Times in Texas* was destined to endure. An earlier book of his, just as meritorious, was *The Adventures of Big Foot Wallace,* a biography of a famous ranger who had come to Texas in 1836 to avenge the death of his brother killed in Goliad. Containing less adventure but associated with a broader scene were Francis R. Lubbock's *Six Decades in Texas* and John H. Reagan's *Memoirs.* Cowper Brann wrote and published in the 1890s, first in Austin and later in Waco, the newspaper *Iconoclast,* in which he purported to combat hypocrisy, intolerance, and other evils.

During this period, books of travel were relatively less important than they were earlier. However, *On a Mexican Mustang through Texas,* by Alex E. Sweet and J. Armory Knox, two newspapermen, is notable. Their writing shows the influence of Mark Twain. N. A. Taylor's *The Coming Empire* or *Two Thousand Miles in Texas on Horseback* contains less satire and is more trustworthy and dependable than the book by Sweet and Knox.

Since the frontier era did not close in Texas until nearly the end of the nineteenth century, for two decades and more following the Civil War, men who sought adventure did not have to leave the state to find it, adventure of the hardest frontier style. Thus, authors continued to write of contemporary experiences, of the exploits of an early period, or of both. J. W. Wilbarger filled a fat volume entitled *Indian Depredations of Texas* with accounts of border tragedies. This book was a precursor of James T. DeShields's *Border Wars of Texas,* published in the twentieth century. Neither book made much effort to present the Indian side of the story. N. A. Jennings, a New York newspaperman who came to Texas and served with the rangers on the frontier in the eighties, wrote of some of his own experiences in *A Texas Ranger.* In 1886 Charles A. Siringo, a real cowboy who could interest readers, published his *Texas Cowboy* or *Fifteen Years on the Hurricane Deck of a Spanish Pony.* As a paperback thriller, its sale ran into many thousands, and it pointed the way for many other writers who have, since that day, dealt with similar themes in books, both of fact and of fiction.

By no means did all Texas literature of adventure in the period deal with legitimate enterprise or with men on the side of the law. The "bad man" theme was popular. The later frontier period brought forth Henry C. Fuller's *The Adventure of Bill Longly,* the story of a notorious killer. Sam Bass, a train robber, who since his death has become the Robin Hood of Texas, was the subject of a biography published anonymously in 1878. The gruesome record of John Wesley Hardin was written by himself. W. M. Walton wrote *The Life and Adventures of Ben Thompson,* sometime city marshal of Austin and noted for fights in which he was not always enforcing the law.

Many poems were written during this period, but few of them bear evidence of talent. John P. Sjolander, a Swedish-American, has been called the "greatest pioneer poet of the Southwest." Crude but genuine and destined to endure was William Lawrence (Larry) Chittenden's "Cowboy Christmas Ball." Sam H. Dixon compiled and edited *Poets and Poetry of Texas,* and Francis L. Allen published a collection known as *Lone Star Ballads.*

The late nineteenth century also was characterized by many works of fiction. Although few of these had any enduring value, there were some notable exceptions. Mrs. Molley E. Moore Davis, the wife of a New Orleans editor, began her writing in Texas, and her best work had a Texas setting. *Under the Man-Fig,* probably her best-known novel, dealt with the destructive effects of gossip in a small town. William Sidney Porter, known as O. Henry, came to Texas from his native North Carolina in 1882. Two years on a ranch in La Salle County and a decade in Austin, where he held various jobs and lost some, supplied much of the experience and setting for the literary work that made him one of the great short-story writers of all time. His collection of stories, *Heart of the West,* published during the first decade of the twentieth century, is based almost wholly on Texas scenes.

Historical writing in Texas took a major step forward in 1897 when the Texas State Historical Association was organized. The association began the publication of the *Quarterly of the Texas State Historical Association*, which in 1912 became *The Southwestern Historical Quarterly*. George P. Garrison and Herbert E. Bolton contributed much to the success of this publication, and, under the editorship of E. C. Barker, which lasted a quarter of a century, it came to be recognized as an important historical journal.

Garrison and Bolton were the vanguard of a group of outstanding Texas historians to be active in the early decades of the twentieth century. In his *Texas, A Contest of Civilizations,* George Pierce Garrison brought to bear on the subject years of research and historical training. Bolton, a noted scholar of the Spanish Southwest, published some studies pertaining to Texas, among them *Texas in the Middle-Eighteenth Century* and *Athanase de Mézières and the Louisiana-Texas Frontier.* A contemporary, Charles W. Ramsdell, earned a place among the authorities on the Old South and the Civil War. Eugene C. Barker's studies on the Austins remain the standard work, and his scholarly articles would fill several volumes. Later in the period relatively lengthy histories of Texas were written by Louis J. Wortham and Clarence R. Wharton.

Among the well-known artists of the period was H. A. McArdle, whose pictures, "Battle of San Jacinto" and "Dawn of the Alamo," attracted much attention when they were hung in the state capitol. A contemporary of McArdle was William H. Huddle, whose "Surrender of Santa Anna" also hangs in the state capitol. Robert Jenkins Onderdonk left some superior portraits and paintings of scenes in the vicinity of both Dallas and San Antonio. His son, Julian, who died in 1922 at the age of forty, was probably Texas's most distinguished painter. Of particular note were his landscape scenes, especially "Dawn on the Hills."

In Texas sculpture one name stood supreme—Elisabet Ney. Ney came to the state with her husband, Dr. Edmund Montgomery, about 1870, from her native Bavaria where she had already attained fame. Best known to Texans were her statues of Stephen F. Austin, Sam Houston, and Albert Sidney Johnston. Of higher quality, however, were her imaginative works: for example, the group that she called *Sursum,* now in the Chicago Art Institute, and her statue of Lady Macbeth, now in the National Gallery in Washington, D.C. After Miss Ney's death, her studio in Austin became a museum and a shrine for Texas artists and lovers of art.

Elisabet Ney—beautiful, talented, and willful—learned sculpture in Munich and Berlin where she cast busts of such famous men as Schopenhauer, Garibaldi, and King William I of Prussia. She moved to the United States with her British husband in 1870 and settled in Texas two years later. Unhappy on a remote plantation, she received commissions from the state for busts of Stephen Austin and Sam Houston which enabled her to move to a studio in Austin. One of her best works, a statue of General Albert Sidney Johnston, is now in the state cemetery, but it was her last work, a statue of Lady Macbeth, that won her the fame she frankly enjoyed. (E. C. Barker History Center, University of Texas)

In the early decades of the twentieth century, Texas musicians contributed to the cultural development of the state. Born in Germany and trained in Europe, Carl Venth had already earned fame when he moved to Texas in 1909, and he contributed much to the musical growth of the state thereafter. The cultural diversity of Texas was otherwise particularly influential in the music of this period. Many of the familiar ballads and folk songs heard reflected the culture of the Mexican-American people. Scott Joplin, son of a slave and born in Texarkana, took part in the development of ragtime music, wrote an opera, and composed other songs. Active in the popularization of jazz were Blind Lemon Jefferson and Huddie ("Leadbelly") Ledbetter. Born in Ballinger in 1895, David W. Guion took the folk music of the Indian, the black, and the cowboy and presented them in popular form.

# SELECTED BIBLIOGRAPHY

There are a number of autobiographical studies that tell much about life at the turn of the century. See Edward Everett Dale, *The Cross Timbers* (Austin, 1966); Bertha McKee Dobie, *Growing Up in Texas* (Austin, 1972); Drury B. Alexander, *Texas Homes of the Nineteenth Century* (Austin, 1966); Adah Robertson Hadlock, *My Life in the Southwest* (ed. Kenneth A. Goldblatt, El Paso, Tex., 1969); C. C. White and Ada Moreland Holland, *No Quittin' Sense* (Austin, 1969); and Robert W. Richmond, ed., "Letter from Wise County, Texas," *The American West,* IX, 42–47. See also Catherine Ikard Carrow, "Amusements of Men and Women in Texas in the 1880s," *West Texas Historical Association Year Book,* XXXV, 77–96; Calvin Dickerson, "Collegiate Life in Nineteenth Century Texas," *Texana,* VII, 313–321; David G. McComb, *Houston: The Bayou City;* and Katherine Hart and others, *Austin and Travis County: A Pictoral History, 1839–1939.* A readable and comprehensive discussion of the Galveston flood is available in Herbert M. Mason, Jr., *Death from the Sea: Our Greatest Natural Disaster, the Galveston Hurricane of 1900* (New York, 1972). For information on medical care, see P. I. Nixon, *A History of the Texas Medical Association;* and B. M. Jones, *Health Seekers in the Southwest, 1817–1900.*

Additional information on women in Texas is available in Lawrence W. Neff, *The Legal Status of Women in Texas* (Dallas, 1895); James M. Day and others, *Women of Texas* (Waco, Tex., 1972); Emily Jones Shelton, "Lizzie E. Johnson: A Cattle Queen of Texas," *Southwestern Historical Quarterly,* LVIII, 315–348; Evelyn M. Carrington, ed., *Women in Early Texas* (Austin, 1975); and Elizabeth York Enstam, "The Frontier Woman As City Worker: Women's Occupations in Dallas, Texas, 1856–1880," *East Texas Historical Journal,* XVIII, 12–28.

Life for black Texans at the turn of the century is described thoroughly in Lawrence Rice, *The Negro in Texas, 1874–1900;* and in Alwyn Barr, *Black Texans.* There is an abundance of literature dealing with specialized topics: See John D. Weaver, *The Brownsville Raid* (New York, 1970); Alwyn Barr, "Occupational and Geographic Mobility in San Antonio, 1870–1900," *Social Science Quarterly,* LI, 396–403; and Mason Brewer, *Negro Legislators of Texas and Their Descendants* (Austin, 1970). Also invaluable is the manuscript of Bruce Glasrud in the Texas Tech library, "Black Texans, 1900–1930: A History"; and that of William J. Brophy, "The Black Texan, 1900–1950: A Quantitative History," in the library of Vanderbilt University.

Useful as a starting point for additional study on Mexican-American history is Juan Gómez-Quinones and Luis Leobardo Arrayo, "On the State of Chicano History: Observations on Its Development, Interpre-

**372**

tations, and Theory," *Western Historical Quarterly,* VII, 155–185. Also see Paul S. Taylor, *An American-Mexican Frontier: Nueces County, Texas* (Chapel Hill, N.C., 1934); Pauline R. Kibbe, *Latin Americans in Texas* (Albuquerque, N.M., 1946); William Madsen, *The Mexican-Americans of South Texas* (New York, 1964); Arnulfo D. Trejo, *The Chicanos As We See Ourselves* (Tucson, Arz., 1979); Clifford Alan Perkins, *Border Patrol: With the U.S. Immigration Service on the Mexican Boundary, 1910–1954* (ed. C. L. Sonnichsen, El Paso, Tex., 1978); and Lawrence A. Cardoso "Labor Emigration to the Southwest, 1916 to 1920; Mexican Attitudes and Policy," *Southwestern Historical Quarterly,* LXXIX, 400–416.

For information on other ethnic groups, see Terry G. Jordan, "The German Settlement of Texas after 1865," *Southwestern Historical Quarterly,* LXXIII, 193–212; Edward J. M. Rhoads, "The Chinese in Texas," *ibid.,* LXXXI, 1–36; and T. Lindsey Baker, *The First Polish Americans: Silesian Settlements in Texas* (College Station, Tex., 1979). The Institute of Texan Cultures has published some studies on individual ethnic groups which are useful introductory materials.

The most valuable sources for the literature of this period are Martin Shockley, ed., *Southwest Writers' Anthology* (Austin, 1967); Mabel Major and others, *Southwest Heritage: A Literary History* (Albuquerque, N.M., 1948); and J. Frank Dobie, *Life and Literature of the Southwest* (rev. ed., Dallas, 1973), and "The Southwest, a Cultural Inventory," *Saturday Review of Literature,* May 16, 1942.

For the fine arts, see Pauline Pinckney, *Texas Artists of the Nineteenth Century* (Austin, 1967); Lota M. Spell, *Music in Texas* (Austin, 1938); and Cecilia Steinfeldt, *The Onderdonks: A Family of Texas Painters* (San Antonio, 1976).

Chapter Seventeen

# CRUSADES
# AND COMPLACENCY
# 1910–1930

Crusades and complacency characterized Texas politics in the score of years between the progressive era and the Great Depression. Many Texans joined the crusade for Prohibition with enthusiasm; practically all supported the great crusade of the First World War; and not a few endorsed the reactionary crusading of the Ku Klux Klan. It was, moreover, an age of dramatic social, technological, and economic change. Yet, it was in some respects an era of complacency. Particularly in the twenties, politics was largely the story of governors who sought reforms, reforms that were in the main moderate and reasonable and generally needed but that indifferent legislators and a still more indifferent electorate would not accept. Prohibition, a world war, the impeachment of a governor, and the rise of a hooded tyranny contributed diversity. But basic problems associated with the rapid pace of industrialization and urbanization and a corresponding decline in the role of agriculture provided an element of continuity.

## OSCAR BRANCH COLQUITT

Having the support of most of the opponents of Prohibition in the Democratic gubernatorial primary of 1910, Railroad Commissioner Oscar Branch Colquitt captured 40 percent of the vote, the nomination, and subsequently the general election. A former Hogg man, the governor nevertheless was generally regarded as the most conservative man in the race. Most assuredly, he was not a crusader and received the support of some corporate interests. Once in office, his record, in part, fulfilled conservative expectations. He attempted to block some labor legislation, vetoed a city charter providing for initiative and referendum, denounced direct democracy as "socialistic, un-American," curbed appropriations for higher education, and frowned on the introduction of free textbooks in the public schools.

Yet the Colquitt years were not without progressive achievements. Additional penal reforms were adopted; two hospitals for tuberculosis patients were authorized and one established; and a training school for delinquent girls was founded. Crude but well aimed was a law permitting counties to provide poor houses and poor farms for indigents. There were laws regulating child labor, promoting factory safety, and limiting the hours of women workers. Most important was the workmen's compensation act requiring that persons employed in most industries be insured against accidents and setting forth rules for compensation in case of injury.

An old vexing problem returned during the Colquitt administration. Provoked by a series of Mexican revolutions beginning in 1910, violence erupted along the Rio Grande, and rumors of a Mexican insurrection in the United States were heard. Ill will and confusion persisted on the border until long after the First World War. An investigating committee of the United States Senate reported that between November 1910 and October 1919 five hundred Americans lost their lives in the Mexican troubles; of these, sixty-two civilians and sixty-four soldiers were killed along the American side of the river. Governor Colquitt twice sent state troops to the Rio Grande; they were soon supplanted by federal soldiers. A thousand Texas Rangers stationed along the border afforded a measure of protection, but violence did not cease until several months after the close of the war. Following a sweeping legislative investigation in which it was charged that the rangers had maltreated peaceful Mexican-American citizens of the United States, a law of March 31, 1919, reduced the force to four regular companies of seventeen men each.

Less dramatic than rumored insurrection but certainly serious were the state's financial problems during the Colquitt years. When the outgoing administration set tax rates too low, Governor Colquitt inherited a deficit of nearly a million dollars. A rising cost of living necessitated an increase in salaries. New departments, new institutions, and repairs on buildings at the older institutions required heavier outlays. Various calamities, especially a fire at the Agricultural and Mechanical College, augmented the normal expenses. The penitentiary seemed the most hopeless of all state institutions, requiring the state legislature in 1913 to authorize additional funds to pay debts, make repairs, and add improvements. Reelected in 1912 without much difficulty, Colquitt during his second administration vetoed some appropriations, but even then it was necessary to raise the state tax rate. State expenditures, in fact, more than doubled between 1903 and 1914.

## PROHIBITION: THE TRIUMPH
## OF A MORAL CRUSADE

Although discouraged temporarily by their severe defeat in 1887, prohibitionists soon renewed their fight, directing their efforts mainly toward local option. The Texas Local Option Association was organized in Dallas in 1903, and in 1907 the Anti-Saloon League entered Texas. To meet their challenge, the powerful Texas Brewers' Association raised between 1902 and 1911, by assessment of its members, more than $2 million. In 1907 the Retail Liquor Dealers' Association was organized, its members pledging themselves to obey all laws as the only way to stop the march of prohibition. Nevertheless, through the extension of local option, the prohibitionists gained ground steadily. During the nineties they drove the saloons out of most of North and West Texas, and in the following decade they began to make inroads into South and Southeast Texas. The constitutional amendment of 1902 requiring a poll tax for voting was regarded as a victory for the prohibitionists. Encouraged by their triumph, prohibitionists turned their aims toward a statewide ban, only to encounter among some of its former opponents a strange and new enthusiasm for local option.

By 1908 Prohibition had become the all-absorbing political issue. In fact, from the primary campaign of 1908 when the question of statewide prohibition was again submitted to the voter until the First World War, there were in effect two Democratic parties in Texas, one prohibitionist, the other antiprohibitionist. True, there was no formal division; there was only one set of party committees; and there was only one Democratic primary. But the factions were so pronounced that every prominent leader was forced to join one side or the other, and the great rank and file of voters took their places in the respective camps to fight one another with greater vehemence than Democrat had ever fought Republican since the time of E. J. Davis.

The forces were evenly matched. In the primary election of 1908 the prohibitionists won by a slender margin, but the brewery interests were able to defeat the submission of a constitutional amendment by the legislature. When the entire question was fought out again in the primary election of 1910, the prohibitionists again committed the party to submission. In the selection of candidates, however, they were not so successful. Better organized than their opponents, the antiprohibitionists centered their votes on Colquitt, who was elected by a large plurality over three opponents, two of them ardent prohibitionists who split the votes. Thus, in its primary the Democratic party called for a prohibition amendment and at the same time made sure of the election of an antiprohibitionist governor.

When the legislature submitted the prohibition amendment to the voters and designated July 22, 1911, as the day for the election, the two factions aligned themselves for another desperate contest. With great fervor, lay leaders and preachers campaigned for the cause, while Governor Colquitt joined others in opposition. By a close vote, 231,096 for to 237,393 against, statewide prohibition again failed.

Although they kept up the fight, the prohibitionists in Texas made little headway for some time. However, suits filed by Attorney General B. F. Looney in 1915 revealed that brewers had violated the state's antitrust laws and had illegally used funds in elections. Then came the impeachment of the governor in 1917 and evidence indicating that the brewers had shown him favors. Moreover, Prohibition became a patriotic issue, a measure with which to win World War I. Women, long a strong voice in the movement, renewed their efforts with the formation of the Texas Woman's Anti-Vice Committee, particularly concerned with conditions for servicemen. A law which became effective on April 15, 1918, forbade the sale of liquor within ten miles of any place where troops were quartered. Shortly thereafter, a statewide law closed all saloons. Then, beginning July 1, 1919, a federal law prohibiting the sale of intoxicating liquor anywhere in the nation went into effect, and on January 16, 1920, the Eighteenth Amendment to the United States Constitution made Prohibition a national policy. Meanwhile, the legislature of Texas had ratified the Eighteenth Amendment, and on May 24, 1919, the voters of Texas had adopted a prohibition amendment to the state constitution by a vote of 188,982 to 130,907. Traces of the rift caused by the issue would linger nearly as long as the experiment. But other dramatic national and state issues had already diverted the interest of both voter and politician alike.

## THE BIRTH OF FERGUSONISM

In 1914 there appeared in Texas politics a man destined to stir the emotions of the people for a generation. Rising from poverty and a meager formal education, by 1914 James E. Ferguson was a successful banker at the Temple State Bank, lawyer, and businessman, but he was a virtual unknown in state politics. Yet, Ferguson, who would be often called "Farmer Jim," was twice elected governor, serving from January

1915 to September 1917. Through his wife, Governor Miriam A. ("Ma") Ferguson, he guided many policies of the state from January 1925 to January 1927 and again from January 1933 to January 1935. In addition to his successful campaigns, he was a candidate for governor in 1918, for president of the United States in 1920, and for the United States Senate in 1922. Besides the years when she was elected, Mrs. Ferguson ran for governor in 1926, 1930, and 1940. Meaning different things to different people, "Fergusonism" became a familiar term to the Texas voter. Critics angrily denounced the Fergusons as unprincipled demagogues, but to their loyal supporters they were undaunted crusaders seeking justice for the oppressed.

Believing that the majority of Texans were tired of the prohibition controversy, Ferguson announced as a candidate for governor in the primary of 1914 with the declaration that he would hold aloof from both prohibition political factions and make this campaign on other and more important issues. Although he posed as a businessman's candidate, the principal plank in Ferguson's platform appealed to tenant farmers. For many decades tenantry in Texas had been increasing. In 1880, 37 percent of all farms were operated by tenants; in 1900 the percentage had increased to 59; and in 1910 it was 62.6 percent. While their number had increased, the lot of tenants was growing harder and their outlook more discouraging. The time-honored custom of the landlord's taking a rental of one-fourth of the cotton and one-third of most other crops was not being followed uniformly in Texas. In the richer farmland regions the practice of charging higher rentals, or the customary one-third and one-fourth plus a money bonus, was increasing. Ferguson proposed to fix by law farm rentals at one-third and one-fourth and to make a higher rate illegal. He opened his campaign in Blum, Hill County, a tenant community. Of the 155 speeches that he delivered before the primary election, only ten were made in towns and cities. In the primary he defeated Thomas H. Ball of Houston, who was supported by the prohibition wing of the party. In November he was elected governor with little opposition.

Ferguson's first administration was characterized by harmony and an imposing list of constructive laws. Of the 160 general laws enacted during the regular session of the Thirty-fourth Legislature in 1915, the governor vetoed only five. Ferguson was easily reelected in 1916, and the first five months of his second administration witnessed a continuation of a constructive legislative program. The governor's rental plank was readily enacted into law in 1915. Apparently never rigidly enforced, however, the law was declared unconstitutional in 1921. Interesting and indicative of a new era was a law setting automobile speed limits at fifteen miles an hour in towns and eighteen miles an hour in the country. More significant and, in view of subsequent developments, more incongruous were a number of laws substantially improving educational services.

Governor Ferguson's popularity declined during his second administration, but he still had a large following both in the legislature and among the rank and file of voters. In March 1917 the house of representatives investigated charges of irregular conduct on the part of the governor and discovered some questionable transactions; the committee, nevertheless, recommended that the charges be dropped. The regular session of the legislature completed its work and adjourned, but developments soon indicated that the governor would not be allowed to finish his second term.

Although charges of corruption and incompetence were leveled at Ferguson, both friend and foe have usually agreed that he would not have been impeached if he had not antagonized the alumni of the University of Texas. The governor's quarrel with the university began as early as 1915 when he attempted to dictate to Acting President W. J. Battle the interpretation of the appropriation law for the school. In the following year he apparently became piqued because he was not consulted by the regents in their selection of a president for the university. Later, he demanded that the regents dismiss President Robert E. Vinson and several other faculty members, threatening to veto the entire university appropriation if they did not. The regents, supported by the powerful alumni association, refused to yield. The governor was not bluffing; in June 1917, just after the legislature had adjourned, he vetoed the appropriation. Although the attorney general declared the veto void on a technicality, the fight between Ferguson and the university was then eclipsed by a movement to impeach the governor.

Another Ferguson foe appeared as impeachment proceedings began. The Texas Equal Suffrage Association looked upon the governor as a man of questionable morality and an obvious opponent of women's suffrage. Led by Minnie Fisher Cunningham, the association's president who went to Austin for the contest, the suffragists enthusiastically urged that the cause not be abandoned.

Responding to rising sentiment for impeachment proceedings, on July 23 the speaker of the house issued a call for a special legislative session. He had no constitutional authority for such an act, but Governor Ferguson made the session legal by issuing a call after it became evident that the legislature was going to meet anyway. When the legislature convened, the house impeached the governor on twenty-one articles. On September 24 the senate convicted Ferguson on ten charges. The most serious counts held that Governor Ferguson had appropriated for his own use certain state funds; that he was guilty of irregularities in connection with deposits of public funds in the Temple State Bank, of which he was a stockholder; and that during his campaign in 1916 he had secured currency in the amount of $156,500 from unknown sources. It was discovered later that most of this money had been borrowed from the brewing interests and apparently had never been repaid. The court of impeachment removed Governor Ferguson from office and prohibited him from holding office in Texas again, a restriction that would bring strange developments in later years.

Despite the ban on his holding office, Ferguson returned to the political wars the following year, contesting Will P. Hobby, the lieutenant governor who had taken his position after his impeachment, for the Democratic gubernatorial nomination. Ferguson campaigned with enthusiasm, venting his ire on the University of Texas in particular. One professor of the school, he declared, had devoted two years to an attempt to grow wool on the back of an armadillo. Faculty members were "educated fools," "butterfly chasers," and "two-bit thieves"; crooks and grafters controlled the school's administration. Governor Hobby was a "political accident." The "political accident" won the nomination with a comfortable margin of almost 70 percent of the vote. But the state had not heard the last of Farmer Jim Ferguson.


## TEXAS IN THE FIRST WORLD WAR

The impeachment of a governor in Texas took place in the midst of a titanic military contest in Europe that was shaking the foundations of civilization. When German submarines took the lives of United States citizens, Texans, along with other Americans, became aroused. When Congress declared war on Germany on April 6, 1917, sentiment in Texas in support of the measure was overwhelming.

Politics determined that Texans would play a prominent role in the world conflict that dominated the second term of President Woodrow Wilson. It was the Texas delegation in the Democratic National Convention in Baltimore in 1912, the "immortal forty," that voted for Wilson first and last and possibly assured his nomination. Later Wilson appointed Thomas Watt Gregory, of Austin, as attorney general and David F. Houston, a former Texan, as secretary of agriculture. Albert Sidney Burleson, of Austin, served as postmaster general and during the war directed government operation of the nation's telephone and telegraph systems. Colonel E. M. House was for some time probably the president's most trusted and important private counselor and personal representative. Thomas Love of Dallas served as assistant secretary of the treasury, and many other Texans held positions of great honor and trust.

Within the state the military demands of war were quite apparent.

Thousands of soldiers trained in four large camps (McArthur in Waco, Logan in Houston, Travis in San Antonio, and Bowie in Fort Worth) and in officers' training schools in Leon Springs and Kelly Field. A number of aviation schools scattered over the state provided many citizens with their first view of an airplane. Almost one million Texans registered for military service. Through the selective service law and voluntary enlistment, 197,389 served in the army, navy, and marine corps, with only a few opposing or evading the draft. Women made their contribution to the services, providing 449 nurses. Of those Texans in the armed services, more than 5,000 lost their lives.

At home the state council of defense sought to make the resources of Texas available for the war effort. Its work was distributed among major committees. Cooperating with it were 240 county councils and approximately 15,000 community councils. The services of these committees were placed at the disposal of the directors of various drives for Liberty Loans and support of the Red Cross. These committees also assisted in promoting wholesome recreation for the soldiers and in doing various other things to add to the comfort of the troops and to improve their morale. The publicity committee of the council directed war information, kept available a staff of "four-minute men" for various campaigns, distributed pamphlets, urged the conservation of food, and remained on the alert for disloyal acts and utterances. After the war, the council aided returning soldiers in securing employment.

Independent of the council of defense but cooperating with it was the Federal Food Administration in Texas. Its first campaign in the fall of 1917, which aimed at getting housewives to sign cards agreeing to conserve flour, sugar, fats, and meats, was not so successful as had been expected. Then the emphasis was shifted from the homes to the merchants, and each dealer was requested to conform to the "fifty-fifty" rule which required the sale of one pound of wheat substitute for every pound of wheat flour. From April 15 to June 15, 1918, a "wheat fast" was imposed on Texas, during which period no flour was shipped into the state. Thus, some Texans found themselves eating corn bread even for breakfast.

The war effected a number of more significant changes. Inflation brought a soaring cost of living not always matched by a comparable increase in incomes, though farm prices generally advanced. A permanent change was the rapid increase in public expenditures, expenditures that failed to decline when the war ended. In 1913 the government of Texas spent approximately $13 million for all purposes; by 1919 this amount had increased to $27 million. Still another change was in the role of women who provided a major part of the additional labor force needed for the war effort. Often they worked in voluntary agencies, but some took jobs formerly reserved for men, such as in law enforcement, real estate sales, and labor union management.

Racial tensions grew during the period, though black Texans gave their support to the war effort. Approximately 25 percent of the soldiers from Texas were black, and blacks took part in Liberty Loan drives, supported the Red Cross, and otherwise demonstrated their patriotism. But a mob lynched a black man at Huntsville who was accused of evading the draft, and before the turmoil was ended, six members of his family were also dead. When rioting broke out in Houston in August 1917, seventeen people were killed, and there were other instances of racial violence scattered throughout the war.

Wartime also saw the triumph of the women's suffrage movement. Organized in 1903, the Texas Woman Suffrage Association gradually gained strength and narrowly missed securing legislative approval of a constitutional amendment granting women's suffrage in 1915. The suffragists resumed their battle in the legislature in 1917, only to see the impeachment of the governor intervene. But in a special session in 1918, the legislature adopted a law granting partial suffrage in that it permitted women to vote in all primary elections. That same year several women were elected to posts in local governments, and Annie Webb Blanton won a race for the state superintendent of education. Voters in 1919 turned down a state constitutional amendment granting women's suffrage, but the cause was triumphant anyway, inasmuch as the decision would be made nationally. Another special session of the legislature in June 1919 ratified the Nineteenth Amendment to the Constitution of the United States, Texas being the ninth state in the union and the first in the South to give its approval.

Predictable but regrettable was a spirit of fear, intolerance, and enforced conformity. Following the example set by the general government, the state legislature in a special session in 1918 enacted a drastic law to promote loyalty. To utter criticisms of the United States government, its flag, its officers, soldiers' uniforms, or to question the wisdom of the entrance or continuance of the United States in the war was an offense punishable by fine and imprisonment. The election law was changed to deny the ballot to foreign-born persons not naturalized. It was required that all classes in the public schools, the study of foreign language excepted, be conducted in English; that all schools devote at least ten minutes each day to the teaching of patriotism; and that the United States flag be displayed from a flagpole in every school yard. The law of 1923 requiring that the Constitution of the United States and that of Texas be taught in all public schools and that all teachers be citizens of the United States was, beyond a doubt, a belated product of the war mood.

Sometimes there were excesses of superpatriotism which ranged from the absurd to the tragic. In keeping with the spirit of the times was a legislative investigating committee's recommendation that all recent books and periodicals in the state library extolling the greatness of Germany be immediately destroyed or securely boxed and put out of the way. Governor Hobby in 1919 vetoed the appropriation for the German department of the University of Texas, observing that elimination of such courses would promote purer Americanism. In some communities the obsession for conformity led to terror. "Influential and esteemed" citizens of a central Texas town, for example, flogged six of their neighbors who declined to join the American Red Cross. A newspaper editor in a nearby community endorsed the action, remarking that "whipping may convert some, while others are beyond conversion and should be shot." Texans found that crusading may beget intolerance.

## THE POLITICS OF COMPLACENCY

"You are assembled here in a new era. You have problems to deal with that concern a new age." Thus did Governor William P. Hobby, in a message to the legislature in 1919, evaluate the importance of that time and occasion. Two years later, in the midst of a short financial depression, Governor Pat M. Neff expressed a similar feeling in language even more startling: "We are pioneering today," he said to the legislature, "amid the rocks and reefs and whirlpools of the most disturbed and uncertain financial ocean the world has ever known. These are testing times. The affairs of men are shifting. Things are abnormal. The world is at a turning point in civilization. . . . "

Indeed, the sense of change was very pronounced in the postwar years. Most Texans seemed to feel that with the defeat of Germany and the triumph of democracy, time had turned a page and begun a new chapter. The old order had passed, and a new era had come bringing sharp changes in the affairs of people and nations. In a sense this was true; it was the dawn of a great boom. As men went from the army and navy back to civilian life, they were easily absorbed by industry. The depression of 1920 was short lived, and Texas shared the general prosperity that soon returned. New plants were erected for the manufacturing and processing of goods, land values doubled, millions were invested in public utilities, and thousands of new oil wells belched forth their black gold. The great state highway system was constructed, destined to be used by an ever-increasing number of foreign and Texan-owned cars. New colleges were built, and thousands of youths crowded into the old ones; the public school system grew larger and more creditable each year. Prices of farm commodities lagged behind those enjoyed by industry, but bountiful crops tended to offset the price handicap. Texas was prosperous during the "mad decade," and people paid no heed to timid prophets here and there who told them that ahead were lean years that would devour the fat ones.

Thus, for business and industry the decade following the close of the First World War did constitute a new era, but in politics and political institutions there was little to distinguish it from the years that preceded it. A few new government agencies were added and some of the old ones were enlarged, but there was little suggestive of the "new era" that Governor Hobby thought he saw ahead. In many respects the governors recognized the political demands of the emerging industrial and urban society. But a reluctant legislature and a complacent electorate refused to respond.

Complacency in politics was apparent even before the end of the war. In February 1918 a legislative investigating committee made a report suggesting various changes in the state government, but nothing except the eventual creation of the state board of control as a budget agency came out of the report. After the war Governor Hobby advocated more aid for education, a civil service commission, judicial reform, and state aid for home buyers, but only some educational improvements were made. The question of a constitutional convention was submitted to the voters in 1919 and defeated as voters rejected ten out of thirteen constitutional amendments. Caught by the spell of the new era, the legislature might propose changes, but the people disposed of them in their own way.

Proclaiming a new democracy, Pat M. Neff entered the race for governor in 1919, subject to the action of the Democratic primary in the following year. The dignified and devout Waco lawyer knew Texas politics firsthand, for he had served as speaker of the house of representatives in 1903 and 1904. His chief opponent in the Democratic primary was Joe Bailey, who returned to politics after eight years of retirement to base his campaign largely on opposition to the Wilson administration, women's suffrage, and most of the trends in government that had appeared during the last decade. Neff championed the great causes Bailey opposed, and he also favored a graduated land tax and other proposals that scandalized the staunch champions of the old Democratic party. Bailey led in the first primary, but in the runoff Neff won by a majority of 79,376. In spite of opposition from organized labor, Neff was renominated and reelected in 1922.

The new democracy was triumphant, but the people were not ready for any drastic changes. Through various messages to the legislature, Governor Neff advocated a number of reform measures and got practically nowhere. Rejected were changes in the state administrative system, a constitutional convention, and more laws to combat what Neff called the worst "crime wave" in the history of Texas. Neff, however, did his part to keep prisoners in the penitentiary. He disbanded the board of pardons, made his own investigations, and granted very few pardons. In this respect his administration was in striking contrast to those of Hobby and the Fergusons.[1]

Otherwise, some permanent improvements were made. Governor Neff, an ardent champion of good roads, must be given a share of credit for the expansion and improvement of the highway system. Likewise, he used his influence effectively to promote the conservation of natural resources. The state park system had its beginning in 1923 with the creation of a nonsalaried park board. A harsh comment on the lack of foresight of those who had gone before is the fact that the state of Texas, which once had owned millions of acres of land, was obliged to solicit donations of a few hundred acres here and there so that its people might have access to recreational facilities.


## THE KU KLUX KLAN
## AND THE RETURN OF FERGUSONISM

In 1921 there appeared in Texas an organization that was the subject of bitter controversy for several years. The Ku Klux Klan had its beginning near Atlanta, Georgia, in about 1915, taking the name of the famous organization of Reconstruction days and making white supremacy one of its slogans. It was, however, more akin to the various nativist movements that have arisen among the American people from time to time than it was to the original Ku Klux Klan of Reconstruction days. In fact, the Klan in Texas was, as much as anything else, an effort to impose social and moral conformity on a society in rapid transition from the farm to the city. The Klan made little headway until after the First World War, when various conditions combined to promote its spread. The nation had been made aware of the presence of millions of foreign-born persons, commonly called "hyphenated Americans," whose loyalty had been impeached, in many cases unjustly, and after the war there arose sharp

---

[1]From January 1915 to September 1917 Governor James E. Ferguson granted 1,774 pardons and 479 conditional pardons; from August 1917 to January 1921 Governor W. P. Hobby granted 1,319 pardons and 199 conditional pardons; from January 1925 to September 1926 Governor Miriam A. Ferguson granted 384 pardons and 777 conditional pardons. The period covered in Mrs. Ferguson's first administration (January 1925 to September 1926) does not include the time during which the governor exercised the pardoning power most liberally.

resentment toward everybody and everything foreign. Protestant in sympathy, the Klan was distinctly anti-Catholic and anti-Jewish. It declared war on crime and corrupt officials, a phase of its program that appealed to thousands of men who had little sympathy for its racial and religious intolerance. It gained its maximum growth in Texas during 1921 and 1922, at a time when Governor Neff (not in sympathy with the Klan) was writing and speaking against the "greatest crime wave" in Texas history and giving credence to the estimate that "not ten percent of those who violated the law were arrested, and not half of those who are arrested are convicted." The Klan went further, assuming for itself the responsibility of protecting "virtuous womanhood," "premarital chastity," "marital fidelity," "respect for parental authority," and "abstinence from alcoholic beverages."

Covertly, the Klan entered politics and soon its power was felt in almost every community. In 1922 it gained control of many local offices and participated in the campaign for the United States Senate. That year several candidates sought to succeed United States Senator Charles A. Culberson, who had served continuously since 1899 but was prevented by poor health from making an active campaign. The strongest contenders were Earle B. Mayfield, member of the Texas railroad commission, and James E. Ferguson, who had left the Democrats in 1920 to run for president of the United States on his own American party ticket but returned to the Democratic party two years later. Mayfield admitted that he had belonged to the Klan, and it was generally understood that he was supported by it, whereas Ferguson attacked the organization severely. Mayfield received the nomination, and disgruntled Democrats, uniting with the Republicans behind George E. B. Peddy, a Houston attorney, failed to defeat him in the general election.

In the election of 1924 the Klan played an even more important part by supporting Judge Felix D. Robertson of Dallas. His opponent, James E. Ferguson, disqualified from holding the governorship by the terms of his impeachment in 1917, entered the race through his wife, Miriam A. Ferguson. Robertson and Mrs. Ferguson survived the first primary, and the race became the keenest the state had seen in many years. The Klan was powerful but it had already lost ground. In their zeal to impose moral conformity, the Klansmen had frequently taken the law into their own hands. From many communities came reports of hooded men, working by night, serving as their own sheriff, judge, and jury, and flogging persons, driving them from their communities, or otherwise terrifying them. The Klan denied their connection with most of these outrages, but it must be said that its masked parades and secret conclaves had inspired many of them. In the primary Mrs. Ferguson defeated Robertson by nearly 100,000 votes. Another minority of the

Democratic party was now dissatisfied, and this group united with the Republicans in an effort to defeat Mrs. Ferguson in the general election. The bolters supported George C. Butte, dean of the University of Texas law school. Mrs. Ferguson defeated him by more than 100,000 votes to become the first woman governor of Texas.

During this second era of Fergusonism (1925–1927), reform took a holiday. James E. Ferguson, who determined the policies his wife followed, was disposed to pursue a conservative course. No drastic proposals appeared in the governor's messages and no outstanding laws were enacted. Ferguson's liberal pardoning policy—two thousand acts of executive clemency, counting furloughs and extensions, during twenty months—evoked much gossip and unfavorable comment. An investigating committee found that most of the governor's pardons were issued on the recommendation of her husband, some of them before the beneficiaries reached the prison. The chief attack by the enemies of the administration was, however, aimed at the highway commission, a body composed completely of Ferguson appointees and dominated by the former governor who sat with it whenever important matters were up for consideration. It was alleged that favoritism, rather than the best interests of the state, was the determining factor in awarding contracts for the construction of roads. Several contracts were canceled as the result of suits brought by Attorney General Dan Moody, who became the chief antagonist of the Fergusons.

A crusader for reform, in 1926 Dan Moody entered the campaign for governor against Mrs. Ferguson. The Fergusons were confident, but the attorney general was able to defeat her by a substantial majority to become the next governor of the state.

## MOODY'S REFORM PROGRAM

In Dan Moody the friends of reform had an able spokesman. Although he was the youngest governor who ever served Texas (elected at the age of thirty-three), he had been seasoned by experience as a local prosecutor and by two years as attorney general. As district attorney in Williamson County, Moody had attained a statewide reputation for his vigorous prosecution of certain members of the Ku Klux Klan who had committed acts of violence, a distinction that brought him the office of attorney general.

He proposed a broad reform program that represented in the main the best ideals of the progressive forces of the day. He advocated a number of measures calling for important changes in the constitution and state laws. He supported a change in the constitution to permit the legislature to enact new laws on taxation. He proposed that the judiciary article of the constitution be rewritten so as to raise the number of justices of the supreme court from three to nine. He would give the governor power to appoint the important executive officers who were not elected under the Constitution of 1876. With these appeals Moody was no more successful than his predecessors who advocated the same or similar reforms, and the governor's most earnest and persistent plea for a civil service law was likewise rejected.

The perennial problem of prisons and prison management demanded attention during this period. The prison population was growing, the system was difficult to manage, and costs were climbing. Pursuant to the recommendation of Governor Moody, who favored a centralized system with fewer farming and more industrial projects, the legislature created a centralization commission to make a study of the Texas system and those of other states and to formulate a plan that would settle the vexing problem. The commission report resulted in a compromise measure that fell far short of the complete reorganization and concentration that the governor and other champions of reform had advocated. However, a previous legislature had created a governing body of nine members to select and employ a manager to be in charge of the entire system and to be responsible to the board. After Lee Simmons, a Sherman business-man, was appointed manager in 1930, the prison system thereafter showed marked improvement.

In the election of 1928, for the first time in history the interest in the contest for the presidential electoral vote in Texas was keener than the interest in state and local races. Governor Moody received a majority vote in the first primary, over Louis J. Wardlaw who was supported by the Fergusons. But early in the year the presidential candidacy of Governor Alfred E. Smith of New York, a Catholic and an outspoken opponent of Prohibition, threatened the unity of Texas Democrats. The Republicans also were, as usual, divided. The "Harmony Democrats" chose Governor Moody as their leader and at the state convention prevailed against the "Constitutional Democrats" led by Thomas Love, who sought to instruct the state delegation against Smith. After Smith was nominated at the national convention in Houston, the anti-Smith forces organized to do battle with the regular Democrats. Most of the party leaders stayed with the regular organization, but they were not able to match the strength of the bolters who united with the major Republican faction in a campaign for Herbert Hoover that resembled the prohibition crusades of other years. Hoover's plurality was 26,000; he was the first Republican to receive an electoral vote in Texas. It has been said that the chief issue in the campaign of 1928 were "the three P's"—Prosperity, Prohibition, and Prejudice. In this election Tom Connally defeated Earle B. Mayfield for the United States Senate.

Moody's first term was, perhaps, the most prosperous period the state had ever known. But during the last year of his administration the state began to feel the pinch of the depression and panic that had begun in 1929 with the collapse of the stock market and spread to all parts of the nation. The brunt of the depression, however, was born by the Sterling and Ferguson administrations (1931–1935).

## LIFE IN THE TWENTIES

The twenties are often remembered as a flamboyant age, replete with "flappers," raccoon coats, speakeasies, real estate promotions, bathtub gin and bootleggers, gangsters, and the Charleston. The image is probably greatly exaggerated for the nation as a whole; certainly it is exaggerated for Texas. But there were dramatic social changes evident in the life of the people.

It was a period of rapid population growth and mobility within the population of the state. With an increase in population from 4,663,228 to 5,824,715, Texas enjoyed one of the most rapid growth rates in the union. Rural Texas gained only 9 percent in population, while urban Texas increased 58 percent. Between 1920 and 1930, the rural farm inhabitants declined from about 48 percent of the population to 40 percent. All cities of more than 25,000, and there were sixteen of them, grew at an average rate of 61 percent. Smaller cities generally grew in a like manner, but not quite as consistently, some with dramatically high rates of increase and a few even showing a decline.

The impact of technology is noteworthy. In urban areas conveniences such as electrical appliances and lights and plumbing facilities became commonplace, and occasionally a radio was seen. In rural areas living conveniences changed but little, inasmuch as electricity was rarely available, and indoor plumbing was the exception rather than the rule. However, the number of farm tractors tripled, signaling the acceleration of the mechanical revolution in agriculture.

Both farm and city shared in the growth of the automobile industry. The number of automobiles in Texas rose more than 500 percent during the decade, to the point at which by 1929 there was an automobile for every 4.3 Texans. Apparent everywhere was the economic impact of the automobile, but there were also many social consequences. By the end of the decade many smaller towns were losing population, and some of the churches and businesses within them were disappearing as the automobile made long distance travel practical. Another consequence, somewhat more intangible, was the belief of some that the morality of the people was declining and that the automobile bore much of the responsibility.

Whether or not immorality increased during the decade is perhaps debatable, but certainly there was a great deal of concern about the matter. Parents, preachers, school authorities, social workers, editors, and others condemned the behavior of society. Concern was frequently expressed over immodest dress, modern dances, smoking, drinking, lewd movies, midnight joy riding, the rising crime rate, and an increasing traffic in narcotics. In addition to the automobile, the movies were often held accountable for the altered pattern of behavior. Surely, the movies were an important part of life in the twenties. By 1920 Texans were spending more than $24 million a year for movie tickets, an average per capita attendance of more than twenty movies per year.

Efforts to regulate morality took many forms. In some instances the violent and lawless methods of the Ku Klux Klan were used to punish suspected evildoers, but more lawful and less violent methods generally prevailed. A number of cities established movie censor boards; other cities passed ordinances prohibiting questionable behavior. One ordinance seems to have banned flirting; there were laws regulating the type and extent of clothing worn by bathers and prohibiting the showing of movies on Sunday. A law was proposed, though never passed, even limiting the height of a woman's shoe heel to one inch. Toward the end of the decade such efforts to regulate behavior tended to diminish.

The changing character of society was reflected in the status of the family. Texans married at a rate generally higher than the national average, but by 1929 the divorce rate in Texas was one of the highest in the nation and had more than doubled since 1916. At the same time, the size of the average family grew smaller, declining from 4.6 in 1920 to 3.5 in 1930, and urban families were even smaller. On a more positive note, the employment of children declined rapidly. Whereas in 1910 more than 40 percent of the boys in Texas were employed, only slightly more than 7 percent of all children were employed in 1930. Compulsory school attendance laws, child labor regulations, and a growing urban population likely accounted for the decline.

Conditions for women suggested some significant changes during the decade. The total proportion of women in the population who worked outside the home rose only slightly, but the nature of their employment changed a great deal, as farm employment declined and more found urban jobs. The number of married women who worked increased almost two-thirds over the state during the decade and even more in larger cities. More and more women engaged in political activity, and by 1929 three women held seats in the state legislature. But the quest for equality still had a distance to go. Wages for women were generally one-half or less than those paid to men. Efforts were made to secure legal equality for women, particularly with respect to laws regarding property management and marriage rights, but to no avail.

Although the decade opened with a considerable amount of violence and oppression, conditions for black people improved in subsequent years. The number of black people in the population increased, though more blacks left the state than moved into it. Likewise, there was a ' movement of black people from rural to urban areas. The violence of earlier years, which often had ended in lynching, almost ceased, and a significant, if temporary, victory in the ongoing battle for the right to vote was won when the United States Supreme Court ruled that the legislature could not, by state law, establish a white primary.

Even against the obstacle of political complacency, the educational system of Texas made substantial progress during these years. To be sure, by most criteria that could be used to evaluate the public schools, Texas continued to lag behind the national norms. But through constitutional reforms, added local responsibility, expanded resources, and consolidation, public education came nearer than before to meeting the needs of a modern society. The creation of new institutions of higher learning and the dramatic growth of older ones were additional evidence of a maturing educational structure.

The legislature on the eve of the twenties took several steps toward providing educational opportunities. In 1915 the legislature approved a special appropriation for rural schools, provided that the rural district itself maintained a certain level of taxation. The measure had the effect of stimulating greatly the levying of local school taxes in rural districts where they were most needed. Legislatures continued the practice until 1949 when more fundamental reforms were made. Ferguson's administration also gave the state a compulsory school attendance law, which went into effect in the fall of 1916. In 1918 a constitutional amendment authorizing free textbooks was adopted; at the same time the constitutional maximum for the state school tax was raised; and in 1920 the voters abolished entirely the limit on the tax rate that communities might levy for school purposes. These measures, and even more generous expenditures in the early twenties, did not lift the Texas school system from its low rank when compared with other states. A survey of the schools, authorized in 1923, revealed deficiencies and brought forth a number of recommendations, most of which the legislators and voters did not see fit to adopt. But a number of changes in education in the twenties did take place.

Consolidation of schools was an apparent trend. The building of a state highway system and the improvements of other roads during this period made it possible for communities to take advantage of a law of 1914 that permitted the consolidation of schools whenever a majority of the voters of two or more districts favored it. A 1925 law permitted trustees to make consolidations under certain conditions, and with the decision to provide transportation at public expense for students who lived at a distance, the beginning of the end of the "little red school-house" was at hand. By 1930, 1,530 consolidations had been made.

A second trend noticeable in the public schools was in the matter of curriculum changes. Especially in the urban schools, the influence of so-called "progressivism" was felt, as some educators insisted that schools must go beyond traditional teaching and prepare the students for life in a wide variety of ways. With the movement came changes in teaching methodology, school health programs, comprehensive student testing programs, and an expansion of vocation training, especially in courses related to business. In another curriculum matter there was an ongoing effort to prohibit by law the teaching of evolution. Beginning in 1923, critics of the theory of evolution fought the battle regularly in each session of the legislature until 1929, but no law was ever passed.

With the pattern of segregation as rigid as ever, black schools, already far behind those for white students, failed to share equally in the educational gains. Between 1905 and 1930 the salaries of white teachers

The lack of a public school system was one of the griev-ances listed in the Texas Declaration of Independence, and the Constitution of the Republic of Texas stipulated that Congress provide such a system. Despite the support of President Mirabeau B. Lamar and Governors E. M. Pease and James S. Hogg, among others, the Texas public education system was relatively poor, and the one-room school house was still very common in 1914 (the date of the photograph). Not until the automobile was in general use was it possible for widely separated families to send their children to larger and better equipped schools that offered more specialized education. (E. C. Barker History Center, University of Texas)

in rural areas increased $8.98 per scholastic; salaries of black teachers per student increased sixteen cents. In 1929 black teachers received about $120.00. Blacks constituted approximately one-third of the scholastic population of East Texas, but more than 97 percent of the high schools of East Texas were for whites only. Nevertheless, progress was made. In 1930 the illiteracy rate for black people was down to 13.4 percent.

During these years the junior college movement, associated with Texas since its infancy, expanded rapidly. In 1897 the Baptist state convention established a correlated system of higher educational institutions, with Baylor University and Mary Hardin–Baylor College as senior schools and Howard Payne College, Rusk College, and Decatur Baptist College as two-year institutions. Other denominations entered the field, establishing by 1920 a number of church-controlled junior colleges. About the same time the state created junior colleges in Stephenville and Arlington, and with the founding of El Paso Junior College in 1920, Texas cities had begun to provide junior colleges.

Four-year colleges and universities also grew in number and size. During the early decades of the twentieth century, the state established a college for women in Denton and acquired, founded, or authorized normal schools in Canyon, Commerce, Kingsville, and Alpine. In 1923 the state normal schools were made into teachers' colleges. The same legislature authorized the establishment of Texas Technological College in Lubbock, thus meeting the demand for a university pressed by citizens of that area for many years.

The twenties saw the most rapid growth the state colleges had known. Each year brought additional thousands of students to tax the facilities of the already overcrowded institutions. In fact, student enrollment grew about 150 percent during the decade. To solve the space problem temporarily, the University of Texas erected flimsy wooden structures dubbed "shacks" by the students. In a sense, the shacks symbolized the position of education in Texas at this point. Progress had been made, and the need for improvement had been recognized, but there remained much to do.

*SELECTED BIBLIOGRAPHY*

General studies on this period are R. Steen in F. C. Adams (ed.), *Texas Democracy* (4 vols., Austin, 1937); S. S. McKay, *Texas Politics, 1906–1944;* Lewis L. Gould, *Progressives and Prohibitionists: Texas Democrats in the Wilson Era* (Austin, 1973); Lewis L. Gould, "Progressives and Prohibitionists: Texas Democratic Politics, 1911–1921," *South-*

*western Historical Quarterly,* LXXV, 5–18; S. Acheson, *35,000 Days in Texas,* and *Joe Bailey: The Last Democrat;* R. Steen, *Twentieth Century Texas; An Economic and Social History;* and S. S. McKay and O. B. Faulk, *Texas after Spindletop.*

Discussion of border troubles are W. P. Webb, *The Texas Rangers;* and C. C. Cumberland, "Border Raids in the Lower Rio Grande Valley, 1915," *Southwestern Historical Quarterly,* LVII, 285–311.

For special studies on the Fergusons, see R. Steen, "The Ferguson War on the University of Texas," *Southwestern Social Science Quarterly,* XXXV, 356–362; Ouida Ferguson Nalle, *The Fergusons of Texas* (San Antonio, 1946); H. G. James, "The Removal of Governor Ferguson of Texas by Impeachment," *National Municipal Review,* VI, 725–726; W. F. McCaleb, "The Impeachment of a Governor," *American Political Science Review,* XII, 111–115; and Octavia F. Rogan, "Texas Legislation, 1925," *Southwestern Political and Social Science Quarterly,* VI, 167–168. Useful also is the manuscript of Jack Lynn Calbert on the Fergusons, located in the library of Indiana University.

Activities of two other governors are described in James Clark, *The Tactful Texan: Governor W. P. Hobby* (New York, 1958); and in Emma M. Shirley, *The Administration of Pat M. Neff, Governor of Texas, 1921–1925* (Waco, Tex., 1938). Also see S. A. MacCorkle, "The Pardoning Power in Texas," *Southwestern Social Science Quarterly,* XV, 218–228; and O. D. Weeks, "The Election of 1928," *ibid.,* IX, 337–348.

Texas's part in the First World War is treated, inadequately, in Army and Navy History Company, *History of Texas World War Heroes* (Dallas, 1919). For the operation of the draft law, see *Second Report of the Provost Marshal General to the Secretary of War* (Washington, D.C., Government Printing Office, 1919). See also James W. Pohl, "Slayden's Defeat: A Texas Congressman Loses Bid as Wilson's Secretary of War," *Military History of Texas and the Southwest* (1972); William E. Nicholas, "World War I and Academic Dissent in Texas," *Arizona and the West,* XIV, 215–230; and Robert V. Haynes, *A Night of Violence: The Houston Riot of 1917* (Baton Rouge, La., 1976).

For additional reading on other crusades, see H. A. Ivey, *Rum on the Run in Texas* (Dallas, 1910), biased but of value; Elizabeth A. Taylor, "The Woman Suffrage Movement in Texas," *Journal of Southern History,* XVIII, 194–215; Charles C. Alexander, *Crusade for Conformity: The Ku Klux Klan in Texas, 1920–1930* (Houston, 1962); and John Carroll Eudy, "The Vote and Lone Star Women: Minnie Fisher Cunningham and the Texas Equal Suffrage Association," *East Texas Historical Journal,* XIV, 52–57.

Texas's place on the national scene is touched upon in Arthur Link, "The Wilson Movement in Texas, 1910–1912," *Southwestern Historical*

*Quarterly,* XLVIII, 169–185; Lewis L. Gould, "Theodore Roosevelt, William Howard Taft, and the Disputed Delegates in 1912: Texas as a Test Case," *ibid.,* 33–56; Dewey Grantham, "Texas Congressional Leaders and the New Freedom, 1913–1917," *ibid.,* LIII, 35–48; R. N. Richardson, *Colonel Edward M. House: The Texas Years, 1858–1912;* W. P. Webb and Terrell Webb (eds.), *Washington Wife: Journal of Ellen Maury Slayden from 1897–1919* (New York, 1962); Lee N. Allen, "The Democratic Presidential Primary Election of 1924 in Texas," *Southwestern Historical Quarterly,* LXI, 474–493; Tom Connally and Alfred Steinberg, *My Name Is Tom Connally* (New York, 1954); and Bascom M. Timmons, *Garner of Texas; A Personal History* (New York, 1948).

Social and cultural affairs in the 1920s are studied in Lynn Ray Musslewhite, "Texas in the 1920's: A History of Social Change," a manuscript in the Texas Tech University library. See also Alwyn Barr, *Black Texans;* and Charles R. Wilson, "Morons, Monkeys, and Morality: Reactions to the Scopes Trial in Texas," *East Texas Historical Journal,* XII, 51–63.

Chapter Eighteen

# THE GREAT DEPRESSION
# 1930–1941

In the early autumn of 1929, after a long period of soaring prices, the New York stock market turned downward. On October 23 a sharp drop precipitated much selling, and on the next day panic seized the exchanges of the nation. Although Texans suffered their share of losses in the stock market crash, their immediate injuries were not as great as those that followed later. Prices fell, business volume declined, unemployment rose, the number of bankruptcies increased, and with the closing of all banks in March 1933, the Great Depression reached every farm and hamlet in the land.

"Prosperity is just around the corner" came to be a trite, sorry joke. President Herbert Hoover, who was unduly optimistic, thought for a time that local relief agencies could supply adequate aid to those in need, but toward the end of his term, he advocated stronger measures. In 1933 newly inaugurated President Franklin D. Roosevelt announced his "New Deal." His positive action in dealing with the bank crisis and his assurance that the general government would apply its vast resources toward relief and recovery restored a measure of confidence, but it did not bring the nation out of the financial doldrums. Meanwhile, state and local governments tried to survive and to offer a degree of assistance in the troubled times.

Progress toward recovery was uneven until midsummer 1935; henceforth improvement was rapid until the autumn of 1937, when a recession that continued through much of the following year wiped out a considerable part of the gain. Not until the gigantic defense program of 1940–1941 stimulated demands for labor and goods did the economic society attain "recovery," and even then many thousands of workers continued to be unemployed.

The times were difficult, but the decade was not without positive achievements. Conservation of natural resources received more attention than ever before, and cultural achievements were rich and varied.


## TEXANS IN HARD TIMES

Although Texans apparently fared somewhat better than people in some other areas, the depression brought worry and concern to most people, and to others it brought suffering, even desperation. An unemployment census taken in 1933 showed that 105,045 families, representing 7.1 percent of the population, were on relief. The next year there were 246,819 relief cases, representing a million people, or about 13 percent of the population. Building construction came almost to a standstill. Cotton, which sold for eighteen cents a pound in 1928, dropped to five cents in 1932. East Texas oil, which was selling for sixty cents a barrel in 1930, fell to five cents in 1931. Food prices declined. Bread cost as little as four cents a loaf; steak sold for eighteen cents per pound; milk sometimes cost as little as four or five cents a quart; and hamburgers cost a nickel.

These statistics, though grim, can tell only a part of the story, for though the prices were meager, many could not afford them. In one West Texas town a citizens' relief association killed, dressed, and stored wild rabbits to be distributed to those in need. The demand soon exceeded the supply. Aransas Pass businessmen donated tons of fish to feed the poor and hungry people of Dallas. Soup kitchens and bread lines appeared in most towns of any size. Many farm laborers and tenants, dispirited and broken, gathered in towns and cities, hoping either to share in direct relief or to draw small wages on public works projects. Merchants, manufacturers, and shopowners laid off workers, adding to the ranks of the unemployed.

In many cases relatives and friends helped for a while and local charity organizations did the best they could, but all such efforts proved to be inadequate. Thousands of individuals and not a few families took to the highways, hitchhiking from place to place. Many were without funds, and persons living near the roads were often compelled either to give them food or turn them away hungry. Swarms of unfortunate people sought protection in abandoned buildings, caves, dugouts, and shanties made of discarded boxes.

Some groups suffered more than others in the depression. The unemployment rate for black people was approximately twice that for the white population, and sometimes relief agencies refused to aid blacks or otherwise discriminated against them. In San Antonio the dependence of Mexican-American people on relief seems to have been in line with that of the general population. In 1933, however, the percentage of Mexican-Americans receiving aid exceeded all other groups. Some emigrants returned to Mexico, apparently because of the hard times they encountered in Texas.

Schools and local governments shared in the hard times, for tax receipts declined. In Houston in 1932 one-half of the street lights were turned off because money to pay for the electricity was not available. Beaumont in 1934 reduced funds for the city library to almost nothing and for the city schools by almost one-half. Street lights were turned off altogether. School teachers in San Antonio whose husbands earned as much as two thousand dollars per year were not rehired. The severity of the budget cuts varied from city to city and from school district to school district, but few, if any, escaped altogether. Even churches suffered from the depression. Other factors were involved, especially the automobile, but financial problems played a large role in the decline of the number of churches by almost four thousand during the period between 1926 and 1936.

Texans' reactions to the depression varied but were not greatly different from reactions elsewhere in the nation. At first, most seemed to believe that there was no cause for worry. By 1930 there was still a considerable amount of optimism, but some were beginning to question the future. From 1931 on, the existence of the crisis was generally accepted and the search for solutions intensified.

On the whole, the solutions supported were of a moderate kind. There were "Buy Now" campaigns, "Give-a-Job" and "Share-the-Work" programs, and most widely discussed of all, a "Back-to-the-Farm" movement. Some worried about socialism or communism, and many believed that capitalism was threatened. But there is little to indicate that revolution or rebellion was a serious possibility. There were demonstrations by the unemployed such as those in Houston in 1930 and in Beaumont in 1931, but these were orderly and peaceable. Sheep shearers in San Angelo and pecan shellers in San Antonio, both desperately poor Mexican-American groups, struck for higher wages. There was some violence, but not of the scale found in labor disputes elsewhere in the nation.

Violence of another kind, however, did afflict the countryside of Texas from time to time. Perhaps to some degree a holdover from the lawless side of Prohibition, or perhaps a reflection of the unsettled conditions of the depression, occasionally notorious and outrageous criminals killed and robbed on a grand scale, apparently relishing the publicity. Of these, none was more flagrant in the disregard for human life and decency than were Bonnie Parker and Clyde Barrow. This pair terrorized large areas of Texas from 1932 until they were finally shot to death in 1934 in an ambush in neighboring Louisiana.

## THE POLITICS OF POVERTY, 1930–1935

The history of the gubernatorial campaign of 1930 in the early stages of the depression sustains the exaggerated statement that the Democratic party in Texas chooses its candidate for governor by lottery. Twelve persons filed for that office, and it seemed that of a half-dozen or more any two might qualify for the second primary. Governor Moody supported Ross Sterling of Houston, who was completing his fourth year as chairman of the highway commission. James E. Ferguson, as usual, was in the race through the candidacy of his wife. In the first primary, Mrs. Ferguson led the ticket and Sterling ran next to her. After a bitter contest preceding the second primary, Sterling was nominated by a majority of about 100,000. His chief claim to the office was the promise of "a business administration to meet the demands of a growing State, by a successful business man." In the general election he defeated without difficulty the Republican nominee.

During Sterling's administration (January 1931 to January 1933), emergency followed emergency, and one crisis had not passed before another appeared in the offing. Taxes were in arrears; state income fell off sharply; expenditures were nearly as high as ever; and Sterling was obliged to use the veto often and to call special sessions repeatedly.

Governor Sterling worked faithfully in the interest of Texas and brought to bear on public affairs the rich experience of a varied business career, but the times bred discontent and in 1932 the voters were ready for a change. Sensing the dissatisfaction, James E. Ferguson again entered the contest. In supporting his wife's campaign he said to the voters: "Two years ago you got the best governor money could buy, this year you have an opportunity to get the best governor patriotism can give you." He added that when his wife was governor he would "be on hand picking up chips and bringing in water for mama." He charged that Sterling had wasted state highway funds; he attacked him for invoking martial law in the East Texas oilfields; and he proposed certain drastic changes in state taxes. Former Governor Moody and other prominent Texans worked diligently for Sterling, but in the second primary Mrs. Ferguson beat him by a few hundred votes out of a total of nearly a million.

The Forty-third Legislature, which convened in January 1933, found that the depression was aggravating old problems and creating new ones. Governor Ferguson recommended a sales tax of 3 percent, but the legislature, like its successors until 1961, refused to adopt such a measure. Despite budget economies, the administration found it difficult to make ends meet, and municipalities and school districts everywhere were impoverished. The urgent need for more revenue accounted in part for a measure, enacted as a rider on an appropriation bill in 1933, making betting on horse racing legal and for the end of Prohibition. Texas joined in ratifying the Twenty-first Amendment to the Constitution of the United States which ended national Prohibition on December 5, 1933. Then the Forty-fourth Legislature submitted an amendment repealing state prohibition, and the voters ratified it in August 1935.

It is difficult to evaluate objectively Mrs. Ferguson's second administration. Relations between the legislature and the executive were not harmonious, as lawmakers distrusted the governor and her husband. The return of the Fergusons' policy of liberal pardons and paroles for state prisoners was attacked from various quarters. It must be said, however, that the administration was economical and apparently met with much greater public approval than did Mrs. Ferguson's first administration as governor.

For the first time since 1914, Texas voters were not confronted directly by "Fergusonism" in 1934, as Governor Ferguson did not seek reelection. Nominated and elected was James V. Allred of Wichita Falls, who was completing his second term as attorney general. Although his platform was more conservative than those of his opponents, Allred was relatively liberal and is sometimes referred to as "Texas's last liberal governor." All candidates favored, or at least refused to oppose, old age pensions, an issue that would dominate Texas politics for the remainder of the decade.

By the beginning of Governor Allred's term, January 1935, the New Deal relief program was well under way and President Roosevelt's plans for national social security had been announced. The governor urged "planned recovery" for Texas, and to that end a Texas planning board was established for a period of four years. It set out to prepare a comprehensive program for the construction and utilization of the resources of the state. No fewer than a dozen boards and commissions were created by the legislature to aid in carrying out projects associated with the program of relief and security in its various forms.

## RELIEF, RECOVERY, AND REFORM

As the depression deepened, it soon became evident that private relief organizations and antiquated public agencies, such as poor farms, could not care for the increasing number of persons who had no means of support. Governor Sterling in 1931 suggested public works as a means of providing indirect relief, but of greater immediate value was his committee for the relief of unemployment.

Meanwhile, the federal government had attacked the problem in a program calling for billions of dollars for direct relief and work relief, much of which was to be spent through state and local agencies. There were two means of approach: the first by making grants to the states for general relief, and the second by carrying out a works program that would serve the double purpose of relieving unemployment and "priming the pumps" of business and industry. The first aid was extended late in 1932 under a law authorizing the lending of Federal Reconstruction Finance Corporation funds to state and local bodies for relief activities. Through various state and local agencies, both public and private, these funds were used to provide work on different projects, supposedly of public value. The RFC insisted that the state should share with the federal government the burden of relief. The legislature accordingly submitted to the voters a constitutional amendment to authorize the issuance of bonds not to exceed $20 million for the relief of unemployment. Issued from time to time, the last of these "bread bonds" were sold during the Allred administration. The legislature also established a Texas relief commission as a coordinating and administrative organization through which the various agencies worked. County relief boards were provided to make plans for roads and other public improvements through which needy persons might be given employment.

The Federal Emergency Relief Administration, the first major New Deal relief agency, provided the states with funds for both direct relief and work relief. Through this agency and through the RFC, which continued to provide funds, Texas received for the aid of its destitute in 1933 and 1934 approximately $50 million. Unfortunately, the number of persons calling for relief did not diminish.

While these agencies were meeting the pressing needs of the people who had neither property nor jobs, a broader program of government spending was launched which was designed both to furnish employment and to revive business and industry. From 1933 through 1938 the Civilian Conservation Corps employed about 110,000 men and war veterans. The National Youth Administration, directed for a time in Texas by Lyndon B. Johnson, was established in 1935 to administer a program of assistance to young people. Under the National Industrial Recovery Act, the Federal Emergency Administration of Public Works (PWA) organized and coordinated a gigantic system of public building. The RFC loaned funds both to private business establishments and to construction firms for the purpose of financing public and public-guaranteed projects. In May 1935 work relief was coordinated in a Works Progress Administra-

*The Great Depression 1930–1941*

tion, which made possible construction and rehabilitation of all kinds of public property and provided hundreds of white-collar jobs. The various works program left some results of enduring value in Texas. For instance, PWA alone listed in its "physical accomplishments" up to 1939, 510 public buildings, 998.7 miles of new highway pavement, and improvements in 135 parks and playgrounds.

For the calendar years 1933 through 1936 the national government supplied through various agencies $10,667,379,186 for relief and works programs. Of this sum $351,023,546, or about 3.03 percent, was spent in Texas. During the same period, state and local funds used for relief and work programs in Texas amounted to $80,268,595. Expenditures continued with some variations but without any substantial decrease. General relief functions were transferred from the Texas Relief Commission to the Welfare Department in September 1939, and during the following four years the administration of general relief cost $1,300,000. For the sound of mind and able-bodied, war industry ended the need for aid from the state.

More permanent reform to cope with the problems of the needy came with the adoption of the National Social Security Act in August 1935. This law provided support for the elderly either through pensions supplied by state and federal taxes (old age pensions) or through funds provided jointly by employee and employer contributions (social security). The law, which also provided assistance to other groups in need, has been amended a number of times over the years.

## INDUSTRY, OIL, AND TRANSPORTATION

The depression that brought uncertainty and worry to so many Texans brought stagnation or even retrenchment to some areas of the state's industrial economy, though not to all. Spurred by business organizations, such as the Texas Manufacturing Association and regional chambers of commerce, manufacturing expanded slowly and steadily in the early decades of the twentieth century. By 1929 industry in Texas employed more than 150,000 people and contributed almost a half-billion dollars annually to the economy. With the onslaught of the depression, almost 30 percent of these factories disappeared by 1933, and with them disappeared almost 40,000 jobs and more than $225 million of annual production. Some industries declined to about one-third of their normal level of activity in 1932. Not until 1939 would conditions return to the level of ten years earlier.

Chemicals, petrochemicals, and oil refining were the most prosperous of Texas industries during the depression. Using a sulfate process, a large paper mill that made paper out of yellow pine began production in a plant near Houston in 1937. The production of alkalies, used in the manufacture of a wide variety of items ranging from stockings to soap, began in a Corpus Christi plant in 1934. Oil refining, in particular, expanded. By 1939 more than 80 percent of the state's oil production was processed in Texas refineries, and volume had almost doubled during the depression decade.

Oil, in fact, became more and more a mainstay of the state's economy in the 1930s. With Texas leading the petroleum-producing states of the nation after 1928, oil production generally edged upward until 1937. Production was increased greatly in the 1930s through the discovery of the East Texas field, one of the most sensational finds in oil history, by Columbus Marion ("Dad") Joiner, a veteran wildcatter. Other discoveries after 1930, though not so sensational, added to the supply. A slowdown in pipeline construction during the depression temporarily impeded the growth of the natural gas industry, but over the decade it too expanded.

Transportation, in some ways, suffered from the impact of the depression. Railroad construction had continued at a slow pace in the early decades of the twentieth century. Mostly, the construction consisted of feeder roads or extensions of trunk lines, with only a few projects of major proportions between 1910 and 1930. In 1932, however, railroad mileage in Texas reached its peak of seventeen thousand miles and began a slow decline. Electric railroads which came into use earlier in the twentieth century likewise began to disappear in the thirties.

Possibly the depression slowed, but certainly it did not stop Texans' growing dependence on the automobile and the highway. Automobiles became commonplace in the twenties and continued to grow in numbers in the thirties in spite of the hard times. While the population was growing scarcely 10 percent, motor vehicle registration grew almost 25 percent between 1929 and 1939.

With the coming of the automobile came the demand for good roads, a demand that would not truly be answered until the 1930s. Until 1907, roads were built and maintained, or not maintained, by the counties, using the personal labor of local citizens who contributed their time. After 1907, counties could vote for bonds and build roads, but the state could not. In 1916 a limited amount of federal aid became available, and the next year the state set aside a small fund for roads under the supervision of a newly created state highway department. But as late as 1923 Governor Neff was quite correct in claiming that there were not a hundred miles of continuously good roads in the state. Texas had no highway system worthy of the name.

Reform and success came with the reorganization of the Texas

Highway Commission through laws enacted in 1923 and 1925 and with energetic and efficient management during the Moody years. Under capable leadership and with sufficient funding from gasoline taxes and federal sources, the state by 1932 began to develop a highway system worthy of pride. In a decade not noted for tangible progress, the number of miles of paved roads in Texas more than tripled.

Although progress was slow and came mostly in the second half of the decade, labor unions gained in numbers and in power in the depression. During the 1920s, labor unions declined somewhat, hampered by determined opposition from management, the competition of company unions, and even by a bit of lethargy. With the advent of the depression, workers were more inclined to turn to unions in search of security, and the federal government lent a friendly hand. The organization of workers especially made headway among oil, chemical, and refinery workers after the Congress of Industrial Organizations (CIO) launched a campaign along the Gulf Coast. In addition to efforts directly affecting workers, unions regularly took stands on public issues. Organized labor aided in the repeal of Prohibition and secured favorable amendments to the Texas eight-hour law. It helped in delaying the adoption of a general sales tax and worked to secure a law prohibiting the sale of prison-made goods.

## AGRICULTURE IN THE DEPRESSION

Despite disasters, such as floods and price fluctuations, the early years of the twentieth century were relatively prosperous ones for Texas farmers. Growing cities and the consequent enlargement of markets brought to them an affluence greater than they had ever known. Sharp price breaks were temporary and prices soon recovered. The value of Texas farms more than doubled between 1910 and 1920. The twenties were more difficult. Mechanization aided production, but prices declined, and the value of Texas farms fell slightly. On the national level Congress passed several acts intended to assist the troubled farmer, but these had little effect.

The depression years, often coinciding with drought, threatened disaster. For the farmer, prosperity was out of the question, and survival was often in doubt. The Roosevelt administration attacked the problem with the most elaborate farm program in history. In fact, it made relief for agriculture a sort of cornerstone for the entire New Deal structure. At the heart of the plan was a concept known as parity—that is, a fair price. Prices for farm products would provide farmers with the purchasing power they had had in the years immediately preceding World War I.

To accomplish this goal, Congress passed the Agriculture Adjustment Act of 1933, commonly called the "Triple A," under which farmers received payments for taking land out of cultivation and for producing small numbers of livestock. Texas growers received more than $44 million under the program, income desperately needed, for low prices were combining with a major drought to bring many perilously close to bankruptcy. The Agriculture Adjustment Act was declared unconstitutional in 1936, but other legislation was passed limiting acreage and providing payments to assure the farmer of at least a portion of parity. In 1939 farmers who complied with the program's requirements were guaranteed 75 percent of parity.

Other New Deal farm programs expanded credit facilities for farmers. This additional credit enabled many farmers to hold onto their homes, when otherwise they would have lost them through foreclosure. Limited in scope but of particular value to low-income farmers was the Farmers Home Administration. It lent money for purchasing livestock, fertilizer, and a small number of farms.

The New Deal farm program was a popular program with most Texas farmers. In the election of 1936, one West Texas town almost totally dependent on agriculture voted for Roosevelt by a margin of eight to one, and this type of support was general across the state. For many, only the government payments enabled them to hold onto their lands.

But the New Deal programs did not solve the problems of Texas agriculture. The value of Texas farms declined 28 percent during the depression decade. Texans talked a great deal about going "back to the farm," and there were a few experiments in rural resettlement. But the actual movement of the population was in the other direction. While the total population of the state increased, the number of Texans living on farms declined. Forty percent of the population lived on farms in 1930; only one-third of the population did so in 1940.

## CONSERVATION

In the depression decade, conservation programs intended to preserve the state's natural resources made considerable headway. Soil, timber, water, and petroleum—all exhaustible resources—were affected by programs either begun or expanded in the midst of the Great Depression.

A survey by the Soil Conservation Service of the United States Department of Agriculture reported that about three-fourths of the area of Texas suffered from soil erosion. A few people had recognized the gravity of the problem at an early date, long before the 1930s. In Newton County a farmer constructed a farm terrace in 1882, and other East Texas farmers imitated his practices. The Farmers Cooperative Demonstration Work, now known as the Extension Service, began to educate farmers on the dangers of soil erosion as early as 1910. In 1927 the Federal Land Bank made terracing a part of its credit extension agreement, and soon the United States Department of Agriculture established erosion control experiment stations in Texas. The United States Soil Conservation Service, created by the Department of Agriculture in 1935, began to apply to the problem the vast resources placed at its command, and the Agricultural and Mechanical College of Texas cooperated with it. Texans generally complied enthusiastically with the Soil Conservation and Allotment Act of 1935 under which farmers of wheat, corn, cotton, and tobacco received government grants for leaving part of their land idle and practicing measures that would conserve the soil. In order that Texas might get the maximum benefit from the federal agencies, the legislature in 1939 passed a state soil conservation law under which landowners may, by their own vote, establish soil conservation districts, and today nearly all of the state has been organized into such districts.

Although there is very little virgin timber left, the more than ten million acres of forest land in eastern Texas represent one of the state's greatest natural resources. Very little was done by way of conserving the timberlands until the Texas Forest Service was created in 1913 and placed under the direction of the Agricultural and Mechanical College. In the following year federal cooperative aid for fire prevention was secured and a skeleton organization was established. Demonstration and research facilities were provided in 1924 when the state acquired its first forest. Later, forest nurseries and research laboratories were established.

But again, it was in the 1930s that a major step was taken in the development of forests in Texas. Pursuant to an invitation extended by the legislature in 1935, the federal government began to purchase forest lands. By 1980, the national forests in the state represented a total of almost 700,000 acres.

Water is another resource of Texas that has long affected the movement of population and the comfort and prosperity of the people. Abundant springs and running streams made easy the settlement of East Texas, but in many parts of Central and West Texas settlement was retarded because of the difficulty of securing water. It will be recalled that the High Plains were not appropriated until well drills and windmills tapped the bountiful veins of underground water.

The problem of flood control and of the equitable distribution for irrigation, municipal supply, and industry brought about the enactment of a number of laws pertaining to the surface waters of Texas. Coincidental with the beginning of the depression, the oldest large Texas conservation district was created. This was the Brazos River Conservation and Reclamation District, created with generous powers for conserving and exploiting the waters of the entire Brazos River watershed. A similarly large and independently powerful water district was the Lower Colorado River Authority. In the depression years LCRA began the construction of a series of dams along the Colorado River which formed the reservoirs now known as the Highland Lakes. Other river systems in the state were developed in a like manner. Anticipating some problems of a later day, the legislature in 1932 passed the Wagstaff-Woodward Law which placed the claims of cities to water ahead of all other interests.

Conservation of oil, which became a reality and attracted the most attention in the 1930s, was actually an old idea, dating back to the time of the Spanish. Under the Spanish and Mexican law, title to minerals remained with the state when land was deeded to individuals, and the Republic of Texas and the state of Texas pursued this policy until adoption of the Constitution of 1866. This constitution and subsequent ones provided that minerals and land were released with the sale of the land by the state. More modifications of the policy followed, until the Relinquishment Act of 1919 gave landowners fifteen-sixteenths of the oil and gas found under the land and retained one-sixteenth of the minerals for the benefits of public funds, particularly for the public schools.

The first Texas law to regulate the production of oil and gas was enacted in 1899, just four years after the first commercial production of petroleum in Corsicana. It required that water be cased off from oil-bearing formations, that abandoned wells be plugged, and that gas not be permitted to escape. More adequate efforts at regulation followed the adoption of the constitutional amendment of 1917 which enlarged greatly the control of legislature over natural resources. The pipeline law of 1917 was enacted, providing for the organization of the oil and gas division of the Railroad Commission, with power to supervise common carrier pipelines and to regulate their rates. Two years later the oil and gas conservation law was enacted. Under its terms, the Railroad Commission issued regulations calculated to prevent waste in the production of oil and gas, and after some delay the rules were enforced through agents and supervisors. Work was confined chiefly to requiring drilling reports of operators, to preventing injury to oil and gas formations by permitting water seepage, and to preventing drilling a well too close to a property line or to another well.

But it was overproduction and collapsing markets that truly brought regulation to the Texas oil industry and led oil operators to turn to the Railroad Commission for aid. At first the commission assisted in making voluntary agreements to limit production, but after trying this method for some three years, the commission in 1930 held a hearing and issued an order limiting the production of the state to a certain number of barrels each day. The order was attacked in the courts on the contention that it was not designed to prevent the waste of oil but to fix the price. It was, however, upheld by the Travis County district court.

Meanwhile, there came a flood of oil from the newly discovered East Texas field. The commission was slow in asserting its authority in the new field, and when it did so, many operators either ignored its orders or attacked by suits in the federal courts. Thus, there was inaugurated a train of litigation over oil production that seemed interminable. During three special sessions the legislature gave much time to the problem. Rules made by the Railroad Commission were modified and repealed repeatedly, and the decisions of the courts were not consistent. For a period in 1931, many wells were opened completely. The production amounted to one-third of the nation's requirements, and the price declined to a few cents a barrel. Then Governor Sterling placed the field under martial law, sent in the National Guard, and controlled production until February 1932, when a three-judge federal court ruled that he was acting without authority.

The cause of conservation was strengthened when the federal government, first by an executive decree and later by an act of Congress, prohibited the shipping of illegally produced oil across state boundaries. The state laws were improved; the courts became more sympathetic to regulation; and the plan of proration set forth in the order of the Railroad Commission in April 1933 was finally upheld by the federal courts. At last proration had become a reality. The purpose of the practice of proration, claimed a senior member of the Railroad Commission, was to leave in the earth "the least possible amount of oil never to be recovered by man." Production limits, however, were generally restricted to the level that would supply the market demand but not result in an oversupply that might depress prices unduly. Later compacts to regulate production were made with other oil-producing states, and although claims were again made that these agreements were not "for the purpose of stabilizing or fixing the price" of petroleum products, market demand was a major factor in determining production quotas.

## LITERATURE AND THE ARTS
## IN THE DEPRESSION

Although the times were hard, jobs were scarce, and life was often insecure, the age of the Great Depression in Texas brought forth a number of outstanding accomplishments in literature and the arts. The Texas Institute of Letters, organized in 1936 in keeping with the observance of the centennial of Texas independence, came to be an effective agency in encouraging writing and improving its quality. Perhaps J. Frank Dobie gave it its watchword when he wrote: "Great literature transcends its native land, but there is none that I know of that ignores its own soil. All great literature plumbs and soars to the elementals. Texas authors need not be antiquarians; in the rich soil of the novel there has not been even a furrow plowed."

Dobie was one of a trio long linked with the Texas Institute of Letters who constituted what is perhaps the nearest thing to a school of writers that Texas has known. The others were Roy Bedicheck, a naturalist, and Walter Prescott Webb, an historian. The range of Frank Dobie's writings was remarkably broad: cowboys and the cattle industry, folklore, and themes of nature. His publication of *A Vaquero of the Brush Country* in 1929 was soon followed by *Coronado's Children, Tales of Lost Mines, Buried Treasure in the Southwest, Tongues of Monte,* and others. Bedicheck twice won awards for his *Karankawa Country* and *Adventures with a Texas Naturalist.* Walter Prescott Webb wrote convincingly on such diverse subjects as *The Great Plains* and *The Texas Rangers,* and later his *Divided We Stand* and *The Great Frontier* would receive national acclaim.

The tradition of scholarly historical writing continued in the depression years. C. C. Rister and R. N. Richardson published studies on the Indian frontier of the late nineteenth century; J. Evetts Haley and W. C. Holden wrote on the same period but turned their attention more to the settlement of western areas and the development of the ranching industry. Carlos Castañeda began his seven-volume study of the Catholic heritage in Texas which would require more than twenty years to complete. Julia Kathryn Garrett featured the filibusters and short-lived Texas Republic in her *Green Flag over Texas.* Twentieth century Texas began to attract some writers as evidenced in S. S. McKay's studies on twentieth century politics and Sam Acheson's biography of the colorful Texas senator, Joe Bailey.

Folklore attracted the attention of a number of creative artists. J. Mason Brewer in prose and Huddie ("Leadbelly") Ledbetter in song captured many of the folk stories and songs of the black people of Texas. Another collector of folklore was John A. Lomax, who began his work in an earlier decade but continued to collect ballads throughout the 1930s.

Texas writers of fiction produced works that received national recognition. Of these, Katherine Ann Porter was the most widely known. A prolific writer, she published stories with a variety of settings, including some within Texas. *The Leaning Tower and Other Stories, The Days Before,* and *Ship of Fools* are her better-known books. Dorothy Scarborough and George Sessions Perry, writing about life in rural Texas in a realistic style, described the struggle for survival in a land where nature often turned harsh, relentless, and unrewarding.

New types of media offered opportunities for creativity. Texas contributed a number of stars to the motion picture industry. Among the actors were Tom Mix, Joan Crawford, Ginger Rogers, Mary Martin, and Gene Autry, and achieving fame as directors were King Vidor and Howard Hughes. Radio, which was little more than a curiosity in Texas in the 1920s, was of great value to the aspiring artists of the 1930s. During the depression decade several network chains were organized, and by the end of the decade, Texas was well covered by radio stations. An important feature of radio programming was hillbilly music, later to achieve a kind of respectability as country music. Ernest Tubb and Bob Wills began their music careers in Texas, as did Leonard Slye, who became better known as Roy Rogers, and there were many others.

## THE POLITICS OF RECOVERY

The Allred administration, which took office in 1935, faced many problems, the most difficult of which was that of old age assistance, more commonly referred to as old age pensions. The constitutional amendment establishing the pension program was vague, not specifying the amounts to be paid or the standards for determining who should receive them. Furthermore, the amendment made no provision for raising additional funds necessary to meet the payments. Pension questions occupied much of the regular sessions of the legislature and led to the calling of several special sessions, but the problems persisted. Applications for aid quickly climbed to more than 80,000; the legislature voted more funds and made conditions for receiving pensions more difficult, but by June 1937 more than 125,000 aged Texans were receiving pensions. At that time the legislature conducted an investigation of the old age assistance commission, and it was evident that the subject of pensions was in politics.

Pensions and taxation, subjects necessarily linked together, drew sharp attention in the gubernatorial campaign of 1936 when Allred sought reelection. Texans had heard a great deal of Huey Long's "share of the wealth" program in Louisiana; they were well acquainted with Dr. Francis E. Townsend's plan to pay a pension of two hundred dollars a month to most persons past sixty years of age; and Father Charles E. Coughlin's National Union for Social Justice was then active. The candidates accordingly leaned toward a more generous pension policy. Governor Allred, who advocated pensions for the aged needy only and but few new taxes, was more conservative than his opponents, and the fact that he was nominated in the first primary by receiving more votes than his four opponents combined indicates that the Texas voters were still in a conservative mood.

The governor was obliged, nevertheless, to appeal to the Forty-fifth Legislature, which convened in January 1937, for additional revenue. Colleges, public schools, and almost all state institutions and agencies needed more money. The voters had, moreover, authorized worker's compensation for state employees, had planned a teachers' retirement fund, and, apparently, would soon authorize the state to care for the needy blind and for dependent children.

Allred proposed to raise most of the additional revenue by an increase in all taxes on oil, gas, and sulfur. The legislature refused to increase taxes, and in keeping with the spirit of the times, it showed a weakness for imposing new burdens on the general revenue fund without providing additional income. In appropriating it was as bold as a lion, in taxing, timid as a lamb.

Some decisions made earlier in the decade brought more problems to the Allred years. An urgent need for revenue accounted in part for a measure, enacted in 1933, making betting on horse racing legal. The act, denounced in the pulpits of the state and by many editors and businessmen, was repealed in 1937 by a special session of the legislature called by Governor Allred for that purpose.

The return of legalized liquor likewise brought problems. When voters in August 1935 repealed the state prohibition amendment, they rejected a plan for state liquor sales. Shortly thereafter, the legislature provided for taxing and licensing dealers, prohibited the sale of hard liquor by the drink, provided for local option elections, and placed the administration of the traffic under a liquor control board. Soon there were complaints of violations by dealers, especially of the provision of selling liquor by the drink, and subsequently each legislature has had to deal with the question in one or more of its phases. The status of liquor in counties and cities that were dry at the time that state prohibition was enacted in 1919 was not affected by the repeal of the amendment, and local option again became an issue in many communities. Revenue from the sale of liquor was of substantial aid in paying social security obligations.

Pursuant to a mandate of the voters in a constitutional amendment in 1932, Texas celebrated in 1936 the one hundredth anniversary of its independence. The state appropriated $3 million for the use of the centennial commission and the United States government matched it with an equal amount. The WPA also made contributions. The public funds were divided between the main exposition at Dallas and various other historical and commemorative projects in different communities. A considerable part of the money was spent in erecting numerous monuments to historical personages and placing markers at historic sites.

In the Texas gubernatorial race of 1938, politics and showmanship combined to produce one of the most spectacular campaigns in the state's history. Among the thirteen candidates there were a number of veteran campaigners, but it was W. Lee O'Daniel, a flour-milling company executive and salesman of Fort Worth, who attracted the most attention. About a month before the election it became evident that he was reaching more people than all other candidates combined.

O'Daniel was a familiar name to most Texans. For several years he had conducted a noonday radio program, replete with a hillbilly band, humor, and homely advice. "Please pass the biscuits, Pappy," and "The Light Crust Dough Boys are 'On the Air' " were words heard by thousands each week. Many thought that O'Daniel's candidacy was only a device to sell more flour, and perhaps it was, at least at first, but he soon became a serious contender. He applied to the race the same tactics he had used in selling flour by radio: a bit of country music interspersed with comments and an occasional short, informal speech filled with blasts at "professional politicians." Whether it was the promise of a business-like administration, the castigation of professional politicians, the music, the candidate's homely philosophy, or the promise of pensions that drew the votes has not been determined; it is only known that for the first time since the Texas primary law was adopted did a candidate for governor, making his first race, poll more than half of the votes.

From the beginning, O'Daniel was a controversial figure in politics. His admirers were as loyal as those of the Fergusons and accepted O'Daniel as the spokesman for the ordinary citizen who had long been victimized by the people in power. His critics were equally determined in their opposition. Many of them looked upon O'Daniel as someone who was more foolish and naive than he was wicked, an innocent who had strayed into politics. Actually, O'Daniel was neither a crusader for the ordinary people nor an innocent. He was a shrewd and tough businessman, a superb actor, and a successful salesman who was one of the early politicians in Texas who hired and relied upon a public relations firm. He was often inconsistent and had the ability to be so without alarming his supporters, but he did have some convictions that never wavered. For example, he was a dedicated enemy of organized labor.

O'Daniel's performance as a governor left much to be desired. His campaign promise to give a pension to every old person was pared down to a proposal to give only to needy persons past sixty-five years of age an amount sufficient to raise their income to thirty dollars a month.

Likewise, the governor soon abandoned the hope, often expressed to the voters, that the new taxes would not be necessary and proposed to the legislature that an enlarged pension program be financed by a tax of 1.6 percent on all transactions. The lawmakers dubbed the proposal a sales tax (anathema in Texas at that time) and attacked it bitterly. The affair widened the breach already existing between the governor and the legislature. The legislature liberalized pensions but failed to provide additional revenue, and the problem became even more vexing. In spite of vetoes the deficit in the general fund continued to increase.

Six candidates challenged O'Daniel's bid for reelection in 1940. Although they attacked his record and his plan for raising revenue, his opponents did not directly attack his proposal for more liberal pensions. Texas had developed a "share-the-wealth" movement of its own, and the candidates did not dare to resist it. O'Daniel was renominated by an overwhelming vote and reelected in November 1940.

Like the lawmaking bodies that had preceded it for a decade, the Forty-seventh Legislature, which convened in January 1941, found that the problem of taxation was its chief worry. It could not, like its predecessor, take up the question, debate it, and drop it. The general fund, which supplied most of the agencies, showed a deficit of $25 million. There were predictions that Texas would be deprived of all federal pension money unless it raised more funds to meet the increasing demand of its own liberal pension laws. The teachers' retirement payments had not been matched by the state; the electorate demanded that it care for its destitute children and the blind. After extended debate there was passed and given executive approval an omnibus tax bill calculated to bring $22 million in additional revenue annually. Approximately one-half of the amount was to come from increased taxes on the production of oil and gas and the remainder from a variety of sources. This measure doubled the old age pension income but did not quiet the agitation over pensions.

When a seat in the United States Senate was made vacant by the death of Morris Sheppard in 1941, the governor appointed as his successor, until an election could be held, Andrew Jackson Houston, the eighty-seven-year-old son of the hero of the Battle of San Jacinto, who was also once a member of the United States Senate. Houston got to Washington but did not live to complete his short appointive term. Meanwhile, several candidates entered the race, one of the last being the governor himself. Although he was elected, his prestige was seriously impaired, for he defeated by only a few hundred votes Congressman Lyndon B. Johnson, an "old friend" of President Roosevelt. Again, in the Democratic primaries of 1942 he defeated ex-Governors Dan Moody and James V. Allred, after a hard-fought campaign in which it was charged that O'Daniel had failed to support adequately President Roosevelt's defense and war policies.

With the election of O'Daniel to the United States Senate, Lieutenant Governor Coke R. Stevenson, formerly a speaker of the house, was inaugurated governor in August 1941. Stevenson's term coincided with the years of World War II, and this, coupled with Stevenson's strong conservative beliefs, would mean that his years in the governorship would see little change in state government, services, and programs. However, the state highway system was given additional funding early in Stevenson's administration.

During the 1930s the influence of Texans in the national government became greater than ever before. John Nance Garner, who had served continuously in the House of Representatives since he first took the oath of office before Speaker Joe Cannon in 1903, was elected Speaker in 1931. In the year following he was nominated and elected vice-president and was reelected in 1936. In presiding over the Senate, his great personal influence and broad acquaintance with legislative tactics were brought to bear on most of the measures that made up the New Deal. A movement was launched to nominate him for president in 1940, but the movement declined as it became increasingly evident that President Roosevelt would again accept the nomination.

There were other influential Texans in Washington. Jesse Jones of Houston was chairman of the RFC from 1933 to 1939. In 1939 he was appointed administrator of the powerful Federal Loan Agency and in 1940 was appointed secretary of commerce. In 1933 Texans held the chairmanships of six major committees in the House of Representatives. Sam Rayburn of Bonham became majority leader and later Speaker of the House of Representatives. Morris Sheppard, mostly remembered for his work on behalf of national prohibition, promoted President Roosevelt's New Deal in the Senate until his death in 1941. The other senator, Tom Connally, became chairman of the Committee on Foreign Relations and was a staunch spokesman for the administration in the enactment of the gigantic defense program and the war measures of the 1940s.

## SELECTED BIBLIOGRAPHY

General accounts of the depression include the writings of S. S. McKay as previously cited: S. S. McKay and O. B. Faulk, *Texas after Spindletop;* Robert C. Cotner (ed.), *Texas Cities and the Great Depression* (Austin, 1973); and the manuscript of Donald Whisenhunt, "Texas in the Depression, 1929–1933: A Study of Public Reaction," in the library of

Texas Tech University. For political affairs toward the end of the decade, see George Green, *The Establishment in Texas Politics, The Primitive Years, 1938–1957* (Westport, Conn., 1979).

The annual reports of the Texas Department of Human Resources give the most complete accounts of the aid given by the state to certain classes of citizens. The *Annual Report* for 1949 is especially useful for the period preceding that date. On federal aid during the depression years, see F. A. Williams, *Federal Aid for Relief* (New York, 1939). On Texas relief, see Booth Mooney, "925,000 Texans Getting Government Aid," *Texas Weekly,* November 11, 1939, pp. 6–7. Also see William R. Johnson, "Rural Rehabilitation in the New Deal: The Ropesville Project," *Southwestern Historical Quarterly,* LXXIX, 279–295.

On national affairs, see Bascom Timmons, *Jesse H. Jones* (New York, 1956), and *Garner of Texas* (New York, 1948); C. D. Dorough, *Mr. Sam, A Biography of Samuel T. Rayburn* (New York, 1962); Lionel Patenaude, "Garner, Sumners, and Connally: The Defeat of the Roosevelt Court Bill in 1937," *Southwestern Historical Quarterly,* LXXIV, 136–151, and "The Garner Vote Switch to Roosevelt: 1932 Democratic Convention," *ibid.,* LXXIX, 189–204; and Richard B. Henderson, *Maury Maverick: A Political Biography* (Austin, 1970).

The best general reference on industrial development is the *Texas Almanac.* The *Texas Business Review,* published monthly by the Bureau of Business Research, The University of Texas, Austin, is invaluable. Especially useful are Edwin J. Foscue, "The Pulp and Paper Industry of East Texas," April 1967, pp. 105–109; and Stanley A. Arbingast, "Notes on the Industrialization of Texas: Synthetic Rubber," September 1952, pp. 16–17. On the history of oil, good references are C. C. Rister, *Oil! Titan of the Southwest* (Norman, Okla., 1949), comprehensive and authoritative; W. Gard, *The First Hundred Years of Oil and Gas* (Dallas, 1966); Craig Thompson, *Since Spindletop* (Pittsburgh, 1951); Henrietta M. Larson, *History of Humble Oil and Refining Company* (New York, 1959); Alfred M. Leeston, John A. Chrichton, and John C. Jacobs, *The Dynamic Natural Gas Industry* (Norman, Okla., 1963). *Texas Highways,* official journal of the Texas Highway Department, Austin, Texas, and *Texas Parade,* published in Austin monthly with the endorsement of the Texas Good Roads Association, are rich sources of information on Texas roads. On railroads, see Everett L. DeGolyer, Jr., "The Railroads: The End of An Era," *Southwestern Historical Quarterly,* LXXIII, 356–364.

Considerable writing has been done on conservation efforts. The beginning of demonstration work in Texas is related in H. R. Southworth, "The Later Years of Seaman A. Knapp," *West Texas Historical Association Year Book,* X, 88–104. A satisfactory account of the New Deal farm program is given in Henry Bamford Parkes and Vincent V. Carosso,

*Recent America, Book II* (New York, 1963). See also *Agricultural Research in Texas since 1888* (College Station, Tex., 1956). For an account of soil conservation, the *Annual Reports* of the Agricultural Extension Service, Texas A. & M. University, are most useful. On water conservation, floods, and droughts, much has been written in recent years. Among the best sources are W. P. Webb, *More Water for Texas* (Austin, 1954); and Robert Lee Lowry, *Surface Water Resources in Texas* (Austin, 1958). The long and involved history of the conservation of oil in Texas is dealt with by R. E. Hardwicke, *Legal History of Conservation of Oil in Texas;* and Maurice Cheek, *Legal History of Conservation of Gas in Texas* (Mineral Law Section, American Bar Association, 1938). A briefer study is that of James P. Hart, "Oil, the Courts, and the Railroad Commission," *Southwestern Historical Quarterly,* XLIV, 303–320. Concerning the East Texas oil field, see Ruel McDaniel, *Some Ran Hot* (Dallas, 1939). The work of the Texas Railroad Commission is brought out in J. A. Clark's *Three Stars for the Colonel* [Ernest O. Thompson] (New York, 1957).

Texas writers are discussed in Mabel Major and others, *Southwest Heritage: A Literary History;* J. Frank Dobie, *Life and Literature of the Southwest;* Ronnie Dugger (ed.), *Three Men in Texas: Bedicheck, Webb, and Dobie* (Austin, 1967); and Lon Tinkle, *An American Original: The Life of J. Frank Dobie* (Boston, 1978). Also, see the publications of the Texas Folklore Society. Country music is featured in two studies: Bill C. Malone, *Country Music U.S.A.; A Fifty-Year History* (Austin, 1968); and Charles R. Townsend, *San Antonio Rose: The Life and Music of Bob Wills* (Urbana, Ill., 1976).

# Chapter Nineteen

# WAR
# AND
# READJUSTMENT
# 1941–1959

On December 7, 1941, the armed forces of Japan attacked Pearl Harbor and drew the United States into the global war that had started in Europe in September 1939 when England and France resisted the German dictator Adolf Hitler. For months the nation had been moving toward hostilities: Congress, short of declaring war, had appropriated funds for a two-ocean navy, had enacted the first peace-time conscription law in American history, and had aided the enemies of Hitler and Benito Mussolini of Italy through almost every agency.

The government of Texas and the people loyally supported the national war effort. In keeping with its finest traditions, the state's men and women responded to the call to arms; its oil kept ships, trucks, tanks, and planes moving against the enemy; and its industries were strengthened and harnessed for the cause of freedom. Everybody was needed in the war effort, and the people loyally did their part. Soon the rate of industrial activity was the highest ever known, and the total income surpassed all previous records. In spite of the many heartbreaking experiences of war, material prosperity generally prevailed, and after the victory was won, the problems of postwar readjustment were made easier by expanding industry, high prices for farm commodities, and a generous federal policy of providing schooling or on-the-job training for veterans. As in most of the rest of the nation, the Texas economy continued to expand; full employment, high wages, and high prices emphasized the abundance of the period.

Prosperity did not bring tranquility to the state, however. Farmers protested that they were not sharing fairly in the general abundance and called for greater freedom in their farming practices or for more controls, as their interest and points of view varied. Labor unions chafed at restraints and penalties they considered unfair and grew stronger regardless of them. The public school system, growing costlier each year and declining in efficiency, was completely reorganized. There were pleas, fervent and often repeated, for better care of children; the friends of the needy aged were not reconciled to the aid accorded them; and the blind and the crippled had their champions. During the war and the decade that followed, minority groups, though not as vocal as they would become in the sixties, began to express their demands for equality of treatment and for expansion of opportunity.

## PUBLIC AFFAIRS DURING THE WAR YEARS

Public affairs in the state reflected the conditions of wartime. Although Governor Stevenson was critical of the rationing program, he sought to promote the war effort. He called for rigid economy in all agencies of government and entered into a no-strike covenant with organized labor that prevented work stoppages in Texas. Attorney General Mann announced that the strict Texas antitrust laws would not be enforced against concerns seriously engaging in production. In its session of 1943 the legislature cut appropriations to most state agencies and reduced substantially expenditures for senior colleges, which were then short of faculty and students.

As the war proceeded, various federal agencies brought their efforts to bear on the people. The War Manpower Commission in Texas, with some twelve regional directors, sought to see that all qualified people were employed and that those deferred from military service worked at essential jobs. The National Office of Price Administration, in charge of rationing and price ceilings, used the staff and pupils of the public schools to implement sugar rationing. Later, rationing was extended to meats, fats (including butter), canned goods, coffee, shoes, and gasoline. One state agency, the powerful Railroad Commission, in charge of the production of from 40 percent to 50 percent of the nation's gas and oil, occupied a strategic position in the nation's war effort. It was effective and managed to cooperate with Harold L. Ickes, secretary of the interior and petroleum administrator for war.

In spite of the "freezing" of rents, salaries, and wages and the restraints on prices, the cost of living rose moderately during the war; but since almost every employable person was busy, family incomes increased by a fourth or a third, and the rank and file of people were in relatively good circumstances.

For the most part, Texans at home accepted the problems of wartime with a minimum of complaints. They collected scrap iron and grew "victory gardens." They bought war bonds and gave to the Red Cross. They practiced blackout and air raid alerts, and generally they complied with the restrictions of rationing, although hoarding certainly was not an unknown practice. Occasionally the tensions of race mixed with the tensions of wartime to produce a crisis. Rioting in Beaumont in mid-June 1943 lasted for twenty hours until national guardsmen, local police, and rangers restored peace. From time to time there were complaints about the stationing of black servicemen in the state, and often they were subjected to discrimination. A signal of the future, however, was the establishment of a civilian and military committee in Houston, charged with the responsibility of ending the mistreatment of black soldiers and lowering the tensions of the community.

It was during the war years that the cleavage between Texas conservative and liberal Democrats developed fully with race having a significant influence in that development. The opponents of President Roosevelt and the New Deal were in evidence as a minority group in 1936. The candidacy for the presidency of the staunch Texas Democrat, John Nance Garner, held the factions together in 1940, but President Roosevelt's determination to seek a third term prevented the Garner-for-President movement from reaching far beyond Texas. Added to their objections to Roosevelt and the New Deal, the conservative Texas Democrats had a grievance against the Supreme Court in 1944: namely, its decision in *Smith* v. *Allwright* (321 U.S. 649) that the Texas Democratic party's rule excluding blacks from its primaries violated the Fifteenth Amendment. When the conservatives in control of the Texas convention sought to make a party test of opposition to the Supreme Court's decision, the convention split, and the conservatives, organized later as "Texas Regulars", made a futile effort against the Roosevelt-Truman presidential ticket.

These factional contests had their repercussions in the state Democratic executive committee and to a limited extent in the legislature. Texas's war governor, Coke R. Stevenson, a conservative Democrat, managed to stay aloof from them. He was easily reelected in 1944.

For the Forty-ninth Legislature, which assembled in January 1945, the problem of state finance was delightfully simple. Income had outrun expenditures so far that a $12 million deficit had been eliminated by economies and increased revenues and had been changed to a surplus. Appropriations surpassed those of any preceding legislature in history; much of the surplus was distributed to the schools; and the legislature submitted to the voters a proposed constitutional change to raise the ceiling of the funds available to spend on social security payments.

Before the legislature adjourned on June 5, 1945, it was evident that the war's end was near. Thousands of veterans had returned home and tens of thousands would follow them. Texas laws allowed them free voting privileges, the renewal of drivers' licenses without examination, and the privilege of attending state colleges without charge. Already the federal G.I. Bill of Rights was in effect, providing aid for schooling or training, and these privileges were later extended to veterans of the Korean War, the cold war, and the war in Vietnam. Texas voters ratified an amendment to the constitution authorizing bonds for the purchase by the state of land to be sold to veterans. The program has since been extended from time to time. These bonds were the Texan answer to the urge for a blanket state bonus to veterans.

The tang of change was in the air. For the new day the old constitution seemed inadequate in many respects. Bales of proposed constitutional amendments were submitted to each legislature after World War II. In the Forty-ninth Legislature, eighty-four proposals were introduced and eight were submitted to the voters (not including one proposing a constitutional convention). The voters approved amendments extending favors to veterans, raising to nine the number of supreme court justices, and raising the ceiling on social welfare payments.

## TEXAS AND TEXANS IN THE WAR

Long before the day of Pearl Harbor, Texas was a huge training field for the armed forces. The first peace-time draft in American history went into effect on October 16, 1940, when seventeen million Americans registered. Of the state army organizations transferred to federal service, the Thirty-sixth Division and the Fifty-sixth Cavalry Brigade were all-Texas units. Texas posts became headquarters of importance. San Antonio, long a soldier's center, was, during a considerable part of the war, the headquarters of the Third Army, which trained men from Arizona to Florida. It was also the headquarters for the Fourth Army, which prepared men for overseas combat service in nine states. The Eighth Service Command, serving as the operating agency for army forces in Texas and adjoining states, had its headquarters in Dallas. For a period the army had as many as fifteen training posts in Texas and prisoner-of-war camps came to number twenty-one. For defense of the Gulf Coast and Mexican border areas, the Southern Defense Command, with its headquarters at Fort Sam Houston, was maintained during most of the war.

Texas became the most active training region in the nation for airmen. Randolph Field, Kelly Field, and Brooks Field, all near San

Antonio, were enlarged; Ellington Field near Houston was rebuilt; and additional air fields were established in Wichita Falls, San Angelo, Lubbock, Midland, San Marcos, Amarillo, and other cities. The national headquarters of the American Air Force Training Command was in Fort Worth, a command that at its peak strength in January 1944 had more than a million men and women under its jurisdiction.

It is estimated that one and a quarter million men in all branches of the service were trained in Texas, among them more than 20 combat army divisions. Probably as many as three-quarters of a million Texans, including 12,000 women, served in all branches of the armed forces. Of these about a fourth were in the Navy, Marine Corps, and Coast Guard combined. More than 8,000 Texas women served in the Women's Army Corps (WAC), about 4,200 in the Women Accepted for Voluntary Emergency Service (WAVES), and others in the women's division of the Coast Guard (SPARS) and the Marines.

The Selective Service Act of September 1940, applicable to men between the ages of twenty-one and thirty-six, was extended after the United States entered the war to include all men between the ages of eighteen and forty-five. Secretary of the Navy Frank Knox stated in December 1942 that Texas was contributing a larger percentage of men to the fighting forces than any other state, a circumstance perhaps caused by the fact that the great majority of Texans were acquainted with the history of their state.

Texas organizations came to be known around the world. The Thirty-sixth Division, a Texan force, sent to Java an organization whose epic experiences caused it to be known as the Lost Battalion. The division landed at Salerno, Italy, the first American force to enter Europe, and in four hundred days of combat advanced through Italy, France, Germany, and into Austria. Texas also had a special claim on the Ninetieth (Texas-Oklahoma) Division, the 112th Cavalry Regiment, the 144th Infantry Regiment in the Pacific theater, and the Second Infantry Division and the First Cavalry Division in the European theater.

Wherever they went Texans seemed to have been very much in evidence. The Thirty-sixth Division carried the Texas flag and often displayed it. Where Texas troops were congregated, natives sometimes spoke of the "Texas army." Many Texans were recognized for valor as well as for enthusiasm. Lieutenant Audie Murphy, of Farmersville, became the "most decorated" soldier of World War II. The Congressional Medal of Honor went to him and some twenty-nine other Texans. Six Texans received the Navy's Medal of Honor, among them Commander Samuel D. Dealey, killed in action, and known as the "most decorated man in the Navy."

Many military officers of renown were Texans or had once called

Texas home. Oveta Culp Hobby was director of the Women's Army Corps. The state could claim at least 12 admirals and 155 generals, among them Chester W. Nimitz, commander in chief of the Pacific Fleet, and Dwight David Eisenhower, Supreme Allied Commander in Europe. Texans fought on every front and paid their share of war's cruel toll. Their war dead for all branches of the service amounted to 23,022. The seriously wounded and permanently injured numbered many more.

## THE JESTER YEARS

As the gubernatorial campaign of 1946 began to take shape, Homer Price Rainey, former president of the University of Texas who had been dismissed from that post after a long, bitter controversy with the board of regents, seemed to be the strongest of a long slate of candidates. Railroad Commissioner Beauford Jester proved to be a better campaigner, however, and was nominated in the run-off primary. Although Jester had the support of the conservative or anti-Truman element of the party, his middle-of-the-road course prevented an open breach with the liberals.

Like his predecessors in office, Governor Jester emphatically opposed any new taxes. Still, the expanding economy and general prosperity that prevailed placed the executive in the happy position of being able to recommend substantial increases in appropriations without being obliged to suggest new sources of revenue. In his "Report to the People" by radio in 1949, the chief executive could point to the doubling of appropriations for hospitals and orphanages and the opening of several other institutions that provided care for the unfortunate. Under the constitutional amendment limiting appropriations to anticipated revenue, which had become effective in 1945, the comptroller refused to certify a number of appropriations made near the end of the session.

Labor unions became the focus of attention in the postwar years. In 1947 a veritable shower of laws regulating unions came to Governor Jester, some of which he had advocated. Chief of these were: The checkoff of the workers' union dues, to be paid directly to the union, was forbidden, except by the assent of the worker; the "right to work" law made it unlawful to require union membership of any employee; picketing was rigidly regulated and mass picketing outlawed; strikes by public employees were forbidden; secondary strikes, picketing, and boycotts were forbidden; the picketing of utilities was prohibited; and labor unions were brought under trust-law regulations. This was the year also that Congress passed the Labor-Management Relations Act (Taft-Hartley Law), which made substantial changes in the body of federal law regarding labor. Even this was not the end. In 1951 a law enacted

Beauford H. Jester (left) was elected governor of Texas in 1946 and again in 1948. He died in office in 1949. Here he is shown with Harry Truman and a fellow Texan, John Nance Garner. In a close national election, 750,000 Texans voted for Truman and 280,000 for his Republican opponent, Thomas E. Dewey. Garner was vice-president from 1933 to 1941. (E. C. Barker History Center, University of Texas)

provided beyond the shadow of a doubt that there be no closed shops in Texas—no sort of labor agreement could require that workers belong to a union.

On the national scene, many conservative Texas Democrats opposed President Truman as they had opposed Roosevelt. Indeed, with Truman they associated the Fair Employment Practice Committee, the CIO Political Action Committee, and other features and groups that they had opposed consistently. Governor Jester worked for harmony, however, and there was no party division when the Democratic National Convention nominated Truman in 1948. The number of those who supported the Republican and Dixiecrat tickets evidently was not large.

Jester was reelected governor without having to campaign. For the seat in the United States Senate to be vacated by W. Lee O'Daniel, who did not seek reelection in 1948, Congressman Lyndon B. Johnson opposed former Governor Coke R. Stevenson, in a contest close, acrimonious, and undecided until a federal court ordered Johnson's name placed on the ballot as the Democratic nominee.

In the longest session the state had known, from January 11 to July 6, 1949, the Fifty-first Legislature enacted many laws, some of them probably of enduring value. In an effort to improve the pitiable conditions in the institutions for the mentally ill, it created the Board for Texas State Hospitals and Special Schools and gave it supervision over state mental hospitals and state schools for handicapped children. A Youth Development Council was set up to take charge of schools for juvenile offenders. The body enacted an antilynching law, adopted a controversial basic science law that set forth minimum requirements for all persons in medical and health work and provided for the licensing of chiropractors.

During this session, state appropriations for the biennium, when supplemented by various federal grants, came to a billion dollars, so the session was the first to be called a "billion-dollar legislature." Like its predecessors the body refused to vote new taxes, and in order to keep expenditures within the limits of income, Governor Jester vetoed second-year appropriations for state hospitals and special schools. Two of its measures were far reaching in effect: the modernization of the state prison system and the reorganization of the state public school system through the Gilmer-Aiken school laws.

Because of limitations brought about by the war and its aftermath, the Texas prison system, never a high-ranking one, had deteriorated rapidly. The growth of the prison population—a gain of one thousand, or 29 percent in 1946 over the preceding year—added greatly to all problems. The board secured O. B. Ellis, an experienced prison administrator, who drew up the Ellis plan for rehabilitating the system. In 1949 the legislature appropriated $4.29 million for improvements; subsequent legislatures continued to improve the morale of the men. In 1957 the name was changed to State Department of Corrections. The prison population continued to grow, necessitating the periodic enlargement and improvement of the plants.

Reorganization of the state public school system was the result of three far-reaching laws sponsored by Representative Claude Gilmer and Senator A. M. Aiken and representing some badly needed reforms. By the end of World War II most school systems in the state had added a twelfth year to their programs. Broadening of the curriculum was a process that had been going on for many years, but one that had accelerated in the postwar years, with added emphasis on vocational subjects, music, and the other fine arts. Most problems centered on funding. Despite enormous increases in appropriations, Texas schools remained near the bottom of the scale of state school systems.

The Gilmer-Aiken laws reorganized state school administration, established a system of minimum standards for programs, and altered the manner in which state funds for education were distributed. One law created an elective board of education with the power to appoint a commissioner and to supervise the Texas Education Agency. Another law required that all persons of school age be given a minimum of nine months of schooling each year, under teachers who met certain minimum training requirements, and in an environment conforming to certain standards. The third law established an intricate formula whereby schools were to be supported by state and local funds, with larger amounts of state aid to be given to poor districts.

Some wholesome effects of the new system were soon in evidence. It eliminated many hundreds of inoperative or "dormant" school districts; it helped to improve school attendance; it placed a premium on academic training and thereby stimulated thousands of teachers to get more schooling; it provided a means for enforcing minimum salary schedules; and it removed much of the political pressure on the distribution of funds.

## SHIVERS AND THE INTERPLAY OF NATIONAL AND STATE ISSUES

When on July 11, 1949, Governor Jester died of a heart attack, Lieutenant Governor Allan Shivers succeeded to the office. Shivers was just forty-one, but ten years in the state senate and two as lieutenant governor had seasoned him. A called session of the legislature in 1950 was made necessary by the failure of the body to complete appropriations for the second year of the biennium.

The governor called for additional taxes as the only way of meeting the demands for increased expenditures. "If we are going to appropriate in the spring," he said, "we must tax in the winter." Shivers pleaded for large appropriations to hospitals to improve old plants and add new. Too many mentally ill people were in jails because of inadequate hospital space. The legislature followed with relatively generous appropriations for the operations of state hospitals and increased taxes slightly.

The next legislature, the fifty-second, meeting in 1951, found that still more taxes were needed. Two agencies worked on the budget for that year: the Board of Control, as it had been accustomed to do for some years, and the Legislative Budget Board, or Council, created by the preceding legislature from its own members. All agreed that additional revenue must be found, and again levies in the Omnibus Bill of 1941 were raised, and a gathering tax on natural gas pipelines was added. Unfortunately the courts later declared this tax unconstitutional, as being in effect a state levy on interstate commerce, and the natural gas interests avoided their equitable share of taxation.

This legislature enacted the first redistricting law in thirty years. Another act, which was the object of much criticism, was the safety inspection and driver responsibility law designed to force unsafe cars off the road and also to give the public a modicum of assurance that drivers were responsible for the damage they might do to others.

More and more the political stage in Texas came to be appropriated by national and international issues and by state-federal relationships. President Truman continued to decline in the esteem of conservative Texas Democrats. Charges of corrupt practice and the infiltration of Communism were hurled at his administration. There was also much criticism of his policies in the Korean War. But it was Truman's tidelands policies that aroused the most criticism of Texans.

The tidelands were areas under the sea but closely adjacent to the coast and believed to be rich in oil deposits. Early opinions held almost unanimously that the state owned the tidelands, until Secretary of the Interior Harold Ickes formally challenged the claim in 1937. In August 1947, the Supreme Court of the United States held that the state of California did not have the right to exploit its tidelands through oil leases and other means because the federal government had "paramount right and power" over this domain. In 1950 the Court by a vote of four to three (two not voting) handed down a similar decision against Texas. It was a heavy blow, for these lands were being leased already for oil and gas development, and nearly $10 million in lease bonuses had been received.

President Truman vetoed an act of Congress in 1946 recognizing the rights of the states to lease these lands, and when a similar act was submitted to him in 1952, he vetoed that also. By way of completing the account of these lands, it may be stated that on May 22, 1953, President Eisenhower signed a quit-claim bill, restoring the tidelands to state ownership and extending ownership to "historic limits." For Texas and the west coast of Florida, where the rule of Spanish law still prevailed, "historic limits" meant three Spanish leagues or about ten and a half miles.

For many Texans the subject of the tidelands became a prime factor in the presidential election of 1952. The Democratic party split that year. The liberal wing bolted; the conservatives led by Shivers kept control of the party organization and refused to support Governor Adlai Stevenson, the Democratic nominee for president, after Stevenson had indicated no sympathy for the claims of the states to the tidelands. That year Texas Republicans also had a breach between the forces supporting Senator Robert A. Taft for president and those supporting General Dwight D. Eisenhower. Later the factions united, joined with the conservative Democrats, and carried the state for Eisenhower. Two million Texans voted that November, the greatest turnout to the polls the state had known. Eisenhower carried the state by a majority of over 100,000, winning the second Republican victory in Texas within a quarter of a century. Shivers was easily renominated that year over his chief opponent, the liberal judge Ralph Yarborough. Most of the Texas state offices were not sought by Republicans in 1952; by a system of "cross filing" they placed in their columns on the ballot the names of the Democratic nominees. That year Attorney General Price Daniel defeated Congressman Lindly Beckworth, a pro-Truman or liberal Democrat, for the United States Senate seat of Tom Connally, who withdrew from the race.

With the support of the conservative Democrats, Shivers, in a campaign for his third full term as governor, defeated Ralph Yarborough

Babe Dedrikson Zaharias, born and reared in Texas, for more than two decades was recognized as one of the outstanding athletes in American sports history. After breaking four world records in track and field and winning acclaim in the 1932 Olympics, she went on to master a number of sports. She became a golf champion in the 1930s and continued to win tournaments in the post–World War II years.

again in 1954 in an acrimonious contest that was settled by the second primary. Yarborough awaited the renewal of the contest in 1956.

## CRUSADES AND SCANDALS:
## POLITICS OF THE FIFTIES

In the turmoil of the sixties and seventies, some observers looked back to the fifties with the nostalgic conviction that the decade was tranquil and complacent, with scarcely a conflict in sight to mar the peace of the day. Actually, the fifties were neither tranquil nor complacent. A Communist "scare" began the decade; black and Mexican-American groups turned to the courts and to other means to claim their rights; and in the second half of the decade, insurance and land scandals alarmed voters and threatened many political careers.

Tensions and frustrations in foreign affairs and fears of subversion at home resulted in a sensational and sometimes less than responsible search for Communists, Socialists, and their sympathizers. Texas shared in this "Red Scare," often termed McCarthyism in keeping with the activities of Wisconsin Senator Joseph McCarthy. McCarthy dominated the headlines of the day with indiscriminate charges of Communism levied against a wide variety of people. In Texas his supporters included right-wing extremists, who were prepared to believe almost anything about almost anybody and who made similar charges, and more moderate groups whose fear of subversion may or may not have been justified but certainly was real.

Except for the legislative requirement of loyalty oaths for public employees, "Red Scare" politics had little effect on state affairs, but in local politics the issue often dominated. Agitated interests demanded that libraries be purged of books sympathetic to Communism, that educators suspected of Socialist tendencies be fired, and that speakers of dubious loyalty be silenced. Such groups were particularly active in larger cities such as Houston, San Antonio, and Dallas, but smaller communities also experienced their crusades. One Communist among the approximately sixty-thousand school teachers of Texas was discovered and discharged, but not much else was accomplished. By the mid-fifties most of the more extreme evidences of the fear had disappeared, though the ubiquitous loyalty oaths would linger in government agencies and public schools for many years to come.

In two areas, suffrage and school desegregation, black people in the fifties made significant progress toward the attainment of their civil rights. The right to vote came more easily than did the integration of the schools. Most significant was the Supreme Court decision of 1944 in *Smith* v. *Allwright,* a Texas case, which outlawed the white primary. Later court decisions applied the rule to local primaries, and thus the principal device whereby blacks were denied an effective voice in politics was removed. Some resistance by white citizens lingered, but black voters became more numerous in the late 1940s. By 1958 more than one-third of the potential black voters of the state were registered; in comparison, almost one-half of the potential white voters were registered. In some areas of the state, however, as much as 70 percent of the eligible black population registered to vote.

Integration of the state's schools was another matter; much was accomplished, but progress was slow and often painful. Again, Supreme Court decisions played a crucial role. Ruling in *Sweatt* v. *Painter* in 1950, the Court directed the University of Texas to admit a black man, H. M. Sweatt, to its law school, thus opening to blacks the graduate and professional schools of the university. Far more sweeping was the decision in *Brown* v. *Board of Education of Topeka* in 1954. Basing its opinion squarely on the Fourteenth Amendment, which guarantees to all persons the equal protection of the laws, the Court held that even if the schools that were maintained by the state for blacks were in every respect just as good as those for whites, segregation itself deprived the children of the minority group of equal educational opportunities and added: "We conclude that in the field of public education the doctrine of separate but equal has no place." The Court indicated a willingness to move slowly in applying its doctrine and left the approach to the lower federal courts.

Reaction to the decision divided along racial lines in Texas. Polls reflected a four-to-one opposition in the white community and a two-to-one support in the black community. Tensions began to build. In the 1954 election Governor Shivers left little doubt of his opposition to the decision, though his stand was not as adamant as that of some southern leaders. In the July 1956 Democratic primary certain segregation issues were submitted on the ballot. A large majority of voters favored stronger laws against intermarriage between whites and blacks, laws exempting white students from attending integrated schools, and interposition by the state to avoid the effects of certain Supreme Court decisions. Here and there in the fall of 1956 there were threats of violence as the schools opened in September. Happily, the serious disturbances were few, though some did occur. In Mansfield near Fort Worth, attempts of black students to attend the local school pursuant to a federal court order brought a threat of mob action, and Governor Shivers sent in state rangers to restore order. No violence occurred, but the black students were not allowed to enroll. Integration proceeded peacefully in some other districts, with more than 120 carrying out at least some integration by the 1957 school term.

Integration of colleges generated less opposition. A mob of outsiders sought to prevent blacks from entering Lamar College in Beaumont in 1956, but without success, though a similar mob had succeeded in their efforts the previous year at Texarkana Junior College. By 1958 approximately two-thirds of the colleges and universities of Texas had integrated their classes.

Opposition to integration did not die easily. Early in 1957 the legislature passed a law making mandatory the assent of the voters of any school district before the races could be mixed in the schools. The penalty provided was the withdrawal of all state aid for the district. Before the year ended, another law was enacted providing for the closing of any public school at which troops, either federal or state, were stationed. But legislation against integration and disapproval of it in many communities only delayed it. Its proponents appealed to the federal courts, and federal judges, by the authority of the Supreme Court of the United States, uniformly ordered school districts to present plans for desegregation. Governor Price Daniel made no effort to interpose state authority against the federal agencies charged with carrying out the judicial decrees.

Mexican-American people also made progress in the 1950s in their struggle for equal civil rights. Although not subjected to the legal discrimination common against black people, Mexican-Americans in Texas frequently were denied opportunities and rights extended to other people in the state. Organized efforts to combat such discrimination began early in the century and picked up momentum after World War I. In 1921 a group known as the Orden Hijos de America was formed to help Mexican-Americans secure the rights enjoyed by other citizens. The League of Latin-American Citizens, eventually to be known as LULAC, was formed in 1927 and continued the struggle. After World War II, a Mexican-American veterans' group, the American G.I. Forum, became very active, promoting poll-tax drive payments, the establishment of scholarships, and otherwise encouraging political involvement. In 1948 a court decision ruled segregation of Mexican-Americans in the public schools to be unconstitutional, and three years later another decision outlawed the exclusion of Mexican-Americans from juries. Mexican-Americans became considerably more active in politics during the decade, and in 1956 San Antonio voters elected Henry B. Gonzales to the state senate, the first Mexican-American in the Texas senate in modern times. Gonzales eventually won a seat in Congress.

Otherwise in public affairs, taxation, spending, administrative reorganization, and scandals occupied the legislature. The Fifty-third Legislature in 1953 held out against a tax increase but saw a voted teachers' pay raise voided for lack of funds. Two years later the legislature established new state commissions to supervise state building construction and higher education; terms of county officials were lengthened; and state employee and teacher retirement systems were improved. This term saw the legislature finally accept the necessity for more taxes, with increases of $100 million applied to certain specialized sales taxes.

But it was insurance, not taxes, that captured the headlines in 1955 and for the next two years. Texas insurance laws were lax and long had left the way open for fly-by-night promoters and operators. Failures of insurance companies, never uncommon, became more frequent after World War II. In 1955, Lieutenant Governor Ben Ramsey reminded the lawmakers that during the last ten years eighty-six Texas insurance companies had failed, largely because of an inadequate insurance code. The legislature enacted twenty-two laws on the subject, providing for more effective regulation generally and placing the sale of insurance stock under the board of insurance commissioners.

Failure continued, however—among them the United Services Trust and Guaranty Company, a concern that controlled some seventy-four insurance and finance companies in twenty-two states and Alaska—and in 1957 the lawmakers complied with the governor's request that he be authorized to appoint an entirely new insurance commission. The legislature also passed sixteen laws designed to improve the insurance situation in the state. Meanwhile, Texas insurance companies were subjected to an audit, and more than a hundred were denied, temporarily or permanently, permits to continue in business. Among other things, investigations of the failures brought before the public an unwholesome relationship between certain Texas lawmakers and some corporations. For instance, nine members of the Texas senate had received legal fees or other income from the United Services Trust and Guaranty Company.

In the midst of the furor over insurance, politics continued, and the line of cleavage in the Texas Democratic party between conservative and liberal elements intensified. The liberals, those loyal to the national organization, controlled the Democratic state presidential convention in 1956, but Governor Shivers again refused to support Stevenson, the Democratic nominee, and threw his strength to Eisenhower. Eisenhower and Nixon carried the state by a majority about twice that of four years before. This year Senator Price Daniel became a candidate for governor, running against Ralph Yarborough and a field of other candidates. Yarborough had the support of organized labor and a majority of the liberal Democrats. In the contest he charged Daniel, along with Shivers, with responsibility for certain irregularities of the veterans' land board, of which Daniel and Shivers were ex-officio members when Daniel was attorney general. The $100-million program, by which the state purchased land for resale to veterans, was placed under the direction of a veterans' land board, composed of the commissioner of the General Land Office, the governor, and the attorney general. Reports of irregularities and frauds in the work of the commission brought investigations by grand juries and senate and house committees. Bascom Giles, commissioner of the General Land Office, who had just been elected to his ninth term, was sent to the penitentiary for six years on charges of misrepresentation and perjury. By a small margin, Daniel defeated Yarborough for governor in a second primary; then over a slate of opponents Yarborough was elected to the United States Senate to take the seat Daniel had vacated to become governor.

The Fifty-fifth Legislature in 1957 worked under trying conditions. It was brought out that many legislators were employed more or less regularly by corporations, some of which maintained very active lobbies in Austin. Charges of bribery were hurled freely, and one representative who resigned in the face of the charge was convicted in court. The legislature adopted annual budgets of well beyond a billion dollars, and voters approved constitutional amendments liberalizing retirement benefits for state employees and increasing the state's share in pensions to the aged.

The final years of the fifties offered hope to liberal Democrats and disappointment to aspiring Republicans. Encouraged by the election of Ralph Yarborough to the Senate, liberal Democrats under the leadership of Mrs. R. D. ("Frankie") Randolph of Houston, a Democratic national committeewoman, and Jerry Holleman, president of the Texas A.F.L.–C.I.O., and others organized the "Democrats of Texas" (DOT). Outstanding among a list of demands they made of the party were the abolition of the poll tax, greater liberal representation in party affairs, and loyalty to the national Democratic party. Joined by other liberals in 1958, the DOT gave Yarborough a decisive victory over his conservative opponent, William A. Blakley (charged with being the candidate of big business), in Yarborough's contest for a regular term in the Senate, and he was elected in November. In contrast, Governor Price Daniel, generally regarded as a moderate conservative, was continued in office by a generous margin, and he dominated the Democratic state convention. Republican hopes for victory after Eisenhower's large margin in 1956 did not materialize. The party elected only one congressman in 1958, Bruce Alger of Dallas.

As the decade drew to a close, the outstanding feature in Democratic circles was the bid for the presidency by Lyndon Baines Johnson, the Texan who was now majority leader in the United States Senate and who had the endorsements of Sam Rayburn, the powerful Speaker of the House of Representatives, and of Governor Price Daniel. To promote Johnson's candidacy, the legislature moved the party primaries up to May and changed the convention system so that Senator Johnson's name could appear on the ballot as the incumbent candidate for senator, while on the same day precinct conventions could endorse him for the presidency.

## SELECTED BIBLIOGRAPHY

Fighting by Texans in World War II is related in *The Infantry Journal,* March 1944, an account of the Thirty-Sixth Division (Paris, France, 1944); and in "The Thirty-Sixth Division at Salerno," by Major James E. Taylor, *Southwestern Historical Quarterly,* XLVIII, 281–285. Also see Robert L. Wagner, *The Texas Army: A History of the Thirty-Sixth Division in the Italian Campaign* (Austin, 1972); Fred L. Walker, "The 36th was a Great Fighting Division"; Robert L. Wagner, "The Odyssey of a Texas Citizen Soldier," *Southwestern Historical Quarterly,* LXXII, 40–87; and Philip Ardery, *Bomber Pilot: A Memoir of World War II* (Lexington, Ky., 1978).

Politics of the era are considered in George Norris Green, *The Establishment in Texas Politics;* James R. Soukup, Clifton McCleskey, and Harry Holloway, *Party and Factional Division in Texas* (Austin, 1964); Sam Kinch and Stuart Long, *Allan Shivers: The Pied Piper of Texas Politics* (Austin, 1974); and Rowland Evans and Robert Novak, *Lyndon B. Johnson: The Exercise of Power* (New York, 1966). For accounts of the tidelands and the issues involved, see Ernest R. Bartley, *The Tidelands Oil Controversy* (Austin, 1953). One aspect of the "Red Scare" is discussed in Don E. Carleton, "McCarthyism in Houston: The George Ebey Affair," *Southwestern Historical Quarterly,* LXXX, 163–176.

Some sources on education in Texas are C. E. Evans, *The Story of Texas Schools* (Austin, 1955); James T. Taylor, "Gilmer-Aiken Program and State Finances," *East Texas,* January 1950, p. 9; Texas Research League, *Texas Public Schools under the Minimum Foundation Program, An Evaluation, 1949–1954.* Recent developments are set forth in the biennial *Report* of the Texas Education Agency.

In connection with scandals in insurance, see: The Texas Legislative Council, "Insolvency in the Texas Insurance Industry; Insurance, Texas' Frauds and Failures," *Time,* May 31, 1954, p. 64; "Those Texas Scandals," *The Saturday Evening Post,* November 12, 1955, pp. 19ff; D. B. Hardeman, "Shivers of Texas: A Tragedy in Three Acts,"

*Harpers,* November 1956, pp. 50–56; and Ronnie Dugger, "What Corrupted Texas?" *Harpers,* March 1957, pp. 58–78.

On developments in black history, Alwyn Barr, *Black Texans,* is very useful, but see Norman V. Bartley, *The Rise of Massive Resistance: Race and Politics in the South during the 1950's* (Baton Rouge, La., 1969); Darlene Clark Hine, "The Elusive Ballot: The Black Struggle against the Texas Democratic White Primary, 1932–1945," *Southwestern Historical Quarterly,* LXXXI, 371–392; Michael L. Gillette, "The Rise of the NAACP in Texas," *Southwestern Historical Quarterly,* LXXXI, 393–416; and Darlene Clark Hine, "Blacks and the Destruction of the Democratic White Primary, 1935–1944," *Journal of Negro History,* LXII, 43–59.

# Chapter Twenty

# REFORM,
# REACTION,
# AND REPUBLICANS

Although Texas politics of the fifties were seldom dull or tranquil, the following decades were even more eventful. Tragic violence marred the sixties, and charges of scandal and corruption brought efforts at reform in the early seventies. Minority interests continued their search for equality, justice, power, and position throughout the period. Much of the attention focused on two groups, blacks and Mexican-Americans, whose efforts of the fifties had resulted in significant change, and others joined the struggle. Women's organizations, youth groups, native Americans, the handicapped, and others grew more active and in some instances more effective in their activities.

Protest and dissent became much more visible. Several cities and a number of college campuses witnessed marches, gatherings, and various other manifestations of dissatisfaction with the "establishment." The aims of the protesters were sometimes poorly defined, but calls for more freedom, more democracy, and more equal treatment seemed to be paramount. Charges of brutality were made against law enforcement officers at times. There were accusations of discrimination, bribery, and embezzlement made against officers in high places and in low, and some of the charges were sustained.

Again and again the state's political system was sorely tried. Within the Democratic party, factionalism persisted throughout the period, and toward the end of the seventies the election of a Republican governor, the first since Reconstruction, brought speculation about a possible new era. But careful observers tempered their speculation with caution. In some respects it appeared that politics were becoming more polarized, with both liberal Democrats and conservative Republicans gaining power, but this was far from certain. Exciting events in considerable number brought interest to the period, but no clear theme emerged to show the way for the prophet of the future.

## THE ELECTION OF 1960

Texas politics in 1960, rarely simple in the post-World War II years, were more complicated than usual. In his race for a third term as governor, Price Daniel easily defeated his more conservative Democratic opponent, Jack Cox, and was elected in November with little opposition. Liberal Democrats gained a few seats in the legislature. The complicating element in the election was the dual candidacy of Senator Lyndon B. Johnson. Johnson had hopes of securing the Democratic presidential nomination, but he had no intention of giving up his Senate seat should he fail in his presidential bid.

The Senate race was much closer than the contest over the governorship. Republican hopes rested on a young teacher at Midwestern University, John Tower. Johnson's vote of 1,306,625 was sufficient to win reelection, but Tower's vote was surprisingly large. Resentment by some voters of Johnson's dual candidacy may account in part for the small margin, but Republican strength was also increasing.

Although there was discontent, the Democratic party in Texas generally supported Senator Johnson's bid for the presidential nomination. With little opposition the state convention chose a delegation pledged to Johnson. The DOT (now calling themselves the Democrats of Texas Clubs) made an unsuccessful fight, not directly against Johnson's candidacy, but in an effort to require of all state convention delegates an individual written pledge that they would support all Democratic candidates in the election of 1960. This was clearly an effort to put an end to party bolting, such as had occurred in 1952 and 1956. However, only a general loyalty resolution could be passed through the convention.

Senator Johnson campaigned energetically for the Democratic presidential nomination, traveling more than thirty thousand miles. He relied heavily on the political strength and prestige of his supporter, Texan Speaker of the House Sam Rayburn, and his supporters emphasized his experience in government, his leadership so well proved in the Senate, and the youth and inexperience of his leading opponent, Senator John F. Kennedy of Massachusetts.

When the Democratic National Convention met in Los Angeles in 1960, the Johnson campaign for the presidency ended quickly. Johnson got only 409 delegate votes, mainly from the South, and John F. Kennedy was nominated on the first ballot. Kennedy then appealed to Johnson to become the vice-presidential candidate for the party. Johnson agreed, a decision that puzzled many who were his followers and alarmed others who were not. On one hand, many Texans were disgruntled with the strong civil rights plank in the national party platform, and, on the other, many liberals were dissatisfied with Johnson. Party discord at home in Texas was apparent in the Democratic state convention held in September. The Texans supported the state's right-to-work law (disliked by organized labor) and the oil depletion allowance (which reduced the federal income tax on oil production) and generally advocated states' rights.

Relative harmony prevailed among the Republicans. The state party organization centered its efforts on carrying Texas for the national Republican ticket, headed by Vice-President Richard M. Nixon with Henry Cabot Lodge, III, as his running mate. Republican efforts were supported by some conservative Democrats, such as Allan Shivers, who campaigned for Nixon and Lodge.

Texas was a pivotal state, with 24 electoral votes, and an electorate divided rather evenly. Both parties had strong organizations in the state, and neither candidate ignored Texas. There was a record vote in November, with the Kennedy-Johnson ticket carrying Texas by a narrow margin of 24,019 votes. The Democratic margin on the national level also was exceedingly close. By slightly more than 100,000 votes, Kennedy and Johnson were elected.

Despite their losses in the election of 1960, Texas Republicans were encouraged. Nixon and Lodge had polled the greatest Republican vote in Texas in history. Party workers set out immediately to increase their strength in the state legislature and in Congress. In a special election held in 1961 to fill the Senate seat vacated by Lyndon Johnson, Republican John Tower defeated a conservative Democrat, William A. Blakley. The victory was evidence of the growth of the Republican party, though the liberal Democrats' refusal to support their conservative candidate likely contributed to the Republican cause. In 1962 the Republicans gained a second congressman and several house seats in the legislature, six of them from Dallas districts.

The election of the governor in 1962 offered additional evidence of a growing Republican party. In the Democratic party there were a number of candidates for the nomination. Price Daniel sought a fourth term; Houston attorney Don Yarborough represented the liberal faction of the party; John B. Connally, who had close ties with Lyndon Johnson, claimed support from both conservatives and moderates; and there were others. Connally suffered to some extent from charges that he was running as the "Johnson candidate," but he won the Democratic nomination in a run-off with Yarborough, possibly because his promise to appoint black executives won some support from black voters. In the general election in the fall he defeated Jack Cox, a conservative Democrat turned Republican, but Cox polled almost 46 percent of the vote.

These and a few other victories raised high hopes in Republican ranks, but dissension soon appeared to plague the party in Texas. Many conservative Democrats were joining the party, which may help to explain a noticeable tendency toward the extreme right. The conservative political philosophy of Senator Barry Goldwater of Arizona, coupled with his opposition to federal intervention in the race issue, gave him a large following in Texas. Goldwater's nomination as the Republican candidate for president in 1964 marked the ascendancy of conservative Republicanism in the nation, and conservative Texas followed him with enthusiasm. Many Republicans were loath to support him, however, and he had no appeal for some of the Democrats who were getting into the habit of voting for Republican candidates for president.

## JOHNSON AND CONNALLY

Tragedy in Texas on November 23, 1963, profoundly affected the course of public affairs in Texas, indeed in the world. While the people of the city and of the state were receiving President John Kennedy with enthusiastic hospitality, a hidden assassin shot and killed him and seriously wounded Governor Connally, who was riding with him. Within two hours after the death of President Kennedy, Lyndon Baines Johnson, a native Texan, took the oath of office that made him president of the United States.

Through the prestige of the presidency, Johnson was able to suppress to a degree the factionalism in Texas Democratic ranks for a period, but the relationship between Senator Ralph Yarborough, Texas's most prominent liberal Democrat, and Governor Connally was cool. There were differences in ideology, and both sought to control the Democratic party in Texas. With President Johnson in office, Governor Connally had a clear advantage, for his ties to the president were close. In the Democratic primaries of 1964 the influence of the president, working through and with Governor Connally, prevailed. Connally was easily nominated and elected governor for another term and defeated his Republican opponent, George Bush. Connally's control of the Democratic state convention was complete, and the delegation was sent to the national convention in Atlantic City with instructions to "put forth every effort" to secure Johnson's nomination. Johnson was nominated with ease.

The second United States President born in Texas (Dwight D. Eisenhower was the first), Lyndon Baines Johnson made his home state the base for a long and distinguished political career. Elected to Congress in 1937, to the Senate in 1948, to the vice-presidency in 1960, he became president when John F. Kennedy was assassinated and was elected for the next term in 1964. The University of Texas awarded him a degree as a distinguished American statesman as well as the state's most illustrious citizen of the day. After deciding not to seek reelection, Johnson returned to Texas in 1969 where he lived quietly until his death in 1973. (E. C. Barker History Center, University of Texas)

Although the Republican candidate Barry Goldwater visited Texas six times during the campaign, and Republicans worked hard otherwise, Johnson's strength proved invincible. Even former Governor Shivers supported the Johnson ticket. Out of a record vote of 2.558 million, the Republicans received less than a million votes.

A determined leader in his first term, Governor Connally gained additional strength in his dealings with the legislature upon his reelection in 1964. State finances, usually a major problem for both governor and legislature, were not as much of an issue during these years. After much wrangling between liberals who wanted additional taxes on business and conservatives who favored some form of a sales tax, the legislature in 1961 adopted a sales tax and some other levies. Governor Daniel, who opposed a sales tax, did not sign the law establishing it, but he allowed it to become law. The sales tax, with some additional levies adopted during Connally's first term, gave the state a firm financial base. When additional funds were needed, the sales tax was increased. Consequently, Governor Connally was free to concentrate on other issues in his administration.

Putting great emphasis on the need for long-range planning, Connally encouraged the legislature in the enactment of an impressive legislative program. New intergovernmental planning agencies, which coordinated the efforts of counties, cities, schools, and other political subdivisions, were created. The legislature established a state Fine Arts Commission. Constitutional amendments liberalizing the state welfare program, expanding teacher retirement programs, increasing building funds for state colleges, and authorizing student loans were adopted. A twenty-five member committee to make a study of education beyond the high school was appointed, and its recommendation led to the strengthening of the Texas Commission on Higher Education, which acts as a coordinator for the colleges and universities. The governor sought to secure greater appropriations for the colleges and universities, to promote the founding of more junior colleges, and to offer greater facilities for vocational training generally. The University of Houston was made a state university, and Angelo State College in San Angelo and Pan American College in Edinburg were made senior colleges.

Two changes in the electoral process during these years had far-reaching implications. In compliance with the mandates of federal judicial decrees, the legislature redistricted the state, drawing new boundaries for the election of members of the state legislature and for the house of representatives. Most agreed that redistricting would diminish the influence of rural areas in the government, but while some thought that the Republicans would benefit from the changes, others believed that liberal politicians would gain an advantage. In another issue, federal courts ruled in 1966 that the poll-tax voting requirement (which Texans had consistently refused to change) was unconstitutional, whereupon the legislature enacted a law eliminating the poll tax. Over the objection of many liberals, the legislature included a provision in the law requiring that voters register annually. Whatever the long-range consequences of these changes might have been, the immediate impact on statewide office holding was limited. In the election of 1966 Governor Connally, who had kept his promise to appoint black executives, was elected overwhelmingly for a third term, and other conservative candidates fared well.

Although Governor Connally was successful in securing the enactment of much of his program, he was not successful in all instances. The legislature refused to license the sale of liquor by the drink or to license betting on horse races, nor would it submit to the voters the question of a constitutional convention to revise the state's constitution. Voters refused to approve constitutional amendments giving the governor a four-year term and providing for annual legislative sessions.

The outlook of Texas politics was changed greatly in 1968 when both Governor Connally and President Johnson announced that they would not seek reelection. Half a score of candidates sought the Democratic nomination for governor, and nearly two million voters took part in the primary. Lieutenant Governor Preston Smith, a conservative, and Don Yarborough, a well-known liberal, entered the run-off. Yarborough advocated a minimum wage of $1.25, a state poverty corps, and increased state aid to the aged, to the disabled, and to dependent children. Some of Smith's billboards read, "Continue Conservative Government."

Results were disappointing to the liberals. The "new voters" they had counted on either did not vote or had fragmented their strength. Smith's vote was 756,909 against Yarborough's 620,726. In November Smith defeated the Republican nominee, Paul Eggars, with a comfortable margin.

Led by Governor Connally, the conservative Democratic forces controlled the state presidential convention and sent to the national convention in Chicago a delegation of 104 instructed to support the governor as a favorite-son candidate. In Chicago the Texas liberals unsuccessfully contested the seating of the regular delegation. Vice-President Hubert Humphrey won the nomination on the first ballot.

Texas Republicans united by supporting Richard Nixon and his running mate, Spiro T. Agnew, who were nominated at the national convention in Miami. George C. Wallace, former governor of Alabama, headed the new American party in the contest. The Democrats carried Texas by a close vote, and, by an even narrower margin, Nixon and Agnew carried the nation. Wallace's vote in Texas and in the nation was relatively small.

## THE SEARCH FOR CIVIL RIGHTS

The civil rights movement, building upon the gains of the fifties, added momentum thereafter. The right to vote was relatively secure and segregation legally was supposedly a policy of the past, but discrimination and socioeconomic inequities persisted. Across the nation, minority groups formed organizations and launched campaigns to correct the problems. Texas, with about one-third of its population made up of two major ethnic minorities, was the scene of much of the activity.

Although their interests were not dissimilar, there was rarely much cooperation between the two groups. Black minorities concentrated their activities in urban areas, particularly in Houston and Dallas, and although there were a number of new black organizations formed, the long-established NAACP remained the most important. Among Mexican-American peoples, a wide variety of organizations, many of them formed in the 1960s and 1970s, reflected basic differences over the proper approach for solving the problems of discrimination and inequality. Some called themselves Chicanos, asserting the distinctiveness of their culture and rejecting that of the Anglos. Some Chicanos, though not all, were militant in their demands and in effect advocated a form of separatism. Other Mexican-Americans rejected both the name Chicano and the idea of militancy, preferring to work "within the system or establishment."

Both minorities launched concerted campaigns to secure the election of their people to important offices, particularly to the legislature. In 1961 only two members of the state senate and five members of the house of representatives were Mexican-Americans, and no member of the legislature was from the black community. With the support of a number of organizations on both the state and the local level, minority candidates entered more contests, and the number of minority office-holders in the legislature moved steadily upward. By 1978 the Texas house of representatives included fourteen blacks and seventeen Mexican-Americans. Four Mexican-Americans served in the senate, and two held posts in the United States Congress. During this period Houston voters elected a black woman, Barbara Jordan, to the state senate, where she served with distinction between 1967 and 1971. Subsequently she won election to the United States Congress where her abilities attracted national attention.

Local politics also felt the impact of the civil rights movement. In a dramatic and hostile contest in South Texas in 1963, Mexican-American activists won control of the Crystal City town government. The election focused on racial discrimination, and victory encouraged similar efforts elsewhere, especially in communities where the Mexican-American population was either in a majority or was quite large. By 1980 almost one thousand Mexican-Americans held public offices in local government. Black politicians on the local level were less successful. In 1970 there were forty-two black officeholders in the state, and while the number increased in the 1970s, it remained small.

Mexican-American political activism on the local level led to the organization of a new political party, La Raza Unida. The party was an outgrowth of the Mexican-American Youth Organization (MAYO), formed in 1967 with Jose Angel Gutierrez as its leader. For a time the party apeared to have prospects of at least some success. Party leaders contributed to Chicano victories in Crystal City and in other local elections, and in the 1972 gubernatorial race, La Raza candidate Ramsey

Muniz polled more than 200,000 votes. But the defection of liberal supporters who tired of one-issue politics, the lack of organization, the inherent difficulties faced by any third party, and the 1976 conviction of the party's gubernatorial candidate on a charge of conspiracy to distribute marijuana brought hard times in the late seventies.

A major issue throughout the period was the strained and often hostile relations between law enforcement officials and minority groups. Blacks and Mexican-Americans had long claimed that they were often subjected to harassment, brutality, and other forms of unfair treatment by police and other law officers. The rise of activism, with the demonstrations and protest meetings, offered more opportunities for conflict, and a number of confrontations occurred. On the campus of Texas Southern University in May 1967, rumors of trouble and a gathering crowd of black students led to violence involving the students and the Houston police. Rocks and bottles were thrown; shots were fired; and a state of siege existed around one of the dormitories for several hours. Before order could be restored, a policeman was shot to death. Three years later in the summer of 1970 there was another shootout resulting in a fatality between the Houston police and a radical black group. Violent incidents took place in Midland in 1968, in Lubbock in 1971, and there were others. Frequently, charges were made that the police resorted to undue force in making arrests and were too quick in the use of their guns. In an effort to add minorities to the police force and thereby lessen the tensions, Houston adopted a special recruiting program in 1971, and other cities followed with similar programs. Special police-community relations councils were established in a number of cities. Still, the problems and charges persisted. Between 1975 and 1978 there were more than thirty official charges of alleged police brutality, and in at least two Houston cases policemen were convicted on serious charges.

Much of the enthusiasm and energy of the civil rights crusade of the sixties and early seventies centered on the student protest movement that brought tensions and unrest to college campuses all across the nation. Underlying the movement was a broad reaction against the unpopular war in Vietnam, but civil rights also was an important goal. Texas students on a number of college campuses took part in these protests. In some instances these were the result of traveling student activist organizers, such as those associated with the Student Nonviolent Coordinating Committee (SNCC). In other instances the demonstrations were altogether the product of local talent. Rarely did the protests assume threatening proportions, except for the tragic affair on the campus of Texas Southern University, but many college administrators had some anxious moments before the momentum of the movement waned in the early seventies.

A completely fair and sound evaluation of the effects of the student protest movement cannot be easily made. No doubt, the demonstrations and the enthusiasm of the students focused attention on the issue of civil rights. However, the movement offered relatively few solutions beyond a host of platitudes, and the fears and frustrations of public reaction may well have hindered the development of solutions.

Women, not a minority in the state since they outnumbered men in the 1960 census and thereafter, but certainly a group subjected to discrimination and unequal treatment, joined the search for civil rights. The National Organization for Women (NOW), formed in 1966, soon had chapters in Texas. In 1971 women's rights workers met in Austin to organize the Texas Women's Political Caucus (TWPC), and shortly thereafter the group organized a successful campaign to secure legislative ratification of the proposed Twenty-seventh Amendment to the United States Constitution, the equal rights amendment. The TWPC promoted greater involvement of women in politics, urging more to seek public office and to take more active roles in party affairs. The cause of women in politics was assisted in 1972 by the gubernatorial candidacy of Frances Farenthold, who ran a strong, though unsuccessful, race. Progress has been painfully slow, but women are gaining more influence in politics. In 1977 almost 8 percent of the elected officials in Texas were women. In 1979 one member of the state senate was a woman, and eleven women served in the house of representatives. Moreover, women have held increasingly influential posts in both Republican and Democratic party organizations.

## SMITH, SHARPSTOWN, AND BRISCOE

While the struggle for civil rights provided some interest and excitement in the final years of the sixties, political affairs in Texas were generally quiet. In style, appearance, and background, Governor Smith was unlike the colorful and aggressive John Connally. Less than dynamic, the governor was not even very articulate, but over a long political career he patiently learned the system, cultivated his supporters, and took advantage of the opportunities that came his way. Rural and small-town voters were his primary strength. Leadership in the legislature was strong but closely tied to business and financial interests and not particularly sympathetic to reform or change. Speaker Gus Mutscher ruled the house of representatives with a firm hand, and Lieutenant Governor Ben Barnes's rule over the senate was almost as complete. Barnes was an able, pragmatic leader, and many regarded him as the politician with the most promising future.

Smith in his first term presented a legislative program that received only limited support. He proposed more funds for vocational education, two new medical schools, higher pay for legislators, a relatively small increase in taxes, and a lower voting age. He supported a comprehensive program to provide additional water supplies, primarily for western areas of the state. Somewhat surprisingly, he endorsed a state minimum wage. The legislature approved increased spending for vocational and medical schools and adopted a state minimum wage. But voters rejected the water plan, and the legislature turned down the governor's proposals for additional taxes.

In the election of 1970, attention focused not on the governor's race but on the contest for the Senate seat held by liberal Ralph Yarborough. Yarborough, who had first been elected in a special election but had won reelection to two regular terms, faced a difficult task. Conservative business and financial leaders in the Democratic party generally supported Lloyd Bentsen of Houston. The primary campaign, which was vigorous and somewhat bitter, ended in victory for Bentsen, who then defeated Republican George Bush in the general elections. Party emphasis on the Senate race perhaps affected Governor Smith's campaign for reelection. Smith defeated Paul Eggars, his Republican opponent of the previous election, but his margin of victory declined. Smith received 57 percent of the vote in 1968 but only 53 percent in 1970. In the election, voters gave their approval to a constitutional amendment making the sale of liquor by the drink permissible.

Scandals and charges of corruption dominated state affairs during Smith's second term. In January 1971 the Federal Securities and Exchange Commission filed charges in federal court against a number of Texas businessmen, alleging illegal manipulation in the sale of securities. Although the original charges did not name any politicians currently holding office, subsequent disclosures did, and charges of scandal, fraud, and bribery were soon heard throughout the state. The affair was complicated, but the essence of it was the allegation that high-ranking officials were given opportunities to profit in stock transactions in which prices were illegally manipulated in order to assure their profits. Frank Sharp, a prominent Houston banker, allegedly organized the scheme. He hoped to secure special legislation that would allow his troubled banking empire to evade the supervision and regulation of the Federal Deposit Insurance Corporation. The politicians involved were expected to see that the legislation desired by Sharp became law.

Several state officers did speculate in the stock, using funds loaned to them by Sharp's bank. Governor Smith and a close associate, Speaker of the House Gus Mutscher and two of his aides, and two other representatives quickly amassed profits that amounted to more than

$300,000. The legislation was introduced in a special legislative session in August 1969 and with the strong support of Mutscher it passed both houses of the legislature. But Governor Smith, who had allowed the measure to be considered in the special session, vetoed it.

The consequences of the so-called "Sharpstown" case were many. After a Travis County grand jury indicted Mutscher and two associates in September 1971, an Abilene jury convicted the trio on charges of conspiracy and bribery the following March. Within the house of representatives a strange collection of liberals, conservatives, mavericks, and members otherwise unclassified, all known collectively as the "Dirty Thirty," led a fight not only to oust the embattled speaker but also to change the rules so that no future speaker could exercise so much power.

The call for reform was strong and not entirely unanswered. The next legislature after Sharpstown, the sixty-third, adopted seven reform bills. The legislation established new rules for regulating lobbying, required financial reports from officeholders, laid down rules for opening public meetings and records, and tightened regulations on campaign financing. Much support developed for a comprehensive revision of the constitution.

The immediate impact of the scandal was felt in the elections of 1972. It was not a good year for incumbents. Less than half of the members of the house of representatives and of the senate would return to take their seats in the next legislature. Among the losers was Gus Mutscher who sought reelection despite his conviction. Members of the "Dirty Thirty" who had challenged the power of the speaker fared somewhat better, especially those who sought reelection rather than new offices. Many factors contributed to the large turnover in the legislature, especially the effects of newly installed, single-member districting, but observers gave the Sharpstown scandal much of the credit.

Several candidates entered the race for governor. Smith, who had profited from the stock deals but who had not been charged with a crime, compaigned for a third term. Other major candidates included Lieutenant Governor Ben Barnes, Representative Frances "Sissy" Farenthold, who was one of the "Dirty Thirty," and Dolph Briscoe, who was a wealthy South Texas landowner. Smith ran a distant fourth and Barnes fared little better. Probably Sharpstown accounted for their poor showing, though there was little or nothing to connect Barnes with the affair. Briscoe, enjoying the support of business and financial interests, in a run-off defeated Representative Farenthold, generally regarded as the candidate of the liberals.

The general election saw triumph for Briscoe, but the vote was close. Briscoe polled slightly more than 100,000 votes over his Republican opponent, Henry Grover, winning with only 47 percent of the vote. The La Raza Unida candidate, Ramsey Muniz, received 6 percent of the vote, and had he received very much more, the election might well have fallen to the Republicans. On the national level Republicans did well in Texas. President Richard Nixon, in his contest with Democrat George McGovern, received 65 percent of the vote and carried 246 counties. Republican Senator John Tower also won reelection.

The election of Briscoe brought little in the way of dramatic change to Texas politics. Briscoe, who had little active experience in political office except for a brief period in the legislature in the fifties, was less than aggressive in his new post. Indeed, he seemed to enjoy being governor but to care little about performing the functions of the office. Although some regarded the governor as a leader of limited political ability, he was not entirely lacking in such skills. While maintaining a conservative reputation and the support of business and financial interests, he also maintained good relations with organized labor and much of the Mexican-American electorate.

"No new taxes," law enforcement, constitutional revision, school finances, and, toward the end of the period, tax revision were the issues of the Briscoe years. Constitutional revision, however, though one of the more important issues, received scant attention from the governor. In fact, he eventually announced his opposition to the effort. Perhaps heard more often than any other during the six years was the governor's promise of "no new taxes." It was a promise well kept, though lack of increased tax levels was not necessarily an indication of frugal public spending. The state budget almost doubled during the Briscoe years, but revenues from existing taxation more than kept pace with the needs. Public school finances was the most persistent budget problem of the period. Solutions adopted were only makeshift and tended in many instances to shift the tax burden from the state treasury to local districts. The legislature spent considerable time on law enforcement legislation, eventually adopting a new criminal code, several anticrime bills, and an act restoring the death penalty.

In the final year of his tenure, after he had lost his primary bid for renomination, the governor called a special legislative session to enact a program of tax relief. The legislature increased inheritance tax exemptions, repealed the sales tax on utilities, and adopted a constitutional amendment, later approved by the voters, that reduced property taxes levied primarily on the local level.

## CONSTITUTIONAL REVISION

Voters in an atmosphere sympathetic to reform in 1972 approved an amendment to the constitution authorizing the legislature to meet in a constitutional convention in January 1974. In the interim a thirty-seven-member constitutional revision committee prepared recommendations calling for a new, shorter, and more general constitution. The committee suggested annual legislative sessions, more power for the governor, reorganization of the judicial system, and other extensive changes.

With Speaker of the House Price Daniel, Jr. as its presiding officer, the legislative constitutional convention met as planned in January 1974. After much debate and compromise, the convention completed an eleven-article constitution in July. Though government reforms were not as extensive as those proposed by the commission, the document did provide for many changes. However, the convention refused, by a three-vote margin, to approve its own work, and the document was not presented to the voters. The controversy over a "right-to-work" provision, the dissatisfaction of some members who wanted more drastic reforms, the opposition of the lobby, and the opposition of those who wanted no new constitution at all accounted for the defeat.

The following legislature which met in 1975 revived the constitutional revision issue. Eight proposed amendments were drafted, and these in effect amounted to a new constitution and were similar to the constitution prepared the previous year. The legislature adopted the amendments and presented them to the voters in the November elections. But interest in reform was waning; certain groups were adamantly opposed; the governor belatedly announced his opposition; and the voters rejected constitutional revision by a margin of three to one.

## REPUBLICAN GOVERNOR—A NEW ERA?

The 1978 elections in Texas provided more than the usual number of political surprises. Governor Briscoe announced for a third term, not an unusual move except that election would mean ten years in office since the governorship became a four-year term in 1974. His opponent for the nomination was John Hill, the attorney general, who was considered by most to be moderately liberal. Supported enthusiastically by the state's teachers who were attracted by Hill's stand on education, the attorney general defeated Briscoe in the Democratic primary. Other factors contributing to Briscoe's defeat included his less-than-aggressive style of leadership, defection of some labor and Mexican-American support, and the reluctance of some voters to have the same governor for ten years.

In the Republican party the contest for the nomination was between Ray Hutchison, a highly respected and able long-time party leader, and William Clements, a wealthy and outspoken Dallas oilman. Relying on an effective, well-financed publicity campaign, Clements won the nomination.

To the surprise of most, he also won the election. By a very narrow margin and with less than 50 percent of the votes, Clements defeated Hill to become the first Republican governor elected in Texas in more than a century. Political observers offered many explanations in analyzing the victory. Voter turnout was light; many conservative Democrats voted Republican; Hill supporters were overconfident; and Clements's campaign, which spent more than seven million dollars on the primary and general elections, was better financed than Hill's. To these may be added the fact that Clements's campaign not only was well financed, it also was shrewdly effective in its appeal to a conservatively inclined Texas electorate. Republican strength in the legislature increased slightly, claiming twenty-three members in the house of representatives and four in the senate.

Governor Clements's first term of office offered many contrasts to that of his predecessor, Dolph Briscoe. Energetic and aggressive, the new governor had an opinion on nearly all issues and a willingness to express it. Whether or not a new era of Republican leadership had developed was not clear, however, even after a legislative session and more than a year had passed. Governor Clements offered a host of proposals to the legislature, and some were adopted but most were rejected. If there were major accomplishments in the session, it was the passage of a new public school finance law and the adoption of a more uniform program for the taxation of property. Both of these laws were primarily the work of leaders within the legislature. On the whole, the relationship between the Democratic legislature and the Republican governor could best be described as proper and polite but cautious and skeptical.

Certainly, Republican fortunes had improved considerably since World War II. Although Republican candidates once had polled only 5 to 10 percent of the vote, as Texas entered the eighties, Republicans in statewide races could ordinarily expect a respectable vote, generally in excess of 40 percent. Success beyond that level remained uncertain, dependent upon improved party organization and a broadening of Republican voter appeal. In 1980 Texas appeared to be some distance away from Republican party domination in politics, but one-party politics likewise seemed to be a thing of the past.

## THE NEW FEDERALISM

If political trends within the state were not exactly clear at the end of the seventies, another development in government was quite obvious. The role of the national government in the lives of Texans was ever more a larger and larger one. Although activities of the federal government have always been important in the state, extensive involvement came with the programs of the New Deal. More programs and more regulations were added after World War II, and the sixties and seventies saw even more. Other aspects were involved, but regulatory functions and financial support were the two primary areas of federal activity.

A number of agencies carried on investigations to determine compliance with federal law and judicial decrees. Many of these stemmed from the civil rights legislation of the sixties, with added emphasis toward the end of the seventies on protection of the handicapped and the elderly. Acting under the authority of the Voting Rights Act of 1965, as amended in 1975, the Civil Rights Division of the Justice Department supervised certain election practices and approved or disapproved any changes in voting procedures. Minority rights, however, by no means accounted for all of the federal regulatory action in the state. Exercising a degree of control over private industry and public activities were two powerful agencies, the Environmental Protection Agency (EPA) and the Occupational Safety and Health Administration (OSHA). And there were others.

Federal courts likewise have become more active. Often the controversies centered on alleged violations of civil rights, but the issues were many and varied. By the end of the seventies a significant number of school districts in the state were functioning under federal court orders calling for busing or some other method to accelerate the pace of integration. Indeed, in many school districts the school attorney was a vital part of the organization, and integration was not always the issue. Tuition for aliens, students' rights, teachers' rights, bilingual education, and other controversies kept the schools in the courtrooms.

Financial support was the other area in which the federal government loomed large in Texas. In the seventies the federal government provided about 11 percent of the money used by the public schools of Texas. Although the level of support declined somewhat toward the end of the decade, federal funds in 1978 provided more than 26 percent of the monies spent by the state government. In addition, there were large sums parceled out through special grants to cities and other governmental units.

The desirability of federal regulation is a matter of personal values, to be determined in large measure by political ideologies and the degree to which one is affected for good or for bad. Supporters argue necessity and justice, but critics claim that, at best, harm is more often done than good.

Federal financial contributions were likely to be more generally welcomed, though not in all instances. State government in Texas provided through the seventies only a minimal level of state services in terms of money, spending at a rate of less than 80 percent of the national average. But even so, the costs were high. Welfare costs in 1976, administered primarily through the Texas Department of Human Resources, required almost 18 percent of the state's budget, but federal funds supplied 70 percent of the need. More than 40 percent of the monies spent on highways and transportation came from federal sources. These two areas together with education accounted for more than three-fourths of the federal monies spent in the state.


## SELECTED BIBLIOGRAPHY

George Green, *The Establishment in Texas Politics,* surveys briefly the politics of the sixties and seventies, but no general study of the period in depth has been published. One aspect, however, has been thoroughly studied: For information on the bank bill scandals, consult Sam Kinch, Jr., and Ben Proctor, *Texas under a Cloud* (Austin, 1972); Charles Deaton, *The Year They Threw the Rascals Out* (Austin, 1973); Jimmy Banks, *Money, Marbles, and Chalk: The Wondrous World of Texas Politics* (Austin, 1971); and Harvey Katz, *Shadow on the Alamo: New Heroes Fight Old Corruption in Texas Politics* (Garden City, N.Y., 1972). Rowland Evans and Robert Novak, *Lyndon B. Johnson: The Exercise of Power;* and Ann Fears Crawford and Jack Keever, *John B. Connally: A Portrait in Power* (Austin, 1973), focus on two of the prominent figures of the period.

Literature on minorities and their politics is becoming more available in recent years. Alwyn Barr, *Black Texans,* provides material up to 1971. Matt S. Meir and Feliciano Rivera, *The Chicanos: A History of Mexican Americans* (New York, 1972) is a useful general study. Typical of more specialized studies are John Stapler Shockley, *Chicano Revolt in a Texas Town* (Notre Dame, Ind., 1974); and Robert W. Talbert, "Poll Tax Repeal in Texas: A Three Year Individual Performance Evaluation," *Journal of Politics,* XXXVI, 1050–1056. See also David W. Brady and Kent L. Tedin: "Religion and Political Ideology in the Anti-ERA Movement," *Social Science Quarterly,* LVI, 464–475; and Jan Meadows, "Woman against Herself," *Texas Parade,* March 1975, pp. 29–33. The lobby, often charged with exercising undue influence in Texas politics, is described and discussed in Lee Clark, "May the Lobby Hold You in the Palm of Its Hand," *Texas Observer,* May 24, 1968 pp. 1–3; and in several studies in the *Texas Monthly,* July 1973.

Chapter Twenty-One

# IN THE AGE
# OF ATOMS
# AND SPACE

Dramatic change, highlighted by the use of atomic power and human flight in space, characterized the economic, scientific, and social development of the United States in the years after World War II. Economic, social, and cultural change in Texas in these years depended only to a limited extent on space and perhaps even less on atomic power, but these were, nonetheless, years of change in which Texas economically and socially experienced a transformation of almost revolutionary proportions.

Industrialization and urbanization, trends long apparent in Texas, accelerated in the years after World War II. By 1978 an estimated 3 percent of the population depended on farms and ranches directly for their income; eight out of ten Texans lived in urban areas; and almost one-half of the people were concentrated in the Dallas–Fort Worth, Houston, and San Antonio areas. For most, living was no longer a matter of wide-open spaces and the smell of the earth, but rather an environment of housing developments, freeways, and shopping centers.

These were the most obvious changes, but there were many others. Though requiring the efforts of a relatively small portion of the population, agriculture by no means assumed an unimportant role. Social and cultural institutions grew in number and scope and added their contributions to the postwar world, as did many individuals in the arts and literature. The population grew, in part because of the attraction offered by the appeal of the so-called "sunbelt." Economically and otherwise, the roles of women and minorities in the society were altered.

Thus, in many respects these were years of change, growth,

progress, and achievement. But all of the changes were not good, and some that were good brought with them new tensions and anxieties. Social tensions and uncertainties, declining petroleum production, and water shortages were among the more important problems facing Texans as they entered the decade of the eighties.

## THE ECONOMY

By any measure, industry grew vigorously in the years after World War II. Employment in manufacturing more than tripled between 1947 and 1979, rising to an estimate of almost a million workers, and the increased value added to goods by manufacturing was even more impressive, amounting to more than $27 billion annually. Oil refining, chemicals, and petrochemicals, all important in the thirties, continued to dominate, but electronics, aerospace components, and other high-technology items also were important. The aircraft industry, located in the Dallas–Fort Worth area during World War II, continued production thereafter, and electronics plants were built nearby in later years. Oil and chemical refining concentrated in locations along the coast, with many plants being established in the Beaumont–Port Arthur and the Houston–Baytown–Texas City areas. The manufacture of oil-field equipment became a major industry in Houston.

Oil production rose more or less steadily after World War II, reaching a peak of slightly more than 1.3 million barrels in 1972. That year the Railroad Commission abandoned its practice, in effect since 1933, of restricting production. Nevertheless, declining reserves and weakening wells brought lowered production, so that in 1979 about one billion barrels were pumped. Declining oil production represents one of the major causes of anxiety as Texas enters the eighties. Without even considering the usual implications of the shortage of this vital source of energy, disappearing oil resources present some problems of special concern to Texans. In 1978 the petroleum industry employed 313,237 people; at the same time, oil and gas production provided slightly more than 20 percent of the tax revenue available to finance state government. Thus, a further decline in oil production will have a marked impact on the economy of Texas.

Agricultural production, in terms of monetary value, more than tripled between 1947 and 1977, with income generally divided more or less evenly between the sale of field crops and the sale of livestock. Cotton continued to be the most valuable field crop, though displaced temporarily in 1975 by grain sorghums, but by a wide margin, cattle was the most valuable single product. With only a small portion of the

Texas was to get its first nuclear powered electric generation with completion of two plants scheduled for the early 1980s. This one is the South Texas Project Unit I, under construction in Matagorda County and jointly owned by Houston Lighting and Power Co., Central Power and Light Co., and the cities of San Antonio and Austin. The other nuclear plant is the Comanche Peak Project being built near Glen Rose by Texas Utilities Co.

population living on farms, the influence of agriculture has declined significantly over the years, but it appears that the voice of agriculture in the state has remained substantially stronger than the number of farmers indicates that it would likely be.

Dominating developments in transportation in the postwar years were automobiles and airplanes. Motor vehicle registration rose from 2,192,654 in 1947 to 11,297,938 in 1978, a rate of growth approximately five times greater than the rise in population. Only California had more automobiles on the highways. Texas ranked first in 1978 in terms of highway and street mileage, with more than 257,000 miles.

Commercial air passenger service began in the state in 1928 with schedules connecting Dallas with San Antonio and Fort Worth with Galveston. Growth was modest during the years of the depression, but military aviation in World War II built interest and support. Air travel rapidly increased in the postwar years, and between 1965 and 1978 the number of people traveling by air each year more than tripled. At the same time rail travel dwindled to almost nothing, and railroad miles continued their decline, falling to 13,035. However, railroad freight tonnage increased almost 50 percent during the postwar years, and railroading in Texas continued to be profitable.

Organized labor shared in the economic growth of the postwar years, for, despite a barrage of laws regulating unions passed in the late 1940s and early 1950s, labor gained strength. Unification of the American Federation of Labor and the Congress of Industrial Organizations in 1957 brought a larger role in politics. Labor's voice in state politics was heard more often, and in local politics of certain areas it was a voice that could not be ignored. Oil refining and chemical industries were, in most instances, unionized, as were most of the construction trades. In the seventies there were a number of instances in which the public employees formed unions or similar organizations. However, toward the end of the decade, union membership was apparently declining slightly. Among the reasons given for the decline was the continued existence of the "right-to-work" law, long opposed by organized labor. In 1978 approximately 13 percent of the Texas work force were union members.

## CHURCHES, SCHOOLS, AND SOCIETIES

The growth of Texas churches has generally kept pace with the population. In 1890, church members represented 30.3 percent of the population, and by 1916 they had increased to 40 percent. In 1968 the Texas Council of Churches reported a total of 4,864,162, but membership was probably higher, inasmuch as not all churches reported their members and some counts were incomplete. The Baptist bodies led, with nearly 1.75 million members; Roman Catholics numbered more than 1.25 million; and United Methodists counted about 800,000. The Church of Christ, Disciples of Christ, Presbyterian, Protestant Episcopal, and Lutheran denominations were represented by large numbers.

Notwithstanding certain distinct differences, the larger Protestant bodies have had many characteristics in common. They have maintained Sunday schools and auxiliary organizations for young people. Certain churches have had special organizations for men, and most of them have had one or more organizations for women. Almost without exception they have emphasized the importance of maintaining a zealous and active laity to aid a ministry that was better trained and better paid than any ministry that had preceded it. Although the state has taken over much of the burden that the churches once bore alone, the churches still carry on extensive work in education, child care, and the maintenance of hospitals.

Public education in Texas benefited significantly from the adoption of the Gilmer-Aiken program shortly after the end of World War II. State leadership in the fifties worked in various ways to emphasize productive living and citizenship. After the Russians placed satellites in orbit in 1957, there was a persistent demand for more study and more effective teaching in the schools, from kindergarten through the university.

Later years saw added emphasis on special programs. Programs for the instruction of retarded children reached a substantial number of the less fortunate young, and programs to assist educationally deprived children were established in many communities. Bilingual education received special attention in the seventies. Toward the end of the decade, declining scores on verbal and mathematical achievement tests generated widespread concern and gave rise to a "back-to-basics" movement.

In higher education the years after World War II were a period of steady growth. The growth rate was especially high in the seventies, with student enrollment almost doubling and the addition of 36 new units of higher education. By 1980 more than 150 institutions in the state provided opportunities for those seeking education beyond the high school. Public-supported senior colleges numbered 24, and there were 47 public community colleges and a number of educational centers. Specialized training was offered by 7 medical schools, 2 dental schools, allied health units, a technical institute, and a maritime academy.

Private institutions, most with church connections, numbered forty-nine in 1980. Rice University was noted for its educational excellence. Largest of a number of Baptist institutions was Baylor University, and Southern Methodist University, established in 1915, was the largest of nine Methodist schools. The Presbyterians had Austin College and Trinity University; the Church of Christ had Abilene Christian College and several smaller schools; the Disciples of Christ maintained Texas Christian University; and Saint Mary's University was the largest Catholic school. Even though their proportion of the enrollment has declined in recent years, the private and denominational schools are still important to Texas higher education, providing in 1978 education for one out of every eight students. In addition to their emphasis on religious training, several of these schools do outstanding work in music, drama, and the other fine arts.

Lodges, clubs, and societies, some with roots far back into pioneer times, have continued to form an important sector of Texas's social and cultural institutions since World War II. The Masonic orders, active in the early nineteenth century, located lodges in practically every city and town in the state. Among other strong organizations are the Odd Fellows, the Knights of Pythias, and the Woodmen. These and other lodges have provided a measure of security for their members and have contributed to the general welfare through the maintenance of homes, orphanages, and hospitals.

Service clubs have assumed a more important role over the years.

First to be established in Texas was the Rotary Club, founded in Dallas in 1911. During the First World War the Lions, an organization dedicated to community service, was founded. It has one or more clubs in practically every town and city in the state. Other organizations with similar purposes are Kiwanis, Optimists International, and Exchange Clubs.

Veterans' organizations have exercised considerable influence in the state. The American Legion, formed first in 1919 by veterans of the First World War, have constructed buildings, provided facilities for recreation, and carried on various programs of community improvement. The American G.I. Forum, a veterans' group formed by Mexican-Americans, has taken an active stand in many state and local matters. The Veterans of Foreign Wars, an organization with purposes similar to the American Legion, has had rapid growth in Texas.

Of particular value in promoting adult education has been the Texas Federation of Women's Clubs. In earlier years the organization played a major role in the establishment of public libraries across the state. In addition to its library work, the federation promoted legislation in the interest of rural education, compulsory school laws, the protection of women and children in industry, and Texas heritage work.

Indeed, Texans are confirmed "joiners." Apparently everyone belongs to at least one organization, and the average for adults of middle and higher incomes is surely three or more. There are hundreds and hundreds of organizations in the state. There is the Texas State Teachers' Association, a powerful group that long has wielded great influence in legislation. Likewise organizations of strength are the state bar and the state medical associations. There are learned societies, such as the Texas Academy of Science and the Texas Philosophical Society, which was founded during the republic and revived in 1936. There are three geological societies and six organizations of engineers, one statewide historical association and half a dozen regional ones. There are organizations as unrelated as barbers and cattle raisers, Indians and skeet shooters, veterans and Zionists. These provide outlets for the innumerable interests and emotions of the people and are channels of communication and cooperation. More perhaps than any other source, they reveal the nature of our civilization. They are the institutions of a free people and could not thrive except in an atmosphere of freedom.

## LITERATURE AND THE ARTS

Since World War II the literature of Texas has grown in volume, in richness, and in diversity. The traditional topics of earlier years have continued to attract the interest of both writers and readers. Ernest

Wallace and E. Adamson Hoebel dealt with both history and ethnology in *The Comanches, Lords of the South Plains;* Mildred P. Mayhall published a historical study of the Kiowas; Charles L. Sonnichsen wrote on the Mescalero Apaches; and W. W. Newcomb surveyed the entire subject in *The Indians of Texas.* In Ernest Wallace's *Ranald S. Mackenzie*, the story of Texas's last great Indian war is well told. J. Evetts Haley, W. C. Holden, J. W. Williams, Tom Lea, Wayne Gard, and others have added to the literature on the cattle industry.

A number of biographies have appeared. Llerena Friend published the authoritative *Sam Houston, The Great Designer.* Ernest Wallace's *Charles DeMorse, Pioneer Editor and Statesman,* Ben Proctor's *Not without Honor* (John H. Reagan), Joe B. Frantz's *Gail Borden, Dairyman to a Nation,* Alvy King's *Louis T. Wigfall,* and Robert C. Cotner's *James Stephen Hogg* deal with prominent nineteenth century figures. The lives of more recent Texans are portrayed in R. N. Richardson's *Colonel House: The Texas Years,* John O. King's *Joseph Stephen Cullinana: A Study of Leadership in the Texas Petroleum Industry, 1897–1937,* T. Dwight Donough's *Mr. Sam* (Sam Rayburn), Rowland Evans and Robert Novak, *Lyndon B. Johnson: The Exercise of Power,* and Ann Fears Crawford and Jack Keever, *John B. Connally: Portrait in Power.*

Interpretative writing on Texas and Texans has increased greatly during the last quarter-century. Some are autobiographical and at times are sympathetic but more often are critical. William A. Owens has produced several works, among them *This Stubborn Soil.* Edward Everett Dale's *The Cross Timbers*, Bertha McKee Dobie's *Growing Up in Texas*, and C. C. White's and Ada Moreland Holland's *No Quittin' Sense* emphasize the rural heritage of the state. Somewhat more critical are Willie Morris's *North toward Home* and David Nevin's *The Texans: What They Are—And Why.* In his *Big Country Texas*, Donald Day has sought to explain the country and its institutions through history, politics, and folklore. Joseph Leach in *The Typical Texan: Biography of an American Myth* has sought to find in history, novels, and biography a true account of Texan character. Frank Goodwyn's *Lone Star Land: Twentieth Century in Perspective* deals with the social changes Texas has known in the light of its culture, geography, and history. T. R. Fehrenbach's *Lone Star* offers some interesting insights into the forces that have molded the state. The cowboy, a type inseparably linked with Texas, is appraised by Joe B. Frantz and Julian Earnest Choate in *The American Cowboy: The Myth and the Reality.*

In fiction during the middle decades of the twentieth century, Texas novelists were writing on an increasingly varied list of subjects. In *Wetback*, Claud Garner attacked the injustice often done to Mexican immigrants who crossed the Rio Grande unlawfully. William A. Owen's *Walking on Borrowed Land* is a plea for better understanding between the races. David Westheimer, in *Summer on the Water*, deals with the humor and tragedy of a family in a summer colony near Houston. Madison Cooper's *Sironia, Texas* discusses the intimate affairs of the people of a town. In *The Brave Bulls*, Tom Lea treats the interplay of courage and fear in the mind of a matador hero. In *Hound Dog Man*, Fred Gipson took a boy and his dogs through commonplace experiences in a style suggestive of Mark Twain and Booth Tarkington. Loula Grace Erdman's *The Years of the Locusts*, a story of farm people, won a prize of ten thousand dollars from a national publisher. In keeping with the spirit of the age, Larry McMurtry's novel, *The Last Picture Show*, set in a fictional Panhandle oil-field and ranching community, is a critical portrayal of personalities limited by a provincial environment. In a similar vein, Garland Roark wrote of the skullduggery of two East Texas oil promoters in *Drill a Crooked Hole*. *North to Yesterday*, a tragicomic novel about a cattle drive written by Robert Flynn, won an award from the Texas Institute of Letters.

In folklore, the pioneering works of John Lomax, John Mason Brewer, and J. Frank Dobie have endured and been joined by others. *Adventures of a Ballad Hunter* by Lomax won a Texas Institute of Letters Award in 1947. J. Mason Brewer's collections of folklore dealing with the lives of black people, recorded in *The World on the Brazos, Aunt Dicey*, and others, continue to be read. One of the first Mexican-American folklorists to be published was Jovita Gonzales, and adding to her contributions have been the works of Americo Paredes. His study of the *corrido* (Mexican-American folk ballad) is particularly noteworthy. "With his Pistol in his Hand," a study of Gregorio Cortez, is probably his most popular work. Moody Boatwright and William Owens have collected many tales that offer much about the culture of the state.

Societies and journals have done much to preserve the literature of Texas. Vital to the preservation of folklore is the work of the Texas Folklore Society, which over the years has published a large number of volumes. Of the two outstanding literary magazines in the state, the oldest is the *Southwest Review*, founded in Austin in 1915 and later moved to Dallas, where it is sponsored by Southern Methodist University. The quality of its articles is high, and it is a worthy exponent of the life and literature of the state. In 1958 the *Texas Quarterly* was established by members of the faculty of the University of Texas. It carries a wide range of narratives, biographies, poems, and art and provides an outlet for a number of talented writers. Through the pages of these journals much of the poetry of recent times has been preserved and made available to readers.

Interest in the theater dates at least back to the days of the Texas republic and has grown in the twentieth century. In 1909 the Curtain Club was organized at the University of Texas, and after the First World War the little theater became a community project in most towns and cities. Of such organizations, the oldest and best-known in Texas is one in Dallas, founded in 1921. Professional drama presented in the Alley Theater in Houston and in the Dallas Theater Center has won national recognition since World War II.

In twentieth-century music Texas has made some substantial contributions. Dallas, Houston, and San Antonio have major symphony orchestras, and interest in ballet has increased significantly in recent years. Beaumont, Dallas, Fort Worth, Houston, and San Antonio maintain opera groups. Since World War II there has been an unprecedented development of music education through the Interscholastic League. North Texas State University and the University of Texas are known nationally for their excellent music programs, and other universities have developed similarly.

Affecting a larger proportion of the population was the growth of country and western and rock music, or combinations thereof. Drawing on the foundations made popular in the thirties by musicians such as Bob Wills and Ernest Tubb, music once termed "hillbilly" by some, evolved into western and thence into country music. The change was more than a matter of names. Lyrics, emphasis, and instrumentations were altered, although many of the basic themes remained the same. In the sixties and seventies elements of rock were added, to produce a combination termed by some as "progressive country."

Austin became a prominent center for country and western musicians: Willie Nelson, a Texan who abandoned Nashville to return to his home state, perhaps won the most acclaim, but there were many others. On occasion large festivals or "Picnics" were held where literally tens of thousands gathered for all-day concerts.

Rock music also attracted a large following in the postwar years. An early pioneer in the development of rock and roll was a Texan, Buddy Holly, whose promising career was cut short in a tragic plane crash. Janis Joplin of Port Arthur, in a brief but hectic career, won national fame for her versions of rock and roll. Touring rock groups regularly attracted large audiences, mostly youth, and in every city and hamlet, rock groups of widely varying abilities were formed. Especially in the late sixties, rock was often viewed as a part of the social protest movement attractive to those who questioned the values of contemporary society, but as the seventies progressed, more seemed to be attracted to rock because they enjoyed listening to it or playing it.

Widespread interest in art in Texas may be measured from the organization in 1911 of the Texas Fine Arts Association. During recent years this interest has grown. Most large Texas cities, and many smaller ones, have art museums. Also, the colleges have art departments, and art is an increasingly popular subject in the public schools. Over the years the state has produced many fine artists, and some have gained national acclaim. Porfirio Salinas is known for his paintings of the Texas hill country, particularly for scenes featuring bluebonnets. Another artist is Jose Cisneros, who is noted for his pen-and-ink illustrations.

Thus in many ways, the cultural progress of Texas in modern times has kept pace with the economic growth of the state. In literature, drama, music, and the arts, Texans have brought enrichment to their lives and to the nation.

## THE PEOPLE

As Texas entered the eighties, the tricentennial of settlement by peoples other than native Americans was at hand, for it was in 1682 that Spanish friars established their first settlement in Texas, the mission of Corpus Christi de la Ysleta, located a few miles east of the modern city of El Paso. Three centuries have brought great changes in the land that is Texas and also changes, perhaps even more dramatic, in the people who inhabit the land.

Estimates in 1978 placed the population at 13,014,000, third largest in the nation, and almost double that of Texas in 1940. Although the growth rate continued to be higher than the national average in the early 1970s, it has declined in recent years. Women have outnumbered men since 1960. The bulk of the population lives in the twenty-five Standard Metropolitan Statistical Areas (SMSAs), but in the seventies, small towns and rural counties began to grow once more. Because of a declining birth rate, Texas was increasingly dependent upon migration for its population growth. Among the many ethnic groups that made up the population in 1976, "Anglos" represented 67.1 percent, blacks 11.6 percent, and people speaking Spanish as a native language or with a Spanish surname 20.8 percent. The distribution of ethnic minorities within the population has spread. By 1970 approximately 20 percent of the Mexican-American population, once concentrated in South Texas, was in the Dallas, Fort Worth, and Houston areas.

Perhaps the most striking change of recent decades has been the altered role of ethnic minorities and women within the society. As progress has been made in the direction of political equality, so has progress been made in social and economic areas. Blacks and Mexican-Americans, once almost automatically relegated to low-paying, common-

The twenty-five Metropolitan Areas of Texas, 1980. These areas are distributed throughout the state, but the bulk of the population is in the eastern third. (Courtesy of the Texas Research League)

labor jobs, today hold responsible and influential posts in industry, business, the professions, and government. Sports and cultural areas likewise have been strengthened by the contributions of the minorities.

Women have assumed a more visible role. In the late seventies women were elected mayor in San Antonio and Austin, and others were appointed federal judges. A woman was appointed as the United States ambassador to Great Britain, and another served for several years as the president of the University of Texas. More and more, women sought employment outside the home, and in the 1970s women made up approximately one-third of the work force. In a variety of ways, the women of Texas struggled for equality and the expansion of opportunities. Regularly, women's groups appeared at state public-school textbook hearings to ensure that a fair image of women and their role was presented to the school children of the state. With the support of grants

The skyline of Dallas in 1980. (Courtesy Dallas Chamber of Commerce)

from a variety of sources, the Texas Foundation for Women's Resources has conducted extensive research and compiled publications and films to present more accurately the role of Texas women in history. Toward the end of the seventies, the National Organization of Women held its national convention in Houston, attended by thousands. Noticeable at the convention was some disagreement over both methods and goals, and this has been apparent in other ways. A group of Texas women, sometimes called the "Pink Ladies," has campaigned tirelessly to secure the repeal of the legislature's ratification of the ERA amendment to the Constitution.

To a considerable extent, the progress of minorities and women in Texas has come through the use of federal regulation. Laws passed primarily in the sixties and administered through federal agencies sought to ensure an open society and an end to ethnic and sexual discrimination. On occasion the courts have taken a role. But even without the regulation of law, opportunities have become more abundant and open discrimination more rare.

Total equality for ethnic minorities and women remained a goal, however, not a reality. The proportion of Mexican-Americans, blacks, and women who held low-paying, lower-status jobs continued to be much higher than that of Anglo males. Among state government employees, for example, in 1976 approximately 37 percent of Anglo males held higher-paying jobs, while slightly less than 4 percent of black and Mexican-American women held such jobs. But the proportion of Mexican-Americans, blacks, and women employed was substantially higher than it had been a decade earlier.

As Texas entered the eighties, its people were relatively well educated. In 1970 Texans had completed an average of 11.7 years of school, slightly less than the achievement for the nation. Approximately 30 percent had not gone beyond the eighth grade, and 3 percent had not completed the first. On the other hand, more than 22 percent had attended college.

In terms of wealth, the stereotype of the fabulously wealthy Texan who flaunted his or her money persisted, and there seemed to always be enough of that sort around to perpetuate the image. Indeed, one of the most popular television programs aired in the late seventies was a fictional account of a rich Texas family whose outrageous wealth was exceeded only by its outrageous behavior. Texans did their part to keep the program high in the ratings. Certainly, there was much wealth in the state—enough to support the Astrodome, two professional football teams, two major league baseball clubs, a long list of leisure-time activities, and general luxurious living. But for the population as a whole, per capita income was only $6,827 in 1977, even with the impact of inflation. In 1976 the state ranked twenty-fifth in the nation, slightly less than the national average in these terms. Disparities in per capita income were striking. In some of the communities in the Rio Grande Valley, income was only a little more than a third of what it was in the city of Midland located in the West Texas oil fields.

As the people of Texas entered their fourth century of modern civilization, many of the problems that had prevailed throughout the previous three were no more. Indian wars, starvation, and back-breaking physical labor were no longer a part of the struggle for survival. For practically all, the standard of living was at an all-time high, though certainly much higher for some than for others.

But the future contained many challenges. City life brought new comforts and conveniences but posed problems in the form of congestion, cultural conflicts, transportation, and pollution. The energy crisis presented by declining petroleum reserves added to the uncertainties in a variety of ways. Sometimes ignored, but perhaps the most serious problem of all for a large part of the western section of the state, was the declining supply of water reserves.

In one way or another, Texas resolved its problems of an earlier day. A free, prosperous, and contented life depends upon its ability to solve those of the present and of the future.

## SELECTED BIBLIOGRAPHY

For information on contemporary industry and business in Texas, *The Texas Almanac* is indispensible, and the *Texas Business Review* is quite valuable. Another excellent source is the issue of *Newsweek* dated

December 12, 1977, which features articles on a variety of aspects of Texas but especially considers economic affairs. See also John A. Burghort, "Trends in Population Growth in Texas," *National Business Review*, June 1978, pp. 112–114; and Donald E. Green, *Land of the Underground Rain: Irrigation on the Texas High Plains, 1910–1970* (Austin, 1973).

References on minorities may be found in the bibliography of the previous chapter; in addition, see Vernon M. Briggs, Jr. and others, *The Chicano Worker* (Austin, 1977).

Art is discussed in Al Lowman, *Painting Arts in Texas* (Austin, 1975); Harold V. Ratliff surveys Texas sports in "A History of Sports in Texas with a Unique Philosophy," *Proceedings of the Philosophical Society of Texas* (1968)). Country music is discussed in the *Texas Monthly* and in a number of other contemporary publications, sometimes in depth. Hubert Rouseel has written *The Houston Symphony Orchestra, 1913–1971* (Austin, 1972).

# APPENDIX

## GOVERNORS OF TEXAS[1]

| | |
|---|---|
| 1691–1692 | Domingo Terán de los Ríos |
| 1693–1716 | Texas unoccupied but included in Coahuila |
| 1716–1719 | Martín de Alarcón appointed governor of Texas on December 7, 1716. (On August 5, 1716, he had been appointed governor of Coahuila.) |
| 1719–1722 | The Marqués de San Miguél de Aguayo, governor of Coahuila and Texas |
| 1722–1726 | Fernando Pérez de Almazán |
| 1727–1730 | Melchor de Media Villa y Ascona |
| 1730– | Juan Antonio Bustillo y Zevallos |
| 1734– | Manuel de Sandoval |
| 1736–1737 | Carlos Benites Franquis de Lugo |
| 1737– | Fernández de Jáuregui y Urrutia, governor of Nuevo León, governor extraordinary and *visitador* |
| 1737–1740 | Prudencio de Orobio y Bazterra *(governor ad interim)* |

[1]The list of governors holding office before the Texan Revolution is based on Herbert E. Bolton, *Guide to Materials for the History of the United States in the Principal Archives of Mexico* (Washington, D.C., 1913) pp. 478, 479. Bolton makes the statement that "there are some imperfections in the results, in spite of care, for the materials for compiling a correct list are still mainly unprinted." In a few instances information made available subsequent to the publication of Bolton's study has removed doubt as to the terms of governors.

| | |
|---|---|
| 1741–1743 | Tomás Felipe Wintuisen |
| 1743–1744 | Justo Boneo y Morales |
| 1744–1748 | Francisco García Larios *(governor ad interim)* |
| 1748–1750 | Pedro del Barrio Junco y Espriella |
| 1751–1759 | Jacinto de Barrios y Jáuregui. Barrios was appointed governor of Coahuila in 1757, but was retained in Texas until 1759 to complete a task. |
| 1759–1766 | Angel de Martos y Navarrete |
| 1767–1770 | Hugo Oconór *(governor ad interim)* |
| 1770–1778 | The Baron de Ripperdá |
| 1778–1786 | Domingo Cabello |
| 1786 | Bernardo Bonavía appointed July 8, but apparently did not serve. |
| 1787–1790 | Rafael Martínez Pachecho appointed February 27; removal approved October 18, 1790. |
| 1788 | The office of governor was ordered suppressed and the province put under a presidial captain. |
| 1790–1799(?) | Manuel Muñoz |
| 1798(?) | Josef Irigoyen, apparently appointed but did not serve. |
| 1800(?)–1805 | Juan Bautista de Elguezábal |
| 1805–1810 | Antonio Cordero y Bustamante |
| 1810–1813 | Manuel de Salcedo |
| 1811 (Jan. 22–March 2) | Juan Bautista Casas (revolutionary governor) |
| 1814–1818 | Christóbal Domínguez |
| 1817– | Ignacio Pérez and Manuel Pardo *(governors ad interim)* |
| 1817–1822 | Antonio Martínez |
| 1822–1823 | José Felix Trespalacios |
| 1823(?)–1824 | Luciano García |

## GOVERNORS OF COAHUILA AND TEXAS

| | |
|---|---|
| 1824–1826 | Rafael Gonzáles |
| 1826–1827 | Victor Blanco |
| 1827–1831 | José María Viesca |
| 1831–1832 | José María Letona |
| 1832–1833 | Juan Martín de Beramendi |
| 1834–1835 | Juan José Elguezábal |
| 1835– | Agustín Viesca |
| 1835– | Ramón Eca y Músquiz |

## PROVISIONAL GOVERNORS
## DURING THE TEXAN REVOLUTION[2]

Nov. 14, 1835–March 1, 1836    Henry Smith
Jan. 11, 1836–March 1, 1836    James W. Robinson[3]


## PRESIDENTS OF THE REPUBLIC OF TEXAS

March 17, 1836–Oct. 22, 1836    David G. Burnet
Oct. 22, 1836–Dec. 10, 1838    Sam Houston
Dec. 10, 1838–Dec. 13, 1841    Mirabeau B. Lamar
Dec. 13, 1841–Dec. 9, 1844    Sam Houston
Dec. 9, 1844–Feb. 19, 1846    Anson Jones


## GOVERNORS AFTER ANNEXATION

Feb. 19, 1846–Dec. 21, 1847    J. Pinckney Henderson
May 19, 1846–Nov.—, 1846    A. C. Horton[4]
Dec. 21, 1847–Dec. 21, 1849    George T. Wood
Dec. 21, 1849–Nov. 23, 1853    P. Hansborough Bell
Nov. 23, 1853–Dec. 21, 1853    J. W. Henderson[5]
Dec. 21, 1853–Dec. 21, 1857    Elisha M. Pease
Dec. 21, 1857–Dec. 21, 1859    Hardin R. Runnels
Dec. 21, 1859–March 16, 1861    Sam Houston[6]
March 16, 1861–Nov. 7, 1861    Edward Clark
Nov. 7, 1861–Nov. 5, 1863    Francis R. Lubbock
Nov. 5, 1863–June 17, 1865    Pendleton Murrah[7]


[2]This list of Texas chief executives is taken in part from the *Texas Almanac,* 1936, p. 317. Later information courtesy Ray Barrera, Secretary of State.
[3]Robinson was elected by the council after Smith had been deposed and the office of governor declared vacant by the council. Thereafter both men claimed the right to exercise the executive authority.
[4]Lieutenant Governor Horton served as governor while Governor Henderson was away commanding troops in the war with Mexico.
[5]Lieutenant Governor Henderson became governor when Governor Bell resigned to take his seat in Congress, to which he had been elected.
[6]Houston refused to take the oath of allegiance to the Confederacy and was deposed. He was succeeded by Lieutenant Governor Edward Clark.
[7]Murrah's administration was terminated by the fall of the Confederacy. Murrah retired to Mexico, and for a period, May–June, 1865, Lieutenant Governor Fletcher S. Stockdale was acting governor.

| | |
|---|---|
| July 21, 1865–Aug. 9, 1866 | Andrew J. Hamilton (provisional) |
| Aug. 9, 1866–Aug. 8, 1867 | James W. Throckmorton[8] |
| Aug. 8, 1867–Sept. 30, 1869 | Elisha M. Pease |
| Jan. 8, 1870–Jan. 15, 1874 | Edmund J. Davis[9] |
| Jan. 15, 1874–Dec. 1, 1876 | Richard Coke[10] |
| Dec. 1, 1876–Jan. 21, 1879 | Richard B. Hubbard |
| Jan. 21, 1879–Jan. 16, 1883 | Oran M. Roberts |
| Jan. 16, 1883–Jan. 18, 1887 | John Ireland |
| Jan. 18, 1887–Jan. 20, 1891 | Lawrence Sullivan Ross |
| Jan. 20, 1891–Jan. 15, 1895 | James S. Hogg |
| Jan. 15, 1895–Jan. 17, 1899 | Charles A. Culberson |
| Jan. 17, 1899–Jan. 20, 1903 | Joseph D. Sayers |
| Jan. 20, 1903–Jan. 15, 1907 | S. W. T. Lanham |
| Jan. 15, 1907–Jan. 19, 1911 | Thomas M. Campbell |
| Jan. 19, 1911–Jan. 19, 1915 | Oscar Branch Colquitt |
| Jan. 19, 1915–Aug. 25, 1917 | James E. Ferguson (impeached) |
| Aug. 25, 1917–Jan. 18, 1921 | William P. Hobby |
| Jan. 18, 1921–Jan. 20, 1925 | Pat M. Neff |
| Jan. 20, 1925–Jan. 17, 1927 | Miriam A. Ferguson |
| Jan. 17, 1927–Jan. 20, 1931 | Dan Moody |
| Jan. 20, 1931–Jan. 17, 1933 | Ross S. Sterling |
| Jan. 17, 1933–Jan. 15, 1935 | Miriam A. Ferguson |
| Jan. 15, 1935–Jan. 17, 1939 | James V. Allred |
| Jan. 17, 1939–Aug. 4, 1941 | W. Lee O'Daniel (resigned to enter U.S. Senate) |
| Aug. 4, 1941–Jan. 21, 1947 | Coke R. Stevenson |
| Jan. 21, 1947–July 11, 1949 | Beauford H. Jester (died) |
| July 11, 1949–Jan. 15, 1957 | Allan Shivers |
| Jan. 15, 1957–Jan. 15, 1963 | Price Daniel |
| Jan. 15, 1963–Jan. 21, 1969 | John Connally |
| Jan. 21, 1969–Jan. 16, 1973 | Preston Smith |
| Jan. 16, 1973–Jan. 16, 1979 | Dolph Briscoe |
| Jan. 16, 1979– | William Clements |

[8]Throckmorton was removed by the military. Pease, provisional governor who succeeded him, resigned September 30, 1869.

[9]Davis was appointed provisional governor after he had been elected governor.

[10]Coke resigned to enter the United States Senate and was succeeded by Lieutenant Governor Hubbard.

# UNITED STATES SENATORS

## Houston Succession

| | |
|---|---|
| Feb. 21, 1846–March 4, 1859 | Sam Houston |
| March 4, 1859–July 11, 1861 | John Hemphill[11] |
| Feb. 22, 1870–March 3, 1877 | Morgan C. Hamilton |
| March 3, 1877–March 3, 1895 | Richard Coke |
| March 3, 1895–March 3, 1901 | Horace Chilton |
| March 3, 1901–Jan. 8, 1913 | Joseph W. Bailey (resigned) |
| Jan. 8, 1913–Feb. 3, 1913 | R. M. Johnson (filled vacancy on appointment) |
| Feb. 13, 1913–April 9, 1941 | Morris Sheppard (died) |
| April 21, 1941–June 26, 1941 | Andrew Jackson Houston (died) |
| Aug. 4, 1941–Jan. 3, 1949 | W. Lee O'Daniel |
| Jan. 3, 1949–Jan. 20, 1961 | Lyndon B. Johnson |
| Jan. 20, 1961–June 15, 1961 | William A. Blakley |
| June 15, 1961– | John G. Tower |

## Rusk Succession

| | |
|---|---|
| Feb. 21, 1846–July 29, 1857 | Thomas J. Rusk (died) |
| Nov. 9, 1857–June 4, 1858 | J. Pinckney Henderson (died) |
| Sept. 29, 1858–Dec. 5, 1859 | Matthias Ward (filled vacancy on appointment) |
| 1859–1861 | Louis T. Wigfall |
| Feb. 22, 1870–March 3, 1875 | James W. Flanagan |
| March 3, 1875–March 3, 1887 | Samuel B. Maxey |
| March 3, 1887–June 10, 1891 | John H. Reagan (resigned) |
| Dec. 7, 1891–March 30, 1892 | Horace Chilton (filled vacancy on appointment) |
| March 30, 1892–March 3, 1899 | Roger Q. Mills |
| March 3, 1899–March 4, 1923 | Charles A. Culberson |
| March 4, 1923–March 4, 1929 | Earle B. Mayfield |

[11]Succession was broken by the secession of Texas. Louis T. Wigfall and W. S. Oldham represented Texas in the Confederate Senate. On August 21, 1866, the Texas legislature elected David G. Burnet and Oran M. Roberts to the United States Senate, but they were not allowed to take their seats.

| March 4, 1929–Jan. 3, 1953 | Tom Connally |
| Jan. 3, 1953–Jan. 15, 1957 | Price Daniel (resigned to become governor) |
| Jan. 13, 1957–April 19, 1957 | William A. Blakley |
| April 19, 1957–Jan. 12, 1971 | Ralph W. Yarborough |
| Jan. 12, 1971– | Lloyd Bentsen |

# INDEX

Barrow, Clyde, 399
Barrymore, Ethel, 360
Bass, Sam, 369
Bastrop, Baron, de, 59, 62, 73, 74
Bastrop (Mina), 96, 97–98
Bastrop Military Institute, 210 *illus.*
Battle, W. J., 379
Battles: Alamo (1835), 109–11, 124, 144; Buena Vista (1946), 168; Mexico City (1846), 168; Monterrey (1846), 167–68, 174–75; Neches (1839), 138; Palmito Ranch, 179, 230, 232; Sabine Pass (1863), 229–30; San Jacinto (1836), 101, 118–20, 120*n*, 124, 129, 134, 137, 143, 300, 413
Baylor, George W., 297
Baylor, John R., 229
Baylor, R. E. B., 146, 164, 177
Baylor University, 209, 362, 393, 456
Bays, Joseph E., 77
Beales, Dr. John, 70
Bean, Peter Ellis, 325
Beaumont (Tex.), 325; riots (1943), 419
Beckworth, Lindly, 427
Bedicheck, Roy, 409
Bee, Barnard E., 153, 157
Belgium, 152–53
Bell, James H., 247
Bell, John, 172, 222
Bell, Josiah H., 60, 61
Bell, Gov. Peter Hansborough, 171, 173 and *illus.*, 175
Benavides, Santos, 193
Benton, Sen. Thomas H., 172
Bentsen, Lloyd, 445
Bernhardt, Sarah, 360
Bexar (San Antonio), 24, 40, 42, 43, 45, 50, 73, 75, 93, 104*n*, 106
Bienville, Gov. Celeron de, 24
Big Tree, Chief, 294
Bird, John, 138
Black codes, 249–50, 252
Blacks, 193, 356, 359, 363, 365–66, 391 (*see also* Free blacks; Slaves, slavery); businesses, 365; civil rights movement, 435, 441–42; education, 365, 393; and the Great Depression, 397–98; labor unions, 363, 365; occupations, 363, 462–63; political parties, 276, 345, 365, 419; in public office, 440, 442; and Reconstruction, 247, 248, 249–51, 261, 264–65; segregation, 366, 392; in state legislatures, 275; voting rights, 248, 249, 256, 262, 272, 276, 348–49, 428–29; and World War I, 382; and World War II, 419
Black schools, 285, 286, 345, 365, 392–93
Blakley, William A., 432, 437
Blanco, Victor, 85
Blanton, Annie Webb, 382
Blondel, Corp. M., 24
Boatright, Thomas, 61
Boatwright, Moody, 459
Bolton, Herbert E., 370
Bonaparte, Joseph, 52
Bonham, James B., 110–11
Bonnell, G. W., 137
Boone, Daniel, 58
Booth, Edwin, 360

Borden, Gail, Jr., 105
Bourland, Col. James, 228
Bowie, James, 97, 102, 109 and *illus.*, 112
Bradburn, Col. John D., 86
Brann, Cowper, 368
Brazoria, 78, 79, 87–89
Brazos Indian Reservation, 186, 187
Brazos River Conservation . . . District, 406–7
"Bread bonds" (1932), 401
Breckinridge, John C., 221, 222
Brenham, Dr. Richard F., 155
Brewer, J. Mason, 409, 459
Briscoe, Andrew, 95
Briscoe, Gov. Dolph, 446–47, 448, 449
Brown, John, raid (1859), 221
*Brown* v. *Bd. of Education* (1954), 429
Bryan, Lt. Francis T., 180
Bryan, Guy M., 223
Bryan, John Neely, 148
Bryan, William Jennings, 345
Buchanan, James, 170
Buell, Lt. Col. George P., 296
Buffalo Hump, Chief, 141
Buffalo slaughter (1873–80), 198–99, 319
Bugbee, Thomas Sherman, 309
Burke, Capt. David N., 124
Burkham, Charles, 58
Burleson, Albert Sidney, 380
Burleson, Edward, 103, 116, 119, 138, 139, 140, 142
Burleson, R. C., 287
Burnam, Jesse, 58
Burnet, Pres. David G., 65, 68, 91, 115, 116 and *illus.*, 117, 121–23, 125, 129, 130, 135, 140, 151, 153, 154, 222, 238, 249
Burr, Aaron, 39
Burton, Maj. Isaac W., 125–26
Bush, George, 445
Bustamente, Anastacio, 67, 87, 92, 153
Butler, Anthony, 85
Butte, George C., 387
Butterfield Mail Line, 203
Byars, Noah, 215

Cabello, Domingo, 37
Cabeza de Vaca, Alvar Núñez, 15–16
Caddo Indians, 7, 9, 186
Cadillac, Antoine de la Mothe, 22
Caldwell, Justice Colbert, 255
Calhoun, John C., 57, 157, 164, 178
Calhoun Democrats, 178
California, 166, 168
Campbell, Gov. Thomas M., 351–54
Cannon, Joe, 414
Carbajal, José María, 87, 94
Carhart, Lewis Henry, 311
Carl of Solms-Braunfels, Prince, 146, 202
Carpetbaggers, 254
Carson, Samuel P., 114, 115
Casafuerte, Marquis de, 25
Cass, Lewis, 175
Castañeda, Carlos, 409
Castañeda, Lt. Francisco, 102
Castrillón, Gen. Manuel Fernandez, 119

# TEXAS

### COUNTIES

Anderson, 27,789 .............J 6
Andrews, 10,372 .............B 5
Angelina, 49,349 .............K 6
Aransas, 8,902 .............H 10
Archer, 5,759 .............F 4
Armstrong, 1,895 .............C 3
Atascosa, 18,696 .............F 9
Austin, 13,831 .............H 8
Bailey, 8,487 .............B 3
Bandera, 4,747 .............E 8
Bastrop, 17,297 .............G 7
Baylor, 5,221 .............E 4
Bee, 22,737 .............G 9
Bell, 124,483 .............G 6
Bexar, 830,460 .............F 8
Blanco, 3,567 .............F 7
Borden, 888 .............C 5
Bosque, 10,966 .............G 6
Bowie, 67,813 .............K 4
Brazoria, 108,312 .............J 8
Brazos, 57,978 .............H 7
Brewster, 7,780 .............A 8
Briscoe, 2,794 .............C 3
Brooks, 8,005 .............F 11
Brown, 25,877 .............F 6
Burleson, 9,999 .............H 7
Burnet, 11,420 .............F 7
Caldwell, 21,178 .............G 8
Calhoun, 17,831 .............H 9
Callahan, 8,205 .............E 5
Cameron, 140,368 .............G 11
Camp, 8,005 .............K 5
Carson, 6,358 .............C 2
Cass, 24,133 .............K 4
Castro, 10,394 .............B 3
Chambers, 12,187 .............K 8
Cherokee, 32,008 .............J 6
Childress, 6,605 .............D 3
Clay, 8,079 .............F 4
Cochran, 5,326 .............B 4
Coke, 3,087 .............D 6
Coleman, 10,288 .............E 6
Collin, 66,920 .............H 4
Collingsworth, 4,755 .............D 3
Colorado, 17,638 .............H 8
Comal, 24,165 .............F 8
Comanche, 11,898 .............F 5
Concho, 2,937 .............E 6
Cooke, 23,471 .............G 4
Coryell, 35,311 .............G 6
Cottle, 3,204 .............D 3
Crane, 4,172 .............B 6
Crockett, 3,885 .............C 7
Crosby, 9,085 .............C 4
Culberson, 3,429 .............C 11
Dallam, 6,012 .............B 1
Dallas, 1,327,321 .............H 5
Dawson, 16,604 .............C 5
Deaf Smith, 18,999 .............B 3
Delta, 4,927 .............J 4
Denton, 75,633 .............G 4
De Witt, 18,660 .............G 9
Dickens, 3,737 .............D 4
Dimmit, 9,039 .............E 9
Donley, 3,641 .............D 2
Duval, 11,722 .............F 10
Eastland, 18,092 .............F 5
Ector, 91,805 .............B 6
Edwards, 2,107 .............D 7
Ellis, 46,638 .............H 5
El Paso, 359,291 .............A 10
Erath, 18,141 .............F 5
Falls, 17,300 .............H 6
Fannin, 22,705 .............H 4
Fayette, 17,650 .............H 8
Fisher, 6,344 .............D 5
Floyd, 11,044 .............C 3
Foard, 2,211 .............E 3
Fort Bend, 52,314 .............J 8
Franklin, 5,291 .............J 4
Freestone, 11,116 .............H 6
Frio, 11,159 .............E 9
Gaines, 11,593 .............B 5
Galveston, 169,812 .............K 8
Garza, 5,289 .............C 4
Gillespie, 10,553 .............F 7
Glasscock, 1,155 .............C 6
Goliad, 4,869 .............G 9
Gonzales, 16,375 .............G 8
Gray, 26,949 .............D 2
Grayson, 83,225 .............H 4
Gregg, 75,929 .............K 5
Grimes, 11,855 .............J 7
Guadalupe, 33,554 .............G 8
Hale, 34,137 .............C 3
Hall, 6,015 .............D 3
Hamilton, 7,198 .............F 6
Hansford, 6,351 .............C 1
Hardeman, 6,795 .............E 3
Hardin, 29,996 .............K 7

### (continued)

Harris, 1,741,912 .............J 8
Harrison, 44,841 .............K 5
Hartley, 2,782 .............B 2
Haskell, 8,512 .............E 4
Hays, 27,642 .............F 7
Hemphill, 3,084 .............D 2
Henderson, 26,466 .............J 5
Hidalgo, 181,535 .............F 11
Hill, 22,596 .............G 5
Hockley, 20,396 .............B 4
Hood, 6,368 .............G 5
Hopkins, 20,710 .............J 4
Houston, 17,855 .............J 6
Howard, 37,796 .............C 5
Hudspeth, 2,392 .............B 10
Hunt, 47,948 .............H 4
Hutchinson, 24,443 .............C 2
Irion, 1,070 .............C 6
Jack, 6,711 .............F 4
Jackson, 12,975 .............H 9
Jasper, 24,692 .............K 7
Jeff Davis, 1,527 .............C 11
Jefferson, 244,773 .............K 8
Jim Hogg, 4,654 .............F 11
Jim Wells, 33,032 .............F 10
Johnson, 45,769 .............G 5
Jones, 16,106 .............E 5
Karnes, 13,462 .............G 9
Kaufman, 32,392 .............H 5
Kendall, 6,964 .............F 8
Kenedy, 678 .............G 11
Kent, 1,434 .............D 4
Kerr, 19,454 .............E 7
Kimble, 3,904 .............E 7
King, 464 .............D 4
Kinney, 2,006 .............D 8
Kleberg, 33,166 .............G 10
Knox, 5,972 .............E 4
Lamar, 36,062 .............J 4
Lamb, 17,770 .............B 3
Lampasas, 9,323 .............F 6
La Salle, 5,014 .............E 9
Lavaca, 17,903 .............H 8
Lee, 8,048 .............H 7
Leon, 8,738 .............J 6
Liberty, 33,014 .............K 7
Limestone, 18,100 .............H 6
Lipscomb, 3,486 .............D 1
Live Oak, 6,697 .............F 9
Llano, 6,979 .............F 7
Loving, 164 .............D 10
Lubbock, 179,295 .............C 4
Lynn, 9,107 .............C 4
Madison, 7,693 .............J 6
Marion, 8,517 .............K 5
Martin, 4,774 .............C 5
Mason, 3,356 .............E 7
Matagorda, 27,913 .............H 9
Maverick, 18,093 .............D 9
McCulloch, 8,571 .............E 6
McLennan, 147,553 .............G 6
McMullen, 1,095 .............F 9
Medina, 20,249 .............E 8
Menard, 2,646 .............E 7
Midland, 65,433 .............B 6
Milam, 20,028 .............H 7
Mills, 4,212 .............F 6
Mitchell, 9,073 .............D 5
Montague, 15,326 .............G 4
Montgomery, 49,479 .............J 7
Moore, 14,060 .............C 2
Morris, 12,310 .............K 4
Motley, 2,178 .............D 3
Nacogdoches, 36,362 .............K 6
Navarro, 31,150 .............H 5
Newton, 11,657 .............L 7
Nolan, 16,220 .............D 5
Nueces, 237,544 .............G 10
Ochiltree, 9,704 .............D 1
Oldham, 2,258 .............B 2
Orange, 71,170 .............L 7
Palo Pinto, 28,962 .............F 5
Panola, 15,894 .............K 5
Parker, 33,888 .............G 5
Parmer, 10,509 .............B 3
Pecos, 13,748 .............B 7
Polk, 14,457 .............K 7
Potter, 90,511 .............C 2
Presidio, 4,842 .............C 12
Rains, 3,752 .............J 5
Randall, 53,885 .............C 2
Reagan, 3,239 .............C 6
Real, 2,013 .............E 8
Red River, 14,298 .............J 4
Reeves, 9,494 .............D 11
Refugio, 9,494 .............G 9
Roberts, 967 .............D 2
Robertson, 14,389 .............H 6
Rockwall, 7,046 .............H 5
Runnels, 12,108 .............E 6
Rusk, 34,102 .............K 5
Sabine, 7,187 .............L 6

### (continued)

San Augustine, 7,858 .............K 6
San Jacinto, 6,702 .............J 7
San Patricio, 47,288 .............G 10
San Saba, 5,540 .............F 6
Schleicher, 2,277 .............D 7
Scurry, 15,760 .............D 5
Shackelford, 3,323 .............E 5
Shelby, 19,672 .............K 6
Sherman, 3,657 .............C 1
Smith, 97,096 .............J 5
Somervell, 2,793 .............G 5
Starr, 17,707 .............F 11
Stephens, 8,414 .............F 5
Sterling, 1,056 .............C 6
Stonewall, 2,397 .............D 4
Sutton, 3,175 .............D 7
Swisher, 10,373 .............C 3
Tarrant, 716,317 .............G 5
Taylor, 97,853 .............E 5
Terrell, 1,940 .............B 7
Terry, 14,118 .............B 4
Throckmorton, 2,205 .............E 4
Titus, 16,702 .............K 4
Tom Green, 71,047 .............D 6
Travis, 295,516 .............G 7
Trinity, 7,628 .............J 6
Tyler, 12,417 .............K 7
Upshur, 20,976 .............K 5
Upton, 4,697 .............B 6
Uvalde, 17,348 .............E 8
Val Verde, 27,471 .............C 8
Van Zandt, 22,155 .............J 5
Victoria, 53,766 .............H 9
Walker, 27,680 .............J 7
Waller, 14,285 .............J 8
Ward, 13,019 .............A 6
Washington, 18,842 .............H 7
Webb, 72,859 .............E 10
Wharton, 36,729 .............H 8
Wheeler, 6,434 .............D 2
Wichita, 121,862 .............F 3
Wilbarger, 15,355 .............E 3
Willacy, 15,570 .............G 11
Williamson, 37,305 .............G 7
Wilson, 13,041 .............F 8
Winkler, 9,640 .............A 6
Wise, 19,687 .............G 4
Wood, 18,589 .............J 5
Yoakum, 7,344 .............B 4
Young, 15,400 .............F 4
Zapata, 4,352 .............E 11
Zavala, 11,370 .............E 9

### CITIES and TOWNS

Abernathy, 2,625 .............B 4
Abilene◉, 89,653 .............E 5
Abilene, 113,959 .............E 5
Alamo, 4,291 .............F 11
Alamo Heights, 6,933 .............F 8
Albany◉, 1,978 .............E 5
Alice◉, 20,121 .............F 10
Allen■, 1,940 .............H 4
Alpine◉, 5,971 .............D 11
Alvarado, 2,129 .............G 5
Alvin, 10,671 .............J 3
Amarillo◉, 127,010 .............C 2
Amarillo, ‡144,396 .............C 2
Anahuac◉, 1,881 .............K 8
Anderson◉, 500 .............J 7
Andrews◉, 8,625 .............B 5
Angleton◉, 9,770 .............J 3
Anson◉, 2,615 .............E 5
Anthony, 2,154 .............A 10
Aransas Pass, 5,813 .............G 10
Archer City◉, 1,722 .............F 4
Arlington, 90,643 .............F 2
Aspermont◉, 1,198 .............D 4
Athens◉, 9,582 .............J 5
Atlanta, 5,007 .............K 4
Austin (cap.)◉, 251,808 .............G 7
Austin, ‡295,516 .............G 7
Azle, 4,493 .............E 1
Bacliff, 1,900 .............K 2
Baird◉, 1,538 .............E 5
Balch Springs, 10,464 .............H 2
Balcones Heights■, 2,504 .............F 8
Ballinger◉, 4,203 .............E 6
Bandera◉, 891 .............F 8
Barrett, 2,750 .............K 1
Bastrop◉, 3,112 .............G 7
Bay City◉, 11,733 .............H 9
Baytown, 43,980 .............L 2
Beaumont◉, 115,919 .............K 7
Beaumont-Port Arthur-
  Orange, ‡315,943 .............K 7
Bedford, 10,049 .............F 2
Beeville◉, 13,506 .............G 9
Bellaire, 19,009 .............J 2
Bellmead, 7,698 .............H 6
Bellville◉, 2,371 .............H 8
Belton◉, 8,696 .............G 7

### (continued)

Benavides, 2,112 .............F 10
Benbrook, 8,169 .............E 2
Benjamin◉, 308 .............E 4
Beverly Hills■, 2,289 .............G 6
Big Lake◉, 2,489 .............C 6
Big Spring◉, 28,735 .............C 5
Bishop, 3,466 .............G 10
Boerne◉, 2,432 .............F 8
Bonham◉, 7,698 .............H 4
Borger, 14,195 .............C 2
Boston◉, 500 .............K 4
Bowie, 5,185 .............G 4
Brackettville◉, 1,539 .............D 8
Brady◉, 5,557 .............E 6
Breckenridge◉, 5,944 .............F 5
Brenham◉, 8,922 .............H 7
Bridge City, 8,164 .............L 7
Bridgeport, 3,614 .............G 4
Brownfield◉, 9,647 .............B 4
Brownsville◉, 52,522 .............G 12
Brownsville-Harlingen-
  San Benito, ‡140,368 .............G 12
Brownwood◉, 17,368 .............F 6
Bryan◉, 33,719 .............H 7
Bryan-College Station,
  ‡57,978 .............H 7
Bunker Hill Village, 3,977 .............J 1
Burkburnett, 9,230 .............F 3
Burleson, 7,713 .............F 2
Burnet◉, 2,864 .............F 7
Caldwell◉, 2,308 .............H 7
Calvert, 2,072 .............H 7
Cameron◉, 5,546 .............H 7
Canadian◉, 2,292 .............D 2
Canton◉, 2,283 .............J 5
Canyon◉, 8,333 .............C 3
Carrizo Springs◉, 5,374 .............E 9
Carrollton, 13,855 .............G 1
Carthage◉, 5,392 .............K 5
Castle Hills■, 5,311 .............F 8
Castroville, 1,893 .............E 8
Cedar Hill, 2,610 .............G 2
Center◉, 4,989 .............K 6
Centerville◉, 831 .............H 6
Channelview, 9,000 .............K 1
Channing◉, 336 .............B 2
Childress◉, 5,408 .............D 3
Cisco, 4,160 .............E 5
Clarendon◉, 1,974 .............C 3
Clarksville◉, 3,346 .............K 4
Claude◉, 992 .............C 2
Clear Lake Shores, 500 .............K 2
Cleburne◉, 16,015 .............G 5
Cleveland, 5,627 .............K 7
Clifton, 2,578 .............G 6
Clute, 6,023 .............J 9
Cockrell Hill, 3,515 .............G 2
Coldspring◉, 500 .............J 7
Coleman◉, 5,608 .............E 6
College Station, 17,676 .............H 7
Colleyville, 3,368 .............F 1
Colorado City◉, 5,227 .............C 5
Columbus◉, 3,342 .............H 8
Comanche◉, 3,933 .............F 6
Commerce, 9,534 .............J 4
Conroe◉, 11,969 .............J 7
Cooper◉, 2,258 .............J 4
Coppell, 1,728 .............F 1
Copperas Cove, 10,818 .............G 6
Corpus Christi◉, 204,525 .............G 10
Corpus Christi, ‡284,832 .............G 10
Corsicana◉, 19,972 .............H 5
Cotulla◉, 3,415 .............E 9
Crane◉, 3,427 .............B 6
Crockett◉, 6,616 .............J 6
Crosbyton◉, 2,251 .............C 4
Crowell◉, 1,399 .............E 4
Crowley, 2,662 .............E 2
Crystal City◉, 8,104 .............E 9
Cuero◉, 6,956 .............G 8
Daingerfield◉, 2,630 .............K 4
Dalhart◉, 5,705 .............B 1
Dallas◉, 844,401 .............H 2
Dallas, ‡1,555,950 .............H 2
Dayton, 3,804 .............J 7
Decatur◉, 3,240 .............G 4
Deer Park, 12,773 .............K 2
De Kalb, 2,197 .............K 4
De Leon, 2,170 .............F 5
Del Rio◉, 21,330 .............D 8
Denison, 24,923 .............H 4
Denton◉, 39,874 .............G 4
Denver City, 4,133 .............B 4
De Soto, 6,617 .............G 2
Devine, 3,311 .............E 8
Diboll, 3,557 .............K 6
Dickens◉, 295 .............D 4
Dickinson, 10,776 .............K 3
Dilley, 2,362 .............E 9
Dimmitt◉, 4,327 .............B 3
Donna, 7,365 .............F 11
Dublin, 2,810 .............F 5

### (continued)

Dumas◉, 9,771 .............C 2
Duncanville, 14,105 .............G 2
Eagle Lake, 3,587 .............H 8
Eagle Pass◉, 15,364 .............D 9
Eastland◉, 3,178 .............F 5
Edcouch■, 2,656 .............G 11
Edinburg◉, 17,163 .............F 11
Edna◉, 5,332 .............H 9
El Campo, 8,563 .............H 8
Eldorado◉, 1,446 .............D 7
Electra, 3,895 .............F 4
Elgin, 3,832 .............G 7
El Paso◉, 322,261 .............A 10
El Paso, ‡359,291 .............A 10
Elsa, 4,400 .............G 11
Emory◉, 693 .............J 5
Ennis, 11,046 .............H 5
Euless, 19,316 .............F 1
Everman, 4,570 .............F 2
Fabens, 3,241 .............B 10
Fairfield◉, 2,074 .............H 6
Falfurrias◉, 6,355 .............F 10
Farmers Branch, 27,492 .............G 1
Farmersville, 2,311 .............H 4
Farwell◉, 1,185 .............A 3
Ferris, 2,180 .............H 2
Floresville◉, 3,707 .............F 8
Floydada◉, 4,109 .............C 3
Forest Hill, 8,236 .............F 2
Forney, 1,745 .............H 5
Fort Davis◉, 900 .............D 11
Fort Stockton◉, 8,283 .............A 7
Fort Worth◉, 393,476 .............E 2
Fort Worth, ‡762,086 .............E 2
Franklin◉, 1,063 .............H 7
Fredericksburg◉, 5,326 .............E 7
Fredonia, 50 .............E 7
Freeport, 11,997 .............J 9
Freer, 2,804 .............F 10
Friendswood, 5,675 .............J 2
Friona, 3,111 .............B 3
Frisco, 1,845 .............H 4
Fritch, 1,778 .............C 2
Gail◉, 150 .............C 5
Gainesville◉, 13,830 .............G 4
Galena Park, 10,479 .............J 1
Galveston◉, 61,809 .............L 3
Galveston-Texas City,
  ‡169,812 .............L 3
Garden City◉, 300 .............C 6
Garland, 81,437 .............H 1
Gatesville◉, 4,683 .............G 6
Georgetown◉, 6,395 .............G 7
George West◉, 2,022 .............F 9
Giddings◉, 2,783 .............H 7
Gilmer◉, 4,196 .............J 5
Gladewater, 5,574 .............K 5
Glen Rose◉, 1,554 .............G 5
Goldthwaite◉, 1,693 .............F 6
Goliad◉, 1,709 .............G 9
Gonzales◉, 5,854 .............G 8
Graham◉, 7,477 .............F 4
Granbury◉, 2,473 .............G 5
Grand Prairie, 50,904 .............G 2
Grand Saline, 2,257 .............J 5
Grapevine, 7,023 .............F 1
Greenville◉, 22,043 .............H 4
Gregory■, 2,246 .............G 10
Griffing Park■, 2,075 .............L 8
Groesbeck◉, 2,396 .............H 6
Groves, 18,067 .............L 8
Groveton◉, 1,219 .............J 7
Guthrie◉, 150 .............D 4
Hale Center, 1,964 .............C 3
Hallettsville◉, 2,712 .............G 8
Haltom City, 28,127 .............F 2
Hamilton◉, 2,760 .............G 6
Hamlin, 3,325 .............E 5
Harker Heights■, 4,216 .............G 7
Harlingen, 33,503 .............G 11
Haskell◉, 3,655 .............E 4
Hearne, 4,982 .............H 7
Hebbronville◉, 4,079 .............F 10
Hedwig Village■, 3,255 .............J 1
Hemphill◉, 1,005 .............L 6
Hempstead◉, 1,891 .............J 7
Henderson◉, 10,187 .............K 5
Henrietta◉, 2,897 .............F 4
Hereford◉, 13,414 .............B 3
Highland Park, 10,133 .............G 2
Highlands, 3,462 .............K 1
Hillsboro◉, 7,224 .............G 5
Hitchcock, 5,565 .............K 3
Hollywood Park■, 2,299 .............F 8
Hondo◉, 5,487 .............E 8
Honey Grove, 1,853 .............J 4
Hooks, 2,545 .............K 4
Houston◉, 1,232,802 .............J 2
Houston, ‡1,985,031 .............J 2
Humble, 3,278 .............J 1
Hunters Creek Village,
  3,959 .............J 1